If you're wondering why you should buy this new edition of *Texas Politics and Government*, here are six good reasons!

1. New "Roots of" and "Toward Reform" sections have been added to the beginning and conclusion of each chapter, highlighting the importance of the history of Texas politics and government, as well as the dynamic cycle of reassessment and reform that allows Texas to continue to evolve. Each "Roots of" section gives a historical overview of the topic at hand, and each "Toward Reform" section is devoted to a particularly contentious, current aspect of Texas politics.

2. New "What Should I Know About" sections begin each chapter with a series of questions tied to major chapter headings and focus your reading on the most important concepts and points. New "What Have I Learned" sections now close each chapter, briefly summarizing the answers to those questions.

3. New "Thinking Nationally" features highlight Texas's differences from and commonalities with other states in the U.S. Examples of this feature include a comparison of legislative and gubernatorial budget preparations in New York and Texas (in Chapter 4) and a comparison of the length of state constitutions (in Chapter 2).

4. New "Ideas into Action" features discuss practical ways for college students to become more involved in their government and communities. Some of the features focus on initiatives on Texas campuses; others relate to state and national-level issues. For example, Chapter 2 discusses the role that Angelo State University students played in a legislative attempt to revise the Texas Constitution.

5. New Timelines appear in selected chapters and provide students with a clear understanding of – and visual study aid for – the development of key topics in Texas politics. For example, Chapter 3 includes a timeline devoted to voting requirements in Texas.

6. Updated "Politics Now" boxes highlight reform through a focus on recent events. News articles about current political personalities or political developments are paired with critical thinking questions to allow students to learn more about the most recent state of Texas politics. For example, Chapter 4's "Politics Now" box focuses on the controversy over "ghost workers" employed by members of the Texas legislature.

PEARSON

Texas Politics and GOVERNMENT

ROOTS AND REFORM

Third Edition

Gary A. Keith
University of the Incarnate Word

Stefan D. Haag
Austin Community College

Longman
New York San Francisco Boston
London Toronto Sydney Tokyo Singapore Madrid
Mexico City Munich Paris Cape Town Hong Kong Montreal

Editor-in-Chief: Eric Stano
Development Editor: Melissa Mashburn
Associate Development Editor: Donna Garnier
Marketing Manager: Lindsey Prudhomme
Media Producer: Regina Vertiz
Production Manager: Eric Jorgensen
Project Coordination, Text Design, and Electronic Page Makeup: Electronic Publishing Services Inc., NYC
Art Studio: Electronic Publishing Services Inc., NYC
Senior Cover Design Manager/Cover Designer: Nancy Danahy
Cover Image: © Darren Greenwood/Photographer's Choice/Getty Immages, Inc.
Photo Researcher: Jody Potter
Image Permission Coordination: Frances Toepfer
Senior Manufacturing Buyer: Alfred C. Dorsey
Printer and Binder: RR Donnelley & Sons Company
Cover Printer: Lehigh/Phoenix Color Corporation

For permission to use copyrighted material, grateful acknowledgment is made to the copyright holders acknowledged throughout the book, which are hereby made part of this copyright page.

Chapter opening image credits: p. 2, Jill Stephenson/Alamy; p. 3, Bob Daemmrich/Stock Boston; p. 32, Library of Congress; p. 33, Bob Daemmrich; p. 60, Austin History Center, Austin Public Library; p. 61, Bob Daemmrich; p. 98, Austin History Center, Austin Public Library; p. 99, Bob Daemmrich; p. 138, AP Photo; p. 139, David J. Phillip/AP/Wide World Photos; p. 176, Bettmann/Corbis; p. 177, Bob Daemmrich; p. 202, Library of Congress; p. 203, Mark Wilson/Getty Images; p. 230, Bettmann/Corbis; p. 231, Courtesy of the author

Library of Congress Cataloging-in-Publication Data
Keith, Gary.
 Texas politics and government / Gary A. Keith, Stefan D. Haag. -- 3rd ed.
  p. cm.
 Includes bibliographical references and index.
 ISBN 978-0-205-73460-3 (alk. paper)
 1. Texas--Politics and government--1951---Textbooks. I. Haag, Stefan D. II. Title.
 JK4816.H33 2010
 320.9764--dc22
                                                                  2008053588

Copyright © 2010 by Pearson Education, Inc.

All rights reserved. No part of this publication may be reproduced, stored in a retrieval system, or transmitted, in any form or by any means, electronic, mechanical, photocopying, recording, or otherwise, without the prior written permission of the publisher. Printed in the United States.

1 2 3 4 5 6 7 8 9 10—DOW—12 11 10 09

Longman
is an imprint of

www.pearsonhighered.com

ISBN-13: 978-0-205-73460-3
ISBN-10: 0-205-73460-X

To Jacqueline,
whose work in public health
is so affected by Texas politics, and
to Gabe and David,
whose choices in life will
similarly be influenced by Texas politics

Gary A. Keith

To my son, Jeffrey,
who shares my love for all things political

Stefan D. Haag

Contents

Preface xi

Analyzing Visuals xvi

CHAPTER 1 Ideas, People, and Economics in Texas Politics 2

Roots of Texas Politics and Government 5
- Native Americans 6
- Hispanics 8
- African Americans 9
- Asian Americans 10
- Anglos 11
- The Contemporary Population of Texas 11
  - Analyzing Visuals Texas Population Projections, 2010–2040 13

The Ideological Context 14
- The Texan Creed 14
  - Individualism 14
  - Politics Now Health Insurance in Texas 15
  - Liberty 17
  - Constitutionalism and Democracy 18
  - Equality 18
  - The Living Constitution Article 1, Section 3A, Texas Equal Rights Amendment 19
- Political Ideologies in Texas 20
  - Ideas into Action Students Protest an Immigration Policy 21
  - Libertarians 21
  - Populists 22
  - Conservatives 23
  - Liberals 23

The Economy of Texas 24
- Cotton 24
- Cattle 24
- Petroleum 25
- The Contemporary Economy 25

Join the Debate How Should Texas Educate Students of Limited English Proficiency? 26

Wealth and Poverty in Texas 28

Toward Reform: Political Culture and Welfare Reform 29

CHAPTER 2 Constitutionalism 32
Timeline: Texas's Constitutions 34

Roots of the Texas Constitution 35
- The 1836 Texas Constitution 35
- The 1845 Texas Constitution 36
- The 1861 Texas Constitution 37
- The 1866 Texas Constitution 37
- The 1869 Texas Constitution 38

The Current Texas Constitution 39
- Reasons for the 1876 Constitution 40
- Provisions of the 1876 Constitution 41
  - The Living Constitution Article 7, Section 1 43
  - Politics Now Wimberly ISD and School Finance 45
  - Analyzing Visuals Constitutional Amendments and Voter Turnout 46
- Criticisms of the 1876 Constitution 46

Constitutional Revision 48
- Piecemeal Revision Efforts 49
  - Ideas into Action Grassroots Engagement in the Amendment Process 50
- Comprehensive Revision Efforts 50
  - The 1974 Constitutional Convention 51
  - The 1975 Constitutional Amendments 53
  - The 1999 Constitutional Revision Effort 54

Toward Reform: The Marriage Amendment 55
Join the Debate Should Texas Adopt the Initiative Process? 56

CHAPTER 3 Voting and Participating: Political Parties, Interest Groups, and Elections 60

Roots of Political Parties, Interest Groups, Elections, and Campaigns in Texas 63

Political Parties in Texas 64
- Party Organization 64
  - Formal Organization 64
  - Functional Organization 67
  - Democratic Party Unity 67
  - Republican Party Unity 68
  - Party Effectiveness: What's at Stake? 68
- Party in the Electorate 70
  - Distribution of Party Attachments 70
  - Party Realignment in Texas 71
  - Contemporary Party Coalitions 72
- The Party in Government 72
  - In the Executive Branch 73
  - In the Legislative Branch 74
  - In the Judicial Branch 75

Interest Groups in Texas 75
- Types of Interest Groups 75
  - Business Groups and Trade Associations 75
  - Professional Associations 75
  - Labor Groups 76
  - Racial and Ethnic Groups 76
  - Public-Interest Groups 76
- Political Activities of Interest Groups 76
  - Lobbying 76
  - Electioneering 79
  - **Politics Now** Hefty Gift to Bailey has Craddick Ties 80
  - Litigation 81

Elections and Political Campaigns in Texas 81
- Types of Elections 81
  - Primary Elections 81
  - Special Elections 82
  - General Elections 82
  - Local Elections 83
- Political Campaigns in Texas 83
  - Money: The Mother's Milk of Politics 83
  - Media: Linking the Candidates and the Voters 84
  - Marketing: Selling the Candidate 84
  - **Ideas into Action** Blogging on Texas Politics 85
  - **Timeline:** Voting Requirements in Texas 86
- The Voters' Decisions 86
  - Voter Turnout 86
  - **The Living Constitution** Article 6, Section 1 88
  - **Join the Debate** Are Electronic Voting Systems Better Than Paper Ballots? 90
  - The Vote Choice: Parties, Issues, and Candidates 92
  - **Analyzing Visuals** Voter Turnout in Texas 93

Toward Reform: Recent Reforms in Elections and Campaigns 95

CHAPTER 4 The Legislative Branch 98

Roots of the Legislative Branch 101
- The State Constitution and the Legislative Branch of Government 102
  - **The Living Constitution** Article 3, Section 25 103
- Constitutional Provisions Affecting Legislators 104
  - Length of Terms 104
  - Temporary Acting Legislators 104
  - Compensation 104
- Sessions of the Legislature 105
  - **Timeline:** Redistricting and the Texas Legislature 106

Who Are the Members of the Legislature and How Do They Represent the Public? 106

Variables Affecting Members' Elections   106
    Redistricting   107
    Reelection Rates and Turnover of Membership   109
    Join the Debate   Would Nonpartisan Redistricting Produce Better (or Different) Results?   110
Personal and Political Characteristics of Members   110
    Occupation, Education, and Religion   111
    Gender, Race, and Age   113
    Political Party   113
    Ideology   114
    Ideology and Partisanship   114
    Analyzing Visuals   Ideological Voting Patterns in the Texas House of Representatives   115

How Is the Texas Legislature Organized?   116

Leaders   116
Committees   117
Organizing for Power and Influence in the Legislature   118
Leadership and Opposition in the House   119
    The Speaker's Race   119
    House Leadership and the Political Parties   120
    The Speaker's Influence Over Committees   120
    Politics Now   "Ghost Worker" Flap Renews Speaker's Feud with Critics   121
    House Opposition and the Political Parties   121
    Organizing in the House Through Nonparty Caucuses   122
Leadership and Opposition in the Senate   122
    The Role of the Lieutenant Governor   123
    Coalition Building in the Senate   123

How Does the Legislature Make Laws and Budgets?   124

What Is a Bill? What Is a Resolution?   124
Rules, Procedures, and Internal Government   124
How a Bill Becomes Law   124
    The House Calendars Committee   126
    The Senate Calendaring Function   126
    The Bill Reaches the Floor   127
    Two Bills Into One: The Final Stages   128
The Budgeting Process   129

How Do Legislators Make Decisions?   130

Growth of Legislative Staff   130
    Ideas into Action   Student Interns Learn Legislative Politics   131
Staffing for Technical Assistance, Specialized Information, and Political Assistance   131
Relations with Lobbyists   132
The Ethics of Lobbying   133

The Legislature and the Governor   133
Toward Reform: The Public and the Legislature   134

CHAPTER 5   The Governor and Executive Branch   138

Roots of the Executive Branch in Texas   141

From President of the Lone Star Republic to Governor of Texas   141
    The Living Constitution   Article 4, Section 14   142
Terms of Office   143
    Length and Number of Terms   144
    Salary   145
    Impeachment   145
    Succession   145

The Constitutional Roles of the Governor   146

The Development of Gubernatorial Power   146

Characteristics of Gubernatorial Power   147
Restriction of Governors' Powers   147
Comparing the Texas Governor with Other Governors   147
    Join the Debate   Should the Texas Governor Have a Cabinet?   148
The Governor's Power to Appoint Executive Officials   150
The Power of Staff and Budget   153

The Governor as Policy Maker and Political Leader   154

Public-Opinion Leadership   154
Relationship with the Legislature   154
    Analyzing Visuals   Ideology and Governors   155
Executive Orders   157

The Plural Executive in Texas   158

Attorney General   158
Comptroller of Public Accounts   159
Land Commissioner   160
Agriculture Commissioner   161
Railroad Commissioners   162
State Board of Education   163

Modern Texas Bureaucracy   164

Secretary of State   165
Public Utility Commissioners   166

Texas Commission on Environmental Quality 166
Insurance Commissioner 167
Health and Human Services Commission 167
Public Counsels 168
Boards and Commissions 168
> Ideas into Action Student Regents 169

Making Agencies Accountable 170
The Sunset Process 170
Staff Size and Pay 171
Regulating the Revolving Door 172
Regulating the Relationship Between Agencies and Private Interests 172

Toward Reform: Gubernatorial and Executive Power 173

CHAPTER 6 The Judicial Branch 176

Roots of the Texas Judiciary 179
> The Living Constitution Article 5, Section 1 180

The Structure of the Texas Judiciary 180
Local Trial Courts 182
County Courts 182
District Courts 183
Intermediate Courts of Appeal 184
The Supreme Courts 184

Judges and Judicial Selection 186
Judicial Qualifications and Personal Characteristics 186
Judicial Selection 187
> Join the Debate Should Texas Elect Its Judges? 188
> Analyzing Visuals Is Justice for Sale in the State of Texas? 190

The Judicial Process in Texas 192
The Criminal Justice Process 192
Arrest and Searches 192
Booking 193
Magistrate Appearance 193
Grand Jury Indictment 193
Arraignment 194
Pretrial Motions 194
Jury Selection 194
Trial 194
> Ideas into Action Defending Actual Innocence 195
Appeals 195

The Civil Justice Process 195
Pretrial Procedures 195
Trial 196
Appeals 196

Toward Reform: Changing the Texas Judiciary 196
Reforming the Court Structure 196
Reforming Judicial Selection 198
Reforming Judicial Campaign Finance 199

CHAPTER 7 Local Governments 202

Roots of Local Government in Texas 205
> Analyzing Visuals Texas Counties and Population 207

Counties 208
Structure of County Government 208
County Commissioners Court 208
> The Living Constitution Article 5, Section 18 209
District Attorneys and County Attorneys 210
Sheriff 210
County Clerk and District Clerk 210
Judges and Constables 211
County Tax Assessor-Collector 211
Treasurer and Auditor 211
Authority of County Governments 211
Finances of County Governments 212

Cities 213
> Join the Debate Should Texas Cities Be Allowed to Photograph Red-Light Runners? 214
Forms of City Governments 216
Weak Mayor-Council 216
Strong Mayor-Council 217
Council-Manager 217
City Commission 217
Authority and Functions of City Governments 218
Finances of City Governments 219
> Politics Now The Border Fence 220
Municipal Annexation 221
Politics and Representation in City Governments 222
> Ideas into Action Students Run for Local Office 224

Special Districts 224
Water Districts 225
School Districts 226

Toward Reform: Local Government and Politics in Texas 227

CHAPTER 8 Public Policy in Texas 230

The Roots of Public Policy in Texas 233

Public Policy Process, Actors, and Outcomes 234
  Policy Process 235
  Policy Actors 236
  Policy Outcomes 237

State Finance 237
  Budgeting and Borrowing 238
   The Living Constitution A Constitutional Cap on Welfare Spending 240
  Revenue 241
    Taxes 241
    Federal Funds 244
    Other Revenue Sources 244
    Level of Taxation 245
    Effects of the Texas Tax System on Individuals 245
  Spending 246
    Policy Areas of State Expenditures 246
    Spending Comparisons 247

Public Education and Higher Education Policy 248
  Public Education: Fulfilling Our Constitutional Mandate 248
    Structure of Elementary and Secondary Education 249
    School Finance: The Class of Economic and Social Policies 249
   Analyzing Visuals Public School Finance 251
  Educational Quality 252
  Higher Education: From Community Colleges to Universities 253
    Funding Colleges and Universities 253
    Access to Higher Education 254
   Ideas into Action The Texas Top 10 Percent Law 255
   Join the Debate Privatizing Public Assistance 256

Health and Human Services Policy 256
  The Federal–State Partnership 257
  Assistance for Food, Shelter, Clothing, and Protection 259
  Health Care 259
  The Adequacy of Health and Human Service Programs in Texas 260

Transportation Policy 261

Toward Reform: Changing Public Policies in Texas 263
   Politics Now Privatization and Texas Government 264

Notes 267

Glossary 281

Spanish Glossary 287

Index 291

Preface

John Steinbeck wrote that "*Texas* is the obsession, the proper study and the passionate possession of all Texans." It certainly is one of our passions as authors and teachers. The politics and government of Texas have not only fashioned much of the quality of civic life in the state, but have also influenced the direction of the nation as a whole. We hope, in our classrooms and in this textbook, to stir in students a healthy intellectual curiosity in all things Texan.

The national presence and profile of Texans during President George W. Bush's administration suggests that Texas has come of age and provides national political and policy leadership to match even Texas bragging rights. Yet, this prominence in national politics should not overshadow the rich past of Texas as a national political contributor, from Sam Houston through Colonel Edward House, Cactus Jack Garner, Jesse Jones, Sam Rayburn, Landslide Lyndon Johnson, Big John Connally, Jim Wright, Lloyd Bentsen, James Baker, and George H. W. Bush.

Though Texas has long been a part of the United States of America, its unique history, vast landscape, diverse population, border-state identity, and other aspects have combined to create a political culture that sets it apart from the rest of the nation. Texans who diverge from each other on characteristics such as ideology, ethnicity, income, and education nevertheless unite under a rallying sense of Texas pride. Texas lore is full of cowboys, oilmen, gutsy frontier women, and colorful political characters. Taken as a whole, Texans have, as the late Governor Ann Richards once remarked, been a little too rowdy for their own good.

We believe that understanding Texas's current socio-economic and political alignment as well as its prominence in national politics requires not only an analysis of what is happening now, but a clear view and comparison with what Texas has been. Thus, our subtitle, *Roots and Reform*, reflects the approach of this book as one that draws on history and contemporary political and governmental dynamics to provide that proper study that Steinbeck suggested.

Highlights of the Text

There is an ample measure of historical roots and significant reforms in Texas politics and government, and students will find numerous examples of the theme throughout the eight chapters of this book. Institutions that were created when Texas was a rural, agrarian state during the late nineteenth century have survived along with a constitution that was created for a society quite different from that of contemporary Texas.

There have also been numerous changes. We doubt that the framers of the 1876 Texas Constitution would recognize that document as it exists today with its more than 450 amendments, but it would not be totally foreign to them either. The continuity that has kept Texas moored to its roots would be evident to them, as would the changes that have been required to make government more relevant to the twenty-first century.

In the politics of Texas, reform is also compelling. At first glance, party competition seems to have been completely turned upside down over a century of change. Democrats ruled Texas from the 1870s to the 1970s with little opposition; today, Republicans are so dominant that no Democratic statewide officeholders were elected in 2002, 2004, 2006, or 2008. Yet, when one looks below the party labels to ideology, voting patterns, and voting outcomes, one finds a battle between a populist (and often lower-income) segment of the population and a business-affiliated, conservative segment of the population. This socio-economic cleavage happened between populists and Democrats in the late nineteenth century; it happened within the Democratic Party during its long period of hegemony; and it persists now in a new two-party configuration.

Each of this book's eight chapters, then, will take the historical roots of the topic covered and use them to illustrate the roots and the reform that Texans have seen over a century and a half. By understanding the time dimension and its influences on current politics, government, and policy, students should be better able to analyze for themselves what is happening in Texas politics now, and as it unfolds in the coming years.

Organization

We first examine the social, economic, and constitutional milieu in Texas, then proceed to the heart of its politics, examining political behavior through interest groups, parties, and voting. Next, we focus on governmental institutions, before concluding with a look at some of the outcomes of Texas politics and government, as evidenced in public policies. Each chapter begins with a vignette exploring a recent event, personality, or group related to the chapter's topic. We then lay the foundation for the reading by looking at the roots and historical development of that topic in Texas.

The first two chapters provide the context for a study of Texas politics and government. **Chapter 1:** Ideas, People, and Economics in Texas Politics discusses the various peoples of Texas (past and present), and the likely trends in population growth and change. It then explores the ideological context, which is essential to the examination of politics in later chapters. A look at the basic economic structure of Texas is next, and the chapter ends with a spotlight on the politics of wealth and poverty. **Chapter 2:** Constitutionalism begins with a brief march through the five constitutions from Texas's independence up to 1876. We lay out a lengthier examination of the politics that led to the 1876 adoption of the current constitution before highlighting its substance, then the dilemmas and problems caused by its statutory nature. Finally, we examine twentieth-century efforts, successful and unsuccessful, to revise the Texas Constitution.

Chapter 3: Voting and Participating: Political Parties, Interest Groups, and Elections combines the *institutions* and *dynamics* of political behavior. No analysis of Texas politics would be complete without a look at the system of one-party dominance for more than a century. We then investigate party organization, party in the electorate, and party in government. Parties' sister organizations, interest groups, are then highlighted, focusing on types of groups in Texas and their political activities. We then focus on the arenas closest to voting Texans: elections and campaigns, including campaign finance, voters' decisions, and voter turnout results.

The next four chapters present Texas's state and governmental institutions. **Chapter 4:** The Legislative Branch describes the roots of the legislature as a series of conclaves engaging the Mexican national government, followed by the Texas Congress and a series of constitutional conventions. The 1876 Constitution then put its stamp on the new Texas legislature, and we examine its structure, powers, pay, and biennial setup. Next, we look at legislative membership, how legislators organize politically, and the law-making and budgeting functions. Finally, we explore how legislators make decisions, including the role of the governor in legislative decision making. **Chapter 5:** The Governor and Executive Branch shows that the Texas governorship is rooted in the Spanish monarchical administration, then the presidency of the Lone Star Republic and the series of expansive constitutions after that. We examine the current constitutional roles of the governor and the slow redevelopment of power that had been stripped away by the original 1876 Constitution. We then describe the governor as policy maker and political leader. Next, we turn to the executive branch that serves alongside the governor, including the plural executive, the modern Texas bureaucracy, and how the legislature attempts to make bureaucracy accountable. **Chapter 6:** The Judicial Branch finds the Texas judiciary rooted in English and Spanish law. We describe the court structure, from local courts to the top appellate courts, and the judges who serve those courts. Next, we examine the debates over reforming the court structure and the judicial selection method. Finally, we outline the judicial process. The last institutional chapter is **Chapter 7:** Local Governments. In nineteenth-century Texas, rural government grew out of the Mexican establishment of districts and the American establishment of counties. For modern times, we look at the structure, authority, and finances of counties, cities, and special districts, then at the politics of local governance.

Once we have explored the context for *Texas Politics and Government,* then looked at the state and local institutions, we conclude the book with a look at what it all means to Texans. **Chapter 8:** Public Policy in Texas finds modern policy rooted in the populist and social welfare policy battles of the late nineteenth and early twentieth century. We then describe the policy process and who the policy actors are, and we put policy outcomes into their political-economy context. The chapter then details modern policy in the areas of state finance, education, health and human service, and transportation.

Features

Tables and figures provide up-to-date data throughout the book. Each chapter also contains a uniform set of features to provide additional depth, context, interest, and opportunities for critical thinking:

- *Roots of* and *Toward Reform* sections highlight the text's emphasis on the importance of the history of Texas politics and government, as well as the dynamic cycle of reassessment and reform that allows Texas to continue to evolve. Every chapter begins with a "Roots of" section that gives a historical overview of the topic at hand, and the chapter ends with a "Toward Reform" section devoted to a particularly contentious aspect of the topic being discussed.

- *What Should I Know About...* sections begin each chapter with a series of questions tied to major section headings. A *What Should I Have Learned?* section at the end of each chapter briefly summarizes the answer to each of the *What Should I Know...* questions.

- *Thinking Nationally,* a new feature, highlights Texas's differences from and commonalities with other states in the United States. Examples of this feature include a comparison of legislative and gubernatorial budget preparations in New York and Texas (in Chapter 4) and a comparison of the length of state constitutions (in Chapter 2).

- *Ideas into Action,* another new feature, discusses ways in which college students can become more involved in their government and communities. Some of the features focus on initiatives on Texas campuses; others relate to state and national-level issues. For example, Chapter 2 discusses the role that Angelo State University students played in a legislative attempt to revise the Texas Constitution.

- *Timelines* appear in selected chapters and provide students with a clear understanding of the development of key topics in Texas politics. For example, Chapter 3 includes a timeline devoted to voting requirements in Texas.
- *Politics Now* highlights reform through a focus on recent events. News articles about current political personalities or political developments are paired with critical thinking questions to allow students to learn more about Texas politics. For example, Chapter 4's *Politics Now* focuses on the controversy over "ghost workers" employed by members of the Texas Legislature.
- *Texas in Comparison* helps put Texas into perspective with its fellow large states. Using variables that measure the chapter's topic, this feature compares Texas with the other three largest states: California, New York, and Florida.
- *The Living Constitution* places the chapter topic into its Texas constitutional context by explaining a topical section, its intent, and how it affects Texas today. For example, Chapter 8 highlights the constitutional ceiling on welfare spending.
- *Analyzing Visuals* is a visual literacy exercise, with graphs, maps, charts, or cartoons that are accompanied by critical thinking questions that ask students to interpret the information provided. (See Analyzing Visuals: A Brief Guide, immediately following this Preface for more information about assessing visual information.)
- *Join the Debate* is a critical thinking exercise that asks students to compare and contrast opposing views of a controversial issue. The feature examines topics like the use of red-light cameras at intersections, which is debated in Chapter 7.
- *Key terms* with page references are provided in a list at the end of each chapter, and each term is also defined in the margin on the page where it is used and highlighted. Key terms are also listed in a glossary at the end of the text.
- *In the Library* sections list books that are relevant to key chapter topics.
- *On the Web* sections list Web sites that students can access to find more information on a chapter's main topics. For example, official Web sites of the Texas legislature are listed in Chapter 4.

The Ancillary Package

The ancillary package for *Texas Politics and Government: Roots and Reform* reflects the pedagogical goals of the text: to provide information in a useful context and with colorful examples. We have tried to provide materials that are useful for instructors and helpful to students.

Instructor's Manual/Test Bank: The Instructor's Manual portion offers chapter summaries, outlines, key terms, teaching suggestions, discussion topics, and Web activities that reflect recent news and political events. The Test Bank portion contains questions in multiple-choice, true-false, short-answer, and essay format, which address all levels of Bloom's taxonomy and have been both reviewed and class-tested for accuracy and effectiveness.

MyTest: This flexible, online test-generating software includes all questions found in the printed Test Bank.

Study Guide: Contains learning objectives, chapter summaries, key terms, and practice tests.

Digital Transparency Masters: These PDF slides contain all maps, figures, and tables found in the text. Available on the Instructor Resource Center.

Study Site: Online set of practice tests, Web links, and flashcards organized by major topics and arranged according to this book's table of contents. www.pearsontexasgovernment.com

Acknowledgments

We would like to thank Eric Stano at Longman for his constant encouragement and support over the years. Our students at the University of Texas, Austin Community College, the University of the Incarnate Word, and other places where we have taught have helped pique our interest in things Texan, hone our skills, and keep us on our toes.

We would also like to thank Rex Peebles, a colleague with whom we collaborated on an earlier book, and other colleagues who have helped enrich our understanding of politics. We are grateful to Karen O'Connor and Larry Sabato for their support on this and other publishing projects.

Finally, we wish to acknowledge our families—Jacqueline, Gabe, and David, and Patricia, Jeff, and Joel, and their integral roles in our writing as one small but important part of our broader lives.

We assume full responsibility for any errors in the textbook.

GARY A. KEITH
STEFAN D. HAAG

Analyzing Visuals

The information age requires a new, more expansive definition of literacy. Visual literacy—the ability to analyze, interpret, synthesize, and apply visual information—is essential in today's world. We receive much information from the written and spoken word, but much also comes from visual forms. We are used to thinking about reading written texts critically—for example, reading a textbook carefully for information, sometimes highlighting or underlining as we go along—but we do not always think about "reading" visuals in this way. We should, for images and informational graphics can tell us a lot if we read and consider them carefully. In order to emphasize these skills, *Texas Politics and Government: Roots and Reform* contains one Analyzing Visuals feature in each chapter. The features are intended to prompt you to think about the images and informational graphics you will encounter throughout this text, as well as those you see every day in newspapers and magazines, on the Web, on television, and in books. We provide critical thinking questions to assist you in learning how to analyze visuals. Though we focus on one visual in each chapter, we encourage you to examine carefully and ask similar questions of all the visuals in this text, and those you encounter elsewhere in your study of and participation in American government.

We look at several types of visuals in the chapters: tables, graphs and charts, maps, news photographs, and political cartoons. This brief guide provides some information about these types of visuals and offers a few questions to guide your analysis of each type.

Tables

Tables are the least "visual" of the visuals, and consist of textual information or numerical data arranged in tabular form, in columns and rows. Tables are frequently used when exact information is required and when orderly arrangement is necessary to locate and, in many cases, to compare the information. For example, a table presenting the requirements in terms of residency, minimum age, citizenship, voting status, and conflict of interest for Texas House and Senate members would make comparisons of the data visually accessible.

Here are a few questions to guide your analysis:

- What is the purpose of the table? What information does it show? There is usually a title that offers a sense of the table's purpose.
- What information is provided in the column headings (provided in the top row)? How are the rows labeled?

TABLE 4.1 Constitutional Requirements Affecting Texas Legislators

	Senate	House
Residency	5 years in Texas, 1 year in district	2 years in Texas, 1 year in district
Minimum age	26 years	21 years
Term of office	4 years	2 years
Citizenship	United States	United States
Voting status	Qualified (registered) voter	Qualified (registered) voter
Salary	$600 per month	$600 per month
Conflict of interest	Must disclose any personal interest in a bill; may not hold any other state office or contract	Must disclose any personal interest in a bill; may not hold any other state office or contract

Source: Texas Constitution, Article 3.

- Is there a time period indicated, such as January to June 2009? Or, are the data as of a specific date, such as June 30, 2009?
- If the table shows numerical data, what do these data represent? In what units? Dollars a special interest lobby provides to a political party? Percentages of men and women responding in a particular way to a poll question about the president's performance? Estimated life expectancy in years?
- What is the source of the information presented in the table?

Charts and Graphs

Charts and graphs depict numerical data in visual forms. The most common kinds of graphs plot data in two dimensions along horizontal and vertical axes. Examples that you will encounter throughout this text are line graphs, pie charts, and bar graphs. These kinds of visuals emphasize data relationships: at a particular point in time, at regular intervals over a fixed period of time or, sometimes, as parts of a whole.

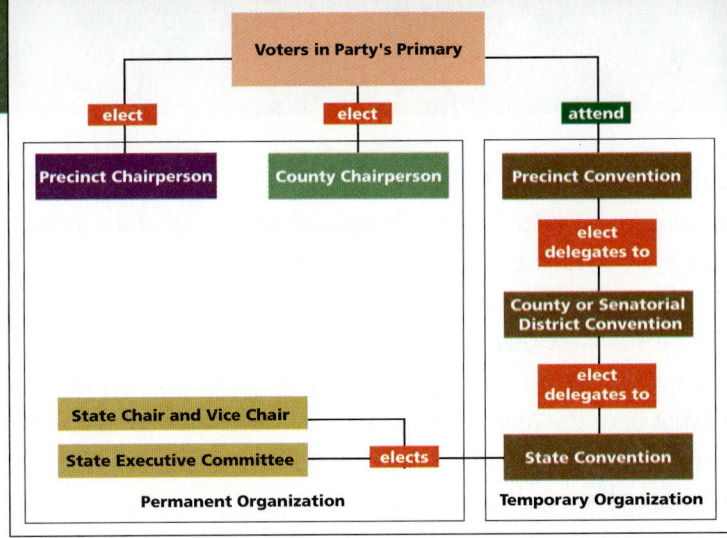

Line graphs show a progression, usually over time (as in Political Party Finances, 1979–2009). Pie charts (such as the distribution of federal civilian employment) demonstrate how a whole (total federal civilian employment) is divided into its parts (employees in each branch). Bar graphs compare values across categories, showing how proportions are related to each other (as in the numbers of women and minorities in Congress). Bar graphs can present data either horizontally or vertically.

Here are a few questions to guide your analysis:

- What is the purpose of the chart or graph? What information does it provide? Or, what is being measured? Usually a title indicates the subject and purpose of the figure.
- Is there a time period shown, such as January to June 2008? Or, are the data as of a specific date, such as June 30, 2008? Are the data shown at multiple intervals over a fixed period, or at one particular point in time?
- What do the units represent? Dollars a candidate spends on a campaign? Number of voters versus number of nonvoters in Texas? If there are two or more sets of figures, what are the relationships among them?
- What is the source? Is it government information? Private polling information? A newspaper? A private organization? A corporation? An individual?
- Is the type of chart or graph appropriate for the information that is provided? For example, a line graph assumes a smooth progression from one data point to the next. Is that assumption valid for the data shown?
- Is there distortion in the visual representation of the information? Are the intervals equal? Does the area shown distort the actual amount or the proportion?

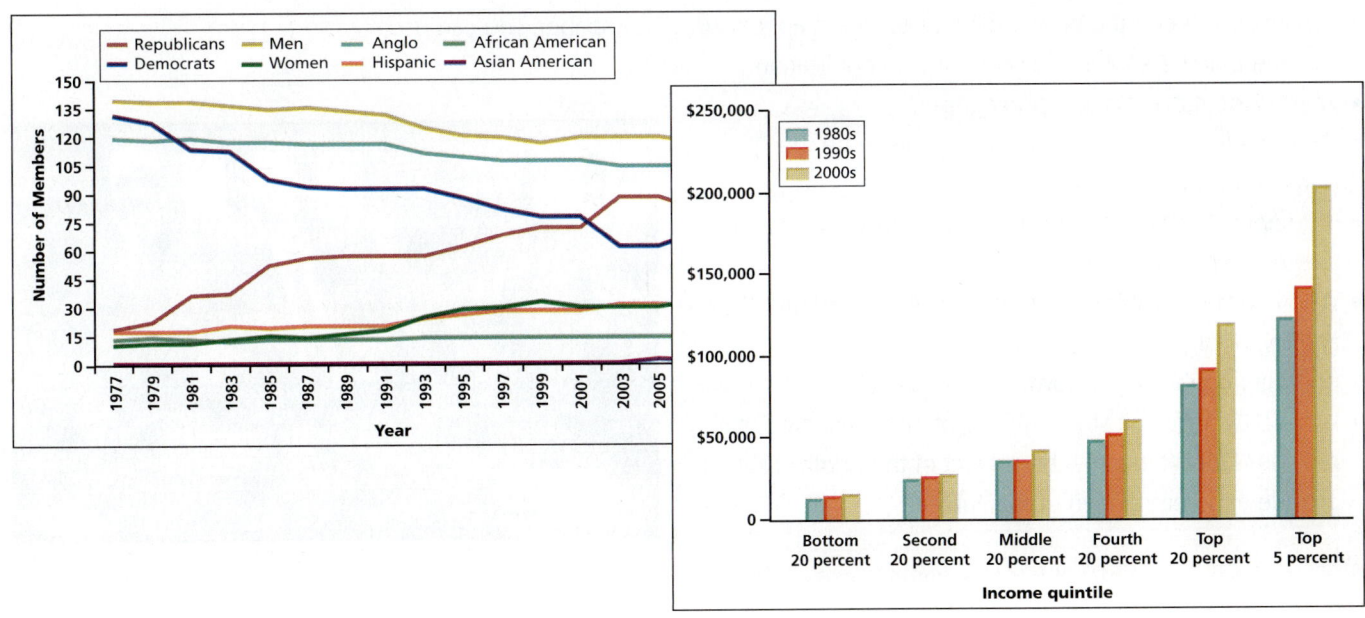

Maps

Maps—of the United States, of particular regions, or of the world—are frequently used in political analysis to illustrate demographic, social, economic, and political issues and trends.

Here are a few questions to guide your analysis:
- Is there a title that identifies the purpose or subject of the map?
- What does the map key/legend show? What are the factors that the map is analyzing?
- What is the region being shown?
- What source is given for the map?
- Maps usually depict a specific point in time. What is the point in time being shown on the map?

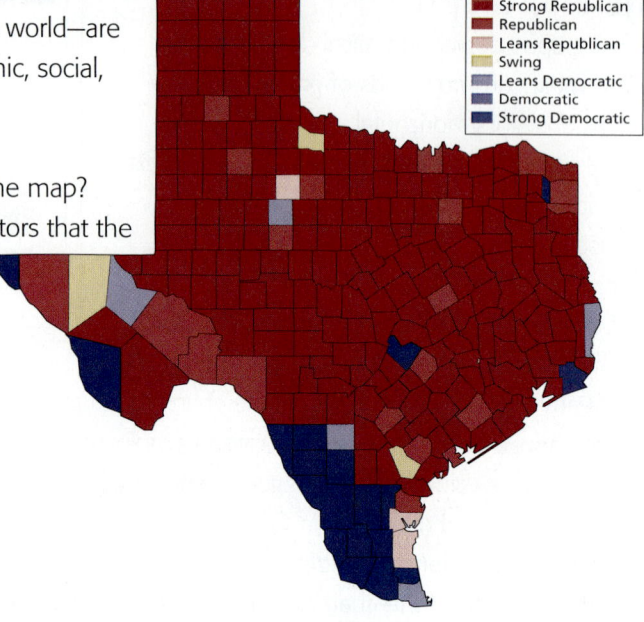

News Photographs

If a picture is worth a thousand words, it is no wonder that our newspapers, magazines, and television news broadcasts rely on photographs as well as words to report and analyze the news. Photos can have a dramatic—and often immediate—impact on politics and government. Think about some photos that have political significance. For example, do you remember photos from the September 11, 2001, terrorist attack on the World Trade Center? Visual images usually evoke a stronger emotional response from people than do written descriptions. For this reason, individuals and organizations have learned to use photographs as a means to document events, make arguments, offer evidence, and even in some cases manipulate the viewer into having a particular response.

Here are a few questions to guide your analysis:
- When was the photograph taken? (If there is no date given for the photograph in its credit line or caption, you may be able to approximate the date according to the people or events depicted in the photo. If the photograph appears in a newspaper, you can usually assume that the shot is fairly current with publication.)
- What is the subject of the photograph?
- Why was the photo taken? What appears to be the purpose of the photograph?
- Is it spontaneous or posed? Did the subject know he or she was being photographed?
- Who was responsible for the photo? (An individual, agency, or organization?) Can you discern the photographer's attitude toward the subject?
- Is there a caption? If so, what kind of information does it provide? Does it identify the subject of the photo? Does it provide an interpretation of the subject?

Political Cartoons

Political cartoons have a long history in America. Some of the most interesting commentary on American politics takes place in the form of political cartoons, which usually exaggerate physical and other qualities of the persons depicted and often rely on a kind of visual shorthand to announce the subject or set the scene—visual cues, clichés, or stereotypes that are instantly recognizable. For example, a greedy corporate executive might be depicted as an individual in professional clothing with paper currency sticking out of his or her pockets. In another cartoon, powdered wigs and quill pens might signal a historical setting. The cartoonist's goal is to comment on or criticize political figures, policies, or events. The cartoonist uses several techniques to accomplish this goal, including exaggeration, irony, and juxtaposition. A cartoonist might point out how the results of governmental policies are the opposite of their intended effects (irony), or two people, ideas, or events that don't belong together might be joined to make a point (juxtaposition). Because cartoons comment on political situations and events, you generally need some knowledge of current events to interpret political cartoons.

Here are a few questions to guide your analysis:

- What labels appear on objects or people in the cartoon? Cartoonists will often label some of the elements. For example, a building with columns might be labeled "Texas Supreme Court." Or, an individual might be labeled "senator" or "Republican."
- Study the cartoon element by element. Political cartoons are often complex. If the cartoon is in strip form, you also need to think about the relationship of the frames in sequence.
- Can any of the people shown be identified? Governors, well-known executive officials, and legislative leaders are often shown with specific characteristics that help to identify them. For example, George W. Bush has been portrayed with large ears and bushy eyebrows in many cartoons, and Ann Richards almost always sported a towering white hairdo. Rick Perry has perfectly coiffed hair, and Carole Keeton Strayhorn is usually depicted as grandmotherly or bearing yet another new last name.
- Can the event being depicted be identified? Historical events, such as the Alamo or contemporary events, such as the 81st legislature's regular session in 2009, are often the subject matter for cartoons.
- What are the elements of the cartoon? Objects often represent ideas or events. For example, a donkey is often used to depict the Democratic Party, and an eagle is often used to represent the United States.
- How are the characters interacting? What do the speech bubbles contribute to the cartoon?
- What is the overall message of the cartoon? Can you determine what the cartoonist's position is on the subject?

1 Ideas, People, and Economics in Texas Politics

The face of Texas is changing. By mid-2004, Anglos no longer constituted a majority of Texans for the first time since the early 1800s. As a result of immigration trends and differential birthrates among the larger minority ethnic groups in Texas—Hispanics, African Americans, and Asian Americans—Texas became a majority minority state (a state in which ethnic and racial minorities constitute a majority of the state's population), joining the states of Hawaii, New Mexico, and California. The changing Texas demographics will probably produce other changes—social, economic, and political—in Texas as well.

The demographic history of Texas involves growth, but the 1990s were exceptional for several reasons. First, the growth of Texas's population by nearly 3.9 million, about equally split between natural increase and immigration, was the largest

■ Texas encompasses a broad geography and wide range of people.

decade increase in population in the state's history. Second, the population growth occurred in all twenty-seven of Texas's metropolitan areas, in 73 percent of its counties, and in 74 percent of its towns and cities. Moreover, the greatest increase in population occurred in the state's large urban centers and in three regions of the state: along the Texas–Mexico border, along the central Interstate 35 corridor of Texas from Dallas–Fort Worth to San Antonio, and the Houston–Galveston area. Third, the population became even more ethnically diverse. During the 1990s, the Anglo population increased by only 7.6 percent, whereas the Hispanic population increased by 53.7 percent and the African American population increased by 22.5 percent. The most important ethnic change involves the Hispanic population, which was the single largest factor in Texas's population growth in the 1990s. Slightly more than 60 percent of the net population increase was a result of the growth in Hispanic residents. According to state demographer Steve Murdock, "For the State of Texas as a whole and pervasively across the state, population change has come to be increasingly determined by change in non-Anglo populations."[1] Finally, Texas's population, like the population of the rest of the United States, is aging, a result of increasing life expectancy and the aging of the Baby Boomers. Another aspect of age structure of the Texas population involves the relationship between youth and ethnicity.

WHAT SHOULD I KNOW ABOUT...
- the roots of Texas politics and government?
- the ideological context for Texas politics and government?
- how the economy of Texas evolved?
- how wealth and poverty in Texas affect Texas politics and government?
- how the context for Texas politics and government influences political culture and welfare reform?

Sixty percent of the Texas population younger than five years of age and 57 percent of the population younger than eighteen years of age are non-Anglos. Thus, issues related to the elderly involve significant numbers of Anglos, and issues related to children and adolescents involve significant numbers of Hispanics, African Americans, and Asian Americans.

> **TO LEARN MORE—**
> **—TO DO MORE**
> To learn more about the changing population of Texas, go to the Texas State Data Center at www.txsdc.utsa.edu/.

As these trends continue in the twenty-first century, what effects will the changing demography of Texas have on the economic, social, and political characteristics of Texas? During the first four decades of the twenty-first century, the labor force will grow significantly, especially for the non-Anglo segments of the population. With the changing ethnic composition and the aging of Texas workers, the Texas workforce will be less educated than in 2000, unless ethnic differences in education levels are addressed quickly. Demographer Steve Murdock states, "If differentials in the socioeconomic characteristics of the labor force do not change, the state's future labor force will be less well educated, less skilled, earn lower salaries and wages, and thus be in greater need of labor force training (with substantial associated costs)."[2]

Increases in the demand for education will also be substantial. Enrollment in public education institutions at all levels will increase by 79 percent by 2040, with most of the increase provided by Hispanic, African American, and Asian American Texans. Community college and university enrollments will also increase dramatically—by 102 percent and 82 percent, respectively. As a result, the cost of providing an education to Texans will increase substantially, as will the requirement for financial assistance for those attending the state's colleges and universities.

In human services, the changes in Texas's population produce an anticipated percentage increase in Temporary Assistance for Needy Families (TANF) recipients (149 percent), an even greater percentage increase in Medicaid recipients (182 percent), and the greatest percentage increase in food stamp recipients (221 percent). As the recipients increase, there is an associated cost to the state to meet the human services needs of Texans.[3]

These demographic, economic, and social changes will produce a form of politics that is different from what existed at the close of the twentieth century. They will also affect what it means to be a Texan.

What does it mean to be a Texan? The beliefs that Texans hold are a product of Texas's roots—its land, its people, and its history. The politics and government of a state are shaped by its inhabitants' ideas about politics and government, by the social and ethnic composition of its population, by its history, and by its economy. These factors, along with its constitution (see chapter 2) and its relationship with the national government, provide the context for politics and government, as well as the continuity and changes.

In this chapter, we describe the ideological, social, historical, and economic context for Texas politics and government. By placing Texas in context, we gain an appreciation for the unique characteristics of Texas politics and government as well as the characteristics shared with other states.

★ First, we will identify and describe *the roots of Texas politics and government*, focusing on the land and people of Texas and indicating how these people have historically influenced and continue to influence Texas politics and government.

★ Second, we will analyze *the ideological context* for Texas politics and government, noting how a set of ideas—shared with other Americans—has been modified by Texas's unique experiences. The ideological context focuses on a core set of ideas that motivate and shape Texas politics and government.

★ Third, we will examine *the economy of Texas,* focusing on the evolution of Texas's economy from a colonial, land-based economy to a modern, information-based economy.

★ Fourth, we will analyze *wealth and poverty in Texas*, indicating how the distribution of wealth and poverty influences politics and government in the Lone Star State.

★ ally, we will describe how the context for Texas politics and government affects *political culture and welfare reform.*

Roots of Texas Politics and Government

The roots of Texas politics and government are found in the early settlers of Texas and in the type of society and government they created. But, even before people inhabited Texas, there was the land. With an area of 267,339 square miles, Texas is larger than most nations and contains every major landform: mountains, plains, plateaus, and hills. West of the Pecos River, in far West Texas, are the Chisos and Davis mountains, a part of the Rocky Mountain chain. Plains constitute the major landform in Texas, covering much of West Texas, North Texas, the Gulf Coast, and northwestern Texas. The Edwards Plateau, in west central Texas, is the major plateau, or tableland, in Texas. Hills are found in many parts of Texas, but they are especially prominent in the German Hill Country, located northwest of San Antonio. The variety of landforms and the geographical size of Texas has an effect on its inhabitants, including their settlement patterns, voting behavior, economic activities, partisan proclivities, and their political ideas. Taming a land of such great size and variety is not accomplished easily, but many different peoples have tried.

Did you think that you were looking at the Grand Canyon? This is Palo Duro Canyon, which is located in the Panhandle and offers magnificent views that rival those of the Grand Canyon.

Photo courtesy: Laurence Parent

CHAPTER 1 Ideas, People, and Economics in Texas Politics

Is this lake the result of an earthquake? Located in East Texas, Caddo Lake, named for the Caddo Indians, was formed by the Caddo Dam in Louisiana. Prior to the dam's construction, Caddo Lake was one of the largest natural lakes in the South. Caddo Indian legend maintains that an earthquake created the lake when a Caddo chief failed to obey the Great Spirit.

Photo courtesy: Laurence Parent

With its nearly 24 million residents in 2007, Texas is the second largest state in population and in territory.[4] Texas's population is almost as diverse as its geography. Whereas the United States in 2006 was 66 percent Anglo, 15 percent Hispanic, 13 percent African American, and 5 percent Asian American, Texas in the same year was nearly 48 percent Anglo, 36 percent Hispanic, 12 percent African American, and 4 percent Asian American and others.[5] The Institute of Texan Cultures identifies twenty-seven ethnic groups in contemporary Texas. From the beginning, Texas's population was diverse. The first inhabitants, of course, were the American Indians, or Native Americans.

Native Americans

There are few Native American tribes in present-day Texas. However, from prehistoric times, Native Americans representing four different cultural traditions established permanent residence in Texas, and members of many more tribes and nations, some of whom are still present in Texas, were brief inhabitants.

In the coastal areas of the state and extending into all of South Texas, the Coahuiltecan and Karankawan tribes maintained an imperiled existence in a harsh environment by hunting and gathering. In central Texas, scattered bands of Native Americans, known contemporarily as the Tonkawa, established themselves during the 1500s. By the eighteenth century, they had become a buffalo-hunting, tepee-using, horse-riding Plains people. To the north of the Tonkawa were the ancestors of the Lipan Apache. Other Plains tribes associated with Texas in those early days were the Kiowa Apache, Kiowa, and especially Comanche.[6] The Jumano, related to the Puebloan culture of the American Southwest, were present from historical times, especially in the Rio Grande Valley from El Paso to the confluence of the Rio Grande and Mexican Rio Conchos. Spanish Fort on the Red River was the headquarters for a group of semisedentary tribes, known today as the Wichita, who extended to Waco in central Texas. The Wichita had much in common with the Caddo, but after their adoption of horses in the eighteenth century, their culture became more Plains-like.

TEXAS IN COMPARISON

The Socio-economic Context in the States

Texas in Comparison compares Texas with the three other most populous states—California, New York, and Florida—in terms of variables pertaining to the chapter's focus. California remains the nation's most populous state. The four largest states vary in the percentage of ethnic minorities, with Texas having the largest percentage of Hispanics and Florida having the largest percentage of African Americans. The four states also vary in poverty levels, with Texas having the largest percentage of population living below the poverty level and Florida having the smallest percentage below the poverty level.

	Resident Population (2007 estimate, in thousands)	African American Population (2006)	Hispanic Population (2006)	Population Below Poverty (2006)
Texas	23,904	11.7%	36.1%	16.9%
California	36,553	6..9%	34.6%	13.1%
New York	19,298	15.3%	13.4%	14.2%
Florida	18,251	16.0%	19.1%	12.6%

Sources: U.S. Census Bureau, *Population Estimates*, July 1, 2007; Texas State Data Center, *2006 Population Projections for the State of Texas*, 2000–2004 scenario, October 2006; U.S. Census Bureau, *Estimates of the Population by Race and Hispanic or Latino Origin for the United States and States*, July 1, 2006; U.S. Census Bureau, *2006 American Community Survey*, Percent of People Below Poverty Level in the Past 12 Months: 2006, Table R1701.

In eastern and northeastern Texas, tribes of Caddo, joined together in confederacies, possessed a complex culture built around intensive farming and agriculture.

The Native American legacy in Texas is substantial. The Caddo established economic and cultural patterns—involving farming, trading, and trotline fishing—on which subsequent inhabitants of Texas expanded. The Caddo also greeted early Spanish explorers as *Tayshas*, meaning "friends." The term was subsequently Hispanicized to *Tejas*, and then Anglicized to *Texas*. Similarly, the most feared and respected Native Americans in Texas, the Comanche, displayed many of the characteristics of individualism that Anglo Texans on the frontier most admired.[7] Also, their resistance to Anglo expansion forced the farmers and ranchers to become horsemen and to adapt to the challenges of existence on the frontier.

By the late 1800s, few Native Americans remained in Texas, a result of epidemics of diseases such as cholera and smallpox, military campaigns, and their forced removal to reservations in other states. Native Americans constitute a small percentage of Texas's population, and their political influence reflects their small numbers. Currently, there are only three Native American tribes on reservations in Texas: the Alabama-Coushatta in Polk County (in East Texas), the Kickapoo near Eagle Pass (in South Texas, on the Rio Grande River), and the Tigua near El Paso (in far West Texas). The oldest, the Alabama-Coushatta reservation, was established in 1854 as compensation for the tribe's neutrality during the war for Texas independence in 1836.

The Tigua first became embroiled in Texas politics when they opened their Speaking Rock Casino in 1993. In 1987, Congress recognized the Tigua, and in exchange, the tribe agreed to prohibit gambling in all forms and to obey Texas laws. Nevertheless, the tribe filed a lawsuit, which they lost, attempting to force the state to negotiate a casino compact with the tribe under the 1988 Indian Gaming Regulatory Act. In 1999, Texas Attorney General John Cornyn sought an injunction to halt gambling on tribal property. In 2001, a federal district court granted a permanent injunction against the tribe's casino and ordered it to close by November 30, 2001. The Tigua appealed his ruling and were allowed to keep the casino open during their appeals. In February 2002, the casino was forced to close.

Do Native Americans profit from gambling? Tigua Indians operated the Speaking Rock Casino until it was closed in 2002. When operating, the casino earned $60 million annually for the 1,200 members of the tribe, allowing them to build houses, fund social and health programs, and provide annual cash payments of $15,000 to each tribe member.

Other tribes in Texas have tried to establish gambling operations. In 1999, the Alabama-Coushatta tribe voted to bring gambling to its Texas reservation and opened a casino in November 2001. In July 2002, a federal district court ordered it to close. Currently, the only tribal gaming facility is the Kickapoo Lucky Eagle Casino in Eagle Pass. In 2007, the tribe received permission from the U.S. Interior Department to offer Class III games (slots, roulette, and black jack), but the U.S. Court of Appeals reversed the department's decision.

The desire for additional revenues to fund public education in Texas fueled efforts by Texas Native Americans to pressure the legislature to authorize video slot machines on their reservations. However, conservative religious groups opposed any additional gambling in Texas and garnered the support of a majority of legislators.

Hispanics

Spaniards explored Texas in the sixteenth century, but only by the early eighteenth century did they establish permanent settlements. An early colony in Nacogdoches was followed by a *presidio*, San Antonio de Bexar, and a mission, San Antonio de Valero, along the San Antonio River. A colony in La Bahia (Goliad) followed. Only in the 1740s and 1750s did Spaniards colonize the Rio Grande, although these were some of their most successful settlements.

The mainstays of Spanish colonization included four institutions: (1) the mission, which performed civilian as well as religious functions; (2) the *presidio*, which provided frontier defense; (3) the *rancho*, which sustained civilian life; and, (4) towns or civilian settlements. By the end of the eighteenth century, only about 5,000 *pobladores* (settlers) inhabited Texas.[8] Nonetheless, their legacy far exceeds what their numbers suggest. They created a culture that valued "egalitarianism, a sense of duty, and a respect for physical prowess and gallantry in the face of adversity."[9] They also provided cultural norms for ranchers, sheep herders, and goat raisers. In addition, Spanish legal traditions, such as those pertaining to women's property rights, endured, as did customs protecting debtors.[10]

After Mexico's independence from Spain in 1821, Mexican colonialization of Texas was no more successful. In 1836, when Texas became an independent republic, no more than 7,000 or 8,000 Spaniards, Christianized Native Americans, and *mestizos* (people of mixed European and Native American ancestry) resided in Texas. In 1850, the U.S. Census revealed a Hispanic population of only 14,000—less than 7 percent of Texas's population. As late as 1887, the state census counted only 83,000 Hispanics, only 4 percent of the Texas population. Concentrated in the border counties along the Rio Grande, Hispanics were outnumbered even by German Americans. However, between 1890 and 1910, a major influx of Mexicans occurred, resulting in a doubling of the Hispanic population of 1887. Between 1910 and the 1980s, the Hispanic population in Texas grew tenfold, caused largely by an explosive birthrate in Mexico and the steady industrialization of Texas. During the late 1940s, Hispanics displaced African Americans as the largest ethnic minority in Texas.[11]

By 2007, Hispanics had achieved considerable political clout in Texas. In that year, there were 2,170 Hispanic elected public officials in Texas, more than in any other state. With Railroad Commissioner Tony Garza's appointment as U.S. ambassador to Mexico, Victor G. Carrillo was appointed to fill Tony Garza's seat on the Railroad Commission. In 2004, Carrillo was elected to a full term on the Railroad Commission, and Governor Perry appointed

Is this the first Hispanic governor of Texas? Rafael Anchía, (far right) currently a Democratic member of the Texas House, could, according to *Texas Monthly* chief political editor Paul Burka, become the first Hispanic governor of Texas before the end of the next decade.

What do the Texas courts want from the Texas legislature? Texas Supreme Court Chief Justice Wallace B. Jefferson delivers his State of the Judiciary address to the Texas legislature.

David Medina, his general counsel, to the Texas Supreme Court to fill the vacancy created when Justice Wallace Jefferson was appointed chief justice of the Texas Supreme Court. In 2007, 36 Hispanics served in the Texas Legislature, 271 were county officials, 595 were municipal officers, 402 held judicial and law enforcement posts, 807 served on elected school boards, and 52 were special district officials.[12]

In 2007, almost all Hispanic elected officials (97 percent) were Democrats. However, the Republican Party made a concerted effort to attract Hispanic voters in recent elections, appealing to Hispanics' desires for educational advancement, personal responsibility, and economic opportunity.[13]

African Americans

African Americans have inhabited Texas since Spanish rule but probably made up no more than 12 percent of the population in Texas prior to 1836. This was due to the Mexican government's opposition to slavery, and most early settlers in Texas came from the southern mountain states, where slavery was less common. In the late 1830s, however, an influx of African Americans accompanied Anglo planters from coastal southern states. With slavery legalized in the Republic of Texas, the number of African Americans increased rapidly, composing 20 percent of the population by 1840. The growth of the African American population in Texas was effectively halted by the Civil War. Between 1865 and 1880, only 6 percent of immigrants were African American, and the percentage of African Americans has continued to decline since 1865, the year in which nearly one-third of Texas's population was African American.[14]

The bulk of the settlement by African Americans in Texas occurred between 1836 and 1865. The states that contributed the largest number of slaves were Alabama, Virginia, Georgia, and Mississippi, and the area of greatest settlement for African Americans lay east of a line connecting Texarkana and San Antonio. This was also the area dominated by Anglos from the lower South. By 1860, thirteen Texas counties had African American majorities. All of these counties were located along the major rivers of eastern and southeastern Texas, especially the lower Brazos, Colorado, and Trinity Rivers. After emancipation, African American freedpeople remained in that area; consequently, in 1887, twelve counties had African American majorities. However, with the decline of the sharecropper system, African Americans abandoned the rural areas of East Texas for the urban centers that were closest to the old plantation districts—Houston and Dallas. In 1930, only four counties had African American majorities, and by 1980, there were none.[15]

African Americans in Texas held fewer elected offices in 2001 than they did in 1993.[16] In 2001, 460 African Americans held elective office, but because the number of African American elected officials in other states increased, Texas dropped from fifth highest to ninth highest among the states in number of African American elected officials. Among the elected officials, two African Americans were U.S. Representatives, two were state senators, fourteen were representatives, twenty were county officials, 282 were municipal officials, forty-four were judicial or law enforcement officials, and ninety-five were elected to school boards and other elected education positions. In early 2009, three African Americans (all Republicans)—Railroad Commissioner Michael Williams and Texas Supreme Court Justices Wallace Jefferson and Dale Wainwright—held statewide elective offices. Williams was appointed to the Railroad Commission in 1998 to fill the position vacated by Carole Keeton Rylander, who was elected comptroller in 1998. In 2000 Williams won the remainder of Rylanders term, and in 2002 and 2008, he won reelection to the commission. Governor Perry appointed Jefferson to the Texas Supreme Court in 2001, and Jefferson and Dale Wainwright were elected to the court in 2002. In 2004, Perry appointed Jefferson chief justice of the Supreme Court, and he won the unexpired two-year term in 2006 and a full term in 2008. Wainwright was reelected in 2008.

Among the prominent African American politicians in Texas is former Dallas Mayor Ron Kirk. In November 2001, Kirk resigned as mayor and later won the Democratic Party's nomination for U.S. senator, but he lost the general election. Houston Democrat Sylvester Turner served as speaker pro tempore during the 78th, 79th and 80th Legislatures. African Americans selected to chair House committees in the 80th Legislature included Helen Giddings (D–Dallas), Harold Dutton (D–Houston), Joe Deshotel (D-Beaumont), and Ruth Jones McClendon (D-San Antonio).

Asian Americans

The first permanent resident Asian Americans in Texas were probably Chinese immigrants who arrived in Houston in 1869 to clear land for the Houston and Texas Central Railway. Chinese laborers also worked for the Southern Pacific Railroad and the Texas and Pacific line during the 1870s and 1880s. In the early 1900s, a distinguished Japanese businessman, Seito Saibara, was invited to the United States to help develop the rice industry on the Gulf Coast. In 1903, Harris County officials invited him to start a colony in Webster, just south of Houston. Saibara bought 304 acres and began bringing families from Japan. Several Japanese colonies were subsequently established in the Rio Grande Valley and in Orange County. During the 1970s, thousands of Vietnamese immigrants came to Texas when the South Vietnamese government neared collapse and ultimately fell to North Vietnam.

In 2000, there were 562,319 Asian Americans in Texas, primarily of Vietnamese, Chinese, Indian, Filipino, Korean, and Japanese ethnicity. The larger cities in Texas contain Asian neighborhoods. In Houston, which has the largest Asian American population, there are two Chinatowns: an historic district near the George R. Brown Convention Center and a newer area on Bellaire Boulevard. In fact, a number of small malls, many along Bellaire, have signs in Chinese, Japanese, Vietnamese, and other Asian languages. In 2003, few Asian Americans held elective political office in Texas. The offices held were mostly at the county or municipal level.[17] Martha Wong, longtime community activist, served on the Houston city council from 1993 until 1999 and won election to the Texas House in 2002 and in 2004. She was the first Asian American woman elected to the Texas legislature. In 2002, Linda Yew Chew won election as a district court judge in

Do Asian Americans inhabit particular neighborhoods in Texas's cities? In Houston, Bellaire Boulevard hosts signs in Chinese, Japanese, Vietnamese, and other Asian languages.

Photo courtesy: John Everett/The Houston Chronicle

El Paso and was reelected in 2006. In 2006, El Paso county court at law judge M. Sue Kurita was also reelected. Jennifer Kim was elected to the Austin city council in 2005. In 2004, Hubert Vo was elected to the Texas House, narrowly defeating veteran Representative Talmadge Heflin. Vo was reelected in 2006 and 2008.

Anglos

As the term is used in Texas, **Anglos** are non-Hispanic whites. During the early period of Anglo settlement in Texas, 1815 to 1836, the Anglo immigrants to Texas were predominantly upper Southerners from Tennessee, Kentucky, Arkansas, and North Carolina. By 1820, these people had firmly established themselves in northeast Texas. During the 1820s, the *empresario* program of the Mexican government, which granted land to contractors who promised to bring settlers, drew additional upper Southerners to the Austin, DeWitt, and Robertson colonies in south central Texas. Missouri, Kentucky, Tennessee, and Arkansas provided most of these settlers.

In the southeastern border area of Texas, known as the Atascosita District, Anglos began drifting in after 1819. These settlers were lower Southerners, mostly poor whites from Louisiana, Mississippi, and Alabama.

North of the Big Thicket, between the Trinity and Sabine Rivers, a few small Anglo settlements developed. Most of these settlers were upper Southerners, although many slave-owning planters were attracted by the fertile Redlands area. Thus, by 1836, more than 60 percent of Anglos in Texas were from the upper South, about 25 percent were from the lower South, and about 10 percent were New Englanders.[18]

From Texas's independence to the Civil War, Anglo immigration increased, drawing more heavily from the lower South. The legalization of slavery in the Texas Republic resulted in the first major wave of lower Southerners, primarily from Alabama, Georgia, Mississippi, and Louisiana. According to the 1850 Census, lower Southerners had become almost as numerous as the upper Southerners. The two groups, however, occupied different areas of Texas. Most of eastern and southeastern Texas was successfully settled by lower southern planters, and the continuing waves of upper Southerners were directed to the western interior of Texas.

In the post–Civil War period, upper and lower southern immigration continued in roughly equal proportions. The western expansion to the New Mexico border by 1880 was primarily an achievement of upper Southerners, who settled most of West Texas, and lower Midwesterners (Illinois, Kansas, and Iowa), who dominated the upper Panhandle.

Anglos have dominated politics and government in Texas since its independence from Mexico in 1836. Since statehood, Anglos have provided all of Texas's governors and lieutenant governors, almost all of its statewide elected officials, an overwhelming majority of its legislators, and almost all of the members of its administrative boards and commissions. However, the changing composition of Texas's population presages a likely challenge to the Anglo dominance in politics and government.

Anglos
Non-Hispanic whites.

The Contemporary Population of Texas

The patterns of settlement established by Texas's first residents are still evident today, providing a measure of continuity, but new patterns are emerging as Texas becomes more heavily populated, more urbanized, and more diverse ethnically. The 2000 Census tallied 20,851,820 residents of Texas. The previous census, in 1990, revealed that Texas's population had grown faster than the population of the United States, although slower than its growth during the 1970s. Also, whereas more than half of Texas's growth during the 1970s was the result of net in-migration (immigration minus emigration), over two-thirds of Texas's growth during the 1980s was due to natural increase (internal population growth). Furthermore, the migration of the 1980s was primarily from other nations, not from other U.S. states. By 1994, Texas's population size had surpassed New York's, making Texas the second most populous state in the nation. Between 1990 and 2000, Texas added nearly 3.9 million people to its population. Texas's population growth during the period was the result of natural increase (50 percent) and immigration from other states (30 percent) and from other nations (20 percent). By 2007, Texas's population had increased by 3.1 million since the 2000 Census and, according to estimates, is expected to increase by as much as 4.3 million by the next census in 2010. This balance between the components of population growth combined with a relatively constant rate of growth through natural increase makes continued population growth in Texas likely.[19]

The urbanization of Texas also continued during the 1990s. The rural population of Texas had fallen to 14 percent by 2000 and fell to 12.8 percent by 2006. Despite the rural image frequently associated with Texas, a majority of Texans have lived in urban areas since the 1940s. In 2000, Texas had twenty-seven metropolitan areas, ranging in size from Victoria, with 84,000 people, to Houston, with 4 million people. During the 1990s, the twenty-seven metropolitan areas accounted for 91 percent of Texas's population growth. The fastest-growing metropolitan areas are in Texas's central core (Austin–San Marcos grew by 48 percent, Dallas by 31 percent, Houston by 26 percent, and Fort Worth–Arlington by 25 percent) or are located along the border with Mexico (McAllen–Edinburg–Mission grew by 48 percent, Laredo by 45 percent, and Brownsville–Harlingen–San Benito by 29 percent). Central Texas and the lower Rio Grande Valley area were the fastest-growing regions of Texas during the 1990s.[20] Three Texas cities (Houston, San Antonio, and Dallas) are among the ten most populous cities in the United States. Since 2000, population growth in Texas has been even more concentrated in the state's central cities and suburban areas, especially in the regions incorporating Dallas–Fort Worth, Houston–Galveston, Austin–San Antonio, and the Texas border from Brownsville to Laredo.[21]

Probably the most important demographic change in Texas between 1990 and 2000 involves the ethnic composition of the population. Texas's minority populations have increased much more rapidly than the Anglo population. Hispanics, the largest minority group, made up 32 percent of the population, increasing by 54 percent during the decade. African Americans, who composed about 11.5 percent of the population, increased by 23 percent. In 2000, Anglos, who still constituted a majority with 52.4 percent of the population, increased by less than 8 percent.[22] However, population estimates for Texas indicate that Anglos ceased to be the majority in 2004, and population projections predict that sometime before 2015, Hispanics will probably outnumber Anglos in Texas. (To learn more about Texas's population, see Analyzing Visuals: Texas Population Projections, 2010–2040.)

Anglos lost their majority status, and as Hispanics become the principal ethnic group, politics and government will definitely change, but political scientists disagree on the effect of the changes. First, most political analysts agree that Hispanics will enjoy greater political clout in Texas. In partisanship, Hispanics are more likely to be Democrats than Republicans (in Texas, Democrats outnumbered Republicans by a two-to-one margin in party identification among Hispanic voters). Nevertheless, in the 2004 presidential election in Texas, George W. Bush increased his percentage of the Hispanic vote, according to exit polls.[23] The one Hispanic group that did strongly support Bush in 2004 was evangel-

Should this city be in New Mexico? El Paso is the fifth largest city in Texas. Located on the western edge of the state, the city is geographically and culturally closer to New Mexico than it is to Texas.

Photo courtesy: Jerry Woodhouse/Getty Images

Analyzing Visuals: Texas Population Projections, 2010–2040

Study the chart depicting population projections for Texas based on data by the Texas State Data Center.

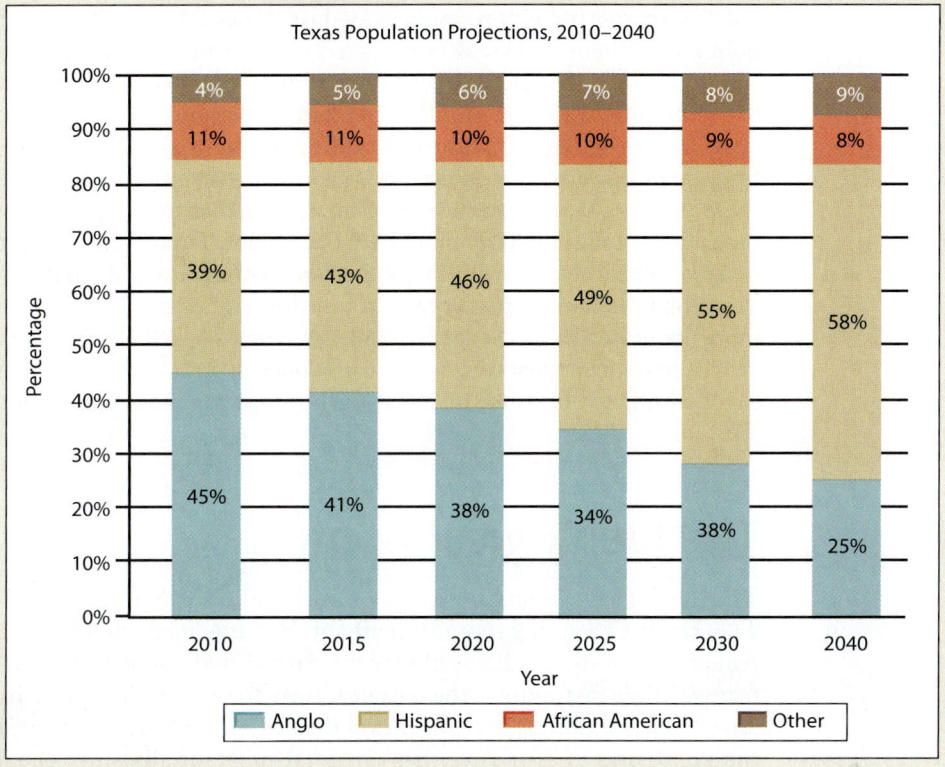

Answer the following questions relating to the population projections:

WHY are the Hispanic and Other population categories increasing in percentage?

WHY are the Anglo and African American population categories decreasing in percentage?

WHAT changes to political agendas, public policy, and partisan control are likely to accompany these population changes?

Source: Texas State Data Center, *2006 Population Projections for the State of Texas*, 2000–2004 scenario, October 2006, www.txsdc.utsa.edu/tpepp/2006projections/2006_txpopprj_txtotnum.php.

---

ical Christians. However, many Hispanics, who were formally or informally excluded from the political process prior to the application of the Voting Rights Act to Texas in 1975, are likely to claim no partisan affiliation or an attachment to some other party.[24]

In ideology, Hispanics in the United States are more likely to identify themselves as conservatives or moderates than as liberals. In terms of the public agenda, Hispanics are more likely than Anglos to mention social issues than economic issues. There is also a difference in how Hispanics approach certain issues. For example, in education, Hispanics want more schools, smaller classes, and more cultural sensitivity. Interestingly, the social issues that Hispanics rarely consider important are abortion, family values, and the death penalty.[25] In policy positions, Hispanics tend to be conservative in terms of government's responsibility for housing, jobs, and income; on abortion; on capital punishment; and on some aspects of language policy. Among the social issues, Hispanics are most concerned about crime, drugs, assistance for the elderly, and responding to prejudice and discrimination. The most important economic issue for Hispanics is jobs. Although self-identified conservatives, Hispanics are willing to pay more taxes for an expanded government role in combating crime, preventing drug abuse, providing public education, increasing health care and child care, and protecting the environment. This is especially true for Hispanic Texans.[26] Furthermore, government is viewed positively by Hispanics as a problem solver in society.[27]

Given the policy preferences of Hispanics and presuming an increase in their political influence, several policy changes can be anticipated. The tax structure in Texas, which takes 11.4 percent of the income of poorest Texans (incomes less than $15,000 annually) and only 3.2 percent of the income of richest Texans (incomes greater than $304,000 annually), will likely be revised to become less regressive.[28] State spending for elementary and secondary education will probably increase, given the need for a better-educated workforce. Furthermore, spending on health care will probably increase. In 2006, more than 5.7 million Texans were without health insurance, making Texas the state with the highest uninsured rate in the nation (24.5 percent), and Texas had the highest percentage of uninsured children (22 percent) in 2006 (To learn more about health insurance, see Politics Now: Health Insurance in Texas).[29]

In subsequent chapters, we return frequently to the topic of Texas's people; however, we now shift our focus to the ideological context for Texas politics and government.

The Ideological Context

The ideological context for Texas politics and government centers on a Texan Creed. The Texan Creed incorporates many of the same ideas that were influential for other Americans: individualism, liberty, constitutionalism, democracy, and equality. The features that distinguish the Texan Creed from the ideas held by other Americans arise from the unique historical experiences of Texas and Texans, especially between the 1820s and 1880s. Texas has changed substantially since the late 1800s, but the repetition of the prior historical experiences, whether mythical or not, keeps the creed alive and perpetuates it in each new generation. Consequently, we first explore how these experiences have shaped the five ideas of the Texan Creed.

The Texan Creed

Texan Creed
A set of ideas—primarily individualism and liberty—that shape Texas politics and government.

The **Texan Creed** consists of a set of ideas that identify Texans and provide the basis for their politics and government. For a majority of Texans, there is a consensus on the importance of the five ideas of the Texan Creed. Contemporary Texas is more heterogeneous than nineteenth-century Texas, but the ideas that were established during that century are still important today. Among the five ideas, individualism holds a special place for most Texans.

individualism
The belief that each person should act in accordance with his or her own conscience.

INDIVIDUALISM For most Americans, **individualism,** which stresses the primacy of the individual conscience as the basis for behavior, is the product of seventeenth-century Protestantism. Historian T. R. Fehrenbach cites individualism as the reason that early Anglo settlers came to Texas in the first place:

> The early Texans descended from clans and families, heavily Scotch Irish, who deserted the panoply of Europe, despising its hierarchies and social organism. . . and who plunged into the wilderness. These folk sought land and opportunity, surely—but they were also consciously fleeing something: a vision of the world in which community and state transcended the individual family and its personal good.[30]

Coming to Texas in the late eighteenth century, these people created a society dedicated to individualism. According to the ideal, the individual is responsible for the

POLITICS NOW

Source: Temple Daily Telegram
August 27, 2008

Health Insurance in Texas

Texas leads nation in people without health insurance

BY JANICE GIBBS | MEDICAL WRITER
PUBLISHED: AUGUST 27, 2008

Texas continues to lead the nation in the number of residents without health insurance, according to a report released Tuesday by the U.S. Census Bureau.

Between 2005 and 2007 the average percentage of uninsured in Texas was 24.4 percent. By contrast, 8.3 percent of Hawaii's and Massachusetts' population were uninsured during the same period.

Other states with sizable Hispanic populations also had percentages of uninsured closer to that of Texas. Arizona has 19.6 percent uninsured, California has 18.6 percent uninsured and New Mexico's uninsured rate is 21.9 percent.

Texas, with its large Hispanic population and the lower-than-average income of people with Hispanic surnames and origins, continues to have a high poverty rate, said Dr. James Rohack, director of Scott & White's Center for Healthcare Policy and president-elect of the American Medical Association.

The number of uninsured dropped from 47 million to 45.7 million nationwide; however that number is disproportionately Hispanic, and will remain so as long as the poverty level of Hispanics remains high, Rohack said.

The official poverty rate in 2007 was 12.5 percent, not statistically different from 2006, according to the Census report.

The poverty rates of non-Hispanics were statistically unchanged, while the poverty of Hispanics rose from 20.6 percent in 2006 to 21.5 percent in 2007.

According to the Census report, 17.6 percent of children living in poverty are uninsured, compared to 11 percent of all children. By race and origin, 7.3 percent of white children are uninsured, compared to 20 percent Hispanic.

Education is the key and plays a role in whether a person can get a job that provides insurance or can achieve an income level making health insurance affordable, Rohack said.

The percentage of the uninsured over the past 20 years has increased from 13 to 15 percent, not all that significant until the increase of population is factored in, Rohack said.

"The number of warm bodies that are uninsured becomes much higher," he said. "Twenty years ago, 19 percent of children were covered by the government. Now the number is up to 31 percent."

The extremely poor qualify for Medicaid, but Texas Medicaid is not all that generous, hence the high number of uninsured children compared to northeastern states with more liberal coverage of children, Rohack said.

Between 6 and 8 percent of the uninsured choose not to get health insurance, he said.

There are tax incentives for businesses to provide health insurance for its employees, but there are none for the individual, Rohack said.

According to recent data, 80 percent of uninsured children live in a household where one of the adults have insurance, which highlights the fact that if that person wanted to buy insurance for his family there would be no tax break, he said.

Since a large segment of the population works for employers who don't provide health insurance, the tax code should change to provide breaks for those looking at purchasing individual coverage, Rohack said.

Discussion Questions:

1. According to the article, why does Texas have the largest number of uninsured residents? Is the number of uninsured Texans an issue of concern? Why or why not?
2. What role, if any, should the state government have in providing health care to Texans? Is adequate health care a right of all U.S. citizens? Why or why not?

---

benefits that she or he receives in life and in the hereafter. In reality, the feeling for the soil that these Texans developed created the society. For Texans, land possesses both a symbolic and a practical meaning. During the nineteenth century, Texans created a social environment in which every person, whether dirt farmer or rancher, could be a landowner, independent and supreme over his or her "country." The landowners' ethos remains in contemporary Texas, a legacy of early Texas individualism. For most Texans, the landowner remains the ideal and is accorded the highest social status.[31]

The individualism created in Texans' attachment to the land was nurtured by the frontier experience. For most Americans, the frontier era was short lived, lasting usually no more than a decade. Civilization advanced rapidly. For Texans, however, the **frontier era** lasted four decades (1830s to 1870s) and involved three distinct challenges: a battle with Mexico for cultural and political dominance, a more dangerous conflict for survival with a Native American population, and a struggle to conquer a difficult land. The frontier era had an enormous impact on Texans.

frontier era
The period when Texas constituted a border between American civilization and an area inhabited by a hostile, indigenous population.

CHAPTER 1 Ideas, People, and Economics in Texas Politics

Are these the good guys or the bad guys? During the 1800s, battalions of Texas Rangers, such as the one pictured here, provided law enforcement on the frontier.

Texas Rangers
A mounted militia formed to provide order on the frontier.

For Texans, the most dangerous frontier was the western, Native American frontier. By 1834, Texan colonists had placed themselves within range of the Comanche. Previous wars between Native Americans and Anglos followed a common pattern: Anglo encroachment engendered Native American retaliation, which incited a military response that subdued the Native Americans. The Plains Indians, such as the Comanche, were not stationary, agricultural peoples. They were nomads who followed the bison herds over the seemingly boundless prairie. They avoided contact with Anglo settlers, except for raids on established settlements. Thus, the conflict involved an Anglo farming population and powerful, warlike Native Americans who held a decided advantage in military tactics, weapons, and mobility. The Comanche were never numerous, but they were defending their territory from intruders and their raids exacted a terrible toll. As historian T. R. Fehrenbach notes, "Between 1836 and 1860, 200 men, women, and children were killed each year by Indians on the Texas border; between 1860 and 1875 at least 100 died or were carried off annually. The trek through central Texas cost seventeen white lives per mile."[32]

In order to survive on the frontier, Anglo farmers and ranchers had to adapt. They became true horsemen, they learned to survive in Native American country, and they adapted their agriculture to raising stock. The most important adaptation, however, involved frontier defense—the creation of the **Texas Rangers,** a mounted force of armed volunteers. Companies of Texas Rangers date from Austin's colony, having been formed as early as 1823. However, only after Texas independence was their presence significant. Characterized as an early state police, the rangers were in reality unique. The state authorized the rangers as a mounted militia, a paramilitary organization, which the state assisted when it could—usually not often. The rangers were composed of farmers and ranchers threatened by the native population; they were young, adventuresome, courageous volunteers. Though the rangers were less numerous than their enemies, they quickly found that the best defense was to attack, dominate, and subdue. Though moral and ethical questions surround their tactics, few have questioned their success in seeking out their enemies' weakness and then attacking it without mercy. These characteristics and the use of Samuel Colt's revolving pistol, which gave each ranger the firepower of six, enabled the rangers to subdue their enemies.[33] However, as Fehrenbach admits,

> The Rangers never halted all the lawlessness and violence, of course, and the Army, not they, waged all the final campaigns against the Indians. . . . But Texans applauded their efforts. . . . For Rangers, born of the frontier, embodied many of the bedrock values of the frontier. They were brutal to enemies, loyal to friends, courteous to women, kind to old ladies; they never gave up, claiming that no power on earth could stop the man in the right who kept "a-coming." These were male values, warrior values.[34]

The final contribution to individualism came from the cowboy, who experienced the closing of the frontier and its way of life. Similar to the ranger in many of his values, the cowhand adopted a semifeudal notion of loyalty to his boss and brand, taken from the Mexican cattle-ranching culture. To herd half-wild cattle over thousands of miles required physical courage, but not recklessness. However, no respectable cowboy backed away from a fight that was forced upon him.[35] In all its manifestations, individualism has produced in Texans "a hard pragmatism and absence of ideology, a worship of action and accomplishment, a disdain for weakness and incompetence, and a thread of belligerence—and finally, a natural mythology stemming from the Alamo."[36] (The Alamo is discussed in the next section on liberty.)

LIBERTY Closely related to individualism and nearly as important to the Texan Creed is the idea of liberty. For most Americans, liberty is a product of the eighteenth century's Age of Enlightenment, with its emphasis on natural rights, the social contract, and a limited role for government. Complementing individualism, **liberty** ensures that a person's inherent rights are free from government infringement. For Texans, a passion for liberty has additional sources: it was the reason for Texas's revolt against Mexico and the battle for the Alamo.

The decision by Texans to declare their independence from Mexico in 1836 had many causes, but the most important ones involved Mexico's attempts to exert greater control over Texas and Texans. Perhaps the cultural differences between the Anglo settlers and their Mexican governors were such that conflict was inevitable. However, Stephen F. Austin's leadership had enabled the settlers to avoid involvement in domestic Mexican factional disputes for many years. Minor problems—religious requirements imposed on the settlers and Mexican opposition to slavery—offered potential areas of greater conflict, but a more serious concern involved the lack of an adequate local government through which the settlers could exercise a voice in the administration of their own affairs and the maintenance of order.[37] This grievance and Mexican suspicions of Anglo motives led the Mexicans to ban further immigration in 1830 and, two years later, to enforce the collection of tariff duties. In response to these Mexican actions, the colonists dispatched Stephen F. Austin to request separate statehood for Texas and other reforms. Until 1835, Texans considered themselves loyal Mexican citizens and were attempting to uphold the principles of the liberal, federal Mexican constitution of 1824. Only when the futility of such a position became evident were the "Texians," as they called themselves, willing to revolt against Mexico itself.[38]

In October 1835, Mexican President Antonio López de Santa Anna replaced the federal constitution of 1824 with the *Siete Leyes* (the "Seven Laws"), which established a centralized government under the president's control. The *Siete Leyes* signaled the end of republicanism in Mexico, converted the states into departments under the central government, and replaced the elected governors with appointed ones. At the same time, Mexican troops took up positions in Texas. When Mexican troops attempted to take a cannon in Gonzales, a skirmish ensued, and Texians prepared for war. A summons to arms in 1835 appealed to the Texians: "Fellow citizens, Your cause is a good one, none can be better; it is republicanism in opposition to despotism; in a word it is liberty in opposition to slavery. You will be fighting for your wives and children, your homes and firesides, for your country, for liberty."[39] With the adoption of this declaration, Texas established the right to revolution and laid the foundation for its subsequent government.

More than any historic event, the loss of **the Alamo** exemplifies Texans' passion for liberty. The Alamo, a former Spanish mission in the heart of San Antonio, once separated Mexican forces from Anglo settlements. In February and March of 1836, Lieutenant Colonel William Barret Travis and his band of about 180 volunteers fought to their deaths there against a Mexican army of more than 5,000. The Alamo defenders lost the battle, but historian Joe Frantz contends that they "set the stage for ultimate Texas unification and victory"[40] and created a legacy that inspires and defines Texans more than a century and a half later. Over the years, fact and legend have intertwined so that the real story of the Alamo is impossible to discover. However, the true story is unimportant, for the power of the Alamo as a symbol of Texan independence and liberty transcends any measure of the truth. To a significant degree, the importance of the Alamo is embodied in the statements and the alleged actions of its heroes: David Crockett, William Barret Travis, and Jim Bowie.

Upon his arrival in Texas in 1836, David Crockett was administered the oath of allegiance by Judge John Forbes, who was forced to pause during his reading. Crockett had "noticed that he was required to uphold 'any future government' that might be established. That could mean a dictatorship. He refused to sign until the wording was changed to 'any future *republican* government.' "[41] Similarly, when he reached the Alamo, Crockett, noted for his verbal excesses, announced that "all the honor that I desire is that of

liberty
The belief that government should not infringe upon a person's individual rights.

the Alamo
A San Antonio mission that was defended by Texans during their war for independence.

defending as a high private, in common with my fellow citizens, the liberties of our common country."⁴² For Crockett and others of his generation, the defining historical event was the American Revolution. To these men, the similarities between the American Revolution and the revolt by Texans were overpowering.

William Barret Travis, the youthful commander of the Alamo, probably best exemplifies the ideal of individual liberty and freedom. In his appeal for assistance, which was addressed "To The People of Texas & All Americans in the World," Travis pledged never to surrender or retreat and called on Americans everywhere "in the name of liberty, of patriotism & everything dear to the American character, to come to our aid."⁴³ In a letter to a friend, Travis explained his stand at the Alamo: "he felt the spirit of the times—the conviction that liberty, freedom and independence were in themselves worth fighting for; the belief that a man should be willing to make any sacrifice to hold these prizes."⁴⁴

Whether Travis really drew a line in the dirt is disputed. Nevertheless, his speech in which he gave his men three choices—surrender, escape, or fight to the end—is a cornerstone of the Alamo legacy. Travis urged his men to fight with him, but he left the choice to each individual. Aware that no reinforcements were coming, all but one man crossed the line, choosing to fight and die with Travis. Jim Bowie, confined to a cot by typhoid-pneumonia, allegedly said, "Boys, I am not able to go to you, but I wish some of you would be so kind as to remove my cot over there."⁴⁵

Who were the heroes of the Alamo? The Alamo Cenotaph, erected on Alamo Plaza in 1939, honors the heroes of the Alamo. At the east panel, depicted in the photo, are statues of James Bowie and James Bonham. Statues of William Barret Travis and David Crockett stand in front of the west panel.

The symbolic power of the Alamo reaches all Anglo Texans, regardless of political ideology. To a conservative, the Alamo symbolizes rugged individualism on the frontier and the need to defend liberty. A liberal sees in the Alamo the struggle for a sense of community, justice, and civil liberties.⁴⁶ Both visions offer insight into Texas and its politics. For *Tejanos* (native Hispanic inhabitants of Texas), the Alamo is an ambiguous symbol. Although Texas independence was the result of an alliance between Anglos and *Tejanos*, who played a crucial role, the ambivalence that *Tejanos* feel "stems from . . . the long use of the Alamo as an everyday symbol of conquest over Mexicans, as a vindication for the repressive treatment of Mexicans."⁴⁷

Tejanos
Native Texans of Mexican descent.

constitutionalism
Limits placed on government through a written document.

CONSTITUTIONALISM AND DEMOCRACY Texans grant nearly equal status to the ideas of **constitutionalism** and democracy. Perhaps Texans give a slight edge to constitutionalism because of its greater harmony with the dominant values of individualism and liberty. Following a tradition established in the United States, Texas has, for each of its governments, adopted a formal, written constitution, which clearly and distinctly limits the authority of government. (To learn more about one limit on government's authority, see The Living Constitution.) In fact, from their first constitution in 1836, Texans created what historian T. R. Fehrenbach considers a "state that did not and could not plan society—they saw this as an immoral intrusion upon personal liberty—and in fact had almost no control over society in general."⁴⁸ Further support for the connection between constitutionalism and liberty is seen in the inclusion, in all of Texas's constitutions, of an extensive Bill of Rights (we will examine the constitutions of Texas and their provisions in detail in chapter 2). Texans' desire for democracy was reflected in their commitment to creating an Athenian or Jeffersonian democracy—that is, a male, slave-owning democracy of property holders.

equality
The belief that all individuals should be treated similarly, regardless of socio-economic status.

EQUALITY The idea of **equality** that developed in Texas during the nineteenth century was a product of the social system. Although there were substantial differences in social and economic statuses of Anglo males, no rigid social or political hierarchy existed. The

The Living Constitution

Equality under the law shall not be denied or abridged because of sex, race, color, creed, or national origin. This amendment is self-operative.

ARTICLE 1, SECTION 3A, TEXAS EQUAL RIGHTS AMENDMENT

In 1957, the Texas Federation of Business and Professional Women launched a fifteen-year campaign to get a Texas Equal Rights Amendment (ERA) proposed by the Texas legislature. In 1971, the group sought the assistance of a lobbyist and the support of women legislators, and their efforts finally succeeded. The amendment was ratified by Texas voters in 1972. Of the fourteen amendments on the ballot that year, the Texas ERA received the largest majority, nearly 80 percent of the vote. In 1973, women legislators took advantage of the amendment to push laws to halt discriminatory practices. Laws that prohibited sex-based discrimination in processing loan and credit applications and prevented husbands from abandoning and selling homesteads without their wives' consent were passed. In 1974, Texas Attorney General John Hill, citing the amendment, struck down laws restricting the hours that women could work. During the 1975 legislative session, a coalition of women's organizations successfully lobbied the legislature when groups attempted to rescind the Texas ERA.[a] Although one scholar argued that the amendment added nothing to the protections of "equal rights" found in the Fourteenth Amendment to the U.S. Constitution and section 3 of the Texas Constitution,[b] the Texas Supreme Court has viewed the amendment differently.

In the first case involving the Texas ERA—*In re McLean*—the Texas Supreme Court established a three-pronged test for cases alleging a violation of the Texas ERA. First, the court had to decide whether equality under the law had been denied. If it had, the ERA's language required the court to determine "whether equality was denied because of a person's membership in a protected class of sex, race, color, creed, or national origin." If the court concluded that equality was denied because of a person's membership in a protected class, the challenged action violated the ERA unless (and this is the third prong) it was narrowly tailored to serve a compelling governmental interest.[c] In essence, the Texas Supreme Court elevated sex discrimination to the strictest scrutiny.

In 1993, three physicians and three clinics filed suit in an Austin district court on behalf of all low-income women in Texas. The suit challenged the Texas Medical Assistance Program (TMAP), which provides public funds for abortions for Medicaid recipients only when the pregnancy is the result of rape or incest or endangers the life of the mother. The plaintiffs argued that a number of conditions may be caused or aggravated by pregnancy and that as a result, women were being denied medically necessary treatments. Men, they noted, had all medically necessary conditions treated under Medicaid. In the Texas Supreme Court opinion, issued in December 2002, the majority stated that although equality of the law had been denied, the reason for the unequal treatment of women was not because of their sex but because the Texas legislature would only cover those treatments for which the state would be reimbursed by the federal government. Because Congress has refused to reimburse states for abortions since the passage of the Hyde Amendment in 1976, the Texas legislature declared it would not fund abortions for Medicaid recipients.

In 1998, John Geddes Lawrence and Tyron Garner were arrested, convicted, and fined $200 in Houston for sodomy. On appeal to the 14th Texas Court of Appeals, Lawrence and Garner argued that since the law prohibited sexual acts only

(continued)

between individuals of the same sex, it violated the Equal Rights Amendment. In 2000, a three-judge panel ruled in favor of Lawrence and Garner and declared the Texas sodomy law unconstitutional. In 2001, however, the full 14th Texas Court of Appeals voted 7–2 to reverse the three-judge panel, declaring that the Texas sodomy law applied both to males and females and did not violate the Equal Rights Amendment. Subsequently, the Texas law was overturned by the U.S. Supreme Court as a violation of the U.S. Constitution's Fourteenth Amendment.[d] Other issues under this amendment will surely arise in the future.

CRITICAL THINKING QUESTIONS

1. Do you agree with the Texas Supreme Court that the TMAP does not violate the Texas ERA? Why or why not?
2. Do you agree with the 14th Court of Appeals that the Texas sodomy law did not violate the Texas ERA? Why or why not?

[a] Sherilyn Brandenstein, "Texas Equal Rights Amendment," *Handbook of Texas Online*, www.tsha.utexas.edu/handbook/online/articles/TT/mlt2.html.
[b] George D. Braden, *The Constitution of the State of Texas: An Annotated and Comparative Analysis*, vol. 1 (Austin: Texas Advisory Commission on Intergovernmental Relations, 1977), 19–20.
[c] *In re McLean*, 725 S.W.2d Tex. (1987).
[d] *Lawrence v. Texas*, 539 U.S. 558 (2003).

commitment to social and political equality reflected a society based on land ownership, and land was a plentiful commodity. However, the equality accorded Anglo males did not extend to other members of the society. For non-Anglos, the inequality was palpable and perverse. Historian T. R. Fehrenbach describes slavery for African American Texans as "a system of the entrepreneurial exploitation of labor for profit, based on a law and society that was explicitly racist, in that the servitude of black people was justified by their racial inequality with whites."[49] The end of slavery was followed by the legal segregation of African Americans. Though no longer supported by law, there are still, in many areas of contemporary Texas, two societies—one Anglo and one African American, separate and unequal. The Anglo response to Hispanics has been similar, and Mexican Americans have been subjected to segregation and discrimination as well.

The Texan Creed is similar to the American Creed. According to political scientist Samuel Huntington, the **American Creed** consists of five ideas—individualism, equality, liberty, constitutionalism, and democracy—that provide Americans with a national identity, limit government authority, and are the foundation for American politics.[50] Like the American Creed, the Texan Creed provides the ideas that are the foundation for politics and government. Though similar to the American Creed, the Texan Creed has been shaped by historical events to place more emphasis on individualism and liberty than does the American Creed. If the Texan Creed is to endure, it must be transmitted from generation to generation, and Texans make a concerted effort to ensure its transmission.

As people acquire additional knowledge about politics and government, there is a growing need to organize that information and make it meaningful. For those who are most involved and active in politics, it means the development of a political ideology. A political ideology is a consistent set of beliefs and attitudes concerning the scope and purpose of government. People who adhere to a particular ideology are called ideologues.

Political Ideologies in Texas

Politics involves conflicts over different ideas about the proper scope and purpose of government. If everyone agreed about what government should do and to what extent it should do it, there would be no need for politics. However, there is limited agreement and extensive disagreement. The Texan Creed allows different conceptions of government's role. Some people may want the government to regulate individual behavior so that greater liberty is enjoyed by all; others may claim that the individual's right should be supreme and absolute. For example, for some Texans, the law that required motorcyclists to wear protective helmets infringed unnecessarily on individualism in the interest of the general welfare. Similarly, some people may want government to promote equal rights and protections for all immigrants, regardless of their

American Creed
A set of ideas that provide a national identity, limit government, and structure politics in America.

Ideas Into Action

Students Protest an Immigration Policy

During the spring of 2006, students from Texas high schools in Dallas, Houston, and Austin participated in protests against proposed U.S. House of Representatives legislation that would make illegal immigration a felony. School districts reacted swiftly to student walkouts by enacting policies that would charge students as truant or suspend or expel them if they continued to miss classes in order to participate in protests.

The protest organizers were aided by modern technology. Students communicated with fellow students through e-mails, postings on blogs, and text messages. The purpose was to organize quickly and efficiently.

"It's a very, very potent form of communication," University of Houston communications professor Garth Jowett said. "In a matter of minutes, literally, they can get a crowd to assemble some place within half an hour, of tens of thousands of people, simply by everybody text messaging five people."[a]

Immigration policy remains a heated topic in Texas and throughout the United States. In January 2008, the National Network for Immigrant and Refugee Rights held its first national conference in ten years. Composed of members of more than 250 community, religious, labor, civil rights, and legal organizations, the group defends the rights of all immigrants and refugees, regardless of their status as documented or undocumented immigrants. Meanwhile, interest groups such as the Federation for American Immigration Reform (www.fairus.org) continue to push for caps on immigration and tougher penalties related to illegal immigration.

Should these students be expelled for skipping school? Protestors in Houston demonstrate against proposed federal legislation that would have criminalized undocumented workers.

- Were high school students justified in skipping classes to participate in the protests? Were high schools justified in penalizing the students who chose to participate? What punishment, if any, was justified in response to students' participation in the demonstrations?
- Communication technology has made political protests and demonstrations easier to organize and implement. Does this dilute the meaningfulness of protests and lessen their impact on the public officials protestors are trying to influence?
- Should undocumented immigrants have the same rights and liberties that documented immigrants receive?

Go to these websites to learn more about immigration and immigration policy:

- The U.S. Immigration and Naturalization Service
  www.uscis.gov/portal/site/uscis
- Immigration Data page at the U.S. Census Bureau
  www.census.gov/population/www/socdemo/immigration.html
- An immigration issue guide from Public Agenda, a nonpartisan opinion research and civic engagement organization www.publicagenda.org/issues/frontdoor.cfm?issue_type=immigration

[a]"Technology Key to Promoting Immigration Protests," Click2Houstin.com, www.click2houston.com/technology/8335647/detail.html.

---

legal status (To learn more about student protests, see Ideas into Action: Student Immigration Protests), whereas others may want government to lower the number of immigrants allowed into the United States.

Figure 1.1 illustrates the kinds of conflict that occur in Texas concerning the proper role of government. The choices that a person makes on these issues indicate his or her idea of the scope of government (how much government should do) and the purpose of government (what goals are legitimate for government). Those choices also determine the person's political ideology: libertarian, populist, conservative, or liberal.[51]

LIBERTARIANS Libertarianism is "a highly individualistic extension of classical liberalism. . . . Libertarians emphasize very strongly the autonomy of the individual and the minimal role required of government."[52] Compared to conservatives, who view

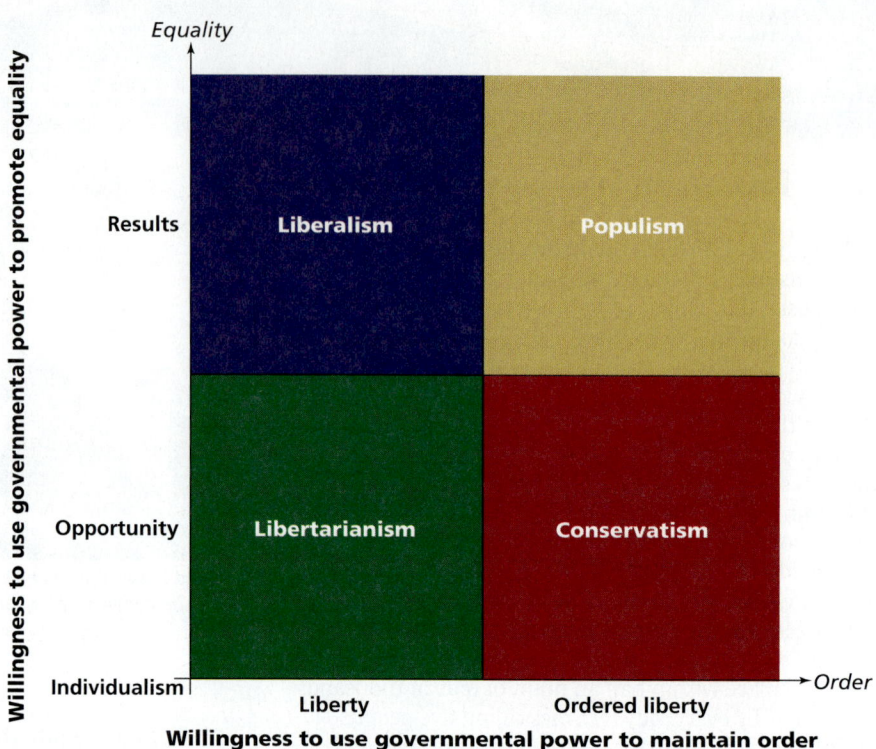

FIGURE 1.1 **The Four Ideologies** The axes represent people's attitudes concerning the use of government to achieve certain goals. The horizontal axis represents a person's willingness to use governmental power to limit personal freedoms in order to maintain order. The vertical axis represents a person's willingness to use governmental power to promote equality. Each ideology reflects a choice between conflicting values. For example, liberals oppose the use of governmental power to limit personal freedoms in order to maintain order, but support the use of governmental power to promote equality over protecting personal freedoms. On the other hand, conservatives support the use of governmental power to maintain order over protecting personal freedoms and support the protection of personal freedom over the use of governmental power to promote equality. Libertarians support the protection of personal freedom over the use of governmental power either to promote equality or to maintain order. Populists support the use of governmental power to maintain order and to promote equality over the protection of personal freedom.

government as a necessary evil, libertarians see government as an evil, limiting the ability of individuals to make choices and achieve their own destinies. In Texas, Libertarian Party candidates have been on the ballot for statewide and local offices since 1980. In most contests, however, the candidates received only 3–5 percent of the vote. The party has never elected a member to state office, and most voters, even if they share the libertarian ideology, consider the Libertarian Party either too extreme or unable to win against a major party candidate. However, this lack of support for the Libertarian Party's candidates is not a valid measure of the support for the ideology.

POPULISTS In contrast to libertarians, **populists** favor government intervention both to promote equality and to establish or maintain an ordered liberty. Populists support the greatest scope of government action. Populism swept the nation in the 1880s and 1890s, becoming one of the largest social movements in American history. Texas has a strong populist tradition. Started in Comanche County by Thomas Gaines in 1886 as a protest against its Democratic Party's leaders, the People's Party led the political struggle for the ideas promoted by the Farmers' Alliance. The fundamental value championed by the People's Party was the equality of humankind. The view was incorporated in the Farmers' Alliance slogan: "Equal rights to all, spe-

populists
People who support the promotion of equality and of traditional values and behaviors.

cial privileges to none." Despite the supposed equality of humans, the People's Party noted that certain economic inequalities existed in America, which placed a burden on all working people and most especially on the agricultural classes. These inequities had to be eliminated, and this could only be accomplished with the assistance of the government's power. Thus, the People's Party sought government intervention to regulate or, if necessary, to control the economy. The economic issues of greatest concern to the populists involved land, transportation, and money.[53]

Concerning the conflict between individualism and an ordered liberty, the People's Party showed less tolerance for diversity and individual choice in matters of morality. The People's Party had a strong Protestant religious flavor and drew few converts in counties where African Americans, Mexican Americans, and foreign-born residents were numerous. The populist movement was essentially a native Anglo movement, which was unsuccessful with foreign-born Texans and ignored Mexican Americans. For example, Germans, who were courted by the populists, viewed the movement as anti-alien, anti-Catholic, anti-liberal, and prohibitionist.[54] The Populist Party no longer nominates candidates for public office, but populism persists to this day as an ideology in Texas.

CONSERVATIVES Conservatives believe that government should not promote equality, but they support government regulation of individual behavior in order to ensure an ordered liberty. The contradiction that conservatives exhibit in terms of the scope of government action can be explained by American conservatism's view of human nature. According to this view, humans are selfish, flawed by original sin, and in need of moral guidance. Thus, American conservatism believes in the necessity for moral principles to guide human behavior and allows government, through legislation and other devices, to apply those principles. Similarly, doubts about the capabilities of humans lead to a reluctance to allow government tampering with natural economic and social laws. Despite their opposition to government intervention in the economy, contemporary conservatives recognize the value of some forms of economic promotion and regulation. This concession to government involvement in the capitalist economy by contemporary conservatives has forced some traditional conservatives to abandon conservatism in favor of libertarianism.

In contemporary Texas, self-identified conservatives are prominent in both of the major political parties and both state and local government, as well as the population generally.[55] Economic issues have provided the basis for Texas conservatism. Conservatives view government programs to provide public services as unnecessary and anti-capitalist. However, some of Texas's most intense confrontations historically have involved the use of government authority to protect traditional values—for example, the prohibition of alcohol in the early 1900s and restrictions on abortions in the 2000s. Increasingly, in Texas as well as in other states, conservatives are joined by libertarians in battles that involve government's regulation of the economy.

LIBERALS Liberalism favors a government that uses its authority to promote equality but that leaves an individual free to make moral or personal decisions. Modern liberalism in Texas is traceable to the effects of industrialization and the economic and social dislocations associated with it. The events that define modern American liberalism are the Great Depression, which promoted the use of government authority to limit the economic effects of dramatic swings in the business cycle, and the civil rights movement, which promoted the use of government authority to ensure equality for all elements of society. While favoring government's promotion of economic, political, and social equality, modern liberals oppose government infringement on each individual's freedom to make personal choices on moral issues, such as the

Thinking Nationally
Conservative and Liberal Cities

According to a study of American cities by the Bay Area Center for Voting Research, the five most conservative cities in the United States in 2005 were Provo, Utah; Lubbock, Texas; Abilene, Texas; Hialeah, Florida; and Plano, Texas. The five most liberal cities in the United States were Detroit, Michigan; Gary, Indiana; Berkeley, California; Washington, D.C.; and Oakland, California.

- What geographic and demographic differences distinguish the conservative cities from the liberal cities?
- What political and governmental differences separate the conservative cities from the liberal cities?

decision by a woman to terminate a pregnancy. In Texas, liberals have always constituted a minority of the population.

We revisit the ideologies frequently in subsequent chapters. For now, understanding the ideologies in Texas is important for two reasons. *First, most issues in Texas politics are expressed in terms of a preference either for individualism or for an ordered liberty or in terms of a preference either for equality or for individualism.* Almost every political issue in Texas politics can be viewed as a conflict over ideas in the Texan Creed. For example, the conflict over affirmative action programs involves the ideas of individualism and equality. As Figure 1.1 illustrates, the choices are usually between individualism and equality or between individualism and social order. Furthermore, although only a small fraction of Texans are ideologues, they are the ones who frame the political debates over issues. They are the most sophisticated and active people politically. Understanding the bases for their views helps you understand political discussions and the positions of the participants and, if you are so inclined, allows you to join in.

Second, most people in Texas have ideological tendencies. Most Texans are not ideologues, but they do hold consistent attitudes in a general policy area, such as social policy or economic policy. Most political debates play to these tendencies because political activists realize that this is how most people organize their political information.

As political scientist V. O. Key Jr. noted more than fifty years ago, Texas politics is about economics, and Texas "voters divide along class lines in accord with their class interests."[56] We will turn next to an examination of the evolving Texas economy.

The Economy of Texas

Until quite recently, the Texas economy was land based and colonial in structure. Texas produced, processed, and shipped its agricultural and mineral products to outside markets. Thus, the Texas economy was dependent on external demand and the prices paid for its cotton, cattle, or petroleum.

Cotton

The first real economy in Texas was created by southern planters and resembled the southern seaboard of the United States in prior centuries. In the 1830s, the economy was based on large slave plantations. The money crop, cotton, was barged down Texas rivers to the Gulf of Mexico because reefs prevented the development of ports at the mouths of Texas rivers. The cotton was then shipped to Europe or the United States, mostly through New Orleans. Later, Galveston was developed as a port, and it was the commercial center of Texas from the 1840s to the 1880s. During Texas's experience as a republic, and during its early statehood, cotton was the economic heart. Consequently, the region flourished during the cotton boom that preceded the Civil War. Cotton survived the Civil War, but the plantation system did not, and it was replaced by sharecropping. Nevertheless, Texas's annual cotton harvest accounts for a fourth of the total cotton production in the United States, providing $1.14 billion in receipts in 2000.[57]

Cattle

The cattle kingdom, inherited from the Mexicans, spread across the entire American West, capturing the fancy of Texas and the world in the late nineteenth century. Initially, the cattle business involved rounding up stray cattle and driving them to the Kansas railheads. The demand for beef created a link between the western frontier and the industrial marketplace. Like King Cotton, the cattle kingdom drew people and money from afar and involved agricultural products shipped to distant markets. For example, the largest ranch in Texas, the XIT, involved a Chicago syndicate, which was given 3 million acres in return for constructing the state capitol in 1881. Covering parts of nine counties in the Panhandle, the XIT ranch, which operated until the early 1900s, featured more than 1,500 miles of fence.[58]

Petroleum

For much of the twentieth century, petroleum was the basis for the Texas economy. From the first major oil discovery in 1901 at Spindletop, near Beaumont, by mining engineer Captain A. F. Lucas, Texas and the production of crude oil have been synonymous. Between 1900 and 1901, Texas oil production increased fourfold. In 1902, Spindletop alone produced 17 million barrels, 94 percent of the state's production. In 1923, the success of Santa Rita No. 1 ushered in the West Texas oil industry. The largest Texas oil field, the East Texas field, was discovered by C. M. "Dad" Joiner in 1930. However, the discovery of the East Texas field created a surplus of petroleum in a depressed economy. After World War II, the United States market sought cheaper oil in the Middle East. However, the oil embargo by the Organization of Petroleum Exporting Countries (OPEC) in 1973, a year after Texas reached its peak in oil production, caused an economic boom during the 1970s as prices were driven upward. This boom was followed by the bust of the 1980s when, in 1986, the price for West Texas crude fell below ten dollars a barrel. In 1981, the petroleum industry contributed 27 percent of the state's gross state product (GSP). Eighteen years later, in 1999, the industry contributed only 7.5 percent to the GSP, due to the lower price for crude oil and America's greater dependence on foreign oil.[59]

The Contemporary Economy

Since the 1980s, the Texas economy, which is projected to produce a GSP of $1,244 billion in 2009, has become more diverse, more nationalized, and more globalized than in the past. The diversity was thrust upon the Texas economy by the decline of the petroleum industry in the early 1980s. Furthermore, the economic regions of Texas that were most dependent on oil and natural gas—the Gulf Coast, West Texas, and portions of South Texas—have substantially altered their economies. The larger regions of Texas, such as the metroplex area of Dallas–Fort Worth, are the most diverse. The importance of increased economic diversity is that it allows regions to withstand economic setbacks in one or more industries.[60] Currently, the greatest economic growth is occurring in a core area anchored by Houston, Dallas–Fort Worth, and San Antonio. According to former Comptroller John Sharp,

> This core triangle of high-growth industries and population tends to dominate the business sections of newspapers and to draw the most attention in plans for future development. Power is shared in a variety of ways by the three largest urban centers. Each is a distinct market and supply center, defining not only itself and the surrounding areas, but serving as a business link to the rest of the world, too. . . .
>
> With just 10 percent of the state's land mass, the core is home to 60 percent of Texans, less than two-thirds of whom were born in Texas. . . .
>
> Economic characteristics draw the most vivid distinctions. With the obvious exceptions of agriculture, forestry, and fisheries, jobs are more plentiful in the central triangle, higher education more readily available and the growth of future industries more assured. The triangle cities are particularly strong in the financial, insurance and real estate sectors, in business and repair services, and in microelectronics, computer technology and biotechnology.[61]

Today, the Texas economy more closely resembles the national economy, although the Texas economy grew faster than the United States economy during the 1990s. During the 1990s, Texas led all states in net job creation. From 1990 to 2000, Texas created 2.35 million new jobs, producing a 3 percent growth in jobs and ranking first in the

Join the Debate

How Should Texas Educate Students of Limited English Proficiency?

OVERVIEW: The Texas legislature adopted the Texas Bilingual Education Act in 1973. The law required school districts to educate non-English-speaking children in their native language to promote learning and to facilitate their transfer into English-only mainstream classes. In 1974, the U.S. Supreme Court decided in *Lau* v. *Nichols* that students were denied a quality education if they could not understand the language in which they were being instructed. In *U.S.* v. *Texas* (1981), U.S. District Court Judge William Wayne Justice ordered the Texas Education Agency to increase bilingual education. In 1982, the U.S. Court of Appeals for the Fifth Circuit vacated Judge Justice's opinion because of new legislation in 1981. In July 2006, Justice reopened the case, based on claims by several civil advocacy groups that Texas is not adequately educating its students of limited English proficiency.

The debate over bilingual education has usually involved how best to ensure that non-English-speaking students learn English and, in the process, do not fall behind their peers in subject-matter instruction, such as the arts and sciences. As the number of students requiring bilingual education has increased, the debate has become more heated. In 1979, Texas public schools enrolled 2.9 million children. Of those students, approximately 198,000 (6.9 percent) were classified as limited English proficient (LEP). By way of contrast, in 2006–2007, approximately 731,304 students (16 percent) were classified as LEP out of a total of 4.6 million students. Estimates place the number of LEP students at 1 million by 2010.

Other states, also facing increasing numbers of LEP students, have decided to eliminate bilingual education. In 1998, California voters adopted Proposition 227, which required public schools to teach primarily in English and ended the state's nearly thirty years of bilingual education. In 2000, Arizona voters passed Proposition 203, eliminating bilingual education in that state. Both measures passed with large majorities. In place of bilingual education, both states use English-only immersion to educate LEP students.

Read and think about the following arguments for and against teaching non-English speakers through bilingual education. Then, continue the debate concerning how Texas should educate students of limited English proficiency by answering the questions posed after the arguments.

Arguments IN FAVOR of Bilingual Education

- Bilingual education is the most effective way to teach limited English proficient (LEP) students. English-only immersion is less effective than teaching LEP students English at the same time as content matter in their native language. By learning content in their native language, the students do not fall behind their peers, and they join mainstream classes sooner.

---

nation in total jobs added. Texas substantially outpaced second-place California, which created 1.79 million jobs, and third-place Florida, which created 1.72 million jobs.

The growth in jobs occurred in most sectors of the economy. Construction jobs increased by 5.7 percent, bolstered by low interest rates and increasing demand for residential and nonresidential construction. Growing by 30 percent during the 1990s, manufacturing jobs in Texas are concentrated in high-technology areas, primarily computers and electronics. The service-producing sectors of the economy accounted for the largest share of the growth in jobs during the decade. Leading the service-producing sectors were business services, engineering, accounting, research, consulting, and management services. Meanwhile, employment in public utilities and in government decreased as a percentage of the total.[62] In 2004, after three years of decline in Texas, the number of nonfarm jobs finally surpassed the March 2001 peak of 9.5 million jobs, growing to 9.8 million jobs by early 2006.[63]

As the 1990s ended, the unemployment rate in Texas was 4.5 percent, the lowest rate in twenty years. The economic strength of the 1990s reduced the number of unemployed Texans by 15 percent. After reaching a peak in 1992, the unemployment rate and the number of unemployed Texans decreased each year during the decade,[64]

- English learners in bilingual classes transition to mainstream classes quickly, and bilingual classes do not impede their acquisition of English. Of Texas students who started early in bilingual education, only 7 percent were still in bilingual classes after the fifth grade. Also, bilingual education is just as effective as large doses of English in the acquisition of English.

- Dual language instruction—a form of bilingual education in which students whose primary language is English are in a class with students whose primary language is not English and both languages are employed—is probably the most effective. The *Bilingual Research Journal* published a study in which Texas schools that employ this method demonstrated improved Texas Assessment of Knowledge and Skills (TAKS) scores for third-grade and fifth-grade students.

Arguments AGAINST Bilingual Education

- Bilingual education is expensive. States have to spend more to educate students in small classes for bilingual education. According to one study, the average additional cost for each LEP student is $1,200.

- Bilingual education separates students by language, segregating and isolating LEP students from the mainstream. Opponents of bilingual education note that LEP students are isolated and develop feelings of low self-esteem, which are similar to the effects of racial segregation on African Americans prior to *Brown v. Board of Education* (1954).

- Bilingual education allows LEP students to resist assimilation and avoid learning English. Whether students resist moving into mainstream classes because the bilingual classroom is more comfortable or teachers are holding them back, opponents of bilingual education maintain that tens of thousands of California students were held back in bilingual classes when they should have been in mainstream classes.

Photo courtesy: Bob Daemmrich

What is the best method for teaching students who have limited English proficiency? Texas students in a dual language class are taught English and Spanish, which is an effective method of teaching non-English-speaking students English while English-speaking students are taught Spanish.

Continuing the Debate

1. What effect would adopting an English-only immersion program have on LEP students in Texas?
2. What effect would continuing to provide bilingual education have on the cost of education in Texas?

To Follow the Debate Online, Go To:

Center for Equal Opportunity
www.ceousa.org/content/blogcategory/62/92/

National Association for Bilingual Education www.nabe.org/

---

but the recession of 2001 reversed that trend. By late 2003, the unemployment rate had reached 6.1 percent, but it dropped to 5.0 percent by January 2006 during the economic recovery and ended 2007 at 4.5 percent.[65]

The Texas economy became globalized during the 1990s, and Texas businesses compete throughout the world. In 2000, Texas exports reached $100 billion, growing by 66 percent since 1993 and accounting for 13.8 percent of Texas's gross product. Four industries—electronics, industrial machinery (which includes computers and oil and gas field machinery), chemicals and petrochemicals, and transportation equipment—accounted for 66 percent of Texas's exports in 2000. In 2001, Texas export revenues declined to $95 billion. After 2001, Texas exports increased until they totaled $150.8 billion in 2006. Since 2002, Texas has been the leading state in export revenues.[66]

For long-term, sustained economic growth, however, competition in the global market requires a commitment to developing a highly skilled, high-wage workforce supported by advanced technology, efficient telecommunications, strong research and development, and innovative marketing systems.[67] This is the economic challenge to Texas in the twenty-first century. (To learn more about bilingual education, see Join the Debate: How Should Texas Educate Students of Limited English Proficiency?)

Wealth and Poverty in Texas

In distribution of income, Texas ranks among the most unequal states. Between 2000 and 2002, Texas ranked second among the fifty states in income inequality between rich and poor families, and first among the fifty states in income inequality between rich and middle-income families. In Texas, the richest 20 percent of families had average incomes that were nearly triple the average incomes of middle-income families. Compared with families in the lowest 20 percent of income, the richest 5 percent of families had fourteen times the average income. (To learn more about income distribution in Texas, see Figure 1.2.)[68]

Despite the unprecedented economic growth in Texas and other states, the gap between the rich and the poor has increased. Contributing factors to the income disparity are that most new jobs are low-paying positions in the service sectors of the economy, incomes have risen fastest for people with the most education, and the minimum wage has not kept up with inflation. Texas ranked fiftieth among the fifty states in percentage of high school graduates and forty-fifth among the fifty states in percentage of college graduates, which means that many Texans are ill prepared to qualify for better-paying jobs.[69]

Poverty is not only more pronounced in Texas than in the nation as a whole but is also more prevalent among certain ethnic groups, among children, and in certain areas of Texas. Among the major ethnic groups in Texas, African Americans (25 percent) and Hispanics (25 percent) have the highest poverty rates, followed by Asian Americans (12 percent) and Anglos (8 percent). Twenty-two percent of children fewer than eighteen years of age in Texas live in poverty; the national average is 18 percent. Also, the poverty rate for young children (under five years of age) in Texas (25 percent) is higher than the national average (21 percent). The poor in Texas live primarily in metropolitan areas and along the border with Mexico.[70]

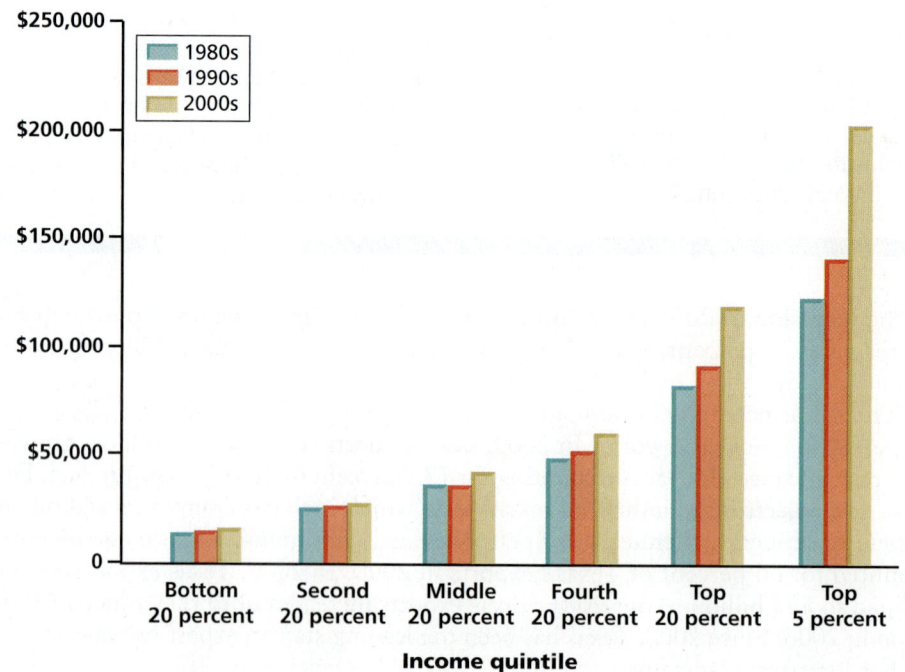

FIGURE 1.2 Texas Family Income by Decade, 1980s–2000s This figure depicts the increase in family income by quintile from 1980 to 2000.

Source: Center on Budget and Policy Priorities, "Pulling Apart: A State-by-State Analysis of Income Trends," January 26, 2006, www.cbpp.org/1-26-06sfp.pdf.

Poor people do not usually participate actively and routinely in politics and government in Texas or in the other states, while the wealthy tend to be more aware of what they could gain or lose through policy changes, so they more actively protect their interests. As we note in subsequent chapters, the economic leaders in Texas engage in many political activities. In the past, wealthy Texans influenced state politics either by recruiting and funding candidates for public office or by seeking public office themselves. In the 1940s and 1950s, Houston-area and statewide politics were heavily influenced by a group of millionaire executives. Houston's "8-F Crowd" met in oilman Herman Brown's Suite 8-F of the Lamar Hotel for poker and politics. They recruited and designated candidates for office, and they raised money and business support for those candidates. One of the 8-F group, George Brown, was a large contributor to Lyndon B. Johnson and to conservative governors, and he was crucial in the successful efforts in the 1950s to pass state laws limiting labor unions.[71]

> ### Thinking Nationally
> #### Income Distribution
> The most recent figures available show that Indiana, Utah, and South Dakota had the smallest gap between low-income and high-income families, while New York, Louisiana, Texas, and California had the largest gap between low-income and high-income families.
>
> - What differences in political culture might explain the differences in income distribution between the states with the largest gap and the states with the smallest gap?
> - What differences in government fiscal policies might explain these differences in income distribution?
> - What other variables could assist in explaining the differences between the states with the largest gap and the states with the smallest gap?

Before becoming president in 1989, George Bush, a Midland and Houston oil millionaire, ran unsuccessfully for the U.S. Senate as a Republican in 1964. He won a U.S. House of Representatives seat in 1966 and 1968 before losing a U.S. Senate race again in 1970 to Democratic business millionaire Lloyd Bentsen. Bush's campaigns received financial help from Dallas oil millionaire Bill Clements.

Both Clements and Clayton Williams—Republican nominees for governor between 1978 and 1990—were among the wealthiest Texans. Robert Mosbacher, another of the wealthiest Texans, served as finance chair for Gerald R. Ford in 1976 and as President George Bush's secretary of commerce. Dallas billionaire H. Ross Perot contributed money to Clements's campaigns before running for president as an independent candidate in 1992 and as the Reform Party candidate in 1996.[72] Other examples of wealthy Texas businessmen taking the leap into electoral politics include Lieutenant Governor David Dewhurst, former Governor George W. Bush, and 2002 Democratic gubernatorial nominee Tony Sanchez.

Toward Reform: Political Culture and Welfare Reform

Political culture affects the adoption and implementation of political reforms. Political scientist Daniel Elazar developed a typology of political culture in the United States that identified three political cultures.[73] He termed the three cultures moralistic, individualistic, and traditionalistic. According to this typology, Texas's political culture is a mixture between the individualistic and traditionalistic political subcultures, reflecting a governing preference for individual responsibility and maintaining traditional social values. Furthermore, states with traditionalistic and individualistic political subcultures feature lower levels of political participation, less professional bureaucracies, and less competitive political parties.

The effect of political culture can be seen in how Texas adopted and implemented welfare reform during the 1990s and 2000s. In 1996, Congress adopted the Personal Responsibility and Work Opportunity Reconciliation Act (PRWOR), which replaced the Aid to Families with Dependent Children (AFDC) entitlement program with the Temporary Assistance for Needy Families (TANF) block grant program. The welfare system was transformed from a cash assistance program to a workforce training program. Although federal guidelines accompanied TANF, each state developed and implemented its own program. A study that compared several states, representing different political subcultures, indicated that states with moralistic political subcultures performed better than states with traditionalistic or individualistic political subcultures in adopting and implementing welfare reform. Texas, for example, performed poorly in developing a coherent policy, in providing the necessary funds for the reforms, and in implementing the reforms.[74]

Although the number of welfare recipients fell by 75 percent between 1996 and 2006, the program cannot be considered a total success. First, Texas requires an income below 14 percent of poverty to qualify for TANF ($2,350 for a family of three in 2006). Second, Texas TANF recipients receive one of the nation's lowest benefits ($213 a month for a family of three in 2003). Third, program rules frequently remove TANF recipients from the program before they find employment. Fourth, a small percentage of TANF recipients are involved in job skills training programs or in educational programs related to employment. Finally, the declining TANF caseload has produced neither a decline in Texas's poverty rate nor an increase in the number of workers who earn above the poverty level.[75]

A political culture that emphasizes individual freedom and responsibility explains why Texas's welfare system provides few benefits while placing onerous demands on its participants.

WHAT SHOULD I HAVE LEARNED?

In this chapter, we examined the context for Texas politics and government and answered the following questions:

- **What are the roots of Texas politics and government?**

    The roots of Texas politics and government reside in the breadth of Texas's geography, in the variety of people who have inhabited Texas, and in the ideas that those people have held about the scope and purpose of government. Native Americans, Hispanics, African Americans, Asian Americans, and Anglos have contributed to Texas's political culture. As the composition of Texas's population has changed, different ideas about politics and government have emerged.

- **What constitutes the ideological context for Texas politics and government?**

    A Texan Creed, based on the ideas that are shared with other Americans but modified by the unique experiences of Texans, provides the foundation for politics and government in Texas. The Texan Creed comprises five ideas: individualism, liberty, equality, constitutionalism, and democracy. In addition, four ideologies—libertarianism, populism, liberalism, and conservatism—influence the responses of Texas politicians and political activists to issues of public policy.

- **How has the economy of Texas evolved?**

    The Texas economy evolved from a land-based, colonial economy to a modern industrial, service, and information-based economy. Dependent first on cotton, then on cattle, and finally on petroleum, the economy of Texas was controlled by external markets. The contemporary Texas economy closely mirrors the U.S. economy in terms of its structure and operation.

- **How have wealth and poverty in Texas affected Texas politics and government?**

    Texas has an image of great economic wealth, but poverty is more common in Texas than in the United States generally. The inequities in wealth in Texas are concentrated ethnically and geographically.

> ■ **How does the context for Texas politics and government influence political culture and welfare reform?**
> Texas's individualistic and traditionalistic political culture affected the adoption and implementation of welfare reforms during the 1990s and 2000s. Emphasizing individual freedom and responsibility, Texas provides little cash assistance and job preparation to the poor while placing large burdens on them in terms of qualifications to receive benefits and program rules to continue receiving benefits.

Key Terms

the Alamo, p. 17
American Creed, p. 20
Anglos, p. 11
constitutionalism, p. 18

equality, p. 18
frontier era, p. 15
individualism, p. 14
liberty, p. 17

populists, p. 22
Tejanos, p. 18
Texan Creed, p. 14
Texas Rangers, p. 16

Researching the Context for Texas Politics and Government in the Library

In the Library

Anderson, Gary Clayton. *The Conquest of Texas: Ethnic Cleansing in the Promised Land, 1820–1875*. Norman: University of Oklahoma Press, 2005.

Barr, Alwyn. *Black Texans: A History of African Americans in Texas, 1528–1995*, 2nd ed. Norman: University of Oklahoma Press, 1996.

Brands, H. W. *Lone Star Nation*. New York: Doubleday, 2004.

Campbell, Randolph B. *Gone to Texas: A History of the Lone Star State*. New York: Oxford University Press, 2003.

Davis, William C. *Lone Star Rising: The Revolutionary Birth of the Texas Republic*. New York: Free Press, 2004.

Fehrenbach, T. R. *Lone Star: A History of Texas and the Texans*, updated ed. Cambridge, MA: Da Capo, 2000.

———. *Seven Keys to Texas*, rev. ed. El Paso: Texas Western Press, 1986.

Himmel, Kelly. *Conquest of the Karankawas and the Tonkawas, 1821–1859*. College Station: Texas A&M University Press, 1999.

La Vere, David. *The Texas Indians*. College Station: Texas A&M University Press, 2004.

Maddox, William S., and Stuart A. Lilie. *Beyond Liberal and Conservative: Reassessing the Political Spectrum*. Washington, DC: Cato Institute, 1984.

Newcomb, W. W., Jr. *The Indians of Texas: From Prehistoric to Modern Times*. Austin: University of Texas Press, 1961.

Tijerina, Andres. *Tejanos and Texas Under the Mexican Flag, 1821–1836*. College Station: Texas A&M University Press, 1994.

On the Web

Institute of Texan Cultures, www.texancultures.utsa.edu/
This institute provides exhibits, programs, and special events to enhance the understanding of Texas's cultural history and people.

Texas State Data Center, txsdc.utsa.edu/
The center provides estimates, projections, and reports on Texas's population.

Handbook of Texas Online, www.tsha.utexas.edu/ handbook/online/
The handbook provides encyclopedic information about Texas. This is an excellent place to get an overview of almost any Texas topic.

Business and Industry Data Center, www.governor.state.tx.us/divisions/ecodev/bidc/
This center, maintained by a division in the governor's office, provides recent data on the economy of Texas.

Center for the Public Policy Priorities, www.cppp.org
This nonpartisan, nonprofit research organization provides information concerning workforce and economic development, access to public benefits, child protection, school finance, state and federal tax and budget analysis, and family economic security.

2

Constitutionalism

The current Texas Constitution is often criticized, and attempts to revise the document have been frequent. The constitution has provided the framework for Texas government since 1876, and to make the document applicable to solving contemporary problems, it has been amended 456 times since its adoption. With each amendment, the Texas Constitution has become longer, more detailed, and more confusing. As the number of amendments mounted, legislators, journalists, political scientists, and citizens became more supportive of a comprehensive revision.

Between 1971 and 1976, the Texas legislature struggled to produce a new constitution that would meet the needs of Texans and provide an acceptable substitute for the current constitution. Their attempts failed miserably, and the impetus for comprehensive reform languished, as legislators would not soon forget the brutal battles during the reform efforts. For members of the legislature, who had served as the Constitutional Convention of 1974, there were few political benefits in

■ The Texas Constitution is the foundation of Texas Government and reflects Texas's unique history. At left, a political cartoon from 1844 depicts the collapse of factional opposition to the annexation of the Republic of Texas (depicted as a ship, at top) into the United States. At right, original versions of Texas's 1836, 1845, and 1869 Constitutions are handled carefully and reverently.

advocating constitutional reform, especially when the political costs of their inability to produce a new constitution for the voters were calculated. Consequently, constitutional revision, except for the constant parade of constitutional amendments, was abandoned for nearly a quarter of a century.

In 1999, House Appropriations Committee Chair Rob Junell, a Democrat from San Angelo, thought that the legislature just might be ready for a major revision to the 1876 constitution. Representative Junell and Senator Bill Ratliff, a Republican from Mount Pleasant, proposed a new constitution that would have reduced the 376 sections and approximately 90,000 words to 150 sections and 19,000 words. Despite a public opinion poll that showed 49 percent of the population thought constitutional revision was a "very important" or "somewhat important" issue, the proposed new constitution never left committee. To this day, former Senator Ratliff believes that the Texas Constitution needs a comprehensive revision. As voters know, he told the *Austin American-Statesman*, "any document that you have to amend twenty times every other year is broke. It's sort of a Texas tragedy, actually, that we can't seem to come to grips with the fact that we need a new, basic document going into the next century and the next millennium."[1] Proponents of a new Texas Constitution continue to wait for that realization.

WHAT SHOULD I KNOW ABOUT . . .
- the roots of the Texas Constitution?
- the current Texas Constitution?
- constitutional revision?
- a recent constitutional reform: the marriage amendment?

Timeline: Texas's Constitutions

1836 Texas declares independence from Mexico and drafts a constitution for the Republic of Texas.

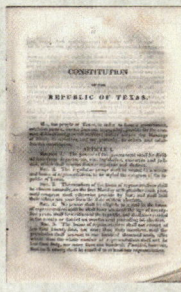

1845 To join the United States, Texas adopts a constitution for statehood, which is deemed Texas's "best constitution."

1861 Civil War commences. Texas secedes from the United States and joins the Confederate States of America, necessitating a new constitution.

1865 Civil War ends with General Lee's acceptance of General Grant's surrender terms at the Appomattox Courthouse.

1866 Texas rejoins the United States, adopting a constitution that complies with the demands of presidential Reconstruction.

1867 Presidential Reconstruction ends.

> **TO LEARN MORE—**
> **—TO DO MORE**
> Learn more about the 1999 constitutional reform proposal at www.capitol.state.tx.us/tlodocs/76R/billtext/html/HJ00001I.htm.

Texas has drafted several constitutions since it declared its independence from Mexico in 1836. Each constitution has been written to deal with changing political conditions in Texas. First, Texas was an independent republic. Then Texas joined the United States as the twenty-eighth state, which required a new constitution. Next, Texas seceded from the United States in 1861 to join the Confederacy during the American Civil War. To reenter the union required two constitutions. Finally, after Reconstruction, Texas adopted its current constitution in 1876. Since then, attempts to modernize the Texas Constitution have represented a political struggle between the roots of the Texas Constitution and efforts to achieve constitutional reforms.

In order to understand the roots of the Texas Constitution and its evolution in the face of a variety of reform efforts, we will examine the following topics.

★ First, we will discuss *the roots of the Texas Constitution*, examining the legacies of Texas's first five constitutions, which established the foundation for the current constitution.

★ Second, we will discuss *the current Texas Constitution*, examining the convention that framed it, its provisions, and the criticisms that continue to dog this document.

★ Third, we will assess *constitutional revision* in Texas, considering both piecemeal reform through constitutional amendments and comprehensive reform efforts through the drafting of a new constitution.

1869 Congressional Reconstruction requires the adoption of a new constitution.

1971 A constitutional amendment that creates a constitutional convention is proposed and adopted by an overwhelming majority of voters.

1975 The legislature attempts to redeem itself by proposing a new constitution through the amending process, but voters reject their efforts.

1876 Democrats regain control of Texas government after congressional Reconstruction. A new constitution is adopted to reflect traditional Texas values.

1974 The constitutional convention, composed of state legislators, meets to adopt a new constitution for submission to the voters. The convention spends millions and fails to produce a constitution, antagonizing voters.

1999 An attempt by two senior legislators to propose a new constitution fails, ending comprehensive reform efforts for at least a decade.

★ Finally, we will analyze *a recent constitutional reform: the marriage amendment*. In an effort to prevent marriage practices from being broadened to include homosexual couples, Texas has joined other states in defining marriage as an explicitly heterosexual institution in the state's constitution.

Roots of the Texas Constitution

Like most other states, Texas has had several written constitutions. Constitutions serve several purposes. First, and possibly foremost, a constitution specifies the civil liberties of individuals by placing limits on government's ability to restrict an individual's basic rights. Constitutions also establish the structures of government and provide their powers. Finally, constitutions provide a method of constitutional change, allowing them to be adapted to changing social, economic, and political conditions. We consider each Texas constitution in turn.

The 1836 Texas Constitution

Prior to its independence, Texas was governed as a part of Mexico under the Mexican Constitution of 1824, which established a federal republic and provided that each state should write its own constitution. Combined as a single state, Texas and Coahuila established a constitution in 1827. Because of escalating tensions between

Mexicans and Texians (see chapter 1), Texas declared its independence in 1836, established the Republic of Texas, and adopted the constitution of 1836.

The 1836 Texas Constitution contained a declaration of rights that consisted of seventeen articles. It also created a bicameral Congress, consisting of a Senate and House of Representatives, whose members were popularly elected and exercised powers similar to those of the U.S. Congress. The executive branch included a president and vice president, whose powers resembled the powers of the U.S. president and vice president. The judiciary consisted of courts at four levels: justice, county, district, and supreme courts. The fifty-nine delegates who assembled at Washington-on-the-Brazos to draft the document borrowed heavily from the U.S. Constitution and contemporary state constitutions and were guided by their political experiences. They produced a document quickly because of the imminent threat of attack by Mexican cavalry troops.[2]

The 1836 Texas Constitution included typical American features: a preamble; the incorporation of a separation of powers combined with checks and balances; recognition of slavery; a definition of citizenship that precluded Africans, the descendents of Africans, and Indians; a bill of rights; adult male suffrage; and an amending process. However, the amending process proved so complex that although several amendments were proposed during the constitution's existence, none was adopted.

Several provisions reflected state constitutions with which the delegates were familiar. For example, clergy were prohibited from holding public office, imprisonment for debt was abolished, and terms of office were short, ranging from one year for representatives to four years for some judges.

Spanish Mexican law also found its way into the constitution. Community property rights were established, homesteads were protected and exempted from taxation, and Texas courts were not separated into distinct courts of law and equity. However, the delegates' preference for English common law prevailed when deciding all criminal cases.[3]

The 1845 Texas Constitution

When Texas ceased to be an independent republic and joined the United States, a new constitution was necessary. In June 1845, President Anson Jones called a meeting of the Texas Congress to discuss offers by the United States to annex the Republic of Texas as a state. At the same time, he called a convention to assemble in July, which approved the offer of annexation with the Texas Congress and drew up a constitution, which the voters ratified in October 1845. The U.S. Congress accepted the 1845 Texas Constitution on December 29, 1845, and Texas became the twenty-eighth state to join the United States. The actual transfer of power occurred in February 1846.

Often cited as among the best of all state constitutions of its time, the 1845 Texas Constitution was noted for its straightforward, simple form. It created a bicameral legislature consisting of a Senate and House of Representatives that met biennially (once every two years). The governor served a two-year term and was limited to serving no more than four years in any six-year period. The attorney general and secretary of state were appointed by the governor and confirmed by the Senate; the comptroller and treasurer were elected by the legislature biennially in a joint session of the legislature. The governor could convene the legislature, was commander in chief of the state militia, granted pardons and reprieves, and could veto legislation, which could be overridden by a two-thirds vote of both chambers. The judiciary included a supreme court, district courts, and additional courts created by the legislature. The supreme court consisted of three judges, appointed by the governor for six-year terms. The constitution created district courts, whose judges were also appointed by the governor and which had a district attorney appointed by a joint session of the legislature for two-year terms.

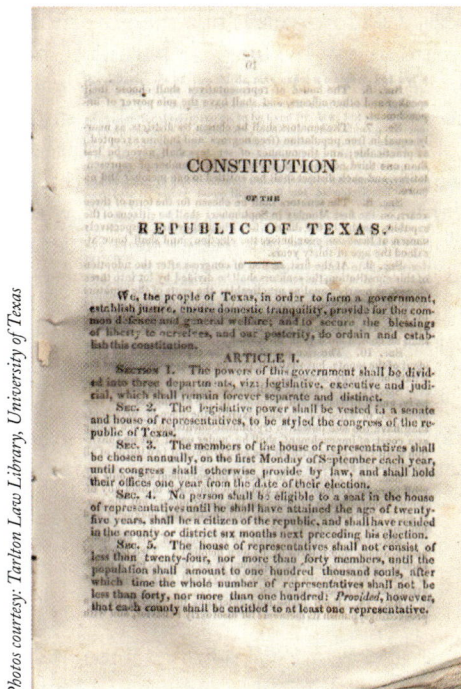 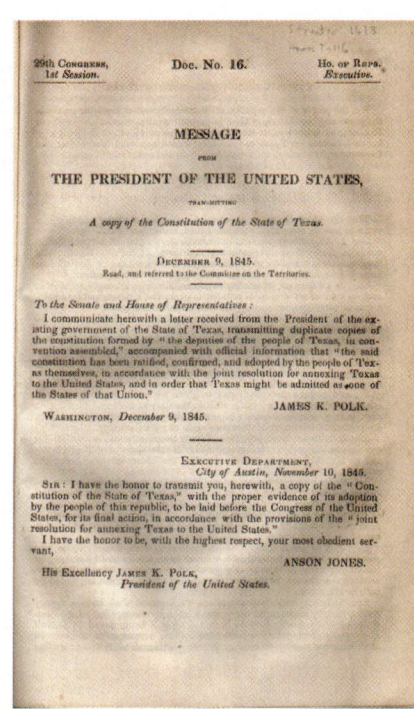 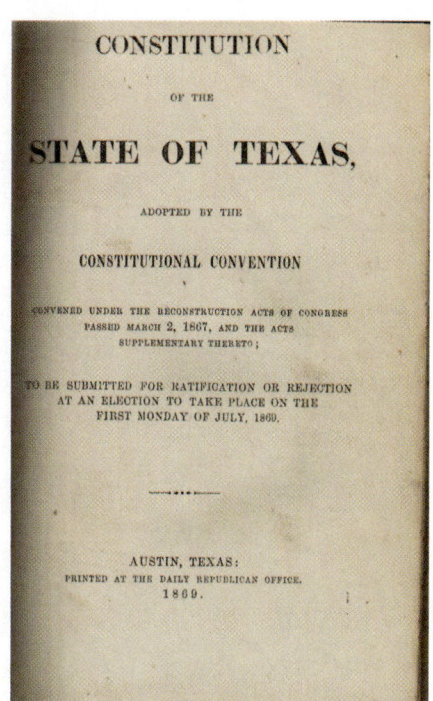

Is the difference in style or substance in the Texas Constitutions? Depicted here are the original constitution of the Republic of Texas (1836), the transmittal letter that accompanied the 1845 Texas Constitution, and the cover page from the 1869 Texas Constitution.

The longest article was entitled General Provisions, which primarily limited the legislature's powers. For example, bank corporations were prohibited; the state debt was limited to $100,000; homesteads and community property of husband and wife were protected. The constitution also created a public school system and Permanent and Available School Funds, and it continued the general land office to oversee Texas's public lands.

Amendments required proposal by a two-thirds vote of both chambers, and ratification both by a majority of voters in an election and by a two-thirds vote of the next legislature. Only one amendment survived these requirements. Adopted in 1850, it provided for the election of state officials who were originally appointed by the governor or the legislature.

The 1861 Texas Constitution

When Texas seceded from the United States in February 1861 at the beginning of the Civil War, the convention that had proposed secession reconvened to direct the transition of Texas into the Confederacy and replace the 1845 constitution. Changes necessitated by secession were made as well as a defense of slavery and states' rights. A provision in the 1845 constitution that provided for the emancipation of slaves was deleted, and the emancipation of slaves was prohibited. However, many changes that some secessionist leaders had advocated were not incorporated, such as legalizing the resumption of the African slave trade, taking an extreme position on states' rights, and making major changes in existing laws.[4]

The 1866 Texas Constitution

When Texas reentered the union after the Civil War, presidential Reconstruction required certain changes in the state's charter, such as the acceptance of the abolition of slavery. In addition to those changes, the constitutional convention of 1866 proposed a series of amendments, which were narrowly adopted in June 1866. In the executive branch, the governor's term was increased to four years, but the governor was prohibited from serving more than eight years in any twelve-year period. The governor was given a line-item veto over appropriations, and the governor's salary was increased from $3,000 to $4,000 annually. The attorney general, comptroller, and treasurer were to be elected to four-year terms. The legislators' salaries were increased significantly, although the structure and powers of the legislature changed only slightly. Only white men could serve as legislators. The state supreme court was increased to five judges, and they were elected for ten-year terms. Also elected were district judges, but their terms were shorter. The jurisdiction of each court was specified in detail.

An additional method of constitutional revision was adopted, which allowed the legislature by a three-fourths vote of each chamber and approval by the governor to call a convention to propose changes. Provisions of the constitution also called for internal improvements in the state and a system of public education, segregated by race and directed by a superintendent of public instruction. State land was set aside to support public education, to create and support a university, and for charitable institutions.[5]

The 1869 Texas Constitution

When the U.S. Congress ended presidential Reconstruction in 1867, additional requirements were placed on Texas's readmission to the union. Texas was required to have another constitutional convention, with delegates elected by all male citizens over the age of twenty-one, regardless of race, color, or previous condition of servitude. In what was called congressional Reconstruction, Congress required that the convention write a new state constitution that would provide for universal adult male suffrage. When the constitution had been written and the state had ratified the Fourteenth Amendment to the U.S. Constitution, Congress would consider the case for readmission to the union. The vote on holding the convention and electing delegates produced a lopsided victory for a convention, primarily due to an overwhelmingly favorable African American vote. A majority of registered voters, however, did not vote.

When the ninety delegates met in June 1868, they represented four different voting blocs, differentiated by geography, party, and issues. None of the four blocs was dominant. The convention's principal task—writing a new constitution—was overshadowed by other issues as each bloc pushed its own agenda. By August, the convention had exhausted its funding without even starting its consideration of a new constitution. A special tax allowed the convention to reconvene, but the delegates still failed to consider the convention's principal task until the last month of the convention. In February 1869, the convention broke up in confusion. Forty-five of the ninety delegates signed a partially assembled constitution. Military officers gath-

---

TEXAS IN COMPARISON

State Constitutions

State constitutions are frequently revised. All four of the largest states have adopted several constitutions. Florida has adopted the most constitutions since statehood, but Texas has the longest constitution. The California Constitution has been amended most frequently.

	Number of Constitutions Since Statehood and (Last Adoption Date)	Number of Words in Constitution (2006)	Number of Amendments (2006)
Texas	5 (1876)	90,000	submitted 614, ratified 439
California	2 (1879)	54,645	submitted 870, ratified 514
New York	4 (1894)	51,700	submitted 291, ratified 216
Florida	6 (1968)	51,456	submitted 141, ratified 110

Source: Council of State Governments, *The Book of the States 2007*, (Lexington, KY: Council of State Governments, 2007).

ered the materials together after the convention and, in July 1869, voters approved the convention's proposals as the 1869 constitution.[6]

The constitution met the requirements of congressional Reconstruction. In addition, it extended the term of senators to six years, increased the governor's salary, and allowed the governor to appoint the attorney general and secretary of state. The number of state supreme court justices and the length of their terms were reduced. All judicial offices were appointive. Overall, the constitution created a strong and expensive state government with annual legislative sessions, a system of centralized public education, higher salaries for public officials, and a lack of controls on state and local taxing powers.[7]

When rank-and-file Democrats regained control of the Texas legislature in 1873 and won the governorship in 1874, the constitution was bound to change once again.

The Current Texas Constitution

The adoption of a new constitution for Texas was shaped by the effects of Reconstruction. Although Texas Democrats agreed that the constitution needed to be changed, there were differences concerning the method and the scope of the change. Governor Richard Coke and the legislature's Democratic leadership favored a constitution written by a legislative committee rather than by a constitutional convention. They believed that only a document drafted by a legislative committee would ensure a short, liberal constitution and allow a more activist government. A majority of House members, however, considered anything but a convention "antidemocratic." Through a series of parliamentary maneuvers, a joint legislative committee was formed to produce a constitution. The result was a constitution that shared many similarities with its predecessors. However, the joint committee's proposed constitution failed when the Texas House rejected it. Public pressure resulted in Governor Coke's calling a special legislative session to assemble a constitutional convention in 1875.[8]

According to most studies of the Constitutional Convention of 1875, the delegates were not a distinguished group. These evaluations were based on contemporary newspaper accounts. However, a reappraisal, based on interviews with the delegates, reveals a group both more experienced and better trained than earlier accounts had indicated. Of the ninety elected delegates, seventy-five were Democrats and fifteen were Republicans. However, one of the Republicans served only a short time and was replaced by a Democrat. Thus, the convention actu-

Were the newspaper criticisms of the delegates justified? Members of the Constitutional Convention of 1875, which drafted the current Texas Constitution, are evaluated more highly today than they were when the convention met.

Photo courtesy: Texas State Library and Archives Commission

ally included seventy-six Democrats and fourteen Republicans. Six African Americans, all Republicans, were originally elected as delegates, but one resigned after the first day and was replaced by an Anglo. Of the ninety delegates, thirty-eight identified themselves as members of the Patrons of Husbandry, or Grange, an organization of farmers created in response to the economic panic of 1873. Seventy-two delegates were immigrants from other southern states, principally Tennessee, Kentucky, and Alabama. Seven delegates were European immigrants. Only four were native Texans.

Among the delegates claiming a single occupation, there were thirty-three lawyers, twenty-eight farmers, three merchants, three physicians, two editors, two teachers, two mechanics, one minister, and one postmaster. The other fifteen delegates pursued two or more occupations. These were usually farmers, lawyers, or physicians who also claimed at least one other occupation.

Averaging forty-five years of age, the delegates had a wealth of political experience. Eleven delegates had been members of a previous Texas constitutional convention—most commonly the 1861 convention. At least thirty members had served at least one term in the Texas legislature. In addition, several delegates had served in other states' legislatures, the U.S. Congress, and the Congress of the Confederate States. Five delegates had been judges, and four had executive and administrative experience. Evaluating the delegates to the 1875 constitutional convention, political scientist Joe E. Ericson concluded, "The convention of 1875 was composed, therefore, of a much abler group of men on the basis of their previous experience and training than is generally conceded. Their background and training compares favorably with that of the delegates to any previous constitutional convention held in Texas. If their product is inferior, then the cause must lie elsewhere."[9]

Reasons for the 1876 Constitution

What accounts for the 1876 constitution, a constitution that is quite different from previous Texas constitutions and the U.S. Constitution? The U.S. Constitution has served as a model for many national and state constitutions, and previous Texas constitutions had followed that example. Three factors explain the adoption of an organic, restrictive Texas Constitution.

First, the 1876 constitution was, to some extent, a reaction to Reconstruction. Certainly the adoption of the 1869 constitution angered many Texans. To many, the 1869 constitution was an illegitimate constitution that Texas had been forced by the Reconstruction government to accept.

Second, the 1869 constitution had led to Governor E. J. Davis's regime. During that administration, power had been centralized in the state government. The Enabling Act allowed Governor Davis to appoint district attorneys, district clerks, sheriffs, mayors, aldermen, and other local officials. In all, Davis appointed more than 8,000 officials. The legislature granted the governor extraordinary powers to maintain public order. For example, the governor controlled a state police that could operate anywhere in the state. Additionally, the Militia Bill allowed the governor to declare martial law in any Texas county, suspend the laws, and assess punishments for violators.

The legislature had also adopted expensive programs that increased taxes dramatically. Universal, compulsory education for all children under the direction of a state superintendent of education was a progressive but expensive policy. In addition, the legislature had provided bond subsidies to railroads. After only two years, state and county property tax rates in Texas had increased from fifteen cents on $100 property valuation to $2.18 on $100 property valuation. In addition, there were occupation taxes, city taxes, poll taxes, and taxes to retire the railroad bonds. Wanting to avoid similar governments in the future, the convention delegates of 1875 attempted to hobble government.

The third factor affecting the 1876 constitution was a movement that swept through the United States in the 1870s, calling for a politics of substantive issues and restrictive constitutionalism.¹⁰ Using the ideological labels explained in chapter 1, the movement had both populist and libertarian elements. As a result of this movement, many states, both southern and northern, revised their constitutions.

In the 1875 Constitutional Convention, this movement took the form of "retrenchment and reform," the motto of the constitutional revision effort adopted by the members of the Grange and their allies, who were anti-Coke Democratic delegates. For these delegates, the 1869 constitution had violated important Texas ideals, including a belief that government should be limited in its purpose. Historian Patrick Williams disputes this emphasis on the existence of two factions at the Constitutional Convention of 1875 to explain the provisions of the 1876 Constitution. Studying the convention journals, he notes: "There were distinct patterns to their [the delegates'] votes, especially when it came to government promotion of economic growth and social welfare."¹¹ The division among Democrats at the convention was more complex than support or opposition to government activism; it also involved the *way* that government should be active, and it resulted in four distinct groupings. One group supported rapid commercial and agricultural growth and believed that the government's principal role was to nurture private enterprise, but that otherwise government's role should be limited. A second group also supported rapid economic growth and believed that government's role should include assistance to private enterprise, but they further believed that government should invest in Texas's human resources, such as schools. A third group wanted government's role to be almost exclusively the promotion of those activities that private enterprise would not or could not accomplish, such as education and frontier defense. A fourth group favored less government generally, whether the purpose of government was economic assistance to private enterprise or to the state's social welfare.¹²

The provisions of the 1876 constitution, therefore, are not only a reaction to Reconstruction and the Davis regime but also the product of a national movement and a complex mix of motives among the convention delegates.

Provisions of the 1876 Constitution

The current Texas Constitution has seventeen numbered articles. (To learn more about the articles of the current constitution, see Table 2.1.) Article 13, Spanish and Mexican Land Titles, was deleted by amendment in 1969.¹³ Consequently, the constitution currently has sixteen operable articles. Many of the provisions of the constitution are nearly identical to the way they were written when ratified in 1876, but others have been amended extensively. Like the U.S. Constitution, the Texas Constitution incorporates many principles of American constitutional theory. However, because the U.S. Constitution is a **liberal constitution**—establishing the basic structure and principles of government—and the Texas Constitution is a **statutory constitution**—creating the structure and powers of government in great detail—the two are quite different.

Article 1 of the Texas Constitution contains the Texas Bill of Rights. Many of its provisions are similar to the U.S. Constitution's Bill of Rights, but the Texas Bill of Rights is longer and in some respects more extensive. Because of the framers' experience during the Davis administration, the Texas Bill of Rights contains provisions that state that the "writ of *habeas corpus* is a writ of right, and shall never be suspended" and that the Bill of Rights

liberal constitution
Constitution that incorporates the basic structure of government and allows the legislature to provide the details through statutes.

statutory constitution
Constitution that incorporates detailed provisions in order to limit the powers of government.

TABLE 2.1 Articles of the Texas Constitution

Preamble		
Article	1	Bill of Rights
Article	2	The Powers of Government
Article	3	Legislative Department
Article	4	Executive Department
Article	5	Judicial Department
Article	6	Suffrage
Article	7	Education
Article	8	Taxation and Revenue
Article	9	Counties
Article	10	Railroads
Article	11	Municipal Corporations
Article	12	Private Corporations
Article	13	Spanish and Mexican Land (repealed August 5, 1969)
Article	14	Public Lands and Land Office
Article	15	Impeachment
Article	16	General Provisions
Article	17	Mode of Amending the Constitution of This State

"is excepted from the general powers of government, and shall forever remain inviolate."[14] Amendments incorporating equal rights for women, ensuring rights for victims of violent crimes, and defining marriage as only the union of one man and one woman were added later.

Article 2 of the Texas Constitution establishes a separation of powers among the legislative, executive, and judicial branches in Texas government and prohibits an individual from holding positions in more than one branch simultaneously.

Article 3 establishes the legislative branch, specifying its structure and powers. The 1876 constitution continued the bicameral legislature, comprising a Senate with thirty-one members and a House of Representatives that can never exceed 150 members. House members' terms continued to be two years, but senators' terms were reduced to four years. To limit the legislature's power, the constitution created regular legislative sessions that are biennial, meeting in odd-numbered years, and attempted to limit the length of the regular legislative session. Originally, legislators received their full pay—a per diem of five dollars a day—only for the first sixty days of a regular session. Their pay was then cut by 60 percent for the remaining days of the session—a powerful incentive for short sessions. The framers of the constitution reasoned that if the legislature is not in session, it cannot pass laws, thereby limiting the government's authority.

Article 3's provisions also include legislative procedures, such as a requirement that a bill's title clearly indicate its content. Other provisions place limits and requirements on the legislature, such as specifying, in great detail, the purposes for which the legislature can levy taxes. Another provision of Article 3 specifies that the legislature is prohibited from passing special or local legislation for certain purposes, such as creating offices and assigning duties for counties, cities, and other local governments.

Article 4 establishes the executive branch. The governor's term was reduced to two years (it was reinstated to four years in 1974), and the governor's salary was reduced. To ensure the independence of other executive officers from the governor's control, the major executive officers—lieutenant governor, attorney general, comptroller, treasurer, and land commissioner—were elected independently. The addition of numerous elected and appointed boards and commissions in Texas by constitutional amendment and legislation has further diminished the governor's control over the executive branch. A seeming anomaly to the reduction of the governor's powers was the retention of the governor's line-item veto. However, the framers probably viewed the line-item veto as another check on the legislature's spending powers.[15]

In Article 5, the constitution created a judicial system that included a supreme court (the highest state court for civil matters), a court of appeals (the highest state court for criminal matters), district courts, county courts, commissioners courts, and justice of the peace courts. The judicial branch was also subject to popular control. Judges for each of the courts are currently selected in partisan elections. The article also specifies in detail the qualifications of judges, the jurisdiction of the courts, and even the operation of the courts.

Article 7, the education article, created a public school system that differed dramatically from the system that the Davis administration had created. (To learn more about the education article in the Texas Constitution, see The Living Constitution.) The superintendent of public instruction's position and compulsory school attendance were eliminated, schools were segregated by race, and the constitution made no provision for local school taxes. The constitution funded public education through a poll tax, general funds, and interest earned on the principal in the Permanent School Fund.

The Living Constitution

A general diffusion of knowledge being essential to the preservation of the liberties and rights of the people, it shall be the duty of the legislature of the state to establish and make suitable provision for the support and maintenance of an efficient system of free public schools.

ARTICLE 7, SECTION 1

In the Constitutional Convention of 1875, no issue was more vigorously debated than public education. In the end, Article 7, section 1, reflects the majority's opinion that "an elaborate and expensive system [of public education] like the one devised by the hated Republicans" should be prevented.[a] The initial result was a return to education as it had existed in Texas in the 1850s.

Beginning in the early 1900s, Texas courts interpreted the terms "suitable," "free," and "public" in such a way as to allow the legislature great latitude in providing a public education to Texas residents. Texas courts began to interpret Article 7, section 1, differently in the late 1980s and early 1990s. In 1987, a state district court judge, Harley Clark, ruled that the Texas system of funding public education violated Article 1, section 3, and Article 7, section 1, of the Texas Constitution. Article 1, section 3, declares that all people in Texas have equal rights. Additionally, Judge Clark ruled that "under our state constitution[,] education is a fundamental right for each of our citizens."[b] When the state appealed, the 3rd Texas Court of Appeals reversed Judge Clark. Viewing the issue as a political question, the court eschewed its ability to interpret Article 7, section 1.

Edgewood Independent School District appealed that decision to the Texas Supreme Court. In 1989, the court unanimously reversed the 3rd Court of Appeals, ruling, in *Edgewood* v. *Kirby*, that Article 7, section 1, "imposes . . . an affirmative duty to establish and provide for the public free schools."[c]

Furthermore, the Texas system of funding public education violated Article 7 because the system "is neither financially efficient nor efficient in the sense of providing for a 'general diffusion of knowledge' statewide"[d] and relies too heavily on local property taxes. Because the value of property varies widely from school district to school district, the state did not make the most efficient use of the state's resources in funding public education.

Over the next four years, the legislature struggled to develop a system that created a more equal distribution of money among the state's more than 1,000 school districts. Finally, in 1993, the legislature developed a plan that met the court's requirement.[e] In 2004, State District Judge John Dietz ruled that Texas's method of funding public education contained several flaws that made the system unconstitutional: the cap on local taxation created a statewide property tax, violating Article 8, section 1; the funding was not adequate for a general diffusion of knowledge, and the funding of school facilities failed to meet the equity standard, violating Article 7, section 1.[f] On appeal, the Texas Supreme Court, in *Neeley* v. *West Orange-Cove CISD* (2005), upheld only Judge Dietz's ruling that the school financing scheme created a statewide property tax and gave the legislature until June 1, 2006, to reform the system.[g] In May 2006, the Texas legislature reduced the maximum property tax for school districts by one-third and created three state taxes to compensate for the lost revenues: a revised franchise tax, an increased cigarette tax, and a revised sales tax for motor vehicles. These revenues were dedicated to property tax reduction.[h]

---

[a]George D. Braden, *The Constitution of the State of Texas: An Annotated and Comparative Analysis*, vol. 2 (Austin: Texas Advisory Commission on Intergovernmental Relations, 1977), 506.

[b]Harley Clark, District Judge, 250th District Court, *Edgewood Independent School District et al. v. William Kirby et al.*, written opinion, April 29, 1987, 2, Travis County Courthouse, Austin, Texas.

[c]*Edgewood v. Kirby*, 777 S.W.2d 394 (Tex. 1989).

(continued)

[d]*Edgewood v. Kirby*, 777 S.W.2d 397 (Tex. 1989).
[e]*Edgewood v. Meno*, 893 S.W.2d 450 (Tex. 1995).
[f]Betsy Blair, "Court Rules School Finance System Unconstitutional," *House Research Organization*, Focus Report No. 79-6 (February 21, 2005).
[g]Sharon Weintraub, "Texas Supreme Court Rules School Finance System Does Not Make the Grade," *Research Spotlight: A Publication of the Texas Senate Research Center*, April 2006.
[h]"Schools and Taxes: A Summary of Legislation of the 2006 Special Session," *House Research Organization*, Focus Report No. 79-13 (May 25, 2006).

CRITICAL THINKING QUESTIONS

1. Given the constitutional demands for public education, who do you think was correct: Judge Dietz or the Texas Supreme Court? Explain your answer.
2. Is the creation of a new business tax to replace the franchise tax the best solution to the educational problems in Texas? What alternatives do you think the legislature should have considered?

Constitutional provisions relating to local governments are found in several articles. In fact, Article 9, which is entitled "Counties," provides no information about the structure of county government and its officials. That information is contained in Article 5, the Judicial Article. In all, four articles must be consulted to find all of the constitutional provisions relating to counties.

In several articles, the 1876 constitution limits the legislature's discretion in enacting fiscal policies—taxing and spending. First, it mandates a balanced budget. Except for war or insurrection, debt is prohibited. Furthermore, the state's debt cannot exceed $200,000. Seventy-four provisions in the original 1876 constitution related to taxation, spending state money, and the use of private property.[16]

As an additional check on government spending, the constitution contains provisions for **dedicated funds**, which require that certain tax moneys be deposited in particular funds. The money in a dedicated fund may be used only for specified purposes. For example, 75 percent of the state portion of the gasoline tax is deposited into the Highway Trust Fund, which may be spent only to build and maintain roads and bridges in Texas. The other 25 percent is deposited into the Available School Fund, which may be spent only on public education in Texas. The balanced-budget and dedicated-fund provisions of the Texas Constitution serve to limit the discretion of the legislature. Funding schemes may also lead to resistance from entities within the state (To learn more about a school finance controversy, see Politics Now: Wimberley ISD and School Finance.)

Article 17 establishes the process for amending the Texas Constitution, limiting it to only one method. Amendments are proposed by a joint resolution, which must receive a two-thirds majority vote of the Texas House of Representatives and the Texas Senate. After the two-thirds vote by each chamber, the secretary of state prepares a statement that describes the proposed amendment. The statement must be approved by the attorney general and published twice in Texas newspapers that print official state notices. Ratification of a proposed amendment requires a simple majority of those who actually cast ballots in an election. The ratification of constitutional amendments may occur in a general election, which is conducted in even-numbered years in November, or in special elections, which are conducted at other times. The legislature determines when the election to ratify a constitutional amendment will be held.

In the 1980s, the legislature established a pattern of conducting constitutional amendment elections primarily in odd-numbered years, in November. At this time, only constitutional amendments and local issues are on the ballot, which results in lower voter turnout and in a lower adoption rate for amendments. (To learn more about constitutional amendment elections, see Analyzing Visuals: Constitutional Amendments

Politics Now

Source: San Angelo Standard-Times · February 9, 2008

Wimberley ISD and School Finance

In-debt district warned of split-up

BY APRIL CASTRO, THE ASSOCIATED PRESS SATURDAY, FEBRUARY 9, 2008

AUSTIN - The Texas education commissioner said Friday that he will dismantle a property-wealthy school district in Central Texas if it doesn't make a legally required payment to the state school finance system known as Robin Hood by next week.

"I can't be any more emphatic to say I have no choice in this case to take action against a district that fails to make a recapture payment," Education Commissioner Robert Scott said. "I took an oath as commissioner of education to uphold the laws of this state, and the laws are very clear."

School officials at Wimberley have refused to make a payment on their $2.3 million debt, which is due by Feb. 15. The school district has been in negotiations with Scott, and the school board will meet Tuesday to discuss the issue.

Scott said state law would require him to remove property from the Wimberley Independent School District and make those homes, businesses and students part of a neighboring district. Enough property would have to be removed so the property wealth per student is reduced to a level that does not require property tax money be sent back to the state for redistribution among poorer districts.

"We cannot afford to get consolidated. That is a terrible outcome for our school district, for our county and particularly for those approximately 2,000 students," said Rep. Patrick Rose, D-Dripping Springs, whose district also includes Wimberley. "We have a week to resolve that."

Wimberley Superintendent Dwain York said the district already is having to cut teachers and reduce academic programs that have helped the schools be considered "recognized," one of the top two levels given by the state.

"We perform well because we have programs in place that don't cost us a lot of money," York said Friday in a hearing before the House Select Committee on Higher and Public Education Finance. "And the key to our success is quality teachers ... I just submitted an '08-'09 budget with 14 less teachers in our district. That's absurd."

York said his district has weathered a "perfect storm" of financial hardships that have led to the budget crisis.

Among them was a projected level of enrollment growth at Wimberley in previous years that didn't hold up. Because school finances are based on a per-student measurement, the district now has to repay about $1 million that they were allowed to keep last year for expected new students who never came.

Rose told reporters Friday that the Texas Education Agency would allow the district to delay the $1 million enrollment debt payment until 2009, but agency spokeswoman Debbie Ratcliffe said the state has not made that offer. She did say that regular payments starting this month would be an option.

"We can stretch it out, but a balloon payment is not an option at this point," Ratcliffe said. "I'm not sure it ever will be, quite frankly, but that's not what's been offered."

The district also must pay a penalty to the state for money they paid to buy out a superintendent's contract. In an effort to discourage districts from spending such money, a clause in state law requires districts to pay a penalty equal to the amount spent in such situations.

But the amount owed to the state also has increased in recent years. The popular retirement community has seen increasing property values as more people move into the town. But because the newcomers are retirees, most don't have school-aged children that would create enrollment growth and the corresponding dollars that would come with additional students.

"Our problem is with the Legislature, seriously, with these sessions that seem to give us no assistance in this area whatsoever," York said, begging the lawmakers to grant the district relief when they next meet for a legislative session.

Discussion Questions:

1. If Texas Education Commissioner Robert Scott removed property from Wimberley Independent School District (ISD), what effect would that have on the education of students in the Wimberley district? Are there other remedies that you would consider more appropriate? Explain your answer.
2. Should the legislature provide relief for Wimberley ISD and similarly situated districts? Why or why not?

---

and Voter Turnout.) Apparently, with the election limited to constitutional amendments and issues of local interest, the small percentage of voters who participate closely scrutinize the proposed amendments.

Having a statutory constitution that requires constitutional amendment to make major and even minor changes in government also means that the constitution has been amended many times. By early 2009, the Texas Constitution had

Analyzing Visuals: Constitutional Amendments and Voter Turnout

This table shows the types of elections—presidential, gubernatorial, or special—where Texans voted on proposed constitutional amendments. It lists the percentage of eligible voters who took part in each election, the number of amendments voted on, and how many of those amendments were adopted.

Decade	Type of Election	Voter Turnout[a]	Considered Amendments	Adopted Amendments	% Adopted
1970s	General: Presidential	45.52	15	12	80.0
	General: Gubernatorial	25.47	16	12	75.0
	Special	5.42	26	16	61.5
1980s	General: Presidential	45.81	20	16	80.0
	General: Gubernatorial	29.44	10	10	100.0
	Special	10.23	77	65	84.4
1990s	General: Presidential	45.31	0	0	0.0
	General: Gubernatorial	30.41	1	1	100.0
	Special	9.47	91	63	69.2
2000s	General: Presidential	45.20	0	0	0.0
	General: Gubernatorial	19.80	1	1	100.0
	Special	8.18	67	65	97.0

[a]Voter turnout indicates the percentage of voting-age people who voted. For the 1970s, special election turnout figures are only for the 1977 and 1979 special elections (no figures were available for 1971, 1973, or 1975).

WHAT do you notice about the difference in voter turnout between general elections and special elections?

WHICH type of election resulted in the greatest percentage of amendments being adopted during the 1980s, 1990s, and 2000s?

IF you were a member of the Texas legislature, during which type of election would you schedule the popular vote for most constitutional amendments (assuming that you favored the adoption of the amendments)?

Source: Secretary of State, Election Results, Turnout and Voter Registration Figures (1970–present), www.sos.state.tx.us/elections/historical/70-92.shtml.; Texas Legislative Library, Constitutional Amendments, updated November 2007, www.lrl.state.tx.us/legis/constAmends/lrlhome.cfm.

---

been amended 456 times. (To learn more about the adoption of constitutional amendments, see Figure 2.1.) In contrast, the U.S. Constitution has survived since 1789 with only twenty-seven amendments. Because the first ten amendments to the U.S. Constitution, the Bill of Rights, were necessary to achieve ratification and because the Twenty-First Amendment repeals the Eighteenth Amendment, there have been only fifteen actual changes to the U.S. Constitution since its ratification.

Criticisms of the 1876 Constitution

With so many amendments, one might think that Texans would have been able to make a nineteenth-century constitution applicable to the twenty-first century. In many respects, however, the constitutional amendments have not fundamentally changed the basic structure of Texas government. For example, the legislature, executive branch, and county government remain quite similar to their original structures. Admittedly, the judiciary was reorganized in an 1891 amendment, and amendments and legislation have created numerous boards and commissions in the executive branch. Other amendments have added various local governments (see chapter 7). Nevertheless, for many Texans, the 1876 constitution does not provide an adequate foundation for governing in the twenty-first century.

With the addition of so many amendments, Texas has earned the distinction of having one of the longest constitutions in the United States (almost 90,000 words). Only Alabama's constitution contains more words. The amendments have

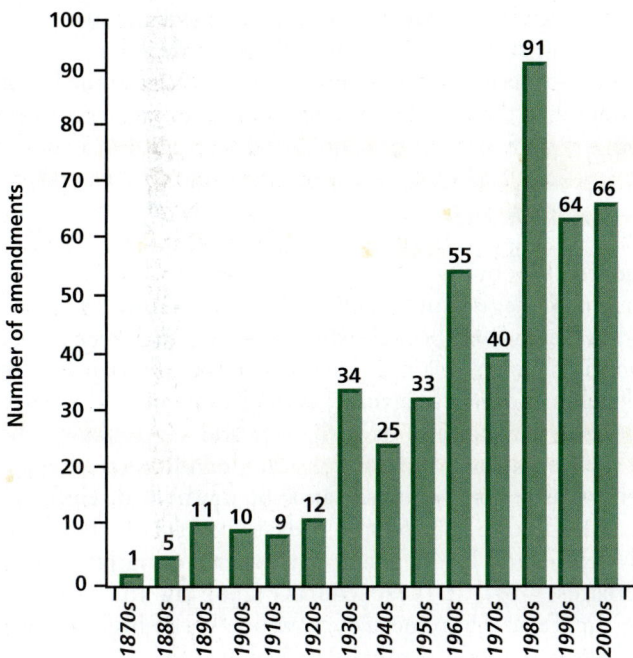

FIGURE 2.1 Amendments to the Texas Constitution, 1877–2008
Source: Texas Legislative Library, Constitutional Amendments, www.lrl.state.tx.us/legis/constAmends/lrlhome.cfm.

also exacerbated the disorganization that plagued the 1876 constitution originally. In the most heavily amended articles, the numbering of sections is almost impossible to follow because of missing letters and duplication. For example, until a 1999 amendment corrected the errors, there was no Article 3, section 48c, but as if to compensate, there were two 48e's, each dealing with a separate topic. Both 48e's were added by the 70th Legislature in 1987. A similar problem existed in section 52. The length and disorganization of the Texas Constitution, however, is far less serious than other concerns.

Some of the most serious concerns relate to the three branches of Texas government. The plural executive has been criticized because it limits the executive power of the governor to implement public policy. By dividing the executive authority among several officials, who are elected statewide to four-year terms (just as the governor is), the constitution makes these officials the co-equals of the governor. Though the constitution declares that the governor is the state's chief executive, it also denies him or her the powers necessary to perform that role. The governor's executive authority is further diminished by the numerous elected and appointed agencies, boards, and commissions that make up a substantial portion of the executive branch of Texas government. Political scientist and Texas Constitution expert Janice May has stated: "Texas has probably the most disintegrated and fragmented administrative organization in the country."[17] Despite efforts in the early 1990s to transfer more control to the governor, the executive branch remains badly fragmented. Consequently, Texas governors are in a much weaker position to influence public policy than are most of their counterparts in the rest of the United States (see chapter 5). For those who wish to see stronger executive authority in the state of Texas, those portions of the constitution that weaken the governor remain troublesome.

In the legislative branch, the most important criticisms relate to the constitutional provisions that make the legislature a part-time, citizen legislature. Among these provisions are the requirement for 140-day biennial sessions and the low, constitutionally mandated salary for legislators. Meeting every two years for such a short time makes governing a large urban state difficult. Particularly burdensome is the need to prepare a budget for a two-year period, anticipating economic conditions so that revenues will cover appropriations and the next legislature will not face a large deficit. A legislator's salary of $7,200 per year, which has not changed since 1975, plus a per diem for expenses, affects who can financially afford to serve and who can afford the time away from their primary occupation to attend regular and special sessions. This helps explain the high percentage of lawyers and businesspeople in the Texas legislature, as well as the influence of lobbyists.

Restrictions on the legislature, such as dedicated funds and specific prohibited activities, have been criticized because they limit the legislature's ability to react to social and economic changes in a modern, urban state. Perhaps the restrictions were more reasonable when Texas was a rural, agricultural state. Currently, however, the legislature needs more flexibility in its budgetary and law-making functions so that it can more easily and quickly respond to events and conditions in Texas.

The structure of the Texas judiciary and the method of selecting judges are also frequently criticized. The court system in Texas consists of a bewildering number of courts, divided into several levels, many with overlapping jurisdictions. The Texas Constitution creates most of these courts. Capping the court system are two supreme courts: the Texas Supreme Court, which is the highest state court for civil cases, and the Texas Court of Criminal Appeals, which is the highest state court for criminal cases. Each court has nine members, elected on a partisan ballot, as are almost all members of Texas courts. Many political scientists, attorneys, and even Texas judges have questioned whether partisan election is the best way to select judges (see chapter 6).

The 1876 constitution places severe restrictions on local governments. First, the structure of county government is established in the constitution, which means that the smallest and the largest counties in Texas have a commissioners court, a county judge, and a number of independently elected officials to run the various county departments. Although the structure may be effective in rural Texas counties, urban counties, where more than 80 percent of Texans currently reside, find the structure inefficient and unable to adapt to the changes that have occurred in their counties. Any change in the structure of a county's government, such as the elimination of an outdated county office (county surveyor), requires a constitutional amendment, which must be approved by a majority of the voters statewide.[18] Also, counties are limited in their ability to raise revenue and provide needed services. The restrictions placed on county and city government in Texas have resulted in the creation of thousands of special districts across Texas (see chapter 7).

With all the criticisms of the 1876 constitution, legislators and citizens have often called for revisions to the document, which is the topic of the next section.

Constitutional Revision

Constitutional revision in Texas can occur through two methods. First, the constitution can be updated through amendments intended to remove obsolete portions, clarify ambiguous sections, or consolidate sections that pertain to a single topic. This is usually referred to as **piecemeal revision.** The other method involves a new constitution for Texas, such as the 1974 constitutional convention or the revision suggested by Representative Junell and Senator Ratliff's proposal during the 76th Legislature in 1999. This is usually called **comprehensive revision.**

piecemeal revision
Constitutional revision through constitutional amendments that add or delete items.

comprehensive revision
Constitutional revision through the adoption of a new constitution.

Piecemeal Revision Efforts

As we noted earlier, the Texas Constitution has been amended frequently, and the addition of amendments occurred almost immediately after its adoption. The first amendment was proposed in 1877. Since then, amendments have been considered by every legislature, but the addition of amendments accelerated in the 1930s, 1960s, and in every decade since the 1980s. (To learn more about the pace at which constitutional amendments have been adopted, see Figure 2.1.)

Ironically, many piecemeal changes in the Texas Constitution have resulted from attempts to produce comprehensive reform. For example, the League of Women Voters became interested in constitutional revision in 1949 and, in 1957, was successful in getting the legislature to direct the Legislative Council to study each section of the constitution and make recommendations. The legislature also created a Citizens Advisory Committee to follow the council's work, do its own research, and report to the legislature. In its report, the Legislative Council found that the 1876 constitution, "despite its age and alleged deficiencies, is still overall a sound document and generally reflects the governmental philosophy of the people of Texas for their government."[19] The Citizens Advisory Committee disagreed with the assessment of the Legislative Council, seeking a constitutional commission to study the need for constitutional revision. The committee also sought the elimination of "deadwood" and repetitive sections, a logical arrangement of contents, and clarification of ambiguous provisions of the constitution.

Similarly, between 1966 and 1969, Governor John Connally led an effort to revise the Texas Constitution. Although Connally's efforts to call a constitutional convention failed, the legislature did create a Texas Constitutional Revision Commission to study the constitution and make recommendations to the legislature in 1969. The commission's proposed constitution was disregarded by the legislature, but the commission provided momentum for the earlier Citizens Advisory Committee's proposal to eliminate the deadwood provisions of the Texas Constitution through a single amendment. The amendment, which removed fifty-two provisions including Article 13 on Spanish Land Titles and reduced the constitution's length by 10 percent, was passed by the legislature and adopted by the voters in August 1969.[20]

In the 1990s, Representative Anna Mowery led an attempt to revise the Texas Constitution by removing sections that are duplicative, archaic, obsolete, previously executed, or ineffective. As a modest beginning, Mowery introduced a constitutional amendment in 1997 that changed the wording in several articles of the constitution. In the next legislative session, Mowery's proposed revisions were more extensive. The 1999 proposal amended sixty-four provisions of the constitution and repealed seventeen provisions. Seventeen sections of the amendment merely changed the archaic word "elector" to "voter" in order to modernize the language. Several sections eliminated provisions that allowed only property owners to vote in certain elections, a restriction that was not enforced and has been held unconstitutional in most elections. The legislative article was the focus for most of the proposed revisions. None of the proposed changes significantly altered the powers of government, the rights of individuals, or the structure of Texas state and local government.[21] In November 1999, voters approved Mowery's amendment. In 2001, another amendment by Mowery that eliminated duplication and clarified provisions of the constitution won legislative approval and was ratified by voters.

But, many Texans believe that only a thorough rewriting of the Texas Constitution will make it more uniformly applicable to modern Texas (To learn more about a grassroots effort on a constitutional amendment, see Ideas into Action: Grassroots Engagement in the Amendment Process). Professor Dick Smith's observations, made nearly forty years ago, seem especially prophetic today: "Even if, in due time, many non-substantive changes are made, through the overworked amending process, it will still be an inadequate, outdated fundamental law for the state."[22]

Ideas Into Action

Grassroots Engagement in the Amendment Process

In 2007, Cathy Setzer, a graduate student at the University of Texas at Austin, taught a Texas State and Local Government course at Austin Community College. While lecturing about the current Texas Constitution and the amending process, she also talked about the sixteen proposed amendments that would be voted on in November 2007. She called the students' attention to proposition 10, which would abolish the constitutional authority of each county's inspector of hides and animals. Interestingly, no one had served as an inspector of hides and animals in Texas for many years and the amendment was essentially intended to reflect current reality by abolishing the office. Setzer and her students started a "Vote No on Prop 10" campaign to draw attention to low levels of public awareness regarding the amending process and the antiquated Texas Constitution. During the campaign, the class members created a Web site, produced videos, held a rally on the capitol steps, and received statewide coverage from newspapers.

On her Web site, Professor Setzer notes, "While this has been a very time consuming project it has been a ton of fun and a great opportunity for me to teach my students about grassroots organizing and civic participation."[a] Was it appropriate to oppose the amendment in order to bring attention to the amending process? Would support for the amendment have accomplished the same goal?

What methods, in addition to those described above, could have been used to raise awareness about the constitutional amendment process? Which methods are likely to be most effective?

What's wrong with proposition 10? The government class taught by Cathy Setzer protested at the capitol in opposition to proposition 10. They titled their publicity campaign against the amendment "Save Our Hides."

A video made by Cathy Setzer's class may be accessed by searching on "Vote No on Prop 10 #2" on YouTube. What grade would you assign this video? What audience do you believe it would be most effective in reaching?

To learn about working with the media to publicize political events, type ehow.com into your browser and search on "how to get publicity for a political event" or go to www.ehow.com/how_2166761_publicity-political-event.html.

[a] Cathy Sayz, October 28, 2007, cathysayz.com/blog/10/what-i-do-in-my-spare-time.html.
Source: Kevin Stutz, "Students Protest Prop. 10," *Accent* (November 12, 2007): 1.

Comprehensive Revision Efforts

The legislature's first attempt to call a constitutional convention for a comprehensive revision occurred in 1877. It was the first in a long series of such attempts. In 1917, the legislature passed a resolution calling for a constitutional convention without referring the question to the voters. Governor James Ferguson refused to issue a proclamation calling for the election of delegates, and the effort failed. In 1919, the legislature tried again, but this time they submitted the call for a convention to the voters. In November 1919, the proposal was soundly defeated by a nearly three-to-one margin.

Despite the defeat, the proposals for constitutional reform continued. Between 1919 and 1949, the legislature regularly considered proposals for a constitutional convention. Four House Concurrent Resolutions, three Senate Concurrent Resolutions, eight Joint House Resolutions, and four Senate Joint Resolutions were introduced. None of the resolutions calling for a constitutional convention or creating a revision commission was approved by the legislature. In 1949, Governor Beauford Jester invited a group of citizens to the capital for a conference. The group formed a Citizens Committee on the Constitution, which requested the legislature to form a Commission on the Texas Constitution to thoroughly study the constitution and to suggest how to proceed if a revision was deemed necessary. The resolution to create the commission received an unfavorable committee report and was never considered by the House.[23]

When the legislature failed to consider the constitution produced by the 1967–1968 Constitutional Revision Commission and voters ratified the 1969 amendment to eliminate the deadwood in the 1876 constitution, most political observers expected constitutional revision to wane in importance. However, the 62nd Legislature, meeting in 1971, created the first constitutional convention in Texas in nearly a century.

THE 1974 CONSTITUTIONAL CONVENTION In 1971, a group of recently elected representatives led the efforts to revise the constitution. They proposed a constitutional amendment that called for the Texas legislature of 1973 to sit as a constitutional convention in 1974 and required the legislature to establish a **Constitutional Revision Commission** to draft a new constitution prior to the legislature meeting as a constitutional convention. The voters approved the amendment in November 1972 by almost a two-to-one margin (61 percent to 39 percent). According to the amendment, the legislature, meeting as a constitutional convention, was authorized to submit either a new constitution or revisions to the old constitution for voter approval. They also were allowed to present alternative sections or articles of either the old or the new constitution. The only substantive limitation on the legislature involved Article 1—the Bill of Rights—which could not be changed. There was also a time limit on the convention. The convention would automatically end on May 31, 1974, unless the convention voted to adjourn earlier or to extend the session for not more than sixty days after the May deadline.

Thinking Nationally
Calling a Constitutional Convention

Only eight states, including Texas, have no constitutional provision for calling a constitutional convention. Among the forty-two states that have a constitutional provision, most states require a two-thirds majority of the legislature to approve of the submission of a convention question, while a majority of eligible voters must vote to authorize the convention. Thirteen states require the periodic submission, ranging from every nine to twenty years, of a constitutional convention question to voters.

- Should the Texas legislature amend the Texas Constitution to include a provision for calling a constitutional convention? What majority should be required in the legislature for the submission of a convention question?
- How should the call for a convention be authorized? Should such a constitutional provision include specification of who the delegates should be?
- Should a periodic submission of a convention be required in the Texas Constitution? If so, how frequently should it be required?

Constitutional Revision Commission
Group established to research and draft a constitution for a constitutional convention.

Does this group appear representative of contemporary Texans? The Constitutional Revision Commission, chaired by Robert Calvert and co-chaired by Beryl Buckley Milburn, prepared a draft constitution for the Constitutional Convention of 1974.

In 1973, the legislature quickly adopted a resolution establishing the Constitutional Revision Commission.[24] A six-member committee composed of the governor, lieutenant governor, Speaker of the House, attorney general, chief justice of the Texas Supreme Court, and presiding judge of the Texas Court of Criminal Appeals appointed the thirty-seven members of the commission, who could not be public officials. The governor chaired the committee, and the votes of four members were required for an appointment. The committee also selected the commission's chair—Robert W. Calvert, a former chief justice of the Texas Supreme Court—and vice chair—Beryl Buckley Milburn, a prominent Republican civic leader. The commission's membership was finalized in March 1973, and the commission began meeting immediately. From April through June, the commission held nineteen public hearings across the state, meeting with citizens and local advisory committees. On November 1, 1973, the commission submitted a draft constitution to the members of the legislature.

The convention started with great expectations. The 181 members of the 1973 legislature (150 state representatives and thirty-one state senators) met as a constitutional convention on January 8, 1974. The amendment authorizing the process had been passed by the voters by a substantial margin. The Constitutional Revision Commission had prepared a draft constitution from which the convention could begin its work. The convention only had to make whatever modifications it desired to the commission's draft and submit it to the voters for ratification. Most political observers expected a revised constitution to be presented to Texas voters at the 1974 general election. However, the convention adjourned on July 30, 1974, without producing a new constitution. The final vote fell three short of the two-thirds vote necessary to submit a revised constitution to the voters. How can the failure of the constitutional revision effort be explained? According to political scientist Janice May, a member of the Constitutional Revision Commission, there are several reasons:

First, the legislature was the constitutional convention. Legislatures propose constitutions or constitutional revisions frequently, but they normally do this as a legislature. The Texas experience was unique in that the members of the Texas legislature met in a separate session, as a unicameral body, and worked to revise the constitution. In some respects, this was helpful because the legislators were not concerned with other issues and could devote their attention to the constitutional issues. However, the legislature as a constitutional convention may bring too much of the politics from the legislative arena into the convention. Being legislators, the convention delegates thought of constitutional revision as "politics as usual." The delegates were influenced by reelection considerations, institutional and personal rivalries between the chambers, pressure from lobbyists, and partisan and ideological differences. The general practice among the states had been to have delegates to a constitutional convention elected by the people. If the convention had been made up of citizen delegates whose

TABLE 2.2 Committees of the 1974 Constitutional Convention

Substantive Committees	Procedural Committees
Finance	Rules
Local Government	Administration
Education	Submission and Transition
Legislature	Style and Drafting
Judiciary	Public Information
General Provisions	
Executive	
Rights and Suffrage	

political careers might have ended with the adjournment of the convention, the final result might have been different.

The second reason for failure involved the decision rules used in the convention, especially the two-thirds rule. The convention delegates were divided into several substantive and procedural committees. (To learn more about the committees at the convention, see Table 2.2.) The substantive committees were responsible for conducting hearings, taking testimony, and drafting the articles or sections of the new constitution. Once the committee reported out a section, the section was then debated and voted on by the entire convention. For a particular article to be approved by the convention, a simple majority vote was required. However, the final document, made up of all previously approved sections and articles, required a two-thirds majority vote for submission to the voters. This was a rare rule in the history of constitutional conventions. On ten resolutions representing a final document, a simple majority of the delegates voted to submit the document to the voters.

The third reason for failure, and the single most important policy issue, was the right-to-work provision. (A right-to-work provision states that membership or nonmembership in a union cannot be a condition of employment.) The Taft-Hartley Act of 1947 allowed states to establish a right-to-work law, and the Texas legislature passed one in that year. Labor union leaders considered the Taft-Hartley Act a "slave labor" law. Delegates supported by business interests came to the 1974 constitutional convention determined to place a right-to-work provision in the Texas Constitution, which would have made it more difficult to repeal. On the other hand, labor unions refused to support any constitutional revision that contained a right-to-work provision. The issue dragged long-standing partisan, faction, and labor–management battles into the convention. According to students of constitutional conventions, right-to-work is one of those controversial issues that can defeat a constitutional revision effort.

The fourth reason for the convention's failure was the lack of exceptional political leadership. As president of the convention, Speaker Price Daniel Jr. probably bears most of the responsibility for the lack of leadership. As some delegates noted, Daniel lost the convention with his committee appointments, which included many freshmen appointments and not enough experienced legislators. Furthermore, Daniel did not attempt to compromise on the right-to-work issue early in the convention by bringing the two sides together for discussions. Having announced before the convention that he would not seek another term as House Speaker in 1975, Daniel was a lame duck, which reduced his ability to influence members of the convention. Of course, other politicians, such as Governor Dolph Briscoe, could have provided leadership, but Briscoe decided to take a neutral public stand on constitutional revision.

The final reason involves cockroaches and revisionists. In the jargon of constitutional revision, a **cockroach** is an obstructionist who opposes any revision of the constitution. About twenty members of the constitutional convention were cockroaches. In addition, several members were **revisionists,** who opposed the constitutional revision effort because the legislature was the convention and the proposed revision did not go far enough toward giving Texas a good constitution. Together, these two groups were large enough to prevent the adoption of a final resolution.[25]

THE 1975 CONSTITUTIONAL AMENDMENTS In 1975, the legislature rewrote the constitution that the 1974 convention had failed to adopt the previous summer as eight amendments, each dealing with a particular portion of the constitution, and presented them to the voters. Voter approval of all eight amendments would have given Texas a new constitution. The amendments would have shortened the constitution considerably and provided for annual legislative sessions, veto sessions, a

cockroach
A member of a constitutional convention who opposes any changes in the current constitution.

revisionist
A member of a constitutional convention who will not accept less than a total revision of the current constitution.

unified judiciary, a single court of last resort, and a flexible structure for county government. Most political observers expected the amendments to pass.

But, on November 4, 1975, Texas voters rejected all eight amendments by a two-to-one margin. Only two of Texas's 254 counties passed all eight amendments. Several explanations account for the amendments' defeat. First, the constitutional revision efforts of 1974 and 1975 were preceded by the Sharpstown scandal in Texas (in which a number of state officials were involved in stock fraud and bribery) and the Watergate scandal at the national level. Both scandals affected the public's trust in government. Second, many Texans feared that the new constitution would make the government too powerful. Of particular concern was the fear that a new constitution would lead to a state income tax. Third, although Lieutenant Governor Bill Hobby and House Speaker Bill Clayton threw their support behind the new constitution, Governor Dolph Briscoe announced his opposition to the document less than a month before the election. Finally, several groups, representing interests that benefited from provisions of the present constitution, actively campaigned against at least some of the amendments. In the end, voters were not convinced that the proposed amendments justified replacing the existing constitution.

THE 1999 CONSTITUTIONAL REVISION EFFORT The constitution introduced in 1999 by Representative Rob Junell and Senator Bill Ratliff, two of the legislature's more powerful members, proposed major substantive changes in the structure and operation of Texas government. In the legislative branch, the proposal increased House and Senate members' terms to four and six years respectively, placed term limits on House and Senate members, and created veto sessions, an opportunity for the legislature to call itself into session to override gubernatorial vetoes.

Under the proposal, the governor would become a true chief executive, heading a Cabinet of nine appointed department heads. Cabinet members would be confirmed

Why was their proposal never even considered? In 1999, Senator Bill Ratliff, left, and Representative Rob Junell proposed a comprehensive revision of the Texas Constitution, which was not even considered by either chamber. Later, President George W. Bush nominated Junell to be a U.S. District Court Judge, and he was confirmed by the Senate in 2003.

by the Senate and serve at the governor's pleasure. Although the lieutenant governor, comptroller of public accounts, and attorney general would remain as independently elected executive officers, the executive branch would be consolidated and placed under much greater gubernatorial control.

The judiciary would be simplified into fewer courts. A merit system—incorporating nominating commissions, gubernatorial appointments, and nonpartisan retention elections—would be used to select judges for district courts, courts of appeals, and a single supreme court. The supreme court would consist of fourteen justices, divided into seven-member civil and criminal divisions, and a chief justice, who could sit with both divisions, and would replace the current two supreme courts.

Other important changes included a definition of an efficient system of public education and an authorization of a statewide property tax to fund public education. (For a discussion of a controversy relating to funding public education, see Politics Now: Wimberley ISD and School Finance.) Also, counties would retain their limited policy-making authority, but individual counties could change their organizational structure. A salary commission would recommend legislative, executive, and judicial pay and per diem, and the legislature would establish the salaries through legislation. Finally, an addition would allow the legislature to call a constitutional convention, subject to voter approval. (For a related issue, see Join the Debate: Should Texas Adopt the Initiative Process?)

> ### Thinking Nationally
> #### Citizen-Initiated Changes
>
> Some states have provisions for citizen-initiated changes to their laws and to their state constitutions. For example, citizens or groups of citizens in a number of states have pushed to raise their minimum wage above the national minimum wage, to place restrictions on undocumented immigrants, and to ban affirmative action programs.
>
> - Although Texas has no provision for citizen-initiated changes to the Texas Constitution, what policy issues would you like to see addressed in the Texas Constitution that the legislature has not addressed?
> - What policy options on those issues would you favor? For example, should the Texas minimum wage be higher or lower than the national minimum wage?
> - Would you want legislators to amend *state law* to include these policy positions or would you want voters to approve them as amendments to the *constitution*? Why?

The legislature never considered the proposed 1999 constitution. In the House, Speaker Pete Laney assigned the proposal to a Select Committee on Constitutional Revision, which held several hearings but did not report the proposed constitutional amendment. Instead, the committee reported favorably on Representative Mowery's proposal for nonsubstantive changes, which were described earlier in the chapter. The Texas Constitution remained substantially unchanged.

Toward Reform: The Marriage Amendment

In 2005, Texas voters approved an amendment stating that "marriage in this state consists only of the union of one man and one woman." The amendment also prohibited the state or any political subdivision (for example, a county or city) from creating or recognizing any "legal status identical or similar to marriage." The latter provision was meant to prevent the creation or recognition of civil unions by the state or any of its political subdivisions. In adopting the amendment, Texas joined seventeen other states that had previously defined marriage in their constitutions. Ironically, the amendment became a part of Article 1 of the Texas Constitution—the Bill of Rights, which usually provides protections from government's infringement on individual rights or liberties.

Join the Debate

Should Texas Adopt the Initiative Process?

OVERVIEW: Texas does not allow citizens to propose legislation or constitutional amendments through initiative petitions. Currently, twenty-four states employ some form of the initiative process, which allows citizens to propose public policies for a state. Among those states, the process varies greatly. In some states, citizens can propose laws or constitutional amendments, either directly or indirectly. In the *direct initiative process*, proposed legislation or constitutional amendments are placed on a ballot for popular approval without going through the state legislature. In the *indirect legislative process*, proposed legislation or constitutional amendments must first be submitted to the state legislature during a regular session.

Since the first statewide initiative appeared on the ballot in Oregon in 1904, the use of the initiative has waxed and waned. A populist idea that was implemented during the Progressive era, the initiative was used with increasing frequency until 1920, when its use fell dramatically until the late 1970s. In 1978, the passage of California's Proposition 13, which cut property taxes in the state by 60 percent, spurred several decades of growth in the number of initiatives. Between 1981 and 1990, 286 measures were placed on ballots through the initiative process. From 1991 to 2000, 389 initiatives were on statewide ballots. According to most scholars, the number of initiatives reached its zenith in 1996 when 93 measures were on statewide ballots and 44 were adopted. Since then, the number of initiatives has remained stable or declined. In 2007, only two initiatives appeared on statewide ballots.

Read and think about the following arguments for and against adopting the direct or indirect initiative process in Texas. Then, continue the debate by answering the questions posed after the arguments.

In 2003, the Texas legislature adopted a Defense of Marriage Act under which same-sex marriages and civil unions are not recognized in Texas because they are in conflict with public policy of the state. The prohibition against recognizing same-sex marriages is extended to any political subdivision in the state, and no public act, record, or judicial proceeding will be recognized that creates, recognizes, or validates a same-sex marriage or civil union. Also, no claim to a legal protection, benefit, or responsibility as a result of a same-sex marriage or civil union is recognized in Texas. The act also narrowly defines a civil union. The act was adopted when several states, such as Vermont and Massachusetts, recognized civil unions or same-sex marriages.

Proponents of the constitutional amendment, such as the amendment's sponsor, Texas House member Warren Chisum (R–Pampa), argued that the amendment was necessary to prevent activist judges from interpreting the Texas Constitution's equal rights amendment or the U.S. Constitution's equal protection clause as allowing same-sex marriage. Proponents also argued that marriage has traditionally been between one man and one woman and that this form of marriage promotes a stable society and the well-being of children. The amendment's opponents argued that amending the constitution was unnecessary and would bind leg-

Arguments IN FAVOR of Adopting an Initiative Process

- Adopting the initiative process, either direct or indirect, increases the involvement of citizens in government and politics. When the initiative is available to the people, they use it to make public policies that they favor by signing petitions and other forms of political involvement.
- Adopting the initiative process reduces the power of special interests in politics and government. When people are empowered, special interests lose out to majoritarian democratic movements.
- Adopting the initiative process makes government more responsive to the people. When people are able to effect policy changes directly, the government is more likely to heed the voice of the people.

Arguments AGAINST Adopting an Initiative Process

- Adopting the initiative process increases the power of special interests. Initiatives can be sponsored by special interests through paid signature collectors and media advertisements.
- Adopting the initiative process subjects the minority to the tyranny of the majority. People who are concerned about protecting minority rights believe that a pluralistic society needs to safeguard minorities from emotional and misguided majorities.
- Adopting the initiative process reduces the power of the legislature and the deliberation and compromise that occur in the legislative process. Politics involves deliberation and compromise. Too frequently, the initiative process involves little deliberation and allows for no compromise.

Continuing the Debate

1. What effect would the adoption of an initiative process have on political participation and democracy in Texas?
2. What effect would the adoption of an initiative process have on the power of special interests in Texas?

To Follow the Debate Online, Go To:

Initiative and Referendum Institute www.iandrinstitutute.org

Initiative for Texas www.initiativefortexas.org

National Conference of State Legislatures www.ncsl.org/programs/legman/irtaskfc/IandR_report.pdf

---

islators and citizens of Texas to a definition of marriage, limiting the ability to promote the health and safety of families, which could take a different form in the future. Also, the section that prohibits the recognition of any "legal status identical or similar to marriage" is so broad that it could be interpreted to nullify common-law marriages or even legal agreements, such as powers of attorney, between unmarried persons.[26]

Proponents and opponents of the amendment were able to raise about the same amount in campaign contributions. Texans for Marriage PAC and Free Market PAC were the primary political action committees supporting the measure. Opponents funneled campaign contributions, mostly in small amounts, into a PAC called No Nonsense in November. The Vote Against the Amendment PAC, which received support from the National Gay and Lesbian Task Force, also contributed to the opponents' efforts.[27]

Although the war of words between the proponents and opponents of the amendment were heated (resulting in a higher voter turnout than is usual in constitutional amendment special elections), the election results demonstrated the overwhelming approval for the amendment in the state, which passed with 76 percent of the popular vote. Only one county—Travis County—voted against the amendment. The greatest support came from rural counties in West Texas.

WHAT SHOULD I HAVE LEARNED?

In this chapter, we discussed the constitutions of Texas and answered the following questions:

- **What are the roots of the Texas constitution?**

Texas adopted five successive constitutions to reflect Texas's changing status from an independent nation (1836), to a state in the United States (1845), to a state in the Confederacy (1861), to a state readmitted into the union (1866 and 1869). Each of these documents, especially the 1869 constitution, provided the roots for the current Texas Constitution.

- **What characterizes the current Texas constitution?**

The provisions of the 1876 Texas Constitution are a product of three forces: the constitution of 1869, the E. J. Davis administration from 1870 to 1874, and a national movement toward substantive and restrictive constitutions. The current constitution has been criticized because of its disorganization, the limits to executive and legislative powers, the structure of the judiciary, and the limits on local government.

- **What are the methods of constitutional revision in Texas?**

Most changes to the Texas Constitution have resulted from piecemeal efforts to adapt the constitution to changing economic and social conditions in the state. The result has been the adoption of 456 constitutional amendments, a long and confusing document, and an impetus for comprehensive constitutional change through a constitutional convention.

- **Why did Texas adopt a recent constitutional reform: The marriage amendment?**

In 2005, Texas joined seventeen other states by adopting an amendment defining marriage as involving only one man and one woman. Proponents and opponents of the amendment voiced their positions and campaigned vigorously. The amendment passed easily, garnering its strongest support from rural counties.

Key Terms

cockroach, p. 53
comprehensive revision, p. 48
Constitutional Revision Commission, p. 51
liberal constitution, p. 41
piecemeal revision, p. 48
revisionist, p. 53
statutory constitution, p. 41

Researching the Texas Constitution

In the Library

Angell, Robert H. *A Compilation and Analysis of the 1998 Texas Constitution and the Original 1876 Text*. Lewiston, NY: Mellen, 1998.

Braden, George D. *Citizens' Guide to the Texas Constitution*. Austin: Institute of Urban Studies, University of Houston, 1972.

Cornyn, John. "The Roots of the Texas Constitution: Settlement to Statehood." *Texas Tech Law Review* 26 (1995): 1089–1218.

May, Janice C. *The Texas Constitutional Revision Experience in the 1970s*. Austin, TX: Sterling Swift, 1975.

———. *The Texas State Constitution: A Reference Guide*. Westport, CT: Greenwood, 1996.

McKay, Seth S. *Seven Decades of the Texas Constitution of 1876*. Lubbock, TX: n.p., 1942.

Tarr, G. Alan. *Understanding State Constitutions*. Princeton, NJ: Princeton University Press, 1998.

Watts, Mikal, and Brad Rockwall, "The Original Intent of the Education Article of the Texas Constitution," *St. Mary's Law Journal* 21 (1990): 771–820.

Williams, Patrick G. *Beyond Redemption: Texas Democrats After Reconstruction*. College Station, TX: Texas A&M University Press, 2007.

Wolff, Nelson. *Challenge of Change*. San Antonio, TX: Naylor, 1975.

On the Web

The 1845 Texas Constitution www.tarlton.law.utexas.edu/ constitutions/text/1845index.html
Often cited as the "best" Texas Constitution, the 1845 Texas Constitution is available for study and comparison with the current constitution.

The 1869 Texas Constitution www.tarlton.law.utexas.edu/ constitutions/text/1869index.html
The text of the 1869 Constitution facilitates a study of its continuity and differences with previous constitutions.

Amendments to the Texas Constitution www.lrl.state.tx.us/legis/constAmends/lrlhome.cfm
The Legislative Reference Library site facilitates searches for proposed and adopted amendments to the Texas Constitution.

Voter turnout in constitutional elections www.sos.state.tx.us/elections/historical/70-92.shtml
The Texas secretary of state provides data on voter turnout in Texas elections, including those involving constitutional amendments.

3 Voting and Participating: Political Parties, Interest Groups, and Elections

When the Republican Party became the dominant political party in Texas, Republican politicians' aspirations for higher office created contests in Republican primaries. In 2004, political pundits envisioned a gubernatorial contest in the Republican primary among Rick Perry, who succeeded George W. Bush as governor in 2000; Kay Bailey Hutchison, the senior U.S. senator from Texas; and Carole Keeton Strayhorn, the comptroller of public accounts who was elected in 1998 and reelected in 2002.

■ Voting, elections, and campaigns are a crucial aspect of democratic governance in Texas. At left, a photograph depicts women registering at the Travis County Courthouse as a result of the primary suffrage bill, which became law seventeen days before the 1918 primary election. At right, voters with disabilities are given ballots during a recent election in Texas.

Perry—a former Democratic state representative who became a Republican agriculture commissioner and then lieutenant governor—definitely wanted another term in 2006. If elected, he would have the longest tenure as governor in the state's history. However, Perry's failure to provide leadership in resolving the battle among legislators over public school financing led to many failed attempts in regular and special sessions of the legislature. Strayhorn, also a former Democrat, had never sought elective office as a Democrat. She had served on the Insurance Board and Railroad Commission before she was elected comptroller, and she sounded like a gubernatorial candidate in her criticisms of Perry. Hutchison had recently adopted two young children, and many pundits speculated that she would much rather raise them in Texas as governor than in Washington, D.C., as a U.S. senator. But, in late June 2005, Hutchison announced her intention to seek reelection to the Senate. Most observers mused that Perry had sewn up financial support within the Republican Party as well as from important interest groups and convinced loyal Republicans to persuade Hutchison to stay in the Senate.

On the same day as the Hutchison announcement, Strayhorn announced her intention to enter the Republican primary against Perry, dubbing him a "do-nothing drugstore cowboy." On January 2, 2006, however, Strayhorn announced a change in plans; she would run for governor as an independent candidate. Although she cited

WHAT SHOULD I KNOW ABOUT . . .

- the roots of political parties, interest groups, elections, and campaigns in Texas?
- political parties in Texas?
- interest groups in Texas?
- elections and political campaigns in Texas?
- recent reforms in political parties, interest groups, elections, and campaigns?

the increased partisanship of politics in Austin as a reason for her decision, most political observers guessed a more pragmatic reason: she knew that she couldn't beat Perry in the Republican primary.

> **TO LEARN MORE—**
> **—TO DO MORE**
> To learn more about the 2006 Texas gubernatorial debate, go to a video of the debate online and watch it at video.google.com/videoplay?docid-4061730804961994829.

To secure a position on the ballot in the November general election, Strayhorn needed to collect 45,540 signatures on petitions from registered voters who had not voted in any political party's primary election. The petitions had to be submitted to the secretary of state by May 11, 2006. Also seeking a position on the ballot as an independent candidate for governor was Kinky Friedman, a well-known author, singer, and songwriter who had never held political office. On May 9, 2006, Strayhorn submitted 101 boxes containing more than 223,000 signatures on petitions to place her on the ballot. Secretary of State Roger Williams reported that verification of the signatures could require up to eight weeks. Earlier, Strayhorn had sued the secretary of state in federal district court, suggesting that he was manipulating the ballot petition process to favor the person who appointed him secretary of state, Governor Perry. Williams had previously announced that he would verify each signature; Strayhorn wanted him to verify only a sample of the signatures. She lost the lawsuit and decided not to appeal.

On May 11, 2006, Friedman submitted more than 169,000 signatures to the secretary of state. Dean Barkley, Friedman's campaign manager, stated that taking two months to certify an independent candidate's position on the ballot would undermine his or her ability to raise campaign funds and to be considered a serious candidate. Ultimately, the secretary of state certified both Friedman and Strayhorn for the ballot.

Thus, before the election campaign really began, the candidates were busy making charges and counter-charges. But, as the saying goes, "Politics in Texas is a full-body, contact sport." Joining in the battle was the Democratic candidate for governor, Chris Bell, who had received the endorsement of the AFL-CIO, a labor group consisting of 220,000 members.

After a single televised debate in October, numerous campaign commercials, and lower voter turnout than in 2002, the election results were what most political observers had expected. Rick Perry was reelected with 39 percent of the vote. In second place was Bell with 30 percent of the vote. Independent candidates Strayhorn and Friedman received 18 and 13 percent of the vote, respectively.

The four-way contest for Texas governor in 2006 illustrates a number of points about the roots of and the reforms affecting political parties, interest groups, elections, and campaigns in contemporary Texas. Interest groups and political parties represent the interests of their members and promote the adoption of certain government policies, but the activities of interest groups focus on *influencing* government, while the activities of political parties focus on *controlling* government. For example, interest groups, through their members and political action committees, made campaign contributions to Democratic candidate Chris Bell and to Republican candidate Rick Perry. The Democratic and Republican Parties nominated them, helped finance their campaigns, and tried to get them elected, hoping to control the office that leads the executive branch of state government. Elections provide the mechanism by which parties gain control of government, and campaigns create a link among the political parties, their candidates, interest groups, and the public.

In this chapter, we will examine political parties, interest groups, elections, and campaigns in Texas and consider them from several vantage points.

★ First, we will consider the *roots of political parties, interest groups, elections, and campaigns in Texas*, noting how reforms in these institutions and processes influenced their development in Texas history.

★ Second, we will examine *political parties in Texas*, describing the party organization, the party in the electorate, and the party in government and analyzing how these components operate in Texas.

★ Third, we will explore *interest groups in Texas*, describing the types of interest groups and the activities that groups employ to influence public policy.

★ Fourth, we will examine *elections and political campaigns in Texas*, exploring types of elections, voting behavior, the role of money, media, and marketing (the three Ms), voter turnout, and vote choice.

★ Finally, we will discuss *recent reforms in elections and campaigns*, examining changes in election and campaign procedures.

Why were so many candidates vying for the governorship? Chris Bell, Kinky Friedman, Rick Perry, and Carole Keeton Strayhorn during the 2006 gubernatorial debate.

Roots of Political Parties, Interest Groups, Elections, and Campaigns in Texas

Political parties and interest groups developed slowly in Texas. As noted in chapter 1, early Anglo settlers in Texas were from the upper and lower South, and many brought their Democratic Party attachments with them. But, until the late 1840s, personality was the dominant force in electoral politics. In 1848, the Democratic Party emerged as a formal organization that actively participated in elections. Until the end of the Civil War in 1865, personalities still strongly influenced party politics in Texas, providing the basis for factions within the dominant Democratic Party. In 1867, in response to congressional Reconstruction, the Republican Party of Texas formed and took control of Texas politics and government from 1868 to 1874 (see chapter 2), when Democrats reasserted their dominance. After Reconstruction, the Democratic Party, though challenged occasionally by the Greenback Party and People's Party, controlled Texas government, making Texas a one-party state.

The era of one-party Democratic dominance (1874–1986) was filled with feuds between contending factions within the party. Issues such as the free coinage of silver and Prohibition caused splits in the Democratic Party during the late nineteenth and early twentieth centuries. In the 1930s, the Great Depression and President Franklin Roosevelt's New Deal created a split over economic policy that resulted in the development of liberal and conservative factions, which would battle for control of the party until the end of the one-party era.

Like political parties in Texas, interest groups developed slowly. The most influential interest groups in the nineteenth century represented agrarian interests, and the influence of the Grange, though not monolithic, was evident in the constitutional convention of 1875. Groups representing oil and gas interests supplanted agrarian groups during the early twentieth century. After World War II, as the Texas economy and society became more complex and diverse, interest groups proliferated, representing a broader array of interests based on ethnic, social, and cultural divisions in the state. However, economic interests, especially those representing businesses, maintained their preeminence.

Campaigns and elections, which originally were centered on personal loyalties to candidates, became partisan or factional contests. Until the early 1960s, the most important elections were the Democratic primaries, which featured candidates of the contending factions. Democratic candidates always won the general elections, and voter turnout suffered because of the lack of competition. Voter turnout was also hampered by legal impediments to voting, some of which persisted until the 1970s.

Political Parties in Texas

Political parties in Texas perform the same functions as the national parties. The parties perform these functions through their three components: party organization, party in the electorate, and party in government.

Party Organization

The party organization consists of the structures that constitute the party organization and the party activists who occupy positions in the party structure. The party organization includes both a formal organization, established in state law, and a functional organization, which describes how the party actually operates. Party activists, such as precinct and county chairs, usually perform their work in obscurity, unknown and unheralded.

FORMAL ORGANIZATION Texas state law, as in most states, establishes the formal organization for political parties. There is both a temporary and a permanent party organization for each political party.

The **temporary party organization** consists of conventions at the precinct, the county or state senatorial district, and the state levels. Held every two years, party conventions are attended by party activists and last only a short period of time, ranging from a few hours to a few days. The conventions meet to select delegates to subsequent party conventions, choose party leaders, and establish party policies. They provide an opportunity for interested party members to select the party's leaders and influence its policies.

Every two years, the first party convention occurs at the voting-precinct level. Election precincts are voting districts that usually contain fewer than 3,000 registered voters. On the date of the primary election (currently the first Tuesday of March in even-numbered years) after the polls have closed, the parties hold their **precinct conventions.** The political parties conduct primary elections to select their nominees for elected public office—governor, state senator, state representative, and county judge, for example. A stamp, indicating which party's primary election the person voted in, is placed on the voter's registration card by the primary election official, and any person with such a stamp may participate in the party's precinct convention. Participation is open, but only about 1 percent of the voters in the party's primary election actually attend the precinct conventions. Even in presidential election years, when the precinct conventions in the Democratic Party have an effect on the selection of delegates to the party's national convention

temporary party organization
Party organization that exists for a limited time and includes several levels of conventions.

precinct convention
Precinct party meeting to select delegates and adopt resolutions.

How do party precinct conventions involve voters in political parties? Houston voters line up to sign in at a Democratic precinct convention on March 4, 2008. Nearly a million voters statewide participated in the 2008 Democratic Party's precinct conventions.

and the choice of the party's presidential nominee, attendance rarely exceeds 10 percent of the eligible participants.

The precinct convention's principal task is to select delegates to the party's **county convention** or, in those counties that are in more than one state senatorial district (which included fifteen counties in 2008[1]), to the **state senatorial district convention.** In both the Democratic and the Republican Parties, each precinct in the county or senatorial district is allocated delegates based on the number of votes cast in the precinct for the party's gubernatorial nominee in the most recent gubernatorial election. The allocation system is designed to reward those precincts that provided the greatest electoral support for the party's gubernatorial nominee by giving them a larger voice in selecting party officials and setting party policy. After delegates to the county or senatorial district convention have been chosen, the precinct convention debates and then either adopts or rejects resolutions; the resolutions that are adopted are forwarded to the county or senatorial district convention. Through this process, the party begins to build a party platform by discussing the concerns of party members on issues of public policy.

On the third Saturday after the primary election, each party holds its county and senatorial district conventions. The delegates and alternates who were selected in the precinct conventions attend the county and senatorial district conventions, which usually are all-day affairs.

The principal purpose of the county or senatorial district conventions is to select delegates to the party's state convention. Like the precincts, each county or senatorial district is allocated delegates based on its support for the party's gubernatorial nominee in the most recent general election. Also, the conventions consider resolutions adopted in the precinct conventions; if these resolutions are adopted at the county or senatorial district level, the resolutions are sent to the state convention for possible incorporation in the party's platform.

In June, on a date selected by the state executive committee of each party, the delegates assemble for the party's **state convention.** The state convention certifies the results of the party's primary (which nominates the party's candidates for public office), drafts and adopts the party's platform, and selects the party's state executive committee, including the state party chair and vice chair. In presidential election years, the state convention also selects the party's slate of presidential electors, nominates the state's members for the party's national committee, and selects the state's delegates to the party's national convention. The Republican Party allocates all of its national convention delegates based on the presidential primary results, and delegate selection committees, whose members are chosen by the presidential candidates, provide lists of delegates for the state convention to select. In the Democratic Party, delegates are allocated on the basis of the presidential primary results (75 percent of the allotted delegates) and on the basis of support for the candidates at the precinct, county or state senatorial, and state conventions (25 percent of the allotted delegates).

county convention
County party meeting to select delegates and adopt resolutions.

state senatorial district convention
Party meeting held when a county is a part of more than one senatorial district.

state convention
Party meeting held to adopt the party's platform, elect the party's executive committee and state chairperson, and in a presidential election year, elect delegates to the national convention and choose presidential electors.

CHAPTER 3 Voting and Participating: Political Parties, Interest Groups, and Elections

permanent party organization
Party organization that operates throughout the year, performing the party's functions.

The **permanent party organization** consists of the party chairpersons and committees, which purportedly work throughout the year performing party-building and electoral functions. Because of their principal activities, the parties' permanent organizations are tied to electoral districts. Each electoral unit, from the smallest (the precinct) to the largest (the state), is represented in the permanent organization. The political party appears hierarchical in structure, with power concentrated at the top, but party organizations are more accurately described as *stratarchies*—organizations with power distributed in layers or strata.[2] Consequently, each level of party organization is relatively independent of the other levels and concentrates on electoral activities within its level or strata.

precinct chairperson
Party leader in a voting precinct.

Each precinct in Texas has a **precinct chairperson** who represents the party in that electoral district. The chairperson is elected for a two-year term in the party's primary election. The chairperson is responsible for informing members of the party's activities and issue positions, getting party members to the polls on election days, and serving on the party's county executive committee.

county chairperson
Party leader in a county.

county executive committee
Precinct chairpersons in a county that assist the county chairpersons.

Each county in Texas has a **county chairperson** and a **county executive committee.** The county chairperson is elected in the party's primary for a two-year term. The county executive committee, consisting of the county's precinct chairpersons, assists the county chairperson. At the county level, the party's duties, which are usually performed by the county chairperson, include conducting the party's primary elections, arranging for the county convention, raising funds for the county organization, campaigning for party candidates, and promoting precinct organization efforts.

state executive committee
Sixty-two-member party committee that makes decisions for the party between state conventions.

Formally, the supreme unit of the party's permanent organization is the **state executive committee,** composed of a chairperson and a vice chairperson (state law requires that the chairperson and vice chairperson not be of the same gender) and one man and one woman from each of the state's thirty-one senatorial districts. The representatives from the senatorial districts are elected at the state convention, based on nominations by the individual state senatorial districts for two-year terms. Consequently, the selection is really made by the delegates from each of the state's senatorial districts. In addition, the Texas Democratic Party allocates committee membership to state party officials and several constituent groups—such as women, Asian Americans, African Americans, Tejanos, and young Democrats—which increases the size of the committee to ninety-two members. The **state party chairperson** and vice chairperson are chosen by the entire convention, but their selection may be influenced by the party's gubernatorial nominee. The state executive committee's duties include certifying the party's candidates for the general election, conducting the state convention, and promoting the party's candidates and issue positions. (To learn more about the formal party organization, see Figure 3.1.)

state party chairperson
Party leader for the state.

Who are the state party leaders? Tina Benkiser (left) and Boyd Richie (right), elected at their respective state conventions in 2008, are state chairs of the Texas Republican Party and Democratic Party, respectively.

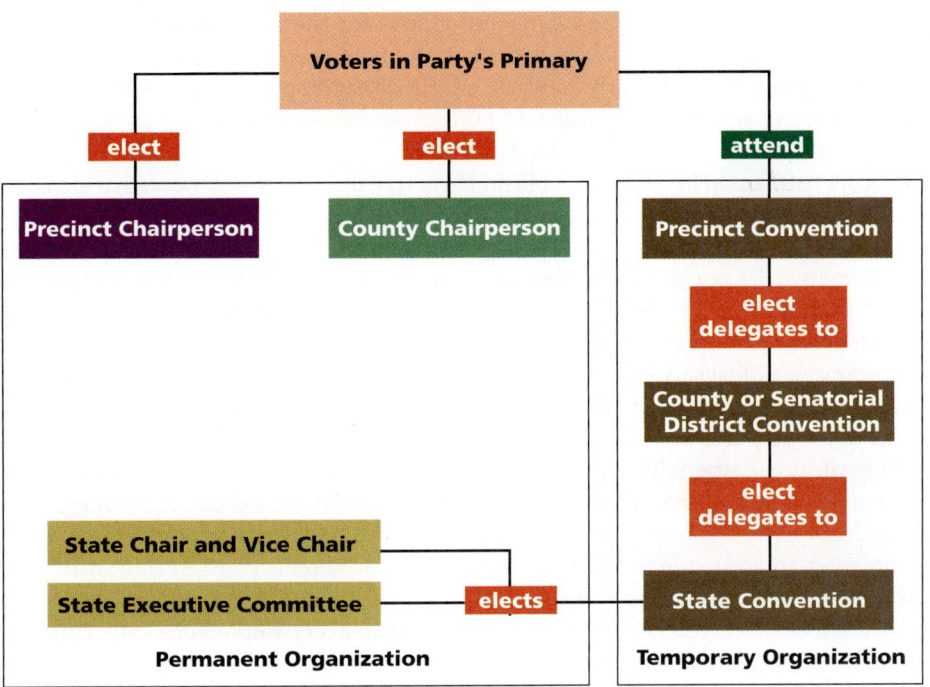

FIGURE 3.1 Party Organization in Texas

FUNCTIONAL ORGANIZATION The formal organizational chart of any organization may not provide the real story of how well the organization functions and where decisions are made. For political parties, although the state chairperson formally heads the party and is elected by the state executive committee, functional leadership may rest with the governor, who can be instrumental in selecting his or her party's state chairperson and shaping party policy. The formal organization provides a skeleton for the party organization, but its performance is determined by the effectiveness of the people who occupy those positions and who use those positions to further the party's political goals. Thus, in this section, we describe and assess the party organizations in Texas in terms of their unity and effectiveness in performing the party's functions.

DEMOCRATIC PARTY UNITY Since 1976, control of the Democratic Party organization in Texas has been in ideological liberals' hands. Their control has affected the number of liberals among Democratic candidates for statewide office, their electoral success, and the party's platform. During the 1950s and 1960s, the only liberal Democrat elected to statewide office in Texas was U.S. Senator Ralph Yarborough. However, in 1982, four liberal Democrats—Jim Mattox, Jim Hightower, Garry Mauro, and Ann Richards— were elected to statewide executive offices. All won reelection in 1986, and Ann Richards was elected governor in 1990. In recent elections, however, liberal Democrats have not fared as well. In 1990, Republican Rick Perry, a former conservative Democratic state representative who switched parties, defeated Jim Hightower for agriculture commissioner. Mattox, who unsuccessfully sought the Democratic gubernatorial nomination in 1990, was replaced as attorney general by moderate Democrat Dan Morales. In 1994, Ann Richards lost the governorship to George W. Bush. In 1998, Mattox lost his comeback bid to become attorney general to Republican Supreme Court Justice John Cornyn. Mauro, who barely won reelection as land commissioner in 1994, lost his bid to become governor to George W. Bush in 1998. Thus, Republicans replaced the liberal class of 1982 in statewide elective offices during the 1990s.

The success of liberal Democrats in the 1980s and early 1990s also had an effect on the Republican Party, as conservative Democrats, having lost control of the Democratic

Party, increasingly abandoned the Democratic Party for the Republican Party. By the 1990s, Democratic Party leaders were overwhelmingly liberal or moderate ideologically. A recent study of Democratic Party activists indicated that 60 percent were self-described liberals, 25 percent were moderates, and 15 percent were conservatives.[3]

REPUBLICAN PARTY UNITY The Republican Party has always been conservative ideologically. Though more cohesive ideologically than the Democratic Party, the Republican Party in Texas also has its intraparty conflicts. Republican Party activists are overwhelmingly conservative (91 percent), with few moderates (7 percent) and even fewer liberals (2 percent).[4] Republican conflicts typically are over goals and policies. Republican *pragmatists* or *economic conservatives* emphasize the party's role in elections and governing and its economic policies. More libertarian in political ideology, the pragmatists seek to expand the party's membership, reaching out to people who have not traditionally been members of the Republican coalition, and to pursue policies that advance the economic well-being of its members. Republican *ideologues* or *social conservatives* emphasize the party's representation function, stressing the party's conservative political ideology over winning elections and controlling the government, and social conservatism. The ideologues are more interested in promoting conservative social policies, especially anti-abortion, than electing Republican candidates to office.

The clash between the factions has been evident in every Republican state convention since 1994, when a coalition of religious conservatives and anti-abortion activists dominated the party's state convention and elected their candidate state party chair. The Christian Coalition, a group that favors what they identify as traditional social values, extended its control by electing the party vice chair, Susan Weddington, and a majority of the state executive committee.[5] In 1996, the issue that divided the convention was abortion. Despite the urgings of former governor Bill Clements to focus on the issues that united Republicans in the past, the social conservatives, who made up more than 80 percent of the delegates, attempted to exclude Senator Kay Bailey Hutchison from the party's national convention delegation because her pro-life credentials were not staunch enough for them.[6]

In 1997, when Susan Weddington was elected state chair, she pledged to unify the party's factions. She reached out to the party's moderates and economic conservatives, many of whom supported abortion rights. However, the election of David Barton, a social conservative like Weddington, as state vice chair raised concerns among some moderate Republicans. Nevertheless, Weddington declared a new leadership and focus for the state party.[7] In 1998, social conservatives initiated a platform provision denying party funding and support to any candidates who refused to endorse a ban on the late-term abortion procedure that social conservatives term "partial-birth abortion." The social conservatives, whose candidates had been unsuccessful in the Republican primary earlier in the year, defied the pleas of Governor Bush and other statewide elected officials not to restrict the party's growth in this manner.[8] In 2002, the social conservatives pushed the Republican platform even further, calling for the deportation of immigrants who do not carry the required ID, stricter requirements for voter registration, and the termination of bilingual education programs in Texas.[9] In 2006, state convention delegates adopted a platform that declares "the United States is a Christian nation" and the Ten Commandments "are the basis of our basic freedoms and the cornerstone of our Western tradition."[10]

PARTY EFFECTIVENESS: WHAT'S AT STAKE? Assessing party organizational effectiveness requires us to examine different factors, depending on the level of party organization being assessed. Consequently, we consider each level of party organization—statewide, county, and precinct—in turn.

At the state level, party effectiveness is related to the complexity of the party's organization and the capacity of the party's organization to perform its party-building functions. Indicators of organizational complexity include an accessible party headquarters, a complex division of labor, a substantial party budget, and a professional leadership. In Texas, both parties maintain fairly complex organizations. A state party's ability to perform its party-building duties is calculated in two areas: (1) institutional support activities such as fund-raising, electoral mobilization programs, public opinion polling, issue leadership, and publication of a newsletter; and, (2) candidate-centered activities such as contributions to candidates, recruitment of candidates, selection of convention delegates, and pre-primary endorsements. A comparison of the contemporary Democratic and Republican Parties in Texas reveals that an advantage in both measures of party building is enjoyed by the Republican Party.

At the county and precinct levels, the party organization's primary task is campaigning for the party's candidates and getting voters to the polls. County and precinct chairpersons are most influential in determining the party's effectiveness at this level.[11] Studies of party activities at these levels reveal that Republican Party activists are more likely to involve their members in party and political activities.

There is also a substantial difference between Republican chairpersons and Democratic chairpersons in their perceptions of changes in their party's organizational strength and effectiveness. A large percentage of Republican county and precinct chairpersons (more than three-fourths on most measures) viewed their organizations as more effective in 2001 than they had been in 1981, 1986, or 1991. On the other hand, few Democratic chairpersons (about one-fourth or fewer on most measures) viewed their organizations as stronger during the same period.[12]

How does the examination of the parties' functional organizations help us understand party politics in Texas? The lack of unity in both parties detracts from their effectiveness as organizations and from their ability to represent a majority of Texans. To become the majority party in Texas, Republicans must effectively deal with the differences between the *ideologues* and the *pragmatists* by becoming less interested in ideological purity and more interested in representing and governing. Although a majority of

TEXAS IN COMPARISON

Political Parties, Interest Groups, and Elections in the States

Political parties in the four largest states vary somewhat in the degree of interparty competition as well as in which party controls the legislature. New York has the largest number of registered lobbyists, and California has the fewest lobbyists. The states also vary greatly in the percentage of registered voters.

	Ranney Measure of Interparty Competition[a] (2002–2008)	Party Composition in the Legislature (2009)	Registered Lobbyists (2006)	Voting-Age Population (2008)	Percentage of Registered Voters (2008)
Texas	0.290	Texas House of Representatives: 76 Republicans, 74 Democrats Texas Senate: 19 Republicans, 12 Democrats	1,489	17,765,083	76.4
California	0.593	California Assembly: 50 Democrats, 30 Republicans California Senate: 26 Democrats, 14 Republicans	1,267	27,596,996	62.7
New York	0.397	New York Assembly: 109 Democrats, 41 Republicans New York Senate: 32 Democrats, 30 Republicans	5,117	14,976,792	80.3
Florida	0.187	Florida House of Representatives: 76 Republicans, 44 Democrats Florida Senate: 26 Republicans, 14 Democrats	2,029	14,451,551	77.8

[a]The Ranney index of party competition actually measures party control. An index of 0.500 indicates that control of government is evenly split between the parties; an index of 1.000 indicates complete Democratic Party control; an index of 0.000 indicates complete Republican control.

Source: Ranney index computed by authors; National Conference of State Legislatures, www.ncsl.org; United States Election Project, elections.gmu.edu/Turnout_2008G.html; Office of the Secretary of State or Board of Elections for the states.

Texans consider themselves conservative politically, they are not as conservative as the Republican ideologues. The challenge for Democrats is to ensure that as conservative Democrats are drawn to the Republican Party, the Democratic Party does not become too liberal to represent a majority of Texans on most issues.

Party in the Electorate

The most important function for the party organization is winning elections, which means mobilizing interest in the party's goals and candidates among the voters—the electorate. The party in the electorate consists of those people who identify with a political party and consider themselves members. In slightly more than half of the states—not including Texas—voters register as members of a particular political party or as independents.

Because Texans don't register by political party, opinion polls are used to determine the party identifications of Texans.[13] Party identification is a psychological attachment that is formed early in life but can be altered by events, issues, and political personalities. Partisan attachments are considered important in determining a party's chances for electoral victory and, consequently, its ability to control government.

DISTRIBUTION OF PARTY ATTACHMENTS In 1952, when survey research began measuring party identification, only 6 percent of Texans identified themselves as Republicans, and 66 percent identified themselves as Democrats. Since 1952, however, the percentage of Democrats has declined and the percentage of Republicans increased. In 1991, the percentages of Republicans and Democrats were identical. In public opinion surveys conducted since 1999, there have been more Republicans than Democrats in Texas. In 2007, 33 percent of Texans identified with the Republican Party, and 28 percent identified with the Democratic Party. (To learn more about the Republican rise and Democratic decline, see Figure 3.2.)

The changes in party affiliation among Texans involve more than just a decrease in Democrats and an increase in Republicans. The percentage of independents—individu-

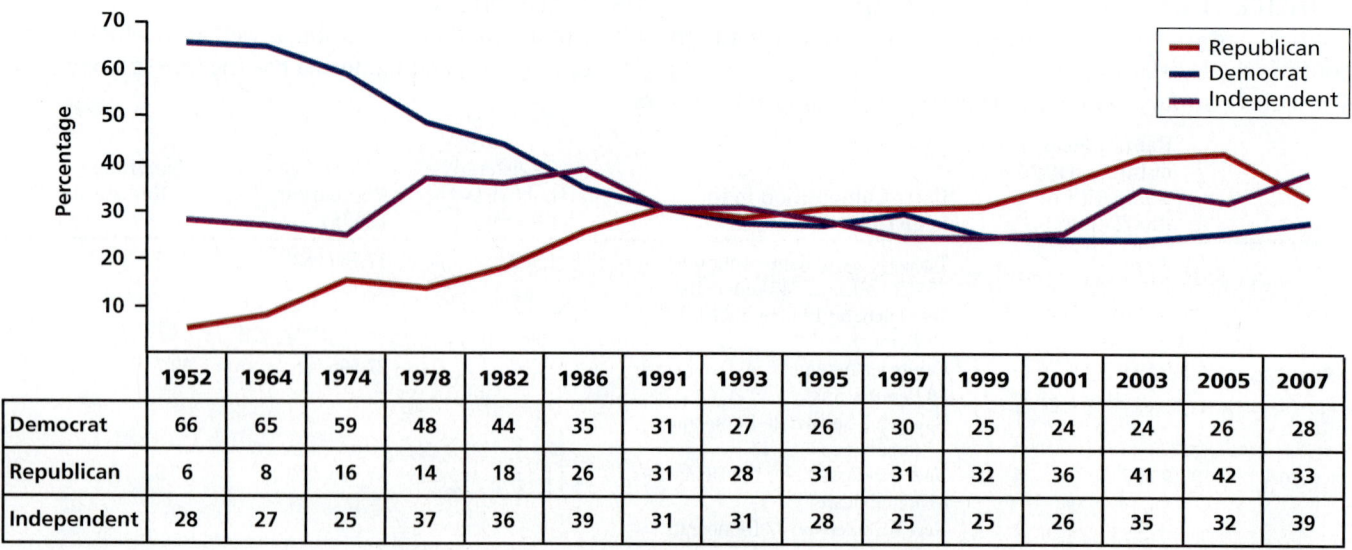

FIGURE 3.2 **Party Identification in Texas: Republican Rise and Democratic Decline** The chart depicts party identification of Texans in selected years between 1952 and 2007. Until recently, Texas was considered a part of the Solid South, a portion of the country known for its one-party Democratic states. The chart shows the changes that have occurred in party identification, reflecting the rise of Republicans in Texas.

Sources: Belden Polls (1952, 1964); Texas Polls (1974–2001); Gallup Poll (2003–2007).

als who identify with neither major political party—has also increased in Texas. In fact, independents constituted a larger percentage of the population (39 percent) than either the Democratic or Republican Party. Thus, whereas 72 percent of the population in Texas identified with one of the major political parties in 1952, only 61 percent did in 2007. Consequently, people with attachments to the Democratic or the Republican Party constitute a smaller percentage of the electorate now than in 1952. This is not a good sign for supporters of strong political parties or for the view that strong parties are essential to democracy.

PARTY REALIGNMENT IN TEXAS Realignments, triggered by critical elections, produce profound changes in the distribution of partisan attachments. According to some political scientists, Texas has experienced an attenuated realignment (or secular realignment). They offer the following evidence:

- Young voters were more likely to identify with the Republican Party than the Democratic Party during the 1980s and 1990s. Among party identifiers, young people—age eighteen to twenty-nine—were much more likely to identify with the Republican Party than were older people. Consequently, generational replacement favored the Republicans. However, surveys conducted in 2007 indicate that nearly half of those age eighteen to twenty-nine are independents. The same percentage of young people (28 percent) identify with the Republican or Democratic Party.
- Some Democrats switched to the Republican Party. These conversions were most likely among conservative Democrats of an upper-level socio-economic status who were bringing their party identification into line with their ideology and status.
- New residents of Texas were more likely to identify with the Republican Party than were native Texans or long-term residents. Between 1970 and 2000, when Texas experienced an influx of immigrants, most of the new residents brought an identification with the Republican Party, which they kept.
- Party identification, especially among Republicans, is important in determining vote choices in elections. Between 80 and 90 percent of Republicans voted for Republican candidates in recent elections. Also, in the two largest counties of Texas, a majority of voters cast straight-ticket ballots, voting for all candidates of one party.
- Republican candidates won more counties (especially the most populous counties) than Democrats in recent presidential, gubernatorial, and other statewide elections. Indeed, a map of voting trends in the 1970s is dramatically different from a map of voting trends from the 2000s. (To learn more about vote choices in the 1970s and 2000s, see Figures 3.3 and 3.4.)[14]

In 2008, Republican candidates won every statewide election, continuing their hold on all twenty-nine statewide elected offices. Republicans also retained control of the Texas Senate, which they have controlled since 1997, and the Texas House, which they have controlled since 2003. Generally speaking, Republican candidates are more successful in large electoral districts. For example, 80 percent of the court of appeals judges were Republicans in 2005, but only 37 percent of the county judges and 36 percent of the county commissioners were Republicans. Nevertheless, the total number of Republican elected officials had increased to approximately 2,166 by 2005.[15] As political scientists Gregory Thielemann and Euel Elliott contend, "The transformation from hard-core 'yellow dog' Democratic Party dominance to Republican supremacy has been thorough and complete."[16]

Another possible interpretation of the surveys on party identification in Texas is that Texans are not realigning but dealigning. In a dealignment, party affiliations weaken, and the importance of party affiliation to the population's political attitudes and behavior also weakens. The dealignment interpretation concludes that although there are more Republican identifiers and fewer Democratic identifiers, the most important fact is the growth

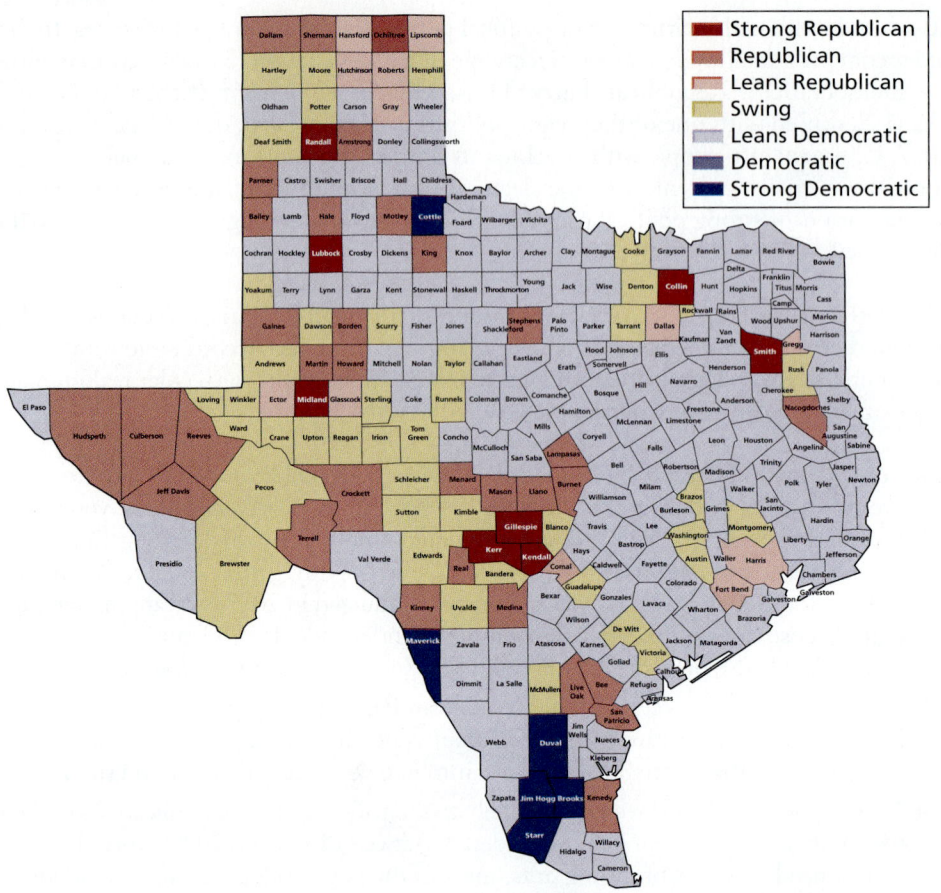

FIGURE 3.3 **Republican and Democratic Party Strength in Texas by County (1970s)** The map reflects the strength of the Texas Republican and Democratic Parties based on votes for Republican and Democratic candidates in selected general election contests during the 1970s.

Sources: Based on county election results from the 1972 presidential election, 1974 gubernatorial election, 1976 presidential election, 1978 gubernatorial election, 1978 lieutenant governor election, and the 1978 attorney general election. Mike Kingston, Sam Attlesey, and Mary G. Crawford, *The Texas Almanac's Political History of Texas* (Austin: Eakin, 1992); *Texas Almanac, 1980–1981* (Dallas: A. H. Belo, 1979).

in independent identifiers, who do not identify with any political party. According to this interpretation, Texas is not becoming a Republican state; it is becoming a no-party state. The large percentage of independents is cited as evidence that party identification is less important, and elections are not about parties but about candidates. However, given the Republican Party's advantage in most elections, this interpretation is more difficult to support.

CONTEMPORARY PARTY COALITIONS As a result of the changes in party identification among Texans, the party coalitions have become more like their national counterparts. Increasingly, people in the upper income categories identify with the Republican Party; people in the lower income categories identify with the Democratic Party. In addition, the Democratic Party is the party of liberals and populists, African Americans and Hispanics, and women; the Republican Party is the party of conservatives and libertarians, Anglos, males, and the Christian Right.

The Party in Government

The party in government is a political party's mechanism for establishing cooperation among the separate branches of government. In theory, all public officials who

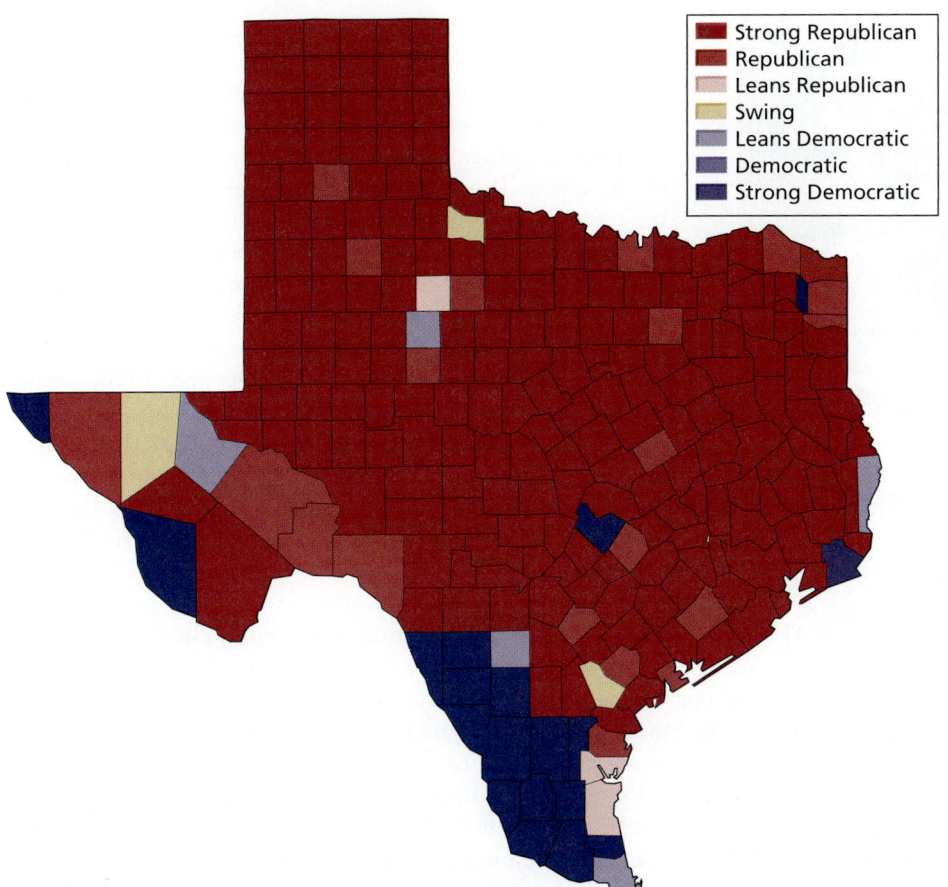

FIGURE 3.4 **Republican and Democratic Party Strength in Texas by County (2000s)** The map reflects the strength of the Texas Republican and Democratic Parties based on votes for Republican and Democratic candidates in selected general election contests during the 2000s.

Sources: Based on county election results from the 2000 presidential election, 2002 gubernatorial election, 2004 presidential election, 2006 gubernatorial election, 2006 lieutenant governor election, and the 2006 attorney general election. Texas Secretary of State Web site, Historical Election Results, http://www.sos.state.tx.us/elections/historical/70-92.shtml.

are appointed or elected under the same party label work together to establish and implement public policies that represent the party's positions on issues. How strong is the party in government in Texas, and how well does it perform this unifying function?

IN THE EXECUTIVE BRANCH For members of the executive branch in Texas, the Texas Constitution establishes several impediments to cooperation. Foremost is the independent election of the most important executive officers in Texas. Even the governor and lieutenant governor do not run as a team on the ballot (see chapter 5). Consequently, the relationship between the governor and lieutenant governor, even when they are members of the same political party, may be strained. Also, because the Texas attorney general's office has often been used as a stepping stone by politicians who aspire to be governor, the relationship between those two officials may not be the most cordial, even when they are members of the same political party. Other statewide elected officials in the executive branch may also harbor such ambitions. For example, shortly after Mark White was elected governor in 1982, Comptroller Bob Bullock, a member of White's party, announced his intention to seek the party's gubernatorial nomination in 1986.[17] More recently, Republican Texas Comptroller Carol Keeton Strayhorn announced her intention to challenge Republican Governor Rick Perry for the party's gubernatorial

Would you raise your right hand and repeat after me? Governor Rick Perry, right, swears in Don Willett, left, as his appointee to the Texas Supreme Court. Tiffany Willett, center, holds the Bible during the ceremony at the Capitol. Perry has appointed five of the nine members of the court.

nomination but later decided to skip the Republican primary and run in the general election as an independent.

Because the executive officers are elected independently, candidates of the same political party have little incentive to campaign together or even to coordinate their campaigns for public office. Typically, each office-seeker establishes his or her campaign organization. This practice further reduces the likelihood of cooperation after the election. In 1982, faced for the first time with Republican opposition in all major executive races, the Democratic candidates showed a greater degree of cooperation than normal and even coordinated portions of their campaigns. In 1990 and 1994, despite strong opposition in many executive contests, the Democrats failed to coordinate their campaigns. In 1998, John Sharp and Paul Hobby, Democratic candidates for lieutenant governor and comptroller respectively, failed to endorse the Democratic gubernatorial nominee, Garry Mauro. Republican candidates for statewide executive offices have usually demonstrated a similar tendency to run independent campaigns.

IN THE LEGISLATIVE BRANCH In the Texas legislature, as noted in chapter 4, partisan considerations are usually minimized. Until recently, Texas was one of only five states that did not hold inclusive party caucuses, elect party leaders, or create party committees. Party caucuses and committees are formed to provide information to party members on policy issues and to formulate the party's position on issues. Party leaders are selected to provide leadership for a party's caucus and committees. In 1981, a group of Democratic members of the Texas House of Representatives formed a Democratic caucus. By 1987, the caucus included all Democrats, including the Speaker of the House and all Democrats on his team, a practice that has continued in subsequent sessions. By 1989, the Speaker's team and the caucus began to work together, reducing the tension that had characterized the earlier years.[18] From 1993 to 2003, while Pete Laney was House Speaker, the Democratic caucus was not very active. In 2003, when Republicans gained control of the House and elected a Republican Speaker, the caucus became more active (see chapter 4). Similarly, since 1999, Senate Democrats, faced with a Republican governor and lieutenant governor, decided to give the caucus a more prominent role. Caucus chairs called frequent meetings, discussed policy and strategy, and held press conferences to publicize the Democrats' position on issues before the legislature.

Prior to 1989, the Republicans avoided party organization in the House, preferring to work with the Speaker and conservative Democrats through the Texas Conservative Coalition. However, in 1989, the Republicans organized a caucus, "formed a policy committee to screen suggested legislation before it went to the full caucus for endorsement, and maintained a political arm called the Republican Campaign Legislative Committee."[19] Also, Governor Bill Clements, who had opposed a Republican organization in the House in 1979, now endorsed it during his second term (1987–1991). As their numbers passed the one-third threshold, Republicans began to feel their independence from the Speaker and conservative Democrats. Breaking the one-third threshold allowed the Republicans to prevent an override of a governor's veto, prevent a constitutional amendment from passing, keep a law from becoming effective immediately, and prevent a suspension of the rules (see chapter 4). More importantly, it allowed the Republicans to create a working majority if they could maintain party unity and attract the votes of only one-fourth of the Democrats.

During recent legislatures, the House Republican caucus has met, but it does not have much influence. Despite predictions to the contrary, the Texas legislature continues to operate with strong institutional leaders, eschewing the opportunity to build strong party organizations.[20]

IN THE JUDICIAL BRANCH In Texas, all judges, except municipal court judges, are elected on a partisan ballot. Consequently, a reluctance to politicize the judiciary, which is evident in some states, is less pronounced in Texas. However, candidates for legislative and executive positions rarely team with members of their party seeking judgeships in a coordinated campaign. Thus, the elections are usually conducted independently.

The influence of party is often dominant in the appointment of judges when a vacancy occurs through a judge's death, resignation, retirement, or removal. Because a large percentage of judges are initially appointed to their positions by the governor, he or she has many opportunities to reward party members with judicial appointments. A comparison of judicial appointments by Governor Clements during his last term (1987–1991) and Governor Richards during her term (1991–1995) indicates that each appointed an overwhelming majority of judges who shared the governor's party affiliation.[21] More recently, when Governor Rick Perry was given the opportunity to fill vacancies on the Texas Supreme Court, he chose Republicans.

Appointments of judges by governors could also be viewed as an attempt to fill the courts with judges who share the governor's political ideology. This assumes that judges, in interpreting the law, can exercise some discretion and that Republican judges and Democratic judges differ in how they interpret the law and decide cases. Evidence in certain kinds of cases indicates that this assumption is correct. In civil suits, Democratic judges are more likely to take the plaintiff's side. Republican judges, on the other hand, are more likely to support the defendant when businesses are being sued. For example, during the 2005–2006 term, the Texas Supreme Court, on which Republicans held all of the seats, decided for the defendant in 82 percent of its cases. In 1985, when Democrats controlled the Supreme Court, defendants won only 28 percent of the cases.[22]

Interest Groups in Texas

Recall that when people form groups, they must decide whether to act as a political party or as an interest group. We now turn from parties to interest groups, considering first the types of interest groups and then their political activities.

Types of Interest Groups

Usually, political scientists classify interest groups according to the type of interest that the group represents. We have adopted a classification that focuses on the policy goals of the group: business groups and trade associations, professional associations, labor groups, racial and ethnic groups, and public-interest groups.

BUSINESS GROUPS AND TRADE ASSOCIATIONS Interest groups representing businesses in Texas are diverse, but business groups and trade associations generally agree that their primary goal is to maintain a favorable climate for businesses in Texas. More specifically, these groups attempt to ensure that business taxes remain low, that labor union influence is restricted, and that favorable business regulations exist. Some *business interest groups* (e.g., Texas Association of Business, and Texas Association of Taxpayers) represent business interests generally. Others, known as *trade associations*, represent specific industries and their interests. Among the more influential trade associations are the Texas Automobile Dealers Association, the Texas Bankers Association, the Mid-Continent Oil and Gas Association, and the Texas Chemical Council. To increase their influence, many corporations (AT & T, for example) also hire their own lobbyists when the legislature is considering a matter of particular importance to their interests.

PROFESSIONAL ASSOCIATIONS Some of the most influential interest groups in Texas represent professional associations, such as trial lawyers, physicians, teachers, and realtors. The Texas Trial Lawyers Association (TTLA) represents the interests of lawyers who make their living representing people in personal-injury lawsuits or product-liability suits. The Texas Medical Association (TMA) represents physicians, and the Texas State Teachers Association (TSTA), the Texas Federation of Teachers (TFT), the Association of Texas Professional Educators (ATPE), and the Texas Classroom Teachers Association (TCTA) compete to represent public-school teachers. The Texas Association of Realtors (TAR) works for realtors in Texas. All of these groups attempt to influence regulations and public policies that affect their professions.

LABOR GROUPS Although labor groups have never been strong in Texas, their influence is greatest in the industrialized areas, such as Houston, Dallas, Fort Worth, and especially in the Golden Triangle area of Beaumont, Port Arthur, and Orange. Labor unions attempt to establish rights for their members to collective bargaining, occupational safety, and increased wages. The membership of the American Federation of Labor–Congress of Industrial Organizations (AFL-CIO) has declined since the 1980s. Within the AFL-CIO, the more influential unions are the American Federation of Teachers (AFT), the American Federation of State, County, and Municipal Employees (AFSCME), and the Communication Workers of America (CWA).

RACIAL AND ETHNIC GROUPS Racial and ethnic groups promote political, economic, and social equality for their members, freedom from discrimination, and representation in public offices. Because they are the largest ethnic minorities in Texas, Hispanics and African Americans have the greatest number of groups representing their interests. The oldest and largest Hispanic group, the League of United Latin American Citizens (LULAC), is involved in efforts to change the method of selecting judges in Texas (see chapter 6), and the Mexican American Legal Defense and Educational Fund (MALDEF) was instrumental in the lawsuit that led to greater equality in funding for public education in Texas. The National Association for the Advancement of Colored People (NAACP) supported the challenge to the Democratic Party's white primary, fought to end segregation in public education, and continues to fight for increased economic and social opportunities for African Americans.

PUBLIC-INTEREST GROUPS Public-interest groups advocate public policies intended to benefit the public interest. Among the more active groups in Texas are the Baptist Christian Life Commission, Common Cause, Clean Water Action, the Sierra Club, Public Citizen, Consumers Union, Texans for Public Justice, Texas Alliance for Human Needs, Texas Citizen Action, the Gray Panthers, and Americans Disabled for Attendant Programs Today (ADAPT). These groups seek public policies that protect consumers, the environment, the poor, the elderly, the young, and the disabled.

Political Activities of Interest Groups

Interest groups usually engage in three distinct, but related, types of political activities: lobbying, electioneering, and litigation. In this section, we identify and explain each of these activities.

LOBBYING When most people think of interest-group activities, lobbying is probably the first thing that comes to mind. Indeed, lobbying may be the universal activity of interest groups. Most groups practice direct and indirect lobbying.

Attempting to influence public officials through direct contacts defines direct lobbying. Because public officials reside in all three branches of government (legislative, executive, and judiciary) and at all levels of government (national, state, and local), we would expect lobbyists (the people who lobby) to attempt to influence all of them. Indeed, lobbyists are evident wherever public policy and political decisions are made.

In 1987, there were approximately 800 lobbyists in Texas. In 2007, there were 1,629 lobbyists registered with the Texas Ethics Commission. In 2007, lobbyists were paid somewhere between $176 million and $348 million for their services. Even so, those figures do not indicate the 2,706 interests with lobbyists working in Austin during the regular legislative session in 2007. The discrepancy between registered lobbyists and the number of interest groups with lobbyists is partially due to the legal requirements for registration in Texas. However, much of the discrepancy arises because many lobbyists have more than one client. For example, Todd M. Smith, the highest paid lobbyist in 2007, had twenty-six contracts.[23]

Texas laws requiring lobbyist registration and placing restrictions on lobbying activity were passed in several legislative sessions since the 1950s. In some respects, the laws are broad and encompassing. Lobbying is defined as efforts to influence the legislative and the executive branches, and the law applies even when the legislature is not in session. Furthermore, individuals who register as lobbyists must indicate their employers, provide information about their expenditures, and indicate the bills or regulations about which they are concerned. Individuals who engage in direct communications with members of the legislature or executive branch of government to influence legislation or administrative action must register as lobbyists if they receive more than $1,000 in any calendar quarter as pay for lobbying, or they spend more than $500 in any calendar quarter for transportation and lodging, food and beverages, gifts, awards, entertainment, or attendance at a political fundraiser or charity event to influence legislation or administrative action.[24] In 1991, the legislature limited the annual amount that a lobbyist could spend on a public official to $500. Pleasure trips and honoraria paid for by lobbyists were also prohibited. In 2001, the legislature established new conflict-of-interest rules for registered lobbyists.

In the late 1980s, two trends characterized lobbyists in Texas. First, there was an increase in the number of contract lobbyists ("hired guns") who work for more than one client. Many of these contract lobbyists were former members of the legislative or executive branches. In the 1990s, that trend continued, as more former legislators and bureaucrats took positions representing interest groups. By 2005, seventy ex-legislators were lobbyists in Texas, the state with the most ex-legislators turned lobbyists.[25] The second trend involved greater ethnic and gender diversity among lobbyists. By 1999, the number of women, Hispanics, and African Americans had increased significantly.[26] This trend reflects the changing ethnic and gender composition of government, as well as the tendency for interest groups to assemble a team of lobbyists who are individually assigned to specific legislators or bureaucrats, based on a number of shared characteristics.

According to lobbyists, their principal job involves access to public officials and presenting information about their issues. To present information to legislators or administrators though, lobbyists first need to gain access to public officials. Access comes from the lobbyist's reputation and from the interest group's contributions to the legislator's campaign (a technique that we discuss more fully in the next section of this chapter). Consequently, many lobbyists are former public officials who have established personal relationships with the people to whom they now want access. Furthermore, their previous experience in public office increases their credibility with current legislators and bureaucrats. As lobbyist and former legislator Bill Messer states, "The real job is to articulate a position and to state a constituency. If you don't have a constituency, then you don't have any influence."[27]

The days when lobbyists could rely on wining and dining public officials in Texas have passed. Currently, lobbyists must rely on their information and integrity. As the late Bill Clayton, former Texas House Speaker and lobbyist, stated, "Integrity is the one thing that counts more than anything. If you lie to one of the members, you won't ever get a

Photo courtesy: Bob Daemmrich Photography

Why are these people on the phone? Texas lobbyists discuss strategy during a recess of a legislative hearing in the Capitol Office Complex in Austin.

job again."28 Despite the personal friendships that many lobbyists have cultivated with legislators and administrators, lobbyists have to make their case on its merits. Currently, with increased personal and committee staffs, legislators are less dependent on lobbyists for information than they were twenty years ago; however, lobbyists still provide information that is useful to legislators because it is processed, interpreted, and packaged.

The information provided by lobbyists can be substantive (usually technical) or political. Substantive information provides details about the content of the legislation. Political information indicates how the legislation will affect the legislator's constituents and supporters. Furthermore, lobbyists can provide experts to testify at legislative hearings. Probably the most persuasive information provided by lobbyists involves what other states have done concerning a particular issue and the effects of those measures. For example, if the legislature is considering welfare reform, lobbyists can provide information on what other states have done and the effects of those efforts. Although the lobbyists represent particular interests, the case for or against a bill must be made in terms of good social policy, not the benefits to the particular interest.29

From legislative session to session, the interests that contracts represent vary according to the legislative agenda, but some interests are always present. Most prevalent are business interests. In 2007, the Texas businesses that employed the greatest number of lobbyists belonged to energy and natural resource companies, establishing 1,101 contracts worth as much as $60 million to the contracts that they employed. In second place among businesses were health industry clients with 1,013 contracts worth up to $42.9 million, and third place belonged to the miscellaneous businesses, which included alcohol and gambling interests and which spent up to $37.3 million on 930 contracts.30

The individuals targeted by lobbyists vary. Some lobbyists pursue a "top-down" strategy, concentrating their efforts on the leadership. Because the Texas Speaker of the House and president of the Senate (lieutenant governor) have considerable powers, lobbying the leadership can be productive. However, most lobbyists focus their efforts on the committees with jurisdiction over legislation that affects the interests of the group. Committee chairs receive more attention than committee members, but lobbyists cannot ignore committee members entirely because committee members' votes can be crucial to their success or failure. As their numbers have increased, legislative staff members are also among the lobbyists' targets, particularly those members who are considered influential with the legislator. Finally, on the House and Senate floors, lobbyists concentrate their efforts on legislators who are undecided, rather than those who have committed to vote for or against a given measure.31

Lobbyists do not confine their activities to the legislature. Interactions between lobbyists and administrators of state agencies and departments are frequent in Texas. A 1982 study of executive agencies in Texas indicated that interest-group-initiated contacts with agencies occurred frequently or very frequently and that half of the contacts were administration initiated. These contacts usually involve an exchange of information or an attempt to influence policies. For example, an environmental group, such as the Sierra Club, might contact the Texas Commission on Environmental Quality (TCEQ) to relay information about water and air pollution in Texas or to lobby the commission for stronger environmental regulations. Administrative agencies contact interest groups to ascertain the effects of their programs on group members and to solicit input on proposed regulations. Interest groups, on the other hand, contact agencies to obtain information about their programs and to influence the agencies' rules and regulations.

Thinking Nationally

Legislators Who Become Lobbyists

Twenty-five states including California, New York, and Florida, but not including Texas, require a waiting period that ranges from six month to two years before former legislators are allowed to register as lobbyists. This "cooling off period" is intended to reduce the likelihood that former legislators' political connections will be used to promote their clients' interests. Among the states, Texas has the largest number of former legislators who are lobbyists.

- Should Texas require a waiting period for former legislators who want to register as lobbyists? Why or why not?
- Would a waiting-period regulation have any effect? Explain your answer.
- Does a waiting period violate an individual's right to earn a living, or should a different set of rules apply to former legislators? Explain your answer.

In addition to direct lobbying, interest groups also engage in a form of lobbying called indirect or "grassroots" lobbying. There are actually two forms of indirect lobbying. In the first form, interest groups attempt to activate their members, urging them to contact their representatives or executive officials to influence public policy. For example, the Texas Automobile Dealers Association (TADA) could encourage its members to write their representatives and senators about pending legislation and could even provide a sample letter. However, the second, increasingly common form attempts to change the climate of public opinion, largely through television advertising. Political activists have termed some of these lobbying efforts "Astroturf" because although they look like grassroots political efforts, they are actually manufactured by interest groups. Despite their artificial quality, they offer a semblance of popular support for a position. In Texas, the commercials by the Texas Partnership for Competition, featuring a "Lady in the Clouds" decrying the charges that Southwestern Bell adds for long-distance access, illustrate the effectiveness of these campaigns in getting an item on decision makers' agendas.[32] In 2003, Astroturf interest groups led the efforts to limit tort liability for doctors, hospitals, and insurance companies.

ELECTIONEERING Electioneering has become a major political activity of interest groups since the mid-1970s. Interest groups maintain that their involvement in political campaigns is to ensure access to public officials. As one lobbyist notes, the price of access is a $1,000 contribution to a senator's campaign and a $250 contribution to a representative's campaign.[33]

Like most states, Texas has experienced a great deal of activity by political action committees (PACs), which are groups formed to solicit funds and then to use those funds to help elect or defeat candidates for public office. In 2006, there were 1,132 general-purpose PACs registered in Texas. Of the $99.2 million spent by PACs in 2005–2006, business PACs spent $57 million (58 percent), ideological and single-issue PACs contributed $37 million (37 percent), and labor PACs contributed $5 million (5 percent).[34] (To learn more about PACs in Texas, see Table 3.1.)

An analysis of the contributions by the Texas Medical Association PAC and the Texas Trial Lawyers Association PAC indicates that PACs in Texas, like PACs in other states, concentrate their contributions on incumbents and committee chairs. The Texas Medical Association PAC revealed an increasing preference for incumbents, contributing 55 percent of its total contributions to incumbents in 1985–1986, 75 percent in 1993–1994, and 85 percent in 1997–1998.[35]

TABLE 3.1 Top General-Purpose Pacs, 2006

Rank 2006	2004	Political Action Committee	2006 Spending	Interest Category
1	1	Texans for Lawsuit Reform	$4,224,428	Ideological
2	2	Texas Association of Realtors	3,334,075	Real Estate
3	—[a]	Texas Rep. Legislative Campaign Com.	2,726,907	Ideological
4	3	Republican Party of Texas	2,604,523	Ideological
5	9	Valero Refining and Marketing	2,347,879	Energy
6	—[a]	Texas Democratic Trust	2,256,378	Ideological
7	9	Texans for Insurance Reform	2,015,611	Lawyers/Lobbyists
8	5	Texas Medical Association	1,896,648	Health
9	4	Texas Democratic Party	1,553,206	Ideological
10	7	Associated Republicans of Texas	1,472,061	Ideological
11	—[a]	Harris Co. Republican Party	1,397,049	Ideological
12	10	SBC Texas Employees PAC	1,253,856	Communications
13	30	Annie's List	1,098,083	Ideological
14	12	Stars Over Texas	1,085,121	Ideological
15	36	House Democratic Campaign Com.	1,051,894	Ideological

[a]The PAC did not exist in 2004.
Source: Texans for Public Justice, "The 100 Biggest PACs in 2006," Texas PACs: 2006 Election Cycle, October 2007, http://www.tpj.org.

Politics Now

Source: HOUSTON CHRONICLE   February 7, 2008

Hefty Gift to Bailey has Craddick Ties

RICK CASEY

In Austin, Democratic State Rep. Dawnna Dukes considers her ties with Republican House Speaker Tom Craddick so sensitive that she turned down a $50,000 contribution from a political action committee tied to Craddick.

But Houston Democrat Kevin Bailey didn't.

Both were among a group of Democrats whose support for Craddick last year helped quell a Republican rebellion that sought to oust him from the speaker's post.

Both face opponents who charge that their ties with the conservative Craddick go against the interests of their low-income, heavily Democratic districts.

Bailey: No hesitations

The political action committee, Texas JOBS PAC, last month contributed to only two other candidates, both Craddick Democrats with primary opponents — Kino Flores of Palmview and Aaron Pena of Edinburg also received $50,000 each.

Dukes says she turned down the contribution because she knew her opponent would turn it into a "distraction."

It was clear she was annoyed to be dealing with a story linking her to Craddick. After all, she turned down $50,000 — more than her campaign had in the bank two weeks ago — to avoid such publicity.

"I hope this will be the last story on this," she said Thursday.

Bailey said he didn't give any consideration to refusing what amounted to the largest chunk of cash he's received in his 17 years in office.

Craddick had 'no control'

"The lawyer who heads (the PAC) called me and he wanted to support me," he said.

"I said that given that the trial lawyers and some of the others are supporting my opponent, I better take it."

Bailey's opponent, Armando Walle, a former staff aide to U.S. Rep. Gene Green, did receive almost $20,000 from lawyers and their PAC. In total, he has collected $37,000, an amount dwarfed by the $103,000 Bailey collected the first three weeks of January alone.

Bailey said he didn't know Craddick was associated with the $50,000 contribution, "but I wasn't surprised."

In fact, at the time the contributions were made to Bailey and the two others, a $250,000 check from Craddick's campaign account was the only money in the PAC's account.

Bailey also said he couldn't remember the name of the lawyer who told him the contribution would be coming.

A spokesman for Craddick emphasized that he had no control over who received the money. If he did dictate to the PAC who should get the money, it would be a criminal violation of the Texas Election Code.

"The speaker donated money to the PAC because it's a bipartisan PAC with a bipartisan board," he said. "He believes supporting candidates who work across the aisle is good for Texas."

It's not the speaker's fault that the PAC decided to give $50,000 each from his quarter of a million to four Democratic Craddick supporters (including Dukes) who face opponents in the March 4 primary.

The PAC does seem to have a rather narrow purpose.

Bailey said the gift was "the biggest I've ever received. I don't think I have ever received one bigger than $5,000."

So soon he forgets. Just last September, Bailey received $10,000 from HillCo, another Craddick-related PAC. HillCo also gave $10,000 to Dukes and Flores, twice as much as they gave to any other recipient that month.

Bailey also received $10,000 in September 2006 from Houston home builder and Craddick supporter Bob Perry.

Speaking of Perry, his spokesman, Anthony Holm of Austin, took issue with a comment I made earlier suggesting the Democrats who Perry supported tended to be minorities. Some Democrats see such contributions and committee appointments of minority Democrats as part of an effort to have the party seen as a minority party.

Perry, one of the nation's most generous conservative political givers, has donated to more than a dozen Hispanic and black Democrats in the Legislature.

Holm sent me a list of Anglo Democratic legislators to whom Perry has contributed. It consisted of Bailey, Houston Sen. John Whitmire and Nederland Rep. Alan Ritter.

In my own research I also found Perry contributions to Austin Rep. Patrick Rose, a Craddick Democrat who broke with the speaker last year.

Holm also included Dallas Rep. Kirk England, who received $57,500 from Perry in 2006. Holm apparently didn't realize England was at that time a Republican and has received nothing from Perry since switching parties in September.

Discussion Questions

1. Why would Republican Speaker Tom Craddick be interested in helping some Democratic legislators running for reelection?
2. Would the Speaker's support be likely to enhance a Democratic incumbent's standing and chances with primary voters or hurt them? Why?
3. Under what, if any, circumstances should state legislators reject campaign contributions?

A study of the campaign contributions of twenty-two Texas PACs that are interested in protecting businesses from civil lawsuits for personal injuries (torts) demonstrated how PACs target their contributions. Although the twenty-two PACs contributed to all but one of the 181 legislators in the House and Senate in 1995 and 1996, the principal beneficiaries of the PACs' largess were legislators involved in close elections, freshmen legislators, Republicans, and the leadership in both chambers. In all, the twenty-two PACs contributed $3.1 million to winning legislative candidates between January 1995 and December 1996.[36] PACs also attempt to influence the selection of the Speaker. (To learn more about PAC activities, see Politics Now: Hefty Gift to Bailey has Craddick Ties.)

LITIGATION Practiced extensively by civil rights and environmental groups in the 1950s and 1960s, litigation recently has become a more common weapon in the arsenal of interest-group activities. Much of the increased use of litigation can be attributed to the new judicial federalism, which has made state courts more likely to entertain such lawsuits (see chapter 6). The purpose of litigation is to effect or prevent changes in public policy. Litigation can also be used as a delaying tactic to slow change.[37] However, because litigation is expensive, the groups that are most likely to pursue litigation are those who are prosperous enough to afford the expense, and who have been unsuccessful in lobbying and campaigning and therefore pursue the legal route as a last resort.

Elections and Political Campaigns in Texas

This section discusses the various types of elections that are conducted in Texas—primary elections, special elections, general elections, and local elections—and examines political campaigns and voting behavior.

Types of Elections

In Texas, elections are frequent, and the ballot tends to be longer than in other states. The legislature has established uniform dates (the second Saturday in May, and the first Tuesday after the first Monday in November) for general and special elections, but elections can occur at other times as well.

PRIMARY ELECTIONS By Texas law, any party whose candidate for governor receives more than 20 percent of the vote must hold a primary election to nominate candidates. Parties whose gubernatorial candidate receives less than 20 percent of the vote can nominate their candidates in primary elections or in party conventions. In Texas, the Democratic Party has held primary elections every two years since 1906. The Republican Party held primaries only five times between 1906 and 1962. Since 1962, the Republican Party has held primaries every two years.

Primaries were established in Texas in 1905 with the passage of the Terrell Election Law, which required a combination of the primary election and a state convention to determine the party's nominees. In 1907, the law was amended to establish a direct primary election, with a plurality vote necessary to secure the nomination. In 1918, the legislature adopted a majority vote requirement to win the primary and established a second, or runoff, primary between the first- and second-place vote-getters if no candidate received a majority of the vote in the first primary.[38] For example, in the 1990 Democratic primary, Jim Mattox, Ann Richards, and Mark White sought the nomination for governor. Because none of the three candidates received a majority of the vote in the primary, the top two vote-getters in the first primary—Ann Richards and Jim Mattox—participated in the second primary.

Although primary elections in Texas are supposedly closed elections, voters can still choose to participate in the opposition party's primary election, making them operate more like open primaries. For example, in the 1994 Democratic gubernatorial primary, incumbent Governor Ann Richards was challenged by Gary Espinosa, a political unknown who received 22 percent of the primary vote. Republicans contended that Espinosa's vote indicated that more than one-fifth of Richards's party members did not support her. However, a county-by-county analysis indicated that a large percentage of Espinosa's vote came from Republicans who "raided" the Democratic primary, attempting to discredit the popularity of the incumbent governor. In the seventy-five counties where few voters (5 percent or fewer) participated in the Republican primary, Espinosa received 27 percent of the vote. In the thirty-six counties where a majority of the voters participated in the Republican primary, Espinosa received only 13 percent of the vote.[39]

Participation in primary elections is usually low in Texas, especially in runoff primaries. However, between 1906 and 1962, a larger percentage of Texas voters participated in the Democratic primary than participated in the general election. Participation in the Democratic primaries was high because they often included contests reflecting the ideological split in the party, making the results more important than the general elections, which were almost always won by the Democratic candidates. In 1962, for the first time in Texas history, the number of voters in the general election in a nonpresidential election year exceeded the number of voters in the Democratic primary election. Since then, as participation in the general election has increased, participation in the Republican primary has increased while participation in the Democratic primary has decreased. This change reflects the rise of the Republican Party in Texas and the resulting increase in the importance of the general election.[40] In 2008, 16.2 percent of the voting-age population voted in the Democratic primary, and 7.7 percent voted in the Republican primary. Only about 2 percent of the voting-age population participated in the parties' runoff primaries in that year.

Because primary elections are party elections, each party is responsible for administering its own primary election, which includes preparing the ballots, conducting the elections, tabulating and certifying the results, and financing the election. Candidates for statewide office file for positions on the ballot with the state party chair; candidates for county or precinct office file with the county party chair; candidates for district office (e.g., court of appeals, state senator) file with each county party chair in the district.

special election
Election held at a time other than general or primary elections.

SPECIAL ELECTIONS **Special elections** are held in Texas to fill vacancies in state legislative and U.S. congressional offices, to approve local bond proposals, and if the legislature chooses, to approve amendments to the Texas Constitution (see chapter 2). Executive and judicial vacancies are filled by gubernatorial appointment. The dates for special elections are set by the legislature for amendments to the Texas Constitution, by the governor to fill legislative and congressional vacancies, and by the local government to approve bond proposals. The parties do not hold primaries to nominate candidates for special elections; thus, access to the ballot for legislative or congressional vacancies is through filing fees or signatures on petitions. Consequently, the number of candidates in special elections tends to be large. For example, the May 1993 special election for U.S. senator drew twenty-four candidates. Candidates who seek an office in special elections are identified by political party on the ballot, and they must receive a majority of the votes cast to win the office. If no candidate receives a majority of the vote, a runoff election between the top two vote-getters is held one month after the first election.

Participation in special elections is usually extremely low but varies, depending on the issues involved in elections to approve constitutional amendments or the competitiveness among candidates in elections to fill vacancies. Bond-approval elections draw even fewer voters.

GENERAL ELECTIONS General elections are interparty contests to determine which candidates will hold public office. In Texas, as in most states, the general election is held on the first Tuesday after the first Monday in November of even-numbered years. Since 1974, when Texas adopted a four-year gubernatorial term, the governor and other statewide elected executive officials who also serve four-year terms are elected in nonpresidential years. Other elected officials in Texas, because of the tenure of their offices, may be chosen in presidential or nonpresidential years. In elections for state, district, and county offices, the person who receives the most votes—a plurality—wins the election.

General elections are administered and funded by the state. The secretary of state, the state's chief election official, is responsible for certifying state and district candidates, ensuring that the county clerks certify local candidates and that the county commissioners court appoints the necessary officials to administer the election, and reporting and maintaining the election results.

LOCAL ELECTIONS **Local elections** are conducted to elect city councils, mayors, school-board members, and special district boards. (In chapter 7, we discuss the unique role of counties as both local governments and administrative arms of state government; county elections are part of the state electoral system.) Cities and special districts may conduct their elections in odd-numbered years, and some cities require a majority vote to win, necessitating a runoff election if no candidate receives a majority. These elections are nonpartisan and are usually conducted in May. Some local elections generate high voter interest and turnout, but most do not.

local election
Election conducted by local governments to elect officials.

Political Campaigns in Texas

As noted earlier, there are ample (some say too many) opportunities to vote in Texas. How do Texans find out about the candidates, their party affiliations, and their positions on issues of public policy in all of these elections? Political campaigns are supposed to perform that function.

Ideally, election campaigns should offer the electorate an opportunity to compare the candidates and their views on the major issues of public policy. Then, armed with this knowledge, voters should choose among the competing political views and, thereby, determine public policy. Unfortunately, contemporary political campaigns do not meet this standard. As political scientist W. Lance Bennett has noted, contemporary political campaigns are about the three M's—money, media, and marketing.[41] We will consider the influence of these factors in Texas campaigns before analyzing voters' decisions in recent gubernatorial campaigns.

MONEY: THE MOTHER'S MILK OF POLITICS Everyone knows that contemporary political campaigns are expensive. In the 2006 gubernatorial campaign in Texas, incumbent Governor Rick Perry raised more than $21 million and spent $29.3 million to win reelection.[42] In 2006, candidates who won election to the Texas House raised an average of $276,298 in campaign contributions to the losers' average of $69,920. Incumbent House candidates raised an average of $267,681 while challengers raised an average of $67,084. In 2006, candidates who won Texas Senate contests raised an average of $938,436 while losers raised an average of $72,620. Incumbent Texas senators raised an average of $766,947 to their challengers' average of $75,385.[43] Money does not guarantee electoral success, but winning candidates generally outspend their opponents. Why are election campaigns so expensive in Texas, and how do the candidates raise the money necessary to be competitive?

The geographic size of Texas makes money important in electoral campaigns. As journalist Kaye Northcott noted, "Money doesn't just talk in Texas elections: it does tap dances and sings the state anthem in three-part harmony."[44] In 1982, Peyton McKnight, a conservative Democratic state senator, spent $1.5 million of his own fortune attempting to win the Democratic nomination for governor. On the filing deadline for the primary election, a media consultant informed McKnight that another $1 million was necessary to raise his name recognition to a winnable percentage. Rather than ante up, McKnight folded. McKnight was replaced by Buddy Temple, son of Arthur Temple Jr., an East Texas timber magnate. The key to name recognition, as Temple learned in an earlier statewide race for a seat on the Texas Railroad Commission, is television advertising. After spending nearly ten months traveling the state, meeting people and giving speeches, Temple had raised his name recognition from 5 to 12 percent. When his television advertising campaign started, two days yielded an increase from 12 to 24 percent. As Temple noted, "That made a believer out of me. If you don't have the money to make a good showing on television, you don't have a chance in Texas."[45]

Individual contributions provide the majority of campaign contributions in Texas, but increasingly, contributions from groups, through their PACs, have become more important, especially to incumbents in state legislative contests. In 2006, of the $27.4 million raised by candidates for the Texas Senate, PACs contributed 55 percent, and individuals contributed 45 percent. Of the $59.1 million raised by Texas House candidates, PACs contributed 55 percent, and individuals contributed 45 percent. On the other hand, Rick Perry received the largest percentage of his contributions in 2006 from individuals (77 percent). PACs provided the remaining 23 percent. Nevertheless, 52 percent of Perry's total contributions came in checks that were written for more than $10,000.[46]

Not only is political money important in Texas, but there are also few restrictions placed on its use in political campaigns. In Texas, campaign finance regulation has usually come as a response to blatant, both legal and illegal, excesses by campaign contributors. A major reform was passed in 1973 in the wake of the Sharpstown scandal (see chapter 4). However, even the scandal did not produce strong legislation. The law merely required candidates to designate a campaign treasurer and to report contributions and expenditures. There were numerous loopholes in the legislation, such as the requirement that only "opposed" candidates must report contributions and expenditures.[47] After Lonnie "Bo" Pilgrim passed out checks for $10,000 to Texas senators in an attempt to influence workers' compensation legislation in 1989, the legislature, at the urging of Governor Richards, attempted to strengthen the regulation of campaign finance in 1991. The legislature created the Ethics Commission, which now receives the contribution and expenditure reports for candidates for state office, and it did close some of the loopholes in the previous law. In 1999, the legislature adopted a law requiring candidates for statewide offices, the state legislature, and many district offices to file their contribution and expenditure reports electronically. Since the 2000 elections, the information has been available on the Ethics Commission's Web site. However, there are still no limits on contributions by individuals or PACs to legislative and executive candidates in Texas.

MEDIA: LINKING THE CANDIDATES AND THE VOTERS Although politicians once believed that campaigning should be conducted personally and should involve face-to-face contacts with the voters at campaign rallies, technology has made personal contacts less effective. Campaign communications are now conducted through the media. This is especially true for statewide political campaigns, but it is also becoming more common in district and local campaigns. In a state the size of Texas, candidates can effectively reach potential voters through the state's nineteen media markets. As political consultant Mark McKinnon noted, "It's impossible to effectively communicate with voters in Texas any other way but television. TV is the next best thing to being there. TV allows the candidate to be in everybody's living room, up close and personal."[48] And, increasingly, campaigns make use of Web sites and blogs. (To learn more about a blog on Texas politics, see Ideas into Action: Blogging on Texas Politics.)

As more people have become detached from their partisan affiliations, party leaders have lost the skills necessary to organize campaigns capable of electing candidates to public office. Thus, candidates have turned to *political consultants*, specialists in the modern campaign technology, to plan and organize their campaigns.[49] The specialized knowledge possessed by campaign consultants has led to the third component of contemporary campaigns—marketing.

MARKETING: SELLING THE CANDIDATE The transition from party-centered to candidate-centered campaigns was facilitated by political consultants. At first, political consultants offered candidates only their technical expertise, probably gained from experience in commercial marketing or advertising. However, as candidates' dependence on media and the techniques of commercial advertising increased, political consultants expanded their influence in the campaign, as well as the specialization of their services to candidates. Despite the proliferation of consultants and their specialization, the most important consultants operate in the area of opinion polling and media services.

Candidates use several techniques to assess the public's concerns and desires, but public opinion polls have become the most commonly used technique. The earliest and most comprehensive opinion survey is the benchmark poll. Conducted a year or more before the election, the benchmark poll is a planning document. The poll typically

Ideas Into Action

Blogging on Texas Politics

In April 2003, Byron LaMasters and Jim Dallas, students at the University of Texas in Austin, started the *Burnt Orange Report*, a blog about local Austin, state, national, and UT politics. When LaMasters graduated in May 2005, he sold the *Burnt Orange Report* to Karl-Thomas Musselman, who added additional contributors.

Byron LaMasters and the *Burnt Orange Report* typifies blogs, bloggers, and the blogosphere. Bloggers are not reporters. They write about whatever interests them and cover topics the mainstream media may not cover. Most telling, bloggers make no pretense of being fair or balanced.

Most young Americans get their news from friends, e-mails, and links to Web sites provided by their friends. As political scientist Gary Chapman notes, "The hyper-linked character of e-mail and the Web lead heavy Internet users to a diversity of information sources that older people find difficult to grasp." According to Joe Trippi, the campaign manager of Howard Dean's 2004 presidential bid, "the power of the Internet to democratically let people come together and link together is going to change everything. And I think bloggers are a big piece of that. It will alter how we consume all media."[a]

The *Burnt Orange Report* won the *Austin Chronicle* readers' poll for Best Local Blog in 2003 and 2004, and it tied with *Pink Dome* in 2005. In 2008, the blog provided a valuable service to Texas voters by explaining the Democratic Party's two-step system for selecting national convention delegates, providing both a thorough description of the process and predicting the results in Texas's thirty-one state senatorial districts.

- How are bloggers different from newspaper or magazine reporters? What objectives and goals differentiate bloggers from journalists?
- Are bloggers beneficial to political discourse? Could newspapers provide the same or better service? For example, could newspapers describe and analyze political processes, such as the selection of national convention delegates, as well as, if not better than, bloggers?
- To see how political bloggers operate, go to any of the following blogs and analyze their content:
  www.pinkdome.com
  www.inthepinktexas.com
  www.perrysworld.com
  rightoftexas.wordpress.com
- Go to one of the blogs noted above and make a comment on one of the posted diaries that interests you.

[a]Quoted in Patrick Beach, "Conventions Ask Bloggers to Join the Convention," *Austin American-Statesman* (July 25, 2004): H4.

---

includes a large number of questions to assess the public's general mood and perception of the candidate's strengths and weaknesses, as well as the strengths and weaknesses of the candidate's likely opponent or opponents. The results of the benchmark poll are used to design the campaign's main themes and to establish the candidate's image.

In 1994, a poll conducted for George W. Bush's gubernatorial campaign indicated that the primary concern of voters was crime. According to Micheline Blum, president of Blum and Weprin Associates, "We had done a poll early in the year about issues, and exactly what voters wanted done.... On crime, they needed to feel that once a criminal was put away for a really serious offense, he was going to stay away. There were certain safety issues people wanted to hear about and Bush addressed them."[50] Bush made crime and citizen safety a centerpiece of his gubernatorial campaign.

During a campaign, the most important polls are tracking polls. Conducted over a period of two or three weeks, the tracking polls are used to determine the effectiveness of the campaign's theme and advertising, to detect shifts in voters' preferences among various segments of the population, and to evaluate the changing image of the candidate. Campaign pollsters compare the daily results to identify changes in the public's opinions and to adjust the campaign strategy accordingly.

To assess the emotional state of the electorate, pollsters employ focus groups, which include a small, not necessarily representative, sample of voters. According to pollsters, these sessions are useful in finding the public's hot-button issues, which evoke the most emotional and intense responses. These groups are also employed to test campaign commercials before the ads are aired on television.[51]

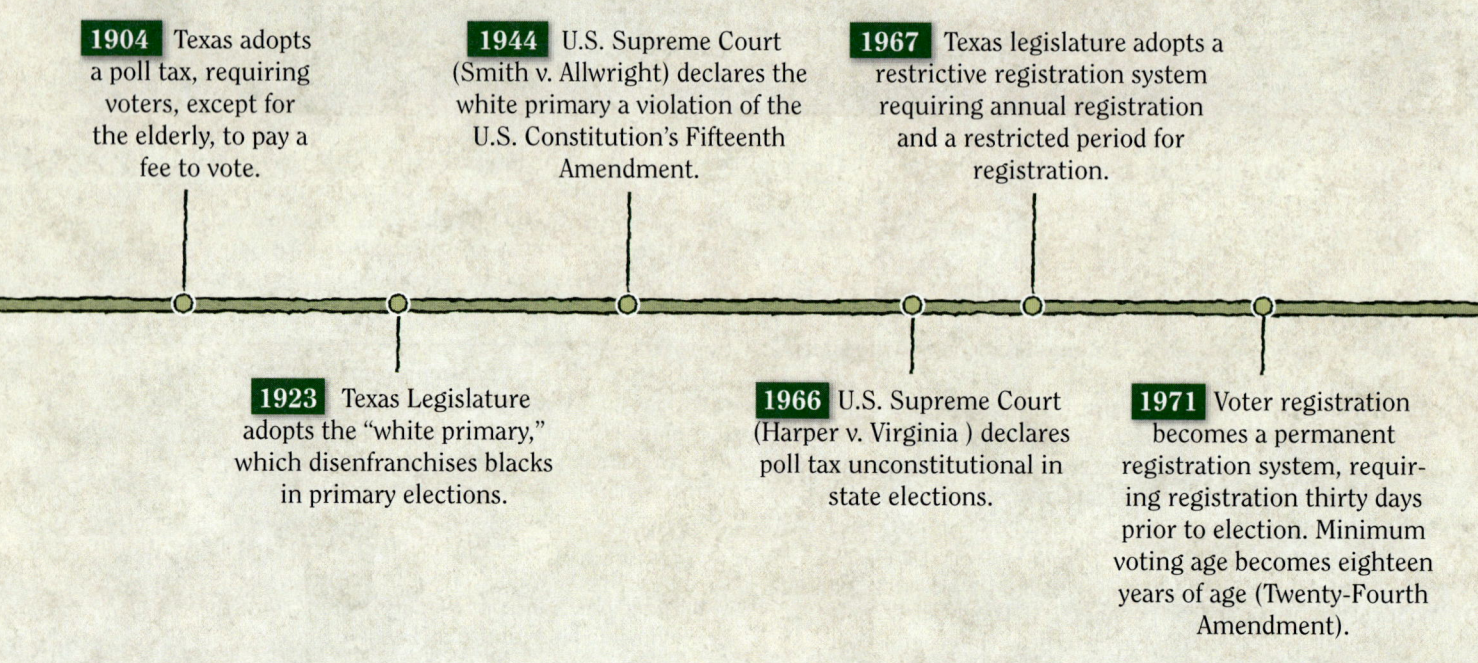

Timeline: Voting Requirements in Texas

1904 Texas adopts a poll tax, requiring voters, except for the elderly, to pay a fee to vote.

1923 Texas Legislature adopts the "white primary," which disenfranchises blacks in primary elections.

1944 U.S. Supreme Court (Smith v. Allwright) declares the white primary a violation of the U.S. Constitution's Fifteenth Amendment.

1966 U.S. Supreme Court (Harper v. Virginia) declares poll tax unconstitutional in state elections.

1967 Texas legislature adopts a restrictive registration system requiring annual registration and a restricted period for registration.

1971 Voter registration becomes a permanent registration system, requiring registration thirty days prior to election. Minimum voting age becomes eighteen years of age (Twenty-Fourth Amendment).

The most important campaign consultants provide media services to their candidates. Media consultants furnish a number of campaign services, such as the creation of the media messages and the coordination of those messages with the campaign theme. The importance of media messages, particularly negative ads, was demonstrated in the 2002 gubernatorial campaign between Rick Perry and Tony Sanchez, when Perry commercials accused Sanchez's Tesoro Savings and Loan of laundering money for drug cartels and contributing to the death of a Drug Enforcement Agency (DEA) agent.[52]

The ultimate goal in a political campaign is winning, which requires that eligible voters who support the candidate participate in the election and vote for the candidate in the election. Thus, our attention in the next section shifts to the factors that influence the voters' decisions during an election.

The Voters' Decisions

In an election, the potential voter faces two decisions. The first decision involves whether to participate. The second decision, which applies only if the person has chosen to participate in the election, involves which candidates to support. In Texas, fewer than half of those age-eligible (people eighteen years of age and older) voters decide to participate in presidential elections, and fewer than one-third decide to participate in gubernatorial elections. Why is voter turnout—the percentage of voting-age people who vote—so low in Texas, ranking forty-ninth among the fifty states in 2008?

VOTER TURNOUT Like most decisions concerning political participation, the decision to vote is the result of a calculation that weighs the costs of voting against the benefits of voting. People vote when they believe that voting will yield benefits.

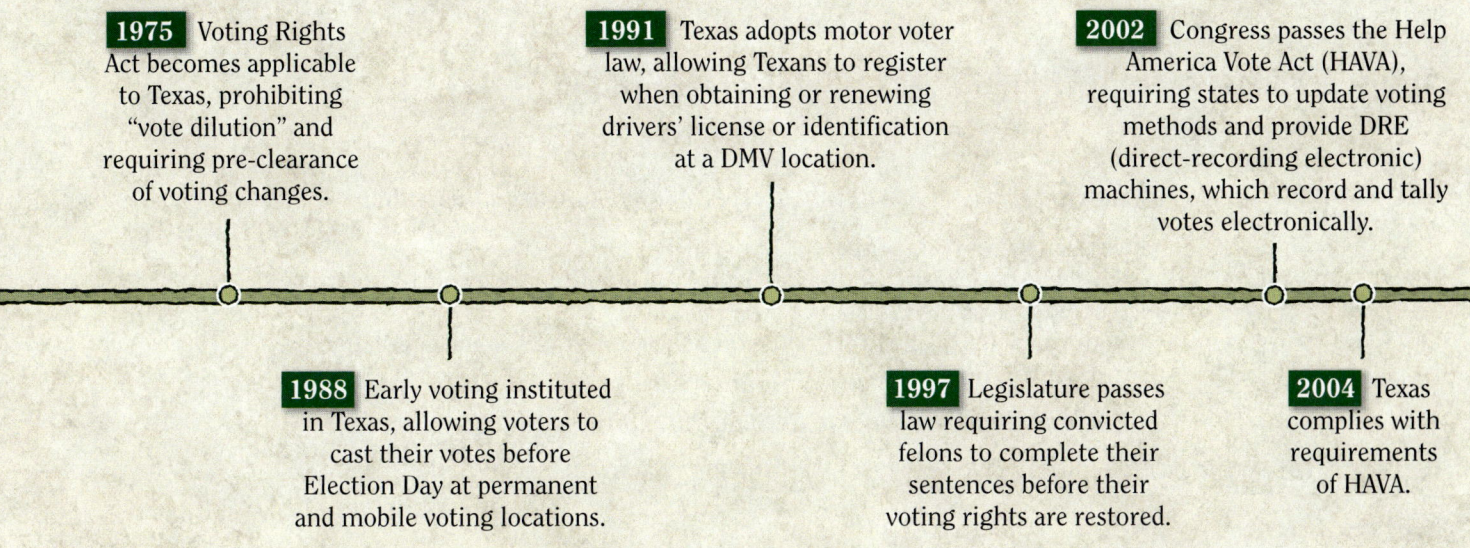

Voting is generally perceived as requiring little effort, but it does involve costs. For example, a voter must find out when the election is held and where the polling place is located, take the time to travel to the polling place, and most importantly, meet the legal requirements to vote. Until the mid-1960s, a number of legal restrictions in Texas, including a poll tax and a white-only Democratic primary, made voting costly, especially for particular groups or categories of Texans. The legal restrictions fell most heavily on the poor, the uninformed, Hispanics, and African Americans.

In contemporary Texas, the legal requirements for voting are minimal. The nominal requirements include U.S. citizenship, being eighteen years of age or older, residency in the state, and registration. The only people who are prohibited from voting are the "mentally incompetent" (as declared by a court of law) and convicted felons who have not completed their sentence, including any term of incarceration, parole, supervision, or probation. (To learn more about the legal requirements for voting, see The Living Constitution.) Thus, the only real legal barrier to voting is registration, which in Texas is relatively easy. A person who wishes to vote must register at least thirty days prior to the election. Once registered, a person is permanently registered and will receive a new registration certificate every two years unless he or she moves during that period, which necessitates completing a new registration form. However, forms are readily available and are printed in both Spanish and English on postage-free postcards.

In 1991, the Texas legislature adopted a motor-voter registration system, which allows a person who is obtaining a driver's license or a Department of Public Safety (DPS) identification card to be registered to vote. Also, registration forms were made even more accessible by placing them in public buildings. The effect of the motor-voter registration system has been to increase significantly the percentage of the population that is registered to vote—from 65 percent before motor-voter in the 1980s to

The Living Constitution

(a) The following classes of persons shall not be allowed to vote in this State:

(1) persons under 18 years of age;
(2) persons who have been determined mentally incompetent by a court, subject to such exceptions as the Legislature may make; and
(3) persons convicted of any felony, subject to such exceptions as the Legislature may make.

(b) The legislature shall enact laws to exclude from the right of suffrage persons who have been convicted of bribery, perjury, forgery, or other high crimes.

ARTICLE 6, SECTION 1

The Texas Constitution establishes the exclusions from the right to vote in Article 6, section 1. Of the various disqualifications, the provisions relating to convicted criminals have the greatest impact. The prohibitions on voting by criminals have appeared in every Texas constitution. In 1836, the constitution of the Republic disqualified persons "convicted of bribery, perjury, or other high crimes and misdemeanors." The 1845 constitution changed the language slightly to prohibit voting by persons "convicted of bribery, perjury, forgery, or other high crimes." The same language appeared in the Texas constitutions of 1861, 1866, and 1869. The constitution of 1869 also disqualified all felons. Although the convention delegates in 1875 debated which crimes should result in disqualification, they retained the felony disqualification. However, they did allow the legislature to make exceptions.[a]

The legislature originally allowed no exceptions, and convicted felons were barred from voting for life. However, in 1983, the legislature allowed convicted felons to vote five years after completing their sentences. Later, the waiting period was reduced to two years. In 1997, the legislature adopted the current provision, which excludes from the disqualification anyone who has not been convicted of a felony, or if convicted, has completed any sentence resulting from the conviction, which includes any incarceration, probation, parole, or supervision. Also, a person is not disqualified if he or she has been pardoned or "otherwise released from the resulting disability to vote." Consequently, without a pardon, convicted felons must complete the sentence imposed by the court before they are eligible to vote.[b]

In Texas, the number of convicted felons who are disenfranchised approaches 500,000 adults. According to political scientist Michael McDonald of George Mason University, there were 172, 116 prisoners, 431,967 probationers, and 101,916 parolees in Texas in 2008. Of those, McDonald estimates that 490,016 are ineligible felons, the largest number in any state in the United States.[c]

CRITICAL THINKING QUESTIONS

1. Should Texas, like some states, prohibit convicted felons from voting for life, or should Texas, like Maine and Vermont, allow convicted felons to vote? Explain your answer.
2. What would be the partisan and electoral effects if convicted felons were allowed to vote? What led you to your conclusions?

---

[a]George D. Braden, *The Constitution of Texas: An Annotated and Comparative Analysis*, vol. 2 (Austin: Texas Legislative Council, 1977), 483.
[b]Juan Castillo, "Did Your Time? Groups Want You to Vote," *Austin American-Statesman* (April 26, 2004): A1.
[c]Michael McDonald, 2008 General Election Turnout Rates, United States Elections Project, George Mason University, http://elections.gmu.edu/Turnout_2008G.html.

a high of 85 percent in 2000. Since then, registration has fluctuated between 75 and 80 percent.

The Texas legislature reduced the cost of voting with the adoption of early voting in 1987. Presently, early voting extends over a two-week period, commencing seventeen days before the election and continuing through the fourth day prior to the election. In most urban counties, there are numerous permanent and mobile early voting sites, such as supermarkets, schools, and churches. The effect of early voting on turnout has been negligible. Early voting has had an impact on the political parties' get out the vote efforts, moving the start of activities to an earlier date and requiring an adjustment in organization and volunteer-recruitment schedules.[53] In the 2006 gubernatorial election, 39 percent of the votes were cast during the early voting period. A comparison of early voters and Election Day voters indicated that early voters are more partisan, older, more conservative, more likely to be male, and require less mobilization than Election Day voters. Candidates can allocate their resources so as to turn out their core supporters early and then concentrate their campaign efforts on those voters who require stronger issue and candidate appeals to obtain their votes on Election Day.[54]

> ## Thinking Nationally
> ### Same-Day Voter Registration
>
> Six states—Idaho, Maine, Minnesota, New Hampshire, Wisconsin, and Wyoming—have same-day voter registration. In other words, you can register and cast your ballot on the day of the election. South Dakota does not require voters to register. In states with same-day voter registration, voter turnout averaged 71 percent of the voting-eligible population (VEP) in the 2004 presidential election; the national average is 61 percent of the VEP.
>
> - Should Texas adopt same-day voter registration?
> - What benefits, in addition to higher turnout rates, might result from same-day voter registration?
> - What problems might same-day voter registration create?

To increase the ease of actually casting a vote, Texas has been introducing electronic voting systems. But, questions have been raised about electronic voting. (To learn more about voting systems, see Join the Debate: Are Electronic Voting Systems Better than Paper Ballots?) Nevertheless, although the costs of voting have been reduced significantly in Texas over the past thirty years, a large percentage of Texans still fail to vote. To complete an explanation of voter turnout, we need to consider the benefits of voting.

The most obvious benefit of voting involves election outcomes—the party and candidates that win the offices contested in the election. Although the results of elections have significant effects on people's lives, an individual person does not have to vote in an election to receive the benefits. The benefits, in terms of the election outcomes, are collective and thus are available to nonvoters as well as to voters. Consequently, the value of a person's vote is not equal to the benefits derived from a given election outcome but to the probability that his or her individual vote will decide a given election. Therefore, the value of voting in most elections is quite small, and it raises questions about why anyone would bother to vote, since there are some costs involved. Apparently, the answer lies in the fact that people derive benefits from voting that are not dependent on deciding the outcome of an election.

In other words, there are selective benefits associated with voting. According to political scientist Ruy Teixeira, the selective benefits are basically expressive, which means that the person must find his or her vote meaningful.[55] For some people, voting expresses a general commitment to a political party, a social category (ethnicity, gender, or social class), or society in general. These benefits are largely symbolic because they are not directly connected to which candidate wins the election. For instance, an individual may find meaning in his or her commitment to the working class and may use the vote to express that commitment. For other people, voting expresses a concern about the election's effect on who holds public office and public policy. These benefits are instrumental because they express a desire to achieve certain results through the election of a particular candidate or political party. An individual who votes because he or she strongly supports the policy goals of a certain candidate would be an example.

Join the Debate

Are Electronic Voting Systems Better than Paper Ballots?

OVERVIEW: Like other states, Texas began eliminating punch-card voting systems and lever machines to comply with the Help America Vote Act (HAVA) of 2002. Texas also decided there should be at least one direct-recording electronic (DRE) voting system at each polling place to accommodate disabled voters. However, some experts have raised questions about the security of electronic voting.

In the 2000 election, Texas's 254 counties employed five election systems for voting. The largest number of counties, 150, employed optical-scan ballots, which are paper ballots that can be scanned and tallied using an optical scanner. Ninety counties used paper ballots, which are marked by the voter and must be tallied manually by individuals. Fourteen counties used punch-card ballots. Three counties used lever-machine voting systems, and four counties used direct-recording electronic systems. Under Texas's plan to comply with the HAVA, the lever-machine voting systems and the punch-card ballots were replaced for 2004.

However, as more states have adopted electronic voting, problems have surfaced. In Muscogee, Georgia, touch-screen voting machines registered "yes" when voters voted "no." In Maryland, a team of computer experts from Johns Hopkins University showed how hackers could determine the password needed to access the Diebold voting machines, break into the results, and program the software to change votes. These problems have caused many states to rethink their plans to adopt electronic voting.

Read and think about the following arguments for and against electronic voting systems. Then, continue the debate by answering the questions posed after the arguments.

Arguments IN FAVOR of Electronic Voting Systems

- Electronic voting systems allow disabled voters to cast secret ballots. Electronic voting systems can be equipped with audio systems that allow visually impaired and blind voters to hear ballot options and select their vote without human assistance, ensuring that their vote is secret.

- Electronic voting systems eliminate some of the problems associated with other voting methods. For example, electronic voting systems can prevent overvoting (voting for more than one candidate for an office) and warn voters of

---

A connection to politics—which is achieved through an identification with a political party, through an involvement in public affairs, and through a sense that government is responsive to people's demands—makes voting meaningful and influences the decision to vote. Many Texans lack a strong connection to politics for several reasons. First, as noted earlier, party identification is weak in Texas. The growing strength of the Republican Party in Texas and the resulting increase in electoral competition have probably increased some people's connection to politics, but there are still many Texans who do not identify with a political party. Second, feelings that the government is responsive to popular demands are low in Texas. Finally, involvement in public affairs—indicated by campaign interest, reading campaign news stories, watching campaign television, and following government and public affairs—is low in Texas.

Voter turnout in gubernatorial elections in nonpresidential years over the past century has exhibited several trends. After reaching its zenith in the 1890s, when more than 75 percent of the eligible voters voted, voter turnout in Texas fell precipitously for the next decade, finally stabilizing at approximately 24 percent of the eligible voters by 1910. In the 1920s, voter turnout dipped again, falling into the low teens and remaining there for the next two decades. During the 1950s and 1960s, voter turnout rose to a twentieth-century high of nearly 35 percent in 1970, before falling into the low 20 percent range during the 1970s. Voter turnout increased during the

undervoting (not voting for a candidate for an office).

- Electronic voting systems are easy to use and allow the results to be tabulated quickly. Some electronic voting machines have a touch-screen computer, similar to an automated teller machine (ATM), which is easy to use and familiar to most people. Also, results from electronic voting machines are available faster than from other voting methods, such as optical-scan systems.

Arguments AGAINST Electronic Voting Systems

- Electronic voting systems do not provide paper tallies of the votes, which are necessary for a recount. Unless votes can be verified, there is the possibility of more disputed elections like the Florida debacle of 2000.
- Electronic voting is not secure. Computer experts have demonstrated that at least some of the current voting systems can be compromised.
- Electronic voting systems are prone to viruses and glitches, just like any computer. Just like any computer, electronic voting systems can freeze up, crash, or lose data.

Continuing the Debate

1. Can electronic voting systems be made secure and reliable enough to ensure that votes are accurately counted? Why or why not?
2. Do you think that using electronic voting systems will solve the problems associated with other voting systems, such as hanging chads or poorly designed ballots, which result in overvoting or undervoting? Explain your answer.

To Follow the Debate Online, Go To:

Reform elections.org,
www.reformelections.org

Voting Machines Pro Con.org,
www.votingmachinesprocon.org

Verified Voting Foundation,
www.verifiedvotingfoundation.org

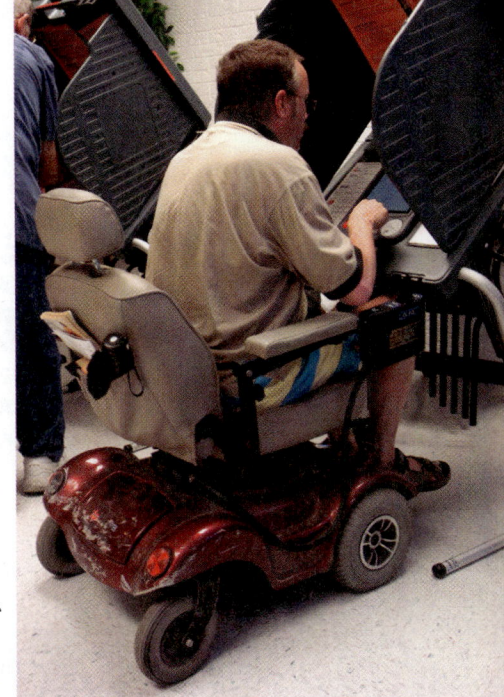

Photo courtesy: Bob Daemmrich

Has HAVA ensured the right to vote? A disabled voter uses an electronic voting machine to cast his ballot. Electronic voting is now prevalent in heavily populated Texas counties.

1980s, but it never exceeded 30 percent until the 1990s. (To learn more about voter turnout, see Analyzing Visuals: Voter Turnout in Texas.)

Several factors, involving both the effort required to vote and the benefits of voting, have contributed to the variation in Texas voter turnout. The initial decline after the 1890s is partly due to the establishment of the poll tax in 1904; however, voter turnout had already declined to approximately 40 percent by the general election in 1902. In 1904, a presidential election year, voter turnout continued its decline to approximately 35 percent. Thus, the increased costs of voting are probably less important than a reduction in benefits in explaining the decline. After 1896, the Populist Party was no longer a threat to Democratic Party dominance. As Texas returned to a one-party Democratic state, general elections became less competitive, and voter turnout declined.

The changing composition of the electorate also affected voter turnout. The decline in voter turnout during the 1920s and the 1970s is associated with the enfranchisement of women and young people, respectively. With the ratification of the Nineteenth Amendment, extending suffrage to women, voter turnout decreased as the number of eligible voters nearly doubled. Similarly, when the minimum voting age was reduced from twenty-one to eighteen in 1972, a large number of former nonvoters were enfranchised, and voter turnout declined. However, when groups who have been disenfranchised have their right to vote restored, as when legal restrictions on

voting are removed, voter turnout increases, as it did during the 1950s and 1960s, after the white primary and the poll tax were eliminated.

Undoubtedly, making voting easier increases voter turnout, but high rates of turnout cannot be achieved solely by minimizing the effort required to vote; people must be motivated by the benefits of voting. During the 1890s, political campaigns in Texas were party centered. Party workers and their supporters marched strong partisans to the polls. The parties were supported by a partisan press, and they distributed campaign literature to a politically active citizenry. Partisan politics occupied a central role in people's lives, both as a social activity and as a statement of personal identity. Obviously, one cannot recreate the society or the politics of the late nineteenth century, but efforts can be made to connect people with politics by providing the institutional means for people to find meaning in political participation. On the other hand, because of attempts to reduce the effort required to vote in Texas, the percentage of Texans who are registered to vote has increased. However, early voting procedures have not increased turnout, as only 45.5 percent of the age-eligible Texans voted in the 2008 presidential election, and only 26.4 percent voted in the 2006 gubernatorial elections.

THE VOTE CHOICE: PARTIES, ISSUES, AND CANDIDATES During the entire nineteenth and first part of the twentieth century, the vote choice was party oriented. Most voters practiced straight-ticket voting, voting for the same party's candidates for all national, state, and local offices. Currently, the vote choice is more office oriented and person oriented, meaning that the basis for the vote choice varies by political office and is more dependent on issues and candidates. Thus, more voters engage in split-ticket voting, voting for some candidates from one party and some from another.

Most explanations of the vote choice focused on three psychological factors: party identification, issues, and candidate characteristics. Party identification was seen as providing stability in the voter's choice, and assessments of candidate characteristics were considered primarily responsible for the variation in the voter's choice. Issues were considered less important. Based on an analysis of voters' choices in presidential elections, the authors of *The American Voter* study implied that vote choices in other elections were motivated by the same factors. However, recent changes in electoral behavior indicate that partisanship is no longer able to structure the vote because of

Analyzing Visuals: Voter Turnout in Texas

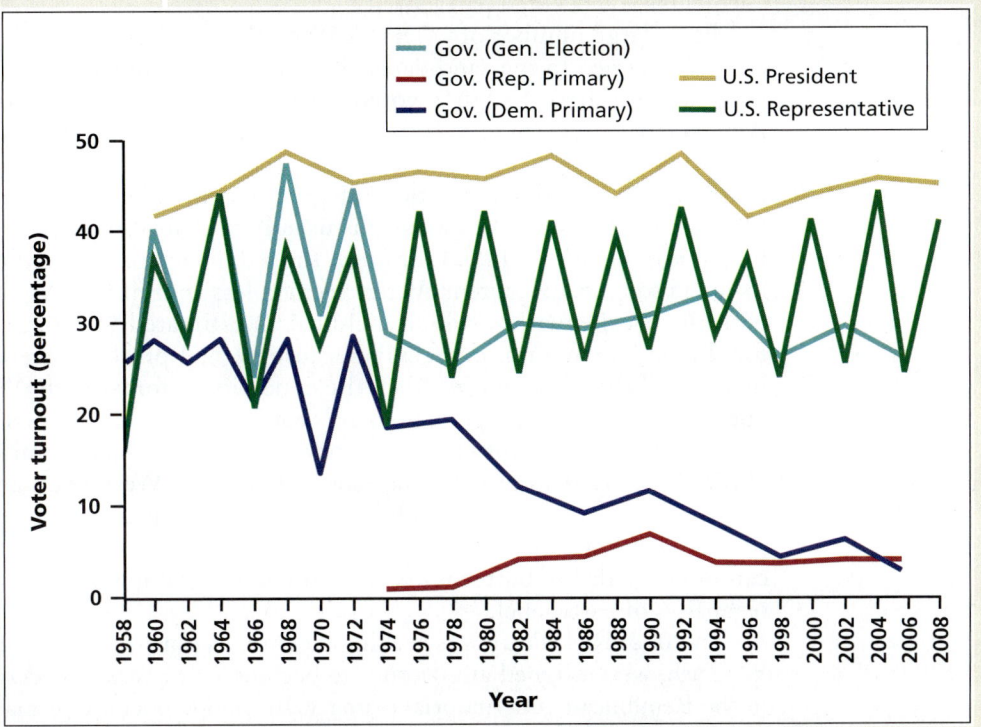

After studying the chart on voter turnout, answer the following critical thinking questions:

WHAT explains the fact that until 1962, voter turnout in the Democratic Party's primary election exceeded voter turnout in the general election for governor?

WHAT caused the changes in voter turnout in the Democratic Party's and Republican Party's primary elections?

WHAT do you think explains the changes in voter turnout in gubernatorial general elections since 1972?

WHY do you think voter turnout was greater in the 1994 gubernatorial election than in the 2006 gubernatorial election?

Sources: For 1958–1968, Clifton McCleskey, Allan K. Butcher, Daniel E. Farlow, and J. Pat Stephens, *The Government and Politics of Texas*, 7th ed. (Boston: Little, Brown, 1982), 41; for 1970–2004, Secretary of State, "Turnout and Voter Registration, 1970–current," www.sos.state.tx.us; authors' calculation.

---

declining partisanship in the electorate and declining strength of partisanship among those members of the electorate who are partisan.[56] Because of the electorate's greater volatility, predicting and explaining the vote choice have become more difficult. Nonetheless, a comparison of the 1986 and 2002 gubernatorial elections in Texas helps clarify the relative importance of the factors.

In 1986, an incumbent Democratic governor, Mark White, was seeking a second term as Texas's governor. In the Republican primary, despite facing a credible challenge, Bill Clements won the first primary handily, avoiding a divisive and expensive runoff election. Meanwhile, in the Democratic primary, White faced five unknown and poorly financed opponents. Winning the first primary with only 53 percent of the vote, White barely escaped a runoff and was embarrassed.

In 1986, party identification favored the Democratic candidate. Nevertheless, among Democratic Party identifiers, White won only 82 percent of the vote, whereas Clements won 92 percent of the Republican vote. Also, among those demographic categories that traditionally support Democratic candidates (low- and moderate-income voters, African Americans, and Hispanics), voter turnout was lower, and support was less enthusiastic than in the gubernatorial election of 1982.[57] Finally, among reasons given for their vote, 20 percent of White's voters and a mere 4 percent of Clements's voters noted party loyalty.

For a large number of voters in 1986, the most important factor in their vote choice pertained to the candidates. The largest percentage of Clements's voters (38 percent) indicated that they voted for Clements as a vote against Mark White. Almost a fifth (19 percent) of White's voters indicated that they voted against Clements.[58] As one study demonstrated, there are several dimensions to candidate characteristics: personal qualities, integrity, reliability, charisma, and competence.[59] Of these dimensions, competence is usually the most important and was the basis for the vote against White. Of course, the judgments of the candidates' competence included some issue content. Voters seemed less confident in White's ability to deal with the fiscal situation, which included an estimated $5.3 billion revenue deficit for the next biennium, especially because he had presided over large tax and fee increases during his tenure. Also, the education reforms that White had championed, especially the "no pass, no play" requirements and the tests for public-school teachers, and his inability to get the pay raises that he had promised educators hurt White in many areas of the state, especially in rural West Texas and the Texas Panhandle. More than anything else, the 1986 election demonstrated that although party labels were still important to at least a portion of the electorate, "the better candidate with the better issues and the better campaign can win in most areas regardless of party label."[60]

In 2002, Rick Perry was seeking election as governor after succeeding George W. Bush, who resigned as governor to become U.S. president. Perry was unopposed in the Republican gubernatorial primary. In the Democratic primary, Tony Sanchez, a wealthy Laredo businessman, expected no opposition, but at the last minute, former Texas Attorney General Dan Morales decided to file for the gubernatorial nomination rather than for the U.S. Senate nomination. As a result, Sanchez had to spend more than $20 million in a highly charged, negative primary campaign. In the end, Sanchez won handily, with more than 60 percent of the vote.

In 2002, the Republican Party held an advantage among Texans in party identification, and the advantage was even greater among voters. Among their respective party identifiers, both candidates did well, but many more Democrats than Republicans defected to the opposition candidate. Sanchez received 78 percent of the Democratic identifiers' votes and Perry received 92 percent of the Republican identifiers' votes. Among independents, Perry received 49 percent of the vote to Sanchez's 33 percent. Sanchez won majorities from several groups that traditionally support Democratic candidates (83 percent of the African American vote, at least 65 percent of the Hispanic vote, and 68 percent of self-identified liberals). Perry won an overwhelming majority of the vote from Anglos; rural, suburban, and small-city dwellers; voters thirty years old and older; voters whose income exceeded $35,000 annually; and Protestants.[61]

Perry and Sanchez voters differed on the issues that were most important to them. Perry voters were more likely to be concerned about taxes than Sanchez voters, who were more concerned about the state of the economy, education, and health care. According to Fox News Election Day polls, Texas voters were equally divided on the factor that most determined their vote choice for governor (47 percent cited positions on the issues, and 47 percent cited personal character and experience). Only 23 percent identified political party as the basis for their vote choice. Regardless of the basis for the vote choice, Perry received an overwhelming majority of the votes.[62]

Election results can be an indication of where the electorate wants to be taken or an indication of satisfaction with the past. If voters base their vote choice on campaign promises, the results indicate what they want public officials to do when they get into office. If they vote on performance, they are endorsing or rejecting the immediate past administration. In Texas, the 1986 gubernatorial election did not endorse Clements's governing vision; it negated White's governing vision.[63] In this sense, the election represented a retrospective judgment,[64] an evaluation of the performance of the incumbent and a decision to approve or reject that performance. The election did not, consequently, provide any guidance for Governor Clements. The 2002 election is probably best explained as a retrospective vote. During the campaign, both candidates tried to label the other candidate with negative advertisements. Perry depicted Sanchez as a businessman who engaged in money laundering for drug dealers, and Sanchez depicted Perry as a professional politician who had failed as a public servant. Neither candidate offered voters substantive reasons to vote for him; rather, both campaigns attempted to increase the negative perception of their opponent. Despite enormous spending by both campaigns, voters were given few reasons to vote for one of the gubernatorial candidates.

Toward Reform: Recent Reforms in Elections and Campaigns

The 80th legislature considered several reforms in campaign and election procedures. The most significant, though unsuccessful, involved moving the primary election date from the first Tuesday in March to the first Tuesday in February. In 2008, the front-loading of presidential primaries and caucuses increased, resulting in more than twenty states scheduling their delegate selection contests on February 5, 2008 (the earliest date allowed by party rules). With so many states holding contests on that date, most political observers thought that the nomination contests would be over before Texas's primary election in March.[65] Consequently, proponents argued that for Texans to have any voice in the nomination of the Democratic and Republican presidential nominees, the date of the primary election had to be moved. The proposal constituted a bipartisan effort endorsed by both major political parties in the House. After sailing through the House, the measure stalled in the Senate, largely because of opposition from the Republican County Chairmen's Association. The association feared that the early primary would cause more turnover in local poll officials. Furthermore, the move would entail "election preparations that would cause county and party staffs to lose Halloween, Thanksgiving, Christmas, and New Years."[66] However, when Hillary Clinton and Barack Obama emerged from the February round of primaries and caucuses with nearly identical delegate counts, the Texas Democratic primary gained added significance.

Additional election reforms included a requirement to notify former prisoners when their voting rights were restored, verification of citizenship or naturalization to register to vote, and additional proof of identification to vote. The notification of former prisoners was vetoed by Governor Perry, who stated that he found it "unseemly that the state would make a greater effort to register former inmates to vote than we would any other group of citizens in this state."[67] The other proposals failed because opponents noted that additional forms of identification in order to vote would create obstacles to voting, especially among certain groups—the elderly, minorities, and low-income citizens. Proponents had argued that the additional requirements were necessary to prevent voter fraud and increase confidence in elections.

Successful reforms involved general-purpose PACs and corporate contributions. One reform requires general-purpose PACs that accept large contributions or make sizeable expenditures shortly before an election to report them before the election occurs, a requirement that already pertains to candidates for public office. Previously, PACs didn't report these contributions until mid-January, long after the election was over. This measure promotes greater transparency and accountability in campaign contributions and expenditures. Also, the ban on corporate campaign contributions to political candidates was amended to ensure that the ban applied to corporations organized under the Texas For-Profit Corporation Law and Texas Nonprofit Corporation Law.

WHAT SHOULD I HAVE LEARNED?

In this chapter, we described and analyzed political parties, interest groups, elections, and political campaigns in Texas, answering the questions posed below.

- **What are the roots of political parties, interest groups, elections, and campaigns in Texas?**

    Political parties developed slowly in Texas, following a period of factional politics based on personalities. With the exception of Reconstruction, the Democratic Party dominated Texas politics until the mid-1980s. Interest groups also developed as economic, social, and ethnic groups organized to influence government.

- **What characterizes political parties in Texas?**

    The party organizations in Texas include a formal organization and a functional organization. At all levels, the Republican Party's organization is stronger than the Democratic Party's organization. Since 1952, the party in the electorate has become more Republican, less Democratic, and more independent in its party attachments. Partisan changes in the 1980s and 1990s made the parties in Texas more like their national counterparts. While some political scientists maintain that Texas has experienced a partisan realignment, others claim that Texans have dealigned. The party in government in Texas is very weak.

- **What distinguishes interest groups in Texas?**

    In Texas, interest groups—representing business groups and trade associations, professional associations, labor groups, racial and ethnic groups, and public-interest groups—engage in a variety of political activities such as direct and indirect lobbying, electioneering, and litigation. The most powerful groups represent business and professional interests.

- **How are elections and political campaigns conducted in Texas?**

    Primary elections, general elections, special elections, and local elections are conducted to nominate candidates, select public officials, fill vacancies, and select local officials. Contemporary political campaigns in Texas are candidate-centered affairs, dominated by the three M's—money, media, and marketing. Voting decisions include a decision to vote, which requires registration, and a choice among candidates, which requires some information about the candidates. Although the costs of voting have been reduced significantly over the last twenty-five years, voter turnout remains low in Texas. Vote choices are less predictable in contemporary Texas than in the past.

- **What recent electoral and campaign reforms have been passed or debated in Texas?**

    The 80th legislature attempted unsuccessfully to move the Texas primary elections to early February. The failure to move the primary, which most political pundits criticized, actually benefited Texas Democrats in 2008. Other reforms involved attempts to require additional identification by voters and proof of citizenship by individuals registering to vote. Also, PACs were required to report large contributions that were made close to the election date more quickly.

Key Terms

county chairperson, p. 66
county convention, p. 65
county executive committee, p. 66
local election, p. 83
permanent party organization, p. 66

precinct chairperson, p. 66
precinct convention, p. 64
special election, p. 82
state convention, p. 65
state executive committee, p. 66

state party chairperson, p. 66
state senatorial district convention, p. 65
temporary party organization, p. 66

Researching Political Parties, Interest Groups, Elections, and Campaigns

In the Library

Black, Earl, and Merle Black. *The Rise of Southern Republicans*. Cambridge, MA: Harvard University Press, 2002.

Davidson, Chandler. *Race and Class in Texas Politics*. Princeton, NJ: Princeton University Press, 1990.

Dryer, James A., Jan E. Leighley, and Arnold A. Vedlitz. "Party Identification and Public Opinion in Texas, 1984–1994: Establishing a Competitive Two-Party System," in Anthony Champagne and Edward J. Harpham, eds., *Texas Politics: A Reader*, 2nd ed., 108–22. New York: Norton, 1998.

Goodwyn, Lawrence. *Texas Oil, American Dreams: A Study of the Texas Independent Producers and Royalty Owners Association*. Austin: Texas State Historical Association, 1996.

Green, George Norris. *The Establishment in Texas Politics: The Primitive Years, 1938–1957*. Westport, CT: Greenwood, 1979.

Hadley, Charles D., and Lewis Bowman, eds. *Southern State Party Organizations and Activists*. Westport, CT: Praeger, 1995.

Martin, Roscoe. *The People's Party in Texas: A Study in Third-Party Politics*. Austin: University of Texas Press, 1970.

Murray, Richord, and Sam Attlesey. "Texas: Republicans Gallop Ahead," in Alexander P. Lamis, ed., *Southern Politics in the 1990s*, 305–42. Baton Rouge: Louisiana State University Press, 1999.

Texans for Public Justice. *The Gated Community: How Texas Incumbents Locked Out Challengers in 1998*. Austin: Texans for Public Justice, 1999.

Thomas, Clive S., and Robert J. Hrebenar. "Interest Group Power in the Fifty States: Trends Since the Late 1970s." *Comparative State Politics* 20:4 (1999): 3–16.

On the Web

Texas Democratic Party, www.txdemocrats.org
Republican Party of Texas, www.texasgop.org
Texas Ethics Commission, www.ethics.state.tx.us/guides/LOBBY%20guide.htm
Secretary of State, Election Division, www.sos.state.tx.us/elections/
Texans for Public Justice, www.tjp.org

4 The Legislative Branch

"Otto Craddick" was sworn in for a third term as Texas House Speaker in January 2007—or at least that is what some started calling Tom Craddick, referencing charges that the Speaker governs with autocratic means, twisting arms and aiding electoral efforts by big donors to get rid of some members. The session went downhill from there, erupting into an unsuccessful, bitter end-of-the-session battle to strip Craddick of the speakership.[1]

Democrats picked up six seats in the 2006 election, leaving Republicans with a slim majority and emboldening Speaker Craddick's opponents. Two Republicans—Brian McCall and Jim Pitts—mounted last-minute campaigns for the speakership, and Democrat Senfronia Thompson dropped her bid and joined them. Over the Christmas break, Craddick and his supporters—including a handful of Democrats—huddled to save the Speaker. Pitts emerged as the candidate catalyzing Republican and Democratic hopes to unseat Craddick, and both sides released vote totals showing their guy winning; clearly, some members were lying and hedging their bets.

■ **Since Texas joined the United States in 1845, the Texas Legislature has convened as the lawmaking body of the state.** The grand Texas capitol has a chamber for the House in the west wing and a chamber for the Senate in the east wing. Recent renovations, seen in the Senate chamber on the right, have restored the chambers as closely as possible to their original state.

Craddick started losing public support as some newspapers editorialized in favor of a change. Three days before the beginning of the session, Pitts guaranteed that he had more than enough votes to win. Then the battle shifted to arguments for and against a secret ballot for the speakership. Was a public, open vote the ideal in a democratic system? Or would a secret ballot enable representatives to vote without fear of retaliation from big-dollar backers of the other side? Craddick's supporters called for an open vote and waged a public relations campaign in favor of it. Yet, public interest groups sided with advocates of a closed ballot, arguing that fear of—indeed, a *history* of—retaliation would taint the election. Of course, the vote on whether to have an open vote would itself be an open vote. "There is the presumption that a vote for a secret ballot is a vote against Craddick," noted Democratic Rep. Scott Hochberg.[2]

When the vote on the balloting system was called, Craddick lost fourteen Republicans but picked up enough Democrats to win, 80–68. With that procedural vote for an open ballot, Craddick's opposition collapsed. Pitts quit, saying "I don't want to put anyone else in jeopardy."[3] Craddick then won the election, 121–27. What happened to Pitts's pledged votes? "I could write a book," he told a reporter, "and everybody would think it's fiction."[4]

When Speaker Craddick made his committee appointments and stripped some of his opponents—including Pitts—of their

★ **WHAT SHOULD I KNOW ABOUT...**
- the roots of Texas's legislative branch?
- provisions of the state constitution that apply to legislators?
- the makeup of the legislature?
- the organization of the legislature?
- how the legislature makes laws and budgets?
- how legislators make decisions?
- the governor's role in the legislative process?
- proposals to reform the legislature?

prime seats, charges of retaliation rocketed around the capitol, and Democrats then defeated a customary motion to set the session's calendar. But the session settled into its routine. Four months later, as usual end-of-the-session pressures mounted, the battle over the speakership exploded again. Speaker Craddick moved a bill to the front of the calendar, sparking a point of order that he rejected. In an almost unheard-of action, the House then overruled his ruling, 87–50.[5] At that point, Republican Jim Keffer began running for Speaker, and disaffected Republicans mounted a campaign for a resolution to vacate the chair immediately. Soon, Republicans Pitts, McCall, Fred Hill, and others tossed their hats into the ring.

How would Craddick react to the attempted coup? He ruled that he would not recognize any motion to vacate the chair. "The Speaker of the House of Representatives has absolute discretion whether or not to recognize any member on any matter," he said. "There is no appeal to that."[6] The chamber erupted into yelling, screaming, and punching, with armed state troopers called in to maintain order, and Craddick's parliamentarian immediately resigned. "This is anarchy!" one member proclaimed. "I thought we elected a Speaker, not a dictator," said another.[7] A Republican legislator then led a walkout from the chamber.

The 2007 session limped to a close, with both sides trying to get the attorney general to vindicate their position on the House rule on recognizing motions. A year later, the AG danced around the question with a murky ruling. More newspapers editorialized for a new Speaker, and Democratic legislators campaigned against the "Craddick D's"—the handful of Democratic members who had supported the Speaker. The 2008 nominations and elections and the 2009 legislative session would renew the battle over leadership and reforms.

> **TO LEARN MORE—**
> **—TO DO MORE**
> Go to the *House Journal* (Jan. 9, 2007, Record Vote #1) and see how your representative voted on the motion for a secret ballot for Speaker: www.tlo2.tlc.state.tx.us/hjrnl/80r/html/0RDAY01FINAL.HTM

constitutional amendment
A change, addition, or deletion to a constitution.

redistrict
Redraw election-district boundaries.

impeach
A vote by the House to formally accuse a government official of official wrongdoing.

The Texas legislature serves the following functions: to represent the people in government; to legislate, budget, and tax; to perform constituent casework; to oversee the bureaucracy (see chapter 5); to consider **constitutional amendments** (proposed changes) for the Texas and U.S. Constitutions; to confirm the governor's appointees; to **redistrict** (redraw election-district boundaries) itself and the U.S. congressional districts in Texas; and to **impeach** (accuse) and remove from office corrupt officials. The agenda considered by the legislature in any given session is influenced by the historical dynamics of the institution, never-ending agitation for reform of the process, and societal power struggles over policy changes.

On Tuesday, January 13, 2009, the 81st Legislature convened in Austin for its session of 140 days. Senators and representatives adopted rules, selected leaders, and started legislating. In 2007, when the 80th Legislature convened in its regular session, it considered 6,190 bills to change public policy, 172 resolutions to amend the Texas Constitution, and 4,628 other resolutions. By the time the legislature adjourned, it had passed 1,481 bills, 17 constitutional amendment proposals, and 4,343 other resolutions.[8] The governor vetoed 51 bills and 3 resolutions. The governor can call the legislature into special thirty-day sessions at any time when the legislature is not in its regular session, as occurred three times in 2005 and 2006. This pattern of regular sessions and occasional special sessions of the Texas legislature has been repeated for more than a century. The 82nd Texas Legislature convenes in regular session on January 11, 2011.

There is much to learn about the Texas legislature's structure, procedures, and members, but were we to study the legislature alone, we would not fully understand its place in the political system. We must also look at external forces that influence its actions—such as elections, lobbyists, governors, and the media.

In this chapter:

★ First, we will examine *what earlier Texas legislatures were like*, focusing on the evolution of the Texas legislature from its roots in Mexico to its contemporary structure.

★ Second, we will look at *provisions of the state constitution that define and limit the legislative branch of government*, indicating how the Texas Constitution affects legislators and their performance.

★ Third, we will focus on *what influences the makeup of the legislative membership and the characteristics of the membership*, including electoral, personal, and political variables.

★ Fourth, we will explore *how legislative leadership and opposition are organized* and how they operate.

★ Fifth, we will study the *vehicles used for passing laws and budgets and the rules and procedures for moving those vehicles forward*, describing the stages of the legislative and budgeting process in the legislature.

★ Sixth, we will examine *what forces influence legislators in their decision making*, focusing on the interactions among legislators and between outside actors and legislators.

★ Seventh, we will look at *the formal and informal powers the governor has in the legislative process*, indicating how the governor wields influence with legislators.

★ Finally, we will look at *some new reforms of the Texas legislative process and some that are being considered*.

Roots of the Legislative Branch

The predecessors to the Texas legislature were Mexican legislatures, a series of elected conventions, and the Congress of the Republic of Texas. Mexico won its war of independence from Spain in 1821, and by 1824 it adopted a constitution that provided for a federal republic. The provinces of Tejas and Coahuila were joined together. The State of Coahuila y Tejas drafted a constitution in 1827 and organized a legislature. Originally, Tejas got only one deputy in the state legislature. As the population of Tejas grew, its representation in the state legislature grew to three.⁹ Texians grew disenchanted with their representation and with Mexican policies, and they met in conventions in 1832, 1833, and 1835 that called for separate statehood and a separate state legislature. Another convention assembled in 1836 and, with civil war erupting, declared Texas's independence.¹⁰

How does a losing candidate concede defeat? Here, Representative Jim Pitts shakes the hand of Speaker Tom Craddock after the 2007 vote that sealed Craddock's reelection as Speaker.

The first Congress of the Republic of Texas convened in 1836 and consisted of thirty representatives and fourteen senators. Members of the Senate served three-year terms, but members of the House were elected for one-year terms, so each Congress lasted one year. The Republic of Texas had nine congresses.[11] When Texas joined the United States in 1846, the Congress of the Republic dissolved and the 1st Legislature of the State of Texas convened. A legislature sat for a two-year period. The numbering of the legislative sessions was not changed when new constitutions were later adopted. Thus, the first legislature to meet under the current constitution (in 1876) was the 15th Legislature.

Texas legislatures have always governed a society of mixed populations, but Anglos have dominated the legislatures. In the 1830s, Anglo immigrants from the United States dominated the series of conventions, though *Tejanos* were also active in both the growing opposition movement and in the official government of Coahuila y Tejas. Some *Tejanos* were leaders in the 1830s conventions, most notably Lorenzo de Zavala, who then served as interim vice president of the Republic of Texas.[12] After the Civil War, African Americans were an integral part of the Texas political process. During Reconstruction, African Americans were elected to the Constitutional Convention of 1868 and to the Texas legislature from 1869 to 1874, then in reduced numbers up to the 1890s. The end of Reconstruction brought about the end of representation for African Americans when white supremacists regained power. The Constitutional Convention of 1875 included a small number of African American delegates, and a few African Americans won election to the legislature into the 1890s; 1895 was the last year that an African American served in the legislature until 1967.[13] The nine African American representatives and two African American senators in the 1871–1872 legislature were not surpassed in number until 1977.

The State Constitution and the Legislative Branch of Government

The Texas legislature, like all state legislatures except Nebraska, is bicameral—it has two chambers. The **bicameral Texas legislature** consists of a Senate of thirty-one members, ranking fortieth in size among the states, and a House of Representatives of 150 members, ranking eighth.[14] The 1876 constitution set the size of the Senate but allowed the House to grow to a maximum of 150, which it reached in 1921. To learn more about representation in the Senate, see The Living Constitution.

Both the House and the Senate must pass a bill for it to become law. Nonetheless, there are a few differences in the duties of the two chambers. The House has the responsibility of initiating action to raise state revenue. The Senate has the responsibility of confirming the governor's appointees to many state offices. Article 15 of the Texas Constitution allows the House to impeach public officials and the Senate to try and, if convicted, to remove impeached officials from office.[15] It does not specify any breach of standards of conduct or any other reasons that must be given for the impeachment. Impeachment requires a majority vote in the House, and conviction requires a two-thirds vote in the Senate.

Article 3 of the Texas Constitution includes numerous rules governing the legislative process, including setting out a designated regular order of business for a legislative calendar. It provides broad rules, but it also contains more specific rules—restrictions so specific that the legislature often overrides them. For instance, the part of the regular order of business limiting the legislature to some types of action early in the session and others later in the session is routinely suspended at the beginning of

---

bicameral Texas legislature
The legislature has two bodies, a House of Representatives and a Senate.

The Living Constitution

The State shall be divided into Senatorial Districts of contiguous territory according to the number of qualified electors as nearly as may be, and each district shall be entitled to elect one Senator; and no single county shall be entitled to more than one Senator.

ARTICLE 3, SECTION 25

The basis for representation in the Texas Senate has changed over time. The Texas Constitution of the Republic (1836) based representation in the Senate on "free population (free negroes and Indians excepted)" and entitled each district to only one senator. The 1845 Constitution based representation on the "number of qualified electors." No change in the provision occurred until the 1876 Texas Constitution, which retained the "number of qualified electors" as the basis for representation but also limited a county, regardless of its population, to one senator.[a]

During the 1960s, the U.S. Supreme Court and lower federal courts issued several opinions that affected Texas. In *Reynolds* v. *Sims* (1964), the U.S. Supreme Court decided that the equal protection clause of the Fourteenth Amendment to the U.S. Constitution requires that both chambers of a bicameral legislature be apportioned solely on the basis of population. In *Kilgarlin* v. *Martin* (1966), a U.S. federal district court, applying the standards set in *Reynolds* v. *Sims*, declared the 1961 Texas Senate redistricting unconstitutional because it limited a single county to one senator, regardless of the county's population. However, basing representation in the Senate on "qualified voters" rather than the "total population" was not affected by the ruling. As Justice William J. Brennan noted, writing for the majority in *Burns* v. *Richardson* (1966), "We start with the proposition that the Equal Protection Clause does not require the States to use total population figures derived from the federal census as the standard by which this substantial population equivalency is to be measured." Continuing, Justice Brennan stated, "Neither in *Reynolds* v. *Sims* nor in any other decision has this Court suggested that the States are required to include aliens, transients, short-term or temporary residents, or persons denied the vote for conviction of crime, in the apportionment base by which their legislators are distributed and against which compliance with the Equal Protection Clause is to be measured."[b] Despite the fact that Texas was not required to use the total population as the basis for representation in the Senate, the legislature employed that figure during redistricting in the 1960s and 1970s, primarily because it was more readily available.

The issue was settled in 1981 when Comptroller Bob Bullock asked Attorney General Mark White whether the legislature was required by the Texas Constitution to use "qualified electors" for redistricting. Attorney General White responded, "The section 25 requirement that the state be divided into senatorial districts on the basis of qualified electors is unconstitutional on its face as inconsistent with the federal constitutional standard."[c] White cited *Kilgarlin* v. *Martin* (1966) as the basis for his assertion. Unless challenged in court and overturned, the attorney general's opinion stands. Nevertheless, the Texas Constitution was not changed until 2001. The section now reads: "The state shall be divided into Senatorial Districts of contiguous territory, and each district shall be entitled to elect one Senator."[d]

CRITICAL THINKING QUESTIONS

1. If the basis for representation in the Texas Senate were "qualified voters" rather than the "total population," which groups would benefit? Why?
2. Which groups would be disadvantaged? Explain your answer.

---

[a]George D. Braden, *The Constitution of the State of Texas: An Annotated and Comparative Analysis*, vol. 1 (Austin: Texas Legislative Council, 1977), 147.

[b]*Burns* v. *Richardson*, 384 U.S. 73 (1966).

[c]Mark White, Attorney General Opinion, Opinion No. MW-320, May 30, 1981, www.oag.state.tx.us/opinions/op46white/mw-350.htm.

[d]Texas Constitution, Article 3, section 25, amended November 6, 2001, www.capitol.state.tx.us/txconst/sections/cn000300-002500.html.

each session. Occasionally tension over the House Speaker's election roils a session, as it did in 1981, 1983, and 2007, when the House was unable to get the four-fifths vote required to suspend the constitutional rule.[16]

Constitutional Provisions Affecting Legislators

The Texas Constitution sets out the length of legislators' terms of office, requirements that a person must meet to serve as a legislator, provisions for legislators' pay, and provisions limiting what a legislator may do in office. To learn more about these constitutional provisions, see Table 4.1.

LENGTH OF TERMS Representatives are elected for two-year and senators for four-year terms, with no limit on the number of terms they may serve. Senate elections are staggered: fifteen seats are up for election, then two years later, the other sixteen are up for election. In the first election after redistricting, all senators must run because new district boundaries are drawn. Senators then draw lots to see who serves a two-year term and who gets a four-year term, so that membership terms return to a staggered system.

TEMPORARY ACTING LEGISLATORS In 2003, the constitution was amended (Article 16, section 72) to provide that a representative or senator who goes into active military service may appoint a temporary replacement legislator (subject to majority approval by the appropriate chamber) for the period of his or her active military duty, up to the remainder of the term. The replacement legislator must meet the same constitutional requirements as other legislators; in addition, the replacement must be of the same political party as the elected legislator. Under this new provision, Representative Rick Noriega (D–Houston) appointed his wife, Melissa, as his replacement when he was deployed to Afghanistan in 2005; Representative Carl Isett (R–Lubbock) appointed his wife, Cheri, as his replacement when he was deployed to Kuwait in 2006; and Representative Frank Corte (R–San Antonio) appointed his wife, Valerie, as his replacement when he was deployed to Iraq in 2006.

COMPENSATION Texas legislators are among the lowest paid in the nation. Legislative salaries are established in the constitution at $600 per month for each month of the term of office (or $7,200 per year). Legislators also get a **per diem,** a per day allowance to cover room and board expenses when they are in session. Nationwide, state legislative annual salaries in 2007 ranged from the top levels of $113,098 in

per diem
Legislators' per day allowance covering room and board expenses while on state business.

TABLE 4.1 Constitutional Requirements Affecting Texas Legislators

	Senate	House
Residency	5 years in Texas, 1 year in district	2 years in Texas, 1 year in district
Minimum age	26 years	21 years
Term of office	4 years	2 years
Citizenship	United States	United States
Voting status	Qualified (registered) voter	Qualified (registered) voter
Salary	$600 per month	$600 per month
Conflict of interest	Must disclose any personal interest in a bill; may not hold any other state office or contract	Must disclose any personal interest in a bill; may not hold any other state office or contract

Source: Texas Constitution, Article 3.

TEXAS IN COMPARISON

Legislatures in the United States

American state legislatures vary considerably, as allowed in a federal system. While only Nebraska varies from the bicameral norm, states do vary on other legislative attributes, such as size of the bodies, length of the sessions, compensation, and membership attributes.

	Regular Sessions	Special Sessions	Number of House Members	Number of Senate Members	Annual Salaries (2007)	Women as Percentage of the Legislature (2006)
Texas	140 calendar days, biennial	30-day limit, called only by governor	150 (8th)	31 (40th)	$7,200 (39th)[a]	19.9 (29th)
California	no limit on length	no limit, called only by governor	80 (35th)	40 (18th)	113,098 (1st)	30.8 (10th)
New York	no limit on length	no limit, called by governor or 2/3 of legislators	150 (8th)	62 (2nd)	79,500 (2nd)	22.6 (25th)
Florida	60 calendar days (extended by 3/5 vote)	20-day limit (extended by 3/5 vote), called by governor, legislative leaders, or legislators	120 (16th)	40 (18th)	30,996 (19th)	23.8 (22nd)

[a]Ranking could be lower; eight states pay by the number of days or weeks in session. If their sessions go long, their pay could exceed Texas pay.
Sources: Council of State Governments, *The Book of the States 2007*, vol. 39, 76–94; National Conference of State Legislatures, www.ncsl.org, 2006.

California, $79,650 in Michigan, and $79,500 in New York, to the lowest level of $100 in New Hampshire (with no per diem).[17] Some states also pay salary supplements to House and Senate leaders.

Texas legislators' pay was last raised, by constitutional amendment, in 1974. In 1991, voters amended the constitution to allow the new Ethics Commission to propose a higher salary, subject to approval by the voters. The commission may also propose higher salaries for the House Speaker and the lieutenant governor. The commission has taken no action under this new authority. The 1991 amendment allows the Ethics Commission to set the per diem rate at an amount no higher than the maximum federal tax deduction for business expenses. The commission adopted the rate of $168 per day for 2009.

Sessions of the Legislature

Texas has a **biennial legislature:** it meets regularly once every two years. Biennial state legislatures were common in the nineteenth and into the twentieth century, out of the belief that "citizen" legislators could tend to the affairs of the state in a short period of time, then return to their jobs and families. Today, forty-four states have annual sessions, and Texas is the only large, urban state that uses biennial sessions.[18]

The constitution calls the biennial session of the legislature a **regular session.** The original 1876 constitution did not say how long a regular session could last, but it contained an economic incentive for short sessions—legislators were paid more for the early part of the session than for the later weeks. In 1960, voters approved an amendment establishing a 140-day limit for regular sessions. The constitution also allows the governor to convene **special (called) sessions** of the legislature lasting up to thirty days each. Despite its pedigree as a biennial, part-time body, the Texas legislature has met so often in special sessions in recent decades, and has upgraded its professional structure so much, that the National Conference of State Legislatures now considers Texas a "hybrid" legislature, with legislators spending more than two-thirds of their time on legislative business.[19] They continue, however, to receive minimal pay.

biennial legislature
A legislative body that meets in regular session only once in a two-year period.

regular session
The biennial 140-day session of the Texas legislature, beginning in January of odd-numbered years.

special (called) session
A legislative session of up to thirty days, called by the governor, during an interim between regular sessions.

Timeline: Redistricting and the Texas Legislature

1962-1964 The U.S. Supreme Court declares in several cases (e.g., Baker v. Carr, Wesberry v. Sanders, Reynolds v. Sims) that states must redistrict, that they must use a one-person-one vote standard, and that courts may hear lawsuits challenging redistricting

1965 Texas legislature redistricts itself and Texas's congressional seats in response to Kilgarlin v. Martin and Bush v. Martin; Bush wins one of the new U.S. House seats in 1966

1971 Texas legislature redistricts after the decennial census; leaders use redistricting to punish Dirty Thirty opponents who wanted to investigate the Sharpstown scandal

1964 George Bush and Bill Kilgarlin lawsuits successfully challenge Texas's congressional and legislative district lines

1971 Court throws out the Sharpstown-tainted district lines for the Texas House and crafts new ones

Who Are the Members of the Legislature and How Do They Represent the Public?

Members of the Texas legislature *represent* the public in government. Differences over the nature of representation, how to achieve representation, and equality of representation are never-ending battles for democracies.

It is the members of the legislature who make the institution work. Thus, it is important to examine qualifications and characteristics of the membership and what influences the selection of those particular members. Another reason to understand who they are is that the legislature often contains future top leaders. Sam Rayburn was elected Speaker of the Texas House of Representatives in 1911 and went on to become the longest-serving Speaker of the U.S. House of Representatives. Recent Texas leaders who served in the legislature include U.S. Senator Kay Bailey Hutchison, Governor Rick Perry, Land Commissioner Jerry Patterson, Comptroller Susan Combs, Agriculture Commissioner Todd Staples, and several of Texas's U.S. congressional representatives.

Variables Affecting Members' Elections

Two election variables are significant in determining who the members of the legislature are. First, members run from districts, so we examine how the lines for those districts are drawn. Second, members may run for reelection to an unlimited number of terms, so we examine the stability or turnover in legislative membership.

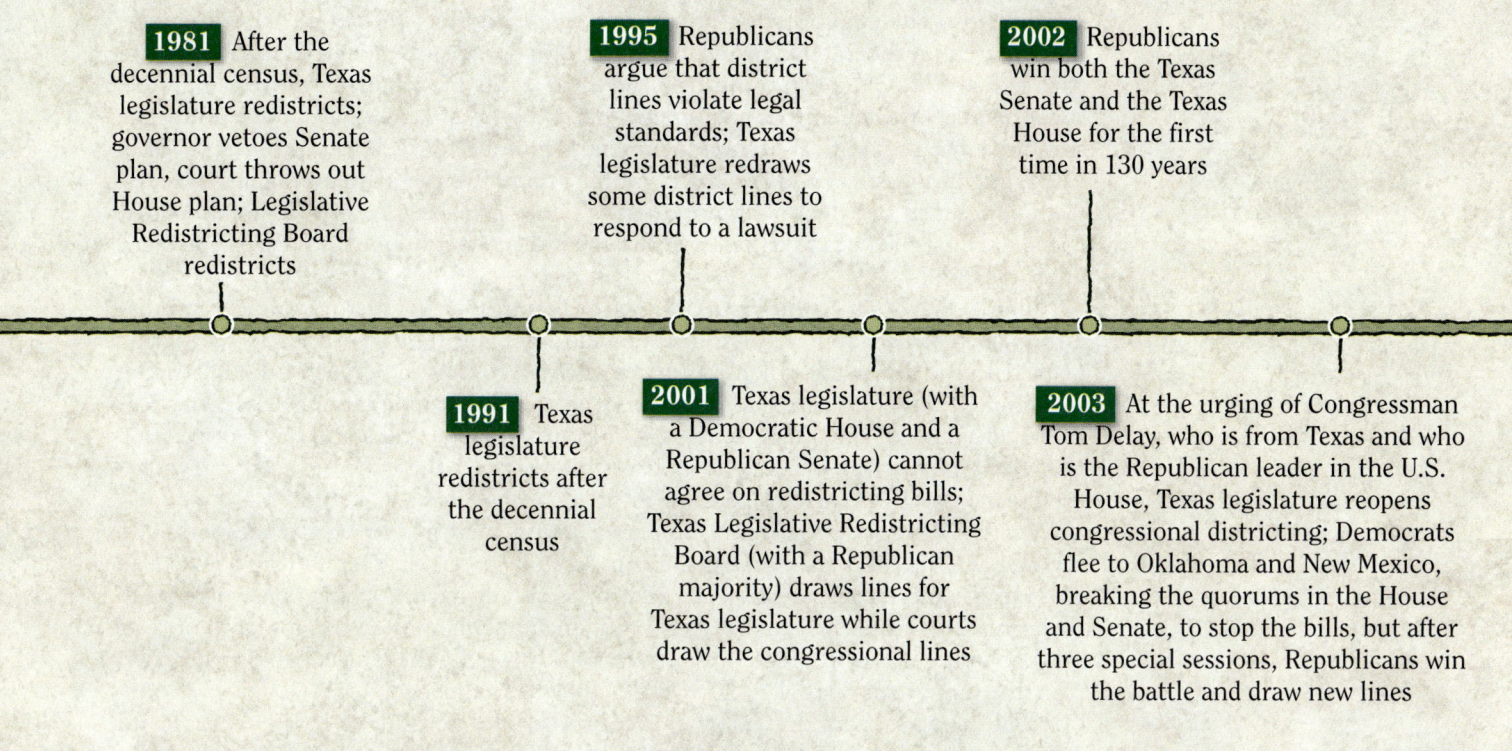

REDISTRICTING Legislators are chosen in single-member districts, where each legislator represents a separate, distinct election district. Because districts become unequal in population size over time, the U.S. and the Texas constitutions require that the district lines be redrawn every decade to assure citizens equal representation, regardless of where they live. (To learn more about legal issues and redistricting in Texas, see Timeline: Redistricting and the Texas Legislature.) The legislature usually redistricts—both itself and Texas's U.S. House seats—in the year after the U.S. Census. Early in the twentieth century, when the rural-dominated Texas legislature was called on to redistrict itself, it faced a dwindling rural population and a burgeoning urban population. When it came time to redistrict, rural legislators simply could not or would not do it, since redistricting meant giving up seats (and incumbent legislators) to urban areas. The result was malapportionment of legislative districts, and those disparities worsened throughout the decades, becoming so extreme that the legislature was forced to act. In 1947, the legislature proposed a constitutional amendment to establish a Legislative Redistricting Board, with the power to act if the legislature ever again failed to pass a redistricting bill after the U.S. Census. Voters approved the amendment in 1948, and it had its intended effect. In 1951, the legislature approved the redistricting bills, rather than let the board redistrict it. Yet, the redistricting still did not effect equal representation. It was the U.S. Supreme Court that finally ended the "rotten boroughs" by making courts watchdogs over legislative redistricting, to assure equalization.[20] Consequently, the Texas legislature was compelled to redistrict in 1965 under the new standards and has adhered more closely to equal representation in recent decades.

The ultimate goal of redistricting is to create districts with equal-sized populations. Based on the 2000 Census of 20.9 million Texans, the ideal Texas Senate district size is 672,639 constituents and the ideal Texas House district size is 139,012 constituents.[21] Reaching that goal of equality is a process laden with political intrigue and hidden traps. Political parties, incumbents running for reelection, courts, the U.S. Department of Justice, and racial and ethnic groups are the primary players in redistricting politics, and their goals are often at odds. Legislators often *gerrymander* districts, drawing the lines to enhance or diminish the power of one party or of one racial or ethnic group.

The U.S. Voting Rights Act declares that states with a history of electoral discrimination against minority groups—including Texas—must preclear redistricting plans with the U.S. Department of Justice or the U.S. District Court of the District of Columbia.[22] Also, the U.S. Supreme Court has ruled that redistricting raises constitutional questions of equal representation, so courts (federal and state) have jurisdiction to review redistricting plans. The Court is divided over the issue of racial gerrymandering and has given mixed signals about it.

In the 1991 redistricting, Democrats had a majority in both chambers, and Democrat Ann Richards had just been elected governor. Republicans, Mexican Americans, and African Americans all proposed redistricting maps that would be to their greatest advantage. Anglo Democratic incumbents wanted to protect their seats but knew that if they protected themselves too strongly, the courts could reject their plan and write their own plan. That is exactly what happened.

The new districts drawn by the courts for 1993 resulted in an increase for Republicans in the Texas Senate and for minorities in both chambers. In 1993, the new Senate redrew lines in a way that would benefit minorities but would not benefit Republicans so much. A federal district court upheld this new plan. In 1994, Republicans still gained an additional seat. In 1995, a group of Republican voters sued the state to overturn the House plan. The House negotiated with the plaintiffs and redrew some districts in metropolitan areas, and the U.S. Department of Justice and a federal court panel approved the new plan. The 1990s redistricting skirmishes led to increased Republican representation, including Republican majority Senates in 1997, 1999, and 2001.

"What do we need to do to win this vote?" Legislators call huddles, much as a football team does before a play. Here, Democratic Senators Royce West, Eliot Shapleigh, Rodney Ellis, and (sitting) John Whitmire confer on the Senate floor.

In 2001, the Democratic-controlled House, Republican-controlled Senate, and Republican Governor Perry did not reach an accommodation on redistricting during the regular session, so the Legislative Redistricting Board (with four Republicans and one Democrat) approved Senate and House plans (by 3 to 2 votes) that distinctly favored Republicans. Several groups sued, and the U.S. Department of Justice objected to one part of the House plan. A three-judge federal panel in Tyler approved the board's Senate plan, then approved its House plan with modifications requested by the Department of Justice.

The 2001 legislature also failed to redistrict the *congressional* lines, leaving that task to the courts. A state district court in Austin established a congressional redistricting plan, but the Texas Supreme Court threw it out. Then the federal judges in Tyler drew their own plan, using as criteria historic district locations, compactness and contiguity of the districts (following city and county boundaries where possible), and protection of incumbents.[23] The panel concluded that additional minority districts were not required by federal law, so it would not impose them, and in 2002 the U.S. Supreme Court approved the plan.

During the regular session of the 78th Legislature, the Republican-controlled legislature tried to redistrict Texas's congressional districts, only to have their plans thwarted by Democrats in the House who fled to Oklahoma to bust the quorum. Later, Senate Democrats fled to New Mexico when Lieutenant Governor Dewhurst announced that he would not observe the traditional calendaring rule (that would have blocked consideration of the bill). Finally, Senator John Whitmire (D–Houston) broke with his fellow Democrats and returned to Austin, ensuring the existence of a quorum and new congressional districts. The remaining Democratic senators then left New Mexico and returned for the remainder of the third called session.[24]

In 2004, the U.S. Supreme Court upheld Pennsylvania redistricting plans (*Vieth v. Jubelirer*) but suggested that partisan issues in redistricting could be so extreme as to render plans unconstitutional. When the Texas congressional redistricting plan got to the Supreme Court, instead of deciding it up or down, the Court sent the case back down with the instruction to reconsider it in light of *Vieth*. The lower court upheld it again, and on a new appeal to the Supreme Court, in 2006 the Court (with two new members) approved most of the plan but required the redrawing of some district lines in south Texas, where Hispanic voting had been illegally diluted. (To learn more about redistricting, see Join the Debate: Would Nonpartisan Redistricting Produce Better [or Different] Results?)

REELECTION RATES AND TURNOVER OF MEMBERSHIP In the early years of the Texas legislature, more than four-fifths of the legislators served a single term and did not seek reelection.[25] Now, most incumbents seek reelection, and most are successful. Around the nation, the average turnover in state legislative races in 2004 was 21 percent in the House and 17 percent in the Senate.[26] The turnover rates for the Texas House were 11 percent in 2004, 18 percent in 2006, and 15 percent in 2008; the turnover rates for the Texas Senate were 6 percent in 2004, 16 percent in 2006, and 6 percent in 2008. Turnover rates typically decline in the election before redistricting because parties push their incumbents to run again (knowing that incumbents usually win), as a strategy to maximize their strength for redistricting. The election after redistricting is often the most volatile; incumbents must run in reconfigured districts, with new voters, and the districts may be drawn in ways to alter party balance in the district. The 2010 and 2012 turnover rates will be the next tests for this pattern.

Today, many legislators make a career of politics. In 2007, the average tenure of incumbents was 13.6 years in the Texas Senate (combining Senate and House experience where present) and 8.0 years in the House.[27] Across the United States, frustration, born out of a sense that the system of representation and election is biased in favor of incumbents staying in office, fueled a 1990s political movement

Join the Debate

Would Nonpartisan Redistricting Produce Better (or Different) Results?

OVERVIEW: In 2005, California and Ohio voters overwhelmingly rejected proposals to strip redistricting away from their legislatures and create nonpartisan redistricting institutions. After the round of redistricting triggered by the 2000 U.S. Census, Pennsylvania, Texas, Georgia, and Colorado all experienced high-profile court cases challenging the results of their redistricting plans. While disagreement over redistricting is as old as the nation, the intense partisan clashes since the election of 2000 have elevated the issue of the consequences—and legitimacy—of redistricting plans drawn by partisan bodies for partisan purposes.

In a representative democracy, political equality is crucial both to the legitimacy of policy outcomes and to the maintenance of a healthy democracy. Legislative bodies must adjust the geographic lines of membership districts every decade to reflect new population figures and to equalize population among the districts. Long ago, legislatures got a reputation for "gerrymandering" their districts—drawing the lines in such a way as to empower one group at the expense of another. One of the consequences of the Voting Rights Act of 1965 was to prohibit legislatures from gerrymandering minority racial or ethnic groups out of legislative representation. Another variety of gerrymandering occurs when the political party that is in the majority in the legislature uses that position to draw district lines with the purpose of keeping themselves in power and minimizing representation for the minority party.

The Center for Voting and Democracy has long pushed nonpartisan redistricting proposals, believing that redistricting in the hands of partisan office holders creates noncompetitive districts that take away real choices from voters. There is evidence that legislative races have become less competitive. In California's 2004 elections, for instance, not one legislative or congressional seat changed parties! New Republican Governor Arnold Schwarzenegger pushed Proposition 77 to create an independent redistricting commission, in an attempt to wrest control of redistricting from the Democratic legislature. Voters defeated it in 2006.

In Texas, the 2001 redistricting helped Republicans in 2002 win majority control of both the House and Senate for the first time in 130 years. Though new congressional districts were in place using the 2000 population figures, the new Republican legislature pushed through another congressional redistricting plan in 2003 with the stated intent of increasing Republican representation. The U.S. Supreme Court ruled in 2006 that the partisan nature of the plan was not a matter for the courts to review.

Read and think about the following arguments for and against the proposition to create a nonpartisan legislative commission that would draw Texas legislative and congressional district lines. Then, continue the debate over nonpartisan redistricting by answering the questions posed after the arguments.

Arguments IN FAVOR of Nonpartisan Legislative Redistricting

- Political parties should not be allowed to use a constitutional process such as redistricting as a tool to maintain or increase political power. Redistricting is an essential element of representative democracy, to keep it from becoming distorted to select groups. When parties use their legislative positions to punish their political adversaries, they have hijacked democracy and turned redistricting into a tool of power.

- Legislatures cannot be expected to be fair in redistricting. Because legislators have an obvious self-

---

term limits
Restrictions that exist in some states about how long an individual may serve in state and/or local elected offices.

for **term limits.** Fifteen states now limit the number of terms that legislators may serve. However, Texas does not have the systems of initiative and referendum—the methods used to force term limits in most states—and it is unlikely that Texas legislators will approve limits for themselves.[28]

Personal and Political Characteristics of Members

An examination of member characteristics such as party affiliation, ideology, occupation, race, gender, and age can reveal who represents Texans in the legislature and can

interest in drawing lines to protect themselves (incumbents) and the majority party, an outside group is essential to fairness in redistricting.

- An independent, nonpartisan body will be more likely to redistrict in a fair, balanced way, minimizing or eliminating gerrymandering. Texas has numerous nonpartisan governing bodies that do a good job. An appointment system with verification for balance and nonpartisanship will assure that redistricting commissioners are fair, and a commission with no self-interest in the outcome will adhere to equality standards and preserve traditional redistricting standards of compactness and keeping communities together.

Arguments AGAINST Nonpartisan Legislative Redistricting

- It is impossible to create a truly independent or nonpartisan redistricting body. Parties and office holders have too much at stake to cede power. They would create the trappings of independence and nonpartisanship, but the process would not likely be transparent, and appointees would be expected to favor their benefactors with districts to benefit one party over the other.
- Commissioners, legislators, and political observers have access to computers and data revealing the consequences (partisan and otherwise) of redistricting plans. It would be a charade to create a process that is ostensibly nonpartisan but in which voting data continue to be a key input in the decision making, producing outcomes similar to the current ones.
- You cannot take politics out of politics. Partisan actions and self-interest should not be hidden behind closed doors or masked in nominally independent entities. Democracy is best served when elected officials make the decisions, with the media and voters watching.

Continuing the Debate

1. Do you support or oppose a nonpartisan redistricting body for Texas? Why?
2. If Texas were to adopt nonpartisan redistricting, how would it affect the next round of Texas redistricting?

To Follow the Debate Online Go To:

League of Women Voters: www.lwv.org/AM/Template.cfm?Section=Redistricting

National Conference of State Legislatures: www.ncsl.org/programs/legis-mgt/redistrict/com&alter.htm

Center for Voting and Democracy www.fairvote.org/redistricting/reports/remanual/frames.htm

Senator Jeff Wentworth reflects on redistricting proposals in the Senate chamber, with redistricting maps in the background.

Photo courtesy: Bob Daemmrich

show whether there are distinctive patterns to that representation. To learn more about party, gender, and race characteristics of the legislative membership over the past thirty years, see Figures 4.1 and 4.2.

OCCUPATION, EDUCATION, AND RELIGION Across the nation in the nineteenth and early twentieth centuries, nearly half of state legislators were farmers and about half were lawyers, businesspeople, and other professionals. The majority of legislators were probably middle class. In state legislatures today, the number of business owners, farmers, and attorneys is declining, and the number of teachers, preachers, public

111

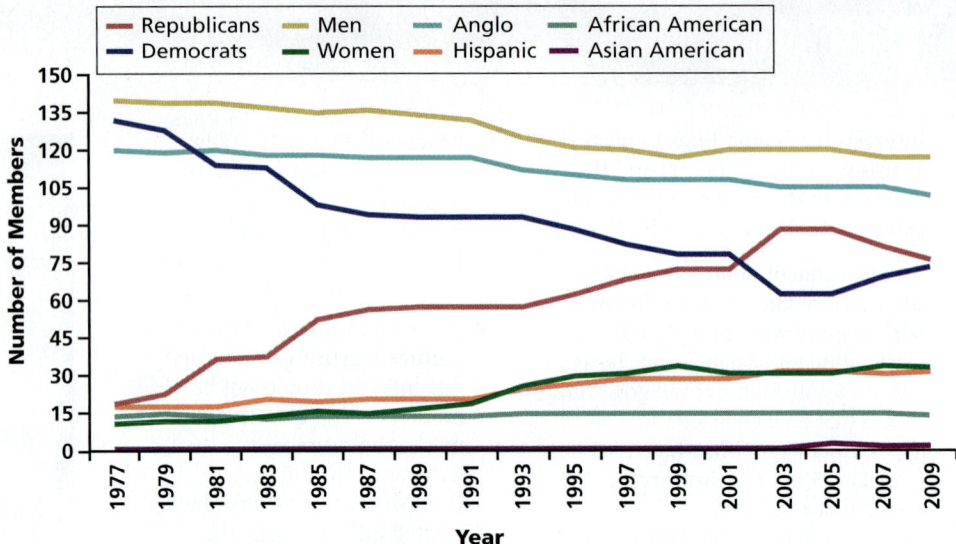

FIGURE 4.1 Texas House Membership, 1977–2009

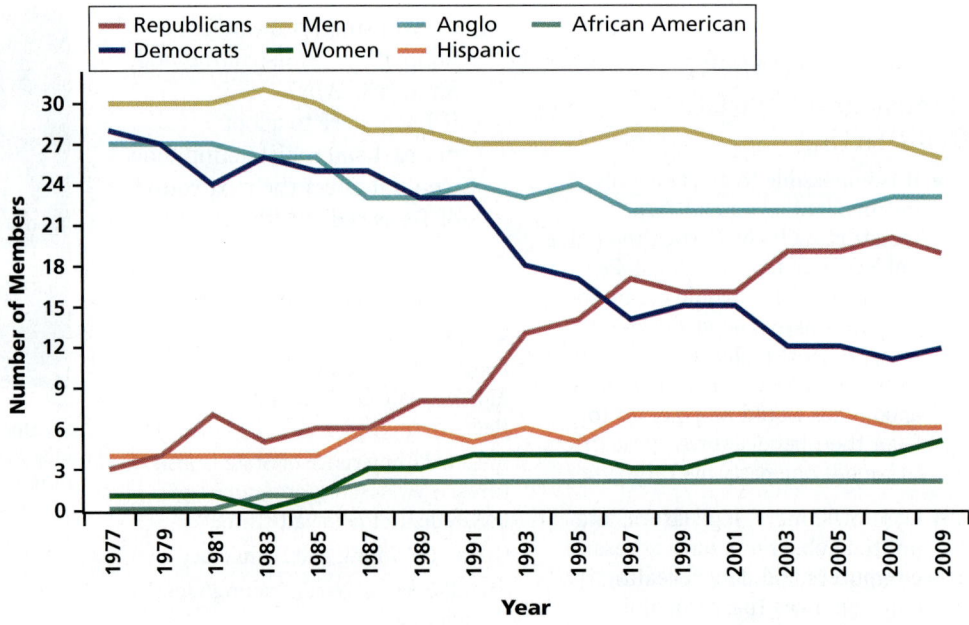

FIGURE 4.2 Texas Senate Membership, 1977–2009

organizers, and former legislative aides being elected to legislatures is increasing. In 2007, 42 percent of Texas senators and 59 percent of representatives were businesspeople, while 32 percent of senators and 33 percent of representatives were attorneys.[29] One possible explanation for continued dominance of lawyers and businesspeople is the low level of pay and part-time nature of the Texas legislature—which ensures that most legislators must have flexible schedules and must be able to take time off from work without losing their jobs and income. The increasing number of Republicans in both chambers also reduced the percentage of attorneys and increased the percentage of professionals and businesspersons.

In 2007, every senator and all but seven House members had attended some college, and a majority of legislators had graduate degrees. Understandably, more Texas legislators have law degrees than any other type of graduate degree, with master's degrees second.

With the diversification of the legislature since the 1970s has come a broadening of the representation of religious denominations. While Baptists traditionally had the highest number of members in the legislature, by the 1990s Catholics were the largest group, followed by Baptists, Methodists, and Episcopalians.

GENDER, RACE, AND AGE Historically, most state legislators across the nation have been Anglo males. The recent trend in legislatures is an increase in minorities and women. By 2008, 23.6 percent of state legislators were women.[30] There is still a tremendous difference among the states, ranging from Vermont (where 37.8 percent of legislators are women), New Hampshire (35.6 percent), Colorado (35 percent), and Minnesota (34.8 percent), to South Carolina, where 8.8 percent are women. Most states with the lowest representation of women are southern or border states. In 2009, the six women in the Texas Senate constituted 20 percent of the membership; the thirty-three women in the Texas House constituted 22 percent of the membership. African Americans constituted only 2.2 percent of the nation's state legislators in 1970; by 2007, 8 percent were African American. In Texas, the figures were 6 percent in the Senate and 9 percent in the House. In 2007, Hispanics constituted 3 percent of the nation's state legislators, though they exceeded 20 percent in New Mexico and California.[31] The figures for 2009 were 19 percent in the Texas Senate and 21 percent in the Texas House.

The demographics of the Texas legislature also vary by party. In the 2009 Texas House membership, of seventy-six Republicans, seventy-five were Anglo and one was Asian American; of seventy-four Democrats, thirty-two were Hispanics, twenty-seven were Anglo, fourteen were African American, and one was Asian American. In the Senate, all nineteen Republicans were Anglo. Of Senate Democrats, six were Hispanic, four were Anglo, and two were African American.

Most Texas legislators are in their forties or fifties in age. House members tend to be young to middle aged, while senators tend to be middle aged to older—though there certainly are exceptions. In 2007, the average House member was fifty-one years old; five House members were under thirty (the youngest was twenty-eight) and five were over seventy (the oldest was eighty-two). The average Senate member was fifty-four; one was under forty, and none were over seventy. The youngest senator was thirty-six and the oldest was sixty-six.[32]

POLITICAL PARTY Historically, Democrats have won far more seats in the Texas legislature than have Republicans. Republicans won a legislative majority only in 1870 until winning a majority of the Senate in 1996 and since, and House majorities since 2002. This Democratic dominance in Texas is overwhelming but also reflects that in the twentieth century, Democrats typically controlled about two-thirds of *all* state legislative chambers. Thus, the strength of Republicans in state legislatures in the 1990s was either an exception or evidence of a new trend. By 2006, the trend started reversing. In 2008, Democrats controlled twenty-seven state senates and Republicans controlled twenty; Democrats controlled thirty state houses of representatives and Republicans controlled nineteen.[33] To learn more about the growth of the Republican Party in the Texas legislature, see Figures 4.1 and 4.2.

In a bicameral legislature, how important is it that House and Senate leaders work well together? Here, House Speaker Tom Craddick and Lieutenant Governor David Dewhurst confer.

IDEOLOGY The four kinds of ideology described in chapter 1 can be useful in analyzing legislative voting patterns in Texas. Different groups rank legislators' votes on ideological dimensions—though they are usually two-dimensional, rather than four-dimensional. The groups or publications simply choose votes on issues that are most important to them, given their policy perspectives, and see whether legislators agreed with them. Of course, these results tend to be skewed, as groups choose issues that clearly divide legislators on their agenda.[34]

It is difficult to find analyses of voting patterns that take into account populism and libertarianism. Recall from chapter 1 that we focused on differences in *equality versus opportunity* and *liberty versus order* in our definitions of ideology. For more than a decade, we have measured ideology of House members based on selected votes. We identified (for legislatures of 1995, 1999, 2001, 2003, 2005, and 2007) five votes on equality and five on liberty measures, based on the description of those ideologies we presented in chapter 1, to test the four-part ideological framework. While the distribution varies some each session, and each session also has its own dynamics that affect voting behavior, there is a general pattern—and that pattern is borne out again in 2007.[35]

To learn about the 2007 voting analysis, see Analyzing Visuals: Ideological Voting Patterns in the Texas House of Representatives. Of the 80 voting Republicans in 2007 (the Speaker does not typically vote), 68 were conservative, 4 were libertarian, 5 were populist, and 3 were liberal. Of the 68 voting Democrats (one member was ill most of the session), 33 were liberal, 33 were populist, and 2 were conservative.

IDEOLOGY AND PARTISANSHIP The data for all the sessions studied reveal a distinct difference between legislative Democrats and legislative Republicans. The center of the House Democratic Party is liberal, with some populist elements, while the center of the House Republican Party is solidly conservative and libertarian (in 1995, 1999, and 2005, it had stronger libertarian elements; in 2001, 2003, and 2007, it had stronger conservative elements). Democrats used to be more ideologically diverse, but as their numbers shrank, they became more unified (liberal). When the Republicans were small in number but growing, they were solidly conservative; once they gained a majority, they exhibited a slightly more diverse membership, with a few liberals and populists.

Partisan differences have become more evident, leading to the Democrats' breaking the quorum in 2003 to prevent adoption of a partisan redistricting plan for Texas's congressional districts. To many observers of Texas politics, the partisan fight over redistricting was simply the culmination of a trend that emerged earlier in the legislative session when Republicans pushed budget cuts for health and human services and for education.[36] The differences between Republican and Democratic Party members are often greatest on government regulation of business, taxing and spending, and social issues (such as abortion and same-sex marriage). Anglo Democrats representing mostly rural, conservative districts often vote with the Republicans in order to reflect their constituents' views on issues such as the Defense of Marriage Act. This group came to be known as the "WD-40s"—white Democrats over forty years of age. The nickname, attributed to Representative Richard Raymond of Laredo, caught on and even provided comedic relief when the WD-40 company sent a letter to the group, complaining that the use of their trademark was illegal. These Democrats represent rural districts that are also swing districts, which normally vote Republican in statewide electoral contests. As a result, the WD-40s may be an endangered species.[37]

Our ideology data demonstrate the party outliers (in terms of ideology) for the past few sessions. In the 1990s, some of the outlying Democrats switched to Republican; in 2007 for the first time, an outlying Republican (Kirk England, populist) switched to Democrat. Additional evidence of increased partisanship and ideological polarization is the willingness of Democratic Party leaders to campaign actively in primary elections against Democratic House incumbents who have been too support-

Analyzing Visuals: Ideological Voting Patterns in the Texas House of Representatives

Examine the distribution of legislators on the ideology quadrant.

Liberal (33 Democrats, 3 Republicans) — top left
Populist (33 Democrats, 5 Republicans) — top right
Libertarian (4 Republicans) — bottom left
Conservative (68 Republicans, 2 Democrats) — bottom right

	8	8	14	7	2
3	2	6 and 1	5	3 and 1	
	3	3 and 2	2 and 1	2	1
		2	2 and 6	3	7
		1	11	10	10
		1	10	6	5

WHICH ideologies are most common among the members of the Texas House of Representatives?

WHAT is the ideological difference between members of the Democratic Party and members of the Republican Party in the House?

IS the difference what you expected based on your understanding of Democrats and Republicans?

Source and Methodology: An ideological voting pattern was identified from five roll-call votes in the 2007 sessions selected on equality/opportunity and five roll-call votes selected on liberty/order. *House Journal* record votes 136, 384, 1022, 1035, and 1438 were used to measure legislators' placement on the liberty/order axis, while record votes 267, 284, 375, 1582, and 1976 were used to measure legislators' placement on the equality/opportunity axis. For instance, on record vote 1976, an aye vote was a vote against the bill to give colleges more flexibility in deciding whom to admit, rather than requiring them to admit the top 10 percent from a high school graduating class; it was categorized as a vote for "equality" and against "opportunity." On record vote 1035, an aye vote was a vote to allow police greater powers to obtain private communications (pen registers); it was categorized as a vote for "order" and against "liberty." Each legislator was then placed on the thirty-six-point grid based on the thirty-six possible combinations of scores, from 0–0 to 5–5.

---

ive of the Republican leadership. Eighteen Democratic House incumbents were challenged in the March 2004 primary elections; seven lost their primary contest either in the first primary election or a runoff election, averaging 38 percent of the vote in the first primary. One of the losing Democrats was Ron Wilson, chair of the House Ways and Means Committee, who had supported Republican Speaker Craddick and the Republican redistricting effort. In 2006 and 2008, additional incumbents lost in the Democratic and Republican primaries. Thus, as party has become more dominant in the House, the voting has become more ideologically polarized, supplanting the old system of bipartisan conservative dominance in the House.

What does the future hold for partisanship in the Texas House of Representatives? According to political scientists Malcolm Jewell and Marcia Lynn Whicker, "strong party cohesion in the legislature depended on polarization of the state party: the two legislative parties should represent distinctly different types of constituencies with different interests."[38] In Texas, as in many southern states, as the number of Republican legislators grew, Democrats became less likely to draw their votes from conservative, rural voters and more likely to draw their votes from lower-income Hispanic, African American, and Anglo voters. If this trend continues, bipartisanship in the Texas House will cease to exist, and partisanship will increasingly provide the basis for political power and conflict.

116 CHAPTER 4 The Legislative Branch

Photo courtesy: Sargent ©2007 Austin. Reprinted with permission of American-Statesman, UNIVERSAL PRESS SYNDICATE. All rights reserved.

How will the Texas House of Representatives address the issues of the Speaker's powers? In 2007, Speaker Tom Craddick quelled a rebellion by claiming absolute power to refuse to recognize legislators for motions that could have stripped him of the speakership. Here, Pulitzer-prize winning cartoonist Ben Sargent spoofs that claim.

How Is the Texas Legislature Organized?

While parties are present in the Texas legislature, they have not played the dominant role that they do in Congress (though as just discussed, with the recent Republican surge and the Democratic rebound, that appears to be changing). Rather, the institutional leaders and the committees are the key organizational units.

president of the Texas Senate
The lieutenant governor of Texas, serving in his constitutional role as presiding officer of the Senate.

pro-tempore (pro-tem)
A legislator who serves temporarily as legislative leader in the absence of the Senate president or House Speaker.

Speaker of the Texas House
The state representative who is elected by his or her fellow representatives to be the official leader of the House.

Leaders

The constitution declares that the lieutenant governor shall serve as the **president of the Texas Senate** and that the Senate shall elect a president **pro-tempore** (or **pro-tem**) to serve in the absence of the lieutenant governor. The constitution states that the House of Representatives shall choose its leader, the **Speaker of the Texas House,** from among its members. At the beginning of each regular session, the House elects a Speaker for the biennium. The Speaker appoints a Speaker pro-tem.

The *process* of selecting the Speaker is the most critical factor in how the House operates (see the section on organizing for power and influence). The *concentration of power* in the hands of the Senate president and the House Speaker provides compelling evidence of a majoritarian rather than a pluralist form of democracy in the Texas legislature.

TABLE 4.2 Types of Legislative Committees

Standing Committee
A committee created at the beginning of a legislative biennium, which continues in existence throughout the biennium.
Substantive Committee
A committee that considers legislation as its primary duty; most are standing committees.
Procedural Committee
A committee that has jurisdiction over such things as legislative rules and calendars and administration of the House or Senate.
Special (or Ad Hoc) Committee
A committee created to study a specific problem or policy area; the committee is given a certain amount of time to complete its work, then it goes out of existence.
Interim Committee
A standing committee (or a commission, including some nonlegislative members), charged by the House Speaker and lieutenant governor to study high-profile issues during the interim between sessions; for instance, the Joint Select Committee on Windstorm Coverage reported to the legislature in 2007 on insurance issues related to Hurricanes Katrina and Rita.
Joint Committee
A committee created by both the House and the Senate, with members from both chambers, for a specific duty; examples include the Legislative Budget Board, the Legislative Council, and the Legislative Reference Library Board.
Conference Committee
A joint committee appointed by the House and the Senate for one specific bill passed by both chambers but with different provisions; it writes a common version of the bill and reports back to both chambers.

Committees

The legislature works through a system of committees. A **committee** is a subunit of the legislature appointed to work on designated subjects. Legislatures use committees because the full House or Senate could not possibly do all the work as one large body. Committees also help legislators develop subject specialties and thus, presumably, make better-informed public policies. To learn more about types of committees, see Table 4.2. *Standing committees* are the basic committees that do most of the work during legislative sessions. They can be either *substantive* (focusing on legislation) or *procedural* (focusing on legislative procedures). At the beginning of a regular session, the House and Senate create standing committees; the chairs of those committees appoint ad hoc subcommittees for specific bills. Some Senate committees also have permanent subcommittees.

In most sessions, the standing committees from the previous legislature are simply recreated. However, when there is turnover in leadership, the committee structure is changed. To learn more about the standing committees and the number of members of each one for the 2007–2008 biennium, see Table 4.3. House members typically serve on two or three committees. Senators serve on four standing committees and possibly an additional standing subcommittee.

Two of the most significant powers of the House Speaker and the lieutenant governor are the powers to appoint legislators to committees and to appoint the commit-

> **committee**
> A subunit of the legislature, appointed to work on designated subjects.

TABLE 4.3 Legislative Committees of the 80th Legislature, 2007–2008

House Committees (number of members)
Substantive Committees:
- Agriculture and Livestock (9)
- Appropriations (29)
    - (six standing subcommittees)
- Border and International Affairs (7)
- Business and Industry (9)
- Civil Practices (9)
- Corrections (7)
- County Affairs (9)
- Criminal Jurisprudence (9)
- Culture, Recreation, and Tourism (7)
- Defense Affairs and State-Federal Relations (9)
- Economic Development (7)
- Elections (7)
- Energy Resources (7)
- Environmental Regulation (7)
- Financial Institutions (7)
- Government Reform (7)
- Higher Education (9)
- Human Services (9)
- Insurance (9)
- Judiciary (9)
- Juvenile Justice and Family Issues (9)
- Land and Resource Management (9)
- Law Enforcement (7)
- Licensing and Administrative Procedures (9)
- Local Government Ways and Means (7)
- Natural Resources (9)
- Pensions and Investments (7)
- Public Education (9)
- Public Health (9)
- Regulated Industries (7)
- State Affairs (9)
- Transportation (9)
- Urban Affairs (7)
- Ways and Means (9)

Procedural Committees:
- Calendars (11)
- General Investigating and Ethics (5)
- House Administration (11)
- Local and Consent Calendars (11)
- Redistricting (15)
- Rules and Resolutions (11)

Senate Committees (number of members)
Substantive Committees:
- Business and Commerce (9)
    - Subcommittee on Emerging Technologies and Economic Development (5)
- Criminal Justice (7)
- Education (9)
    - Subcommittee on Higher Education (5)
- Finance (15)
- Government Organization (7)
- Health and Human Services (9)
- Intergovernmental Relations (5)
    - Subcommittee on Flooding and Evacuations (3)
- International Relations and Trade (7)
- Jurisprudence (7)
- Natural Resources (11)
    - Subcommittee on Agriculture, Rural Affairs, and Coastal Resources (5)
- State Affairs (9)
- Transportation and Homeland Security (9)
- Veterans Affair and Military Installations (5)
    - Subcommittee on Base Realignment and Closure (3)

Procedural Committees:
- Administration (7)
- Nominations (7)

tee chairs. In the 1970s, the House created a weak seniority system for assignment to committees. Each member selects one committee that he or she wants to serve on, and the more senior requesters get the spots—a maximum of one-half of a committee's members (excluding the chair and vice chair) may be determined by seniority, with the other half completely within the power of the Speaker to name. (Seniority does not apply on procedural committees or the Appropriations Committee.) House committee chairs appoint subcommittee members and chairs; in the Senate, the lieutenant governor appoints chairs of the standing subcommittees.

Committee work can be a long, painstaking examination of policy matters, leading to markup or to redrafting and amending bills. Public hearings can be educational for the committee members, who may not know much about the subject, but who must become proficient enough in it to defend the committee's work. On the other hand, decisions are often made before the hearing, and public hearings can become what legislators derisively refer to as "dog-and-pony shows," with no real chance to affect the outcome. (To learn more about legislative lingo, see Table 4.4 for a glossary.)

Organizing for Power and Influence in the Legislature

In order to pass bills, legislatures must have vehicles for organizing the leadership and its supporting coalition; if the legislature is open and democratic, there will also be vehicles (and resources) for organizing opposition. In most legislatures and in the U.S. Congress, political parties serve as those vehicles, but not in Texas. In the absence of parties, strong factions and strong leaders rule. An organization of legislators who are all affiliated with the same political party is called a **legislative party caucus** (e.g., the House Republican Caucus). There were no party caucuses in Texas until the 1980s. The result is that a strong party system is now antithetical to the system of strong Speakers and lieutenant governors that has evolved in its absence.[39] It remains to be seen whether party caucuses will merely coexist in a subservient position with the leadership or will manage to become a new power center.

legislative party caucus
An organization of legislators who are all of the same party, and which is formally allied with a political party.

TABLE 4.4 A Glossary of Legislative Lingo

Legislators often use colorful words and phrases in their debates—terms that may be unfamiliar or confusing to casual observers.

Backscratching: Helping another legislator with a vote, with the expectation that he or she will return the favor.
Carrying water: Sponsoring a bill or an amendment at the request of a lobbyist.
Cockroach: A legislator known as an obstructionist, opposing any significant change.
Dog-and-pony show: Lengthy committee hearings, featuring scores of witnesses who tell emotional and personal stories to persuade legislators to vote a bill out of committee or to kill it.
Gerrymandering: Drawing redistricting lines to help or hurt either an incumbent or a group of voters, such as Democrats, Republicans, Anglos, African Americans, or Mexican Americans.
Gutting: Amending a bill in such a way that it severely weakens the bill or changes its original purpose.
Keying (or cueing): Watching another legislator to see which way he or she is voting before deciding how to vote. Floor leaders extend an arm with the index finger held high to indicate that followers should vote "aye" or with two fingers held high to indicate that followers should vote "nay."
Lite guv: The term lieutenant governor is often abbreviated as "lt. gov." In a verbal takeoff of this abbreviation, the office is humorously abbreviated, in comparison to the governor, of course, as the "lite guv."
Logrolling: Supporting and voting for another member's "local" bill (affecting only the author's district), with the assumption that he or she will then support you when you have a bill coming up.
Pork barrel: Appropriations of money to a project in a single legislative district.
Sine die: Legislators use this Latin phrase to describe the 140th day (the last day) of a regular legislative session.
Taking a walk: Leaving a committee hearing or the floor to avoid voting on a controversial bill if such a vote would hurt the legislator with one group or another.
That dog won't hunt: A debating point suggesting that the legislator does not believe another member's argument.

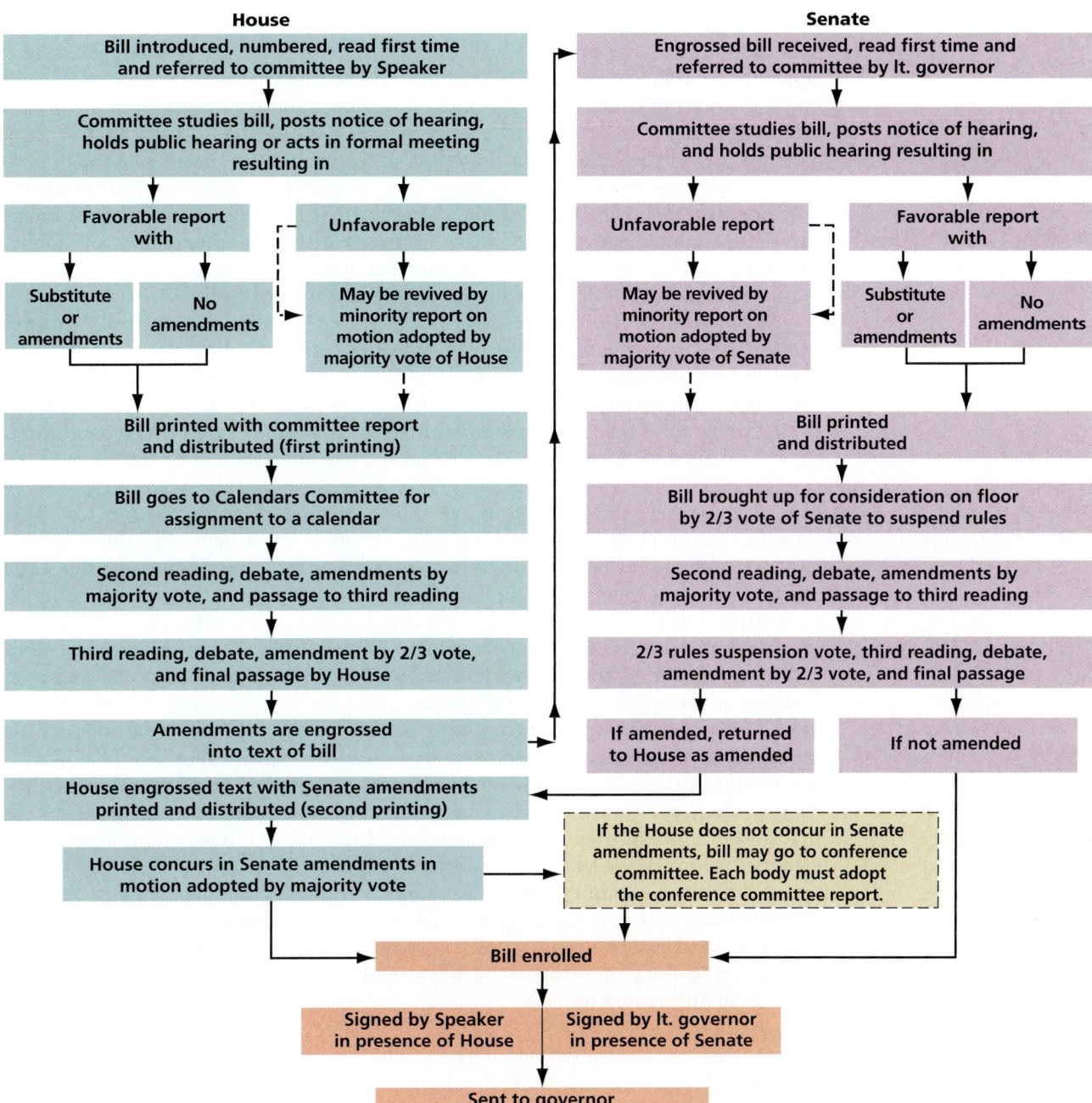

FIGURE 4.3 Basic Steps in the Texas Legislative Process The graphic displays the sequential flow of a bill from the time it is introduced in the House of Representatives to final passage and transmittal to the governor. A bill introduced in the Senate would follow the same procedure in reverse.

Note: If the governor signs the bill or refuses to sign it, it becomes law. If the governor vetoes the bill, it takes a two-thirds vote of both the House and the Senate to override the veto and make the bill law.

Source: Legislative Budget Board, Texas Legislative Council, *Texas Fact Book, 2006* (January 2006): 14. Revised by the authors.

Most bills are considered in *public hearings*, in which citizens may testify for or against the bill, but House committees may consider bills in *formal meetings*, in which testimony is usually not accepted. Because of the reforms following the 1971 Sharpstown scandal and the demand for a more open process, a House committee must post notice of a public hearing at least five days in advance of the hearing. Public hearings must be open to all, and votes must be taken in open meetings. The chair will lay out the bill and call on the author to explain it. The committee hears testimony from witnesses for the bill, witnesses against the bill, and neutral witnesses.

If the chair or committee refers a bill to a subcommittee, the subcommittee chair decides whether to have a public hearing or a formal meeting. Often, subcommittee meetings are brief huddles at the floor desk of the chair. Such meetings, though public, are rarely tape-recorded and frequently occur with no one present other than the subcommittee members and staff members. There is little discussion, and the members often simply ratify decisions made in private meetings of legislators and lobbyists. Action by the subcommittee is in the form of recommendations by majority vote to the full committee, which usually adopts them as drafted.

At this point in the legislative process, the House and the Senate diverge considerably. In both chambers, all bills reported from committee are referred to a procedural committee. Bills in the House go to the Calendars Committee or, if the substantive committee requests it, to the Local and Consent Calendars Committee.[49] In the Senate, bills reported from committee are referred to a procedural committee, but it is an informal process that determines the fate of legislation in the Senate.

THE HOUSE CALENDARS COMMITTEE The Calendars Committee sets the daily calendar for the House.[50] How a bill makes it onto—or is kept off—the daily calendar is one of the more controversial topics in the Texas House. Under 1993 reforms, several aspects of Calendars Committee operations changed. While the committee had been required to lay out the calendar at least twenty-four hours in advance, this requirement was sometimes violated. One reform requires the committee to distribute the daily calendar to each representative at least thirty-six hours in advance, and the committee has complied with the rule. Other reforms include requirements of advance public posting of the meetings and opening the meetings to the public and other members. Another reform requires the committee, within thirty days of receiving a bill, to take a public vote on whether to place it on a calendar. The committee circumvents this requirement by setting the bills that it wishes to set, then adopting a universal motion to not set all other bills on a calendar. Our review of the committee's minutes in the years after the reform revealed that the committee went through the formal procedures required to meet the new rules without changing the real decision-making process. The meetings typically lasted one to five minutes, as the members quickly ratified the list of bills brought in by the committee chair. Clearly, the real decision making was done in the behind-the-scenes process.

THE SENATE CALENDARING FUNCTION The Senate Administration Committee sets a Local and Uncontested Calendar to consider noncontroversial bills, but for significant bills, there is no committee to advance or kill bills approved by the standing committees. Instead, as a means of controlling the flow of legislation, the **Senate two-thirds rule** requires every bill to win a vote of two-thirds of the senators to take up the bill out of the regular order of business. A senator whose bill has been approved by committee must give written *notice of intent* to move to suspend the regular order of business. This daily listing of notices is called the **intent calendar.**

By tradition, at the beginning of each legislative session, a senator will introduce a frivolous bill with no intention of ever asking for a vote on it in the full Senate. For example, in 2007 Senator Kim Brimer introduced SB 259, proposing a county park beautification and improvement program, as the bottleneck bill. The bottleneck bill is the first bill to be approved by any committee, so it is then placed at the top of the order of business. Thus, *every* bill except that one is always out of order, so long as the author of that bill does not request a vote on it. Therefore,

Senate two-thirds rule
The rule in the Texas Senate requiring that every bill win a vote of two-thirds of the senators present to suspend the Senate's regular order of business, so that the bill may be considered.

intent calendar
The Senate calendar listing bills on which the author or sponsor has given notice of intent to move to suspend the regular order of business in order that the Senate may consider them.

before any other bill can be considered, the Senate must first vote to suspend the rule governing the regular order of business. That motion requires a two-thirds vote and must be made for each and every bill, both on second reading and on third reading.

The two-thirds rule is a method by which the Senate assures deliberation and compromise. It protects any minority that has at least one-third of the senators, because they can block passage of a bill. So if an opposition bloc has at least one-third of the senators, the leadership bloc must bargain with it to get the bill passed. This rule makes the leadership–opposition blocs more fluid in the Senate. This protection of minority rights enhances pluralist democracy in the Senate, in stark contrast to the House. The 1979 Killer Bees incident, when twelve senators hid out in order to break the quorum and prohibit a vote, provides a colorful example of what can happen when that norm is violated.[51]

The two-thirds rule also figured in 2003 when Democratic senators hoped to prevent a congressional redistricting bill. During the first called or special legislative session in 2003, Lieutenant Governor Dewhurst observed the two-thirds rule, which allowed Democratic senators to prevent consideration of the bill. However, as the session neared its end, eleven of the twelve Democratic senators, fearing that Governor Perry would immediately call another special session and that the lieutenant governor would lock down the Senate and prevent the senators from leaving the chamber, fled to New Mexico. The Democrats vowed to stay in New Mexico until Governor Perry agreed to remove redistricting from the special session agenda or Lieutenant Governor Dewhurst agreed to abide by the two-thirds rule. According to Dewhurst, the two-thirds rule is merely a Senate "tradition" that is followed or abandoned at the will of the lieutenant governor, citing the "Bullock precedent." (In 1992, then Lieutenant Governor Bullock abandoned the two-thirds rule so that the Senate could consider a court-ordered redistricting bill.) When Senator John Whitmire returned to Texas, he ensured an end to the Democratic senators' holdout in New Mexico and the ultimate passage of the Republican-sponsored redistricting bill.[52]

THE BILL REACHES THE FLOOR Both chambers of the House and Senate are often referred to as the "floor" where legislative action occurs. At the beginning of each legislative day, the Speaker or president calls the members to order and the roll is called to ascertain whether a **quorum,** a required minimum of two-thirds of the members, is on the floor. After housekeeping measures (such as a prayer, announcements, introductions) and **first reading** of bills, the members consider the bills on **third** (final) **reading** (i.e., bills that have already been approved on second reading and require only the usually perfunctory final vote), then bills on **second reading** (when the real debate occurs).

In the House, the Speaker calls a bill from the calendar for second reading and recognizes the bill's author (or, in the case of a Senate bill, the House sponsor), who explains the bill from a podium at the front of the chamber. Any member may go to the microphone in the back of the chamber and ask the author questions. After the author's opening statement, any member may speak for or against the bill or offer amendments, and any other member may question that member. The author is limited to twenty minutes to open debate on the bill and twenty minutes to close it. All other members are limited to ten minutes, including any interruptions from questioners. Members take the full allotment of time only on major or controversial bills. Conceivably, debate on a bill could take days. In reality, this rarely happens.

In the Senate, the president recognizes a senator to suspend the regular order of business so that the Senate may consider a bill on second reading. The senator explains the bill, standing at his or her desk. There could be discussion at this point, if

quorum
The minimum number required to conduct business (as in a legislative body).

first reading
The Texas Constitution requires three readings of a bill by the legislature; first reading is when the bill is introduced, its caption is read aloud, and it is referred to committee.

third reading
The Texas Constitution requires three readings of a bill by the legislature; third reading is the final reading in a chamber, unless the bill returns from the other chamber with amendments.

second reading
The Texas Constitution requires three readings of a bill by the legislature; the second reading is when debate and consideration of amendments occur before the whole chamber.

What does testifying before legislative committees accomplish? Commissioner Carey Cockerell of the Texas Department of Family and Protective Services, in foreground, testifies before members of the Senate Committee on Health and Human Services. Cockerell's testimony was regarding the 2008 raid on a polygamist sect that resulted in many children being placed in state protective custody.

filibuster
A formal way of halting action on a bill by means of long speeches or unlimited debate in the Senate.

germane
Related to the topic.

engrossed bill
A bill that has been given final approval on third reading in one chamber of the legislature.

the bill is controversial. Otherwise, the rules-suspension vote is taken quickly, followed by further explanation, any amendments, and the second-reading vote. Unlike the House, the Senate has no time limits on debate, creating the **filibuster** as a tactical tool: a senator may hold the floor for an unlimited amount of time and thus can try to kill a bill by refusing to allow a vote on it.

An amendment must be **germane** to the bill—that is, related to the topic—but germaneness is a matter of interpretation by the Speaker of the House or Senate president. Amendments can drastically alter a bill and thus become powerful tools in the hands of opponents. The consideration of amendments is a critical part of the legislative process for both sides, and a controversial bill has the potential of lengthy debate and twists and turns in tactical victories and defeats.

In the chamber in which the bill originated, when the final vote on a bill on third reading is favorable, the bill is considered to be an **engrossed bill** and is then sent to the other chamber by a staff messenger. It then goes through the referral and committee process and may or may not ever make it to the floor of the second chamber.

TWO BILLS INTO ONE: THE FINAL STAGES The Texas Constitution requires that, in order to become law, a bill must be adopted by both houses in exactly the same form. Many bills are amended in the second chamber, so an additional step is required to meet this requirement. The original chamber could simply vote to *concur* with the amendments placed on the bill by the other chamber, or it may vote to *not concur* and request a conference committee to adjust the differences between the two versions of the bill.

Conference committees have five House members appointed by the Speaker and five senators appointed by the lieutenant governor. If conferees cannot reach a compromise, the bill is dead. If they do reach a compromise, this new version of the bill is presented to each chamber, which must approve it with no further amendments, by majority vote.[53] For instance, in 2007, the House passed HB 1, the state appropriations bill. The Senate then passed its appropriations bill, but with different amounts of money for many programs. The conference committee worked for weeks to adjust the differences. It finally produced a compromise bill, which the House and Senate then approved in floor votes.

If a bill achieves final approval, it is then an **enrolled bill** and is sent to the governor. The governor may sign the bill into law, ignore it (in which case it goes into effect without his or her signature), or veto it, as discussed in chapter 5.

The Budgeting Process

Biennial legislative sessions necessitate biennial budgets, but some legislatures with annual sessions also adopt biennial budgets. Twenty-nine states prepare annual budgets, while twenty-one, including Texas, have biennial budgets.[54] The budgeting process is complex, largely because many of the numbers used to create the budget are projections and estimates, and state constitutional requirements limit what the legislature can do in Texas. (Chapter 8 discusses state finance in more detail.)

In 1931, the legislature designated the governor as the state's chief budget officer—but the same law gave the State Board of Control the responsibility of preparing the budget. The governor had no budget staff. Through the 1940s, the governor typically just gave the legislature the Board of Control's budget, with a few comments.[55] In 1951, the legislature and Governor Allan Shivers moved the budget function directly into the governor's office, where it has remained.[56] However, that was also the first session for the new Legislative Budget Board (LBB), and the legislature has consistently ignored the budget developed by the governor's office, in favor of the budget developed by legislative leaders in charge of the LBB.[57]

The LBB and the Governor's Budget Office prepare budgets for the legislature to consider. Before a regular session begins, the two offices hold joint hearings for state agencies to present their requests and for the public to comment. In the end, however, each prepares a separate budget proposal to submit to the legislature. For instance, for the 2008–2009 biennium, Governor Perry proposed a budget of $167.3 billion, and the LBB proposed a $161.8 billion budget.[58]

In the budgeting process, legislators must adhere to a constitutional requirement for a **balanced budget**—balancing spending with expected revenues (as estimated by the comptroller of public accounts), and thus avoiding deficit spending. **Deficit spending** is spending in the current budget cycle (in Texas's case, the biennium) above and beyond incoming revenue, while **debt** is the total outstanding amount owed from past borrowing. Thirty-three states, including Texas, have a constitutional balanced-budget requirement.[59] In 1978, Texas adopted an additional constitutional spending limit. Article 8, section 22, of the constitution now imposes a limit on state spending, calculated by a complex formula tied to the state's economic growth. The legislature is prohibited from spending more state tax revenue (from funds not constitutionally dedicated) than a formula-calculated amount above the previous budget. The LBB determines the spending limit by estimating the rate of growth of the state's economy. This can be a subjective process, subject to much second-guessing and criticism. The LBB established the estimated rate of growth of the Texas economy at 9.14 percent for 2010–2011. The constitution also caps welfare spending and limits tax-supported debt.[60]

Thus, in the budgetary process, Texas legislators must consider the constitutional balanced-budget requirement, the comptroller's revenue estimate, proposed budgets submitted by the governor and the LBB, constitutional spending limits, and in the end, the governor's veto authority.

In 1985, voters approved a constitutional amendment (Article 16, section 69) creating **budget execution authority**. During an interim, the governor and the LBB are authorized to move money from one program to another or even from one agency

enrolled bill
A bill that has been given final approval in both chambers of the legislature and is sent to the governor.

balanced budget
A budget in which the legislature balances expenditures with expected revenues, with no deficit.

deficit spending
Government spending in the current budget cycle that exceeds government revenue.

debt
The total outstanding amount the government owes as a result of borrowing in the past.

budget execution authority
The authority to move money from one program to another program or from one agency to another agency.

> **Thinking Nationally**
>
> **Governors and the Budget**
>
> New York's governor prepares a state budget and presents it to the legislature as the working document for the legislative committees. Executive agencies fall in line with the governor's budget and defend it before the legislature.
>
> - How does the Texas Legislative Budget Board alter the balance of power between the governor and the legislature?
> - Why are Texas agencies able to plead their case directly to the Texas legislature, sidestepping the governor?
> - What changes might be required for Texas to adopt a stronger gubernatorial role in budget making, and what might be necessary for the Texas legislature to cede such power?

to another. Because the lieutenant governor is the chair and the Speaker the vice chair of the LBB (and they appoint the members), this budget execution authority allows the governor, lieutenant governor, and Speaker the flexibility to handle some budget crises without having to call the legislature into special session. Budget execution authority has been used but sparingly.

How Do Legislators Make Decisions?

In making decisions on how to vote, legislators interact with executive branch officials, judges, voters, lobbyists, reporters, staff members, party officials, and officials from the federal government and from other states. The legislature is also a social system and must be understood in the context of the norms of behavior and roles that legislators take with each other, from "backscratching" to "logrolling" (to learn more about legislative lingo, see Table 4.4).

The influences on how a legislator votes and provides leadership on policy issues are many and often conflicting. In deciding either how to vote on a particular bill or which bills to sponsor, a legislator asks such questions as these: Do I support it philosophically or in terms of good public policy? Which of my constituents will benefit from or be harmed by this bill? How much support will I get from them for the bill and in my reelection campaign? Will it generate opposition in my district? Whom can I gather into a coalition of support for the bill? Which lobbyists will support me, and which will oppose me? Will they be more or less likely to finance my campaign or an opponent's because of this bill? How will the media play the issue? Does the leadership support the bill? Can I win support from my fellow legislators? Will the bill help or hurt my reputation with them? What do I need to do to get the governor's support? Often, such legislative decision making must be made quickly and can come back to haunt a legislator later, as happened in the Sharpstown scandal.

Growth of Legislative Staff

Staffing and information have been a focal point in institutional development of state legislatures. Legislators do not have the time or resources to do all the work required to conceive, develop, and pass legislation. Staff members can do much of the work in developing information. Deliberative democracy can be enhanced with increased availability of information, though a burdensome staff structure could also thwart access to lawmakers.

Some large states, such as Michigan and California, have significant party staff capabilities. In Michigan, most of the legislative staff is organized along partisan lines. In California, partisan professionals staff most of the committees.[61] In recent years, the Texas House Democratic Caucus had no staff members, and the Texas House Republican Caucus had only one; in the Senate, neither the Democratic nor the Republican caucus had staff members (though members' staff may serve the caucus).

The result of increased use of individual, institutional, and group staffing is that legislatures have much larger staffs than in the recent past (though Texas still has substantially fewer staff members than New York or California). However, there has been a political backlash against the larger staffing levels. As term limits took hold in California in the 1990s,

Ideas Into Action

Student Interns Learn Legislative Politics

For students interested in politics and government, internships in the state capital provide a great opportunity to explore the workings of the legislature from the inside and to make contacts that can be valuable in a government or political career. Many Texas political leaders got their first taste of politics and government by volunteering or working in part-time jobs in Austin. For some students, spending a semester at the legislature can be an interesting, eye-opening experience, enriching their undergraduate and graduate education. Others can get bitten deeply by the political bug and find the power and opportunities that the capital offers so alluring that they continue working there—or even go home and run for the legislature.

Legislative internships can be sponsored by private entities (such as the Texas Public Policy Foundation), colleges and universities, or legislators or groups associated with the legislature. One such program is the Gregory Luna Memorial Scholars Program, a full-time internship sponsored by the Senate Hispanic Caucus and its Research Council. Students receive college credit plus a monthly stipend. The Moreno-Rangel Legislative Leadership Program, a similar internship program in the House, is sponsored by the Mexican American Legislative Caucus's Foundation. Students work full-time in a House office during a legislative session and attend weekly seminars.

Since 1990, Senator Rodney Ellis (D–Houston) has coordinated the Texas Legislative Internship Program, placing students from numerous colleges around the state into internships. The program is sponsored by the Mickey Leland Center on World Hunger and Peace at Texas Southern University. During legislative sessions, undergraduate, graduate, and law students are placed in legislative offices; when the legislature is not in session, internships are in other state and local government offices.

Some political science departments sponsor and coordinate their own internship programs in the capital. The Department of Government at the University of Texas at Austin takes applications and selects a limited number of students each semester to register for the course GOV 374N, Political Internship. Students spend about ten hours a week working for a political, government, or policy entity. Interns have been placed with interest groups, political parties, and think tanks (e.g., Campaigns for People, the Texas Public Policy Foundation, and the Texas Republican and Democratic Parties), but most students choose to work in the legislature. The class meets once a week, and students have reading and writing assignments.

- As a college student, learn what internship programs your college promotes. This information should be available in a student services office, in each college dean's office, or by department.
- In your chosen field of study, find some successful, experienced professionals and interview them to find what job experiences they pursued while in college.
- Visit your college's political science department and ask about internships that the department sponsors. Then discuss with the department the possibilities of expanding internship possibilities in local or state policy areas that interest you. Determine what practical issues would have to be resolved to make new internship possibilities a reality.
- Visit these Web sites to see what legislative internship programs are like:

www.rodneyellis.com/tlip/
www.mallfoundation.org/program.html
www.tshrc.org/program.html
www.texaspolicy.com/pdf/2007-Internship-Description.pdf

---

new legislators cut staffing substantially.[62] There are now just over 2,000 full-time-equivalent legislative staff members in Texas (including those in the representatives' and senators' offices, committees, and groups; the Legislative Council; the State Auditor's Office; the Legislative Budget Board; the Sunset Commission; and the Legislative Reference Library).

Staffing for Technical Assistance, Specialized Information, and Political Assistance

Early efforts at increasing legislative information were aimed at establishing state libraries, interim committees to gather information between sessions, and legislative

Legislative Council
A joint legislative committee (with a large staff) that provides legal advice, bill drafting, copyediting and printing, policy research, and program evaluation services for members of the legislature.

Legislative Budget Board (LBB)
A joint legislative committee (with a large staff) that prepares the state budget and conducts evaluations of agencies' programs.

councils. The councils were centralized staffing operations to provide bill drafting, policy research, and program evaluation services.

The Texas legislature created its **Legislative Council** in 1949. It is a joint committee chaired by the lieutenant governor. The council operates only during the interims, though its staff operates year-round. The Legislative Council has ten representatives, five senators, and the lieutenant governor and Speaker as members. The council's attorneys and other staff members draft bills, conduct policy studies during the interim between sessions, produce documents such as committee schedules, legislative calendars, and bill-status information, and manage the legislature's computer systems. The legislature also established the **Legislative Budget Board (LBB)** in 1949. The LBB has four representatives, four senators, and the lieutenant governor and Speaker as members. The LBB's staff analysts prepare the state budget and conduct evaluations of agencies' programs.

By the 1960s, most state legislatures found centralized staffing inadequate. One staff office could not be specialized enough or attentive enough to the needs of individual legislators or committees, so legislatures began providing staff members for standing committees, individual legislators, and caucuses. By the 1970s, committees in the Texas legislature were typically served by two or three staff members, hired by the committee chair. The expertise and duties of committee staff members vary considerably, with each chair having different priorities. In 2003, new Speaker Craddick abolished the four-year-old House Bill Analysis Office and returned to the committee staff members the job of analyzing bills.

Individual representatives did not have staff members—or offices—until the 1960s. Before then, they used a common pool of secretaries. Now legislators receive a monthly account to pay for office expenses, including staff. A typical representative hires three to five staff members in Austin plus one or two district staff members. Senators hire about five to ten capitol staff members plus district staff. The staff provides constituent services (casework), administrative support, and assistance drafting legislation, negotiating with staff and lobbyists, and preparing support materials.

Relations with Lobbyists

A recurring issue in public policy is the proper role of lobbyists and their relationship with legislators. In the 1960s and 1970s, state legislatures passed many "open-government" measures, including stricter requirements for lobbyists to register, so that the public would know who was seeking to influence state government. In 2007, 1,629 lobbyists registered with the Texas Ethics Commission—more than nine for every legislator—representing more than 4,000 clients.[63]

Lobbyists legitimately approach the legislature to protect the interests of the members of their group through public-policy changes. In trying to persuade legislators, they provide information that legislators need to evaluate—and thus lobbyists can be an invaluable resource to legislators in their quest for deliberative democracy. For instance, in the 2005–2006 battles over public education, the legislature got technical information from private groups such as the Texas Public Policy Foundation and the Equity Center, as well as from public officials and groups such as superintendents, teachers, and school boards. Everyone knew that the information came from groups with different goals, and thus had to be balanced, or compared with particular policy proposals that different legislators favored.

That role as an information source also makes lobbyists power players, and they can become protective of their influence with legislators by monopolizing access to legislators. One lobbyist justified his opposition to a stronger legislative staff by saying to one of the authors: "as long as the representative has analysis, he abdicates [decision-making responsibility] and doesn't need to talk to me." Party caucuses and leaders can also present competition for lobbyists. Upon the formation of the Senate Democratic Caucus in 1983, a senator said: "when the party starts taking positions on issues, lobby influence will be diminished."[64]

The Ethics of Lobbying

Most lobbyist–legislator contact happens with complete legitimacy, but the many questionable contacts and practices raise recurring questions about ethics.[65] Exposure of Frank Sharp's bribery of legislators in 1971 led to the largest wave of Texas government reforms in modern times. Since the Sharpstown scandal, a number of other cases have raised questions about ethical violations related to lobbying. The federal government attempted to ensnare corrupt legislators through its "Brilab" sting operation (Speaker Clayton was accused of accepting a bribe but was acquitted in 1980). Stories circulated about outlandish spending by lobbyists on the "wining and dining" of legislators. Chicken magnate Lonnie "Bo" Pilgrim walked around the Senate floor in 1989 handing out checks to senators after talking with them about his support of Governor Clements's workers' compensation proposals. News reports described legislators creating and maintaining privately funded "officeholder accounts" for political and personal expenses.[66] Speaker Lewis garnered misdemeanor convictions for failure to report all his private financial holdings.

Often, the questionable activities concern blurring the line between lobbying activities and election and campaign activities. The same individuals who are the most successful lobbyists (primarily business representatives) are also deeply involved in raising and contributing money for legislative campaigns and for officeholder accounts. Legislators need money for the next campaign, and interest-group leaders want access to and influence with legislators, so the campaign-finance game is a symbiotic relationship. Legislators and lobbyists both get what they need; the prosecutions of the Texas Association of Business may provide different boundaries for the two.

Questions recur about whether campaign finances, wining and dining, and officeholder accounts taint public policy and political equality. In the wake of repeated news stories about lobby-paid junkets to Mexico, Las Vegas, and various resorts; stories about legislators paying their mortgages or buying cars with political funds; demands from public-interest groups for limits on lobbyists' expenditures; and Governor Ann Richards's successful 1990 campaign that capitalized on perceived unethical conduct, the 1991 legislature passed an ethics reform bill. The new law restricted the amount of money that lobbyists can spend, increased their reporting requirements, and established the Texas Ethics Commission.

The Legislature and the Governor

Texas governors may be weak in their control of the executive branch (see chapter 5), but they are stronger players in the legislative process. Governors have leverage to push their agenda through the give-and-take of legislative politics because they have some things that legislators want—such as an emergency declaration for their bills (which allows the bills to be heard early in a legislative session), adding their bills to a call for a special session, or signing their bills into law.

Except for unusual circumstances, only the governor may call the legislature into special session.[67] This is a significant power of the governor because he or she may call one at any time for any purpose. The governor must specify what issues the legislature is being called to consider, although the governor can add subjects to the call of the session after it has begun. During special sessions, governors may refuse to add a bill to the agenda until or unless the legislator pledges support of the item that the governor is pushing the legislature to adopt. Thus, the governor is in complete control of the agenda of a special session. A special session may last no longer than thirty days. However, there is no limit on how many sessions a governor may call, and indeed they have been called back to back. Governor Ann Richards called four special sessions in the 1991–1992 biennium. There were none again until Governor Perry called four special sessions during the 2003–2004 biennium, and he called three during the 2005–2006 biennium.

Party loyalty is a new factor in gubernatorial–legislative relations. During the long Speakership of Gib Lewis (1983–1992), opposition virtually disappeared except when Republicans left the leadership coalition on selected issues. When the legislature was fighting Republican Governor Bill Clements on tax or school-finance issues, Republican legislators would oppose the Speaker's bills. It put a strain on Lewis's leadership coalition, because seven committee chairs were Republicans.

At the end of the legislative process, the governor may sign the bill into law, veto the bill (nullify its passage), or ignore it, in which case it becomes law without his or her signature. In chapter 5, we examine governors' vetoes more closely. If the governor vetoes a bill, the legislature may consider a motion to override the veto, which requires a two-thirds vote. However, most vetoes happen late in the session or after the legislature has adjourned, so there is no chance to attempt an override. Vetoes of regular-session bills may not be overridden by a subsequent special session.

Toward Reform: The Public and the Legislature

Some element of the Texas citizenry is always agitating for reform of the political system—and those demands for change are often directed at the legislature. Such demands are often deflected or defeated, but sometimes they bear fruit. Current challenges to Tom Craddick's speakership may subside when the next Speaker is sworn in, or they may rise to the level of a challenge to the powers of the office itself. Will his ruling that the Speaker has absolute power to recognize a motion prevail or be overturned? A change in leadership powers may also change the role of party caucuses in the legislature. Such a push for reform at this level strikes at the very heart of the legislative process and the balance of power and, thus, is more difficult. Toward the end of his speakership, Pete Laney championed campaign finance reforms, but those proposals, too, mobilized outside power centers that might be threatened by changes—and thus, the proposals died.

Other efforts at reform may have more strength. They are more likely to triumph if the public has been

Texas governors have clout in the legislative process. Governor Rick Perry meets with legislators to discuss his legislative agenda.

stirred up—as happened with the Sharpstown scandal and the ensuing reforms of legislative process and leadership powers in the 1970s. Over the past several years, the news media and public interest groups stirred interest in the voting procedures in the legislature. They were frustrated at how many votes on the House and Senate floor are nonrecord votes. Thus, they—and their legislative allies—pushed measures to require record votes. Legislative rules have allowed members to request record votes, or triggered automatic records of an "aye" vote unless the individual member registers opposition with the clerk, but these rules did not abate the demand for a more transparent process.

In 2007, those reform efforts succeeded. The legislature approved HJR 19, which voters then ratified as a constitutional amendment. This new constitutional rule requires a record vote on final passage of a measure. Proponents argued that such a requirement will help open up government to scrutiny, and thus encourage responsibility. Opponents argued that the legislative process could be slowed dramatically and, more significantly, that a record vote on final passage is often a charade—the real action on a bill is on the amendments and on second reading. Those votes can still be voice votes. A member could by voice vote try to weaken a bill with amendments or to kill a bill on second reading, then, if it survives, vote for it on final reading and be able to claim support for it despite his or her earlier efforts. Still, the new measure became effective for the 2009 and future sessions.

The next push for reform may be over the phenomenon of "ghost voting" in the House, where members vote by machine. Each member has a control device on his or her desk, by which the member hits a green button for yes, a red button for no, or a white button for present-not-voting. By House rule, each member may vote only from his or her own device (or by individually signaling the chair to record the desired vote). But what happens when a member is across the floor when a vote is called—or even out of the chamber? Often, a fellow member reaches over and votes for the neighboring member, even though the rules forbid it. The colleague might have been asked to do so and instructed which vote the member wanted, but it raises the possibility of one member casting a "yea" vote for other members when the absentees would have voted "nay." When that happens—and it does—a member can enter a statement in the *House Journal* stating that the voting machine "malfunctioned" and his or her intent was to cast a different vote—though the original vote still counts. The *Journal* is replete with such entries. Every once in a while, someone objects from the back microphone, and the Speaker will warn members not to do it—but the rule is not enforced, and everyone knows it. In 2007, YouTube brought the issue to public attention. An Austin TV channel aired a news segment on the issue, and someone uploaded the segment to YouTube (http://youtube.com/watch?v=b-uorcf6Uzs). Hits on the entry spiked and the issue burst into the open, increasing demands that the House stop the practice. Will the YouTube sensation trigger reform? Part of the answer may lie in whether the issue stays alive and whether some organized interest pushes it. A private citizen took the issue to a grand jury in 2008; the grand jurors issued a report calling for the House to enforce its rules, but did not issue an indictment.[68]

WHAT SHOULD I HAVE LEARNED?

- **What are the roots of the Texas legislature?**

  The modern Texas legislature evolved from its Mexican and Republic of Texas predecessors—bicameral institutions that met annually. The state legislature's membership has varied over the years, but the legislature has always been dominated by Anglos.

- **What provisions of the state constitution define and limit the legislative branch of government?**

  The Texas Constitution places limits on the legislature by setting the structure of the two chambers, establishing specific rules for the legislative sessions, prescribing the members' qualifications and salary, and limiting the legislature's power.

- **What influences the makeup of the legislative membership and what are the characteristics of members?**

  Legislators are more likely than the general population to be Anglos, male, lawyers and businesspeople, middle aged, and well educated. They are often conservative in political ideology. However, the composition of the legislature is changing to include more Hispanics, African Americans, and women, as well as a broader ideological array.

- **How are leadership and opposition organized in the Texas Legislature?**

  Like most states, the Texas legislature has leaders and a committee system to structure its activities. Unlike most states, the Texas legislature does not choose its leaders or create its committees in a partisan fashion. Consequently, conflicts are between the legislative leaders' teams and their opposition rather than between political parties—though partisanship is growing. Nonparty caucuses are also influential in the Texas legislature.

- **How are laws and budgets made, and what are the rules and procedures for moving them forward?**

  The Texas legislature makes laws and establishes the state budget during each biennial session, using a variety of resolutions and bills. The legislative process involves several stages, all of which provide an opportunity to halt or modify legislative proposals.

- **What forces influence legislators in their decision making?**

  Texas legislators are influenced by several sets of political actors, including staff members, lobbyists, and members of the executive branch.

- **What formal and informal powers does the governor have in the legislative process?**

  The powers of the Texas governor include legislative powers (such as the veto and emergency declarations) and dictate that the governor and the legislature interact frequently and regularly during legislative sessions.

- **What reforms of the Texas legislative process have been adopted or are being actively considered?**

  Recent efforts led to a new requirement for recorded votes. Speaker Craddick's ruling that the Speaker's powers to recognize members are absolute will trigger calls for repeal of the ruling or change of the rules. Finally, public calls for an end to "ghost voting" may spark legislative debate over enforcement of rules.

Key Terms

balanced budget, p. 129
bicameral Texas legislature, p. 102
biennial legislature, p. 105
bill, p. 124
budget execution authority, p. 129
committee, p. 117
concurrent resolution, p. 124
constitutional amendment, p. 100
debt, p. 129
deficit spending, p. 129
engrossed bill, p. 128
enrolled bill, p. 129
filibuster, p. 128
first reading, p. 127
germane, p. 128
impeach, p. 100
intent calendar, p. 126
joint resolution, p. 124
Legislative Budget Board (LBB), p. 132
Legislative Council, p. 132
legislative party caucus, p. 118
nonparty legislative caucus, p. 122
per diem, p. 104
president of the Texas Senate, p. 116
pro-tempore (pro-tem), p. 116
quorum, p. 127
redistrict, p. 100
regular session, p. 105
second reading, p. 127
Senate two-thirds rule, p. 126
Sharpstown scandal, p. 119
simple resolution, p. 124
Speaker of the Texas House, p. 116
Speaker's lieutenants, p. 120
Speaker's race, p. 119
Speaker's team, p. 120
special (called) session, p. 105
term limits, p. 110
third reading, p. 127

Researching the Texas Legislature

In the Library

Bickerstaff, Steve. *Lines in the Sand: Congressional Redistricting in Texas and the Downfall of Tom DeLay.* Austin: University of Texas Press, 2007.

Bowser, J. Drage, K. Chi, and T. Little. *Coping with Term Limits: A Practical Guide.* Denver, CO: National Conference of State Legislatures, 2006.

Brewer, J. Mason. *Negro Legislators of Texas*, 2nd ed. Austin: Jenkins, 1970 (1st ed., 1935).

Ivins, Molly. *Molly Ivins Can't Say That, Can She?* New York: Random House, 1991.

Kousser, Thad. *Term Limits and the Dismantling of State Legislative Professionalism.* New York: Cambridge University Press, 2005.

Moncrief, Gary F., Peverill Squire, and Malcolm E. Jewell. *Who Runs for the Legislature?* Upper Saddle River, NJ: Prentice Hall, 2001.

Monmonier, Mark. *Bushmanders and Bullwinkles: How Politicians Manipulate Electronic Map and Census Data to Win Elections.* Chicago: University of Chicago Press, 2001.

Niven, David. *The Missing Majority: The Recruitment of Women as State Legislative Candidates.* Westport, CT: Praeger, 1998.

Pittman, H. C. *Inside the Third House: A Veteran Lobbyist Takes a 50-Year Frolic Through Texas Politics.* Austin: Eakin, 1992.

Rosenthal, Alan. *The Decline of Representative Democracy: Process, Participation, and Power in State Legislatures.* Washington DC: CQ Press, 1998.

———. *Engines of Democracy: Politics and Policymaking in State Legislatures.* Washington, DC: CQ Press, 2008.

———. *Third House: Lobbyists and Lobbying in the States.* Washington, DC: CQ Press, 1992.

Squire, Peverill. *101 Chambers: Congress, State Legislatures, and the Future of Legislative Studies.* Columbus: Ohio State University Press, 2005.

Vega, Arturo. "Gender and Ethnicity Effects on the Legislative Behavior and Substantive Representation of the Texas Legislature." *Texas Journal of Political Studies* 19: (1997): 1–21.

On the Web

Texas legislature, **www.capitol.state.tx.us**
This portal opens to the Senate, the House, and the legislative agencies, and provides links to executive Web sites as well.

House Research Organization, **www.hro.house.state.tx.us**
The HRO serves as a quasi-independent research office for House members.

Texas Conservative Coalition, **www.txcc.org**
The TCC is a long-standing nonparty caucus of the legislature.

Texas Legislative Reference Library, **www.lrl.state.tx.us**
The library not only houses books and documents, but through the Web site is also a valuable source for information on legislative action (such as the status of bills under consideration).

Texas Legislative Council, **www.tlc.state.tx.us**
The Legislative Council gives legal advice to legislators, drafts bills, proofreads and prints documents, and does policy research.

5

The Governor and Executive Branch

Was Rick Perry a brave and principled leader, acting to advance the public interest? A lame-duck state officeholder seeking to leapfrog to a federal office? A scheming governor, arrogantly sidestepping constitutional restrictions to thwart the legislature? The public was abuzz with all these opinions when, shortly after the 2007 legislative session started, Governor Perry issued an executive order to the Health and Human Services Commission to require girls entering sixth grade to be vaccinated against human papillomavirus (HPV)—the most common sexually transmitted virus, and one that causes almost all cervical cancer.[1] His action created a classic case study of gubernatorial power engaged with executive agencies, legislators, interest groups, and the media.

In Texas alone, HPV causes nearly 400 deaths a year (and thousands of illnesses). Gardasil, manufactured by Merck, is the first vaccine to protect against some (though not all) HPV strains. It is effective only if received before any potential infection. A vaccination could cost up to $600 for the required dosage. In 2006, the federal Food

and Drug Administration approved Gardasil, and the Centers for Disease Control and Prevention recommended it for females age eleven to twenty-six.

Governor Perry decided that the state could act to stop or reduce HPV-related deaths and illnesses. His Executive Order RP-65 commanded the Health and Human Services Commission to adopt rules requiring the vaccine (with some opt-out provisions) and to make the vaccine available immediately.[2] Perry's order would cost $29 million in state funds, not counting federal funds and private insurance coverage.

The reaction to the order was not what the governor had expected. All twenty of his Republican and six of eleven Democratic senators signed a letter to Perry urging him to rescind the order. Senator Jane Nelson asked the attorney general to rule on the legality of the order.[3] The senators were not convinced that the governor had the power, without legislative authorization, to order a program that would commit state funding. More importantly, though, ideological and interest group politics drove the legislative reaction. Texas Eagle Forum, a conservative political advocacy group, opposed the order, arguing that it would encourage sexual activity. Senator Leticia Van de Putte, a supporter of vaccination, countered that even if a girl abstained from premarital sexual activity, she could later get the virus from her husband, and that early vaccination was the proper and moral policy. But the Republican governor had just won reelection from a conservative political base,

■ **Governors are the most obvious embodiments of Texas government.** Miriam "Ma" Ferguson, at left, became the first woman governor of Texas in 1925. Her husband, James E. "Pa" Ferguson, served as governor for two years, then was impeached, convicted, removed from office, and barred from serving again. Governor Rick Perry, at right, became Texas's longest-serving governor in 2008. Perry was reelected to office in 2006.

WHAT SHOULD I KNOW ABOUT . . .
- the roots of the executive branch in Texas?
- the constitutional roles of the governor?
- gubernatorial power?
- the governor as policy maker and political leader?
- the plural executive in Texas?
- modern Texas bureaucracy?
- making agencies accountable?
- reforming gubernatorial and executive power?

and the Republican legislative majorities were also responsive to that base—and their voters and support organizations such as Eagle Forum were adamantly opposed.

Moreover, reporters and opponents quickly learned that Merck's lobbyist was none other than Mike Toomey, Governor Perry's former chief of staff. Merck had met with Perry's staff before the session and had donated thousands of dollars in campaign contributions to Perry and legislative leaders—had, indeed, donated money to Perry's campaign on the same day that the governor's chief of staff initiated action to push forward on Gardasil. Merck had also given money to Women in Government, an advocacy group including women legislators, to push for state-mandated vaccinations in numerous states. Governor Perry insisted that his action had been proper and that it was the right thing to do. He brought in Heather Burcham, a Houston woman who was gravely ill with cervical cancer, to urge acceptance of the program.

The legislature and the public were not mollified. The House Public Health Committee heard two bills to block the governor's action. Newspapers across the state editorialized against the governor, arguing that even if vaccination was a good policy, it should be debated in the legislative process and approved there—not mandated by an executive order. As the pressure mounted, Merck announced that it was ending its efforts to get states to mandate vaccinations.[4] The committee approved a bill to block the order, and the House quickly passed it.

In the meantime, a judge ruled in an unrelated matter that the governor did not have the power to order a state agency to act on an environmental matter the way that he had ordered it to. Then, the attorney general ruled that a governor's executive order can only be a "suggestion" to an agency, not an order. The Senate soon approved the House bill forbidding the commissioner from requiring HPV vaccination. It was clear that Perry would be unlikely to prevail if he vetoed it—the House and Senate votes for the bill were far more than the required two-thirds support for overriding a veto. So, Governor Perry let the law go into effect without his signature but expressed his regret that without the vaccination, women would be needlessly at risk.

The issue of the extent of gubernatorial power over executive agencies will likely be debated and litigated for some time. Meanwhile, the legislature and the health and human services commission continue to grapple with the issue of HPV. The public health issue is clearly a real one. A few months after the 2007 session ended, Heather Burcham died.

> **TO LEARN MORE—**
> **—TO DO MORE**
> Go to the Centers for Disease Control and Prevention's Web site for HPV www.cdc.gov/STD/HPV/STDFact-HPV.htm to learn more about HPV.

T he top political leader and top official of the executive branch of Texas state government is the governor. However, power and policy implementation are not centralized in the Texas governor's office; rather, Texas has a **plural executive,** with power divided among several independently elected officials, appointed officials, and more than one hundred executive boards and commissions. The governor has little direct power over state agencies. This fragmented government is a double-edged sword: it increases the chance for conflicts over policy making, but it enhances the opportunity for policy innovation and experimentation.

Because Texas governors are not assured of control of state government, they must build strong outside support. That could consist of support from economic powers, popular support among voters, or both. In this chapter, we will explore the governorship and the executive branch, or bureaucracy, in Texas.

plural executive
An executive branch in which power and policy implementation are divided among several executive agencies rather than centralized under one person; the governor does not get to appoint most agency heads.

★ First, we will examine the *roots of the executive branch in Texas*, indicating how the Texas governorship and division of executive authority developed.

★ Second, we will describe the *constitutional roles of the governor*, emphasizing the roles of chief of state, chief executive, and commander in chief.

★ Third, we will look at *gubernatorial power*, comparing the powers of the Texas governor with those of other state governors and describing the powers of the Texas governor in political roles.

★ Fourth, we will assess the *governor as policy maker and political leader*, describing how Texas governors use personal and political skills to achieve their policy goals.

★ Fifth, we will explore the *plural executive in Texas*, describing the elected officials that make up the plural executive and their duties.

★ Sixth, we will look at the structure of the *modern Texas bureaucracy*, examining the organization and operation of Texas's executive boards and commissions.

★ Seventh, we will discuss *making agencies accountable*, describing the methods that the legislature and executive use to ensure bureaucratic accountability.

★ Finally, we will highlight calls for *reforming gubernatorial and executive power*.

Roots of the Executive Branch in Texas

The issue of how executive power should be organized and manifested in Texas has its roots in decisions made long ago, in the emerging political systems of the United States and Mexico. Spanish kings sent representatives of the crown to what is now Texas in the 1500s. In 1691, the king designated the first *Governador de Tejas*—Don Domingo Teran de los Rios—who, in addition to governing, drove cattle from interior Mexico and established the first herds in Texas.[5] After the Mexican Revolution against Spain, the Mexican Constitution of 1824 and the 1827 Constitution of the State of Coahuila y Tejas established a governor and an executive council and gave the governor the power to rule by decree.

Before the American Revolution, governors of the British colonies represented and served at the pleasure of the British monarch. Only two of the governors were elected. These early American governors were weak. They shared power with executive councils and with other statewide officials and were subordinate to the colonial legislatures.[6]

From President of the Lone Star Republic to Governor of Texas

After the Texas Revolution against Mexico, from 1836 to 1845, under the Republic of Texas, the chief executive was the president, who ruled with a *cabinet* (top officials appointed by and responsible to the chief executive). When Texas joined the United States in 1845, it was with a relatively powerful governor. The governor, who was elected to a two-year term, appointed almost all state officials, including judges; the comptroller and the treasurer were elected by the legislature. By 1850, the constitution was amended to provide for the direct election of judges, the attorney general,

The Living Constitution

> *Every bill which shall have passed both houses of the Legislature shall be presented to the Governor for his approval. If he approve he shall sign it; but if he disapprove it, he shall return it, with his objections. . . . If . . . two-thirds of the members present agree to pass the bill, it shall be sent . . . to the other House . . . and, if approved by two-thirds of the members of that House, it shall become a law. If any bill shall not be returned by the Governor . . . within ten days . . . the same shall be a law…unless the Legislature, by its adjournment, prevent its return, in which case it shall be a law unless he shall file the same, with his objections, in the office of the Secretary of State. . . . If any bill presented to the Governor contains several items of appropriation he may object to one or more of such items, and approve the other portion of the bill.*
>
> ARTICLE 4, SECTION 14

The Texas Constitution provides for gubernatorial vetoes in Article 4, section 14. The 1836 constitution of the Republic of Texas is the basis for this provision. The provision has remained largely intact through the various Texas constitutions, with several notable exceptions. First, until the constitution of 1876, the governor was allowed only five days to return vetoed bills. Second, under the constitution of the republic, the president could exercise a pocket veto (if the legislature adjourned during the five days allotted the president to sign or veto a bill, then the Texas president, by refusing to sign the bill, could exercise a veto). None of the constitutions of statehood have allowed the pocket veto. Furthermore, the constitutions of 1845, 1861, 1866, and 1869 did not allow post-adjournment vetoes. The current constitution extended the time to return objectionable bills to ten days and permitted the post-adjournment veto, giving the governor twenty days from adjournment to sign or veto bills. The line-item veto for appropriations measures originated with the 1866 constitution.[a]

If the governor vetoes a bill and the legislature is in session, the provision requires that the chamber of origin must first consider the bill and that a two-thirds majority of the members present is necessary to send the bill to the other chamber. However, because the constitution does not specify whether the vote in the second chamber must be two-thirds of the members present or of the members elected, the chambers differ on their interpretations. According to Senate rules, "A vote of two-thirds of all members elected to the Senate shall be required for the passage of House bills that have been returned by the Governor with his objections, and a vote of two-thirds of the members of the Senate present shall be required for the passage of Senate bills that have been returned by the Governor with his objections."[b] In the House, on the other hand, a two-thirds vote of the members present is required, regardless of the bill's chamber of origin. The constitution is clear that on line-item vetoes, a two-thirds vote of the members present in each chamber is required.

Other states' veto provisions vary greatly. Some states require only a majority vote to override a veto, others require a three-fifths majority, and some require a three-fourths majority. Many states allow the governor a pocket veto. Some states allow an "amendatory" veto, which allows the governor to return an objectionable bill to the legislature with suggested changes that would make the bill acceptable. If the legislature agrees, the bill is returned for the governor's signature.

The veto is the Texas governor's most significant constitutional power. The line-item veto, because the governor's budgetary powers are weak, is almost the only power that the governor has over the amounts and purposes of expenditures by the state.

> **CRITICAL THINKING QUESTIONS**
> 1. Should the governor's veto power be enhanced through the "amendatory" veto, or does the Texas governor have sufficient veto powers currently? Explain your answer.
> 2. Should the legislature be permitted to call itself into session to consider governor's vetoes that were issued after adjournment of a session? Why or why not?

[a] George D. Braden, *The Constitution of the State of Texas: An Annotated and Comparative Analysis*, vol. 1 (Austin: Legislative Council, 1977), 333.

[b] Texas Senate, Rules of the 80th Legislature, Rule 6.20.

comptroller, treasurer, and land commissioner. The state's Confederate constitution of 1861 was similar to the 1845 one in terms of the governor's powers.[7]

The 1866 constitution included a four-year term for the governor, with a limit of two consecutive terms, and gubernatorial (meaning of or by the governor) appointment of all officials but the comptroller and the treasurer. A new power for the governor was the line-item veto, which had been used in the Confederacy. The 1869 constitution retained a four-year term and allowed the governor to appoint local officials and state police and impose martial law. However, as one scholar of the Texas governorship wrote, "more disintegration of the executive power than ever was effected." The lieutenant governor, comptroller, treasurer, land commissioner, and public-instruction superintendent were all elected to four-year terms.[8]

The 1876 constitution further decentralized and limited state government, as we note in chapter 2. The governor's term was reduced to two years and the salary was reduced from $5,000 to $4,000. While Texans have amended this constitution many times since its adoption, the basic structure of executive power remains the same: a weak governor who must share power with others in the executive branch and with a strong legislature. Texas has had thirty-one governors under this constitution. (To learn more about the history of Texas governors, see Table 5.1.)

Terms of Office

The state constitution sets the length of the term of office for the governorship, methods for removing a governor from office, and the line of succession in the event of a vacancy in the office. The constitution originally set the governor's salary, though the legislature now does so.

Photo courtesy: CORBIS

> **Who was Sam Houston?** Sam Houston served as commander in chief of the Texas armies during the Texas Revolution. He then served as the first president of the Lone Star Republic. When Texas joined the United States, he served as U.S. senator from Texas. Finally, he served as governor of Texas—only to be ousted in 1861 when he refused to support the move to secede from the United States and join the Confederate States of America.

TABLE 5.1 Texas Governors, 1876–2009

Number	Governor	Party	Age	Terms	Years Served	Left Office	Occupation
1	Richard Coke	D	43	1	2+ (1874–1876)	resigned	lawyer/farmer
2	Richard B. Hubbard	D	44	1+	3+ (1876–1879)	defeated	lawyer
3	Oran M. Roberts	D	63	2	4 (1879–1883)	retired	lawyer/educator
4	John Ireland	D	56	2	4 (1883–1887)	retired	lawyer
5	Lawrence Sul Ross	D	48	2	4 (1887–1891)	retired	farmer/soldier
6	James S. Hogg	D	39	2	4 (1891–1895)	retired	lawyer/editor
7	Charles A. Culberson	D	39	2	4 (1895–1899)	retired	lawyer
8	Joseph D. Sayers	D	57	2	4 (1899–1903)	retired	lawyer
9	Samuel Lanham	D	56	2	4 (1903–1907)	retired	lawyer
10	Thomas M. Campbell	D	50	2	4 (1907–1911)	retired	lawyer/railroad exec.
11	Oscar B. Colquitt	D	49	2	4 (1911–1915)	retired	lawyer/editor
12	James E. Ferguson	D	43	1+	2+ (1915–1917)	impeached	banker/lawyer/farmer
13	William P. Hobby	D	39	1+	2 (1917–1921)	retired	editor
14	Pat M. Neff	D	49	2	4 (1921–1925)	retired	lawyer/educator
15	Miriam A. Ferguson	D	49	1	2 (1925–1927)	defeated	housewife
16	Dan Moody	D	33	2	4 (1927–1931)	retired	lawyer
17	Ross Sterling	D	55	1	2 (1931–1933)	defeated	president of Mobil Oil
	Miriam A. Ferguson[a]	D	57	1	2 (1933–1935)	retired	housewife
18	James V. Allred	D	35	2	4 (1935–1939)	retired	lawyer
19	W. Lee O'Daniel	D	48	1+	2+ (1939–1941)	resigned	business/salesperson
20	Coke Stevenson	D	53	2+	5+ (1941–1947)	retired	lawyer/banker/rancher
21	Beauford Jester	D	54	1+	2+ (1947–1949)	died	lawyer
22	Allan Shivers	D	41	3+	7+ (1949–1957)	retired	lawyer
23	Price Daniel	D	46	3	6 (1957–1963)	defeated	lawyer/educator/rancher
24	John Connally	D	45	3	6 (1963–1969)	retired	lawyer/rancher
25	Preston Smith	D	56	2	4 (1969–1973)	defeated	businessperson
26	Dolph Briscoe	D	49	2[b]	6 (1973–1979)	defeated	rancher/banker
27	Bill Clements	R	61	2	4 (1979–1983)	defeated	oilman
28	Mark White	D	42	1	4 (1983–1987)	defeated	lawyer
	Bill Clements[a]	R	69	1	4 (1987–1991)	retired	oilman
29	Ann Richards	D	57	1	4 (1991–1995)	defeated	teacher/campaigner
30	George W. Bush	R	48	1+	6 (1995–2000)	resigned	oilman/businessperson
31	Rick Perry	R	50	2+	8+ (2000–?)	—	farmer

[a] Miriam Ferguson and Bill Clements served nonconsecutive terms as governor.

[b] Briscoe served one two-year term and one four-year term. The governors after Briscoe served four-year terms.

Sources: Authors; Garland Adair, *Texas Pictorial Handbook* (Austin: Texas Memorial Museum, 1957); William Atkinson, *James V. Allred: A Political Biography* (Ph.D. diss., TCU, 1978); Biographical Files—Governors of Texas (Austin: Center for American History, University of Texas); Robert A. Calvert and Arnoldo DeLeon, *The History of Texas* (Arlington Heights, IL: Harlan Davidson, 1990); Council of State Governments, *The Governors of the States, Commonwealths, and Territories 1900–1980* (Lexington, KY: Council of State Governments, 1981); *Dallas Morning News* (March 7, 1991); Fred Gantt Jr., *The Chief Executive in Texas: A Study in Gubernatorial Leadership* (Austin: University of Texas Press, 1964), appendix 3; Ross Phares, *Governors of Texas* (Gretna, LA: Pelican, 1976); *Texas Almanac* (Dallas: A. H. Belo, 1992); Marquis Who's Who, *Who's Who in the South and Southwest*, 16th ed., 1978–1979, and 18th ed., 1982–1983 (Chicago: Marquis Who's Who).

LENGTH AND NUMBER OF TERMS The length of the term of office for the governor is four years. It was established as a two-year term in the original 1876 constitution and remained two years until it was amended, effective with the 1974 election.[9] There is no limit to the number of terms that the governor may serve.

Until the 1940s, no Texas governor served more than two terms (see Table 5.1). Virtually all governors won two terms when the terms were two years long. Then, from the 1940s to the 1970s, a three-term tradition was maintained. Dolph Briscoe was elected governor in 1972. When he won reelection in 1974, it was for the new four-year term. In 1978, he ran for another four-year term but was defeated in the Democratic primary—partly on an appeal by his opponent against having an unprecedented ten-year governor. Bill Clements served one four-year term and was defeated by Mark White, who served a single four-year term before being defeated by Clements. Clements then served another four-year term.[10] Ann Richards served a four-year term, then in 1994 lost to George W. Bush, who won reelection in 1998. He is the first governor to win back-to-back four-year terms, though he did not serve out his second term, as he resigned to become president in 2000. Rick Perry served out Bush's term, won election to a full term in 2002, then won reelection in 2006. Thus, in 2008, Perry became the longest serving governor in Texas history.

SALARY In all of Texas's constitutions until 1954, the governor's salary was set in the constitution. It was originally $4,000 in the 1876 constitution.[11] Voters repeatedly defeated salary increases before a $12,000 salary was approved in 1935. In 1953, the constitution was amended to allow the legislature to set the governor's salary. It quickly became one of the highest governor's salaries in the nation. The salary level stagnated in the 1990s, and the comparative ranking slipped. In 2006, the governor was paid $115,345, which ranked twenty-eighth in the nation; the highest governor's salary was California's, at $206,500.[12] By 2009, the Texas governor's salary had increased to $150,000, ranking about tenth.

IMPEACHMENT Texas executive officials, like federal officials, are subject to impeachment by the legislative branch. One Texas governor has been impeached, convicted, and removed from office. In 1917, Jim Ferguson angered legislators and University of Texas (UT) alumni by vetoing UT appropriations in order to force changes that he wanted. Legislators resurrected old allegations that he had misused public money, impeached him, and convicted him. He was removed from office and barred from holding office again. Later, his wife, Miriam, successfully ran for governor under the slogan "Two Governors for the Price of One."

SUCCESSION Article 4, section 17, of the constitution provides for **succession**. The lieutenant governor succeeds to the governorship if there is a vacancy. Voters approved a constitutional amendment in 1999 to assure that in the event of a vacancy in the governorship, the lieutenant governor would have to resign that office upon succeeding to the governorship, and the Senate would select a new lieutenant governor. Since 1876, five lieutenant governors have succeeded to the governorship: Richard Hubbard, William Hobby, Coke Stevenson, Allan Shivers, and Rick Perry.[13]

> **succession**
> The constitutional declaration that the lieutenant governor succeeds to the governorship if there is a vacancy.

TEXAS IN COMPARISON

Governors and the Executive Branch

State governments grew considerably throughout the twentieth century, and most of the growth was in the executive branches. States vary considerably, though, in the attributes and powers of the chief executive—the governor—and in the relative size of the executive agencies under the governor.

	Governor's Salary, 2006	Frequency of Meetings of Governor's Cabinet	Governors Who Became President of United States	Number of Consecutive Terms Allowed	Joint Election of Governor/ Lieutenant Governor	Number of FTE State Employees (2004)	Number of State Employees per 10,000 Population (2004)
Texas	$115,345 (28th)	(no Cabinet)	George W. Bush	unlimited	no	268,172 (2nd)	119
California	206,500 (1st)	Every 2 weeks	Ronald Reagan	2	no	393,057 (1st)	110
New York	179,000 (2nd)	Governor's discretion	Martin Van Buren Grover Cleveland Theodore Roosevelt Franklin D. Roosevelt	unlimited	yes	246,385 (3rd)	128
Florida	132,932 (19th)	Every 2 weeks	none	2	yes	183,265 (4th)	105

Sources: Council of State Governments, *Book of the States 2006* and *Book of the States 2007*, Tables 4.1, 4.3, 4.6, 163–167, 173; Kathleen O'Leary Morgan and Scott Morgan, eds., *State Rankings 2007: A Statistical View of the 50 United States*, 18th ed. (Lawrence, KS: Morgan Quitno Press, 2007), 345.

The Constitutional Roles of the Governor

The roles that the governor plays are set by constitutional and legislative mandates and by custom. Some of these roles encompass real powers and functions of the governorship; others appear to be little more than ceremonial.

The Texas Constitution designates the governor as the **chief of state, chief executive officer,** and **commander in chief** of Texas. Article 4, section 9, of the constitution empowers the governor to conduct "all intercourse and business of the State with other States and with the United States," which is the function of chief of state. Article 4, section 7, designates the governor as the "commander-in-chief of the military forces of the State." Article 4, section 1, designates the governor as the chief executive officer, which is further defined in section 12, giving him or her the authority to appoint people to fill vacancies in state offices in certain circumstances. The fragmented organization of executive power, however, makes the position of chief executive officer one that depends largely on the political and personal skills of the governor.

The governor plays other roles that are alluded to in the constitution but not spelled out specifically. Article 4, section 9, requires the governor to "present estimates of the amount of money required to be raised by taxation for all purposes." In 1931, the legislature institutionalized this role by designating the governor as the state's **chief budget officer**—presumably the official responsible for preparing the budget proposal and for overseeing its implementation. However, the same law gave the State Board of Control the responsibility of preparing the budget, and in 1949, the legislature created the Legislative Budget Board, which prepares a budget proposal that becomes the basis for the state appropriations act (see chapter 4). Thus, the governor's role as chief budget officer is greatly circumscribed.

Because of the governor's limited constitutional powers over judicial vacancies (Article 5, section 28) and pardons, parole, and clemency (Article 4, section 11), he or she has a narrow role in law enforcement. The original 1876 constitution gave the governor almost absolute power in **clemency,** the power to reduce prison terms. Governors received and granted thousands of requests for clemency and pardons, and there were recurrent rumors of bribery. The legislature created a Board of Pardons and Paroles in 1929, thus reducing the governor's powers, as well as the pressure on governors.[14] Article 4, section 11, gives the governor the power to grant reprieves and commutations of punishment and pardons "on the written signed recommendation and advice of the Board of Pardons and Paroles."

The governor has become a powerful figure in legislative politics. Article 4, section 8, of the constitution gives the governor the authority to call the legislature into special sessions and set the agenda for those sessions; section 9 requires the governor to deliver **governor's messages** to the legislature, such as the state-of-the-state message and the budget message; section 14 creates the authority to **veto** (negate) acts of the legislature; section 15 empowers the governor to sign bills and resolutions. These constitutional powers, plus the ability to *threaten* to veto bills (and thus gain a seat in negotiations over bills), make the governor an ever present force in legislative affairs.

The Development of Gubernatorial Power

How much power and what kinds of power a governor has depend on constitutional provisions, the era and political times in which a governor serves, and the relative power of other governmental officials. Regardless of how these factors have changed, Texas governors have always been weaker than governors in most other states.

---

chief of state
The governor in his or her role as the official head representing the state of Texas in its relationships with the national government, other states, and foreign dignitaries.

chief executive officer
The governor as the top official of the executive branch of Texas state government.

commander in chief
The governor in his or her role as head of the state militia.

chief budget officer
The governor, who is charged with preparing the state budget proposal for the legislature.

clemency
The governor's authority to reduce the length of a person's prison sentence.

governor's message
Message that the governor delivers to the legislature, pronouncing policy goals, budget priorities, and authorizations for the legislature to act.

veto
The formal, constitutional authority of the chief executive to reject bills passed by both houses of the legislative body, thus preventing their becoming law without further legislative action.

Characteristics of Gubernatorial Power

Political scientist Joseph Schlesinger devised a scale to measure the power of governors, using data from 1960–1961. These data have been updated periodically since then. Schlesinger used four variables: *tenure* (length of term of office, limits on number of terms), *appointments* (power to appoint heads of executive agencies), *budget* (budget-preparation power), and *signing and vetoing of bills* (veto and line-item veto authority, time to consider legislation before signing or vetoing it, difficulty of legislative ability to override). Schlesinger found that strong governorships were typically in large, urbanized, wealthy, nonsouthern states, with a strong level of party competition.[15]

Restriction of Governors' Powers

Nationwide, distrust of government and governors in the eighteenth and nineteenth centuries led to restrictions on the power that governors could wield and on their terms of office. In the Jacksonian era, the powers of governors were increased somewhat: terms were extended to four years, and appointment, veto, and clemency powers were increased. Their powers were checked, though, by the increasing election of other executive officials.[16] Gradually, throughout the twentieth century, states lifted many of the gubernatorial restrictions and empowered their governors. Early in the twenty-first century, most governors possess significant powers.

Texas was a practitioner of restrictions on gubernatorial power, especially in reaction to the strong government set up during Reconstruction. Under the 1869 constitution, the governor had complete control over voter registration, the militia, and the state police, and could appoint the governing bodies of towns and cities. Under Republican Governor Edmund J. Davis, the militia and the state police were despised by some. (Of course, racial politics also influenced people's attitudes.) A much later historical analysis argued that "the police force was used so often to enforce the arbitrary will of the governor that it became an emblem of despotic authority."[17] In 1872, voters rebelled and elected an anti-administration legislature, which triggered adoption of a new constitution. The desire to punish Davis and to prohibit future governors from becoming powerful led constitutional convention delegates in 1875 to adopt provisions that reduced the governor's salary, elected a plethora of other officers independent from the governor, and restricted the governor's appointment and removal powers.[18]

Comparing the Texas Governor with Other Governors

Today, a comparison of the fifty governors around the United States reveals substantial differences among them, particularly some interesting contrasts with the Texas governorship. Whereas forty-one states have some kind of Cabinet system in which the major agency directors are selected by and responsible to the governor, Texas does not.[19] Rather, Texas has a plural executive: most agency directors are appointed by boards, rather than directly by the governor; some agency directors are elected; there is no systematic, ongoing process for the governor to coordinate executive policies; and it is virtually impossible for the governor to fire a board member or an agency head. (To learn more about this issue, see Join the Debate: Should the Texas Governor Have a Cabinet?)

On Schlesinger's 1960–1961 scale, the Texas governor tied for the weakest of the forty-eight governors when the variables of tenure, appointments, budget, and signing and vetoing bills were combined. (To learn more about comparative gubernatorial power, see Table 5.2.) When he updated his scale using 1968–1969 data, Texas ranked fiftieth, leading Schlesinger to comment that "Texas is the only populous state where the governor's formal strength is low."[20] Political scientist Thad Beyle has updated the rankings numerous times since then; in his rankings, Texas was always forty-eighth or forty-ninth, until he changed the variables in 1999 (Texas ranked

Join the Debate

Should the Texas Governor Have a Cabinet?

OVERVIEW: As president of the Republic of Texas, Sam Houston governed with a Cabinet. In the ensuing decades, governors maintained significant control over the executive branch of state government in Texas, but the 1876 constitution then stripped the governor of many powers, including controls over the executive branch. Attempts since then to reconvene Cabinet-style executive authority have been short lived, often accompanied by high-profile clashes among executive officials. In 1931, the legislature created a committee to reorganize state government. Its reorganization plan suggested a Cabinet-style government to strengthen executive coordination, but the Cabinet proposal was killed.[a] The idea lives on with governors, though. Texas's longest-serving governor, Allan Shivers (1949–1957), waited until his final inauguration in 1955 to proclaim:

> I believe we should begin giving serious thought to reorganizing the executive branch. If the governor is to be held accountable for the conduct of the executive branch, future governors should have direct authority over—as well as responsibility for—the performance of administrative functions which are not policymaking in character, [including] appointment and removal.[b]

Today, forty-one states have some kind of Cabinet system in which the major agency directors are selected by and responsible to the governor. Texas does not.[c] The idea of a more unified executive in Texas, with a governor's Cabinet, is not dead—but such proposals have been defeated for more than a century, and their chances do not seem to have improved.

Arguments IN FAVOR of Allowing the Governor to Convene a Cabinet

- If the title "chief executive officer" is to be meaningful, the governor must have tools with which to direct the executive branch. If other executive officials realize that the governor has no or little power, they will respond to other pressures and downplay or ignore the governor's entreaties.

- Texas's fragmented, plural executive guarantees that executive officials will clash with each other to the detriment of good public policy. If the governor can convene regular meetings of the heads of major agencies and coordinate policy initiatives and implementation, Texans will experience more uniform and consistent policies and will be better able to hold governors accountable for executive actions.

- A strong governor, acting with a Cabinet whose members are loyal to the governor, is essential to Texas exercising its role as a modern, energetic state government, able to respond effectively to other power centers in the political economy. Whether it is corporations seeking to find the best place to expand or relocate, states vying with each other for federal funding, or citizens needing a transparent, efficient, and accountable bureaucracy to serve them, a coordinated executive branch will perform better for Texas than the chaotic and contradictory system of numerous independent executive officials.

Arguments AGAINST Allowing the Governor to Convene a Cabinet

- Texans have long valued small, limited government, and a strong

---

twenty-eighth). Texas is also a weak-governor state on the four individual variables. For instance, only the Texas and South Carolina governors have weak budget-making power, and only Texas, Georgia, Mississippi, and Oklahoma governors are weak in appointment powers.[21]

The legislature and the voters have strengthened the Texas governorship in recent years. Today, the governor can appoint more high-level positions than ever before, and he or she has (limited) budget execution authority. Also, a 1980 amendment (Article 15, section 9) allows the governor, for the first time under the current

governor with a Cabinet system goes against that rich tradition. Stronger governors create stronger government. A Cabinet system would allow governors to wield too much power in the executive branch, with fewer checks on that power.

- **Having multiple, independent executive officers, elected by the people, serves to stimulate policy innovations.** If only the governor is elected and powerful, other executive officials will become followers, bureaucrats. By electing seven executive officials independent from the governor, Texas is more likely to get creative, innovative, and energetic policy leadership in the executive branch.

- **The legislature and the voters have expanded gubernatorial power in recent decades, giving the governor specific tools of authority; a broad-brush grant of power over all agencies is unneeded.** Texas governors now have budget execution authority, an expanded list of officials to appoint, and the power to remove officials in extreme circumstances, with legislative participation. Thus, Texans have responded to specific needs without abandoning the general concept of limited and checked governmental authority.

Continuing the Debate

1. Do you favor or oppose the Texas governor using a Cabinet system? Explain your answer.

2. What are some likely consequences resulting from the establishment of a Cabinet system for the Texas executive branch?

To Follow the Debate Online Go To:

The Florida governor's site explaining Cabinet issues and broadcasting live audio feeds of Cabinet meetings: www.myflorida.com/myflorida/cabinet/

The Milwaukee Journal–Sentinel discussion of the 2007 debate over inclusion or exclusion of an officer from the governor's Cabinet: www.jsonline.com/story/index.aspx?id=681975

[a]Joint Advisory Committee on Government Operations, "Final Report to the Governor of Texas and Members of the 65th Texas Legislature," January 1977.

[b]Fred Gantt Jr., *The Chief Executive in Texas: A Study in Gubernatorial Leadership* (Austin: University of Texas Press, 1964); *House Journal*, 54th Legislature, 70.

[c]Council of State Governments, *Book of the States 2005*, Table 4.6, 225, and Table 4.10, 233.

In 2006, the Western Governors' Association met in Austin. Here, four governors speak in the Texas capitol. From left to right, they are New Mexico Governor Bill Richardson (D), California Governor Arnold Schwarzenegger (R), Arizona Governor Janet Napolitano (D), and Texas Governor Rick Perry (R).

---

constitution, to remove from office gubernatorial appointees—but only with a two-thirds vote of the Senate, and only his or her own appointees, not previous governors' appointees. No governor has yet used this power. Other states, too, have increased their governor's powers, so by comparison, Texas governor still appears weaker than others.

Constitutionally, it is apparent that the Texas governor is weak. Governors may be able to amass and exercise more strength, though, in the political arena, where appearance, charisma, and bluff may count more than constitutional reality. In 1994

TABLE 5.2 Powers of the Texas Governor Compared to Other Governors

Four snapshots of governors in the United States show that Texas governors have long been weaker than governors in other states.

	Number of Points (and Comparative Rank)			
Characteristics	1960–1961	1968–1969	1990	2002
Tenure	2 (33rd)	2 (41st)	5 (1st)	5 (1st)
Appointments	1 (38th)	1 (41st)	2 (46th)	1.5 (46th)
Budget	1 (41st)	1 (45th)	1 (50th)	2 (49th)
Veto	3 (14th)	3 (41st)	5 (1st)	5 (1st)
Budget changing			1[a]	
Legislative strength			2 (33rd)	
Separately elected officials				1 (41st)
Gubernatorial party control				4 (3rd)
Combined	7 (48th)	7 (50th)	16 (49th)	18.5 (38th)

[a] For 1990, Beyle added a new category comparing the governor's power with respect to legislative budget-changing power. He found only four states where the governor had any significant power over the legislature, and forty-three states, including Texas, where the governor was "very weak."

Sources: Joseph Schlesinger, "Politics, the Executive," in Herbert Jacob and Kenneth Vines, eds., *Politics in the American States: A Comparative Analysis* (Boston: Little, Brown, 1965), 220–9, and 2nd ed. (1971), 225–34; Thad L. Beyle, "Governors," in Virginia Gray, Herbert Jacob, and Robert Albritton, eds., *Politics in the American States*, 5th ed. (New York: HarperCollins, 1990), 574; Thad L. Beyle, "The Governors," in Virginia Gray and Russell Hanson, eds., *Politics in the American States*, 8th ed. (Washington, DC: CQ Press, 2004), 194–231.

and 1999, Beyle compared "personal power" of the governors. Texas's governor ranked significantly higher on personal power than on the institutional powers rankings. Indeed, when Beyle looked at ambition, future office possibilities, and electoral mandates, he concluded that the Texas governor ranked third, behind only Delaware and Kansas. When he then combined the personal rankings with the lower institutional rankings of the governors, he ranked the Texas governor ninth in the nation.[22]

The Governor's Power to Appoint Executive Officials

Article 4, section 12, of the constitution details the method for filling vacancies in the executive branch: "All vacancies in State or district offices, except members of the Legislature, shall be filled unless otherwise provided by law by appointment of the Governor." The governor appoints more *agency heads* today than ever before. (To learn more about top agency officials, see Table 5.3.) Recent additions to the governor's appointment powers include education commissioner and health and human services executive commissioner. However, most appointments are to *boards, commissions*, and *advisory panels*. The governor makes several hundred appointments a year.[23]

A 1933 court case determined that the legislature may designate someone other than the governor to make an appointment, and no Senate confirmation would be required. However, if the legislature does not provide an alternative means, the governor appoints.[24] Some analysts argue that the legislature can specify a gubernatorial appointment without requiring Senate confirmation. Indeed, there are several positions that the governor fills without confirmation, though there are others that the Senate does confirm, without express provisions for confirmation.[25] Custom and the balance of political power seem to dictate on a case-by-case basis whether confirmation will be required.

While presidential appointment requires only a simple majority confirmation in the U.S. Senate, Texas gubernatorial appointments require consent of the Texas Senate in a vote of at least two-thirds of those present (Article 4, section 12c). Because most appointments are made while the legislature is not in session, when the Senate convenes in regular or special session, it may take up appointments made during the interim. Thus, some appointees may serve for a year or more before the Senate meets and confirms or rejects the nomination. **Senatorial courtesy** is a norm that requires the governor to preclear a nominee with the senator in whose district the nominee resides. Senatorial cour-

senatorial courtesy
A process by which a governor, when selecting an appointee, defers to the state senator in whose district the nominee resides.

TABLE 5.3 State Agency Heads Appointed by the Governor

As recently as the 1970s, Texas governors appointed only a handful of the heads of executive agencies. While most agency heads are still not appointed by the governor, the list of those who are appointed by the governor is growing longer.

Adjutant General
Chief Administrative Law Judge
Executive Director, Children's Trust Fund of Texas Council (nomination by Executive Commissioner of Health and Human Services)
Executive Director, Texas Council on Alcohol and Drug Abuse (nomination by Executive Commissioner of Health and Human Services)
Executive Director, Criminal Justice Policy Council
Commissioner of Education
Fire Fighters Pension Commissioner (nomination by State Firemen's and Fire Marshals' Association and Texas State Association of Fire Fighters)
Executive Commissioner of Health and Human Services Commission
Executive Director, Department of Housing and Community Affairs (nomination by Board of Housing and Community Affairs)
Chair, Regional Mobility Authorities
Insurance Commissioner
Executive Director, Interagency Council on Early Childhood Intervention (nomination by Executive Commissioner of Health and Human Services)
Presiding Officer, Private Sector Prison Industries Oversight Authority
Public Insurance Counsel
Public Utility Counsel
Secretary of State
Executive Director, Office of State–Federal Relations

Source: Marilyn Duncan and Shirley Beckwith, *Guide to Texas State Agencies*, 11th ed. (Austin: LBJ School of Public Affairs, 2001); author.

tesy and the recent growth of a two-party legislature mean that a governor must be sensitive to senatorial concerns or risk either embarrassment or a political battle.

A 1999 appointment attempt by Governor George W. Bush demonstrates how senatorial courtesy actually works. Bush wanted to reappoint Public Utility Commissioner Judy Walsh, who was from Austin. However, opponents of Walsh convinced Austin's Senator Gonzalo Barrientos to oppose the nomination. Governor Bush recognized the norm of senatorial courtesy and assumed that the Senate would then reject the nomination if he submitted it. However, since the legislature was not in session, the governor simply did not appoint anyone, which left Walsh in the position until the Senate convened next (and Governor Perry made a new appointment).[26]

The election of Republican Bill Clements provided the first test of how party clashes would affect appointments. Governor Clements made 105 lame-duck appointments after he was defeated in 1982, but early in 1983, new Democratic Governor Mark White and the Democratic Texas Senate found a way to negate most of the appointments. The Senate returned fifty-nine to White unconfirmed; two more were later rejected. White then reappointed eleven of Clements's picks but ignored the others and made his own nominations.[27] The legislature then approved, and voters ratified, a constitutional amendment shifting the dates of some appointments to take away the chance of so many lame-duck appointments. When George W. Bush became governor, the Senate Nominations Committee—chaired for the first time by a Republican—stalled several of Ann Richards's unconfirmed interim appointees, refusing them hearings, so Bush could fill those positions.

Analysis of appointees reveals that governors tend to appoint people like themselves and their allies. Because all but two governors have been male, all but three have been Democrats, and all have been Anglo, it should not be surprising that Anglo, male Democrats have historically dominated state boards and commissions. **Overrepresentation and underrepresentation** are higher and lower numbers, respectively, than would be expected based on a group's numbers in the general population.

overrepresentation and underrepresentation
Higher and lower numbers, respectively, than would be expected from a group in comparison with that group's numbers in the general population.

For governors' appointees, those who have been overrepresented in appointments are Anglos and males, while women, African Americans, and Mexican Americans have been underrepresented.

The pattern of appointments has changed only marginally in the past three decades, with the significant exception of Ann Richards (1991–1994). Governor Clements (1979–1982, 1987–1990) brought in more Republicans but reduced the number of minorities appointed. Governor White (1983–1986) appointed more women and minorities than did his predecessors,[28] though still in numbers far below their presence in the population. Richards made a public issue of the gender and race of appointees. She is the only governor to appoint numbers of women and racial and ethnic minorities in approximate proportion to their presence in the population. By the end of her term, 45 percent of her appointees were women, 19 percent were Mexican American, and 14 percent were African American. Governor Bush did not appoint as many women and minorities; after four years in office, 37 percent of his appointees were women, 13 percent were Mexican American, and 9 percent were African American. Governor Perry's appointments pattern is in between Richards's and Bush's: in his first five years of office, about 37 percent of his appointees were women, 16 percent Mexican American, and 10 percent African American.[29]

When Ann Richards announced her gubernatorial campaign in 1989, she promised that her administration would "look like Texas." She and her supporters argued that a government truly responsive to the concerns of Texas must take into account the wide variety of groups in the population, and that one way of doing that is to have executive agency officials reflect that population diversity. Her pledge to do so gave a boost to her 1990 campaign. As data in Table 5.4 indicate, Governor Richards did appoint officials who more closely reflected the population demographics in the state.

Moreover, those appointees not only provided new voices inside government but also served to break down barriers and expand public service opportunities for the broader groups from which they came. Ron Kirk served as Governor Richards's secretary of state, then became the first African American mayor of Dallas. Susan Rieff served as the governor's environmental coordinator, became regional director for the Audubon Society, and later became executive director of the Lady Bird Johnson Wildflower Center. Former legislative Dirty Thirty reformer Zan Holmes became the first African American to serve on the University of Texas Board of Regents. Lena Guerrero was appointed to the Railroad Commission, which had previously been almost exclusively male and Anglo. While Guerrero lost her bid to win election to the seat, several Hispanics and women have served on the commission since then.

In addition to the significance of gender and race homogeneity or diversity of appointees, another issue has also dominated the debate over who gains a seat at the table of policy making and administration: the role of campaign donations. Often, key

TABLE 5.4 Gender and Race in Gubernatorial Appointments

	Texas Population (2000)	Appointees of Governor:				
		White	Clements	Richards	Bush	Perry
Gender						
Male	49.5%	78%	82%	55%	63%	62%
Female	50.5	22	18	45	37	37
Race/ethnic group						
White	52.4	82	89	65	77	71
Mexican American	32.0	12	7	19	13	16
African American	11.5	6	3	14	9	11
Other	4.1	n/a	n/a	2	n/a	2

Sources: Clements, White, and Bush appointees from Peggy Fikac, "Bush Appointing Many Females, Minorities," *San Antonio Express-News* (July 9, 2000); Richards appointees from list supplied by Office of Governor Ann Richards, October 13, 1994; Governor Perry's appointees from three years of data, Texans for Public Justice, "Governor Perry's Patronage," April 1, 2006, http://www.tpj.org; and from Office of Governor Rick Perry, May 19, 2006.

appointments go to the governor's largest campaign contributors. Of Governor Mark White's early appointments, 27 percent were campaign contributors.[30] Governor Richards appointed her largest contributor to the Parks and Wildlife Board. Another large contributor was appointed chair of the UT Board of Regents. George W. Bush kept this tradition alive by appointing big contributors to key posts. In his gubernatorial campaigns, Bush collected about $2.4 million in contributions from people he appointed to state positions,[31] including Allan Polunsky (chair of the Board of Criminal Justice), David Laney (chair of the Transportation Commission), Donald Evans (chair of the UT Board of Regents, and later President Bush's secretary of commerce), Tony Sanchez (UT Board of Regents, and later Democratic candidate for governor), Tom Loeffler (UT Board of Regents), and Richard Heath and Mark Watson (Parks and Wildlife Commission).

Photo courtesy: Texans for Public Justice

Governor Bush's contributor-appointees typically gave about $25,000 to his campaigns, with Tom Loeffler giving the most at $141,000. Governor Perry's appointments continued this pattern at an even higher level, according to figures analyzed by the group Texans for Public Justice. For 2003, 2004, and 2005, one-third of Perry's appointees were campaign contributors, and seventeen gave more than $100,000. Texas Tech Regent Larry Anders gave the most at $220,304, followed by UT Regent Robert Rowlings at $207,262 and Parks and Wildlife Commissioner Peter Holt at $206,000.

However, not all contributions in Texas are individual contributions. Texans for Public Justice also documented another dynamic: contributions from corporation political action committees compared with gubernatorial appointment of corporate officials. PACs from Perry Homes, SBC, Pilgrim's Pride, Dell, Reliant Energy, TXU, Hance Scarborough, and H.E. Butt Grocery all gave more than $100,000 to Perry's campaigns, and executives from their companies were appointed to executive offices.[32]

> Is a governor's appointment of campaign contributors to boards and commissions equivalent to "patronage"? Texans for Public Justice has documented and correlated campaign contributors and gubernatorial appointments.

The Power of Staff and Budget

The responsibilities of the governor's staff are broad: developing the governor's budget proposal and policy recommendations; performing public relations; serving as liaison with local, state, and federal agencies and with the legislature and party officials; answering correspondence and visiting with citizens who call on the governor; contacting and negotiating with lobbyists. These duties change with the priorities and organizational preferences of each governor.

Nineteenth-century Texas governors typically had two or three staff members. The growth in the number of boards and commissions, with the governor as an ex officio member of many of them, brought an increase in the governor's staff to about eight in the 1920s. Since the 1950s, the governor's staff size has grown tremendously. Recent governors have had about 200 staff members. Measuring staff size, though, is difficult, because governors can persuade agency heads to pay for staff members that are then loaned to the governor and do not appear on the governor's payroll.

The amount of money that the legislature appropriates for the operations of the Office of the Governor depends on what functions the legislature and the governor choose to place under the office. While the governor's appropriations may exceed $100 million a year, usually less than $10 million is for the narrower Governor's Office (in 2009 it was $9.5 million), and the remainder is for discretionary funds, trusted programs, and suboffices included in the governor's budget, such as the governor's mansion, music and film industry marketing, information on disability policies, women's groups, criminal justice, and workforce issues. For fiscal years 2008 and 2009, the budget for the broad Office of the Governor was $754 million and $143 million respectively—including large amounts for the Texas Enterprise Fund and bond proceeds.

The Governor as Policy Maker and Political Leader

If the Texas governor is constitutionally weak, then the governor's skill in wielding political power becomes even more important in his or her success at governing. As political scientist Fred Gantt points out in his study of the Texas governorship through the middle of the twentieth century, "Instead of the 'Chief Executive of Texas,' under existing laws he might more accurately be labeled the 'Chief Persuader of Texas.' "[33] In more recent years, an analysis of Ann Richards's governorship concluded that she "pushed the powers of a weak office to their limits,"[34] and George W. Bush was perceived as a governor with strong personal skills that made him a strong governor. The political leadership that a governor is able to provide flows from the governor's skills and previous experience, as well as similarity in party, philosophy, and ideology with other decision makers. (To learn more about governors' leadership styles, see Analyzing Visuals: Ideology and Governors.)

These skills must be honed in the electoral arena in order to win the governorship. All Texas governors have sought reelection; governors must, then, maintain those electoral connections while in office. Because Texas political parties have been weak, governors have had to build and sustain personal followings and organizations. Of course, campaign money is essential, and governors must raise money while they are in office, both to pay off any previous campaign debt and to prepare for the next campaign. These electoral linkages help build the visibility of the governor as well as an image of strength—which in turn helps him or her in wielding governmental power in battles with other officials and private interest groups.

The Texas Governor's Mansion was built in 1854. Here is what the mansion looked like before a fire severely damaged it in 2008. The state is attempting to save and restore it.

Public-Opinion Leadership

Because of their weak constitutional powers, Texas governors resort to public-opinion leadership to increase their power with other office holders. Invariably, their opponents see such initiatives as public relations efforts to boost the governor's political fortunes. Governors have sometimes had their own television shows. When Governor Clements developed a tense relationship with the media and stopped showing up for the taping of "The Governor's Report," the show was renamed "Capitol Report." Governor White ran television commercials to build support for higher teacher salaries.

Governors hold news conferences either on a regular basis or whenever they believe such conferences will be beneficial to them. Sometimes they go outside Austin to try to stir up public support for their policies. Governor Clements tried an anti-tax tour during a legislative session. Governor White made trips during legislative sessions to key legislators' districts. Governor Richards tried a "tour of state government" to promote dialogue between state officials and citizens in several locations across the state. Governors Bush and Perry spoke around the state about their tax and education proposals.

Relationship with the Legislature

To be a successful governor, one must succeed in pushing a program through the legislature and in killing unwanted legislative measures. To do so, a governor must develop

Analyzing Visuals: Ideology and Governors

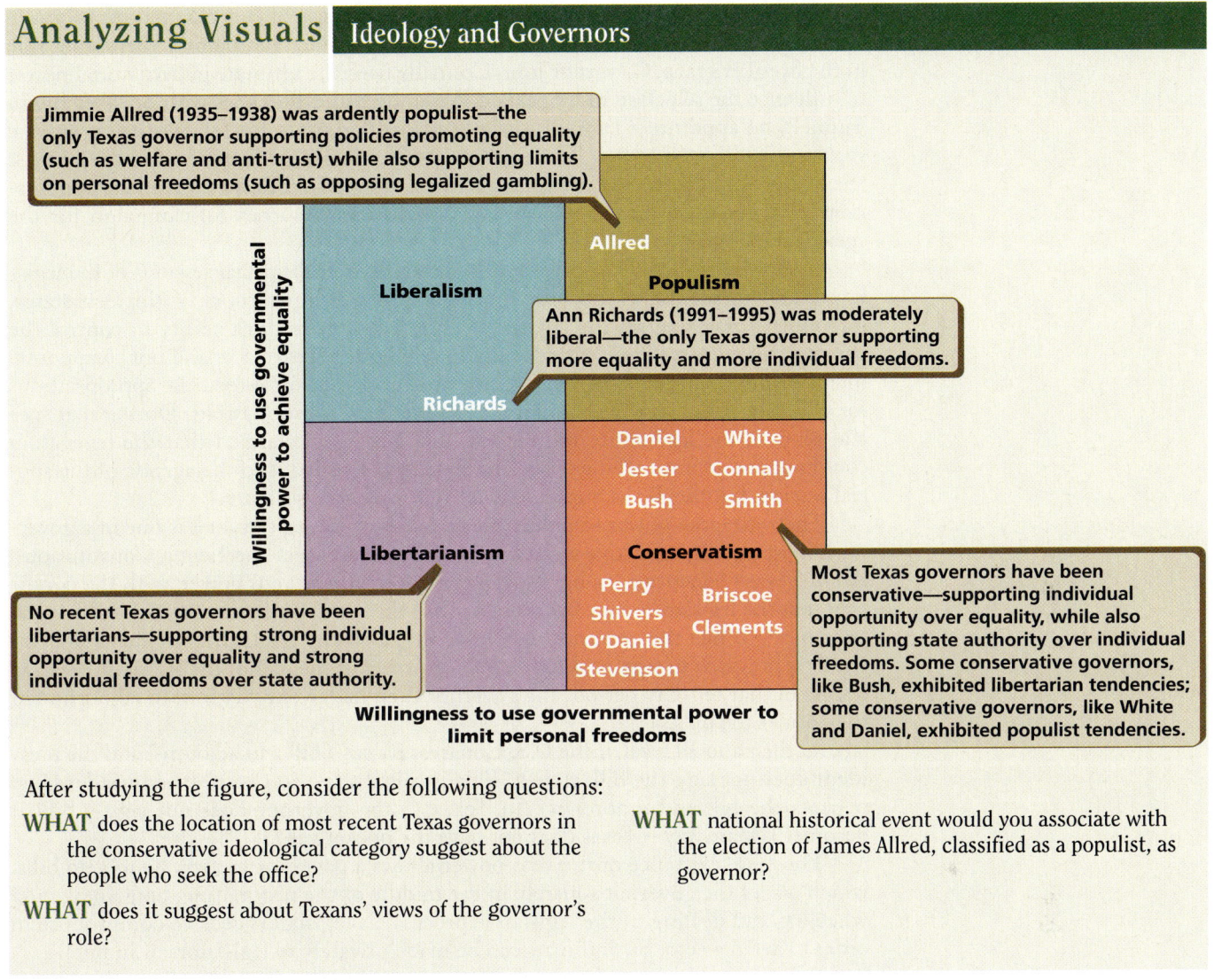

After studying the figure, consider the following questions:

WHAT does the location of most recent Texas governors in the conservative ideological category suggest about the people who seek the office?

WHAT does it suggest about Texans' views of the governor's role?

WHAT national historical event would you associate with the election of James Allred, classified as a populist, as governor?

good personal or working relationships with key legislators and must use the powers of the governorship to assist the legislative process and, sometimes, to thwart it.

A governor uses a grab bag of tools to win his or her legislative agenda, including direct appeals to voters, pleas from citizen study groups, pressure from lobbyists, breakfasts for legislators, entertainment (including evenings at the governor's mansion), individual legislative conferences, floor leaders, and staff representatives working the floor.[35] The "state of the state" message and budget message are the formal vehicles governors use to convey their wishes to the legislature. Governors also make "emergency proclamations," which serve to put governors' favored bills ahead of others on the legislative schedule.

A hostile lieutenant governor or House Speaker could, of course, seriously damage the governor's chances of success. (Such a possibility was an underlying theme in the 1998 lieutenant governor's race.) The governor has no role in the selection of the lieutenant governor because the office is elective. Governors can try to influence the 150 House members who select the Speaker, but to do so is politically risky. In the early twentieth century, governors sometimes became involved in House Speaker races. Governors Colquitt, Sterling, and Allred supported unsuccessful candidates for Speaker. As Miriam Ferguson began her term as governor in 1933, her husband, former Governor Jim Ferguson, successfully supported Coke Stevenson for Speaker.[36]

Since the 1930s, no governor has openly endorsed or campaigned for a House Speaker candidate, although they sometimes play a quiet and behind-the-scenes role in the Speaker's race. Governor John Connally used the ultimate gubernatorial power to influence the selection of a Speaker. When he had differences with Speaker Byron Tunnell, he appointed Tunnell to the Railroad Commission, thus opening up the speakership. To ensure that he would get a new Speaker he liked, he and his lobbyist friend Bob Bullock tipped off young Representative Ben Barnes about the appointment. Barnes used the tip to gear up his ultimately successful campaign for the speakership.[37]

A key power of all U.S. governors is the ability to call special sessions of the legislature and to set the agenda for the special session (governors of thirteen states, including Texas, can set the agenda).[38] The Texas governor's ability to control the agenda of special sessions extends only to regular legislative acts and not to appointments or impeachments. In 1917, Governor Jim Ferguson vetoed the appropriations for UT, then called a special session to consider new appropriations. During that special session, the legislature impeached him. Ferguson claimed that the legislature could not act on impeachment because he had not added it to the agenda of the special session, but the Texas Supreme Court upheld the legislature.[39]

The veto—the power to nullify bills passed by the legislature—is one of a governor's most potent legislative weapons. (To learn more, see The Living Constitution.) All of Texas's constitutions have given the governor the veto power, with the condition that the legislature may override (cancel) the veto by a vote of two-thirds in each chamber.[40] When the governor receives a bill passed by the legislature, he or she has ten days in which to sign or veto the bill. However, if the end of the legislative session occurs in that ten-day period, the governor then has twenty days from adjournment to consider the bills.

At the national level, if the U.S. Congress passes a bill and adjourns, and the president does not sign the bill, it dies. This is called a "pocket veto" (the president just pockets the bill and ignores it). In Texas, if the governor does not sign a bill, it becomes law anyway—Texas does not have the pocket veto.[41]

The mere existence of the veto power allows a governor to *threaten* to veto bills, which places the governor squarely in the middle of the negotiating, bargaining, and wheeling and dealing of the legislative process, as legislators seek to compromise in order to avoid a veto. Such threats can be made privately to legislators or in public.

Republican Governor Clements often resorted to vetoes and threats to veto in his dealings with the Democratic legislature. In his total of eight years as governor, Clements vetoed more bills and resolutions than any other governor—184—a figure that Governor Perry surpassed with his vetoes in 2007 (for a term total of 200). Ann Richards wanted to maintain good relations with her fellow Democratic leaders in the legislature. She told the legislators that she would not resort to such threats and constant use of the veto. By her second legislative session, however, she was publicly and frequently threatening to veto a concealed-handgun bill. The legislature amended it in response to her threats and passed it, but she vetoed it as unacceptable. The legislature passed the bill again in 1995, and Governor Bush signed it. Governor Bush vetoed twenty-four bills in 1995, thirty-six in 1997, and thirty-one in 1999—numbers typical of his predecessors. Then came Governor Perry's 2001 "Father's Day Massacre," when Perry vetoed seventy-eight bills in one day, to make his total of vetoes for the session eighty-two, a new record for one session. In so doing, he touched off a storm of protest. He vetoed forty-eight bills in 2003, nineteen in 2005, and fifty-one in 2007.[42]

In Texas, most bills are passed in the last ten days of the session. Consequently, most vetoes occur after adjournment, as did Governor Perry's Father's Day vetoes in 2001, and the legislature has no chance to vote to override. There have been only seventy-seven veto override attempts under the current constitution, and only twenty-six of these have been successful. Governor Clements had one veto overridden in 1979. There has been only one override attempt since then; in 1990, the Senate voted to override Governor Clements's veto of school finance legislation, but the House vote did not reach the required two-thirds.[43]

A variation of the veto authority is the line-item veto. For bills that appropriate money, this power allows the governor to select one or more lines of appropriations and veto them, while signing the rest of the bill into law. Line-item veto authority has been in the Texas constitutions since 1866. Forty-two governors now have this power.[44] While the power is usually used to void a program that the governor opposes, Governor Clements used it in 1989 to abolish an entire agency, the Advisory Commission on Intergovernmental Relations. In some legislative sessions, the governor vetoes only a handful of line items; in others, governors have vetoed up to twenty-six items. In 2005, Governor Perry's line-item vetoes totaled a whopping $35.3 billion, as he vetoed all funds to the Texas Education Agency, in an (unsuccessful) attempt to force the legislature to reform school financing provisions.[45] In a special session that summer, the legislature reappropriated funding for the agency but was not able to reach agreement on substantive reforms to the school finance provisions.

Because the major appropriations bill is always passed at the end of a session, the legislature adjourns and then has no chance to override any line-item vetoes. Thus, the line-item veto can be a powerful weapon, and every recent governor has used it. However, the legislature has learned to mitigate against it by organizing material in the appropriations bills in such a manner as to limit the usefulness of such a veto (by lumping programs together and by using "riders" to describe programs and funding levels, rather than line items for those programs).

Executive Orders

To exercise effective policy leadership, the governor must have significant influence over executive agencies. As the next section demonstrates, Texas's chief executive may be "chief" in name only. Presidents and governors in strong-governor states often steer executive agencies to act according to their will by issuing executive orders. Texas's weaker governors have used the executive order primarily for two purposes. The first is to force a gubernatorial voice in policy debates through the creation of governor's task forces, interagency councils, and so forth. The second is for emergency management. In fact, this latter area may be the only arena in which the governor has strong constitutional and statutory footing to order action by other executive officials. Section 418.012 of the Government Code states that under its emergency management provisions, "the governor may issue executive orders . . . [with] the force and effect of law." An executive order could declare a state of disaster, establish an emergency management council, or temporarily reassign resources.

Yet, modern governors have issued executive orders on a much broader array of policy issues, as this chapter's opening scenario demonstrates. Perry has made extensive use of them, generating controversy and litigation. In August 2005, he issued Executive Order RP-47, ordering the commissioner of education to establish a requirement that at least 65 percent of school districts' revenue be used for direct classroom instruction, riling superintendents, teachers, and legislators who argued that it was an arbitrary, damaging, and illegal initiative.

Under what authority do governors issue these orders? Whereas emergency management executive orders cite the specific statute that authorizes their issuance, other executive orders seem to have weaker legal footing. Bill Clements's Executive Order WPC-1, for instance, states that the governor is supposed "to be the chief spokesman for the State of Texas," and that the order is issued "under the authority vested in me." Ann Richards's Executive Order 92-1 also falls back on "under the authority vested in me." Rick Perry has expanded the language but not the specificity of the authority. For instance, Perry's Executive Order RP-65 for HPV vaccination was made "by virtue of the power and authority vested in me by the Constitution and laws of the State of Texas as the Chief Executive Officer." Yet, broad reference to the constitution and the laws masks the reality that the constitution deliberately created a weak governor and does not mention specific gubernatorial authority over the other executive officials.

The Plural Executive in Texas

Americans place a high value on elections. We assume that elected officials are more responsive to citizens, and thus more democratic, than nonelected officials. Elected officials may not have any more authority than appointed officials, but election seems to give them more legitimacy in the eyes of citizens—and certainly being a part of the electoral process gives them more political power than appointed officials. Texas elects nine statewide officials[46] (plus the State Board of Education, whose fifteen members are elected from districts). Nearly half the states have reduced the number of elected state officials in recent decades. Texas reflected this trend in 1995, abolishing the position of state treasurer.

While most agency directors cooperate with the governor in policy implementation, there have been hostilities. Attorneys general are often seen as "governors-in-waiting," and many of them have feuded publicly with a governor, then run against the governor in the next election. Democratic Attorney General John Hill clashed with Governor Dolph Briscoe, then defeated Briscoe in the Democratic primary in 1978. Democratic Attorney General Mark White clashed with Republican Governor Bill Clements, then beat Clements for the governorship in 1982. Democratic Land Commissioner Garry Mauro and Governor George W. Bush squared off over coastal and other issues, then Mauro ran as the Democratic nominee against Bush in 1998 but lost. Comptroller Carole Keeton Strayhorn clashed repeatedly with Governor Rick Perry before running a losing race against him in 2006.

Thinking Nationally
Elected State Officials

On the national level, we elect only the president (and his or her hand-picked vice president); the president appoints all the other highest-level executive officials. In Maine, New Hampshire, New Jersey, and Tennessee, only the governor is elected, and those governors have extensive appointment powers. Most other states elect a governor, a lieutenant governor, an attorney general, a secretary of state, and a treasurer/comptroller. Texas ranks fourth among the states in its number of elected state officials. In Texas, the land commissioner, agriculture commissioner, railroad commissioners, and state board of education members are elected, whereas other states' governors appoint officials like these.

- What are the implications of popular election of these officials?
- Should the governor be allowed to appoint them?

Attorney General

attorney general
The elected official who is the chief counsel for the state of Texas.

Next to the governor and the lieutenant governor, the **attorney general** is the most significant elected state official. The attorney general serves as the chief counsel for the state of Texas. Because the attorney general is elected, he or she is independent from the governor (and, indeed, the governor has his or her own legal adviser). In about half of the years since 1978, governors and attorneys general have even been from different parties. Often, attorneys general have ambitions to run for governor, which can impede cooperation.

As chief counsel to state agencies, the attorney general and the hundreds of assistant attorneys general represent most agencies in litigation. When an agency sues a private individual or organization to force compliance with a state law or agency regulation, the attorney general's office usually provides the attorney for the agency. When someone sues a state agency, the attorney general must defend the agency. For example, in 1993, several mothers sued Medicaid officials from the Texas Department of Health and other state agencies, claiming that the agencies had denied their children Medicaid services that Congress had intended to be made available. The attorney general defended the state, arguing that its actions were legal and that state laws were legal. In 2000, a federal judge ruled against the state. In 2002, the federal appeals court upheld the state's actions, but the U.S. Supreme Court ruled against the state in *Frew* v. *Hawkins*, and the district judge then imposed remedies.

While election campaigns for attorney general often focus on criminal issues, the attorney general has little authority in the field of criminal law and focuses instead on civil law. The attorney general may commence civil proceedings in areas where the legislature has given him or her jurisdiction. For instance, the attorney general is authorized in some cases to sue under the state's Deceptive Trade Practices Act. In criminal matters, he or she may assist local prosecutors on request, but only if a state interest is involved.

As the state's chief lawyer, the attorney general may issue advisory opinions to state and local officials on the legality of their actions, as Attorney General Dan Morales did in response to the *Hopwood* v. *Texas* (5th Cir., 1996) decision, forbidding colleges and universities from enforcing some affirmative action plans, and as Attorney General John Cornyn did in 2000, forbidding local governments from using public funds to provide health services to undocumented immigrants. Public officials request an Attorney General Opinion when they are uncertain about a law or when they think that the attorney general will rule in their favor in a dispute with private groups or other public officials. Attorney General Opinions have the force of law for agency officials, until or unless a court rules otherwise.

Attorney General Greg Abbott has been the state's lawyer since 2002. He is the second Republican to hold the office.

The attorney general has continuous opportunities to provide public-policy leadership by deciding what kinds of cases to emphasize and by being pulled into public-policy areas. Jim Mattox (1983–1991) sued numerous companies to force compliance with consumer safety, anti-fraud, and environmental statutes. Dan Morales (1991–1999) sued tobacco companies on health-related issues, winning a huge settlement for the state. Mattox and Morales devoted a massive amount of staff time to resolving the *Ruiz* v. *Estelle* case concerning prison management, and to a new policy area, child-support collection. Also, Morales's staff members spent much time on redistricting issues, as a result of numerous lawsuits over the legislature's 1990s redistricting plans for the U.S. Congress and the Texas legislature (see chapter 4).

In 1998, Jim Mattox won the Democratic nomination for attorney general in a comeback attempt but lost the general election to John Cornyn, the first Republican so elected. Cornyn served on the Texas Supreme Court from 1990 to 1998. In 1999, Attorney General Cornyn attacked the tobacco settlement that Morales had agreed to, trying to undo attorney fee provisions and trying to get courts to investigate the state's attorneys, including Morales. He also issued an opinion rescinding Morales's *Hopwood* opinion. In 2002, the Texas Watch Foundation—a consumer public-interest group—published an analysis showing that Cornyn used the Deceptive Trade Practices Act far less than his predecessors.[47] Cornyn served only one term, choosing in 2002 to run for the U.S. Senate. Republican Greg Abbott, also a former Texas Supreme Court Justice, won the office of attorney general in 2002, then won reelection in 2006. Both Cornyn and Abbott elevated open records requirements as a public-policy issue.

Comptroller of Public Accounts

The **comptroller of public accounts** is the state's tax collector. The comptroller has offices across the state, and even in other states, to ensure that Texas collects what is due it. As of 1996, with the constitutional amendment abolishing the office of state treasurer, the comptroller is also the state's money manager. What makes the comptroller a powerful statewide official, though, is that he or she is responsible for

comptroller of public accounts
The elected official who is the state's tax collector.

160 CHAPTER 5 The Governor and Executive Branch

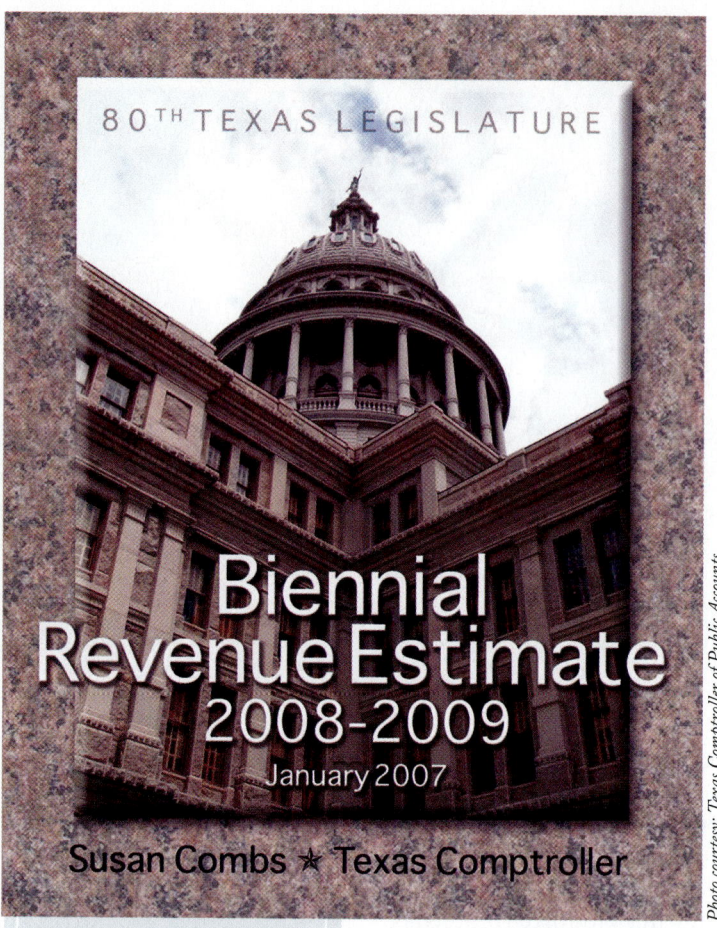

How much money will the state have to spend? The Comptroller of Public Accounts must provide legislators a revenue estimate before each regular session.

estimating the amount of revenue that the state will have coming in, and the legislature may not appropriate more than that amount (except by a four-fifths vote). Thus, the comptroller becomes a significant legislative player.

The revenue-forecasting function requires the comptroller to have a sophisticated economic-analysis capability. The agency includes a large economic and policy research staff, which has become one of the state's most respected economic forecasting centers. Still, part of the comptroller's power in the legislative process is that the forecasts are built on assumptions, and those assumptions can be changed. For instance, the comptroller can increase or decrease the projected state revenues by increasing or decreasing the assumed price of a barrel of oil. Thus, if the comptroller wants to influence the amount of money available to the legislature, the revenue estimating process can accommodate those tactics.

Longtime Comptroller Bob Bullock (1975–1991) used the high-profile nature of the office to boost his standing with voters and then served as lieutenant governor (1991–1999). His comptroller's staff, known as "Bullock's Raiders," was aggressive in collecting overdue taxes from delinquent business taxpayers. Bullock was also an important voice in modernizing the tax laws in the 1980s.

John Sharp served as comptroller from 1991 to 1999, after service as state representative, state senator, and railroad commissioner. Governor Richards and the legislature turned to him for assistance with a wide range of activities, demonstrating the scope, flexibility, and influence of this statewide elected office. Much of Sharp's energy was focused on performance evaluations of state agencies. His office was also given the task of starting up the state lottery, which was later reorganized into the new Lottery Commission.

In 1998, Republican Carole Keeton Rylander narrowly defeated Democrat Paul Hobby (son of former Lieutenant Governor Bill Hobby) to become the first Republican comptroller. She rose from local politics, having served on the Austin school board and as mayor of Austin. She lost a race for Congress, was appointed to the Insurance Board, then won a seat on the Railroad Commission. As comptroller, she emphasized the school district audits that the office was responsible for. In 2002, she easily won reelection as comptroller. After her reelection, she remarried and changed her name to Strayhorn. In 2006, she ran unsuccessfully for governor. In 2007, she was succeeded by fellow Republican Susan Combs, who had served as a state representative, then for eight years as agriculture commissioner.

Land Commissioner

land commissioner
The elected official responsible for managing and leasing the state's property, including oil, gas, and mineral interests.

The **land commissioner** is more significant in Texas than in most states because the state owns so much land. The Republic of Texas validated all Spanish and Mexican land grants, recognized existing property rights, established the General Land Office, and commissioned surveys of the state.[48] The 1845 terms of annexation to the United States gave to the state "all the vacant and unappropriated lands lying within its limits."[49] The land commissioner is responsible for managing and leasing the property.

As oil was discovered in the early twentieth century, the land commissioner enjoyed newfound importance—oil revenues from state-owned land pumped up funds for schools and universities, to which the land-generated revenues are constitutionally committed. Also, the land commissioner was given responsibility for the new Veterans Land Program in 1946, a program that loans money to veterans for the purpose of buying a homestead. Now the program includes loans for houses as well as land.

Land Commissioner Jerry Patterson manages state-owned lands, has a voice in natural resource policymaking, and runs loan programs for veterans to buy land and homes.

Recent land commissioners have enjoyed long tenures. Democrat Bob Armstrong served from 1971 to 1983. He later served on the Parks and Wildlife Commission, Governor Richards appointed him as her energy adviser, and President Clinton appointed him as assistant U.S. secretary of the interior. Garry Mauro, former executive director of the Texas Democratic Party, served as land commissioner from 1983 to 1999. Mauro expanded the scope of the office by focusing on natural gas resources. He promoted the use of natural gas, winning passage of a new state law requiring state and local vehicle fleets to purchase vehicles that can use multiple fuels, including natural gas. Mauro also aggressively turned the land-management responsibilities of his office into environmental protection programs, such as beach cleanups, corporate recycling programs, and coastal zone management. In 1998, Mauro won the Democratic nomination for governor but lost the general election to Governor George W. Bush.

In 1999, Mauro was succeeded by David Dewhurst, the first Republican to win the office. Dewhurst had served in the U.S. Air Force, Central Intelligence Agency, and State Department, then founded a Houston energy and investments company. He had not previously held an elective office. Dewhurst served as head of Governor Perry's Task Force on Homeland Security in 2001–2002 and was instrumental as a member of the Legislative Redistricting Board that redrew state legislative district lines in 2001. Dewhurst served only one term, choosing to run for lieutenant governor in 2002. He was replaced as land commissioner by fellow Republican Jerry Patterson, who won the office in 2002. Patterson had earlier been a state senator and in 1998 had lost to Dewhurst in the Republican primary for land commissioner. Patterson won reelection in 2006. As land commissioner, he has pursued a major wind-energy project off the coast of Texas, on state-owned lands. In 2007 and 2008, he generated controversy by his proposals to sell the state's 9,000-acre Christmas Mountain land in the Big Bend area.

Agriculture Commissioner

The **agriculture commissioner** is the only one of the statewide elected officials whose job was created by the legislature instead of by the constitution. The job of the commissioner is to promote and regulate agricultural interests. The Texas Department of Agriculture administers promotion campaigns for Texas commodities and encourages use of Texas products through labeling them Texas made. Traditional regulatory programs include monitoring the accuracy of weights and measures, regulating the safety of grain warehouses, and ensuring compliance with pest-control regulations and egg- and seed-labeling requirements.

agriculture commissioner
The elected state official in charge of regulating and promoting agriculture.

In 1982, Jim Hightower defeated the incumbent commissioner in the Democratic primary and won the general election. Hightower had been head of an agricultural-policy think tank in Washington, then had been editor of the *Texas Observer*, putting a populist voice to its coverage. Hightower was reelected in 1986, leading the Democratic ticket with more votes than any candidate received for any office. As agriculture commissioner, Hightower initiated and won legislative approval for new programs such as tighter regulation of pesticide use, a right-to-know law for farmworkers who use pesticides, organic food certification, revitalization of farmers' markets, and national promotion of Texas foods. He was narrowly defeated by Rick Perry in the general election in 1990, the first time that a Democrat other than governor had lost an executive office to a Republican; Hightower has gone on to become a nationally known speaker, radio show host, and author of several books on politics.

Perry, a Democratic state representative who had led an effort to limit Hightower's powers and his pesticide regulatory authority, switched to the Republican Party to run against Hightower. Perry deemphasized Hightower's new programs and reemphasized the traditional role of the department. He won reelection easily in 1994. In 1995, Perry and the Farm Bureau urged the legislature to repeal the farmworker right-to-know law, but they failed.

When Perry was elected lieutenant governor in 1998, he was succeeded as agriculture commissioner by Republican Susan Combs, a lawyer-rancher who served in the Texas House from 1993 through 1996 from Austin. She co-authored the state's private property rights act. Combs then served as U.S. Senator Kay Bailey Hutchison's state director. She was the first woman to hold the post of agriculture commissioner. Combs sought and won reelection in 2002. In 2006, she won election as state comptroller. Republican state Senator Todd Staples (R–Palestine) won election as agriculture commissioner, taking office in January 2007.

Railroad Commissioners

The three railroad commissioners are elected in statewide elections. Whereas other state officials are elected to four-year terms, railroad commissioners are elected to six-year **staggered terms,** where one seat is up for election every two years. The **Railroad Commission** was the highest achievement of populists in the 1890s. Populists demanded regulation of railroads, and they insisted that the people have direct control over those regulators by electing them. Over the years, other regulatory duties have been added to the agency's responsibilities.

In the early twentieth century, oil companies wanted to produce, transport, refine, and sell oil and gas but were stymied by another populist victory, a state law forbidding monopoly market concentration.[50] The compromise that was finally reached allowed them an integrated business operation, with the trade-off of having regulation of the pipeline transportation of the oil and gas. Because the Railroad Commission already regulated a form of transportation, it was given authority over the oil and gas industry. Regulation of trucking and mining came later. Today, the federal government has usurped much of the agency's regulatory responsibilities for railroads and trucking, leaving oil and gas regulation as its primary function—and today, it is the oil and gas industry that has the most influence at the agency. In the 1960s, longtime Commissioner Ben Ramsey stated flatly that the Railroad Commission was "industry's representative in state government," and Commissioner Jon Newton stated in the 1970s that the commission was captive of the oil and gas industry.[51]

After the 1994 elections, for the first time in Texas history, all three railroad commissioners were Republicans, and that has remained the case since then. In 2008, the commission included Michael Williams, Elizabeth Ames Jones, and Victor Carrillo. Williams, who served President George Bush as assistant secretary of education for civil rights and had served as general counsel to the Texas Republican Party, is the first

staggered terms
Terms of office for members of boards and commissions that begin and end at different times, so that a governor is not usually able to gain control of a majority of the body for a long time.

Railroad Commission
A full-time, three-member paid commission elected by the people to regulate oil and gas and some transportation entities.

African American to serve as railroad commissioner. Governor George W. Bush appointed him in 1998, and with his election to an unexpired term in 2000, he is the first African American elected to statewide executive office in Texas. In 2002, he won election to a full six-year term and won reelection in 2008 (for 2009–2014). In 2003, Governor Perry appointed Victor Carrillo to fill a vacancy on the commission. Carrillo won a full term in 2004 (for 2005–2010). In early 2005, Governor Perry filled another vacancy by appointing State Representative Elizabeth Ames Jones (R–San Antonio) to the position. In 2006, she won election to a new six-year term (for 2007–2012).

State Board of Education

The **State Board of Education** (SBOE) is an excellent example of the fragmentation of institutions and authority in Texas state government. Public education is governed by the elected fifteen-member SBOE, a commissioner of education appointed by the governor, a large bureaucracy called the **Texas Education Agency** (TEA), and local and regional entities. Since the 1990s, those entities have sometimes warred with each other, with the legislature, and with interest groups.

Although the state has always had a presence in education, the nature of state leadership has evolved.[52] Beginning in 1866, Texas had a superintendent of public instruction, who was usually elected statewide. There was also an advisory Board of Education. Superintendent Annie Webb Blanton (1919–1923) was the first woman elected to statewide office in Texas. In 1949, the Board of Education was enlarged and made an elected board, with the new commissioner of education to be appointed by the board, with Senate confirmation. As a part of Governor White's education reforms developed by the Perot Commission in the early 1980s, the board was reduced in size from twenty-seven to fifteen members. It was also changed to an appointed board, because the elected board members were viewed as hostile to the reforms. The legislature (and later the voters) required, though, that the board revert to an elected board (from districts) once the reforms were in place. The elected board recommended to the governor a person for appointment as commissioner of education. In 1995, the governor was given sole authority to appoint the commissioner, with Senate confirmation.

The SBOE became a lightning rod for public attention in the 1990s as elections to the board became a battleground between religious right and traditional public education forces. Those differences carried over into policy battles about curriculum standards, sex education, phonics, public vouchers for private school education, creationism and intelligent design theories, and textbook content. The controversy was heightened in the 1990s when San Antonio millionaire businessman James Leininger helped fund and elect six religious right candidates to the board. In 1997, Governor Bush, the board chair, and the education commissioner supported adoption of new curriculum standards. Religious conservatives said that the new curriculum would lead to a federal takeover of Texas public schools and opposed the effort, but the board approved the new standards.

In 2000, Republicans won more seats, but religious conservatives lost influence, as one Leininger-supported member went to Iowa to campaign against Bush in Iowa's presidential caucuses; Bush's allies then defeated the incumbent in the Republican primary. The SBOE battles illustrate the uneasy ideological tensions in the Republican Party. Governor Bush and his allies, though conservatives, battled throughout his governorship and his presidential campaign to keep the religious conservatives in check. Governor Perry's new chair was defeated in the 2002 Republican primary by a Republican supported by the religious conservative faction. In 2002, with newly redistricted lines, Republicans increased their number on the board to ten, which they have since retained. In recent years, the SBOE, its supporters, and its critics have battled over evolution, religion, and health and sexuality issues in textbooks.

State Board of Education
The fifteen-member elected body that sets some education policy for the state and has limited authority to oversee the Texas Education Agency and local school districts.

Texas Education Agency
The state agency that oversees local school districts and disburses state funds to districts.

Modern Texas Bureaucracy

The purpose of government bureaucracy is implementation—to put into effect, to *execute* legislative policy, hence the term *executive* branch. Legislatures are chiefly responsible for creating public policies (policy making). Bureaucracies are supposed to translate legislative intent into actual, working public policy—that is, to implement the wishes of the legislature. Agencies do so by rule making (adopting standards and processes by which they operate and make decisions), regulation of private activities, and provision of services and products. However, as they attempt to understand and to implement legislative intent, agency officials often must fill out the details that are missing in legislation and thus sometimes also *make* policy. Texas's rule-making process, spelled out in the **Administrative Procedures Act,** requires agency officials to seek written public comments, and agencies sometimes have public hearings before adopting rules and regulations.

Administrative Procedures Act
A statute containing Texas's rule-making process.

Legislatures create executive agencies to respond to particular problems. How they organize the agencies is determined by the nature of the problem, the personalities and political dynamics at work, and the organizational structure that is in vogue at the time. The ongoing question of how much power the governor should have over executive agencies is often entwined with questions of reorganizing the executive branch. Though the Texas governor is chief executive, he or she has little direct authority over executive agencies and may not reorganize them. Texas executive agencies are organized in a host of ways, but there are two basic patterns. (To learn more about the organizational schemes, see Figure 5.1.)

First are the agencies headed by one person (the head position is called different things in different agencies). Eight agency heads are appointed by the governor, such as the secretary of state. Five agencies have directors elected by the people, as noted earlier (Office of the Attorney General, Office of the Comptroller of Public Accounts, General Land Office, Texas Department of Agriculture, and Railroad Commission). Those statewide elected officials are significant because of their prominent role in policy making and in public-opinion leadership. Though the governor appoints few directors of state agencies (to learn more about gubernatorial appointments, see Table 5.3), the number has grown in recent years. A person appointed directly by the governor is generally seen as more powerful than those appointed by boards or commissions, by virtue of access to the governor and of being part of the governor's political team. However, the distribution of elected versus appointed officials is not based on rational assumptions as much as it is on political power and personalities in power at the time the decisions are made.

Following the second pattern are agencies run by multimember boards or commissions—the two terms are used interchangeably. About one hundred agencies are run by a part-time, unpaid board or commission.[53] The members of most governing boards

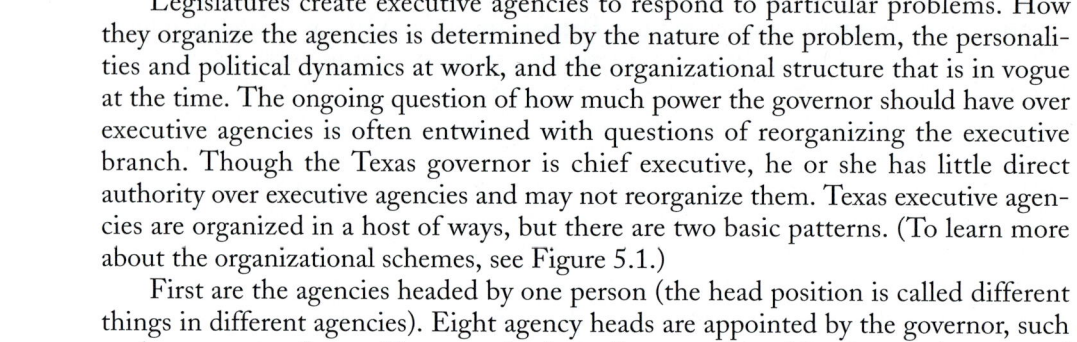

FIGURE 5.1 Texas State Agency Organizational Leadership Schemas State agencies have different leadership structures and different ways of being authorized. Two basic patterns are shown here.

The Texas Capitol. The "capitol complex" consists of all the state office buildings in the area around the capitol. In the distance is the campus of the University of Texas at Austin.

and commissions are appointed by the governor. In most cases, the board or commission hires a person to run the agency. The Texas Alcoholic Beverage Commission is an example of such an agency. The commission's members, appointed by the governor, make policy and hire an administrator.

Five agencies are run by a full-time, paid commission. These include the governor-appointed Public Utility Commission (PUC), Texas Commission on Environmental Quality (TCEQ), Texas Workforce Commission, the Board of Pardons and Paroles, and the elected Railroad Commission. Commission members usually hire an executive director to assist them in running the agency.

Secretary of State

The first appointment made by an incoming governor, and a key one, is the **Texas secretary of state.** This officer is the keeper of the state records: election data and filings, state laws and regulations, public notifications through the *Texas Register*, and corporate charters are managed by the secretary of state.

The secretary of state serves as the state's chief elections officer—registering voters, making sure that counties conduct the elections properly, and collecting and certifying election results. In this capacity, the secretary is one of the most important political officials inside state government. The secretary is a key liaison between the governor, political parties, and elected officials across the state.

Secretaries of state have a golden opportunity to create a political base. In fact, many secretaries run for elective office after serving the governor. After stints as secretary of state, Crawford Martin, John Hill, and Mark White ran successfully for attorney general, and Bob Bullock ran successfully for comptroller and lieutenant governor. Ann Richards's Secretary of State Ron Kirk ran successfully for mayor of Dallas, then won the Democratic nomination for U.S. Senate; President Obama appointed Kirk U.S. Trade Representative in 2009. George W. Bush's Secretary of State Tony Garza ran successfully for railroad commissioner. Later, Bush appointed Secretary of State Alberto Gonzales to the Texas Supreme Court; Gonzales won election to that seat in 2000 but resigned to become President Bush's chief counsel, then U.S. attorney general.

Rick Perry has had a series of secretaries of state, including Democratic State Representative Henry Cuellar, Republican State Representative Gwyn Shea, Geoffrey

Texas secretary of state
The state official appointed by the governor to be the keeper of the state's records, such as state laws, election data and filings, public notifications, and corporate charters.

Connor, Roger Williams, and Phil Wilson. Williams, a Weatherford businessman, is a longtime associate of George W. Bush and a key Republican fundraiser, and he is often mentioned as a possible candidate for elective office. In 2008, Perry appointed Esperanza "Hope" Andrade to be secretary of state.

Public Utility Commissioners

The **Public Utility Commission** (PUC) has jurisdiction over telephone and electric power companies, while the Railroad Commission retains authority over gas companies. The three members of the PUC are appointed to staggered six-year terms by the governor. The public utility commissioners have a role that is largely **quasi-judicial**. They have the authority to hold hearing and issue rulings. The agency was created in 1975 in a storm of public sentiment to limit rapidly rising utility rates. But the governor did not support utility regulation, and the early commissioners were generally perceived as sympathetic to utility companies.

Governor Perry appointed several members who served only briefly. Former investment banker and local prosecutor Barry Smitherman was appointed to the commission in 2004 and became chair in 2007. In 2008, Perry appointed Kenneth Anderson, Jr., and Donna Nelson as commissioners.

In 1995, the legislature redrafted the PUC's statute. Technological developments and congressional support for deregulation framed the debate. In 1995, the legislature passed a bill deregulating telecommunications, and in 1997 passed a bill deregulating public utilities. Under the 1997 bill, most monopoly electric utilities were split into transmission and distribution companies, power-generating companies, retail providers, and independent-system operators. One goal is to guarantee residential customers choice of providers (though the PUC must maintain a no-call list for customers who don't want telephone solicitation about electric service). The PUC still regulates transmission and distribution, but rates for power generating and retail are deregulated. The PUC also oversees some activities of ERCOT—the Electric Reliability Council of Texas.

Texas Commission on Environmental Quality

In 1991, the legislature combined many of the state's environmental programs into a new agency, the Texas Natural Resource Conservation Commission (TNRCC), and abolished the Air Control Board and the Water Commission. In 2002, TNRCC assumed a new name, the **Texas Commission on Environmental Quality** (TCEQ). Its three commissioners are appointed by the governor to staggered six-year terms. Larry Soward, who had served as executive director of the old Texas Water Commission, was appointed TCEQ commissioner in 2003. In early 2007, Governor Perry appointed to the commission Buddy Garcia, who had served as his aide and as deputy secretary of state. Later that year, he appointed Texas A&M engineering professor Bryan Shaw to the third position.

Commissioners have a quasi-judicial role in contested cases, but they have significant policy roles that make them the real powers in running the agency. Businesses that will be emitting pollutants into the air or water must seek permits from the commission and must comply with regulations to limit the amount of those emissions. Thus, the commission becomes a lightning rod for conflicts between environmental and neighborhood groups seeking to restrict activities that could pollute, and businesses seeking to keep costs down while using modern industrial techniques and expanding or beginning new operations supplying products to the marketplace. One such controversy was over several facilities that were emitting air pollutants but did not have to comply with the state's air quality law because of their "grandfathered" status. Those who wanted to end the grandfather status lost 1997 and 1999 battles with Governor Bush but won in 2001.

The legislature has considered scores of bills to scale back the environmental authority of the agency, and some of them were adopted. The 1995 "property rights" law requires state agencies to evaluate the costs of environmental regulation to property owners, and it could force the state to abandon regulations that might lower private-property values. The legislature also scaled back the public participation provisions that the agency must follow. A 1999 bill would have abolished contested case hearings but was passed in a modified version that keeps most contested case hearings and changes public-comment provisions. Another significant change in legislative policy is that the agency must now consider not just the environmental impacts of a specific business that is applying for a permit but also the cumulative impacts of concentrated facilities in an area.

Insurance Commissioner

Because of the need to know whether insurance companies have assets sufficient to pay their claims, and because out-of-state companies proved difficult to pursue if customers had complaints of fraud, Texas has long had a public official or public body to oversee or regulate the insurance industry. The legislature has periodically reorganized the state agency, sometimes having a multimember body of commissioners and sometimes a single commissioner. In 1993, the three-member State Board of Insurance was replaced by a single commissioner, appointed by the governor. The **insurance commissioner** runs the Department of Insurance and is one of the few single executive heads appointed directly by the governor, but the commissioner has a high level of independence because the governor could remove the commissioner only under extraordinary circumstances. The commissioner's job is to monitor the health of the insurance industry and, within new confines voted in by the legislature, to regulate insurance rates. In 2005, Governor Perry appointed Mike Geeslin as insurance commissioner. Geeslin, a former Perry budget and policy adviser, had been serving as deputy insurance commissioner.

insurance commissioner
The official appointed by the governor to direct the Department of Insurance and regulate the insurance industry.

In 1995, the legislature passed a bill regulating health maintenance organizations (HMOs). Insurance companies (the primary owners of HMOs) fought against the bill. When it passed, they persuaded Governor Bush to veto it. Bush then requested his insurance commissioner to write new rules governing HMOs. In 1997, the legislature passed a bill requiring prompt HMO payment of claims to doctors. By 2001, doctors were convinced that the law was not working and persuaded the legislature to pass a tougher law. Governor Perry vetoed it and then requested the commissioner to aggressively enforce the 1997 law.

Between 1997 and 2002, homeowner's insurance premiums increased by more than 100 percent, stoking a major battle over the role of the department. In 2003, the legislature authorized the insurance commissioner to force insurance companies to lower their rates on homeowners' insurance. However, two of the largest insurers in Texas, State Farm and Farmers, fought the commissioner's attempt to lower their rates 12 percent and 17.5 percent respectively. The companies insisted that their rates were fair and contested the commissioner's attempt to force lower rates in court. In December 2004, after extended negotiations, Farmers agreed to lower its future rates and agreed to a $117 million settlement with ratepayers. Ratepayers and policyholders, however, argued that they were due $1 billion and refused the settlement. They got a court to agree and throw out the settlement the commissioner had negotiated.[54]

Health and Human Services Commission

Health and human service programs are administered in Texas by numerous state agencies. Governor Richards proposed consolidating and merging these services into one agency, using the slogan "one person, one trip." Comptroller Sharp, in urging consolidation, wrote: "This fragmentation produces well-documented agency-wide problems such as a failure to maximize federal funds, inconsistency in rate-setting and contracting and a failure to coordinate client transportation services."[55] In 1991, the legislature partially agreed by creating the commissioner of health and human services. The commissioner did not run the agencies but was supposed to *oversee* the massive health and human services programs scattered across the agencies. The commissioner was appointed directly by the governor. In 1999, voters rejected a constitutional amendment that would have increased the tenure and powers of the commissioner and allowed the governor to fire him or her.

In 2003, the legislature completely reorganized the health and human services agencies to create a new system. The legislation merged twelve agencies into four new departments under the Health and Human Services Commission (HHSC), which is headed by an **executive commissioner of health and human services** appointed by the governor and confirmed by the Senate. In 2003, Governor Perry appointed Albert Hawkins, who had worked for the Legislative Budget Board and then served as Governor Bush's budget director; he then went to Washington to work with President Bush as secretary to the Cabinet. The HHSC is also given additional duties, such as centralizing eligibility requirement for several programs, including Medicaid, Temporary Assistance for Needy Families, and the Children's Health Insurance Program. In addition, HHSC is responsible for consolidating administrative services for all health and human services agencies. The four new departments, each headed by a commissioner who is selected by the executive commissioner with the governor's approval, are:

- Department of Family and Protective Services, which reconstitutes the Department of Protective and Regulatory Services.
- Department of Assistive and Rehabilitative Services, which assumes the powers and duties of the Texas Rehabilitation Commission, Commission for the Blind, Commission for the Deaf and Hard of Hearing, and Interagency Council on Early Childhood Intervention.
- Department of Aging and Disability Services (DADS), which consolidates mental retardation and state school programs of the Department of Mental Health and Mental Retardation (MHMR), community care and nursing home services programs of the Department of Human Services, and aging services programs of the Texas Department of Aging.
- Department of State Health Services, which takes over programs from the Texas Department of Health, the Texas Commission on Alcohol and Drug Abuse, and the Health Care Information Council. It also assumes the community and state hospital programs from MHMR.

By merging the agencies, the legislature hopes to improve service, enhance accountability, increase efficiencies, and reduce costs.

Public Counsels

In recent years, as conflicts grew over regulatory policies, public-interest groups charged that regulatory agencies had become **captured agencies.** They were seen as consistently making decisions favorable to business interests and not adequately protecting consumers. A concept that gained some acceptance is that of **public counsels** to serve as advocates for the public before governmental agencies. The legislature gave the governor power to appoint a public insurance counsel and a public utility counsel. These attorneys are heads of small agencies separate from the Department of Insurance and the Public Utility Commission. The counsels and their staffs examine rate-hike requests and other regulatory matters before the agencies. Then they go before the regulators to argue for their position, which is usually for rate reductions or for lower rate increases than the private companies have requested or the regulatory agency staff has recommended.

Boards and Commissions

Most state agencies are organized with a multimember policy-making body and a staff under the direction of the policy-making body. Some of these bodies are called

Ideas Into Action

Student Regents

Perhaps the most obvious and immediate interest that college students have in government is the governance of their own college or university. If you are a student at a state college or university, you are a part of the executive branch of state government, and the leaders of those institutions—presidents and boards of regents—are state executive officers. After decades of effort, student lobbyists finally persuaded the Texas legislature in 2005 to create seats on the state's university boards of regents for student representatives. Thus, if you are a student at a state college or university now, you have representation on the governing board. The new student regents are nonvoting members of the boards of regents. Although other regents serve six-year terms of office, students serve a one-year term.

After Governor Perry signed the Texas measure into law in 2005, each state university system or stand-alone university began the process of recruiting interested students. Candidates are screened by student government organizations, which submit names to the chancellor. The chancellor forwards his or her top choices to the governor. The governor then appoints the student regents. In early 2006, Governor Perry named the first student regents, and he has named student regents each year since then.

As a result of the legislation, students whose college or university is in the University of Texas System, Texas A&M System, Texas State University System, University of Houston System, and Texas Tech System have one student regent on the board, and students at universities that are not part of a university system—Texas Southern University, University of North Texas, Texas Woman's University, Stephen F. Austin University, and Midwestern State University—each have a student on their board of regents.

- Find out whether your institution has a student representative on the board of regents or board of trustees; if so, ask the student trustee how he or she got the position.
- What kinds of student groups engage in policy discussions with the administration or with regents? Find a group concerned with issues that appeal to you and engage with it to influence the outcome of debates on campus.
- Find out when the next regent selection process takes place. Are there student organizations involved in recruiting interested students?
- Application materials for some student regent positions may be accessed on the Internet. For example, see the following:

University of Texas System schools, www.utsystem.edu/aca/files/StudentRegent-Application-form.pdf

University of Houston System schools, www.uhv.edu/pdf/Student_Regent_App.pdf

Texas State University System schools, www.tsus.edu/regents/Student%20Regent%20Application%202007.pdf

---

boards, some are called commissions, and a very few are called councils or authorities. Collectively, these bodies are often referred to as the "board and commission" system of government. Some boards or commissions govern more than one agency. For instance, the ten boards of trustees of the state's colleges and universities run thirty-seven general academic institutions, nine medical schools, and nine major services.

Boards and commissions are used for large and small agencies. The most common sizes of the boards or commissions are three or nine members, though a few have more members. A 1999 constitutional amendment standardizes most boards at three, five, seven, or nine members. A board or commission may have no staff, a handful of staff members, or a large bureaucracy. The Board of Criminal Justice, for instance, hires a full-time, well-paid, and powerful executive director, who oversees a staff of more than 40,000.

In almost all cases, members of these policy-making bodies are appointed by the governor, with Senate confirmation. (A few have statutorily designated membership from agency heads or elected officials.) These appointments to boards and commissions constitute the bulk of the governor's appointments. However, for most boards, the terms of members are six years, and the terms are staggered, so a governor is not usually able to gain control of a majority of a board until late in his or her term of office. Even then, there is no assurance that members will do as the governor wishes, because the governor may not fire the members. The governor may request the removal of an official that he or she appointed, but it requires approval of two-thirds of the Senate, and no such removal has ever occurred.

Other than the full-time, paid members of the PUC, TCEQ, Workforce Commission, Board of Pardons and Paroles, and Railroad Commission, the members of these boards and commissions are not paid. They are volunteer, part-time positions. Members' expenses are reimbursed when they travel to meetings. Most boards or commissions meet monthly or quarterly. They may work through smaller committees of members, with additional meetings of those committees.

Making Agencies Accountable

Legislatures may delegate decision-making authority to executive agencies—a practice long recognized by courts. In creating agencies and programs, and in delegating authority to agencies, legislatures do not then wash their hands of responsibility for those programs. Rather, they have a duty to oversee what they have created and delegated. Legislative oversight of the bureaucracy includes review of expenditures, review of rules and regulations, performance reviews, audits, sunset review (in which the continuing need for an agency is evaluated), review of staff sizes and functions, and response to constituent complaints about agencies. Although Texas has not done so, some states have adopted legislative vetoes of administrative rules and regulations (though several state courts have thrown them out as unconstitutional violations of separation of powers).[56]

The Sunset Process

sunset law
A law that sets a date for a program or regulation to expire unless reauthorized by the legislature.

good government
A term used for policies that open up agencies to public participation and scrutiny and that minimize conflicts of interest.

A **sunset law** establishes a date for programs or regulations to expire (the *sun* will *set* on them) unless the legislature renews them. The sunset concept is used in Texas to force a review of executive agencies and programs. It was first adopted in Colorado in 1976 and is now in use in about two-thirds of the states.[57] The Texas Sunset Act was adopted in 1977. While the motivation for the movement was to review and abolish some agencies, ironically the first step was to create a new agency—the Sunset Advisory Commission. It consists of five state senators, five state representatives, one public member appointed by the lieutenant governor, and one public member appointed by the House Speaker. Under the Texas system, each state agency is given a twelve-year life span. If the commission recommends continuation of an agency, it drafts legislation, always with changes in the structure or procedures of the agency.

In addition to agency-specific recommendations, the first commission adopted a set of across-the-board **good government** recommendations for all agencies to open themselves up to public participation and scrutiny and to minimize conflicts of interest. Early Sunset Advisory Commission analyses clearly reflect that the staff, and perhaps commission members, believed that agencies had been captured by private interests. The first two commissions, appointed in 1977 and 1979, focused on breaking the hold that trade associations had over professional licensing agencies and reestablishing an arms-length relationship between the regulated and the regulators. The commission recommended imposing controls on agencies that for years had escaped serious legislative oversight. Commission actions to impose these controls were fiercely opposed by lobby groups and trade associations surrounding the agencies.[58]

Sunset has become a target for those wary of the repeated battles that ensue as interest groups, agencies, and

> **Thinking Nationally**
> **Legislative Review of Agencies**
>
> Several states allow the legislature a formal role in reviewing executive agency rules and regulations—and vetoing rules and regulations that they disapprove of. Congress, too, has mechanisms for blocking executive agency actions. Courts have sometimes ruled against specific manifestations of such "legislative vetoes."
>
> - In a democratic system, should elected legislators have the final say on rules and regulations that citizens must follow? Why or why not?
> - What are the separation of power implications if the Texas legislature were to have unfettered power to block agency actions?

their defenders and detractors clash over how programs will be organized and implemented. Because of those intense battles, in 1993 Governor Richards, Lieutenant Governor Bullock, and Speaker Laney supported repeal of sunset, but the effort died. In 2007, the commission reviewed twenty agencies, recommending that thirteen be continued, one abolished, two abolished and have their functions transferred, and four have no sunset date.[59] By the end of the legislative session, the legislature had allowed the Texas Historical Representation Advisory Committee to expire and had abolished the Structural Pest Control Board and transferred its functions to the Texas Department of Agriculture. The Office of State–Federal Relations was continued for only two years, meaning that the 2009 legislature will battle over it again.[60]

Staff Size and Pay

Since World War II, state and local governments—not the national government—have grown considerably in size. Across the nation, state government employment grew from 1.5 million in 1960 to 4.3 million full-time equivalent workers by 2006.[61] A favorite method of legislative review and control of agencies is to monitor and then to increase or reduce staff size. Legislators and governors often vow to cut the number of state employees as a way of reducing the budget and as a way of controlling bureaucracy. Governor Clements vowed to cut 25 percent of the state workforce; when he left office, it was larger than when he took office. More recently, the legislature has adopted caps on numbers of employees that an agency may employ. One result of this policy is increased outsourcing of services; the state is currently contracting with thousands of private entities.

Numbers of employees are usually measured in units known as **full-time equivalent (FTE)** workers. That is, if you have five full-time employees and two half-time employees, then you have six FTEs. In 2005, the number of FTE state workers in Texas was approximately 274,352.[62] Another measurement is the number of government employees per person in the state. In 2005, the number of FTE state workers per 10,000 population in Texas was 120. Smaller states generally have larger numbers. Of course, these numbers can be skewed by more heavy reliance on private contractors.

The legislature adopts pay scales, titled the Classification Salary Schedule and the Exempt Salary Schedule, as a part of the appropriations bills. The bottom of the salary schedule for fiscal year 2008–2009 is $16,176, while the top is $203,935. The top earners are physicians, highest-level investment managers and actuaries, and the deputy comptroller. Some top officials, however, are also allowed to accept private pay supplements. While such a policy raises questions of conflicts of interest, state leaders have decided that they will not get qualified people for some positions without extremely high pay levels, and they do not want to be on record as approving those pay levels, so they authorize officials to raise private money as a pay supplement. Typically, college football coaches, physicians at state hospitals and medical facilities, university chancellors, university presidents, some professors in endowed chairs, and the heads and investment officers of pension funds get supplements from private funds, making them the highest-paid state employees.

full-time equivalent (FTE)
A unit of measurement for number of employees.

The Sunset Advisory Commission meets during the interim between legislative sessions to develop recommendations on abolishing, continuing, or changing state agencies up for sunset review. It submits a report of its findings at the beginning of a legislative session.

Regulating the Revolving Door

One practice that tends to reinforce close relations between private interests and public regulators, and thus to influence the direction of change, is the **revolving door,** the ongoing exchange of personnel between the two. Most often, employees of an agency quit and go to work for the industry that they had regulated; then they often turn around and lobby the agency for their new private employer. Sometimes it happens in reverse, or even in a revolving fashion, as in the 1970s, when a Texas Air Control Board official quit, worked for a company regulated by the agency, then returned to the agency as its executive director. Industry and many agency officials argue that such exchanges help to ensure that regulators know the industry they are regulating. Critics charge it is a key method that private groups use to capture agencies: employees hoping to get better-paying jobs with the industry will be tempted to make decisions for personal or industry benefit, not for public benefit. Also, businesses have ready access to decision makers if their lobbyists are former agency officials.

The revolving door periodically becomes a public issue, particularly when an explicit decision benefiting a private interest can be tied to the role of one individual, first as a regulator, then as a representative of private industry. Governor Richards and numerous state officials proposed to "lock" the revolving door at most agencies, as it was already locked at the PUC, by prohibiting officials from working for a regulated industry for a period after leaving the agency. The legislature extended the revolving door lock to TCEQ and the Department of Insurance. Then the legislature applied a limited revolving door restriction to all regulatory agencies. The general revolving door statute applies only to officers and employees with exempt or high-end pay classifications.[63]

revolving door
An exchange of personnel between private interests and public regulators.

REGULATING THE RELATIONSHIP BETWEEN AGENCIES AND PRIVATE INTERESTS

Executive agencies have the primary role of implementing decisions made by the legislature. However, they also play key policy-making roles, and their freedom to interpret legislative intent makes them policy powerhouses. In the 1950s, political scientist Marver Bernstein described the evolution of agencies, from their creation in an atmosphere of public outrage at perceived abuses at the hands of private industry to their original role as independent watchdogs over the industry, to an unintended role as an agency captured by the private interests, consistently making decisions favorable to those interests. This final stage "is marked by the commission's surrender to the regulated. Politically isolated, lacking a firm basis of public support, lethargic in attitude and approach, bowed down by precedent and backlogs, unsupported in its demands for more staff and money, the commission finally becomes a captive of the regulated groups."[64]

The Texas Railroad Commission fits Bernstein's model. Born as the fruit of populists' anger at railroad company rates and practices, the commission at first responded to the public's demand for lower rates. By the time the agency's largest role was to regulate the oil and gas industry, it was so fully captured by that industry that it ran an ad (sponsored by two industry associations) claiming, "Since 1891 the Texas Railroad Commission has served the oil industry."[65] The PUC has had a history similar to that of the Railroad Commission. Attempts at creating a new state agency had stalled for years. In the 1970s, the populace was stirred up over high utility rates and the appearance of favoritism to utility companies by government institutions. This popular participation, triggered by economic crisis, brought about political change and the creation of the PUC. However, key state leaders still opposed an adversarial regulatory relationship with the industry, governors appointed commissioners sympathetic to the industry, and the agency quickly became captured by the industry.

A recent example of an agency that has gained public attention for its closeness to the industry it regulates is the Texas Residential Construction Commission (TRCC). In 2003, with the support of the Texas Association of Builders, the legislature passed a "lemon law" for home building and created the TRCC to resolve complaints. The new law sets building and performance standards detailing how a home must perform upon its completion. Even before the ink was dry on the statute, critics blasted the agency and the law, claiming that the nature of the agency made it impossible to be a neutral arbiter, that it served to block consumers from real relief, and that the legislative process that led to its creation and the appointments of the commissioners were grossly tainted by the undue influence of campaign contributions. In 2007, the legislature strengthened the agency's powers. Critics still argued, though, that the legislature had protected builders and stymied consumers.[66] In 2008, the sunset commission staff members recommended abolishing TRCC.

The iron triangle is a model that includes the role that agencies play in the policy process. The closeness of private interests in Texas to legislators (through lobbying and campaign contributions) and to executive agencies (through influence on gubernatorial appointments and through the revolving door) lends strength to the iron-triangle model. If one follows the proposed rules and regulations as first published by agencies in the *Texas Register*, the written comments received, and the revisions and final rules, it appears that in many cases the agencies merely go through the motions of including the public, but the decisions have already been made or are made in consultation with key private interests, out of the public eye. Indeed, that is what a Texas court ruled in 1999 in a case invalidating some rules of the TNRCC.[67]

Toward Reform: Gubernatorial and Executive Power

The 1990s was a decade of extensive executive branch reorganization in Texas. Since then, agency structures have generally been left alone. Associated with the reorganization were efforts to allow governors to appoint some state agency heads; a few of those changes were made, and again that reform effort has not continued. Governor Perry's expanded use of executive orders—and the swirling opposition to his 2005 education order and 2007 HPV order—may well stir efforts to explicitly limit the reach of gubernatorial executive orders.

A recent and ongoing reform effort is over the issue of gubernatorial vetoes that are issued late in a legislative session or after the legislature has adjourned. Especially with the large number of vetoes that Governor Perry has signed in his long tenure, many legislators have begun moving to expand their opportunities to override those vetoes. The constitutions of 1845, 1861, 1866, and 1869 did not allow post-adjournment vetoes, but the current constitution does. In 2007, Representative Gary Elkins introduced HJR 59 proposing a state constitutional amendment for a legislative session to override governor's vetoes that are issued at the end of or after a regular session. The resolution was approved by the House by the requisite two-thirds vote but was not acted on in Senate committee. A version of it will likely be debated again in 2009.

WHAT SHOULD I HAVE LEARNED?

Texas governors are weak, compared with other governors, and they must share political power with other executive leaders (the plural executive), with the legislature, and with an array of state agency leaders who may not be appointed by or controlled by the governor. In this chapter, we have examined the following questions:

■ **What are the roots of the executive branch in Texas?**

The powers held by Texas governors and other executive officials fluctuated considerably with changes of constitutions in the nineteenth century. This history has influenced the array of elected and appointed executive officials, the terms of office for the governorship, and the governor's salary.

- **What are the constitutional roles of the governor?**

  The constitution and the legislature have created gubernatorial roles, including chief of state, chief executive officer, commander in chief, chief budget officer, and more informal roles in law enforcement and in legislative politics. Some constitutional powers are significant, though most are weak.

- **What powers does the Texas governor have?**

  Texas governors have always been weaker than governors in other states. Governors may be able to amass and exercise more strength, though, in the political arena, where appearance, charisma, and bluff may count more than constitutional reality. Texas gubernatorial power, however, has increased over the past two decades. The governor appoints more agency heads today than ever before.

- **How does the governor act as a policy maker and political leader?**

  The political and policy leadership that a governor is able to provide flows from the governor's skills, previous experience, and similarity in party, philosophy, and ideology with other decision makers. At the base of that leadership is electoral skill. Texas's governors resort to public-opinion leadership to increase their power with other office holders. Still, to be successful, a governor must succeed in pushing a program through the legislature and in killing unwanted legislative measures. To do so, a governor must use a grab bag of tools and must develop good personal or working relationships with key legislators.

- **What is the plural executive in Texas?**

  Texas elects nine statewide officials—more than most states. These include governor, lieutenant governor, attorney general, comptroller of public accounts, land commissioner, agriculture commissioner, and three railroad commissioners, as well as fifteen education board members elected from districts. There are frequent clashes between governors and other executive officials.

- **How is the Texas bureaucracy organized and how does it operate?**

  Texas executive agencies are organized in two basic patterns: agencies headed by one person and agencies run by a board or commission. The distribution of elected officials, appointed officials, and boards and commissions is not based on rational assumptions as much as it is on political power and personalities in power at the time the decisions are made.

- **How do we make agencies accountable?**

  Legislatures have a duty of legislative oversight of executive agencies and programs. Oversight tools include review of expenditures, review of rules and regulations, performance reviews, audits, sunset review, and review of staff sizes and functions.

- **What initiatives are being considered to reform gubernatorial and executive power?**

  Texas recently underwent a series of agency reorganizations and expansion of gubernatorial appointment powers. A current reform being debated in the legislature is a proposal to slow gubernatorial vetoes by creating legislative sessions to consider override of post-session vetoes.

Key Terms

Administrative Procedures Act, p. 164
agriculture commissioner, p. 161
attorney general, p. 158
captured agency, p. 168
chief budget officer, p. 146
chief executive officer, p. 146
chief of state, p. 146
clemency, p. 146
commander in chief, p. 146
comptroller of public accounts, p. 159
executive commissioner of health and human services, p. 168
full-time equivalent (FTE), p. 171
good government, p. 170
governor's message, p. 146
insurance commissioner, p. 167
land commissioner, p. 160
overrepresentation and underrepresentation, p. 151
plural executive, p. 140
public counsels, p. 168
Public Utility Commission, p. 166
quasi-judicial, p. 166
Railroad Commission, p. 162
revolving door, p. 172
senatorial courtesy, p. 150
staggered terms, p. 162
State Board of Education, p. 163
succession, p. 145
sunset law, p. 170
Texas Commission on Environmental Quality, p. 166
Texas Education Agency, p. 163
Texas secretary of state, p. 165
veto, p. 146

Researching the Governor and the Bureaucracy

In the Library

Beyle, Thad, ed. *Governors and Hard Times*. Washington, DC: CQ Press, 1992.

Comptroller of Public Accounts. *Challenging the Status Quo: Toward Smaller, Smarter Government*, 1999.

Duncan, Marilyn, and Shirley Beckwith. *Guide to Texas State Agencies*, 11th ed. Austin: LBJ School of Public Affairs, 2001.

Forsythe, Dall W., ed. *Quicker, Better, Cheaper? Managing Performance in American Government*. Albany, NY: Rockefeller Institute Press, 2001.

Gantt, Fred, Jr. *The Chief Executive in Texas: A Study in Gubernatorial Leadership*. Austin: University of Texas Press, 1964.

Hendrickson, Kenneth, Jr. *The Chief Executives of Texas: From Stephen F. Austin to John B. Connally Jr*. College Station: Texas A&M Press, 1995.

House Research Organization. "Fact or Faction: The SBOE's Role in Textbook Adoption," *Focus Report*, no. 77-17 (February 22, 2002).

———. "Health and Human Services Reorganization: Changes to the Delivery of Mental Health Services," *Focus Report*, no. 78-10 (November 3, 2004).

Lauderdale, Michael. *Reinventing Texas Government*. Austin: University of Texas Press, 1999.

Light, Paul C. *Sustaining Innovation: Creating Nonprofit and Government Organizations That Innovate Naturally*. San Francisco: Jossey-Bass, 1998.

McNeely, Dave, and Jim Henderson. *Bob Bullock: God Bless Texas*. Austin: University of Texas Press, 2008.

Prindle, David. *Petroleum Politics and the Texas Railroad Commission*. Austin: University of Texas Press, 1981.

Sunset Advisory Commission. *Guide to the Texas Sunset Process*, January 2008.

On the Web

Texas governor, **www.governor.state.tx.us**
This portal opens to the Texas governor's office and the programs associated with the governor.

National Governor's Association, **www.nga.org**
All fifty governors are members of this association, which provides services to the governors, news about governor's initiatives, and a forum for the governors to gather and share information and experiences.

Texas Records and Information Locator (TRAIL), **www.tsl.state.tx.us/apps/lrs/agencies/**
The Texas State Library and Archives maintains this Web site with links to all Texas executive agencies.

Texas Sunset Advisory Commission, **www.sunset.state.tx.us**
The commission analyzes state agencies and recommends to the legislature reform of agency structure and programs.

Gubernatorial Power, **www.unc.edu/~beyle/gubnewpwr.html**
Prof. Thad Beyle's comparisons of the 50 governors' powers.

6 The Judicial Branch

At 9:30 p.m. on September 25, 2007, the State of Texas executed Michael Richard, who had been convicted of the 1986 rape and murder of Marguerite Dixon. His execution was not unusual—Texas leads the nation with more than 400 executions in the last thirty years—but the decision by the Texas Court of Criminal Appeals to let the execution proceed stirred a nationwide controversy.[1]

In early September 2007, the U.S. Supreme Court halted a planned execution and agreed to consider the legality of lethal injections. Then, on September 25, the Supreme Court accepted an appeal of another case on similar grounds. The legal community presumed that the two actions constituted a de facto moratorium on executions while the Supreme Court grappled with the issue.

Upon hearing the news of the Supreme Court's action, Michael Richard's attorneys immediately began preparing a request to stop his execution, which was planned for later that day. They had to first file with the highest Texas court—the

■ **The judiciary in Texas has changed a great deal in the last century.** At left, Justice of the Peace Roy Bean tries a horse thief on the front porch of his Pecos County saloon in 1900. At right, a sign in the Supreme Court of Texas building emphasizes the gravity of judicial proceedings.

Texas Court of Criminal Appeals—before they could go to the federal courts. When the attorneys tried to print out their appeal, their computer malfunctioned. As the clock was nearing the 5 p.m. closing time for the Texas Court of Criminal Appeals, they quickly called to explain their problem and request the court to stay open for twenty minutes until they could get their appeal printed off and rush the filing over.

The court's policy was that a specific judge was to be available on the day of a scheduled execution to receive any filings; Judge Cheryl Johnson had been assigned Richard's case. Several of the judges, including Johnson, were in the offices when the phone rang. The clerk who answered the phone went to Presiding Judge Sharon Keller to ask what to do about the request. Keller instructed the clerk to tell the appellate lawyers "we close at 5." She did not consult Judge Johnson or the other judges in the offices. Richard was executed.

Lawyers and legislators have been in a long-running battle over capital punishment policies, including provision of competent counsel for defendants, how long it takes for executions to be carried out, and the number of appeals and filings that defense attorneys make. Sharon Keller had been a Dallas prosecutor before being elected as a Republican to the Texas Court of Criminal Appeals in 1994. She had campaigned as a law-and-order candidate, and as a judge, she gained a reputation of siding consistently with prosecutors. Keller led the

WHAT SHOULD I KNOW ABOUT . . .
- the roots of the Texas judiciary?
- the structure of the Texas judiciary?
- judges and judicial selection?
- the judicial process in Texas?
- reform proposals related to the Texas judiciary?

> **TO LEARN MORE—**
> **—TO DO MORE**
> Legal actions can take years to be resolved. Go to a library or to the Internet to research what has happened with the Supreme Court's decision on lethal injection and with the wrongful death lawsuit and requests for disciplinary action regarding Judge Sharon Keller.

court to support policies speeding executions. Though the court has been all-Republican since she joined it, the Republican justices do not all side with her. One suggested that the bad publicity the court received after an earlier case in which Keller had rejected DNA evidence had turned the court into a "national laughingstock."

When the Richard execution—and the phone call—made the news, conservative bloggers and commentators praised Judge Keller, while civil rights activists angrily denounced what they saw as her callous disregard of due process. "This isn't a liberal or conservative matter—no matter what your opinion is on the death penalty, you've got to have due process," argued Jim Harrington, head of the Texas Civil Rights Project.[2] Richard's family filed a wrongful death suit against Keller. The National Association of Criminal Defense Lawyers, hundreds of Texas lawyers (including former presidents of the state bar), and Texas State Representatives Lon Burnam and Harold Dutton filed complaints with the State Commission on Judicial Conduct, asking it to take disciplinary action against Judge Keller, arguing that she had violated Richard's constitutional rights and damaged the reputation of the judiciary. Some newspapers editorialized against her decision and noted that other states had halted executions to await the U.S. Supreme Court's decision on lethal injections.

In the wake of the controversy, the Texas Court of Criminal Appeals stopped the next scheduled execution, to await the U.S. Supreme Court's decision on the issue of lethal injection. It also implemented an e-mail filing system for emergency pleadings, with any such e-mails to be routed to all judges.

Under what circumstances should a judge be disciplined? Presiding Judge Sharon Keller of the Texas Court of Criminal Appeals became a lightning rod for public criticism in the wake of the execution of Michael Richard.

Photo courtesy: Erich Schlegel/Dallas Morning News

The judiciary differs from the other branches of Texas government—the legislative and the executive—in two respects. First, the judiciary is the least familiar branch of Texas government. Most Texans have little knowledge of the structure and operation of the courts and even less knowledge of the judges who hold positions on them. The election of judges may ask too much of Texas voters. Second, unlike the other branches, the judiciary cannot initiate action. It must wait for an individual or group to seek its assistance by initiating a lawsuit. Even then, the court must determine whether it is an issue that can be settled by the application of state law or is a matter that must be considered by another branch of government.

As in other states, the principal function of courts in Texas is to settle disputes by applying the law. The dispute may involve the state's acting on behalf of the community to prosecute suspected criminals or it may involve individuals who disagree about the terms of a contract. In both kinds of disputes, the courts examine the facts, interpret the law, and attempt to settle the conflict.

In this chapter, we will examine the Texas judiciary to understand how the courts apply and interpret the law to settle disputes.

★ First, we will examine the *roots of the Texas judiciary*, describing how the structure and operation of the judiciary evolved since the early 1800s.

★ Second, we will describe the *structure of the judiciary* in contemporary Texas, indicating the various types of courts and their responsibilities.

★ Third, we will describe *judges and judicial selection* in Texas, indicating who settles disputes in Texas and how they are chosen.

★ Fifth, we will describe the *judicial process in Texas*, examining how criminal cases and civil cases are handled.

★ Finally, we will explore *reforms of the judiciary in Texas*, analyzing persistent problems that affect the ability of the judiciary to settle disputes fairly and impartially and proposals for solving those problems.

Roots of the Texas Judiciary

The first courts in Texas were established in the Austin colony when Stephen F. Austin appointed a provisional justice of the peace for the province of Texas in 1822. Since Texas was a part of Mexico, the Mexican governor subsequently replaced the justice of the peace with three elected officials who applied Spanish law in Austin's colony. The judiciary was a point of contention between the Anglo settlers and the Mexican government.

As an independent republic, Texas created a judiciary that primarily reflected English tradition, although some features of Spanish law were retained. Under the 1836 constitution, the Republic of Texas created a supreme court, which had appellate jurisdiction only, and allowed Congress to create inferior courts. Judges were elected by Congress. Counties also had county and justice of the peace courts, whose judges were popularly elected.

In subsequent constitutions, Texas retained the basic judicial structure established in the 1836 constitution. Almost every constitution provided for the popular election of judges. As caseloads increased, additional courts were created, especially at the appellate level. In the 1876 constitution, the judiciary consisted of the supreme court, with appellate civil jurisdiction; the court of appeals, with criminal jurisdiction and limited civil jurisdiction; and an array of district, county, and justice of the peace courts. To learn more about the constitutional basis for the judiciary, see The Living Constitution. In 1891, the constitution was amended to provide an intermediate level of courts of civil appeal. The amendment also changed the name of the court of appeals to the court of criminal appeals and limited its jurisdiction to criminal cases. With the addition of the intermediate courts, whose numbers could be increased by the legislature, the Texas Supreme Court was allowed to exercise discretion in accepting appeals. However, the additional civil appeals courts did not affect a growing caseload for the Texas Court of Criminal Appeals. A constitutional amendment in 1945 increased the number of justices on the supreme court from three to nine, and amendments in 1966 and 1978 increased the number of judges on the court of criminal appeals, but it still could not keep up with the growing number of criminal appeals. In 1980, the courts of civil appeals became courts of appeals, and their jurisdiction was extended to criminal cases. Thus, the remedy that had cured the supreme court's caseload difficulties was applied to the court of criminal appeals.[3]

Over the years, constitutional amendments and legislative acts have added courts and changed the structure of the Texas judiciary, creating a system that is among the most complicated and confusing in the United States, if not the world. In the next section, we describe the current array of courts and their responsibilities.

The Living Constitution

The judicial power of this State shall be vested in one Supreme Court, in one Court of Criminal Appeals, in Courts of Appeals, in District Courts, in County Courts, in Commissioners Courts, in Courts of Justices of the Peace, and in such other courts as may be provided by law.

ARTICLE 5, SECTION 1

The Texas judicial system reflects both Spanish and Anglo-American traditions. The earliest courts were based on Spanish traditions. The 1836 constitution of the Republic of Texas provided for a supreme court, which consisted of a chief justice and all of the district judges, who served as associate justices. Subsequent constitutions, including the 1876 constitution, provided for one supreme court. However, the 1876 constitution, unlike other constitutions, stripped all criminal jurisdiction from the Texas Supreme Court and gave it to a Texas Court of Appeals. In 1891, an amendment created an intermediate court of civil appeals and a separate court of criminal appeals with criminal jurisdiction. The court of criminal appeals, which originally consisted of three judges, was enlarged to five members in 1966 and to nine members in 1977. In 1980, a constitutional amendment extended intermediate appellate jurisdiction in criminal cases to the courts of civil appeal and renamed them courts of appeals. Only one other state, Oklahoma, has two supreme courts.[a]

There are several criticisms of Texas's system of two supreme courts. Some critics stress the inefficiency of having two highest state courts and the possibility of conflicting rulings from the courts. Others argue that judges who deal exclusively with either civil or criminal law are unlikely to possess the broad perspective that judges who deal with both types of law develop. Some critics note the tendency for the court of criminal appeals to overturn convictions based on technicalities or procedural matters that have no bearing on the convicted person's guilt or innocence. Supporters of the two supreme courts counter that the two courts have rarely disagreed or issued conflicting opinions, that specialization in criminal or civil law is a benefit because judges cannot be experts in both types of law, and that what critics call technicalities are really constitutional and statutory rights that protect all citizens from abuses by the judicial system.[b]

QUESTIONS

1. Are two supreme courts necessary and advisable, or would the merger of the two courts into one supreme court, exercising both criminal and civil jurisdiction, be better? Explain your answer.
2. What problems might result from the merger of the Texas Supreme Court and Texas Court of Criminal Appeals?

---

[a] George D. Braden, *The Constitution of the State of Texas: An Annotated and Comparative Analysis* (Austin: Texas Advisory Commission on Intergovernmental Relations, 1977), 363–8; "Texas Court of Criminal Appeals," *Handbook of Texas Online*, www.tsha.utexas.edu/handbook/online/articles/view/TT/jpt1.html.
[b] See William L. Willis, "The Evolution of the Texas Court of Criminal Appeals," *Texas Bar Journal* (September 1966); and Paul Burka, "Trial by Technicality," *Texas Monthly* (April 1982).

The Structure of the Texas Judiciary

The Texas judiciary incorporates five levels of courts, some created by the constitution and others created by the legislature. To learn more about the courts at each level, see Figure 6.1.

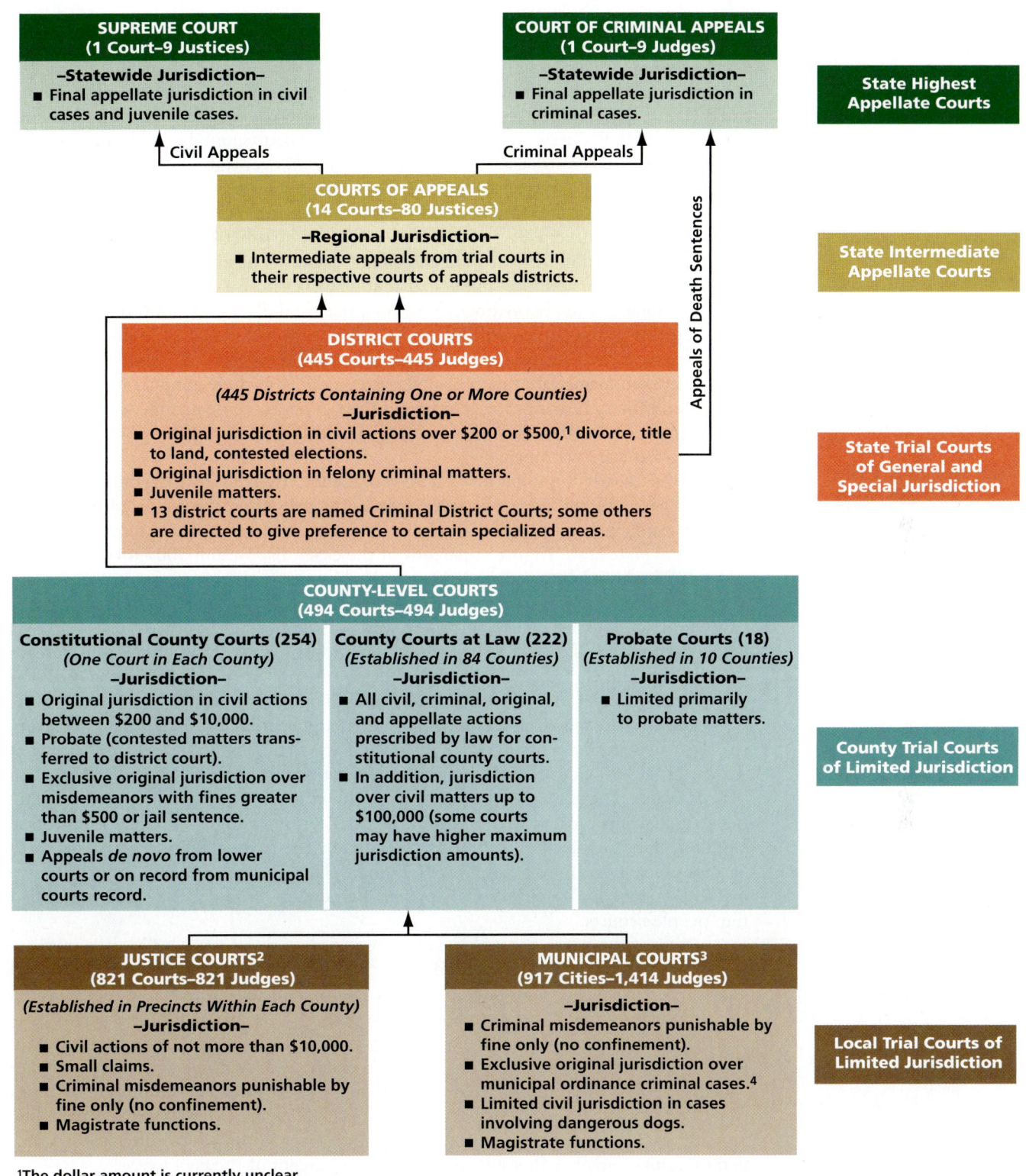

FIGURE 6.1 **The Court Structure of Texas** This figure shows the jurisdictions, levels, and different courts in the Texas judiciary.

Source: Office of Court Administration, Austin, Texas, November 2008.

Local Trial Courts

At the lowest level are local trial courts of limited jurisdiction, which include municipal courts and justice of the peace courts. By statute, the legislature allows each incorporated city in Texas to create a municipal court. Some larger cities are allowed several courts. In 2008, 917 cities had established municipal courts, employing just over 1,400 judges. **Municipal courts** exercise original jurisdiction over traffic misdemeanors, such as speeding, failure to wear a seat belt, and parking on a sidewalk. The maximum penalty in these cases is a fine or sanction that does not include confinement to jail or imprisonment. Municipal courts also have original jurisdiction over Class C misdemeanors, such as public intoxication and simple assault. The penalty in these cases cannot exceed $500. In addition, municipal courts have exclusive original jurisdiction over criminal violations of city ordinance—which may include a maximum fine of $2,000 for violations of fire safety, zoning, and public heath ordinances. Finally, municipal courts exercise civil jurisdiction in cases involving dangerous dogs, and municipal judges perform magistrate functions. Magistrate duties include conducting examining trials (preliminary hearings for county and district courts to determine whether sufficient evidence exists to hold someone for trial), issuing search and arrest warrants, and providing statutory warnings.

In 2007, nearly 8 million new cases were filed in Texas municipal courts. Of those cases, 82 percent involved traffic and parking offenses—thus, the name "traffic courts" given to municipal courts. The remaining cases involved violations of municipal ordinances and state laws. Eighteen percent of the cases disposed in 2007 involved a trial and a decision by a judge or jury, and fewer than 1 percent of those cases were appealed.[4]

The other local trial court in Texas is the justice of the peace court. Most states have eliminated justice courts, but there were 821 justice of the peace courts in Texas in 2008. Each of Texas's 254 counties, depending on its population, must create between one and eight justice precincts. Depending on the population of the precinct, each justice precinct in a county has one or two judges.

Justice of the peace courts have both civil and criminal jurisdiction. They exercise exclusive original jurisdiction in civil cases involving less than $200, and concurrent original jurisdiction with district and county courts in civil cases involving less than $10,000. The justice of the peace courts function as small claims courts: the parties in a civil suit present their sides in the case before a judge, who decides the case based on the evidence and testimony provided by the parties. Neither party needs to be represented by an attorney. Because small claims courts provide an inexpensive method of resolving disputes involving small amounts of money, they are often called the "people's courts."

Justice of the peace courts have original jurisdiction over Class C misdemeanors throughout the county. However, if municipalities within a county have municipal courts, the justice courts usually only hear cases that occur within the unincorporated areas of the county. Justices of the peace also perform magistrate duties—such as issuing search and arrest warrants, conducting preliminary hearings, performing marriages—and have jurisdiction over forcible entry and detainer actions, which are usually attempts by landlords to remove tenants. In 2007, nearly 3.5 million new cases were filed in justice of the peace courts. Of those, 89 percent were criminal cases. The remaining 11 percent were civil cases, of which 51 percent involved forcible entry and detainer suits. Small claims suits constituted 13 percent of the civil cases.

County Courts

At the next level of the Texas judiciary are county courts of limited jurisdiction. There are two major categories of county courts: constitutional county courts and county courts at law.

---

municipal court
City court with limited criminal jurisdiction.

justice of the peace court
Local county court for minor crimes and civil suits.

The Texas Constitution establishes a constitutional county court in each of the state's 254 counties. **Constitutional county courts** have concurrent original jurisdiction in civil matters with justice of the peace courts (suits between $200 and $10,000) and with district courts (suits between $200.01 and $10,000). They also have jurisdiction over probate cases (legal matters primarily involving wills and estates), unless the probate is contested, in which case they are transferred to a district court. Constitutional county courts exercise criminal jurisdiction over Class A and B misdemeanors, which carry penalties of a fine greater than $500 and/or a jail sentence.

Constitutional county courts also exercise appellate jurisdiction over cases from municipal and justice of the peace courts. Since few municipal courts and no justice of the peace courts are courts of record, there is no transcript of the trial. Without a transcript, there is no record of the proceedings for the county court to review for procedural errors. Consequently, appeals from most municipal courts and all justice of the peace courts take the form of a completely new trial—termed a **trial *de novo.***

Statutory county courts—**county courts at law**—were created to relieve county judges in urban counties of their judicial functions so that they could concentrate on their duties as presiding officer of the commissioners court (see chapter 7). In 2008, there were 222 county courts at law in eighty-four counties. Some counties have several county courts at law.

The state legislature has created county courts at law to meet the needs of each county's court system. Since the courts cost the state nothing, if the state legislators from a county want a court at law created, the legislature will probably accommodate them. Since each court is established by statute, a county court at law may have concurrent jurisdiction with other statutory county courts or may exercise original subject-matter jurisdiction in a limited field—such as civil, criminal, or probate—or appellate jurisdiction. Eighteen probate courts, whose jurisdiction is limited to probate, have been established in ten counties in Texas. The original civil jurisdiction of these courts varies greatly, although most exceed the $10,000 limit placed on the constitutional county courts, and at least one court has no limit.[5]

The effect of these statutes is a bewildering array of county courts at law, making meaningful generalizations about these courts and their jurisdictions difficult. Nevertheless, most county courts at law have limited original jurisdiction in civil cases, usually in those cases that involve less than $100,000. They also have limited original jurisdiction in criminal cases involving Class A and B misdemeanors. Most county courts at law have the same appellate jurisdiction as constitutional county courts.

County courts of all types added nearly 884,000 cases to their dockets in 2007. Of that number, 76 percent were criminal cases—including theft or worthless checks, driving while intoxicated or under the influence of drugs (DWI/DUID), traffic violations, drug law violations, and simple assault. The remaining cases were civil cases, probate cases, and cases involving juveniles and mental health commitments.

constitutional county court
Constitutionally mandated court for criminal and civil matters.

trial *de novo*
New trial, necessary for an appeal from a court that is not a court of record.

county court at law
Statutory county court to relieve county judge of judicial duties.

Thinking Nationally
Court Security

Court buildings can be scenes of tragedy. In 2005, a defendant in an Atlanta courtroom got a gun and killed the judge, a court stenographer, and a sheriff's deputy. In recent years, several states have increased court security. For instance, some California courts require all persons, including lawyers, to go through two metal detectors before entering a courtroom. In 2005, the National Center for State Courts recommended ten steps states should take to protect judges, juries, and courts. One of the recommendations is to have only one entrance to a court building.

- Do you think Texas court buildings should have only one entrance? Explain your answer.
- Should metal detectors be mandatory at court building doors? Why or why not?
- How might Texas's concealed handgun policies be affected by increased security measures at courthouses?

District Courts

The state courts of general and special jurisdiction are the district courts, which numbered 445 in 2008. The **district courts** have original civil jurisdiction in cases involving more than $200 or $500, all suits over the title to land, divorce proceedings, election contests, and contested probate matters. The district courts also have original criminal jurisdiction in all felony cases.

district court
Court of general jurisdiction for serious crimes and high-dollar civil cases.

Most district courts exercise both criminal and civil jurisdiction. However, in metropolitan areas, the district courts tend to specialize in criminal, civil, juvenile, or family matters. A total of twelve district courts in Dallas, Tarrant, and Jefferson Counties are designated criminal district courts and hear only criminal cases. In other counties, there are district courts that hear civil or criminal cases almost exclusively.

District courts added more than 904,000 new cases to their dockets during 2007. About two-thirds of the district court caseload is civil cases, nearly one-third criminal cases, and a small percent were juvenile cases. The largest category of criminal cases on the docket involved drug-related offenses—32 percent—either for drug possession or drug sale or manufacture. Homicide (including capital murder) cases constituted the smallest category of criminal cases at 1 percent. Among civil cases, the largest category—43 percent—was family law cases.

Intermediate Courts of Appeals

court of appeals
Intermediate appellate court for criminal and civil appeals.

There are fourteen **courts of appeals** in Texas and a total of eighty justices. Other than the 1st and 14th Courts of Appeals, which are located in Houston and serve the same area, each court serves a distinct geographic region. Each court includes a chief justice, who is elected as chief justice by the voters in a general election, and between two and twelve justices. Cases are usually heard by a panel of three justices. Certain cases, however, are heard *en banc,* which means that all of the justices assigned to the particular court of appeals participate. Since the courts are reviewing the record of the trial court, no testimony is taken, and no juries are involved. Decisions are rendered by a majority of the justices participating in the case. These courts exercise appellate jurisdiction over civil and criminal appeals from district and county courts in their respective regions. Only death penalty cases, which go directly from a district court to the court of criminal appeals, escape the courts' jurisdiction.

More than 11,000 new cases were filed in the courts of appeals during 2007. Of those cases, 53 percent were criminal cases, and 47 percent were civil cases. The courts disposed of criminal appeals in an average of 8.8 months and civil cases in an average of 8.1 months. To equalize the number of cases heard by each court, the Texas Supreme Court transfers cases between the courts. In 2007, a total of 457 cases were transferred.

The Supreme Courts

Texas Supreme Court
Court of last resort in civil and juvenile cases.

Texas Court of Criminal Appeals
Court of last resort in criminal cases.

The state's highest appellate courts include the **Texas Supreme Court,** for civil matters, and the **Texas Court of Criminal Appeals,** for criminal matters. Both courts have limited original jurisdiction, but most of their cases involve appeals from the courts of appeals. Both are courts of last resort, meaning that they are the last state courts to which a person can appeal a case. Of course, a person who claims that a "federal question" is involved may petition the U.S. Supreme Court for a writ of *certiorari.*

Texas Court of Criminal Appeals (2008). Front row: Paul Womack, Lawrence E. Meyers, Presiding Judge Sharon Keller, Tom Price, Cheryl Johnson. Back row: Charles Holcomb, Michael Keasler, Barbara Hervey, Cathy Cochran.

District Court Judge Bob Perkins presides over the 331st District Court in Austin, Texas. The 331st District Court is one of the fourteen district courts in Travis County.

The Texas Supreme Court includes a chief justice and eight justices. The Texas Court of Criminal Appeals also has nine members, a presiding judge and eight judges. The Texas Supreme Court always hears cases *en banc,* with all nine justices participating in the case. The constitution allows the Texas Court of Criminal Appeals to sit in panels of three judges, except for capital murder cases, but it almost never does. For both courts, decisions are reached by a majority vote. Both courts are located in Austin, but they are allowed to hear cases in other locations in Texas. The Texas Supreme Court, only recently given the authority to hear cases outside Austin, has traveled to Waco and to Lubbock to hear cases.

The operations of the two highest state courts in Texas are similar. Each court exercises some discretion in reviewing cases, although the Texas Court of Criminal Appeals is required to review all capital cases from the district courts. To secure a review by the Texas Supreme Court, a party in a suit files a **petition for review**—a request for the supreme court to review the decision of the court of appeals. In conference, the nine justices consider the request, and if four justices agree, the petition is granted. The case is then scheduled for oral argument before the court, and the parties to the suit submit legal briefs.[6] In 2007, the Texas Supreme Court disposed of 919 petitions for review, granting 111 (12 percent) of them. A refusal to grant a petition for review allows the ruling of the lower court to stand. The Texas Court of Criminal Appeals reviews **applications for discretionary review,** following the same procedure as the Texas Supreme Court in reviewing its petitions for review. If four judges concur, the petition is granted. In 2007, the Texas Court of Criminal Appeals considered 1,558 petitions for discretionary review and granted 173 (11 percent).

After the courts hear the oral arguments in a case, they decide the case in conferences. Once the court has reached a decision, one of the justices is assigned the task of writing the court's opinion. The Texas Supreme Court justices wrote 170 opinions in 2007, an average of more than eighteen per justice. Of those opinions, 133 (78 percent) were deciding opinions, including sixty-two majority opinions, and sixty-nine *per curiam.* The remaining opinions were concurring opinions, dissenting opinions, or concurring and dissenting opinions. During that same period, the Texas Court of Criminal Appeals judges issued 575 opinions, of which 36 percent were signed opinions and 41 percent were *per curiam.* The remaining opinions were concurring and dissenting opinions and one denial of rehearing.

The Texas Supreme Court performs several administrative duties in addition to its judicial responsibilities. It is responsible for establishing the rules and procedures that govern trials and appeals in civil and juvenile cases in Texas. It also establishes the rules for the operation of state agencies in the judicial branch, such as the Office of Court Administration, Commission on Judicial Conduct, and State Bar of Texas.

petition for review
Request for Texas Supreme Court review, which is granted if four justices agree.

application for discretionary review
Request for Texas Court of Criminal Appeals review, which is granted if four judges agree.

Judges and Judicial Selection

There are more than 3,200 judges in Texas. Except for municipal judges, they are selected in partisan elections. Trial judges—justices of the peace, constitutional and statutory county court judges, and district court judges—serve four-year terms, while appellate judges and justices—courts of appeals, supreme court, and court of criminal appeals—serve six-year terms. After describing the qualifications for Texas judges, we will examine judicial selection.

Judicial Qualifications and Personal Characteristics

The Texas Constitution establishes the qualifications for most Texas judges, which vary by judicial office. (To learn details on judicial qualifications see Table 6.1.) Consequently, Texas judges vary greatly in education and training. In personal characteristics, however, the judges are quite similar.[7]

For municipal courts, the municipality's legislative body or the city charter establishes the qualifications for its judges. These qualifications vary widely among the municipalities in Texas. In 2007, slightly more than one-half were graduates of law schools, and half were licensed to practice law. In ethnicity, 79 percent were Anglo, 14 percent were Hispanic, and 5 percent were African American. Sixty-seven percent of the judges were males.

Justices of the peace are required to be registered voters, but there are no educational, age, or experience requirements. As a result, in 2007 few (8 percent) had graduated from law school, and even fewer (7 percent) were licensed attorneys. Seventy-seven percent of the judges were Anglos, 20 percent were Hispanic, and 4 percent were African American. Sixty-seven percent of the justices of the peace were males.

The Texas Constitution requires constitutional county judges to be "well informed in the law of the State," but no law degree or license to practice law is required. However, county judges who perform judicial duties are required to complete at least thirty hours of instruction in the administrative duties of the office and in substantive, procedural, and evidentiary laws. Among the county court judges in 2007, 13 percent had graduated from law schools, and 11 percent were licensed attorneys. Eighty-eight percent of the judges were Anglo males.

A statutory county court judge must be at least twenty-five years old and a licensed attorney with a minimum of four years experience either as a judge or a prac-

TABLE 6.1 Judicial Qualifications

Court	Term of Office	Salary, 2008	Qualifications
Municipal courts	2 or 4 years	Set by city, highly variable	Determined by the city; varies by city
Justice of the peace courts	4 years	Set by county, highly variable	None
Constitutional county courts	4 years	Set by county, highly variable	Must be "well informed in the law"
County courts at law	4 years	Set by county, highly variable	25 years of age, county resident for 2 years, licensed attorney in Texas, served as judge or practiced law for 4 years
District courts	4 years	$125,000–$173,000	Age 25 to 74, citizen, district resident for 2 years, licensed attorney in Texas, practicing lawyer or judge for 4 years
Courts of appeals	6 years	Chief justice: $140,000–$147,500; Justices: $137,500–$145,000	Age 35 to 74, citizen, practicing attorney or judge of a court of record for at least 10 years
Texas Court of Criminal Appeals	6 years	Presiding judge: $152,500; Judges: $150,000	Same as courts of appeals
Texas Supreme Court	6 years	Chief justice: $152,500; Justices: $150,000	Same as courts of appeals

Source: Office of Court Administration, "Annual Statistical Report for the Texas Judiciary," December 2007, 14, http://www.courts.state.tx.us/pubs/AR2007/published-annual-report-2007.pdf and "Judicial Qualifications, Selection, and Terms of Office," http://www.courts.state.tx.us/pubs/AR2007/jud_branch/5-judge-qualifications-chart-07.pdf.

ticing attorney. Because of the qualifications, nearly all of the judges in 2007 had graduated from law school and were licensed attorneys. In ethnicity, 76 percent of the judges were Anglos, 18 percent were Hispanic, and 3 percent were African American. Sixty-eight percent were males.

A district court judge must have resided in the judicial district for two years and have been a licensed attorney in Texas or judge for four years. Almost all of the district judges are licensed attorneys. In 2007, 81 percent of the judges were Anglos, 13 percent were Hispanic, 3 percent were African American, and 71 percent were males.

The constitution requires all appellate court judges—those on the courts of appeals, supreme court, and court of criminal appeals—to be at least thirty-five years of age and no more than seventy-four years of age and have been a practicing attorney or a judge of a court of record for at least ten years. In 2007, judges for Texas's fourteen courts of appeals were predominately middle-aged (average age of fifty-five), Anglo (80 percent) males (58 percent). The judges had served on the court for an average of more than six years, and a majority (55 percent) had been lawyers in private practice before becoming a judge on the court. Nineteen percent had previously served as a judge on a trial court, and 18 percent had been prosecutors.

The members of the state's two highest courts also share similar personal characteristics. In 2009, there were eight males and one female on the Texas Supreme Court, five males and four females on the Texas Court of Criminal Appeals, their average age was fifty-four years old on the supreme court and sixty-six on the court of criminal appeals, and the members were overwhelmingly Anglos. All nine members of the court of criminal appeals were Anglo, while on the supreme court, Justice David Medina is Hispanic and Justice Dale Wainwright and Chief Justice Wallace Jefferson are African American. The average tenure was nearly six years on the supreme court and more than eight years on the court of criminal appeals.

Judicial Selection

For more than a century, Texas has chosen its judges in partisan elections and is currently one of only eight states that elect all or most of their judges through partisan elections. There are two exceptions to partisan elections: municipal judges, and filling vacancies in other judicial offices. Municipal judges may be elected or appointed by the city council. If vacancies occur in statutory county judgeships, the county commissioners court appoints a judge. For district courts, courts of appeals, and the Texas Supreme Court and Texas Court of Criminal Appeals, vacancies are filled by gubernatorial appointment. Appointed judges serve until the next general election, when they must compete in a partisan election (except for municipal judges) to retain their positions. In 2008, one-third of the eighteen top judges were initially appointed to the courts, as were 54 percent of the seventy-eight court of appeals judges and 38 percent of the 445 district court judges.

Most of the time, however, potential judges have to compete in partisan contests. First, one must win the nomination of a political party in a primary election or state convention, which requires a political campaign. For the appellate courts in Texas, where the judges are selected in large districts or statewide, a primary election campaign can be time consuming and costly. Then, another campaign must be waged in the general election. Again, getting voter attention requires more campaign contributions. Opinion polls indicate that a majority of Texans favor an electoral system and the accountability of judges that it promotes. They believe that they should be able to choose the people who make decisions that affect their life, liberty, and property. To learn more about the arguments for and against election of judges, see Join the Debate: Should Texas Elect Its Judges?

Over the last two decades, several incidents have raised questions about to whom the judges are accountable and whether judges who depend on campaign contributions to get elected can remain fair and impartial. Since the early 1970s, when the

Join the Debate

Should Texas Elect Its Judges?

OVERVIEW: Judges are expected to be well qualified, fair in making their decisions, and independent from political and public pressures. In a democratic system, we also expect some degree of judicial accountability to the public, though some judicial systems stress accountability more than others. Texas selects its judges in partisan elections—a system intended to stress accountability. Especially with the growth of party competition in Texas, judicial campaigns have become high-dollar affairs, requiring judicial candidates to solicit funds. But, some campaign contributions raise concerns about future undue influence. For example, among the major contributors to judicial campaigns are lawyers—the very people who come before the courts asking for favorable decisions in cases. Such campaign finance dynamics have fueled movements in Texas, as well as across the nation, to reform state-level judicial selection processes in an attempt to increase judicial independence.

Arguments IN FAVOR of Judicial Elections

- **Texans favor the election of judges.** In public opinion polls in Texas, 70 percent of those polled want to continue to elect their judges.

- **Electing judges promotes democracy.** Texans mistrust government and favor popular control. Keeping the partisan election of judges promotes popular control and democracy—government by the people.

- **Elected judges are as competent and qualified as judges selected by other methods.** There is no empirical evidence to indicate that any method of judicial selection results in more competent and better-qualified judges. A high percentage

---

Texas legislature passed a strong Deceptive Trade Practices–Consumer Protection Act, a battle for control of the Texas Supreme Court has raged between plaintiffs' lawyers, who represent injured parties in civil suits, and defense lawyers, who defend businesses, doctors, and insurance companies. During the late 1970s and early 1980s, plaintiffs' lawyers and their association, the Texas Trial Lawyers Association, were the presumptive winners, electing judges who sided with plaintiffs in medical malpractice and product liability suits. Although the Texas Supreme Court did not always decide for the plaintiffs, trial lawyers were more likely to be successful than defense lawyers. In 1985, for example, the supreme court decided for the plaintiffs in 69 percent of the court's cases and for the defendants in only 28 percent of the cases.[8]

In 1986, two justices who had received campaign contributions from trial lawyers were the subjects of investigations. The House Judicial Affairs Committee investigated Justices C. L. Ray and William Kilgarlin for alleged improper contact with attorneys. The House panel made no recommendations concerning the allegations against Ray and Kilgarlin, but the State Commission on Judicial Conduct, the state agency responsible for disciplining judges, also investigated the charges and issued public sanctions against both justices in 1987. Ray received a reprimand for multiple violations of the Code of Judicial Conduct. Kilgarlin received an admonition, the commission's mildest punishment.

The Texas Supreme Court received national attention in 1987 when journalist Mike Wallace devoted a segment of *60 Minutes* to the question "Is Justice for Sale?" Wallace focused on the campaign contributions of Houston trial lawyer Joe Jamail, who won an $11 billion settlement against Texaco for interfering with Pennzoil's

of Texans with experience in Texas courtrooms (82 percent) were satisfied with the judicial process and the judges that they encountered.

Arguments AGAINST Judicial Elections

- **Judicial elections are costly.** In 2002, a political consultant estimated that a statewide judicial contest would cost a candidate $2 million.
- **Judicial elections turn judges into partisan politicians rather than impartial judges.** The judiciary is supposed to be fair and impartial in their decisions about cases and controversies. As a result of the U.S. Supreme Court decision in *Republican Party of Minnesota* v. *White* (2002), the Texas Supreme Court repealed the canon in its Code of Conduct that prevented judges or judicial candidates from commenting on issues that might come before their courts. If judges conduct issue-oriented campaigns, they become politicians rather than fair and impartial jurists.
- **Judicial candidates funded by special interests are less likely to be independent as judges.** In a 1998 Texas public-opinion poll, 83 percent of those polled stated that judicial decisions were "very significantly" or "fairly significantly" affected by campaign contributions. This lack of confidence in the courts undermines the public's confidence in the rule of law—a bedrock of American jurisprudence.

Continuing the Debate

1. Do you think judges in Texas should be elected? Why or why not?
2. What can be done to reduce the possibility that elected judges will show favoritism toward lawyers and their clients who contributed to the judges' political campaigns?

To Follow the Debate Online Go To:

The Federalist Society, www.fed-soc.org
Texans for Public Justice, www.tpj.org/index.jsp

---

attempt to purchase Getty Oil Company in 1984. Jamail, who contributed $10,000 to the district court judge who tried the case shortly before the trial began, gave thousands more to supreme court justices. Wallace questioned the ethics of a judicial system that allowed lawyers to contribute to the political campaigns of judges before whom they appear. To learn more about how the issue was addressed in the media, see Analyzing Visuals: Is Justice for Sale in the State of Texas? Later in 1987, Democratic Chief Justice John Hill and Democratic Justices Robert Campbell and James Wallace resigned from the supreme court. Republican Governor William Clements appointed three Republicans to fill the vacancies on the court, including Thomas R. Phillips as chief justice.

While a cloud of suspicion hung over the supreme court, a group pushing "tort reform," the Texas Civil Justice League (TCJL), initiated an attack on the Deceptive Trade Practices–Consumer Protection Act in the Texas legislature. In the 1987 and subsequent legislative sessions, TCJL convinced the legislature to limit punitive damages, change the state's workers' compensation program to limit lawsuits, limit the liability of manufacturers of products, and protect firearm manufacturers against suits. The group would be particularly successful in the 1995 legislative session, assisted by another group, Texans for Lawsuit Reform, and Governor George W. Bush's support for tort reform in his gubernatorial campaign.[9]

With six supreme court positions on the ballot in 1988, business interests saw an opportunity to reverse the supreme court's preference for plaintiffs, and judicial campaigns became more expensive as the competition increased. Twenty candidates seeking the six positions on the supreme court in 1988 raised more than

Analyzing Visuals: Is Justice for Sale in the State of Texas?

In November 1998, CBS's *60 Minutes* aired a report on judicial selection in Texas. Days after the *60 Minutes* segment aired, the Ben Sargent cartoon reprinted here appeared in the *Austin American-Statesman*. Look at the political cartoon and answer the following questions:

WHAT political event, situation, or politicians are depicted? What message is conveyed by the image?

WHAT message do the words in the speech bubble and labels in the cartoon convey?

WHAT position does the cartoonist appear to take on the issue?

WHAT effect is the cartoonist attempting to achieve: exaggeration, irony, or juxtaposition? How does the cartoon achieve that effect?

$10 million for their primary and general election campaigns. Two supreme court candidates raised more than $2 million.[10] Also, nonlawyer special-interest groups, especially the Texas Medical Association, became major contributors to judicial candidates through their political action committees (see chapter 3). The Texas Medical Association supported a slate of four Republicans and two conservative Democrats. Only one candidate, Paul Murphy, was defeated by a plaintiff-backed candidate, Lloyd Doggett.

During the early 1990s, the cost of judicial elections continued to rise. In 1990, six candidates for three seats on the court spent $6 million. A study of fund-raising by Texas Supreme Court justices during the 1994 and 1996 election cycles indicated that a significant percentage of campaign contributions came from lawyers, law firms, and PACs with interests before the court. The seven justices raised more than $9 million in contributions over $100 for their most recent reelection campaigns, and 40 percent of the contributions came from lawyers and parties who had cases on the court's docket between 1994 and 1997. The report argued that "today's justices continue to sully the court's reputation by raising millions of dollars from parties and lawyers who have business before the court."[11]

The 1994 election was also the last time that Democratic candidates were able to mount competitively financed campaigns for the Texas Supreme Court. Democrat

Jimmy Carroll actually raised more money than his Republican opponent, Priscilla Owen, but he lost anyway. Democrat Alice Oliver-Parrott raised over $1.5 million, but her Republican opponent, incumbent Nathan Hecht, raised more than $2 million. Conservative Democrat Raul Gonzalez, who was backed by doctors and business interests, also raised more than $2 million. He faced two opponents in the Democratic primary and barely defeated Rene Haas in the runoff primary, but he easily won the general election. In 1998, three Republican incumbent justices raised an average of $1 million to their Democratic opponents' average of $96,000. Incumbent Democratic Justice Rose Spector raised $563,931 to her Republican opponent's $1,214,450.[12]

As Republicans replaced Democrats on the Texas Supreme Court, the court became more likely to rule in favor of defendants. Between 1995 and 1998, 70 percent of the supreme court cases that pitted consumers, patients, and crime victims as plaintiffs against corporate, professional, and government defendants were won by the defendants. In 2005–2006, defendants won 83 percent of the cases. With Republicans holding all nine supreme court seats and more firmly in control of conservatives led by Nathan Hecht and Priscilla Owen, the court in 2006 reached a zenith in its support of insurance companies and other defendants in civil suits.[13]

The large sums of money necessary to compete in judicial races and the sources of those contributions have created an image problem for Texas judges. As Chief Justice Thomas R. Phillips told the Texas legislature in 1999, "Neither party label nor campaign war chests necessarily compromise a judge's ability to be fair and impartial. . . . But these attributes of Texas justice *do* compromise the *appearance* of fairness. When judges are labeled as Democrats and Republicans, how can you convince the public that the law is a judge's only constituency? And when a winning litigant has contributed thousands of dollars to the judge's campaign, how do you ever persuade the losing party that only the facts of the case were considered?"[14]

Indeed, in a poll of Texans, 83 percent thought that campaign contributions have a significant effect on judges' decisions. Only 7 percent stated that the contributions have no effect on their decisions. Furthermore, nearly half of the state judges and 79 percent of Texas attorneys stated that campaign contributions have a significant influence on judicial decisions. Only 14 percent of the judges and 1 percent of the attorneys believed that campaign contributions have no influence on judicial opinions.[15]

The high cost of judicial campaigns, racially polarized voting in statewide and countywide contests, and the small numbers of Hispanics and African Americans who are licensed attorneys mean that one consequence of Texas's judicial selection process is that minorities have had only limited success in gaining representation in the judiciary. With increasing Republican strength in judicial elections, minority candidates, who almost always are Democrats, are even less likely to win judicial contests today.

Xavier Rodriguez's case illustrates a problem that minorities face in judicial elections even when they are members of the Republican Party. Governor Rick Perry appointed Rodriguez to the Texas Supreme Court in 2001. In the 2002 Republican primary election, he had the support of state Republican leaders, endorsements from major newspapers, and a $700,000 war chest, yet he lost to a little-known Anglo lawyer, Steven Wayne Smith. As political scientist Richard Murray noted, "In a primary where there are so many white voters who know little about either candidate, the default goes to the Anglo over the Hispanic. . . .He might have survived if his parents had named him Billy Bob."[16] In district court contests in large urban counties, where all district judges compete in countywide elections, straight-ticket Republican voting in judicial elections has virtually eliminated any minority judges who were appointed or elected.

The effect of partisan preferences has been dramatic. In 1997, among the eighty judges on the courts of appeals, forty-four were Republicans and thirty-six were

Democrats. Of the fourteen courts of appeals, six courts had a Republican majority, six courts had a Democratic majority, and two courts were evenly divided. On the state's top courts, seven of the nine supreme court justices were Republican, and six of the nine court of criminal appeals judges were Republicans. In 2008, all eighteen members of the two highest courts were Republicans, and about three-fourths of the courts of appeals judges were Republicans.[17]

The Judicial Process in Texas

Most Texans will experience the judicial system as a potential juror or in municipal court for a traffic offense. Others, however, may experience the criminal or civil justice process as a plaintiff or defendant. For every Texan, a general understanding of the judicial process is helpful. We start by describing the criminal justice process and then consider the civil justice process.

The Criminal Justice Process

In Texas, the legislature has established a graded penalty system, classifying criminal offenses into eight categories: capital murder, four degrees of felonies, and three classes of misdemeanors. To learn more about these graded penalties, see Table 6.2. The legislature also adopts the code of criminal procedure, which regulates how criminal trials are conducted.

ARREST AND SEARCHES In many cases, an individual will be arrested after an arrest warrant has been issued by a magistrate. To issue the warrant, a magistrate will require sufficient information in the form of a complaint. The officer seeking the arrest warrant must satisfy the requirements of probable cause: tangible evidence that a crime was committed and that the person named in the complaint committed the offense. In most cases, however, police officers arrest an individual without a warrant but based on probable cause because the officer sees an offense being committed or receives a credible report of the commission of a felony and the officer does not have time to procure a warrant. Upon arrest, a person and his or her possessions may be searched. Again, a search warrant is usually necessary, but there are conditions under which a warrantless search is reasonable and evidence seized may be admissible in court. In

TABLE 6.2 The Texas System of Graded Penalties

Offense	Maximum Punishment	Examples
Capital felony	Execution	Capital murder
First-degree felony	5–99 years or life; $10,000 fine	Aggravated sexual assault; theft of property valued at $200,000 or more
Second-degree felony	2–20 years; $10,000 fine	Tampering with a consumer product; theft of property valued at $100,000 or more but less than $200,000
Third-degree felony	2–10 years; $10,000 fine	Drive-by shooting without injury; theft of property valued at $20,000 or more but less than $100,000
State jail felony	180 days to 2 years; $10,000 fine	Credit-card or debit-card abuse; theft of property valued at $1,500 or more but less than $20,000
Class A misdemeanor	1 year; $4,000 fine	Burglary of a vehicle; abuse of a corpse; theft of property valued at $500 or more but less than $1,500
Class B misdemeanor	180 days; $2,000 fine	Silent or abusive calls to a 911 service; DWI; theft of property valued at more than $20 but less than $500
Class C misdemeanor	$500 fine	Assault without bodily injury; attending a dog fight; theft of property valued at less than $20

Texas, search warrants are not required for searches pursuant to a lawful arrest and for seizures of evidence in plain view of an officer. Of course, searches conducted with the consent of the person under arrest are considered reasonable.

BOOKING Booking establishes an administrative record of a suspect's arrest. At this time, the suspect is usually fingerprinted and photographed, has the charges explained, and is allowed to make a phone call. For minor offenses, a suspect is usually released on "station house bail." For serious offenses, a suspect is placed in a holding cell until his or her appearance before a magistrate.

MAGISTRATE APPEARANCE If the district or county attorney decides to charge the suspect, he or she becomes a defendant and is brought before a magistrate. The magistrate informs the defendant of the charges, his or her rights under *Miranda* v. *Arizona* (1966), and his or her right to an examining trial. An examining trial is conducted by a magistrate to determine if there is sufficient evidence to continue the criminal proceedings. If the magistrate decides that there is not sufficient evidence, the defendant is released. The examining trial is also used to set bail and take the testimony of witnesses. If the defendant makes bail, he will be released until his trial.

GRAND JURY INDICTMENT Unless defendants waive their right, a grand jury review will be held. In Texas, grand juries consist of twelve people, chosen by a judge from a list provided by a jury commission. The prosecutor presents the evidence to the grand jury, and if nine members are convinced that sufficient evidence exists to justify a trial, the grand jury issues a "true bill." In that case, an indictment accusing the defendant is prepared by the prosecutor and signed by the grand jury foreperson. Otherwise, the grand jury issues a "no bill," and the defendant is released. The indictment is filed with the court's clerk, and a copy is delivered to the defendant, notifying him or her of the court date. If the defendant is free on bail, the judge may issue a warrant for the defendant's arrest.

TEXAS IN COMPARISON

Crime, Courts, and Judges

Criminal justice has been a fast growing area of state governments. The largest states have prison populations that dwarf the number in the federal system. Three of the four largest states practice capital punishment. In 2004, the New York Court of Appeals declared the New York death penalty statute unconstitutional. The structure of the state court systems, method of judicial selection, and compensation of judges vary considerably, with Texas having the largest number of justices on the highest court and the lowest salaries, until the legislature increased the salaries in 2005.

	Number of Prisoners on Death Row (2008)	Courts of Last Resort (2008)	Compensation of Judges (2007)	Prison Population (2006)
Texas	370	2, Supreme Court and Court of Criminal Appeals, 9 justices each, partisan election	Supreme courts, $150,000 (19th among the states)	172,116
California	669	1, Supreme Court, 7 justices, appointed by governor, retention election	Supreme Court, $209,521 (1st among the states)	175,512
New York	0	1, Court of Appeals, 7 justices, appointed by governor from Judicial Nomination Commission, senate confirmation	Court of Appeals, $151,200 (18th among the states)	63,315
Florida	388	1, Supreme Court, 7 justices, appointed by governor with nomination commission	Supreme Court, $161,200 (12th among the states)	92,969

ARRAIGNMENT After an indictment in felony cases and in misdemeanor cases that can result in a jail sentence, an arraignment is required. If the defendant is indigent and requires a court-appointed attorney, the judge will either appoint one or a public defender will be provided. After the defendant is represented by counsel, the judge will again read the charge and take the defendant's plea. At this time, the defendant may plead guilty as a result of a plea-bargain agreement. The prosecutor provides the court with a victim's impact statement, which indicates how the defendant's acts have affected the victim's life and which may be used by the judge or jury during sentencing.

PRETRIAL MOTIONS Pretrial motions establish the scope of the trial, determining, for example, what evidence is admissible, what witnesses may testify about, and what issues can and cannot be raised. Pretrial motions can also be used by the defense attorney to request a jury trial or bench trial, request a continuance, determine if the defendant is competent to stand trial, change the trial's location, or discover evidence held by the prosecution that could prove the defendant's innocence.

JURY SELECTION Defendants have a right to a jury trial but can waive that right unless the charge is capital murder. If either the prosecution or defense requests a jury trial, a group of potential jurors, known as the *venire* or jury pool, is assembled. The potential jurors are assigned numbers randomly and seated in the courtroom. The prosecution and the defense question the potential jurors in a process known as *voir dire*. Each side gets a number of peremptory challenges, depending on the seriousness of the offense, which allow the attorneys to dismiss jurors without cause. The only limitation is that neither side may use their peremptory challenges to exclude potential jurors based on their race or gender. Any potential juror may be challenged for cause, such as prejudice against the defendant, but the judge must agree to eliminate the potential juror from the jury pool. After *voir dire*, if the case involves a felony, the first twelve potential jurors will constitute the jury; if the case involves a misdemeanor, the first six will form the jury. Jury verdicts must be unanimous.

TRIAL In Texas, trials are conducted in two distinct phases—a guilt determination phase and a sentencing phase. There are seven stages in the guilt determination phase. First, the prosecution reads the indictment or information. Then the defense attorney, acting for the defendant, responds by entering a plea. Second, the prosecution provides opening remarks, telling the jury the nature of the offense, the facts that it plans to establish, and how it plans to prove the charges against the defendant. The defense attorney may deliver opening remarks or wait until the prosecution has presented its case to make remarks. Third, the prosecution presents the state's case, calling witnesses and entering evidence in an attempt to prove the defendant guilty beyond a reasonable doubt. Fourth, after the prosecution has presented its case, the defense presents its case. In rebuttal, the prosecution can call additional witnesses to discredit the defense's witnesses. The defense is also given an opportunity to rebut the state's rebuttal witnesses. Fifth, the judge reads the jury its charge, a set of instructions for reaching a verdict. Sixth, the prosecution and defense are given a last chance to convince the jury during final arguments. Finally, the jury retires to the jury room to deliberate and reach a verdict. If the jury cannot reach a unanimous verdict, the judge may declare a mistrial. If the jury finds the defendant not guilty, he or she is released from custody. If the defendant is found guilty, the second phase begins—the sentencing phase.

During the sentencing phase, the defendant's prior convictions are admitted as evidence. The stages are similar to the guilt phase but abbreviated into five steps. In capital murder cases, the sentencing phase involves the jury considering whether the defendant is likely to commit further violent crimes and is a threat to society and whether the defendant actually caused, intended, or anticipated that a human life

Ideas Into Action

Defending Actual Innocence

Sometimes individuals who have long been in prison are released when it is discovered that they are actually innocent of the crime for which they were convicted. Who ensures that those who are actually innocent are released from prison? In 2003, the Texas Center for Actual Innocence (TCAI), a nonprofit, tax-exempt corporation, started the Actual Innocence Clinic in cooperation with the University of Texas School of Law. The clinic allows law students, who earn law school credit and are supervised by TCAI officials, to screen and investigate claims of actual innocence by Texas prisoners.

According to TCAI, there are only two ways to meet the definition of "actual innocence": (1) the prison inmate did not engage in the conduct or participate with others in the conduct for which the inmate was convicted; (2) the inmate was falsely accused of the offense. Since the law considers a criminal conviction final, the inmate must (1) show that he or she is actually innocent with clear and convincing evidence that was not introduced and was not available for introduction at the trial, and (2) show that an error prevented evidence that might have proven the inmate's innocence from being introduced at the trial.

The Actual Innocence Clinic receives between five and fifteen letters a day from inmates who proclaim their innocence. A defense attorney alleging an incarcerated client's actual innocence must show convincing evidence to exonerate the inmate. The investigation of innocence claims involves locating court documents, securing physical evidence, and finding witnesses. DNA testing is an important component of actual innocence claims.

- How would a law student judge the merits of prisoners' claims of innocence?
- Do you think that projects such as the Actual Innocence Clinic stimulate abuse of the judicial system? Explain your answer.

For more information on the Actual Innocence Project, see

- University of Texas School of Law, Clinical Programs, Texas Center for Actual Innocence, www.utexas.edu/law/academics/clinics/innocence
- The Innocence Project, www.innocenceproject.org

---

would be taken. If the jury answers both questions affirmatively, then the jury must consider whether mitigating circumstances warrant a sentence of life imprisonment rather than the death penalty. The jury's responses determine whether the defendant receives life in prison without parole or death by lethal injection.[18]

APPEALS Except in capital murder cases, which are automatically reviewed by the Texas Court of Criminal Appeals, convicted criminals may appeal the trial court's decision to a court of appeals. The court of appeals will review the records of the trial to determine if a reversible error was committed, considering the bases for the appeal in written briefs by attorneys and oral arguments before the court. A further appeal is possible, but the court of criminal appeals determines whether to accept an application for discretionary review and hear the appeal. To learn more about issues in appealing criminal convictions, see Ideas into Action: Defending Actual Innocence.

The Civil Justice Process

The Texas Supreme Court establishes civil procedures, which tend to be less formal than criminal procedures.

PRETRIAL PROCEDURES To initiate a civil suit, the plaintiff, the person who has been injured, files a petition with the clerk of the court that will hear the case. The petition indicates the plaintiff's complaints against the defendant and the remedy sought in the case, usually a monetary award. The court clerk informs the defendant of the charges filed and indicates that the defendant can provide a written answer to the complaint, indicating why the plaintiff is not entitled to the requested remedy. Before the judge sets a trial date, if the parties have not settled the suit out of court, the parties file their petitions, answers, and other documents pertinent to the case. Either party to the suit may request a jury trial; otherwise the judge conducts a bench trial, determining the facts and applying the applicable law.

TRIAL As in a criminal trial, a civil trial begins with the plaintiff's attorney presenting the evidence and witnesses to prove the bases of the complaint. The defendant's attorney may challenge the evidence presented and cross-examine the plaintiff's witnesses. The defendant's attorney then presents evidence, which may be challenged by the plaintiff's attorney, and witnesses, who may be questioned by the plaintiff. If a jury is deciding the case, the judge will issue a charge to the jury, instructing the jury on how to conduct their deliberations and specifying the relevant law in the case. After the charge, the lawyers make their final arguments. The judge then issues the jury a set of questions that the jury will answer. The jury's answers will provide the basis for the judgment in the case. In district courts, ten of the twelve jurors must agree on the answers. In county and justice of the peace courts, five of the six jurors must agree. Based on the jury's answers or verdict, the judge issues a judgment, indicating the remedy to the complaint.

APPEALS Appeals in civil cases, as in criminal cases, involve the record from the trial court, written briefs by the attorneys, and oral arguments before the judges. Appeals from district and county courts are reviewed by a court of appeals and possibly by the Texas Supreme Court.

Toward Reform: Changing the Texas Judiciary

The Texas judicial system is often the recipient of criticism—from lawyers and judges, politicians and criminal justice specialists, businesses and public-interest advocates, and victim advocates and prisoner advocates. Often these criticisms result in attempts to reform court structure, judicial selection, or campaign finance. We consider each criticism and the possible reforms in turn.

Reforming the Court Structure

As indicated earlier, the Texas judicial system is complex and confusing, consisting of five layers of courts. Numerous proposals for judicial reform advocate simplifying and unifying the court structure.

Because of the addition of courts over the years, Texas trial courts present a tangle of mixed jurisdictions where overlapping jurisdiction is the rule rather than the exception. For example, a civil suit involving more than $200 but less than $10,000 falls within the jurisdiction of the justice of the peace courts, the constitutional county court, the statutory county courts, and the district courts. Moreover, the statutory county courts' jurisdiction often overlaps the civil jurisdiction of the district courts. This allows an attorney to shop for justice, seeking a judge that is more likely to decide favorably for a client.

The constitutional revision efforts in 1974 and 1975 (see chapter 2) included a proposal for a new structure for the court system, based on the work of the Texas Chief Justice's Task Force on Judicial Reform.[19] In the early 1990s, the Texas Research League studied the Texas judiciary and published an extensive report with recommendations for a new court structure.[20] The constitutional revision efforts of Representative Rob Junell and Senator Bill Ratliff in 1999 also included changes in the Texas judiciary, which were endorsed by Chief Justice Phillips.

Although the proposals vary, all simplify and unify the court structure. Figure 6.2 illustrates such a proposal. At the local level, municipal courts would operate as they do currently. Constitutional county courts and statutory courts would be eliminated. Consequently, jurisdiction of the justice of the peace courts would be expanded to cover the jurisdiction of the county courts presently, and the judges would be required to be licensed attorneys.

The district courts would be the state's only trial courts, except for the specific jurisdiction assigned to justice of the peace courts. The state would be divided into judicial districts, which would have one district court but could have more than one judge. Specialization could be retained so that some district judges could handle specific cases, such as family cases or criminal cases. The advantage of one district court with several judges would be in equalizing caseloads among the judges. The courts of appeals would be retained, but the geographic districts would be redrawn to equalize the courts' caseloads and prevent the necessity for shifting cases from one court to another, as is the current practice.

Most reforms would merge the Texas Supreme Court and the Texas Court of Criminal Appeals into one supreme court. However, a Texas Research League study argues that the two courts should be retained.[21] The proposal by Junell and Ratliff contemplated one supreme court consisting of a chief justice and fourteen justices, who would be divided equally between a civil division and criminal division. The chief justice could, by court rule, sit with either or both divisions. The most recent effort for reforming the court structure, with many of the provisions discussed here, was Senator Robert Duncan's SB 1204, which passed the Senate in 2007, only to die in the House.[22]

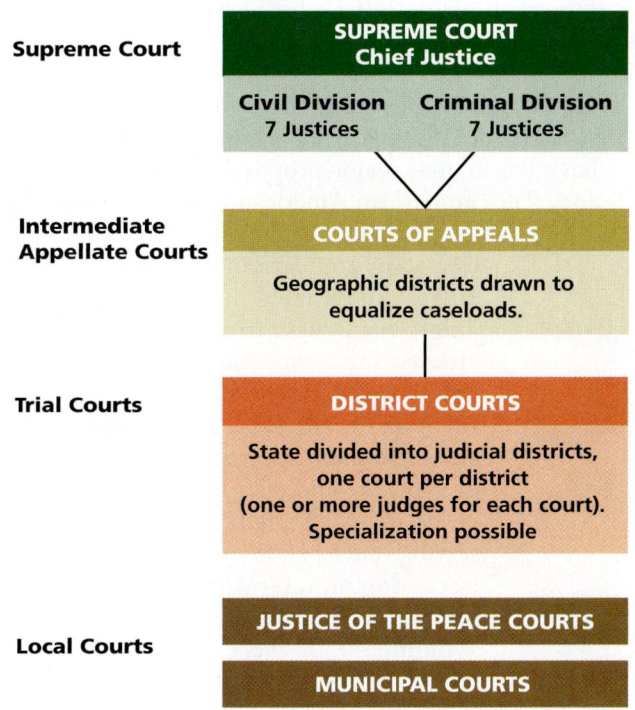

FIGURE 6.2 Proposal for a Unified, Simplified Texas Judiciary

Reforming Judicial Selection

Since at least 1946, various groups, including the Texas State Bar and a series of task forces on judicial selection, have recommended that Texas adopt a merit system for selecting judges. The election of Steve Mansfield, who misrepresented his judicial experience and qualifications, to the court of criminal appeals in 1994 reinvigorated the reform efforts. In 1994, Lieutenant Governor Bob Bullock appointed a committee of state senators and judges to study judicial selection and make a recommendation for reform. After many meetings, the committee produced a compromise that attempted to accommodate the conflicting interests involved in judicial selection—the political parties, lawyers for plaintiffs and defendants, ethnic minorities, and judges. The compromise called for the governor to appoint appellate judges. Trial judges in urban counties would be elected from county commissioner precincts. After serving for a period of time, they would have to run in countywide retention elections. Later, they would have to be reelected from county commissioner precincts. The elections would be nonpartisan. The Texas Senate easily passed the proposal in 1995, but opposition in the House surfaced from Hispanics and Republicans, who had the support of Governor Bush.

A major hurdle in these battles to reform the judicial selection process has been that Hispanics and African Americans have never been represented on the Texas courts in proportion to their percentages of the population. In the 1980s, minority plaintiffs challenged the method of selection of district court judges in countywide elections as violating the U.S. Voting Rights Act, which prohibits states from using voting procedures that dilute minority voting strength. In late 1989, U.S. District Court Judge Lucius Bunton ruled that the countywide election of judges in nine counties violated the act. However, after several appeals, the case was finally settled in 1993, when the U.S. Supreme Court refused to review a U.S. Court of Appeals ruling that the results in Texas's countywide, partisan elections were explained by the partisan affiliations or preferences of the voters rather than vote dilution. Also, the court indicated that because the judges could hear cases from anywhere in the county, the state had an interest in maintaining a link between the court's jurisdiction and the at-large electoral base by allowing all voters in the county to vote for each judge in the county.[23]

In 1996, a Texas Supreme Court task force considered judicial selection but was unable to agree on a substitute for the current system. In every legislative session since 1997, legislators have considered major proposals for judicial selection reform. In 1997, Senator Rodney Ellis, an African American Democrat from Houston, proposed that appellate judges be appointed and trial judges be elected in nonpartisan elections. Both appellate and trial judges would later run in retention elections, but trial judges would have to run in regular nonpartisan elections after two retention elections. In urban counties, district judges would be elected from commissioners precincts.[24] In more recent sessions, Senator Robert Duncan, an Anglo Republican from Lubbock, proposed that judges of appellate and district courts be appointed by the governor and confirmed by a two-thirds Senate vote. After serving one term, the judges would run in retention elections, determining whether the judge should remain in office for another term or be replaced by a new appointee.[25] In every session, the proposed legislation passed the Senate but failed to win House approval. A compromise that accommodates the varied interests in judicial selection has not proven possible so far.[26]

Thinking Nationally

Judicial Election by the Legislature

In South Carolina, the legislature elects judges from candidates submitted by a Judicial Merit Selection Commission. Legislatures in Connecticut and Virginia also select their state judges.

- What factors do these three states have in common that might have influenced their judicial selection method?
- If Texas's legislature is now more diverse than in the past, and if electoral dynamics favor male, Anglo, and wealthier candidates, might a legislative selection of judges produce a more diverse judiciary? Explain your answer.

Reforming Judicial Campaign Finance

Faced with the cost of judicial campaigns and its effect on the judiciary's imputed fairness, the legislature enacted a Judicial Campaign Fairness Act in 1995. The act limits contributions to judicial candidates, depending on the judicial office sought.

For supreme court justices, individuals can contribute $5,000 per election under the act. Thus, an individual can give a supreme court candidate $5,000 for the primary election, $5,000 if there is a runoff primary, and another $5,000 for the general election. However, a candidate who is unopposed either in the primary or in the general election faces reduced contribution limits. Law firms and their political action committees can contribute $30,000 to a supreme court candidate, which includes individual contributions from the firm's attorneys. Candidates are also limited in the amount of contributions that they can accept from general political action committees not affiliated with law firms. For supreme court candidates, the PAC limit is $300,000. Voluntary expenditure limits are also established for judicial campaigns ($2 million for supreme court candidates). In addition, judicial candidates must file disclosure reports with the Texas Ethics Commission. Failure to comply with the law results in civil and possibly criminal penalties.

There are several loopholes in the act. Most importantly, there is no requirement that a judge who has received a large contribution from a lawyer or party to a suit before the court recuse himself or herself from the case. Also, the penalties for violating the contribution limits apply only to the candidate who accepts the contribution and not to the contributor. Incumbent judges who face little or no opposition in primary or general elections can still amass large war chests that intimidate potential candidates in future elections.[27] In other words, the Judicial Campaign Fairness Act faces many of the same dilemmas that confront attempts to regulate campaign finance for legislative or executive offices (see chapter 3).

In 1997, Texans for Public Justice (TPJ), a self-proclaimed judicial watchdog group, formed to spotlight the role of money in Texas judicial campaigns and to press for stronger campaign finance reforms. To influence public opinion, TPJ analyzes public campaign finance reports and unleashes high-profile press releases. TPJ argues that Texas Supreme Court justices raise money from court litigants and that their decisions are tainted as a result.[28] TPJ continued its campaign to convince citizens and policy makers that stricter limits are necessary to ensure justice in the courts. Some legislators, too, have taken up the reform agenda. For example, in 2001, Representative Pete Gallego introduced a bill to change Texas's judicial election system by prohibiting contributions to unopposed candidates. It failed. However, in 2003, the contribution limits to judicial candidates who are unopposed in either the primary election or the general election were reduced.

WHAT SHOULD I HAVE LEARNED?

The Texas judiciary is probably the least familiar of the three governmental branches to most Texans. The system is complex, disorganized, and caters to attorneys, who use phrases and terms with which most Texans are not familiar. In describing and analyzing the judiciary, we have answered the following questions:

- **What are the roots of the Texas judiciary?**

Texas's first courts were established in the Austin colony but were replaced by Mexican courts using Spanish law. Over the years, the court system has evolved through several constitutions. In most cases, there were few courts, and judges were elected by popular vote. The original court structure under the 1876 constitution changed through constitutional amendments to accommodate a growing population and number of lawsuits. The result has been the establishment of additional courts and adjustments to the courts' jurisdictions, creating the complex and confusing court system of today.

■ **What is the structure of the Texas judiciary?**

Five levels of courts make up the Texas judiciary. At the lowest level are local courts of limited jurisdiction, municipal courts and justice of the peace courts, which handle less serious criminal cases and some small civil suits. The county trial courts include constitutional county courts in every Texas county and statutory courts in many counties. These courts exercise original jurisdiction and some appellate jurisdiction. The trial courts of general and special jurisdiction have original jurisdiction in serious criminal cases and higher-dollar civil suits. The courts of appeals are intermediate appellate courts for criminal and civil cases. Texas has two courts of last resort: a supreme court for civil cases and a court of criminal appeals for criminal cases.

■ **What qualifications are necessary to be a part of the Texas judiciary, and how are judges selected?**

The qualifications necessary to be a judge vary by court. The qualifications for justice of the peace and constitutional county courts are minimal. For appellate courts, a license to practice law and experience as an attorney or judge are required. Most judges in Texas are middle-aged, Anglo males. Texas uses partisan elections to select most of its judges. Within the last two decades, judicial campaigns have become more expensive, and as Texas Supreme Court justices rely on contributions from lawyers and groups that have cases before the court, the public has come to question whether those judges can be fair and impartial in deciding cases.

■ **How does the judicial process work in Texas?**

The procedures in a criminal case are more formal and rigorous than in a civil case, but the process is similar. Criminal cases proceed through several identifiable stages from arrest to trial. At each stage, there are opportunities for the defendant to raise doubts about his or her guilt and end the process. In civil cases, which usually take longer to resolve, the process follows similar stages that lead to a settlement and possible award of damages.

■ **What reform proposals are receiving attention in Texas?**

Many suggest that the judicial structure could be unified and simplified so the public could understand the judiciary and its operation. The Texas legislature has considered establishing some variation of merit selection for judges. Several groups representing minorities have sought reforms to increase the number of Hispanic and African American judges in Texas. The legislature passed the Judicial Campaign Fairness Act of 1995; the act could be expanded and strengthened to achieve its goal of reducing the influence of campaign contributions on judicial elections.

Key Terms

application for discretionary review, p. 186
constitutional county court, p. 187
county court at law, p. 183
court of appeals, p. 184
district court, p. 183
justice of the peace court, p. 182
municipal court, p. 182
petition for review, p. 185
Texas Court of Criminal Appeals, p. 184
Texas Supreme Court, p. 184
trial *de novo,* p. 183

Researching the Texas Judiciary

In the Library

Anderson, Ken. *Crime in Texas,* revised ed. Austin: University of Texas Press, 2005.

Champagne, Anthony. "Interest Groups and Judicial Elections." *Loyola of Los Angeles Law Review* 34 (June 2001).

Champagne, Anthony, and Judith Haydel, eds. *Judicial Reform in the States.* New York: University Press of America, 1993.

Cook, Kerry Max. *Chasing Justice: My Story of Freeing Myself After Two Decades on Death Row for a Crime I Didn't Commit.* New York: William Morrow, 2007.

Dow, David R. *Executed on a Technicality: Lethal Injustice on America's Death Row.* Boston: Beacon, 2005.

Dow, David R., and Mark Dow, eds. *Machinery of Death: The Reality of America's Death Penalty Regime.* New York: Routledge, 2002.

Horton, David M., and Ryan Kellis Turner. *Lone Star Justice.* Austin: Eakin, 1999.

House Research Organization. *Focus Report: Should Texas Change Its Laws Dealing with Sex Offenders?* (October 18, 2006).

James, Tom. "Reforming Judicial Elections: The Case for Judicial Elections in Texas." *Veritas* 3 (March 2002).

Johnson, Orrin, and Laura J. Urbis. "Judicial Selection in Texas: A Gathering Storm?" *Texas Tech Law Review* 23 (1992): 525–69.

Marquart, James W., Sheldon Ekland-Olson, and Jonathan R. Sorensen. *The Rope, the Chair and the Needle: Capital Punishment in Texas, 1923–1990.* Austin: University of Texas Press, 1994.

Texans for Public Justice. *Supreme Spending: Political Expenditures by Texas' High-Court Justices.* Austin: Texans for Public Justice, 2008.

Texas Research League. "Texas Courts: A Study by the Texas Research League." Austin: Texas Research League, 1990–1992.

On the Web

Texas courts: **www.courts.state.tx.us**
This Texas Courts Online site is a portal to all the official Texas judicial Web pages.

Texas Court of Criminal Appeals **www.cca.courts.state.tx.us**
The Texas Court of Criminal Appeals posts information on cases, procedures, and the judges.

Texas Supreme Court: **www.supreme.courts.state.tx.us**
The Texas Supreme Court posts information on cases, procedures, the judges, and its administrative functions as the head of the judicial branch.

Office of Court Administration: **www.courts.state.tx.us/oca**
The Office of Court Administration provides resources, technical information, and information to and about Texas courts and judges.

Texas Civil Justice League and Texans for Lawsuit Reform: **www.tcjl.com** and **www.tortreform.com**
These two organizations represent business litigators and research and advocate for policy changes to reduce litigation against business interests.

Texans for Public Justice and the Texas Watch Foundation: **www.tpj.org** and **www.texaswatch.org**
These two organizations research the issue of money and judicial politics and advocate for policy changes to reduce the influence of money in judicial selection and judicial decision making.

7 Local Governments

On August 29, 2005, Hurricane Katrina walloped Louisiana and Mississippi with devastating consequences. In the midst of the chaos, Hurricane Rita formed in the Gulf of Mexico and took aim at Houston. Rita ultimately hit land on the Texas–Louisiana border just twenty-six days after Katrina. Harris County, the City of Houston, and other local governments along the Gulf Coast had to spring into emergency management mode to deal with the one-two punch of Katrina and Rita.

Tens of thousands fled New Orleans in the days after Katrina, spreading out across Louisiana, Texas, and other states. Harris County Judge Robert Eckels opened the Houston Astrodome to house evacuees. When it quickly filled with 12,000 people, he opened additional facilities. Mayor Bill White canceled events at the city's George Brown Convention Center so it could be used for people being bused in from New Orleans. Mayor White called Houston's State Representative Rick Noriega—who had just returned from a year spent in Afghanistan as Lt. Col. Noriega—and asked

him to coordinate the Brown Center. In two days, it was ready. Then, Rita threatened, and White and Eckels had to plan responses to the new threat.

Local officials all along the upper Texas coast announced evacuation plans, advising people to leave the areas most in danger from Rita. They also announced that there would be no emergency public transit, 911 service, or major shelters available. White asked Noriega to set up a series of last-resort shelters but to keep the plans quiet so that people would not be lulled into staying behind. In two days, the shelters were ready, and planners let police, fire, and rescue personnel know about them. With the horror of Katrina evident to anyone tuned in to media, coastal residents responded to the evacuation pleas. More than 2.5 million Texans fled Hurricane Rita. In what has been described as the biggest traffic jam in history, highways out of Houston and throughout southeast Texas became parking lots. Eventually, the state ordered "contraflow"—southbound lanes on some Interstate highways were converted to northbound lanes to relieve the congestion. Troops were sent in, and the Federal Emergency Management Agency delivered fuel, but the tankers had difficulty getting to motorists stranded on the highways without gasoline. When Rita finally hit, it had slowed somewhat, and it veered east of Houston. It still did extensive damage to southeast Texas and Louisiana, but

■ Devestating hurricanes repeatedly ravage the Texas coast, killing people, destroying property, and creating nightmarish problems for local governments. Galveston's 1900 hurricane, at left, is still the deadliest natural disaster in U.S. history, and resulted in the creation of the commission form of city government. In 2008, Hurricane Ike, at right, killed scores of people and caused billions of dollars of damage.

WHAT SHOULD I KNOW ABOUT . . .
- the roots of local government in Texas?
- Texas counties and how they operate?
- Texas cities and how they are governed?
- the creation and functions of special districts in Texas?
- proposals for reforms of local government and politics?

the heavily populated Houston area was mostly spared. The city's last-resort shelters in local school buildings took in 5,000 people the night the storm hit.

Local residents praised Mayor White and Judge Eckels for their proactive response to Rita. Others criticized the mass evacuation orders as unwise, preferring staged evacuation of the most vulnerable areas and people first. The Katrina and Rita dynamics exposed holes in the local, state, and federal emergency response systems. Governor Rick Perry set up an evacuation task force to study what had happened. Mayor White told the task force that the most urgent needs that local governments could not provide were fuel and management of people and traffic on highways. Galveston officials contended that the plan for sequenced evacuation had not been followed, and that finding inland shelters for evacuees was as big a problem as transportation. In early 2006, Governor Perry issued an order to set up regional evacuation management. But local authorities objected, saying that a regional plan would take away local control from mayors and county judges. By 2007, Mayor White had been awarded the John F. Kennedy Profiles in Courage award for his leadership, and by 2008, Rick Noriega was well known enough that he won the Democratic nomination for the U.S. Senate. Katrina and Rita, then, demonstrated the importance of the role of local governments in Texas, the tensions between state and local authority, and the potential for local government leadership to blossom into statewide political leadership.[1]

> **TO LEARN MORE—**
> **—TO DO MORE**
> Is your local government ready to respond to an emergency? Go to your city or county's emergency response Web site, such as Houston's Office of Emergency Management, www.houstontx.gov/oem/index.html, and familiarize yourself with plans for emergency response in your area.

How often have you heard someone, perhaps a politician, say that we ought to return power to the governments closest to the people? Such statements imply that local governments are more likely than other levels of government to reflect the will of the people. Such a proposition is interesting, as well as difficult to prove. Indeed, most people know less about their local governments than they do those farther away, and they do not even bother to express their will by voting in local elections! Yet, people come into contact with their local governments every day.

Texas has three basic categories of political subdivisions that can be characterized as local governments. There are 1,209 city governments, 254 county governments, and 3,372 "special district" governments, including 1,082 school districts.[2] These are all local governments, though some are also connected to state government (e.g., counties) and some are regional (e.g., hospital authorities), rather than strictly local in nature. (Texas also has twenty-four regional planning councils, or Councils of Governments—COGS—that are consortiums of local governments.) Some local governments are established directly in the Texas Constitution, while some are established in statute. The voluminous Local Government Code creates some political subdivisions and establishes rules for all of them.

In this chapter, we will discuss the forms and roles of local government and politics in Texas:

★ First, we will examine *the roots of local government in Texas,* including historical and constitutional influences.

★ Second, we will describe the structure, role, and function that *counties* play as local governments and administrative arms of the state government in Texas.

★ Third, we will look at the governance of *cities* in Texas and how forms, powers, and politics of city government have changed.

★ Fourth, we will explore the myriad *special districts* in Texas, with an emphasis on water districts and school districts.

★ Finally, we will look at *proposals for reform of local government* structures, interactions, and policies.

Roots of Local Government in Texas

The roots of governance for counties, cities, and schools in Texas go back to the colonial period. Few people lived in Texas when Spain and then Mexico governed the area, and there certainly were no settlements of any size. Thus, local governments that were created were expected to govern vast rural territories. Twenty-three large districts, or municipalities, were governed by a council, a judge, an attorney, a sheriff, and a secretary.[3] The 1827 Constitution of the State of Coahuila y Tejas also directed these local governments to establish schools to educate the young.[4]

When the Republic of Texas was formed, it continued using the local districts (municipalities) that Mexico had established, but it called them *counties.* In nineteenth-century rural America, including Texas, counties were the governmental point of contact for most people.[5] Texas copied the form of county government that was then prevalent in southern states of the United States. The Congress of the Republic also enacted laws creating cities as **municipal corporations.** By the end of the Republic, the Texas Congress had created thirty-six counties and incorporated fifty-three cities.

municipal corporation
A city.

These county and city governments became involved in protracted battles over the politics of education. Until the middle of the nineteenth century, education of children was a private or even church matter in the United States. Texas was forming its political structures and policies at the time that the idea of public education was gaining hold. One of the grievances cited by Texians in 1836 was that the Mexican government had failed to establish a system of public education. The 1836 Constitution of the Republic of Texas required the Texas Congress to establish a general system of education, though little was done.

TEXAS IN COMPARISON

Local Government in the States

Texas does not have some local governments, such as townships that a number of other states have. But, states can be compared on the basic forms of local governments—cities, counties, and special districts (2007 Census estimates).

	Number of Cities	Number of Counties	Number of Special Districts	Largest County (population in millions)	Largest City (population in millions)
Texas	1,209	254	3,372	Harris (3.9)	Houston (2.1)
California	478	57	3,809	Los Angeles (9.9)	Los Angeles (3.8)
New York	618	57	1,799	Kings (2.5)	New York City (8.2)
Florida	411	66	1,146	Miami-Dade (2.4)	Jacksonville (0.8)

When Texas joined the United States, the Republic's form of government for counties was brought forward with few changes. As Texas's population grew in the 1840s and 1850s, so did demands for smaller counties. The legislature obliged, passing laws carving the large counties that had originated with Spanish and Mexican governments into smaller counties and requiring that county courthouses be so centrally located that each citizen could travel to the seat, vote, and return home in a day. By 1861, there were 122 counties.[6] During those early days of statehood, the legislature continued to incorporate cities; it also wrote a new general state law providing rules for the incorporation of small cities, though the legislature still wrote their charters.[7]

Texas's early state constitutions carried forward the republic's constitutional support for public education through local governments, though with varying degrees of support. Some Texans believed that the state should provide free education through locally controlled schools, while others believed that education was a private function. In 1854, the legislature made state funds available to local (mostly private) schools. The 1869 constitution mandated a strong public education system, but the taxes levied to support the system generated intense opposition, fueling the fires against the Reconstruction constitution.[8]

Texas's statutory constitution of 1876 (see chapter 2) spells out powers and policies for various local governments. Article 9 of the Texas Constitution of 1876 is "Counties." Yet, in Article 11, "Municipal Corporations," the first section is "Counties as Legal Subdivisions. The several counties of this State are hereby recognized as legal subdivisions of the State." Through statutes passed under this constitution, the legislature has also filled in additional details for local governments.

The constitution of 1876 continued the basic form of county government but increased the number of county officers. The legislature continued to expand the number of counties until 1931, when Loving County (along the New Mexico border) was organized as the 254th county. As the number of counties grew, disputes over boundaries inevitably arose, pitting one county against another. The legislature responded by passing specific bills affixing the boundaries of counties in dispute and by passing new laws in a (futile) attempt to avoid future boundary disputes.[9]

Under the constitution of 1876, a general state law still allowed local incorporation of small cities, but the legislature found itself writing numerous municipal charters for growing cities. As a result of a nationwide municipal **home rule** movement, Texas adopted a constitutional amendment in 1912 that allowed some cities to decide their own structure and, with some limits, their powers.[10] In 1933, the constitution was amended to allow *counties* home-rule authority also, but the conditions under which a county could qualify for home-rule status were so stringent that no county successfully converted to home-rule status. Moreover, the attorney general ruled that

home rule
The right and authority of a local government to govern itself, rather than have the state govern it.

What is the Texas Association of Counties? The Texas Association of Counties represents county governments at the state capitol and provides professional services to them and their employees. Its headquarters is located just blocks from the capitol.

Analyzing Visuals: Texas Counties and Population

Study this map depicting the counties with the largest populations, smallest populations, largest percentage increase in population, and largest percentage loss in population.

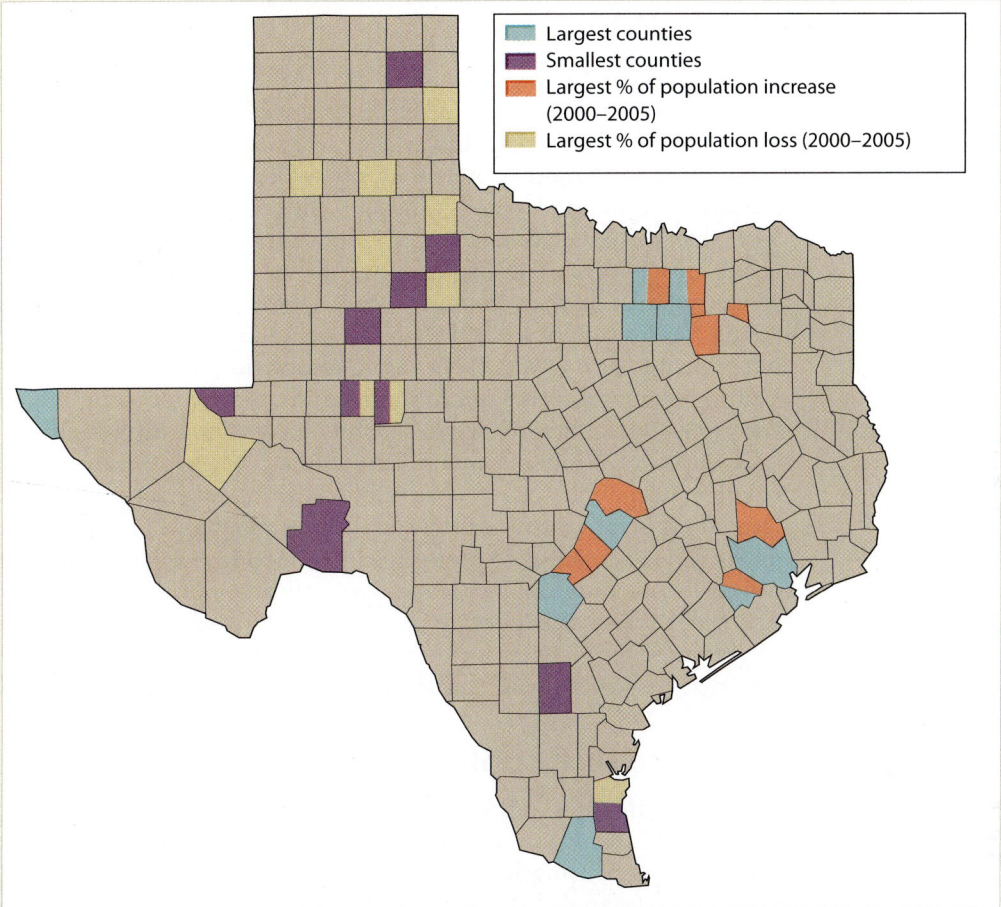

Consider the following questions:

WHAT pattern do you see in the location of counties with the greatest percentage increase?

WHAT pattern do you see in the location of counties with the largest percentage loss?

WHAT effect do you think these differences in populations and growth or loss rates have on the ability of a county government to meet the needs of the residents?

WHAT changes in structure would allow counties to operate more effectively?

Source: Texas State Data Center, *2004 Total Population Estimates for Texas Counties*, Table 1 (2000 and 2005 data), txsdc.utsa.edu/tpepp/2004_txpopest_county.php.

---

no county could abolish any of the offices that were constitutionally established for counties. The provision was repealed from the constitution as "deadwood" in 1969.[11]

Finally, the 1876 constitution (Article 7, section 1) requires the legislature to "establish and make suitable provision for the support and maintenance of an efficient system of public free schools." When Texas embraced the concept of public schools in the late nineteenth century, first county commissioners were empowered to run the schools, then cities, then separate school districts. What resulted was a patchwork of systems around the state. In 1900, the legislature required that independent school districts be governed by seven-member boards of trustees, whose members must be elected in at-large elections.[12]

Counties

Texas has by far the largest number of counties of any state: 254. Brewster County, the largest with 6,204 square miles of territory, is larger than Connecticut, Delaware, or Rhode Island. Harris County is the most populous, with nearly 3.9 million people. It also is the third most populous county in the nation—behind Los Angeles County, California, and Cook County (Chicago), Illinois. The population of Harris County is larger than the population in twenty-four states. Loving County is the least populous, having dropped to only fifty-nine residents in 2007.[13] (To study the population change patterns in Texas counties, see Analyzing Visuals: Texas Counties and Population.) Texas's counties have formed an organization to facilitate communication and to represent their interests. The **Texas Association of Counties,** with headquarters in Austin, provides information, training, and other services for Texas county officials. The group also lobbies the legislature on behalf of county governments.[14]

Texas Association of Counties
Professional association and lobbying arm for county governments.

County governments are multifunctional. Their primary areas of responsibility include roads, public safety, jails, public health, and elections. In Texas, counties are both administrative arms of the state government and locally elected governmental bodies. The state needs to perform some functions—such as elections, public health initiatives, and automobile registration—throughout the state but cannot staff state offices all across this large state. So, counties serve as local offices to administer some programs for the state government. At the same time, counties perform many functions that are strictly local, so their officers are selected locally.

Structure of County Government

When delegates met in the constitutional convention in 1875, a primary goal was to limit government's power. Chapter 2 discussed how they limited state government power by fragmenting it, and they did the same with county government. County authority is fragmented into offices consisting of a county judge, commissioners, county attorney, district attorney, sheriff, treasurer, auditor, tax assessor-collector, county clerk, judges, district clerk, justices of the peace, constables, and other offices.

County officers (except for the auditor) are elected to four-year terms. The county runs the state's elections, so county offices are on the general election ballot at the same time as state elections, with officials elected in partisan elections. All are elected county-wide, except for the four commissioners, the justices of the peace, and constables.

COUNTY COMMISSIONERS COURT The primary governing entity for the county is the commissioners court,[15] whose form is prescribed by the constitution as consisting of one county judge and four county commissioners. (To learn more about the constitution's language, see The Living Constitution.) The **county judge** is formally the judge for court cases heard in the county (through the "constitutional county court"), but modern-day county judges have turned over many judicial functions to district courts and county courts-at-law (see chapter 6). Some county judges, primarily in rural counties, retain nonlitigation judicial matters, such as wills. Despite the name, though, today's county judge is actually the chief executive officer of the county. He or she also serves as a voting member and the chair of the commissioners court.

county judge
Elected official who is the chief administrative officer of county government, serves on the commissioners court, and may also have some judicial functions.

commissioners court
The legislative body of a county in Texas.

county commissioner
Elected official who serves on the county legislative body, the commissioners court.

The **commissioners court,** as the legislative body for the county, is responsible for adopting the budget for all county offices, setting tax rates, overseeing county programs, and redistricting. The four **county commissioners** perform both legislative

The Living Constitution

Each county shall…be divided into four commissioners precincts in each of which shall be elected by the qualified voters thereof one County Commissioner, who shall hold office for four years. . . . The County Commissioners . . ., with the County Judge as presiding officer, shall compose the County Commissioners Court, which shall exercise such powers and jurisdiction over all county business, as is conferred by this Constitution and the laws of the State, or as may be hereafter prescribed.

ARTICLE 5, SECTION 18

The Texas Constitution establishes the structure for county government and its powers in Article 5. The principal problems for counties are their constitutionally mandated structure and their lack of powers. As former Yale law professor George D. Braden notes, "Notwithstanding several constitutional provisions concerning powers of counties. . ., numerous statutes spelling out county powers, and a great many court cases, it is easy to explain the constitutional powers of counties: there are hardly any."[a] Many argue that the answer to these problems is home rule for Texas counties.

In 1933, the legislature proposed a constitutional amendment to Article 9 to allow county home rule, and a majority of citizens supported the amendment. Purportedly adopted during the Great Depression to reduce the cost of government, the amendment proved unworkable. In practice, the requirement that a county home-rule charter be adopted by *a majority of qualified electors in the county*, *a majority of those voting in the incorporated areas of the county*, and *a majority of those voting in the unincorporated areas of the county* made county home rule impossible.[b]

In El Paso County, shortly after the amendment's adoption, a group pushed for a home-rule charter. They produced a charter that most considered an improvement for county government, and the proposal was endorsed by the *El Paso Herald-Post*, which ran a series of articles preceding the charter election. The voters in the city of El Paso approved the charter by a 1,143 vote margin in the May 1934 election, but voters outside the city defeated the charter by a margin of 848 votes. Although the countywide margin for approval was 295 votes, the charter was defeated because the charter failed to receive a majority of rural El Paso County votes.

Also in 1934, Travis County initiated a home-rule campaign, but legal questions about the charter commission's authority ended the movement. The third county to seek home rule in 1934 was Tarrant County, which failed because the county commissioners court ignored the home-rule charter convention's proposal. Home-rule movements in Bexar, Dallas, and Harris Counties in 1934 failed for various reasons.[c] In 1969, the home-rule amendment was removed from the Texas Constitution.

Home rule for Texas counties would permit each county's residents to create a government that would fit the residents' specific needs. A merger of county and city governments and offices could occur. Counties also could make and enforce local ordinances, as home-rule cities do now. As a result, the legislature would no longer be required to solve individual county problems with amendments to the Texas Constitution or state laws.[d]

CRITICAL THINKING QUESTIONS

1. If a workable amendment allowing Texas counties to establish home rule were adopted, what changes would you anticipate in your county? Would governments (city, county, and special districts) be merged?
2. What problems would your county face in establishing a home-rule charter? Why?

---

[a] George D. Braden, *The Constitution of the State of Texas: An Annotated and Comparative Analysis*, vol. 1 (Austin: Texas Legislative Council, 1977), 448.
[b] Braden, *The Constitution of the State of Texas*, 652.
[c] Robert E. Norwood, *Texas County Government: Let the People Choose* (Austin: Texas Research League, 1970), 72–74.
[d] Braden, *The Constitution of the State of Texas*, 652.

What buildings serve county government functions? Potter County has the largest population (115,000) of any county in the Texas Panhandle. The county courthouse, pictured here, is in Amarillo, the seat of county government.

and executive functions and are elected from single-member districts called precincts. Commissioners serve four-year, staggered terms. Every two years at the general election, two commissioners are elected. Each commissioner is responsible for building and maintaining county roads in his or her precinct. Throughout much of the twentieth century, the commissioners' primary job was to provide roads for farmers to get to and from town. In fact, they are still known in some areas as "road commissioners."

The commissioners court must perform redistricting functions for county commissioner precincts. Since counties have historically been governments for rural Texans, and since commissioners wanted to divide up the road duties equally among the four precincts, commissioners courts often drew precinct district lines to produce four districts that were geographically fairly equal sized. Thus, each commissioner had a sizeable rural area in his or her precinct. After the U.S. Supreme Court declared that congressional and state legislative district lines must be drawn to produce equal population districts,[16] a resident of Midland County, Texas, sued the county, arguing that equal representation should also apply to this local legislative body. In 1968, the U.S. Supreme Court agreed, in *Avery* v. *Midland County*,[17] declaring that the one-person, one-vote standard applied to counties as well. Since then, Texas county commissioners courts have had to base their redistricting on the population count in the decennial U.S. Census. As a result, in Texas's metropolitan areas, county commissioners courts are now elected by the majority urban residents, rather than by rural residents.

DISTRICT ATTORNEYS AND COUNTY ATTORNEYS Counties elect district attorneys, county attorneys, and/or criminal district attorneys. There is no uniform system applied across the state. The chief prosecutors for violations of state laws are usually district attorneys. A **district attorney (DA)** or a **criminal district attorney** may be elected from and serve one county, but in areas of small population, the DA may be elected from and serve a judicial district that encompasses more than one county. Most counties also elect a **county attorney,** who provides legal advice and services to the county government. If there is no district attorney serving the county, the county attorney also prosecutes criminal cases and represents the county in civil cases. If there is a district attorney, the county attorney prosecutes less serious criminal cases (misdemeanors), though again, the practices are not uniform across the state.

SHERIFF The **sheriff** serves as chief law enforcement officer in the county. While sheriffs' departments have countywide jurisdiction, generally they operate in the unincorporated areas of the county and leave law enforcement in the cities to municipal police departments. Sheriffs may also contract to provide law enforcement for small cities. The sheriff hires deputies, and together they provide general public safety protection for citizens, serve warrants and civil papers, conduct criminal investigations, arrest offenders, and operate the county jail (which holds alleged and convicted county offenders, and where alleged felons who are not released on bond await trial in district courts).

COUNTY CLERK AND DISTRICT CLERK The **county clerk** keeps records for the county commissioners court and for county courts. He or she is also the official keeper of records such as real estate titles and marriage licenses. County clerks are responsible for conducting county and state elections, except where the county has a separate elections administrator. **District clerks** keep records for district courts. In large counties, the district clerk may serve several courts; in other areas, the district clerk may

district attorney (DA)
Elected official who prosecutes criminal cases.

criminal district attorney
Elected official who prosecutes criminal cases.

county attorney
Elected official serving as the legal officer for county government and also as a criminal prosecutor.

sheriff
Elected official who serves as the chief law enforcement officer in a county.

county clerk
Elected official who serves as the clerk for the commissioners court and for county records.

district clerk
Elected official who is responsible for keeping the records for the district court.

serve one district court that covers several counties in a judicial district. In some small counties, one clerk may perform the duties of the county and district clerk.

JUDGES AND CONSTABLES District judges, county court-at-law judges, justices of the peace, and constables provide judicial and court services. The number of each varies from county to county, as the legislature has adopted a crazy-quilt pattern of institutions and officials, county by county, depending on population size and on local initiatives asking the legislature for special consideration. (These officials are discussed more in chapter 6.)

COUNTY TAX ASSESSOR-COLLECTOR The **county tax assessor-collector** is responsible for an array of functions. These include collecting local property taxes, registering voters, registering automobiles, and collecting motor vehicle sales taxes and registration fees. Because the legislature created county central appraisal districts in the 1970s, tax assessor-collectors do not actually assess property values anymore. Instead, the central appraisal district assesses the value of property for all taxing entities in the county and the tax assessor-collector collects the taxes.

> **county tax assessor-collector**
> Elected official who collects taxes for the county (and perhaps for other local governments).

TREASURER AND AUDITOR The **county treasurer** is the county's money manager. The treasurer deposits revenue collected by the county, signs checks, disburses funds, keeps accounts of receipts and expenditures of county funds, and invests county funds. All but the smallest counties are also required to have a **county auditor** who audits records of all county officers and departments, helps prepare the county budget, and sets up and administers the accounting systems. Unlike other county officials, the auditor is appointed for a two-year term by the district court. Because auditor and treasurer functions are similar, many counties have decided that they do not need both. Several counties have asked the legislature for constitutional amendments to abolish the requirement that they have a treasurer. The legislature and voters have obliged—amending the constitution to repeal the requirement for some specific counties but not for others.[18]

> **county treasurer**
> Elected official who serves as the money manager for county government.
>
> **county auditor**
> Official appointed by a district judge to audit county finances.

Authority of County Governments

County authority is established, in excruciating detail, both in the Texas Constitution and in statute. Article 9 of the constitution is devoted to counties, and other articles also address county structure and power (for instance, Article 16, section 44, is devoted to county treasurers and surveyors). The **Local Government Code** devotes Chapters 71–88 to counties, plus scattered provisions in other chapters (for instance, Chapter 111 designates the county judge as the county budget officer).

> **Local Government Code**
> The Texas statutory code containing state laws about local governments.

Counties are limited to the specific grants of power and areas of responsibility spelled out in the constitution and statutes. Consequently, when new problems arise, or when counties have difficulty administering existing laws, they must seek new or clarified authority from the legislature. For instance, Chapter 231 of the Local Government Code grants county regulatory zoning authority limited to a few specific places where severe problems have arisen, such as Padre Island. Another example is that the constitution requires counties to provide health care for those who cannot afford to pay for it themselves. As health care costs soared, counties had more and more difficulty meeting this obligation. In 1985, the legislature responded with a major initiative for indigent health care, providing expanded authority for counties to address the problem. Now, counties are pursuing regionalization to provide mandated indigent care and other services.

Of course, another method of responding to county-level problems would be to grant them **general ordinance-making authority,** the legal right to adopt ordinances covering a wide array of subject areas—an authority that cities have. The Texas Association of Counties has lobbied the legislature in favor of expanded authority numerous times, but developers and realtors have opposed the counties, and the legislature has repeatedly defeated the effort. In 1999, however, in the wake of the boom of suburban and rural development and the court decision in *Elgin Bank* v. *Travis County*, the legis-

> **general ordinance-making authority**
> The legal right to adopt ordinances covering a wide array of subject areas, authority that cities have but counties do not.

Who runs the city of Houston? Houston's mayor is the only "strong mayor" in Texas's largest cities. Here, Mayor Bill White confers with citizens. White's leadership in the wake of Hurricanes Katrina and Rita in 2005 earned him a "Profiles in Courage" award in 2007, and he is a potential candidate for statewide office in 2010.

lature approved a new law (in Chapter 232 of the Local Government Code) that allows counties significant authority to regulate subdivisions. The law requires platting and drainage in new subdivisions and gives counties authority to enforce those requirements.[19] (Platting is the process by which land is subdivided for development, and the county's review ensures that the proposed subdivision provides adequate roads and other amenities to serve the proposed development.) Since then, numerous counties have begun using the new powers.[20]

A key function of county governments is administering elections. As the whole nation learned from Florida's 2000 elections, counties have independent authority to make many election decisions, and uniform election procedures do not always exist from county to county. Following the 2000 Florida fiasco, in which confusing butterfly ballots and faulty punch-card systems made some votes invalid, the Texas legislature in 2001 revamped county election authority and procedures: punch-card ballots would be phased out; any new voting system must meet accessibility needs of disabled voters; butterfly ballots are prohibited; ballots must be hand inspected; ineligible-voter lists must be verified by the county.[21] In response to Congress's Help America Vote Act of 2002, the Texas legislature adopted additional measures in 2003 to ensure compliance with the act, including the creation of a statewide voter registration list and the provision of at least one direct recording electronic (DRE) voting device at each polling place.[22]

Finances of County Governments

While most property tax revenues go to school districts (see the section on special districts), counties have relied heavily on the property tax to fund the myriad services they provide. Skyrocketing taxes have led the legislature to impose more and more requirements on counties for hearings, notice, and reports of votes on actions that raise the effective tax rate—even prescribing the exact words that a county commissioner must recite in a motion to change taxes.[23] In 1987, the legislature allowed counties to collect a sales tax, but only if the county is not part of a metropolitan area with a metropolitan transit authority that collects a sales tax. The effect of this arrangement is that rural counties and those with medium-sized cities can collect sales taxes, but metropolitan area counties cannot.

In recent years, counties have increased their reliance on fee revenues. Some fee revenues (for instance, motor vehicle registration fees) are pass-through: counties collect the state-imposed fees and send the money on to Austin, retaining a small portion allowed for county overhead. Counties are authorized to collect other fees that are totally county revenues. The legislature has created numerous new fees in recent years, especially in the area of criminal justice. These include jury fees, processing fees, hot check fees, crime-stopper fees, video fees, witness summons fees, breath-testing fees, courthouse security fees, and others. The collection and distribution system for these fees is complicated and confusing for offices throughout the courthouse. Moreover, the 2005 legislature mandated that counties implement a court fee collection program.[24] Counties collect more than thirty different fees for state government, plus about thirty fees for local services. In 2001, voters approved a constitutional amendment to consolidate local fees.[25]

In the 2003 legislative session, with the state facing a $10 billion deficit, the legislature cut services, increased fees, and passed the costs of programs to the counties. In response, county officials pushed (unsuccessfully) for a constitutional amendment to prohibit the state from imposing underfunded or unfunded mandates on the counties.[26]

Cities

Texas has 1,209 cities. Houston is the largest, with 2.1 million citizens. Most cities, however, are small, and size matters in the type of government that the city may have. As Texans moved off the farms and into cities in the late nineteenth and early twentieth centuries, burgeoning cities found it difficult to manage the new growth and to respond to social, economic, and infrastructure problems that the growth brought. They turned to the state legislature for new authority and new governmental forms. As rural populations dwindled, the rural-dominated legislature sometimes violated requirements to redistrict, thus keeping incumbents in power. Cities often could not get what they wanted from the hostile state legislature.

Other states faced similar dynamics. In 1875, Missouri decided to allow cities to adopt their own charters and decide how to govern themselves, thus triggering a movement across the nation for municipal home rule. Home-rule proposals became a part of the agenda of the Progressive movement in the early 1900s. In 1911, the Texas legislature proposed a constitutional amendment for municipal home rule, and voters approved it in 1912. In 1913, the legislature passed a law implementing home rule, stipulating generally that home-rule cities may adopt any provisions that are not inconsistent with the state constitution or statutes. Today, forty-eight states have some form of municipal home rule.[27]

When the municipal home-rule amendment was added to the constitution in 1912, it authorized cities with more than 5,000 people to write their own city charter and decide what structure and authority to give their city government. Today, 315 cities are home-rule cities. The others are called **general-law cities,** because they are governed by the general state laws regarding municipalities, rather than by a locally adopted charter.[28] For small general-law cities, the Local Government Code spells out the form and powers of the city government, and even specific actions that the city must follow. For instance, the code stipulates that general-law cities contract with a newspaper in the municipality to publish all ordinances, notices, and other matters required to be published.

The idea behind home rule is that city leaders need tools to address their local problems, and that one-size-fits-all state provisions deny cities the flexibility they need. For any city that qualifies for home rule, the Local Government Code stipulates that the city "may adopt and operate under any form of government" and that "the

general-law cities
Cities with fewer than 5,000 residents, governed by a general state law rather than by a locally adopted charter.

Join the Debate

Should Texas Cities Be Allowed to Photograph Red-Light Runners?

OVERVIEW: Running red lights is a national problem. In 2002, as many as 207,000 crashes, 178,000 injuries, and 921 fatalities in the United States were attributed to red-light running.[a] The problem is particularly acute in Texas. In the 1990s, Texas had the fourth highest total of fatalities attributed to running red lights, and five Texas cities (Dallas, Corpus Christi, Austin, Houston, and El Paso) were among the top thirty cities in the nation in red-light-running fatalities. According to Texas Department of Public Safety crash records, the number of people killed or injured in crashes attributable to red-light running increased from about 10,000 in 1975 to about 25,000 in 1999.[b] Although several factors contribute to red-light-running crashes, such as poorly designed intersections and human error, many cities have adopted one method to combat the problem: photographing red-light runners with automated cameras. More than one hundred communities have installed cameras at traffic lights to record the license plates of red-light runners, most extensively in California, Maryland, and North Carolina. In Texas, Garland led the way, followed by Houston, El Paso, and others, including Austin.[c]

The application of new technology such as automated cameras to apprehend red-light runners has been controversial. Some argue that such "big brother" government techniques are dangerous to civil liberties. Lobbyists for cities, uncertain about the status of state law over this new policy area, tried for years to get explicit authorization from the Texas legislature for traffic camera systems. In 2003, their bill was again defeated, but a different version was then added to another bill and passed, with opponents angry that the measure was slipped in without people knowing what it would do. The 2007 legislature passed a measure to further regulate the use of red-light cameras.

Read and think about the following arguments for and against using cameras at traffic lights to identify red-light runners. Then, join the debate by answering the questions posed after the arguments.

Arguments IN FAVOR of Using Red-Light Cameras

- **Red-light cameras reduce the number of fatalities resulting from vehicles running red lights.** Several cities using red-light cameras, including Washington, D.C., and San Francisco and Oxnard, California, have experienced a significant reduction in intersection crashes and fatalities.

---

municipality has full power of local self government." Thus, some home-rule cities decide, for instance, to operate their own electric company, while others do not; some allow citizens to recall city officials from office, while others do not. The city of Austin decided (via a voter initiative) to place limits on local campaign finances.

A century of statutory amendments prevents home-rule cities and general-law cities from falling into neat categories. The Local Government Code is full of convoluted statutes and terminology for Type A general-law municipalities, Type B general-law municipalities, Type C general-law municipalities, special-law municipalities, and home-rule municipalities.

Even home-rule municipalities sometimes have state laws passed to restrict their authority to govern themselves or to give them special authority. For instance, the Local Government Code stipulates that if the city of Houston does not adopt a voter-approved local ordinance providing for some single-member districts, then it must

- Red-light cameras allow law enforcement personnel to concentrate on other matters. Freed from the necessity of watching for red-light runners, police can concentrate on other serious threats to public safety, such as rapes and murders.
- Red-light cameras are a constitutional method of enforcing traffic codes. When operating a motor vehicle in open view of the public, one cannot expect privacy. No constitutional guarantee is being violated by the use of red-light cameras.

Arguments AGAINST Using Red-Light Cameras
- Red-light cameras violate an individual's right to privacy protected by several amendments to the U.S. Constitution and the Texas Constitution. Among the concerns are that the wrong person can get the citation, vehicle owners are assumed to be guilty, and the driver cannot tell his or her side of the story. These concerns are based on constitutional protections afforded by the Fourth Amendment (protection against unreasonable searches and seizures), the Fifth Amendment (the right to remain silent), the Sixth Amendment (the right to confront accusers), and the Fourteenth Amendment (due process and equal protection of the law).
- Red-light cameras are used by cities to generate income and not to achieve safety goals. In Garland, Texas, tens of thousands of drivers have been photographed running red lights, and the city has taken in more than $2.5 million in fines. Moreover the cameras can be calibrated to shorten the yellow-light period, quickening revenue, but not safety.
- Red-light running can be reduced through methods that do not infringe on individual liberties. Traffic safety engineers note that redesigning intersections, synchronizing traffic signals, larger traffic signal heads, and longer yellow lights reduce red-light running.

Continuing the Debate
1. Do you favor or oppose the use of red-light cameras? What other methods might curtail the problem of red-light running?
2. Is the invasion of privacy resulting from the use of red-light cameras an acceptable outcome in order to save lives and reduce the number and cost of intersection crashes? Why or why not?

To Follow the Debate Online Go To:
National Campaign to Stop Red-Light Running www.stopredlightrunning.com

American Civil Liberties Union aclu.org/privacy/spying/15718pub20010821.html

Highway Robbery Red Light Cameras www.highwayrobbery.net

---

[a]National Campaign to Stop Red-Light Running, "The Problem," March 22, 2006, www.stopredlightrunning.com/html/problem.htm.

[b]James Bonneson, "STOP! Running That Red Light Could Be Deadly," *Texas Transportation Researcher* 39:2 (2003), tti.tamu.edu/researcher/newsletter; Cesar Quiroga, Edgar Kraus, Ida van Schalkwyk, and James Bonneson, "Red Light Running: A Policy Review," Texas Transportation Institute, Texas A&M University, Report No. CTS-02/150206-1, March 2003, tti.tamu.edu/cts/reports/cts-02.pdf.; House Research Organization, "Red-light Cameras in Texas: A Status Report," *Focus Report* July 31, 2006.

[c]National Campaign to Stop Red-Light Running, "Red Light Cameras," February 11, 2006, www.stopredlightrunning.com/html/redlight.htm.

---

follow a specific form spelled out in the statute. (The city responded to the pressure and adopted its own system.) Other sections of the law apply only to the city of Austin. The legislature, however, must be careful. Laws aimed at one specific local government are unconstitutional,[29] so legislators devise laws that apply to cities in a particular population bracket. Of course, they can try to create a population bracket that encompasses only one city, so long as no one challenges it in court.

Why does the legislature pass laws seemingly at odds with home-rule provisions of the Texas Constitution and Local Government Code? When local battles become unresolvable or one party does not like the outcome of a local decision, one party will turn to the legislature and ask for relief. The legislature then has to decide between, for instance, local developers lobbying for a law to restrict municipal authority, and city officials opposing the bill. For an example of this tension between local and state authority, see Join the Debate: Should Texas Cities Be Allowed to Photograph Red-Light Runners?

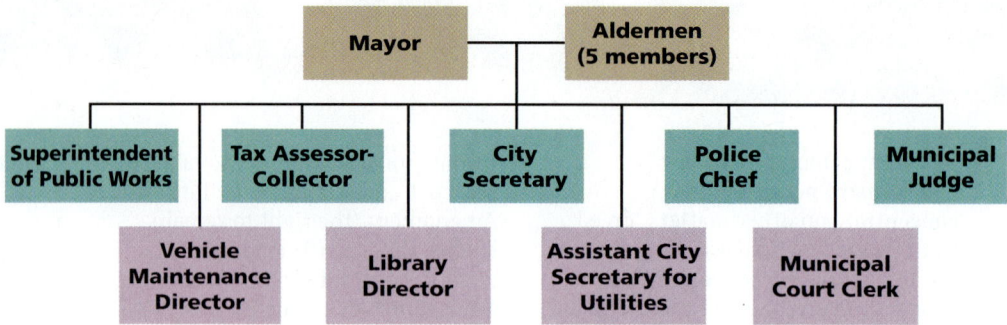

FIGURE 7.1 Organizational Chart: City of Waller (General Law) Waller, Texas, is an incorporated city with about 2,000 residents, requiring it to be a general-law city.

Source: Derived by authors from City of Waller Web site, www.wallertexas.com.

Forms of City Governments

For most general-law cities, the Local Government Code mandates a mayor–council or commission form of government, depending on the class of the general-law city.[30] To learn more about general law cities, see Figure 7.1, depicting the organizational scheme for Waller, a general-law city in Waller County, outside Houston.

For home-rule cities able to decide their own form of government, what are the options available? The four general types are **weak mayor–council, strong mayor–council, council–manager,** and **city commission.** The details of these forms, however, vary from city to city. About 290 Texas home-rule cities have chosen the council–manager form of government, fifteen have chosen weak mayor–council, and four have chosen strong mayor–council. To learn more about types of cities in Texas, see Table 7.1.[31]

WEAK MAYOR–COUNCIL The mayor could be elected at large or by the city council from among their members. The mayor has authority to preside over city council meetings, is the symbolic head of government, and presides at ribbon-cutting ceremonies, but is essentially equal in power to other city council members. The collective council hires, manages, and fires city staff. To learn more about weak-mayor cities, see Figure 7.2, which shows the city organizational chart for White Oak, a weak-mayor home-rule city in Gregg County, bordering Longview.

weak mayor–council
A form of city government in which the mayor has no more power than any other member of the council.

strong mayor–council
A form of city government in which the mayor has strong powers to run the city by hiring, managing, and firing staff and controlling executive departments; the mayor also serves on the council.

council–manager
A form of city government in which the city council and mayor hire a professional manager to run the city.

city commission
A form of city government in which elected members serve on the legislative body and also serve as head administrators of city programs.

TABLE 7.1 Type of Government and Election Systems in Texas's Top Ten Cities

Texas home-rule cities may choose any form of city government: mayor–council, commission, or council–manager. A city's election system, however, must conform to the requirements of U.S. and Texas constitutions and laws. Since the 1970s, many Texas cities have been sued under the federal Voting Rights Act to force changes in the manner of election of city officials.

	Type of Government	City Council Election System	Estimated Population 2007 (thousands)
Houston	Strong Mayor–Council	9 single-member districts, 5 at-large, mayor at-large	2,075
San Antonio	Council–Manager	10 single-member districts, mayor at-large	1,236
Dallas	Council–Manager	14 single-member districts, mayor at-large	1,210
Austin	Council–Manager	6 at-large-by-place, mayor at-large	682
Fort Worth	Council–Manager	8 single-member districts, mayor at-large	603
El Paso	Council-Manager	8 single-member districts, mayor at-large	592
Arlington	Council–Manager	5 single-member districts, 3 at-large, mayor at-large	359
Corpus Christi	Council–Manager	5 single-member districts, 3 at-large, mayor at-large	281
Plano	Council–Manager	4 single-member districts, 3 at-large, mayor at-large	245
Garland	Council–Manager	8 single-member districts, mayor at-large	217

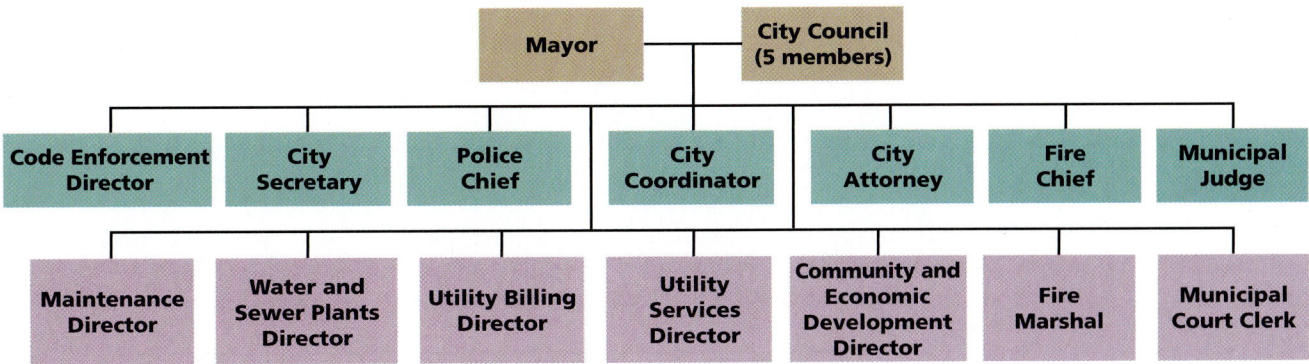

FIGURE 7.2 **Organizational Chart: City of White Oak (Weak Mayor)** White Oak, Texas, is an incorporated city that grew to just over 5,000 residents by 1990 and converted to home-rule status. Its population grew to more than 5,600 by 2000. So far, it has retained a weak mayor–council structure.
Source: Derived by authors from City of White Oak Web site, www.cityofwhiteoak.com.

STRONG MAYOR–COUNCIL The strong mayor is distinguished from a weak mayor by his or her executive powers. The mayor is elected citywide, presides at city council meetings, hires, manages, and fires city staff, and may have the power to veto actions of the city council. Most large American cities have strong mayors. In Texas, few cities have strong mayors, and among Texas's ten largest cities, only Houston uses the strong mayor–council form; Dallas defeated strong-mayor proposals twice in 2005. To learn more about strong-mayor cities, see Figure 7.3, showing the city organizational chart for the city of Houston.

COUNCIL–MANAGER Progressive-era reform empowers a professional manager, hired by the city council, to run the city (hire, manage, and fire staff), while the city council and mayor set policy, adopt budgets and tax rates, and oversee the manager. Most home-rule cities in Texas have city managers. To learn more about the city manager form of government, see Figure 7.4, which depicts the city organizational chart for Austin, a council–manager system. The mayor and city council hire their own staff as well as the municipal judges, court clerk, city clerk, city auditor, and city manager. The city manager hires all other city employees and directs their activities.

CITY COMMISSION On September 8, 1900, the deadliest natural disaster in U.S. history devastated Galveston, the wealthiest city in Texas at the time. A hurricane killed an estimated 8,000 to 10,000 people and wiped out three-fourths of the city. Human remains were still being found five months later. In attempting to cope with the disaster, the legislature allowed Galveston to revamp its city government, giving authority to specific individuals (commissioners) to govern particular policy areas (such as public health, public safety, public improvements). The city managed to build a major sea wall, prop up houses and buildings, and clean up and rebuild the city.[32] In this form of government, the commissioners meet as a body to adopt budgets, set tax rates, and perform other communal functions, but each individual member has authority in the specified functional area. After Galveston's experience, the commission form of government spread quickly to nearly 500 cities across the nation, but the form has since fallen into disuse amid charges of turf battles and lack of coordination among the officials. Today, no Texas city uses the commission form of government.[33] Some cities use the term "commission" rather than "council" for the governing body, but they do not have the commission form of government.

FIGURE 7.3 Organizational Chart: Houston (Strong Mayor)
Source: City of Houston, www.houstontx.gov.

Thinking Nationally

Strong Mayor Government

New York City, Los Angeles, Chicago—the great (and large) cities of the United States are governed by strong mayors who hire, direct, and fire city staff and sometimes have veto authority over city council actions. New York City has a population of 8.2 million—larger than the population of most states—and a strong mayor is seen as essential to effective government there. Houston, Texas's largest city, is governed by a strong mayor. Yet, other large cities—including Dallas and San Antonio, the ninth and tenth largest cities in the nation—are not. Dallas, in fact, defeated strong mayor proposals twice in 2005.

- Why would the strong mayor form of government be unpopular in Texas?
- As the big cities of Texas become giant cities, will current governmental structures be able to govern them effectively?
- Would Houston Mayor Bill White have been able to respond as quickly and decisively to Hurricane Rita if he had not had strong mayor powers?

Authority and Functions of City Governments

Cities are multifunctional governments, providing police, fire, public works, recreation, health, and other services. Cities have wide authority to provide services directly to citizens. Some decide to give franchises to private companies to provide services in the city. For instance, you may live in a city where a private company picks up your garbage, or you may live in a city where the city itself runs the garbage pickup service.

Municipalities have broad regulatory authority. When cities use regulatory authority in the areas of zoning, buildings, signs, nuisances, and subdivision development, public needs and private property rights often collide. The **Texas Municipal League** serves as the voice of cities in the capital, lobbying to defend cities' authority and powers. Sometimes, of course, cities do not agree with each other or choose not to join in an effort to protect a city. Other times, cities and their association fight battles against counties and the Texas Association of Counties.

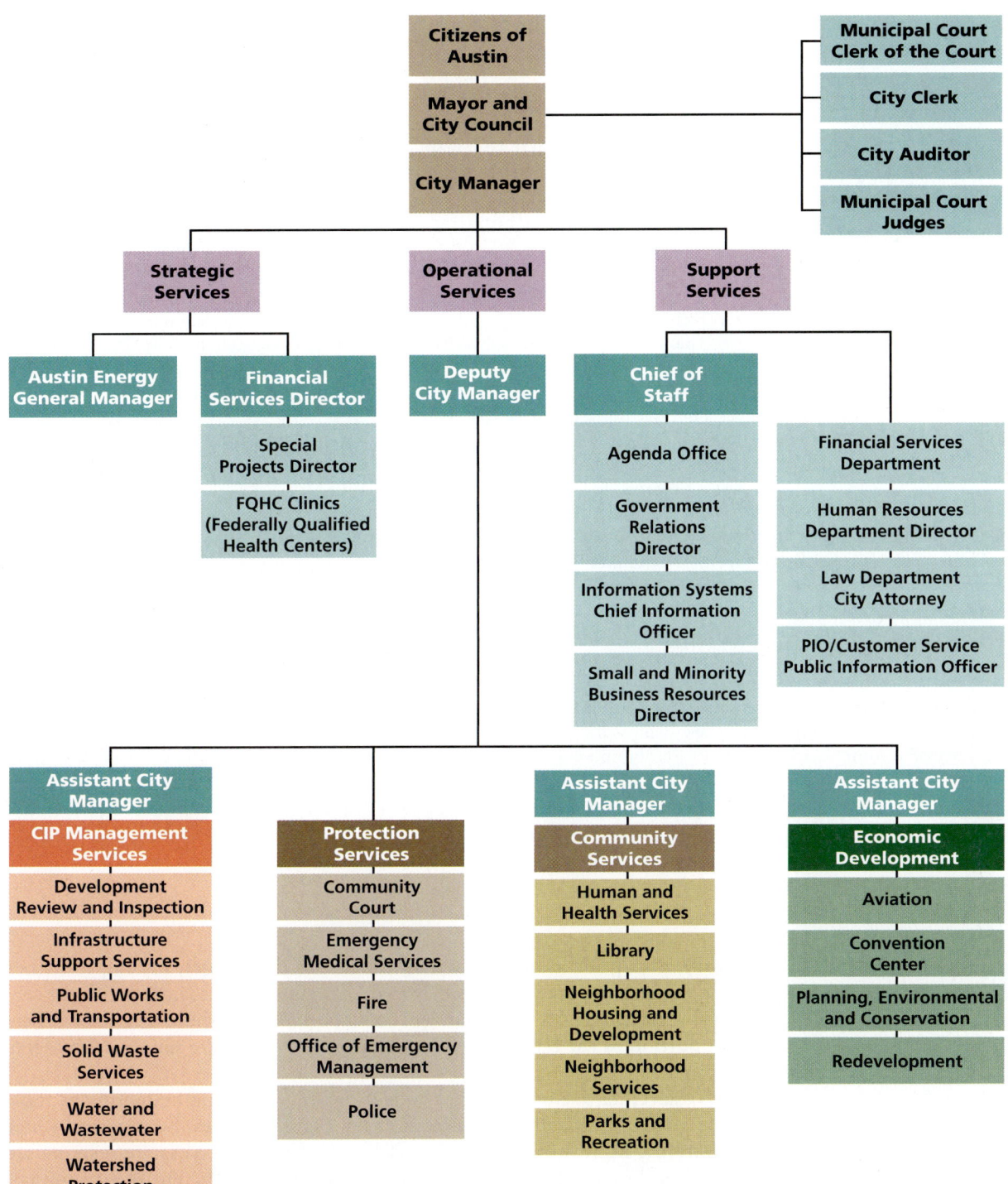

FIGURE 7.4 Organizational Chart: City of Austin (Council–Manager)
Source: City of Austin, www.ci.austin.tx.us/help/orgchart.htm.

Finances of City Governments

Cities raise revenues from several sources, including the municipal sales tax, property taxes, occupation taxes, fees, state and federal revenues, and borrowing (bond sales). Federal funding dropped at the beginning of Ronald Reagan's presidency

Texas Municipal League
Professional association and lobbying arm for city governments.

Politics Now

Source: THE ASSOCIATED PRESS   October 3, 2007

The Border Fence

"Border mayors not letting fence go up on cities' lands"

JUAN A. LOZANO. ASSOCIATED PRESS. SAN ANTONIO EXPRESS-NEWS, OCTOBER 3, 2007

BROWNSVILLE—Some mayors along the Texas-Mexico border have begun a quiet protest of the federal government's plans to build a fence along the boundary: They are refusing access to their cities' land.

Mayors in Brownsville, Del Rio and El Paso have denied or limited access to some parts of their city property to Homeland Security Department workers assigned to begin surveys or other preliminary work on the fence Congress has authorized to keep out undocumented immigrants. And Eagle Pass has denied a request from federal officials to build a portion of the wall within its city limits.

Brownsville Mayor Pat Ahumada said Tuesday that he refused two weeks ago to sign documents granting federal workers permission to begin work if it was to be on city property.

Del Rio granted limited access, and El Paso allowed workers only on its outskirts, said Monica Weisberg Steward of the Texas Border Coalition, a group that represents local officials.

"This is exercising our rights. This is our property," Ahumada said.

In Eagle Pass, Mayor Chad Foster said his city has refused the Border Patrol's request to build 1¼ miles of fencing as part of a project that includes light towers and a new road for border patrols.

But he added that although border communities are at odds with the government, they remain committed to finding solutions to these disagreements.

"All of us are in opposition to physical barriers, but we want to work with (Homeland Security) so everybody walks away happy," said Foster, who is chairman of the Texas Border Coalition.

"We will work with everybody. We plan to accommodate any credible concerns with regard to the environment. Our mission at the end of the day is to secure the border."

David Crump, a law professor at the University of Houston Law Center, said that for now, landowners can keep anybody out of their property for any reason.

"But it's subject to being breached by legislation, and either the Texas Legislature of Congress can give power to an agency to do it," said Crump, who specializes in real property law.

Critical Thinking Questions

1. What seems to be driving local opposition to federal border security initiatives?
2. Do you think that local governments should be able to refuse directives from the federal government? Why or why not?
3. How do you think that the border fence issue will affect state and national elections?

(1981–1989), then grew more slowly than the rest of the budget, leading to higher city taxes in many cities around Texas.[34] If a city has chosen to provide its citizens services such as electricity, water, and garbage collection, fees for these services can be a significant portion of the budget, making it difficult to compare municipal budgets around the state.

Most Texas cities use both capital budgeting and operating budgeting as tools for long-range planning and management of debt and revenues. Sewage and water treatment are the highest priority in capital budgeting.[35] Mayors are responsible for final approval of capital budgets in some cities, though the entire city council does so for most. Most cities use public hearings to involve the public in the planning process.

In the 1980s and 1990s, to attract development, Texas cities turned to innovative policies involving tax incentives, such as tax increment financing, reinvestment zones, tax abatement agreements, and economic development corporations. These policy initiatives can result in decreases in tax revenues, though the intent is to use those tax breaks to stimulate economic activity that would not otherwise occur and to then recoup tax revenues from the new activity.

Municipal Annexation

One of the most controversial and tortuous areas of municipal government and politics is the issue of municipal boundaries and **annexation** of territory to expand those boundaries. The unilateral power of home-rule cities to annex dates back to the 1912 home-rule constitutional amendment. Absent any state restrictions, cities could decide on their own whether and how to grow. In 1963, the legislature passed the Municipal Annexation Act to restrict home-rule cities' leeway in annexing. The 1963 act is an arena for legislative battles nearly every session, sometimes with minor changes, sometimes, such as in 1999, with major changes.[36] The most significant areas of controversy in annexation policies include how the annexation occurs, services that cities must provide in newly annexed areas, and the status of areas beyond the city limits known as **extraterritorial jurisdictions (ETJs).**

Under the Municipal Annexation Act, a city may expand its municipal boundaries by an area up to 10 percent of its geographic area in any one year.[37] The city is not required to obtain the consent of anyone for annexation, though it must hold public hearings. A city also controls an ETJ of up to five miles from its city limits, depending on its population size.[38] The act states that the purpose of limited municipal controls in areas beyond city limits is "to promote and protect the general health, safety, and welfare."[39] For instance, if developers were allowed to simply cross over a city boundary and build a subdivision immediately outside the city without complying with local street and sewer standards, then when the city later annexed the area, it could have a significant cost to upgrade the area to meet standards. When a city decides to annex territory, it may not include any area within the existing ETJ of another municipality. When cities annex territory, they must provide services to those areas within timelines specified in the act.

To complicate matters, some cities use what is called limited-purpose annexation. A home-rule municipality with a population greater than 225,000 may annex an area for the limited purposes of applying its planning, zoning, health, and safety ordinances in the area, without the consequences of full annexation. In essence, limited-purpose annexation provides stronger municipal controls than ETJ restrictions but less than full annexation. Still another variant is called strip annexation. Some cities have used annexation powers to annex narrow strips along highways in order to extend city boundaries (and ETJs) to outlying areas rapidly. In 1973, the act was amended to prohibit the annexation of strips less than 500 feet, and in 1987 the minimum permissible width was increased to 1,000 feet.[40]

In 1998, a Senate interim committee made several recommendations for amendments to the Municipal Annexation Act.[41] The committee's bill was designed to

annexation
Enlargement of a city's corporate limits by incorporating surrounding territory into the city.

extraterritorial jurisdiction (ETJ)
The area outside a city's boundaries over which the city may exercise limited control.

What will building a wall along the Texas-Mexican border accomplish? While many Texans support building a barrier to reduce illegal immigration, others, like these protestors in Laredo, Texas, do not.

provide protection for those to be annexed. The 1999 legislature amended numerous provisions of the proposal, then passed it. As a result of those 1999 amendments, in order to annex, a city must now take the following steps:

- Develop a three-year plan for annexation, and not annex the targeted area during that three-year period.
- Make an inventory of the current services in the area.
- Provide to the annexed area all services currently provided in its full-purpose boundaries no later than two and one-half years (or four and one-half years in some circumstances) after annexation.
- Require negotiations and arbitration regarding services.
- Conduct at least two public hearings.
- Not reduce level of services in the area from what they were before annexation.

Citizens may enforce a service plan by applying for a writ of mandamus (an order to perform a certain act). If the court finds that the service plan is not being implemented, it must provide an option of disannexation, or it must order compliance, a refund of taxes, or civil penalties. The law grandfathers existing land uses or planned land uses at the time of annexation.[42]

Politics and Representation in City Governments

Unlike county elections, municipal elections in Texas are nonpartisan, and they are held on election dates separate from state and county elections. With political parties absent from the nominating process, who then is influential in the socialization, recruitment, and financing of city candidates? The answer to that question is different today from what it was up to the 1970s.

Traditionally, city council elections in Texas have tended to be at-large or **at-large-by-place** elections, where all candidates had to run for office across the entire city. The general pattern of competition was that the business community in the city would coalesce, plan strategy for the elections, recruit candidates, keep other candidates out of the race if possible, and fund the candidates. Some of the business coalitions created formal organizations, while others operated informally. They included such groups as the Dallas Citizens Charter Association/Citizens Council, San Antonio Good Government League, Committee for a Greater Fort Worth, Austin Citizens League, and Houston's "8-F Crowd."[43] Because it was difficult to mount a serious campaign across an entire large city without substantial resources, these business coalitions held nearly monopoly power on municipal politics for decades. Not surprisingly, the candidates that they recruited to fill city council and mayoral seats typically came from the business community and reflected business community leadership: They were white, male, and conservative politically.

The business monopoly over municipal politics in Texas was weakened in the 1970s with the coming of **single-member districts,** in which a legislator runs from and represents one district rather than the entire geographic area encompassed by the government. The League of United Latin American Citizens (LULAC), the Mexican American Legal Defense and Educational Fund (MALDEF), the National Association for the Advancement of Colored People (NAACP), and Texas Rural Legal Aid began using the federal Voting Rights Act as a basis for

at-large-by-place
An election system in which all positions on the council or governing body are filled by city-wide elections, with each position designated as a seat, and candidates must choose which place to run for.

single-member districts
Election system in which a legislator runs from and represents one district rather than the entire geographic area encompassed by the government.

lawsuits challenging the validity of at-large municipal elections that usually resulted in all-white city councils. As courts handed down decisions overturning at-large elections, and as some cities responded to the pressure by making changes on their own, most large cities in Texas abandoned at-large elections in favor of either single-member districts or a mixed system of some single-member districts and some at large. Not all have done so. A variety of systems are demonstrated in Table 7.1.

With the advent of single-member districts, candidates who previously could not mount an effective campaign throughout the entire city became viable. Neighborhood groups, ethnic and racial groups, and other community groups joined the business community in recruiting, endorsing, funding, and socializing candidates for city councils. The most visible result of the change in election systems has been the ethnic and racial make-up of city governments. Whereas it was difficult to find any minority city council members in Texas up through the 1960s, by the 1990s, African Americans and Mexican Americans constituted majorities or near majorities of the city councils in some of the largest cities. Minorities have been winning citywide races, such as mayoral races and at-large city council seats. The best known has been Henry Cisneros, who served as mayor of San Antonio in the 1980s and 1990s and then served in President Bill Clinton's Cabinet. Recent Mexican American mayors include Ed Garza (San Antonio), Gus Garcia (Austin), and Raymond Caballero (El Paso). Former mayors Lee Brown (Houston), Ron Kirk (Dallas), and Elzie Odom (Arlington) are African American.

> ### Thinking Nationally
> **Partisan Ballots for City Offices**
>
> Cities in California have often been governed by officials who were leaders in their political parties and elected on partisan ballots. Sometimes they have even been state officials who went back down to the local level and continued their electoral careers there. House Speakers Willie Brown and Antonio Villagarosa, both Democrats, became mayors of San Francisco and Los Angeles respectively. Governor Jerry Brown, also a Democrat, became mayor of Oakland. In Texas, city officials are elected on a nonpartisan ballot. Party officials can—and do—run for local office, but they may not run as party leaders, with party nominations. The state chair of the Democratic Party, Bill White, won election as mayor of Houston. Travis County Democratic Party Chair Kirk Watson won election as mayor of Austin.
>
> - Would it make a difference if city officials in Texas were elected on a partisan ballot?
> - Why does Texas use a nonpartisan ballot for city offices but a partisan ballot for county offices?
> - Which system do you think Texas cities should use, and why?

Of course, the selection of single-member districts as a means of addressing imbalance in city politics is not the only option. Both cumulative voting and proportional representation would likely yield results that more closely reflect a city's population than is the case with at-large elections, without the redistricting dilemmas that single-member districts raise. **Cumulative voting** allows a voter in a multimember or at-large system to cast a number of votes equal to the number of seats being filled; the voter may cast his or her votes all for one candidate or split them among candidates in various combinations. Some small Texas cities and some school districts are experimenting with cumulative voting (see the discussion of school districts). **Proportional representation** awards seats based on the proportion of the vote that a political party receives for a legislative body. Since Texas cities are nonpartisan, cumulative voting, rather than other types of proportional representation, is used to address imbalances.

Additionally, women have won considerable support in recent city elections. Women winning mayoral elections in recent decades include Dallas Mayors Laura Miller and Annette Strauss, Houston's Kathy Whitmire, San Antonio's Lila Cockrell, Austin's Carole Keeton Strayhorn (later state comptroller), and Fort Worth's Kay Granger (now U.S. Representative). For a look at how youth voting and candidacies have changed city politics, see Ideas into Action: Students Run for Local Office.

cumulative voting
A method of voting in which voters have a number of votes equal to the number of seats being filled, and voters may cast their votes all for one candidate or split them among candidates in various combinations.

proportional representation
A voting system that apportions legislative seats according to the percentage of the vote won by a particular political party.

Ideas Into Action

Students Run for Local Office

College students sometimes literally live in two places—the home where they grew up and their new residence in their college town. The Twenty-Sixth Amendment to the U.S. Constitution gave eighteen-year-olds the right to vote in 1971, raising the question of which residence they would use for voting purposes. The U.S. Supreme Court ordered local officials in Texas to let college students vote in their college town, if they so chose. Then the question shifted to whether a wave of new young voters would influence city politics in college towns.

With the newly won right to vote, some college students have gone even further than voting by running for local offices in their adopted hometowns. In recent years, students around the nation—at Yale, Cornell, and other colleges—have won local office.[a] In 2005, an eighteen-year-old high school student was elected mayor of Hillsdale, Michigan, and was a college student while serving as mayor.[b] In Texas, too, college students have sometimes run for office, and as voters they have sometimes provided the margin of victory for new candidates. In 1970, Jeff Friedman graduated from the law school at the University of Texas and in 1971 won a seat on the Austin City Council. He won the mayor's seat in 1975. Bob Binder, student president at the University of Texas in 1971–1972, won a seat on the city council in 1973. UT students provided critical support for Friedman and Binder in these elections.

Today, college students continue the tradition of running for office in their college towns. In 2006, two University of Texas students ran for Austin city council. Kerdon Rouvell, age twenty-nine, and Colin Kalmbacher, twenty, campaigned on campus, setting up information tables and distributing leaflets, and they hit the campaign trail around the city. "We are 50,000 strong," Kalmbacher said of UT students, "and we don't have a proper voice in city politics. The University might be getting bigger, but it's not getting stronger, at least not in the city's eyes."[c] Both Rouvell and Kalmbacher lost to the incumbent. Student candidates don't always win, but they sometimes energize political participation on campus. And those efforts are likely to continue, as groups such as Young People For and Young America's Foundation provide campaign and leadership skills training on campuses.[d]

- Have you chosen to register to vote in your college town? In the town you grew up in? Why did you make that choice?
- Visit the clerk's office in your city and ask whether college students or young voters have recently run for city council. Does the candidate filing material indicate age or current occupation of the candidate?
- Research the requirements for getting on the ballot in your city. What are the biggest barriers to students running?

---

[a] Gillian Gillers, "Politics 101: Some Students Aren't Just Rocking the Vote. They're Campaigning for It," *Current* (December 5, 2005), www.msnbc.msn.com/id/10298874/site/newsweek/.

[b] "Newest Mayor, 18, Will Juggle City's Work with School Work," *Toledo Blade* (November 9, 2005), toledoblade.com.

[c] Richard Lozano, "Two Students Vie for Council Seat," *Daily Texan* (March 29, 2006).

[d] Young People For (YP4), www.youngpeoplefor.org; Young America's Foundation, www.yaf.org.

Special Districts

Not only does the Texas Constitution set up the state, county, and city governments; it also sets up some political subdivisions of the state that are collectively known as special districts. The constitution allows the legislature, counties, and cities to set up additional special districts. Texas has more than 3,300 special districts, far outstripping the number of counties and cities. In Harris County alone, there are 356 special districts![44] Whereas state, county, and city governments are multifunctional, a special district usually performs just one function. It is established, by the constitution or by a government, to perform a single function. To learn more about types of special districts, see Table 7.2.

Why not simply let the multifunctional counties and cities perform these duties? There are different reasons, of course, for each type of special district. Some policy areas (such as river management) must be addressed on a basis larger than a single county or city. In other policy areas (such as road construction), the constitutional tax limitations placed on counties and cities have made it difficult or impossible for those governments to take on new tasks, so a special district is created to circumvent the con-

TABLE 7.2 Special Districts in Texas

The Texas Constitution creates some special districts. It also authorizes the legislature, counties, and cities to create some special districts. There is no comprehensive list of all special districts in Texas. Following is a list of some types of special districts, with an example of each.

Constitutional Special Districts	Example
Road district	Travis County Road District No. 1
School district	Lubbock Independent School District
Junior college district	North Harris Community College District
Hospital district	Tarrant County Hospital District
Airport authority	Dallas–Fort Worth Airport Authority
Tax appraisal district	Erath County Appraisal District
Conservation and reclamation district	Southeast Texas Agricultural Development District

Statutory Special Districts	Example
Sports facility district	Nueces County Sports Facility District
Crime control and prevention district	Fort Worth Crime Control and Prevention District
Municipal utility district (MUD)	Circle C MUD No. 3
Metropolitan transit authority	Dallas Area Rapid Transit Authority
Soil conservation district	Webb County Soil and Water Conservation District
Waste disposal authority	Gulf Coast Waste Disposal Authority
Municipal power agency	Texas Municipal Power Agency
Groundwater subsidence district	Harris–Galveston Coastal Subsidence District
River authority	Brazos River Authority
Underground water district	High Plains Underground Water Conservation District
Water conservation and improvement	Harris County WCID No. 91 district (WCID)
Flood control district	Harris County Flood Control District

Source: Authors; Virginia Marion Perrenod, *Special Districts, Special Purposes: Fringe Government and Urban Problems in the Houston Area* (College Station: Texas A&M Press, 1984).

stitutional tax ceiling. Finally, some policy areas (such as education) are created out of a belief that the need would be better addressed by a government focusing on that one issue, rather than in competition with other needs that a county or city must address.

Water Districts

Growing population pressures and recurrent droughts make water management a hot potato in Texas politics and policy. The state and local governments often address water policies by creating and empowering special districts. The constitution authorizes the legislature to create special districts for water management (Article 3, section 52) and for conservation and development of natural resources (Article 16, section 59). The legislature also creates other types of water districts. For instance, water issues were at the top of the legislative agenda in 1999, and the legislature created thirteen water districts that session.[45] The Water Code regulates the creation of groundwater conservation districts and the election of their local boards. A district may be composed of all or part of other political subdivisions, such as counties or cities. If the district encompasses several counties, voters in each county must approve it. In cases where there is

How can we best conserve and protect our water supply? Local water districts serve to monitor and regulate water quantity and quality.

Photo courtesy: Ralph Lauer/MCT/Landov

no local action to create a district, the Texas Commission on Environmental Quality (TCEQ) can designate a priority groundwater management area and force hearings and elections to create a district. If voters still do not approve it, the TCEQ could manage the priority area itself or ask the legislature to create a district. For instance, the TCEQ designated part of Comal County as a priority area.[46]

School Districts

The most common type of special district is a school district. Texas has 1,082 local school districts, second only to California's 1,102.[47] Elected school trustees are unpaid government officials. They set the policies for the districts (within federal and state guidelines and requirements), set the district property-tax rate, decide where and when to build new schools, and hire the superintendents to run the schools.

All of Texas is divided among the school districts. There is no uniformity in either geographic size or population size of the districts. Some districts are small—San Vicente Independent School District in Brewster County had fourteen students in 2006—while the largest, Houston Independent School District in Harris County, had 208,879 students.[48] Texas has more than 8,800 public elementary and secondary schools, second in the nation to California,[49] and the number grows every year. Almost all of those schools are operated by local school districts. Local schools and school districts operate under a shifting degree of state oversight and regulation. The State Board of Education, the commissioner of education, and the Texas Education Agency (TEA) have some jurisdiction over school districts. In 1995, the Texas legislature enacted an entirely new education code, recreating the TEA, the State Board of Education, and the commissioner of education, but abolishing some state policies and allowing school districts more leeway in deciding policies.

The 1995 act also set out a process for creating home-rule school districts, free from many state requirements and TEA guidance, if local voters so choose. So far, no districts have attempted to convert to home rule. However, the act also authorized the creation of **charter schools,** which are public schools operating under a contract granted by the state (with the intention of trying different educational methods) rather than under the control of the local school district. By 2005, Texas had 295 public charter schools.[50] There is both strong support for and strong opposition to charter schools. More than a dozen charter schools have failed, some experience rapid teacher turnover, and some have operated with no school transportation and no school lunches. As a consequence, in 2001 the legislature placed a cap on the number of charter schools and mandated management and financial controls over charter schools.

In 1900, the legislature mandated at-large elections for school districts. Later, it began authorizing at-large-by-place elections, and as early as 1950, it authorized the Dallas Independent School District to elect some trustees from single-member districts.[51] Just as at-large elections in cities have been challenged under the Voting Rights Act, so have at-large elections in school districts. Some districts made themselves vulnerable to challenge by failing to submit election changes to the Department of Justice for pre-clearance. Litigation began in the 1970s, but there were still only six systems with single-member districts by 1980. In 1983, the legislature authorized, but did not mandate, local school districts to use single-member districts. More than one hundred school districts were sued or threatened with a suit in a twelve-year period in the 1980s and 1990s. By the late 1990s, 135 school districts elected at least some trustees from single-member districts.[52]

On being challenged, some districts entered into negotiated agreements with plaintiffs, and some of those districts approved "cumulative voting systems" rather than single-member districts. As a result of lawsuits and negotiated settlements, Texas has more governments that use cumulative voting systems than any other state in the nation. By 2008, thirty-five school districts (as well as a community college district and seventeen small cities) had held elections with cumulative voting.[53] The largest

charter school
Public school sanctioned by a specific agreement that allows the program to operate outside the usual rules and regulations.

such system is the Amarillo school district, which has used cumulative voting in its trustee elections since 2004.[54] When the legislature redrafted the Education Code in 1995, after an intense House floor fight, it specifically authorized the use of cumulative voting in conjunction with at-large elections, and additional lawsuits since then have been settled using cumulative voting.

For more than three decades, the big policy issue in Texas concerning school districts has been school finance. Texas relies heavily on the local property tax collected by school districts to fund public education, with additional money from the state. As a result of this heavy reliance, in some recent years, Texas led the nation in local property tax increases. After protracted court battles, the legislature adopted a revised school finance system in 1993. In 2006, the legislature modified the system again, after the courts declared the system unconstitutional. (See chapter 8.)

Toward Reform: Local Government and Politics in Texas

This chapter has examined the roots of local governments in Texas, how the governments are structured, and how the politics have worked. The state legislature, the state's voters (through constitutional amendments), and local governments and voters are constantly considering reforms of local government structures, politics, and policies. Should counties be granted greater powers to respond to suburban and ex-urban sprawl? Do we need all the county officials that the constitution mandates? What taxing authority should special districts be allowed? Reform debates, though, are usually focused on specific governments and specific problems, rather than general reforms.

In Austin, the city council is elected in an at-large-by-place system. As other cities shifted to single-member districts (often by court order) in an attempt to provide more equal (and diverse) representation, Austin successfully resisted such reforms. It did so by an informal "gentleman's agreement" to reserve one seat for African American candidates and one for Mexican American candidates. Indeed, for thirty years, the council has had one African American and one Mexican American member. On several occasions, pressure built to the point of triggering charter-revision elections to force a single-member district system. Each time, voters defeated the proposals. In 2008, city council member Mike Martinez spearheaded an effort to again call an election on a single-member district plan. This time, however, the African American community was divided over such a reform proposal. By 2008, the Latino population of Austin had grown proportionally, while the African American population was a smaller percentage of the total population (and more diffuse); thus, it might be difficult to draw district lines in a way to create a majority African American district. Conceivably, single-member districts could result in the loss of any African American representation on the council. Austin's charter revision proposals for single-member districts failed to come to a vote in 2008.

For counties in Texas, the 1990s reforms of land-use regulation led to marginally greater county power to pass ordinances for platting and subdivision controls. Marginal change in county powers is likely the most change that will happen, given the power dimensions in land-use policies. In another arena affecting counties, recent efforts to abolish some county offices for specific counties may continue. In 2007, though, the legislature and the state's voters went further by amending the constitution to abolish the position of hide inspector that had been in place since the adoption of the constitution in 1876.

Finally, the question of how best to fund public schools in Texas often triggers heated political and policy debates over what changes are truly *reforms* of the system and what changes are patchwork to fix an immediate problem without altering the overall picture. Inevitably, these debates involve school districts. The pressures that built into the 2005–2006 legal battles between the better-off districts and the poorer districts forced the legislature to increase state education spending and reduce reliance on local property taxes. Few believed, though, that the changes reformed the system enough to provide long-term relief. Indeed, by 2007, the Wimberley school trustees voted to defy the state law and refuse to make its required payment to the state for redistribution to poorer districts. The Texas Education Agency and education commissioner responded by beginning plans to consolidate Wimberley with other nearby districts. Though that solution is unlikely to be implemented, these developments illustrate the ongoing tensions over school district powers and school funding that will certainly fuel new reform proposals in the next legislative sessions.

WHAT SHOULD I HAVE LEARNED?

- **What are the roots of local government in Texas?**

    Spain and Mexico established what are now known as counties in Texas. The Republic of Texas and the state of Texas carried forward counties in the series of Texas constitutions. The legislatures also created municipalities. The constitution of 1876 was written to include counties and municipalities and eventually included school districts and other special districts.

- **What are county governments and how do they operate?**

    County governments are both local governments and administrative arms of state government. Their form is spelled out in the constitution. Counties are limited to exercising the authority granted them by the state.

- **How are cities governed and what election systems do they use?**

    Cities with fewer than 5,000 residents are limited to exercising the authority granted them by the state, while the constitution grants larger cities home-rule authority. Home-rule cities choose their form of government. Texas cities vary in the type of election systems they use, though federal Voting Rights Act lawsuits have forced many cities to adopt single-member districts, with a resulting diversification of city government.

- **How are special districts created and what functions do they perform?**

    The constitution, the legislature, and other local governments have created more than 3,300 special districts in Texas. Special districts perform a single function, providing services in areas as diverse as water conservation, health, and rapid transit. The best-known type of special district is the school district.

- **How do local political reform measures fit into the political process?**

    The recent charter revision proposals in Austin, school district consolidation proposals, and abolition of the counties' hide inspector officers illustrate that constitutional, statutory, and administrative reforms aimed at local government structures, politics, and policies are an ongoing part of the political process in Texas.

Key Terms

annexation, p. 221
at-large-by-place, p. 222
charter school, p. 226
city commission, p. 216
commissioners court, p. 208
council–manager, p. 216
county attorney, p. 210
county auditor, p. 211
county clerk, p. 210
county commissioner, p. 208
county judge, p. 208
county tax assessor-collector, p. 211
county treasurer, p. 211
criminal district attorney, p. 210
cumulative voting, p. 223
district attorney (DA), p. 210
district clerk, p. 210
extraterritorial jurisdiction (ETJ), p. 221
general-law cities, p. 213
general ordinance-making authority, p. 211
home rule, p. 206
Local Government Code, p. 211
municipal corporation, p. 205
proportional representation, p. 223
sheriff, p. 210
single-member district, p. 222
strong mayor–council, p. 216
Texas Association of Counties, p. 208
Texas Municipal League, p. 219
weak mayor–council, p. 216

Researching Local Governments

In the Library

Blodgett, Terrell. *Texas Home Rule Charters*. Austin: Texas Municipal League, 1994.

Brischetto, Robert, and Richard Engstrom. "Cumulative Voting and Latino Representation: Exit Surveys in Fifteen Texas Communities." *Social Science Quarterly* 78 (December 1997): 973–91.

Hill, Patricia E. *Dallas: The Making of a Modern City*. Austin: University of Texas Press, 1996.

Houston, Scott. "Municipal Annexation in Texas: 'Is It Really That Complicated?' " Texas Municipal League, January 2008.

Jones, Laurence F., Edward C. Olson, and Delbert A. Taebel. "Change in African American Representation on Texas City Councils: 1980–1993." *Texas Journal of Political Studies* 18 (Spring/Summer 1996): 70.

Neu, Carl. "Change Is in the Air: Five Mega-Trends Redefining the Future of County Government." *County* (September/October 2004): 31–33.

Olson, Edward C., and Laurence F. Jones. "Change in Hispanic Representation on Texas City Councils Between 1980–1993." *Texas Journal of Political Studies* 18 (Spring/Summer 1996): 53–74.

Orum, Anthony. *Power, Money, and the People: The Making of Modern Austin*, revised ed. Houston: Gulf, 1991.

Perrenod, Virginia Marion. *Special Districts, Special Purposes: Fringe Governments and Urban Problems in the Houston Area*. College Station: Texas A&M Press, 1984.

Rosales, Rodolfo. *The Illusion of Inclusion: The Untold Story of San Antonio*. Austin: University of Texas Press, 2000.

Saxe, Allan A. *Politics of a Texas City: Arlington, Texas, an Era of Continuity and Growth*. Austin: Eakin, 2001.

Sprow, Maria. "Regionalization: Some See the Missing Piece. Others See Red." *County* (January/February 2006): 14–17.

Stinebaker, Joe. "Special Districts a Cause of Houston Tax Revolt." *County* (March/April 2005): 22–23.

Texas Senate Research Center. "Invisible Government: Special Purpose Districts in Texas." *Research Spotlight* (October 2008).

On the Web

Counties in the United States: www.naco.org
The National Association of Counties represents county governments in Washington.

Texas counties: www.county.org
The Texas Association of Counties represents Texas counties in Austin and provides services to their members.

Local prosecutors: www.tdcaa.com
The Texas District and County Attorneys Association lobbies for prosecutors before the Texas legislature.

City development processes:
www.ci.austin.tx.us/development/default.htm
City development processes can be complex. This Web site explains the City of Austin's requirements.

Texas Association of Regional Councils:
www.txregionalcouncil.org/
The Texas Association of Regional Councils assists the twenty-four regional councils in Texas.

8 Public Policy in Texas

Beneath the nondescript name Texas Public Policy Foundation (TPPF) lies a powerful engine of twenty-first-century Texas politics and policy. Like the Texas Research League of the mid to late twentieth century, TPPF is a serious policy analysis center, an advocacy group for the business community's public agenda, and a champion of conservative ideology. TPPF's story begins with the rise of the Republican Party and the religious right in the 1980s and 1990s. It is a story of the interstices of private economic powers, think tanks, ideology and party, campaign finance, lobbying, state officials, and public policy outcomes.

James Leininger, a San Antonio doctor who made a fortune with his design of a hospital bed, started putting his wealth to work in the 1980s on behalf of conservative, religious right, and Republican candidates. At first, he focused on electing members to the State Board of Education (SBOE), with an agenda of

■ **Handshakes, Conferences, and Public Policy.** Officeholders work with each other and with policy entrepreneurs and political actors to mold public policy outcomes. In the 1936 photo on the left, Governor Jimmie Allred looks on as President Franklin Roosevelt shakes hands with Congressman Lyndon Johnson. Above, Lt. Governor David Dewhurst addresses the Texas Public Policy Foundation prior to the 2007 legislative session.

promoting private school vouchers and reviewing textbook content. Leininger founded the Texas Public Policy Foundation in 1990 in San Antonio to promote those issues. Soon, TPPF expanded its position to support the business community's agenda on such issues as lawsuits ("tort reform") and tax policy. Candidates supported by Leininger have won SBOE seats since the early 1990s. As the Republican Party strengthened throughout the 1990s, Leininger expanded his funding to legislative and statewide candidates.

In 1995, the legislature reacted to the turmoil caused by the ensuing ideological battles on the SBOE by stripping the board of much of its power, including the power to review content of textbooks other than for factual errors. In 2001, board members whose campaigns Leininger financed continued to review textbooks and voted to remove environmental science textbooks from the approved list. TPPF supported the action, calling the books "full of vitriol against Western civilization," and having "a penchant for Native Americans." Instead, TPPF endorsed a competing book that it said "speaks well to the American system of government."[1] The next year, TPPF reviewed social studies and history books, finding some factual errors but labeling some items as errors that were instead matters of ideological interpretation.

WHAT SHOULD I KNOW ABOUT . . .
- the roots of public policy in Texas?
- the public policy process, actors, and outcomes?
- state finance?
- public education and higher education policy?
- health and human services policy?
- transportation policy?
- policy reforms?

Today, TPPF is closely interwoven with both state government and national conservative leaders. One SBOE member and former chair, Geraldine "Tincy" Miller, is married to Vance Miller, one of the TPPF board members. For a while, Leininger and Rick Perry owned a plane together, and Perry invested in his company. David Dewhurst served on his board; Wendy Gramm (wife of former Senator Phil Gramm) is a current board member. Two former Republican legislators, Talmadge Heflin and Arlene Wohlgemuth, are now on staff. TPPF is aided in its research by associates of the American Legislative Exchange Council, a national conservative think tank. TPPF also coordinates initiatives with national conservative spokesperson and organizer Grover Norquist, famously known for saying, "I'm not in favor of abolishing the government. I just want to shrink it down to the size where we can drown it in the bathtub."[2] Modeled after Norquist's forums in Washington, D.C., TPPF hosts scores of people meeting in regular strategy forums.

> **TO LEARN MORE—**
> **—TO DO MORE**
> What can you learn about the current issue positions of the Texas Public Policy Foundation from their Web site? Can you find who is currently on its board and staff? Go to www.texaspolicy.com/.

After Leininger and other business leaders heavily funded Republican campaigns in 2002, and Republicans won both the Texas House and Senate for the first time in 130 years, TPPF moved to Austin. It then held a four-day seminar at the beginning of the 2003 legislative session, with specialists articulating the conservative position on a broad array of policy issues. Governor Perry, Lieutenant Governor Dewhurst, and other top Republican officials were featured speakers. TPPF sent out a letter soliciting large contributions from lobbyists to pay for the conference, with endorsements from Perry, Dewhurst, and incoming Republican Speaker of the House Tom Craddick. Some lobbyists perceived the letter as a threat that if they did not contribute, their clients would not fare well with the new government. At first, TPPF insisted that the action was okay but soon retreated, admitting that it "was inappropriate for it to appear that the governor, lieutenant governor-elect and speaker-apparent [were] involved in fund raising" for TPPF.[3]

After the 2003 sessions, Governor Perry used his campaign funds to pay for a private plane trip to the Bahamas. He was joined there by Leininger (who had contributed heavily to his campaign), Brooke Robbins (executive director of TPPF, and Perry's former aide), Grover Norquist, and Perry campaign contributor John Nau. Perry was criticized for inappropriate use of campaign funds, but the dustup soon passed, and in the 2005, 2007, and 2009 legislative sessions, the TPPF was back at the capitol with briefing conferences (Perry, Dewhurst, and Craddick were speakers) and a full array of its solutions to the state's policy dilemmas. As the legislature wrestled with tax and school finance policies, TPPF aggressively advocated its positions—in favor of spending down the surplus, privatizing some public schools, and reducing taxes on businesses.[4]

P ublic policies in Texas are the outcomes of societal dynamics, political processes, and governmental institutions that we have examined throughout this book. The public policy *process* is similar across the nation; public policy *outcomes* are more dependent on power balances, traditions, and trends in the state.

In this chapter, we examine:

★ *The roots of public policy in Texas*, describing historical policy developments.

★ *Public policy processes, actors, and outcomes*, presenting the policy cycle and participants.

★ *State finance*, describing the revenue and spending patterns of state government and the public policy implications of battles over public money.

★ The endless skirmishes over equity and quality in Texas's *public education and higher education policy*.

★ *Health and human services policy*, detailing the state's policy posture toward welfare and health care.

★ *Transportation policy*, detailing the ups and down of types of transportation policy and financial support for those systems.

★ *Potential policy reforms*, highlighting proposals that legislators, opinion leaders, and others are debating.

Roots of Public Policy in Texas

State governments in the twentieth century focused much of their attention on economic and social policies. **Economic policies** are public actions that affect economic activity or have economic consequences for individuals or groups (e.g., regulations, subsidies, taxing, and spending).

Social policies are actions that guide our development as human beings and our relationships to other humans and to our broader environment (e.g., education). Sometimes policies have both dimensions (e.g., welfare or environmental protection). Modern Texas public policy is rooted in nineteenth- and early twentieth-century dynamics, as illustrated by the politics of regulation and welfare.

Texas has been both a leader and a straggler in economic regulation. Chapter 3 described the intense populist movement of the 1870s through 1890s that spurred creation of a political party and election of populists to the legislature. With the

economic policies
Public actions that affect economic activity or have economic consequences for individuals or groups (e.g., regulations, subsidies, taxing, and spending).

social policies
Actions that guide our development as human beings and our relationships to other humans and to our broader environment (e.g., education).

What is the best way to provide quality education? School voucher and charter school advocate James Leininger, who is one of the top Republican campaign financiers and the founder of the Texas Public Policy Foundation, visits an elementary school.

creation of the Texas Railroad Commission in 1891, populists won their battle for regulation of the economic powerhouse of the era, as Texas became one of the first states to regulate railroads. Utilities were the next industry to gain the attention of state governments. In 1907, New York and Wisconsin were the first states to regulate utilities.[5] The Texas legislature considered such legislation as early as 1915. In the 1920s and 1930s, Jimmie Allred (first as attorney general, then as governor) picked up the populist banner and successfully pursued anti-trust initiatives against public utilities, insurance companies, and oil companies. He also championed regulation of utilities but was not successful. (Utilities continued to fend off state regulation until 1975.)

As governor, Allred also had to steer the state's economy during the hard Depression years. President Franklin D. Roosevelt's new administration championed initiatives on the federal level, creating federal-state partnerships and much of the social welfare and economic regulatory programs that we still have today. Allred urged the legislature to approve a broad social security program, including unemployment insurance, pensions for the elderly, and aid to dependent children, disabled children, and the blind. He fought through three special sessions before winning aid to the elderly and unemployment insurance.[6]

Those programs, plus new programs of President Lyndon Johnson's Great Society, increased the levels of support that Texas (with federal carrots and sticks) gave to social welfare and economic regulatory programs. By the 1980s and 1990s, however, the pendulum had swung in the opposite direction. In 1995, the legislature passed a new welfare program, with significant reductions in support, and the U.S. Congress followed the next year with restructuring and reduced federal funding. In 1999, the legislature deregulated utilities, and each session now is a forum for additional deregulation in the new world of telecommunications and utility consolidation.

In the policy arena of education, our attention goes back to grievances cited by Texians in 1836 in their disagreements with the Mexican government. Local governments were directed to establish schools, yet one grievance of Texians was that the government had not done so. Upon winning independence, the new Texans wrote into the 1836 constitution of the Republic of Texas a requirement that the Texas Congress establish a general system of education. Yet, little was done. In 1854, the legislature made state funds available to local (mostly private) schools.[7]

Across the United States, though, a strong public movement was stirring to provide free education to all children. Many Texans came to embrace that philosophy, while others continued to support the idea of private education. Public education even became a partisan battleground in the Reconstruction era. The Republican legislators and governor passed a law requiring mandatory education for children and they approved taxes to fund that program. Democrats opposed both the mandatory (integrated) public education and the taxes to pay for it.[8] Still, even Democrats placed in the 1876 constitution a requirement that the legislature "establish and make suitable provision for the support and maintenance of an efficient system of public free schools."

Public Policy Process, Actors, and Outcomes

public policy
What members of a society actually experience, as a result of government action or inaction.

Public policy, in its most basic form, can be described as what members of a society experience as a result of government action or inaction. It is produced from a wide array of dynamics, including public opinion, campaigns and elections, private economic interests, media, and governmental institutions and processes. There is a *policy process*, there are numerous *actors* in that process, and there are *outcomes* felt by a broader public. The outcomes are not necessarily what the actors intended, or what the public believed would result from a policy change.

TEXAS IN COMPARISON

Social and Economic Demographics

Gross state product, 2005 (billions)

Texas	$845.5 (3rd)
California	$1,471.0 (1st)
New York	$867.1 (2nd)
Florida	$595.9 (4th)

Poverty rate, 2006

Texas	16.4% (7th)
California	12.2% (20th)
New York	14.0% (13th)
Florida	11.5% (24th)

State government general expenditures, 2004

Texas	$ 67.7 billion (3rd)
California	$171.1 billion (1st)
New York	$108.2 billion (2nd)
Florida	$54.1 billion (4th)

Estimated per pupil public elementary/secondary school current expenditures, 2006

Texas	$7,397 (41st)
California	$8,205 (29th)
New York	$13,551 (2nd)
Florida	$7,650 (39th)

Sources: Kendra A. Hovey and Harold A. Hovey, *Congressional Quarterly's State Fact Finder 2008: Rankings Across America* (Washington, DC: CQ Press, 2007), 187; Kathleen O'Leary Morgan and Scott Morgan, eds., *Education State Rankings 2007–2008*, Congressional Quarterly, 41; U.S. Department of Commerce, Bureau of the Census, *Statistical Abstract of the United States 2006* (Washington, DC: Government Printing Office, 2005), 446, 468, 471.; U.S. Census Bureau, "State Government Finances: 2004," www.census.gov/govs/www/state04.html.

Policy Process

The public policy process is best described as a cycle. It is never really finished. The policy cycle consists of four basic stages: agenda setting, policy making, implementation, and evaluation. Both private actors and government officials negotiate ideas through these stages to adoption as official policy goals and actions. Then agencies make them real policy that citizens experience. Those same actors and others then look at those consequences and evaluate the success or failure of the policies, setting the agenda for another round of policy making.

Agenda setting is the process of forming the list of issues to be addressed by government decision makers. While it is conceivable that an individual could be an agenda setter, it is more likely that an organized effort will be needed. Media, interest groups, corporations and unions, government officials, academic institutions, and think tanks (policy centers) often play this role of agenda setting. They work up information on a policy topic, try to influence public opinion in that area, and develop avenues of access to decision makers to press the issue.

Once a proposal has been pushed onto the unofficial agenda, **policy making** begins, a process that can include passing legislation (covered in chapter 4), winning gubernatorial support and leadership (chapter 5), passing agency rules and regulations (chapter 5), even winning judicial decisions (chapter 6) that alter the policy, or local ordinances with variations on the structure of the policy (chapter 7). Many of the same actors in the agenda-setting phase are still active in this policy-making phase, though government officials now take the center stage.

After decision makers officially agree on a policy (through legislation, rules, regulations, executive orders, or court orders), it is up to the elected officials and the bureaucracy to make it so: to carry the intent of the policy makers to reality. **Implementation** is action by those agencies in executing the adopted policy: for example, providing services, funding programs, or building facilities or infrastructure.

agenda setting
The process of forming the list of issues to be addressed by government decision makers.

policy making
The creation of public policies (through passage of legislation or local ordinances, winning gubernatorial support and leadership, passing agency rules and regulations, or winning judicial decisions).

implementation
The process of carrying the intent of the policymakers to reality.

We will look at implementation of some Texas policies in the areas of public education, health and human services, and transportation.

Finally, **evaluation** follows. Often policy implementers evaluate the results of their actions and come to conclusions about whether goals are met or not. Other evaluators, though, include legislators (through their oversight function), media (through investigative reporting), academic institutions (critiquing policy ideas and outcomes, and developing hypotheses about alternatives), and of course, private actors affected by the policies (businesses, unions, interest groups, think tanks). These evaluators then don their hats as agenda setters to push (sometimes against each other) for the attention of policy makers to alter the policy anew.

evaluation
The process of examining the results of policy actions and coming to conclusions about whether goals are met or not.

Policy Actors

Just who are these actors in the policy process? While any Texan (and even non-Texans, for that matter) can be involved in the policy process, the institutionalized policy actors include economic, political, and governmental elites; foundations and think tanks; media; and academia. For instance, for several decades, the Texas Research League served as a key agenda setter in Texas, producing policy papers from staff members and academic consultants, then developing legislative proposals for state government, funded by key business leaders. There is probably a wider array of agenda setters today than in the past. The Texas Public Policy Foundation, however, serves as a worthy successor to the Research League in a modern political setting, combining policy analysis with economic backing, lobby clout, party connections, and electoral savvy to influence what is on the plate of decision makers.

TPPF is the modern-day incarnation of a long line of business-allied policy actors. Economic leaders in Texas have long influenced policy making by either recruiting and funding political candidates or becoming candidates themselves, as described in chapter 1. These efforts are often tied to an ideological agenda. A poll of business officials in the 1950s, for instance, showed that they overwhelmingly supported conservative candidates for office and that they were anti–federal government, anti–U.S. Supreme Court, and anti-labor.[9] Dallas billionaire Nelson Hunt was a leader in the right-wing John Birch Society in the 1960s. In the 1940s and 1950s, Houston-area and statewide politics were heavily influenced by a group of millionaire executives. Houston's "8-F Crowd" met in oilman Herman Brown's Suite 8-F of the Lamar Hotel for poker and politics. They recruited and designated candidates for office, and they raised money and business support for those candidates. One of them, George Brown, was a large contributor to Lyndon Johnson and to conservative governors. The successful efforts by economic leaders to influence or control who won office then led to critical influence in economic and social policy. George Brown was crucial in efforts in the 1950s to pass state laws limiting labor unions.[10]

Of course, policy actors go beyond the economic elite. Elected officials (described in chapters 4–7) are the most visible policy actors. Texans see them in action, either in person or as the media cover the policy-making process. Since public opinion can affect agenda setting and policy development, we could even argue that all Texans are potential policy actors.

Who are the public policy actors influencing policy outcomes in Texas? This old *Houston Post* sketch illustrates the role of the economic elite in policy making. Herman and George Brown, brothers who were oilmen and construction company owners and longtime benefactors of Lyndon Johnson, gathered the business leaders of Houston in Suite 8-F of the Lamar Hotel to play poker, talk business, and plan their recruitment and financing of political candidates.

Photo courtesy: Houston Chronicle

Policy Outcomes

We have looked at the policy process and policy actors. Now we turn to the question of what policy outcomes Texans experience. In this chapter, we focus on describing and analyzing an array of Texas policy outcomes (and the processes that produce those outcomes). These policy dynamics produce alterations in the distribution and redistribution of resources for Texans, in the state's power balances (economic and political), in the quality of life, and even in the physical environment. The state's $150 billion to $160 billion biennial budget produced through the policy process plays a role in stimulating the economy. Just as significantly, it sets economic and social priorities that influence Texans' everyday activities.

The state's southern, one-party, conservative, and libertarian heritages influence Texas toward limited government, providing minimal social services. Yet, the large, increasingly diverse, and predominantly urban population has created pressures and demands for Texas to provide both *more* social services and a more *equitable* distribution of health services, educational opportunities, and income-support services.

Policy outcomes are a component of the **political economy**—the whole web of economic, social, governmental, and political institutions and processes. In this chapter, we see that the state plays numerous roles in the political economy. Government uses many tools to interact with private entities in the economy. A **subsidy** is a grant of economic resources. The state subsidizes businesses to encourage certain economic activities. Tax breaks, for example, are used to lure new businesses to Texas. A **regulation** is a government restriction on certain economic activities; for example, the state may set a minimum wage for workers. Whether intentional or not, changes in economic policy redistribute income. A new highway means transportation options for travelers, profits for construction companies, and income for their workers. A freeze on welfare benefits while population continues to increase means smaller checks for each recipient. An increase in the sales tax means that a larger share of a working-class family's budget goes to the state than is true for an upper-class family. These are policy outcomes. Much of the debate we hear in the media, legislative deliberations, or political campaigns revolves around a core issue of political economy: who wins and who loses with changes in economic policies.[11]

Political scientist David Osborne argues in *Laboratories of Democracy* that government's primary roles are to nourish the elements that make innovation possible, and to bring the poor into the growth process.[12] Both agendas affect who gets how much of the state's economic resources. Through its taxing and spending policies, its regulatory and economic development policies, and its education and human services policies, the State of Texas plays a significant role in that redistribution. In the nineteenth century, states subsidized railroads with land, and in the twentieth century they subsidized the automobile industry with highways. Contemporary subsidies by states include tax breaks, location incentives, debt financing, venture capital, higher-education research entities, and trade promotion. In recent years, Texas has created subsidy programs such as industrial development zones (with tax reductions) and finance authorities (with reduced interest rates for business loans). Some see a modern paradigm "built around new roles for government in the economy and new partnerships between the public and private sectors," according to Osborne, with problems attacked "by using the public sector—in partnership with business, academia and labor—to reshape the marketplace."[13]

political economy
The web of economic, social, governmental, and political institutions and processes.

subsidy
A grant of economic resources.

regulation
A government restriction on certain economic activities.

State Finance

Increasingly, state government is a significant player in shaping economic behavior. When governments decide whom to tax, whom to spend money on, how much money to spend, where to place subsidies, and whom to regulate, some people gain and some people lose economic resources. Political scientists Virginia Gray and Peter Eisinger argue that state governments' policy choices have important economic consequences. If natural resources are squandered, then a resource is depleted and the state loses a source of income. If tourists shy away because of pollution or crime, then the government loses revenues. If roads and schools are in poor shape, high-tech and other industries will leave the state.[14] Any of those decisions create dilemmas for policy makers. Substantive policy decisions often are tied to state finance issues; thus, state finance becomes an integral part of understanding economic and social policies in Texas.

Budgeting and Borrowing

A **budget** is a plan for how much money one expects to take in and how one proposes to spend that money. Individuals, families, organizations—sometimes even college students—use a budget as a tool to manage money, pay bills, and avert crises. Governments do the same thing, on a much larger scale. Texas uses a **biennial budgeting system**, covering a two-year period. The state's **fiscal year (FY)**, the period used for accounting, begins September 1 and ends August 31. For instance, the 2010–2011 biennium began September 1, 2009, and ends August 31, 2011. Biennial legislative sessions necessitate biennial budgets, but some legislatures with annual sessions also adopt biennial budgets. Thirty states prepare annual budgets, while twenty states have biennial budgets.[15]

The Legislative Budget Board (LBB) and the Governor's Budget Office prepare budgets for the legislature to consider. (See chapter 4 for more detail on the legislative process of adopting the budget.) As legislators then work on the budget, they must be mindful that the state constitution (in Article 3, section 49a) requires a balanced budget (spending must be limited to incoming revenue). Texas refers to this requirement as a "pay as you go" policy, though that policy has now been compromised by many constitutional amendments. Sometimes the legislature decides that there will not be enough money to pay for a large program, and legislators are unwilling to raise taxes to pay for the program or want to spread the financing out over a long period, so they turn to **bond programs** (borrowing) instead. The state can go into debt (i.e., sell bonds to banks or investors) only if specifically authorized to do so by the state constitution.

Texas now has numerous constitutional bond programs: land and housing programs for veterans; construction projects for the University of Texas and the Texas Agricultural and Mechanical (A&M) University; water development; student loans; farm and ranch loans; park development; construction of prisons and state buildings; roads in South Texas colonias; military enhancement projects; and state highways. Most of these are revenue bonds, to be repaid from revenues generated by the programs (such as the veterans' loan programs). Some programs, such as construction projects, are funded through general obligation bonds and repaid from general revenues dedicated to repayment.

These constitutional bond programs allow a legislature to spend money in a way that does not violate the balanced-budget requirement. As a result, Texas now has a sizable debt (accumulated amount of money owed). In 2006, Texas had a debt of $24.5 billion (ranking near the bottom of the fifty states in a per capita comparison).[16] In the last few decades, Texas has been relying more heavily on general obligation and revenue bonded indebtedness. In 1997, however, voters approved a constitutional amendment limiting state debt from general revenue bonds and obligations.

As a vehicle for achieving a balanced budget, the constitution requires the comptroller of public accounts to provide the legislature with an estimate of how much revenue the state will collect in the coming biennium. When the legislature passes appropriations bills, the comptroller must compare the spending levels with that **revenue estimate** and certify that the budget adopted by the legislature will be within

budget
A plan for how much money one expects to take in and how one proposes to spend that money.

biennial budgeting system
A budget covering a two-year period.

fiscal year (FY)
The period used for accounting purposes (September 1 to August 31 for the State of Texas).

bond programs
Specific programs for which the state borrows money by selling bonds to investors.

revenue estimate
A prediction of how much revenue the state will collect in the coming biennium, made for the legislature by the comptroller of public accounts.

expected revenues. This is called the **comptroller's certification**. The comptroller almost always certifies the appropriated amounts. In 1990, though, the comptroller refused to certify an appropriations bill.[17] After the 2003 legislature adjourned, Comptroller Carole Strayhorn said that she could not certify the appropriations bill; Governor Rick Perry then vetoed some appropriations items, and she certified the appropriations bill with the lowered amounts, thus narrowly avoiding a special legislative session to rewrite the budget. If the comptroller refuses to certify a spending bill that the legislature passes, the bill goes back to the legislature and does not become law. The legislature may override a revenue estimate with a four-fifths vote, but that has never happened.[18]

The comptroller issues a revenue estimate at the beginning of each regular session to guide the appropriations process and to indicate what he or she will be inclined to certify. At the beginning of the 2007 session, Comptroller Susan Combs estimated total 2008–2009 revenues at about $156.9 billion.[19] Sometimes the comptroller will issue a revised estimate during the session, either because of changed economic conditions or because of political considerations, such as a larger amount being needed for required spending, and estimates could be updated for special sessions.

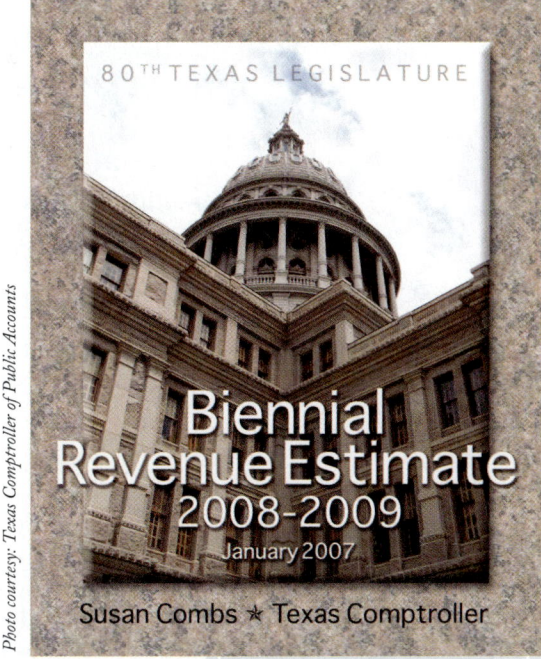
Photo courtesy: Texas Comptroller of Public Accounts

Even after knowing the amount of money that it has to plug into a budget, the legislature still faces immense difficulties in balancing the budget. Legislators and analysts often charge that "legislators' hands are tied"— that legislators are not free to decide how to spend the money and how much to spend. For example, over the past few decades, courts have ordered Texas to spend money in the areas of prison management, mental health/mental retardation, and health benefits to bring those programs into compliance with constitutional principles or federal requirements. Another restriction the legislature faces is the existence and extent of **dedicated funds.** These are monies that are restricted to designated programs (e.g., highways, or the "rainy day" savings account), and the legislature may not spend them for anything else. Funds can be dedicated constitutionally, statutorily, or, if federal funds, by federal requirements.

In 1978, Texas added another restriction (described in chapter 4) by adopting a constitutional spending limit tied to the state's economic growth. There is also a newer limit on tax-supported debt, and a constitutional ceiling on welfare spending. (See The Living Constitution.)

After the legislature passes a budget, the comptroller certifies it, the governor signs it, and the legislature adjourns, what happens in the event of a budget emergency with a state agency or program? Until recently, the agency would have to handle the problem on its own, or the governor would have to call the legislature into special session. In 1985, voters approved a constitutional amendment (Article 16, section 69) to give the governor authority to move money from program to program or agency to agency in an emergency. Under this budget execution authority, the legislature authorized the governor and the LBB, during legislative interims, to move money from one program to another or even from one agency to another. Because the lieutenant governor is the chair and the Speaker is the vice chair of the LBB (and they appoint the members), this budget execution authority, in essence, allows the governor, lieutenant governor, and Speaker the flexibility to handle some budget crises without having to call the legislature into special session. This budget execution authority has been used sparingly. A 1991 constitutional amendment puts the LBB and the governor on equal footing in budget execution. If the governor proposes an alteration, the LBB must ratify it, reject it, or require changes; if the LBB proposes an alteration, the governor must ratify it, reject it, or require changes. In 2005, for example, Governor Perry proposed an alteration to shift money to textbook purchases, payments to nursing homes, and other needs, but the LBB did not act on it, so it died.[20]

> **How does the state coordinate its revenue collections with its appropriations process to keep within the constitutional requirement for a balanced budget?** During each regular session of the legislature, the comptroller of public accounts submits to legislators an estimate of incoming revenue to guide their appropriations—and must then certify that the final appropriations are within estimated revenues.

comptroller's certification
A document signed by the comptroller certifying that the budget adopted by the legislature will be within expected revenues.

dedicated funds
Monies restricted to designated programs.

The Living Constitution

(a) The Legislature shall have the power, by General Law, to provide . . . for assistance grants to needy dependent children and the caretakers of such children, ... (b) . . . The maximum amount paid out of state funds for assistance grants to or on behalf of needy dependent children and their caretakers shall not exceed one percent of the state budget.

ARTICLE 3, SECTION 51-a

This provision of the Texas Constitution has been amended numerous times as the U.S. Congress has changed legislation affecting public assistance to the needy. Initially, the 1876 constitution prevented cash payments to individuals. Section 51-a was added in 1933 to allow the state to provide cash assistance to the aged, the blind or disabled, and dependent children and their caretakers. Through amendment, the limit was set at $80 million per fiscal year in 1969. In 1971, voters rejected a proposed amendment that would have reduced the maximum to $55 million per fiscal year but made it applicable only to cash payments for Aid to Families with Dependent Children (AFDC). In 1972, Congress amended the federal welfare statutes to relieve the states of providing cash payments to the aged, blind, and disabled, thus making the Texas constitutional limit applicable only to the payments to needy dependent children and their caretakers.[a]

In 1982, voters approved another change. According to the amendment, the limit would be $160 million for the 1982–1983 biennium but would become 1 percent of the state budget total after that. The total would include all funds appropriated by the legislature, including federal funds. When the amendment was proposed, Texas ranked forty-ninth among the fifty states in the size of AFDC cash payments, providing a maximum of $85 a month to a parent with one child.[b]

Proponents of the amendment argued first that with projected increases in AFDC recipients, the limit would soon be reached, forcing the state to reduce welfare benefits or change the eligibility requirements. Either action would be unconscionable, given the low benefit level and the strict requirements in Texas at the time. Also, President Reagan's New Federalism program proposed a swap that entailed the states assuming the total cost of AFDC in exchange for the federal government's assumption of the total cost of Medicaid and food stamps. If Reagan's proposal was adopted, the state could not cover the total cost of AFDC unless it raised the ceiling.

Opponents of the amendment argued for elimination of the constitutional limit on welfare spending and noted that President Reagan's proposed New Federalism swap was being revised. Furthermore, the 1 percent limit could prove inadequate if the president's proposal was enacted, requiring another amendment.

Since the 1990s, Texas has seldom approached the spending limit. In fiscal year 2006–2007, the spending limit was $1.4 billion. Allocated spending for Temporary Assistance for Needy Families (TANF)—the cash assistance program that replaced AFDC in 1996—was $134 million, nearly 1 billion less than the limit and 0.15 percent of the total state budget.[c]

CRITICAL THINKING QUESTIONS

1. Should the Texas Constitution retain a constitutional limit on welfare spending, since the limit is unlikely to be exceeded or even approached? Explain your reasoning.
2. What does the Texas welfare limit demonstrate about statutory constitutions?

---

[a] George D. Braden, *The Constitution of the State of Texas: An Annotated and Comparative Analysis*, vol. 1 (Austin: Texas Legislative Council, 1977), 236–40.

[b] See House Research Organization, "Constitutional Amendments," *Focus Report* (July 26, 1982): 7–9, for an analysis of the amendment.

[c] House Research Organization, "Writing the State Budget: 80th Legislature," *State Finance Report* 80-1 (February 14, 2007): 14.

Thus, we see that in the budgetary process, Texas legislators must consider the constitutional balanced-budget requirement, the comptroller's revenue estimate and certification, proposed budgets submitted by the governor and the LBB, dedicated funds, constitutional bond programs, and constitutional spending limits. Now we turn directly to the issues of state revenues and spending.

Revenue

The state has numerous sources of revenue. These include state taxes, federal funds, licenses and fees, lottery income, interest, and other sources. The particular mix of sources of revenue is often a matter of political battles. The choices of what sources of revenue to use and what levels of taxes and fees to exact have wide-ranging effects on the political economy, including the distribution of economic resources and incentives or disincentives for economic activity. To learn more about Texas revenues by source, see Figure 8.1.

TAXES The federal, state, and local governments rely on some common forms of taxation and some that are unique to one level of government. In the nineteenth and early twentieth centuries, state governments relied heavily on property taxes. During the Great Depression of the 1930s, local governments started monopolizing the property tax, while the federal government grabbed the income tax. In 1932, Mississippi became the first state to adopt a sales tax. By the end of World War II, the sales tax had become the top tax producer for state governments. Hawaii began collecting a state income tax in 1901, and other states gradually followed, primarily in the 1930s. No states adopted an income tax after 1976 until Connecticut did so in 1991.[21]

Income taxes and sales taxes are about equal as the largest producers of tax revenues in the fifty states—general sales taxes account for about 33 percent and motor

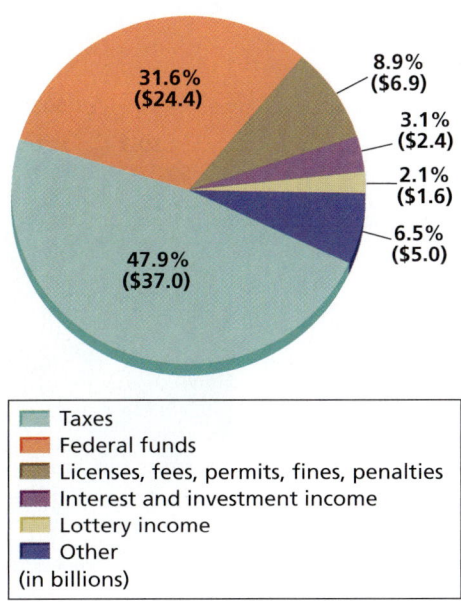

FIGURE 8.1 Texas State Revenue by Source, FY 2007 Just under half of the state's revenue comes from state taxes. Grants from the federal government account for about one-third of the state's revenues, with the remainder from licenses, fees, interest, lottery, and other sources.
Source: Comptroller of Public Accounts, *State of Texas 2007 Annual Cash Report*.

Thinking Nationally
The Value Added Tax in Michigan

A value added tax (VAT) taxes the additional value added to a product at each stage of its production and marketing. The VAT system is common in Europe, where each component of a product is taxed once. Michigan adopted the VAT to lower its corporate income tax. Several other states, including Texas, have considered shifting from the traditional sales tax to a value added tax.

- Who might gain and who might lose from the adoption of a VAT? How might you research the question?
- Should a structural change in the taxing system, such as adoption of a VAT, be revenue neutral, or should it be designed to increase state revenues? Explain your reasoning.
- From what you have learned about sales taxes, income taxes, and the VAT, what do you think the public opinion reaction would be to creating or raising such taxes?

fuels sales taxes 6 percent of state tax revenues; individual income taxes 35 percent; and corporate income taxes 5 percent.[22] The tax distribution in Texas is very different. To learn about the tax revenue spread in Texas, see Figure 8.2.

Forty-three states have *both* income taxes and sales taxes, relying on different mixes of those taxes. Forty-three states have an individual income tax. Forty-six states have a corporate income tax.[23] Texas has neither an individual nor a corporate income tax. If Texas did have income taxes, how much revenue could it produce? To learn more about how income tax revenues of the twelve largest states compare, see Figure 8.3. Texas and New York produce the closest comparison, as Texas's economic base is closest in size to New York—New York's gross state product was $963.5 billion (third largest in the nation), and Texas's was $982.4 billion (second largest).[24] In 2005, New York received a total of $30.9 billion from income taxes. Other than Texas (and Florida, which has a corporate income tax but no individual income tax), the largest states received from 35 percent to 58 percent of their state tax revenues in income taxes. Given the size of the state's economy, Texas could expect to collect anywhere from $12 billion to $30 billion a year in individual and corporate income taxes if it adopted them with rates and in a proportion similar to other large states.

In the absence of income taxes, Texas relies heavily on consumption taxes—taxes on the consumption of goods. Sales taxes were adopted by more than half the states in the 1930s, and others in the following decades. Currently, all but five states have sales taxes. The range of rates for the state general sales tax is from 2.9 percent to 7 percent.[25] Michigan is the only state with a different kind of sales tax, called a value

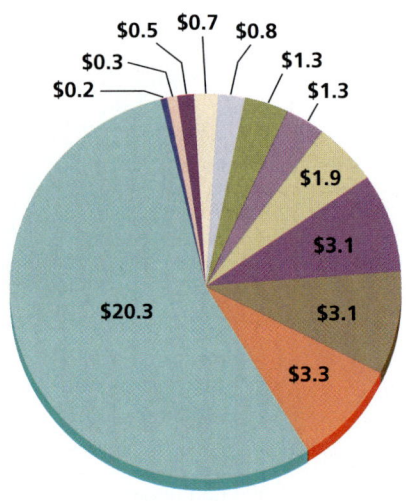

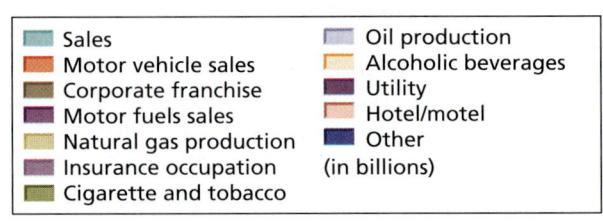

FIGURE 8.2 Texas Revenue from Taxes, FY 2007 The state has more than a dozen taxes—but no income tax. The general sales tax brings in more than half of all the state's tax revenues. Sales taxes on motor fuels and motor vehicles are the next most productive taxes, as well as the newly revamped corporate franchise (business) tax.

Source: Comptroller of Public Accounts, *State of Texas 2007 Annual Cash Report*.

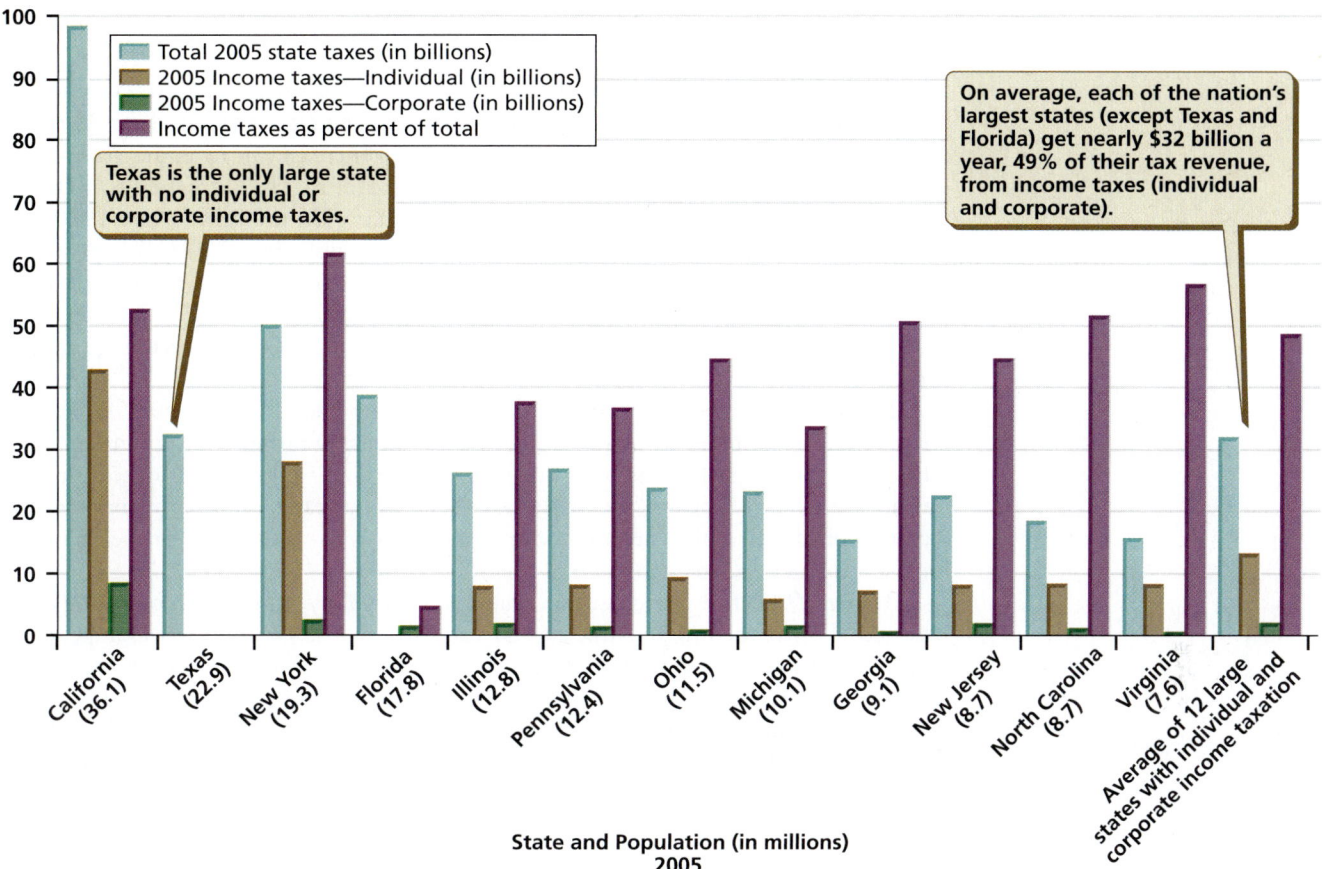

FIGURE 8.3 Income Tax Revenues in the Largest States, 2005

Sources: Kathleen O'Leary Morgan and Scott Morgan, *State Rankings 2006*, 14th ed. (Lawrence, KS: Morgan Quitno Corp., 2005), 317, 320, 322; U.S. Department of Commerce, Bureau of the Census, *Statistical Abstract of the United States 2007*, July 1, 2005 population estimate, 20, and Table 439, State Government Tax Collections, by State: 2005, www.census.gov.

added tax or the single-business tax. This tax (used throughout Europe) imposes a tax on a product at each step in its travel through the marketplace, as "value" is added to it. Governor Bush proposed a similar tax in 1997, but the legislature did not adopt it.

Legislative battles were fought repeatedly in Texas over whether to pass a sales tax or an income tax. Sales tax proponents won in 1961, over the objections of both the governor and the Speaker of the House. The Texas sales tax started at 2 percent. It has been raised seven times since 1961.[26] In 1999, however, the legislature narrowed the sales tax by increasing exemptions to it. In 2007, the rate was 6.25 percent, the seventh highest in the nation. Some communities in Texas also have a local sales tax (see chapter 7.)

Texas has other consumption taxes besides the sales tax. Special sales or excise taxes apply to some products instead of the general sales tax. Texas has a motor fuels tax, currently 20 cents per gallon. The motor vehicle sales tax is currently 6.25 percent. Tobacco tax amounts, which were raised dramatically in 2006, vary from product to product, and alcoholic beverage tax amounts vary from beverage to beverage. The hotel-motel occupancy tax is 6 percent.

Another category of taxes that Texas relies on is severance taxes. These are taxes on "severing" natural resources from the ground. Texas has such taxes on cement, sulfur, oil, and gas. Intense, protracted political battles were fought in the early and mid-twentieth century over creating and then raising the rates of these taxes. Severance taxes are often taxes on people outside Texas. Everyone in the United States consumes oil and gas, but most states have to import those substances from and pay taxes to the few producing states.

From the 1950s through the 1970s, severance taxes provided a growing percentage of Texas revenues. In 1957, oil and gas severance taxes accounted for 31 percent of all tax revenues.[27] There were particularly sharp increases in revenues from oil and gas in the 1970s. Oil prices peaked at $39 per barrel in 1982, crashed to $10, then whipped back and forth between $10 and $18 a barrel in the mid to late 1980s. The state had come to rely on oil and gas revenues so much that the crash caused state budget shortfalls. In 1981, oil and gas severance-tax revenues accounted for 28 percent of all tax revenues. In 2007, they accounted for only 7.3 percent of tax revenues—though with the steep spike of oil prices in 2008, the percentage may rise for the first time in a long time.

Texas has several business taxes. The comptroller has estimated that 58 percent of all state and local taxes in Texas are paid by businesses rather than by individuals.[28] The largest business tax has been the corporate franchise tax, paid by corporations, but not by other businesses. Business taxes such as insurance-company taxes and utility taxes produce smaller amounts of revenue. Businesses also pay property taxes to local governments (see chapter 7).

Before 1991, the franchise tax was assessed solely on capital, or money value invested. This tended to penalize capital-intensive firms. With a 1991 change, capital or net earned surplus was taxed, whichever is higher. Thus, corporate income was taxed, even if it was under another name. But the biggest problem with the tax was that so many business entities organized themselves into legal entities that allowed them to avoid the tax altogether. Thus, when the legislature was forced to reconsider the state's role in funding public schools, in 2006 it restructured the franchise tax to apply more broadly to business enterprises.

FEDERAL FUNDS The federal government contributes a considerable amount of money to the Texas economy. Indeed, the amount of federal expenditures in Texas—$141.9 billion in FY 2004—dwarfs the size of the entire state budget.[29] Most of those are direct expenditures for such things as salaries of federal employees. Part of that federal spending is in grants of **federal funds** to state governments for them to spend. In fact, the most significant non-state-tax source of revenue for states, including Texas, is federal funds.[30] In 2007, Texas received about $24.4 billion in federal funds. Most federal grants are either categorical grants for designated categories of spending or **block grants** for a general group or block of programs. Today, Texas gets federal funds through several block grants, including the Social Services Block Grant, Child Care and Development Block Grant, Temporary Assistance for Needy Families Block Grant, and others.

Federal funds are made available primarily for health and human services, education, and transportation. Texas puts so little state resources into welfare that federal funds make up about 60 percent of all health and human service spending by the state. More than two-thirds of federal aid in Texas goes to health and human services (about $16.8 billion in 2007). Significant amounts also go to education ($4.4 billion) and transportation ($2.0 billion).[31] The largest single programs receiving federal grants are Medicaid and highway construction and planning.

OTHER REVENUE SOURCES The state lottery began selling tickets in 1992, and it started strong. In 1993, it produced $1.1 billion in net lottery proceeds. In 1995, it produced $1.7 billion, but by 2001, it had slipped to $1.4 billion and climbed slightly to $1.6 billion in 2007. Lotteries typically do not produce significant proportions of total state revenue. In its first year, Texas lottery proceeds accounted for 3.3 percent of all state revenues. In 1994 and 1995, the lottery produced 4.3 percent of all state revenues, but by 2007, it was down to 2.0 percent.

federal funds
Grants of money from the federal government to the states.

block grants
Federal grants of money for a general group or block of programs, rather than a specific program.

The state also receives significant amounts of revenue from licenses and fees, such as the motor vehicle registration fee, and from interest income. In FY 2007, Texas received $6.9 billion from license and fee income and $2.4 billion from interest and investment income.

The newest source of state revenue for Texas is tobacco settlement money. As a result of settlement of a lawsuit by the state against tobacco companies, Texas will receive $15 billion over twenty-five years (though the amount can be adjusted, based on sales and inflation). In 1999, Texas received the first installment of about $1.5 billion, and by the end of FY 2005, it had received more than $3 billion.

LEVEL OF TAXATION Many Texans, other Americans, and probably people around the world believe that governments take too much of their incomes in taxes. On average, the federal government took 20.5 percent of Texans' personal income in 2006, while Texas state and local governments took 9.3 percent (which ranked forty-third).[32] How much is too much is, of course, a matter of personal judgment. What we do know is that Americans pay less in taxes than citizens in most other industrialized countries, and Texans pay considerably less than citizens in most other states. In the late 1990s in the United States, taxes took up about 28 percent of the **gross domestic product (GDP)**, or the economic value of the total amount of goods and services produced. Taxes took up about 50 percent in Sweden, 45 percent in France, 39 percent in Germany, 37 percent in Canada, and 35 percent in Great Britain.[33]

gross domestic product (GDP)
The economic value of the total amount of goods and services produced in a state or nation.

Despite the unpopularity of tax increases, pressure for Texas tax increases grew in the 1970s and 1980s with the state's burgeoning population, increased demands for such services as education, health care, and welfare, and a more diverse legislative membership. Special legislative sessions in the 1980s enacted "temporary" tax increases, many of which were later made permanent. In 1986, Bill Clements campaigned for the governorship on a no-new-tax pledge; in 1987, he signed a $5.7 billion tax increase. These significant tax increases do not always spell political doom for public officials. After her first legislative session, Governor Ann Richards signed a bill increasing state taxes $2.4 billion; her approval rating after the session increased to its highest level to that date.[34] In 2006, Governor Perry pushed through a combination of state tax increases and local tax decreases.

Texas relies heavily on the sales tax. On a per capita basis, the state and local sales tax in Texas in FY 2005 was $1,362—the fifteenth highest in the nation.[35] Yet, while Texas has high tax rates for many of its consumption taxes, overall Texas is a low-tax state. Examining state sources of tax revenue only (omitting federal revenues, interest income, etc.), the per capita amount of state taxes Texans paid in FY 2006 was $1,557, ranking forty-ninth among the states; the per capita mount of state and local taxes combined that Texans paid in FY 2005 was $3,015, ranking thirty-seventh.[36]

Increases and decreases in taxes have the potential of stimulating or depressing the economy, of attracting businesses or chasing them away. Whether state tax changes actually do have these effects is a matter of intense debate. David Osborne wrote in *Laboratories of Democracy* that "tax levels are far less important than most of us assume. Extremely high tax rates obviously scare some investors away, and extremely low taxes just as obviously inhibit government's ability to pay for quality schools, highways, and the like."[37] Political scientist Paul Brace argues that high taxation does hurt economic growth, but high-tax states can lower taxes to stimulate growth, "while a state with low taxes has nowhere to go with its taxes during bad economic times. Furthermore, research by economists has shown that a dollar of expenditure may stimulate more growth than that lost by a dollar of taxation."[38]

EFFECTS OF THE TEXAS TAX SYSTEM ON INDIVIDUALS The potential effect of the tax system on businesses and on the economy in general is certainly important, but its effect on us as individuals seems more immediate and important to us. Our state tax system, by design or by default, affects individual citizens differently, depending on their economic status and circumstances.

progressive tax
A tax in which the percentage of a person's income paid for the tax increases as the person's income increases.

regressive tax
A tax in which the percentage of a person's income paid for the tax decreases as the person's income increases.

proportional (or flat) tax
A tax that collects the same percentage of each person's income for the tax, regardless of level of income.

A tax is **progressive** when the percentage of one's income paid for the tax increases as one's income increases. For instance, the federal income tax is designed to be progressive. A tax is **regressive** when the percentage of one's income paid for the tax decreases as one's income increases. A tax is **proportional (or flat)** when everyone pays the same percentage of their income for that tax, regardless of level of income. The Legislative Budget Board is now required to provide a "tax equity note" for tax legislation, and the comptroller is required to analyze the tax burden in Texas each biennium. In 1999, the comptroller suggested that the Texas tax system was "slightly to moderately" regressive; in 2007, the comptroller declined to characterize the system overall but reported data showing that nearly every one of Texas's major taxes was regressive.[39] Sales tax regressivity in Texas has been limited—by providing exemptions for food and prescription drugs, widening the base to cover more services, and adding new exemptions in 1999 (when the issue of regressivity played a prominent role in legislative debates). Yet, the sales tax is still steeply regressive. The 2007 report showed that the poorest 10 percent of Texas households pay a far higher percent of their total income in state sales taxes than the highest 10 percent income earners pay.

Coupled with the absence of a progressive income tax, the result of heavy reliance on sales taxes is that poor and middle-class Texans pay a higher proportion of their incomes to the state in taxes than do the upper-middle and upper classes. Indeed, Texas's overall tax system is one of the most regressive in the nation.[40] To learn more about tax incidence in Texas, see Figure 8.4.

Why do some states have progressive and other states regressive tax systems? It depends on the type and mix of taxes that the state chooses. Of course, that depends largely on the strength of private interests and political factors that lead to adoption of those taxes. One study has shown that the more limited the electorate (low voter turnout), the more regressive the tax system.[41] Also, wealthier, growing, and manufacturing-based states tend to have more progressive systems.[42] Income taxes can be designed to be progressive, if policy makers want a progressive system. Other taxes are more difficult to make progressive.

Spending

In the 2006–2007 biennium, Texas spent $143 billion. By the end of the 2008–2009 biennium, the state will spend approximately $168 billion (about $85 billion per year). Texas spent $3,442 per capita in 2004, which ranked fiftieth among the fifty states.[43] In examining how Texas spends its money, we could use any of several categories. We could look at spending by policy area, by state agency, or by object, such as salaries or capital expenditures.[44] Analysis of spending by agencies is not very helpful, though, in comparing Texas to other states, because several agencies may perform similar tasks, some agencies may perform different tasks in different states, and some functions may be performed at the local level in some states and the state level in others. Thus, comparison by policy areas is more useful.

POLICY AREAS OF STATE EXPENDITURES For state governments, the largest policy categories of spending are education, public welfare, health and hospitals, and highways. To learn more about Texas's spending pattern, see Figure 8.5. It shows that Texas spends about 37 percent of its budget for health and human services and about 35 percent for education.

In 1999, Texas received the first installment of money from tobacco settlement funds. The rationale for the lawsuit was that the state had spent money on health care that it would not have had to spend were it not for tobacco use. The legislature decided to use the money indirectly, by creating twenty-one trust funds and endowments. Only annual interest from those funds is available, plus newly arriving monies. For instance, the Tobacco Settlement Permanent Trust Account yields interest

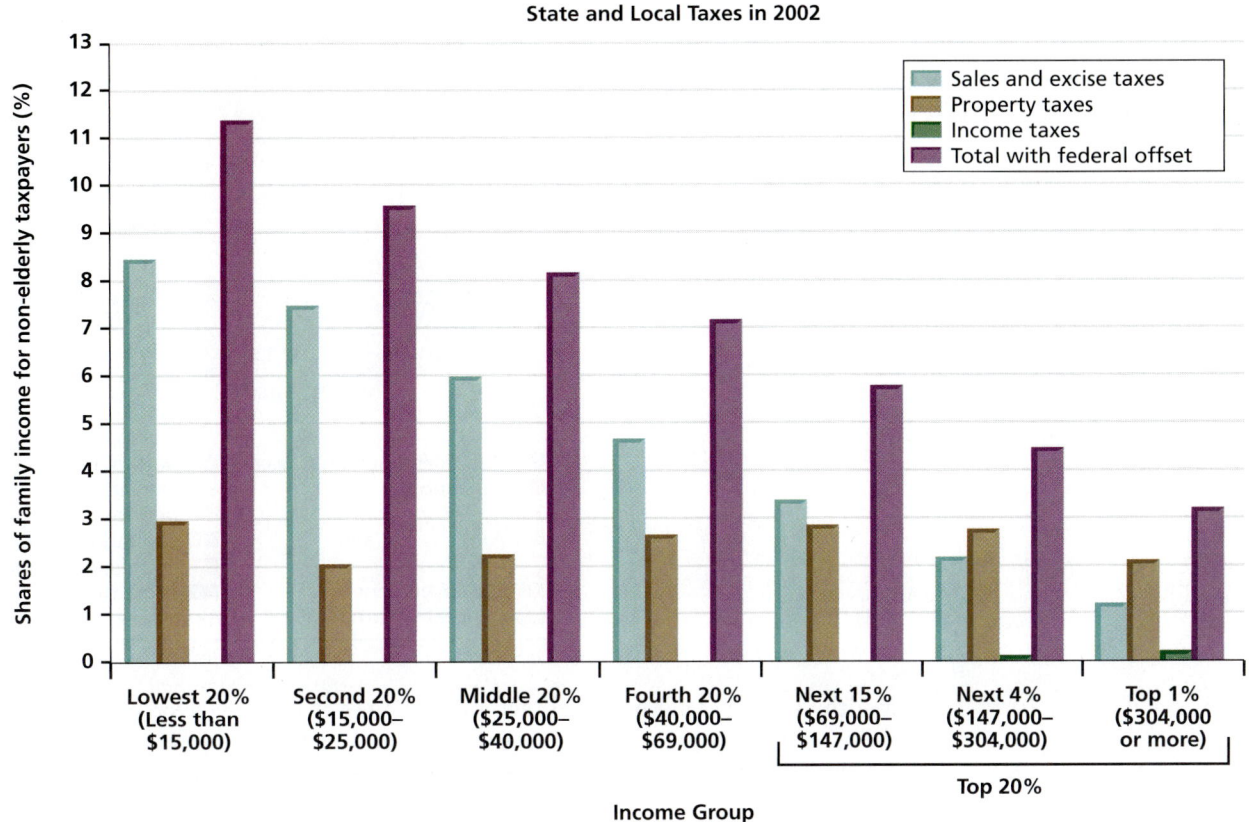

FIGURE 8.4 **Tax Incidence in Texas** One principle of taxation requires equity in taxes. But, there are different ideas of what constitutes tax equity. Some people think it requires those taxpayers who earn more income to pay a greater percentage of their income in taxes. Others maintain that taking a higher percentage of income from those who earn more has a harmful effect on economic growth and penalizes people who earn more. The chart depicts the effect of Texas taxes in 2002 on different income levels, a measure of the *tax burden* or *incidence*. The chart indicates that Texans who earn less than $15,000 annually pay 11.4 percent of their income in state and local taxes, and Texans who earn $304,000 or more annually pay 3.2 percent of their income in taxes.

Source: Robert S. McIntyre et al., *Who Pays? A Distributional Analysis of the Tax Systems in All 50 States*, 2nd ed. (Washington, DC: Citizens for Tax Justice and the Institute on Taxation and Economic Policy, 2003).
Note: Figure shows 2002 tax law at 2000 income levels.

income to reimburse counties and public hospitals for health expenses. Most of the money goes to the Health and Human Services Commission for the Children's Health Insurance Program (CHIP) and to the Department of State Health Services. In 2006–2007, the legislature appropriated about $1.1 billion from tobacco-settlement funds to these programs.[45]

SPENDING COMPARISONS Texas's annual budget of about $80–85 billion seems a huge amount, yet it is dwarfed by state spending in California (now more than $200 billion) and New York (about $130 billion). When calculated on a spending per capita basis, the level of state spending in Texas is typically forty-ninth or fiftieth in the nation.[46] Texas per capita *state and local spending* combined ranked forty-first in one recent ranking.[47] The most important determinant of state expenditures is personal income; wealthier states spend more than poorer states.[48] Texas *is*

FIGURE 8.5 State Spending by Policy Area, FY 2007

The State of Texas spends money on a wide variety of policies, yet more than four-fifths of the state's spending is in three broad policy areas. Health and human services is the policy area that the state spends the most money on, followed closely by education, then transportation.

Source: Comptroller of Public Accounts, *State of Texas 2007 Annual Cash Report*.

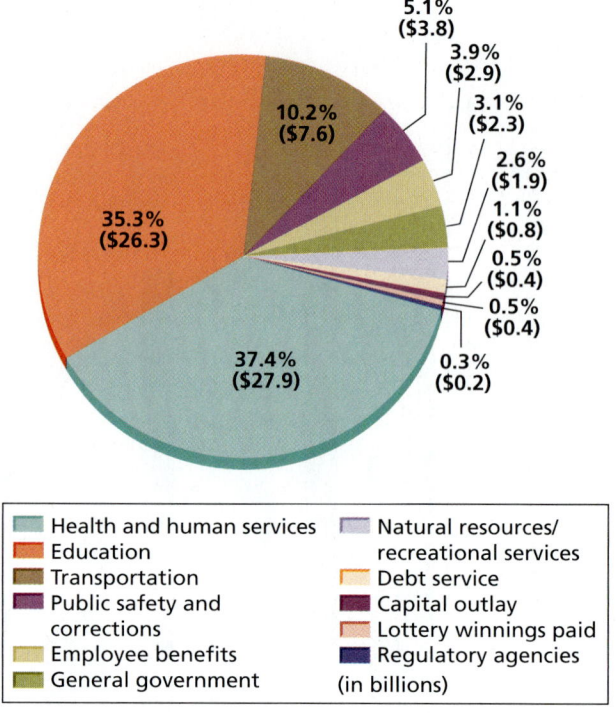

a wealthy state in total personal income, although it is below average in per household personal income. Per capita spending, however, is the lowest of the states in total, and among the lowest in many categories.

Public Education and Higher Education Policy

Public education is widely accepted as public policy—indeed, even as a fundamental human right that the political system must provide for. Texas has embraced this philosophy, supporting a large public school system. Texas has 4.5 million children in public schools, with 620,000 employees. Of those employees, 302,000 are teachers, which is the second highest number in the nation. California has 6.4 million students and 309,000 teachers.[49] This long-standing consensus in support of public education, however, is now being challenged by some on the religious right who question the concept of public education, call for churches to take over the schools, and lobby for public money for private schools in the form of **vouchers**. Even within the context of public education, we experience unending disagreements about the proper roles for the state, local, and federal governments and for parents in administering and paying for public education.

vouchers
Appropriations of public money for use in payment of tuition and expenses at private schools.

Public Education: Fulfilling Our Constitutional Mandate

Article 7, section 1, of the Texas Constitution creates a fundamental right to education and an obligation for the legislature to establish and pay for a public education system, declaring that schooling is to be free to all students. The legislature has created a statutory education code to accomplish these goals. State courts have interpreted the broad language of the constitution to mandate legislative support of an equitable public education system. Some legislators in recent years have proposed amending the constitution to ease the requirement.

The constitutional mandate has resulted in the establishment of public schools throughout the state to meet the goal of making education available to all. Texas parents send their children to these public schools at greater rates than parents in most states. Only 5.5 percent of elementary and secondary school students are in the private schools in Texas, ranking Texas forty-second among the states. Delaware has the highest percentage of private-school students: 17.8 percent.[50]

STRUCTURE OF ELEMENTARY AND SECONDARY EDUCATION Texas provides public education to its citizens from the time they enter elementary school at age five or six until they graduate from high school, usually around age eighteen. Children must be in public, private, or home school from age six to seventeen. The state provides kindergarten, elementary, junior high, high school, and some pre-kindergarten programs.

Local schools and school districts operate under a shifting degree of state oversight and regulation. Today, the Texas Education Agency (TEA) is the largest state agency in terms of funding, though most of its budget is pass-through money that the TEA allocates to school districts. In 1995, the Texas legislature enacted an entirely new education code, recreating the TEA, the State Board of Education, and the commissioner of education but abolishing some state policies and allowing school districts more leeway in deciding policies.

Texas has 1,082 local school districts, ranking first in the nation in the number of these districts. There is no uniformity in either geographic size or population size of the districts. Some have fewer than a dozen students, while the largest—Houston Independent School District in Harris County—has more than 200,000 students. These public school districts are local governments (see chapter 7). Texas has 8,517 public elementary and secondary schools, second in the nation to California, and the number grows every year. Almost all of those schools are operated by local school districts. However, in the 1995 revision of the education code, the legislature authorized the creation of **charter schools,** which are public schools operating under a contract granted by the state rather than under the control of the local school district (see chapter 7). By 2006, there were 319 public charter schools in Texas, which ranked fourth in the nation.[51]

charter schools
Public schools operating under a contract granted by the state rather than under the control of the local school district.

SCHOOL FINANCE: THE CLASH OF ECONOMIC AND SOCIAL POLICIES Across the United States, states respond in different ways to demands for educational equity. In Hawaii, the state assumes nearly all costs of education; in New Hampshire, local districts pay for almost all. The State of Texas supplies just over one-third of school district budgets, while the federal government provides less than 10 percent, and school districts more than half. The legislature and governor have struggled to increase the state's proportion to half or better, but they have not boosted overall spending enough to achieve and sustain that level.

Much of the school finance debate has centered on the level of resources that Texas spends. Though the relationship between spending levels and educational quality is a matter of unresolved debate, spending is one variable used to measure adequacy of educational systems. Across the nation in 2004–2005, total per pupil expenditures in public elementary and secondary schools averaged $10,071 per year. Counting all resources (local, state, and federal), Texas ranked thirty-fourth in expenditures at $8,891. The state spending the most on education was New Jersey at $15,934 per pupil, while Utah spent the least at $6,301. In 2005–2006, the average salary of classroom teachers in Texas was $42,824, which ranked thirty-sixth. The national average was $50,379, and Connecticut had the highest average at $61,038.[52]

> **Thinking Nationally**
> **School Vouchers**
>
> In 1995, Cleveland, Ohio, adopted a school voucher program to distribute tax revenues to parents, who could then choose which school to enroll their children in and pay the money to. In a 5–4 ruling, the U.S. Supreme Court upheld the voucher program in 2002, against charges that it was state-sponsored religious education. Now, about a dozen states have some form of school vouchers. Legislative proposals for vouchers in Texas have been intensely debated for a decade, pitting religious school advocates and others against teacher unions and public school advocates, with repeated defeats of the voucher proposals.
>
> - Why are vouchers controversial?
> - What groups have supported vouchers in Texas and what groups have opposed them? Why?
> - Would the passage of vouchers have implications for the state budget? For local school budgets? Explain.

Permanent School Fund (PSF)
The state fund consisting of revenue from state-owned lands (often paying lucrative oil and gas royalties), dedicated to public education.

Available School Fund
Annual investment income from the Permanent School Fund, used to pay operating expenses of schools.

Where does the public money for schools come from? The state's lottery revenues help but are woefully insufficient. General revenues also help. But primarily, revenue from 13 million acres of state-owned lands in Texas is dedicated to the **Permanent School Fund (PSF),** and thus lucrative oil and gas wells provide much of the money for public education. However, this money is an endowment and may not be spent. Only the annual investment income from the fund, the **Available School Fund,** may be spent, so local resources are critical.

Until the 1950s, the philosophy of local control of schools ensured a minimal state role in financing public education. With 1949 reforms, the state established a minimum level of state support to local schools. As a result, the state's portion of school funding jumped to around 80 percent of the total. However, that level was still so low that most districts must raise and spend money—from property taxes—at rates far above the state aid. The result has been gross disparities in school financing capabilities across the state, and never-ending political, legal, and legislative battles. Some districts have vast resources to tax for school purposes, while others have little. One consequence of local control has been that wealthier districts have repeatedly fought attempts to provide uniform services across the state, fearing that resources in their districts would be siphoned off.

In 1968, San Antonio resident Demetrio Rodriguez filed a lawsuit, arguing that Texas's school finance system violated the U.S. Constitution's guarantee of equality. His children attended school in the Edgewood school district, a poor district that had only $5,960 in property value per student. Students who lived just a few miles away, in the Alamo Heights school district, had $49,000 in property value per student—and far superior educational facilities and services.[53]

Rodriguez v. *San Antonio Independent School District*
U.S. Supreme Court case resulting in a decision that the Texas school finance system did not violate the U.S. Constitution.

In 1973, the U.S. Supreme Court overturned a lower court decision and ruled in ***Rodriguez* v. *San Antonio Independent School District*** that the state's school finance system did not violate the U.S. Constitutions guarantee of equal protection. The Court agreed that it was inequitable but held that education was not a fundamental right under the U.S. Constitution. School finance, the court declared, was a matter for states to resolve within their own courts.

In 1975, the legislature did pass a reform bill, though reform advocates voted against it as being far too little. Since 1975, the legislature has tinkered with the school finance formulas but left intact the basic system of local property taxes supplemented by state appropriations. In 1987, the Edgewood school district sued the state in state court, claiming that the school finance system violated the state constitution's provision for "an efficient system of public free schools." In its unanimous 1989 ***Edgewood* v. *Kirby*** decision invalidating the school finance system, the Texas Supreme Court ruled that the state had to achieve substantial equity, meaning a fair and equitable distribution of resources, among school districts.

Edgewood v. *Kirby* (1989)
Texas Supreme Court case resulting in a decision that the state's school finance system violated the state constitution's provisions for "an efficient education system of public free schools."

The *Edgewood* v. *Kirby* decision created a flurry of legislative activity, court orders, legislative gridlock, and voters' decisions for four years. Ultimately, in 1993, new Governor Ann Richards and the legislature produced a plan requiring some redistribution of tax resources across the state. Opponents dubbed the plan "Robin Hood," but the courts accepted it in 1995. The 1993 school finance reform recaptures and redistributes some local school tax revenues by limiting district revenues, capping tax rates in districts, and adjusting the state aid formula to guarantee a specified yield per tax effort for districts.

With a school finance system based on district-by-district property taxes, the overall amount of property wealth in a district determines how much money a district can raise at any given tax rate. In 1992–1993, the ratio of property wealth per student, from the richest to the poorest district, was 1,035 to 1 (a completely equalized system would have a 1 to 1 ratio). In 1994–1995, after the new reforms took place, the ratio was 489 to 1.[54] Even discounting for the extremes, the system is far from uniform. In 2004, the forty-one poorest districts had an average of $71,358 in wealth (taxable value of property) per student, while the 100 wealthiest districts had $1.3 million per student.[55] The state then provides additional funding, based on formulas and the designation of "Tier 1" and "Tier 2" schools for the amount of state revenues plus guaranteed tax yield. In

Analyzing Visuals: Public School Finance

In 2004, Governor Rick Perry announced his support for additional revenue sources for financing public education, including a fee on adult entertainment (e.g., "gentlemen's clubs"). Analyze the Ben Sargent cartoon (from the *Austin American-Statesman*, April 11, 2004) by answering the following questions:

WHAT political event, situation, or politicians are depicted?

WHAT message is conveyed by the images?

WHAT message is conveyed by the words in the speech bubble and labels in the cartoon?

WHAT position does the cartoonist appear to take on the issue?

WHICH effect is the cartoonist attempting to achieve: exaggeration, irony, or juxtaposition?

HOW does the cartoon achieve that effect?

Source: Sargent, © 2004 *Austin American-Statesman*. Reprinted with permission of Universal Press Syndicate. All rights reserved.

2007, the state provided 65 percent of the funding for those poorest districts and only 9 percent for those wealthiest districts. Still, compared to the wealthiest districts, those poorest districts *received* lower total revenues per student ($9,291 versus $11,298) and *spent* lower amounts ($8,132 versus $8,885) in operating expenses.

In 1997, the legislature examined alternatives to the 1993 system, and Governor George W. Bush proposed a new consumption tax and higher sales taxes to replace some local property tax revenues. Instead, in 1997 and 1999, because the budget surpluses were high, the legislature used them to increase state spending for education and to encourage local school districts to lower their property tax rates. Still, after the 1999 session, many districts raised taxes.

Then, in 2004 and 2005, the whole system imploded again. While the Texas Supreme Court upheld the new system in 1995, it also wrote that future challenges could be brought if the state did not provide the education demanded by the state constitution. In 2001, the state was sued in ***West Orange-Cove Consolidated ISD v. Alanis*** and in *Hopson* v. *Dallas ISD*. By 2004, nearly 300 school districts had joined the lawsuits, in a battle between property-poor districts and property-rich districts, challenging the tax cap and the equity of distribution. A state district court judge ruled that the system had become so unequalized, and did not allow districts true ability to control their tax rates, that it again violated the constitution.

The 2005 regular session of the legislature witnessed fierce battles over the state's taxing system and its school finance system, with classic standoffs between the House

West Orange-Cove Consolidated ISD v. Alanis (2004)
A school finance case pitting property-poor districts, property-rich districts, and the state against each other in state court, challenging the state's tax cap and the equity of revenue distribution, litigating the question of whether the system had become so unequalized that it again violated the state constitution.

and Senate, as Republican leaders clashed among themselves (and with Democrats) over how to restructure the systems. Governor Perry first proposed a series of "sin taxes," but they were not adopted. (See Analyzing Visuals: Public School Finance.) Ultimately, the chambers could not come to agreement, and the session ended with no school finance reform bill and no significant change in the tax structure. The legislature simply funded the existing school system through the appropriations act. Governor Perry decided to force action by using his line-item veto authority to delete all expenditures for public education. He then called a special session for the summer, hoping that legislators would agree to compromises on taxes and school finance before the first day of school in August. It didn't work.

In December, the Texas Supreme Court upheld key parts of the lower court ruling and ordered the legislature to correct it by June 1. By spring 2006, the legislature was back in special session and decided to replace the franchise tax with a new business tax, expected to bring in $3.4 billion more than the old tax, and to increase cigarette taxes dramatically, with an expected revenue increase of more than $1 billion. The new tax revenues are designed to replace some local property tax revenues. Property tax cuts totaling billions of dollars were planned for 2007 and 2008. Additionally, the legislature increased teacher salaries by more than $800 million and other school expenses by $319 million. The Center for Public Policy Priorities predicted the net result of the tax and spending changes: the "expected deficit in 2008–09 is $10.48 billion, growing to $11.12 billion in 2010–11," forcing the legislature to cut spending in other areas, or raise taxes further.[56] School districts that had sued, meanwhile, were glad to get some relief, but they warned that the legislature had not fixed the "fundamental structural problem" with the system, as they would again be forced up to taxing caps, and they hinted at new lawsuits. By 2007, more than 100 districts had raised taxes above the rate set by the legislature.[57]

Educational Quality

While national attention focused on the question of school finance in the 1970s, since then the question of educational quality has emerged as a first-priority issue. Do students get the quality of education they should? How do we measure quality? What kinds of policy changes encourage and discourage high quality? What is the relationship between educational quality and the level of school dropouts?

In the 1980s, legislatures and governors increased their role in educational policy making in an effort to address these questions. Forty-five states increased the number of courses required for graduation; half instituted minimum competency tests; most established minimum grade point averages for participation in sports; thirty-five required standardized testing for teachers; nearly half provided merit-pay incentives for teachers; most raised teachers' salaries.[58]

In 1983, Governor Mark White appointed a Select Committee on Public Education, chaired by H. Ross Perot. The legislature adopted much of the Perot committee's recommendations in 1984. The changes increased state equalization aid, increased teacher salaries, established a career ladder for teachers, mandated teacher testing, adopted the no-pass/no-play rule for athletes, and established an extensive program of testing for students, including an exit test for high school graduation. In the late 1990s, educational quality initiatives focused on testing, school safety, and social promotion. Texas adopted new curriculum standards and statewide assessment programs. In 2003, those tests were revamped and newly named the Texas Assessment of Knowledge and Skills (TAKS). Now, some districts have started "high school redesign" projects in an effort to increase standards and performance.

When George W. Bush went from the Texas governorship to the presidency, he pushed through the U.S. Congress amendments to the Elementary and Secondary Education Act. His No Child Left Behind Act (NCLB) established federal accountability requirements, triggering sanctions if goals are not met. States are required to use achievement tests, and Texas has had to adjust its testing and accountability systems to meet the federal requirements. The state (and individual districts and schools) must demonstrate "adequate yearly progress" or federal funds will be reduced, with increasing sanctions in different stages of measuring progress. Yet, the NCLB was not fully funded, and Texas (and other states) have been pressing for changes and additional federal funding to meet requirements.[59]

Higher Education: From Community Colleges to Universities

Texas has a vast public higher education system—1.1 million of Texas's 24 million citizens are enrolled in 101 public institutions of higher education.[60] (In addition, there are forty-four private institutions of higher education in Texas, with more than 100,000 students.) There are thirty-eight general academic teaching institutions, fifty community/junior/lower-two-year colleges (with multiple campuses), nine medical schools and health science centers, four campuses of the Texas state technical colleges, and nine affiliated agencies, such as Texas AgriLife Research (formerly the Agricultural Experiment Station). These public facilities have 57,000 faculty. Just over half of the students attend two-year institutions, with community college freshmen outnumbering freshmen at four-year institutions by more than 3 to 1. The public institutions are loosely regulated by the Texas Higher Education Coordinating Board. All but five of the public universities are organized into five senior university systems: the University of Texas System, the Texas A&M University System, the University of Houston System, the Texas State University System, and the Texas Tech University System.[61]

FUNDING COLLEGES AND UNIVERSITIES Public colleges and universities get appropriations from the legislature, tuition and fees from students, money from private sources, and funding from the federal government. For institutions affiliated with the University of Texas and Texas A&M University, the legislature appropriates money from the **Available University Fund** investment income, off the endowed **Permanent University Fund (PUF).** Revenue from more than 2 million acres of West Texas land owned by the state is dedicated to the PUF.

Available University Fund
Annual investment income from the Permanent University Fund, used to pay expenses for the University of Texas and Texas A&M Systems.

Permanent University Fund (PUF)
The fund consisting of revenue from state-owned lands (often paying lucrative oil and gas royalties) dedicated to the University of Texas and Texas A&M Systems.

How does Texas provide quality higher education? Students have more than 100 public institutions and scores of private schools to choose from. Here, students visit on the campus of Texas A&M University, the state's original land-grant college.

Higher Education Fund
A constitutionally dedicated fund providing money for capital projects for colleges and universities not a part of the University of Texas or Texas A&M Systems.

The 1876 constitution stipulated that the legislature should establish a "university of the first class." Thus, the University of Texas and later the Texas A&M University were created and funded from the proceeds of the PUF. Both are often ranked among the top universities nationally. Over the past century, other universities and colleges were created, funded from general revenues and from a much smaller new fund created in the 1940s. In the 1980s, the constitution was amended to replace that fund with a new **Higher Education Fund** and to require the University of Texas System to use the PUF for its campuses that had previously been excluded.[62] Today, the PUF funds two dozen institutions, and the Higher Education Fund funds nearly three dozen others. In 1999, voters approved a constitutional amendment that allows some of the PUF investment funds to be used in some circumstances, rather than just the interest income.

A typical annual cost for a student in a Texas public university (tuition, fees, and living expenses) is just over $15,000.[63] Historically, the legislature set tuition rates for state colleges and universities. Tuition has always been low in Texas, compared to public higher education in other states. (But, colleges and universities also have a plethora of fees that can outstrip the cost of tuition.) In the mid-1980s, the legislature began a series of regular increases in tuition. However, in 2003, the legislature "deregulated" tuition, allowing boards of trustees to set tuition rates for their academic institutions (with set-asides for financial aid), and then allowing experimentation with some cost-saving/cost-sharing approaches, such as reducing costs to students who graduate in a timely manner. Thus, each college or university now has different tuition levels. In the 2005–2006 academic year, the lowest level of tuition and fees was at Texas A&M at Texarkana ($3,184), while the highest was at the University of Texas at Austin ($7,438). Nationally, Texas's average cost for in-state tuition and fees ($5,414) ranked twenty-third in the nation in 2005–2006, compared to the highest state, Vermont, at $9,494, and the lowest, New Mexico, at $2,854.[64]

ACCESS TO HIGHER EDUCATION Higher education in Texas was formerly available almost exclusively to Anglos, particularly Anglo males, for economic reasons and because of policies that legitimated segregation and discrimination. College students in Texas now can avail themselves of both federal and state financial aid. Texas has long provided the Hinson-Hazlewood student loan program and, to help pay the difference in costs between tuition at private institutions and public institutions, the Tuition Equalization Grant Program. In addition, 1999 legislation established two new financial aid programs for lower-income students: Toward EXcellence, Access, and Success (TEXAS), and Teach for Texas. The 2003 legislature passed a "Texas B-on-Time" program to forgive loans for students who graduate in a timely manner with at least a B average.

Today, college education is available to a broader spectrum of people, though African Americans and Mexican Americans still do not make up a percentage of students proportional to their numbers in the Texas population. The Texas Higher Education Coordinating Board has set a goal of 5.6 percent of Texas's population to be enrolled in higher education. In 2006, the rate for African Americans was 5.4 percent and for Hispanics, 3.9 percent, with both groups increasing enrollments in recent years, though Hispanic enrollment has not increased as much as projected.[65] Indeed, after the *Hopwood* v. *Texas* case invalidating affirmative action, minority enrollment in Texas colleges and universities fell. To counter the effects of *Hopwood*, in 1997 the legislature passed a law stating that all Texas students in the top 10 percent of their graduating class automatically gain admission to a public college or university. (To learn more about the Top 10 Percent Law and controversy surrounding it, see Ideas into Action.) The Higher Education Coordinating Board reported on the effects of *Hopwood*, noting that minority enrollment was already falling prior to *Hopwood*, but that:

> The *Hopwood* decision has had a negative impact on the number of African-Americans and Hispanics applying for, being admitted to, and enrolling in . . . undergrad-

Ideas Into Action

The Texas Top 10 Percent Law

Texas colleges and universities, responding to public opinion and to increased political participation by African Americans and Hispanics, began using affirmative action programs to diversify their previously all-white student bodies. But in 1996, a U.S. Court of Appeals ruled in *Hopwood* v. *Texas* that the University of Texas Law School's admissions policy was unconstitutional, and Texas Attorney General Dan Morales then applied the *Hopwood* decision "to all internal institutional policies, including admissions, financial aid, scholarships, fellowships, recruitment and retention, among others."[a] Affirmative action programs at Texas's public colleges and universities ended.

In 1997, the Texas legislature passed a law guaranteeing students in the top 10 percent of their high school graduating class admission to any public college or university in Texas. The bill's goal was to provide alternative admissions criteria that ensured a diverse student population—and there is little doubt that ethnic, geographic, and economic diversity has increased under the Top 10 Percent Law.[b] Yet, since then, the legislature and the state's colleges and universities have debated scrapping the law or limiting it (perhaps to the top 5 percent, or up to no more than 50 percent of an incoming class). Top 10 Percent proponents (led by minority legislators) note that retention rates, SAT scores, and graduation rates have increased since the law was passed.[c] In addition, studies by admissions offices indicate that top 10 percent students have performed better than students who scored significantly higher on standardized entrance examinations.

The law's opponents (some university officials and some students and parents) argue that it is unfair to students who attend exemplary, highly competitive high schools and take challenging courses. Some argue that it creates an unhealthy academic environment. For example, talented students in certain fields, such as arts and music, may not be admitted, and "admissions departments have little incentive to aggressively recruit students who are best suited to their campuses."[d] But, perhaps the biggest driving force to change the law is that at the state's flagship universities, the percentage of students offered admission under the Top 10 Percent Law has now reached 50, 60, and even 70 percent.[e]

- What effect would the proposed changes have on diversity at Texas's flagship universities?
- What shift in participation patterns influenced the change in university admissions policies over the past few decades?
- Would increased participation in the policy-making process affect the outcome in this current debate? How?

---

[a] Dan Morales, Office of the Attorney General of Texas, Letter Opinion No. 97-001, February 5, 1997.

[b] House Research Organization, "Should Texas Change the Top 10 Percent Law?" *Focus Report* (February 25, 2005). Texas Higher Education Coordinating Board, "First-time Undergraduate Applicant, Acceptance, and Enrollment Information, Summer/Fall 2005," www.thecb.state.tx.us/.

[c] "Is the 'Top 10' Plan Unfair?" CBS News.com, October 17, 2004, www.cbsnews.com.

[d] House Research Organization, "Should Texas Change," 4–5.

[e] Higher Education Coordinating Board, "First-time Undergraduate Applicant Acceptance"; see also Ralph K. M. Haurwitz, "Tough Fight Shaping Up on State College Admission Law," *Austin American-Statesman* (March 30, 2005).

---

uate and graduate programs at the most selective universities, medical schools, and law schools. . . . As a result of *Hopwood*, both the University of Texas at Austin and Texas A&M University restructured their admissions procedures to eliminate race or ethnicity as a factor and to consider the alternative admissions criteria offered in House Bill 588, which provides automatic admission at public universities to any student in the top 10 percent of his or her high school graduating class. Both institutions also report that they increased their recruitment efforts to help compensate for the effects of *Hopwood*.[66]

The effect of the 10 percent rule has been to broaden the geographic, socioeconomic, and race/ethnic representation on campuses. Yet, in its most recent sessions, the legislature has battled whether to remove or restrict the 10 percent admission criterion, and campuses were divided on its impact. To further roil the waters, in 2003 the U.S. Supreme Court ruled in a pair of University of Michigan affirmative action cases that affirmative action *could* still be used, if structured properly. The University of Texas and other campuses began reinstating redesigned affirmative action programs.

Privatizing Public Assistance

OVERVIEW: In 2003, the Texas legislature consolidated several agencies that provided public health and human services programs into four agencies. In addition, to deal with a $10 billion budget shortfall, the legislature included numerous changes in the programs and the services that recipients received. One of the more controversial provisions of the legislation involved the method of determining eligibility for Temporary Assistance for Needy Families (TANF), food stamps, Medicaid, the Children's Health Insurance Program (CHIP), and Supplemental Security Income (SSI). The bill transferred the determination of eligibility function for the programs from several agencies to the Health and Human Services Commission (HHSC). The bill also required HHSC "to establish a call center for eligibility determination and recertification for TANF, food stamps, and Medicaid, if cost-effective."[a] Finally, the bill authorized HHSC to contract with a private company to operate the call centers, and it has done so.

The privatization of public service is controversial. Governments have frequently contracted with private companies for the delivery of services ranging from garbage collection to prisons. However, privatization is now expanding to include areas of policy making and program design. In Texas, the use of call centers to qualify applicants for public assistance ranging from food stamps and TANF to CHIP and Medicaid means private-sector operators have access to financial data housed in a computer system.

Proponents of privatization include legislators and executive officers anxious to increase efficiency and reduce costs. According to a survey conducted by the Council of State Governments, privatization has increased in recent years as revenues have been outpaced by spending. The principal reason for privatization among budget/legislative directors was cost savings. Among executive agency officials, the principal reason was a lack of personnel or expertise. Savings from privatization ranged from 5 to 15 percent.[b] The principal opponents of privatization are public employees and their representatives. As many as 2,500 state health and social services jobs in Texas could be eliminated through contracts with private companies under HB 2292.[c] Opponents also maintain that hidden costs of privatization, such as a new layer of bureaucracy to administer the bidding process and contracts, result in little or no cost savings through privatization. Furthermore, privatization decreases opportunities for women and ethnic minorities in the workforce, since state agencies traditionally have provided more opportunities for minorities both in numbers hired and in advancement to professional and managerial positions.[d]

Health and Human Services Policy

The broad category of health and human services includes health care, housing, food, income, and employment assistance. Sometimes these policies are referred to as social welfare or socio-economic policies. Health and human services competes with education as the policy area that the State of Texas spends most on. Compared to other states, however, these services in Texas are minimal.

Poverty rates drive social welfare policies. The greater the number of people who lack the resources to provide for themselves and their families, the greater are the demands placed on the state. Texas's poverty rate is usually among the highest in the nation. According to David Osborne in *Laboratories of Democracy*, "The integration of economic and social programs is particularly important in poor communities."[67] Without such integration, programs designed to improve living conditions for those in poverty are likely to have only a temporary effect.

Read and think about the following arguments for and against the privatization of determining eligibility for public assistance. Then, join the debate by answering the series of questions concerning whether private companies should determine eligibility for public assistance.

Arguments IN FAVOR of Private Companies Determining Eligibility for Public Assistance

- Private call centers reduce the amount of time and personal expense required to apply for and receive services. A single access point to determine eligibility for all services saves clients time and ensures that they receive all of the services to which they are entitled.

- Private call centers allow clients to recertify without taking time off from work. Call centers make it easier to accommodate working people, who could contact the centers after hours and would not have to take off from work for a face-to-face interview.

- Private call centers increase the accuracy of eligibility determination, certification, and recertification. When clients have to contact different eligibility workers and understand the guidelines for each program, they become confused and frustrated, and may not receive all of the services they need.

Arguments AGAINST Private Companies Determining Eligibility for Public Assistance

- Private call centers raise questions about the state's ability to protect clients' rights and hold the companies accountable for their performance. Private companies employ low-paid, hourly workers who are not likely to perform as well as state employees.

- Private call centers result in a loss of state jobs, especially in rural areas. The resulting loss of jobs raises questions about client access to services in rural areas of Texas. Also, state jobs are very important to the economies of rural Texas.

- The limited number of call centers is not sufficient to meet the customer service and performance standards established by HHSC. Companies, interested in profits, are not willing to spend the money necessary to train their employees to perform adequately, as has been demonstrated by the early record of the call centers in Texas.

Continuing the Debate

1. Do you favor the operation of call centers by private companies or state employees? Why or why not?
2. Does government abdicate its responsibility and accountability to the public when private companies make the decisions about who receives public benefits, such as TANF, CHIP, and Medicaid? Explain your answer.

To follow the Debate Online Go To:

- Texas Conservative Coalition Research Institute: www.txccri.org/index.html
- Center for Public Policy Priorities: www.cppp.org

[a] House Research Organization, *Bill Analysis*, HB 2292 (April 23, 2003): 18, www.capitol.state.tx.us/.

[b] Reason Foundation, "Annual Privatization Report: 2004," April 2004, www.rppi.org.

[c] Jonathan Walters, "Going Outside," *Governing* (May 2004).

[d] Center for Policy Alternatives, "Privatizing Public Services," 2004, www.stateaction.org.

The Federal–State Partnership

Since the 1930s, the federal government has had anti-poverty programs, such as food stamps, that are known as "entitlement" programs. If a person or family meets the criteria, usually being below the official poverty-level income, then the person or family is entitled to the benefits of that particular program. The federal government typically gives the states money for the programs, and the states run the programs. States also put in some money. For some programs, states have leeway in setting entry criteria. For other programs, the federal government imposes requirements on the states for being eligible for federal funds. For some programs, states can choose the level of support they will provide to recipients. To learn more about some of the best-known social welfare programs, see Table 8.1. Two federal programs, Social Security and **Temporary Assistance for Needy Families (TANF)**, demonstrate some of the different arrangements between the federal and state governments in funding and administering social welfare programs.

Temporary Assistance for Needy Families (TANF)
Federal–state cash assistance program adopted in 1996 to replace Aid to Families with Dependent Children.

TABLE 8.1 Snapshots of Key Social Welfare Programs

Children's Health Insurance Program (CHIP). A federal–state program providing health insurance for children who live in low-income families.
Food Stamps. A federal program providing a monthly allotment to eligible low-income people, which can be used to purchase food (via an electronic card, the Lone Star Card).
Head Start. A federal educational, health care, and social service program for low-income pre-school children, designed to improve their skills so that they do not begin school so far behind other children.
Medicaid. A federal program administered by the states, reimbursing health care providers for costs of caring for eligible low-income and disabled people.
Medicare. A federal health care program for the elderly.
Social Security. A federal social welfare program, including retirement benefits for most American workers, disability benefits, and supplemental income for the aged or disabled. Jointly with the states, it also provides unemployment compensation.
Temporary Assistance for Needy Families (TANF). A federal cash assistance program, enacted in 1996 to replace the long-standing Aid to Families with Dependent Children (AFDC).
Women, Infants, and Children Nutrition (WIC). A federal program providing nutrition education and a monthly food grant to low-income women with young children.

The federal Social Security Act incorporates numerous programs. Its best-known program, Social Security, which is also one of the largest entitlement programs, provides benefits for workers no longer employable due to age or disability. These Social Security recipients are also eligible for Medicare, a health care program. Although Social Security retirement and Medicare are federal programs, the Social Security Act also includes unemployment compensation, which is financed jointly by the federal government, state governments, and employers and is administered by states. Social Security also includes Supplemental Security Income—federal aid to the aged, disabled, and blind, which can be supplemented by states.

In the 1980s and early 1990s, states began pressing for changes in the federal welfare programs, including instituting "welfare to work" programs to reduce the welfare rolls by placing more of the recipients in jobs. The Texas legislature adopted welfare changes in 1995, including limits on the amount of time that people could collect benefits. In 1996, the U.S. Congress abolished Aid to Families with Dependent Children (AFDC), the longtime joint federal–state program to provide cash assistance to low-income families with children, and replaced it with the new TANF program. To achieve its goal of removing people from welfare and encouraging them to work, it established a five-year lifetime limit for benefits. In 1997 and 1999, the Texas legislature revised its 1995 welfare reform act to implement the new federal program. Congressional reauthorization of TANF was required in 2002, though Congress did not get it fully reauthorized until 2006.

As a result of the initial changes, the Texas TANF caseload declined more than 42 percent from 1995 to 1998.[68] Caseloads then flattened and began increasing gradually as the economy slumped. In 2001, the legislature passed several bills with the intent of better coordinating TANF and other programs, better utilizing federal funds, and improving access. In his "Father's Day Massacre" (see chapter 5), Governor Perry vetoed three of the bills revising welfare-to-work policies. In the 2003 budget crunch, the legislature cut spending for many of the state's health and human services programs. The 2005 legislature struggled to restore some funding but did not restore all of it. To cut costs, the legislature began privatizing some of the services, including closing hundreds of state offices and replacing them with "call centers" operated by a private company that would do assessment of needs over the telephone. Opponents argued that privatization would hurt recipients. Indeed, by 2006, Health and Human Services Executive Commissioner Albert Hawkins began penalizing the multinational company that runs the centers for poor performance.[69] (To learn more about privatization, see Join the Debate: Privatizing Public Assistance.)

Assistance for Food, Shelter, Clothing, and Protection

When a family or individual is in a crisis situation and needs food, shelter, or clothing, the availability of government assistance depends on the state in which the family or person resides. Large, urban, and politically competitive states typically provide higher levels of social welfare services. About two-thirds of the states (not including Texas) supply short-term relief programs, but the number has dropped, as several states have abolished their programs.[70] Families in Texas must rely on TANF, food stamps, or Social Security programs. The state is also involved in policy and funding battles over how best to protect children in homes without adequate resources, or with abusive parents.

The federal government has long provided surplus food commodities to the poor and also provides coupons, known as food stamps, which recipients can redeem only for food. The Food Stamp Act is federally funded but is administered by the federal and state governments. In the early 1990s, Texas started using an electronic card, called the Lone Star Card, instead of paper stamps, in an effort to reduce theft, fraud, and administrative costs. (The card is now used for food stamp and TANF benefits.) A third type of food assistance is the federal Women, Infants, and Children nutrition program (WIC), which targets funds for food specifically to young children and their mothers.

The Texas Department of Housing and Community Affairs is Texas's lead agency responsible for affordable housing. The federal government provides money for construction of low-income dwellings and for rent supplementation. The U.S. Department of Housing and Urban Development administers the program, but it is implemented through local housing authorities. One provision of the act, Community Development Block Grants, provides money for rehabilitation of housing. A separate Emergency Shelter Grants Program provides limited money for emergency shelters. The agency also helps with energy costs. Texans with physical or mental disabilities may also be eligible for housing assistance. In 1999, the U.S. Supreme Court ruled, in the *Olmstead* case, that states must place disabled persons in community care facilities, rather than institutions.[71]

Health Care

Skyrocketing costs for doctor and hospital care, increasingly sophisticated medical treatments, the AIDS crisis, the coming-of-age of managed health care insurance programs, President Bill Clinton's failed initiative to adopt a national health insurance program, and soaring pharmaceutical prices combined to make health care policy one of the most salient issues of public opinion. Texas's indicators of public health suggest a continuing need for resources. For instance, in 2005, Texas was fourth in the nation in the number of new AIDS cases; in 2006, Texas ranked only forty-third in the number of doctors per 100,000 population.[72] Chapter 5 explains the array of state agencies that administer health policy in Texas and the reorganization that the 2003 legislature mandated.

Traditionally, individuals have been responsible for their own health care. For many, coverage under a health insurance plan is essential to surviving health crises. Many are covered by insurance provided by their employer, but in 2006, Texas ranked first in the nation in the percentage of its population not covered, at 24.1 percent.[73] In the impoverished communities along the Rio Grande, the figure is higher—about one-third of the

Thinking Nationally
Health Care Costs

Health care costs have been a critical political issue nationally for two decades, but no national solution has been adopted. In 2006, Massachusetts implemented a new health insurance policy, providing health care access to all residents. Texas has the highest percentage of its population uncovered by health insurance.

- Massachusetts provides free coverage for its poorest citizens and negotiated premiums for others. What budgetary implications might this system have?
- What factors could influence a state like Massachusetts to adopt broad health care access policies? What factors might influence Texas to adopt or reject such policies?
- Should individual states continue to experiment with health care policy innovations, or should the crisis be resolved nationally? Why?

population is not covered by health insurance.[74] Because of the gaps in private coverage, there are numerous federal and state programs to assist with health care.

People who do not have health insurance are often unable to afford it. Just as the state constitution requires that education be available for all, it also authorizes counties to make health care available to all, and state law requires them to pay for indigent care. They may do so by operating a public hospital, creating a hospital district, or operating an indigent health care program. County hospitals have become responsible for more and more care for impoverished Texans. As other hospitals started turning away people who had no insurance, the legislature stepped in. After the 1985 defeat of a bill requiring hospitals to provide more health care to the indigent, Governor White called a special legislative session, which enacted a bill that requires hospitals to treat emergency cases, rather than simply sending critically ill patients to county hospitals.[75] More recently, legal and political skirmishes have erupted over the question of whether indigent health care programs can serve undocumented immigrants.[76]

Medicaid is a joint state–federal health care program that pays doctor and hospital bills for those who qualify for the program. Texas has converted Medicaid into a managed care system, as virtually all states have done. It is available to people with incomes below the poverty level and to medically needy people who have lost their insurance or whose insurance cannot cover long-term care needs. In 2007, 2.9 million Texans were in Medicaid, about 2.1 million of whom are children. Many more are eligible but are not covered. Nationally, 15 percent of the population is covered by Medicaid; in Texas, the figure is 12.1 percent, with Texas ranking thirty-fourth among the states.[77] After welfare reform in 1996, there was a significant decline in the number of Texas children on Medicaid. The legislature sought to address numerous problems with the Medicaid program in an omnibus bill in 2001, but Governor Perry vetoed it. The 2003 and 2005 legislatures tried again, including changes to reduce the number of optional services available through Medicaid and reducing reimbursement rates for health care providers.[78]

The legislature has initiated several programs in response to the large number of uninsured children. The U.S. Congress also created a **Children's Health Insurance Program (CHIP)** as a federal block grant program, with states providing matching revenue. People who qualify for Medicaid cannot get CHIP. In 1999, the Texas legislature approved legislation implementing CHIP. As a consequence of the welfare reform focus on employment rather than welfare, the Texas Health and Human Services Commission now administers the "Texas Works" initiative to coordinate the food stamp, CHIP, and Medicaid programs.

In creating CHIP, there was intense controversy over how broad to make the coverage. Those seeking broad coverage won, and CHIP in Texas covered children through age eighteen who live in families with incomes up to 200 percent of the poverty level. Of about 1.2 million children eligible for CHIP or Medicaid coverage, by 2003 the state insured about 726,000 of them. However, the new Republican legislature in 2003 cut back the CHIP program by 22 percent and partially funded the reduced program from the state's "rainy day" fund. Legislators then battled over the effects of those cuts, how much to restore to the program, and whether to turn over elements of the program to private companies. Only about 409,000 were covered by 2007.[79]

The Adequacy of Health and Human Service Programs in Texas

Texas spends an enormous amount of money on TANF, CHIP, and food stamps, though most of it is federal funds. The 1990s program changes are having an effect. In 1996, Texas had 726,000 TANF recipients; by 2006, there were 154,153 TANF

Medicaid
Joint state–federal health care program that pays doctor and hospital bills for those who qualify for the program (primarily those with income below the poverty level).

Children's Health Insurance Program (CHIP)
Federal block grant program, with states providing matching revenue to provide health care to children in low- to medium-income families who have no other insurance.

recipients (or 0.7 percent of the population, ranking Texas forty-first among the states). The number dropped 76 percent from 1996 to 2006.[80] The typical Texas TANF family got $220 per month in 2006, which ranked Texas forty-fourth in the nation in TANF benefits. Food stamp enrollment in Texas dropped from its high of 2.7 million participants in 1994 to 1.4 million in 1999, though it rose to 2.4 million in 2006. Texas is more generous with assistance in the form of food stamps than it is with TANF. The average monthly food stamp benefit per recipient in Texas in 2005 was $90.31, twenty-third highest in the nation.[81]

Transportation Policy

With 24 million Texans on the roads, plus heavy truck and interstate traffic and inadequate public transportation alternatives, Texas highways and roads have become highly congested. The state is now trying a potpourri of responses to the gridlock (with a much heavier emphasis on highways than on public transportation). The Texas Transportation Commission, Texas Department of Transportation, and Governor Perry proposed a **Trans-Texas Corridor** plan for a statewide network of new and existing transportation routes designed to better carry passenger, freight, and utility traffic.[82] They also began increasing reliance on toll roads and contracting out to corporations the right to build private for-profit highways.

In 1917, the legislature created the Highway Department to provide coordination of road building, largely because such state coordination was required to gather federal dollars. The agency has been renamed and reorganized over the years. In 1991, it was named the Texas Department of Transportation (TxDOT), and its jurisdiction broadened to encompass all transportation modes. Its primary focus, though, remains highways, as Texas has developed the largest road system in the nation. Counties and cities have responsibilities for local roads and streets, and the state builds and maintains state and U.S. highways, with state tax dollars and federal funds.

Texas traditionally had a "pay as you go" philosophy behind much of its programs, including transportation. Pushed by a coordinated campaign led by a powerful interest group allied with government officials and local businesses, the state constitutionally dedicated funds for highways and used that money, plus extra appropriated by the legislature for roads. In 1911, the Texas Good Roads Association (TGRA) was founded to promote roads for motor traffic, and it became a powerful voice in the transportation policy discussions. TGRA often had elected officials and civic notables as officers of their interest group.[83] The group proved its mettle in 1923 by winning a dedicated stream of state funds for highways, from the state's motor fuel tax. Then in 1946, TGRA won a "Good Roads" constitutional amendment dedicating the motor vehicle sales tax to highways, soon followed by an additional legislative commitment to spend general revenues for farm-to-market roads.

The Federal Highway Act of 1956 began President Eisenhower's Interstate Highway program, with federal monies and regulations. TxDOT now works with regional and local planning councils to coordinate the federal, state, and local negotiations and agreements on transportation policy. In the 1970s and 1980s, the legislature tinkered with the funding systems, doubling some of the taxes and fees that went to highways. In the 1990s, the state began relying more heavily on bond funding for transportation.

Tolling roads as a means of paying for them has never been widespread in Texas, though it has been used some. The state created the Texas Turnpike Authority and built the Dallas–Fort Worth Turnpike in the 1950s as a toll road,

Trans-Texas Corridor
A proposed statewide network of transportation routes for passenger vehicles, large trucks, rail, and utilities.

tolling
Financing highway construction or operations by requiring motorists who use them to pay tolls (fees).

How do you want to pay for that trip? Historically, the state paid for highways with state and federal tax dollars. Over the past decade, the state has turned to tolls to pay for roads.

then converted it to a freeway when the bonds were paid off. A new toll road was later built in Dallas. In the 1980s, the state authorized three toll roads in Houston, and connector toll roads went out beyond Houston. Regional toll authorities were created in the Dallas and Houston area. But the constitution prohibited using state money to build or maintain toll roads, so those local authorities had to rely only on the toll revenues.[84]

Then in the 2000s, new leadership at the Texas Transportation Commission and TxDOT started adding more toll roads to the mix, in an effort to address the increasing congestion and gridlock on Texas roads. Voters at first rejected efforts to permit more state involvement in toll roads, then in 1991 they approved a constitutional change allowing some state monies to be used in toll roads. In 2001, the legislature proposed, and the voters ratified, an amendment to the Texas Constitution to create the Texas Mobility Fund, a revolving bond fund that would finance the construction of state highways, toll roads, and other transportation projects. The legislature also passed legislation allowing the conversion of existing highways to toll roads and legislation creating the Texas Mobility Fund.[85] In addition, the legislature authorized the creation of Regional Mobility Authorities (RMAs) to construct, operate, and maintain turnpike projects in the state. In 2003, the legislature expanded the powers of Regional Mobility Authorities, and voters approved constitutional amendments to create additional bonding authority and to allow the agency to borrow money from any source to pay for its expenses.[86]

The new RMAs are a form of special district, created to perform a limited government role, approved by the Texas Transportation Commission. An RMA is governed by a seven-member board (three board members are appointed from each of the counties, and the governor appoints the presiding member). Although it has no taxing authority, it can undertake a myriad of transportation projects, issue bonds, condemn land and take it for public use, and convert roads to toll roads.

As a consequence of this new policy environment, the Transportation Commission and TxDOT now aggressively push toll roads as the preferred method for transportation expansion. In 2003, the commission and TxDOT began evaluating all controlled-access highway projects as possible candidates for toll roads. Moreover, officials began planning a Trans-Texas Corridor as a multi-use, statewide network of routes, incorporating new and existing highways and railways. As envisioned, each route will include:

- Separate lanes for passenger vehicles and large trucks.
- Freight railways.
- High-speed commuter railways.
- Infrastructure for utilities, including water lines, oil and gas pipelines, and transmission lines for electricity, broadband, and other telecommunications services.[87]

Plans call for the corridor to be completed in phases over fifty years, with TxDOT overseeing the planning, construction, and ongoing maintenance, and private companies getting contracts to perform daily operations. In March 2005, the Texas Transportation Commission appointed a twenty-one-member Trans-Texas Corridor citizen's advisory committee. Plans are for an Oklahoma to Mexico route and a northeast Texas to Mexico route. Federal environmental studies began for those routes in 2004. The first phase of the planning was contracted out to Cintra-Zachry, a privately owned engineering, construction, and financing firm based in Spain, working in partnership with numerous other companies. Cintra-Zachry plans to maintain and operate the first highway in the corridor as a toll road for fifty years.

Toward Reform: Changing Public Policies in Texas

Public policies are always undergoing changes. Whether those changes are *reforms* or not depends on one's point of view—and often whether one is benefitting from the changes (let's call them reforms) or being hurt by them (let's call them special interest politics). For instance, have the highway tolling policies been reforms? Or is the brewing opposition to tolls reform? The answer probably lies in who wins the battle and gets to claim the victory.

Across the state, the reaction to the new approach to state transportation policy has been mixed. Regional groups pushed ahead with tolling projects, as they have been encouraged or mandated to do (tolling is sometimes a condition for receiving mobility bond funds). Opposition from residents has organized in several areas of the state. Particularly in El Paso, Austin, and northern suburban Dallas, toll-road opponents have been adamant enough to organize political opposition to the projects. That opposition led the 2005 legislature to agree to some modifications in tolling practices; in 2006, anti-tolling candidates ran for various offices, with some of them winning and proposing reforms to the new tolling policies.

Reform in the arena of education policy and education finance is also a matter of perspective (and power). Early in Texas's history, children were educated in private schools. Today, 95 percent of Texas children go to public schools. After 150 years of strong support for public education, a new movement is now challenging the structure of public education, and some even question its worth, arguing for reforms such as vouchers, charter schools, and home schooling. Public school advocates voice strong support for the role of public education in pursuing the value of equity in society. Advocates for flexibility and resources to provide more choices to parents and students voice strong support for the value of parental control over education choices. Sometimes they also criticize values taught in public schools, and thus champion the growth of private education. The values battle is often depicted as a zero-sum game: increasing support for private education (through vouchers, for example) could mean no increase or reduced funding for public education.

Additionally, as school safety issues, teacher turnover and quality, dropout rates, and quality of education issues mounted, coupled with a growing home school movement and strong ideologically driven campaigns against taxation, public schools found themselves in an intense firefight with legislators and interest groups. In 1993, the legislature sunsetted the Education Code, then came back in 1995 for a major rewrite of the state's policy toward public education. The legislature allowed the state to charter schools directly, independent of a school district. Each session, the legislature now battles over whether to provide funds for private education of students through vouchers, which would likely further reduce state funding of public schools. But the

Politics Now

Source: DALLAS MORNING NEWS
November 18, 2008

Privatization and Texas Government

Accenture, Texas Officials Soon to Settle Call-Center Contract That Soured

ROBERT T. GARRETT

Texas and the one-time contractor that operated state call centers are close to a financial pact that will settle their ugly breakup 20 months ago, state social services czar Albert Hawkins said Monday.

Mr. Hawkins told lawmakers that the state and Accenture LLP should agree by Dec. 31 on how to put to rest what began as a five-year, $899 million contract but soon went sour and was suspended—by mutual consent—in March 2007, before the end of its second year.

"There's a mutual interest among all parties to resolve it, and I think we're close," said Mr. Hawkins, who runs the Health and Human Services Commission, testifying before a legislative panel created to oversee public assistance eligibility screening.

In an interview, he declined to elaborate. Accenture spokesman Joe Dickie also declined to discuss the talks.

In December 2006, Accenture and the state scaled back the contract—to $543 million over five years. The reduction came with the return of some call-center duties to state workers.

The partial privatization of the state's call centers was plagued by complaints of slow service and the wrongful denial of help to Texans who were eligible for benefits because their information had been misplaced. Accenture blamed some of the problems on tighter eligibility rules imposed by the state.

Commission spokeswoman Stephanie Goodman said Monday that the state has paid the Texas Access Alliance—a group led by Accenture—$242.6 million for services. The state also paid Accenture $25.8 million for computers, software, furniture and phones purchased by the vendor.

The state is rebidding all of the outsourced duties. Maximus Inc., a former Accenture subcontractor based in Reston, Va., continues to run the call centers

Discussion Questions

1. What role is the Texas legislature playing in taking testimony from Commissioner Hawkins regarding the privatization of health and human service call centers? What other actions could the legislature take?

2. Why might privatization of state services continue in spite of the apparent failure of the Accenture call centers?

3. What triggered quick reconsideration of call-center privatization?

---

legislature was not the only arena for these battles. As noted in chapter 5, since the early 1990s, elections to the State Board of Education have stirred the voices for and against private school vouchers, control of textbook content, and state chartering of schools. James Leininger and his Texas Public Policy Foundation are the most visible advocates for those changes. Yet, supporters of public education, such as the advocacy group the Equity Center, still appear strong enough to win many policy battles—and to keep public schools open.

WHAT SHOULD I HAVE LEARNED?

- **What are the roots of public policy in Texas?**

    Texas's populist tradition of the late nineteenth century, carried forward into the New Deal era initiatives of Governor Jimmie Allred, and the Great Society programs of Texan President Lyndon Johnson created and sustained social welfare and economic regulatory policies in the twentieth century. In the last decade, though, the state has been restructuring those programs and reducing its program support and policy involvement in those areas.

- **What is the public policy process, what actors are involved in it, and what are its outcomes?**

    The public policy process is a four-part cycle of agenda setting, policy making, implementation, and evaluation. Involved in that process are actors such as government officials (elected and nonelected), economic and political elites, interest groups, think tanks, and even the public, expressed through public opinion. Policy outcomes—the action or inaction of government—produce changes in the distribution of resources in society.

- **How does state finance work in Texas?**

    The Texas Constitution includes numerous restrictions on the legislature's power to raise revenues and to spend those monies. Political and governmental processes further shape Texas's budget dynamics. The revenue system relies heavily on consumption taxes, with a regressive tax incidence. Texas spends most of its money on education and health and human services. Overall, both taxes and spending are among the lowest of all the states.

- **What are key public education and higher education policy issues in Texas?**

    Texas has large public school systems, from kindergarten through higher education. K–12 schooling has faced recurring policy battles over funding levels and quality of education issues. Higher education is realigning both its funding systems and its entry programs, addressing tuition levels and campus diversity issues.

- **What are key health and human services policy issues in Texas?**

    In policy and funding partnerships with the federal government, the state provides assistance to citizens for food, shelter, clothing, and health care. Recent state and federal program changes and funding reductions have cut the number of Texas recipients dramatically. Though the state's overall spending for health and human services has increased, the state remains near the bottom among all states in health and human services funding.

- **What are key transportation policy issues in Texas?**

    Highway congestion in a steadily increasing population has challenged Texas's traditional pay-as-you-go approach to transportation funding. For decades, the state relied on dedicated state funds plus federal funds to build and maintain highways. Now, the state is turning to toll roads and a broad vision of a Trans-Texas Corridor in response to heavy commercial traffic through Texas.

- **How are reform efforts affecting key policy issues in Texas?**

    Reform of public policy is a contentious matter of values and power. Policy changes to rely on highway tolls trigger countermovements to increase public transportation and public funding for transportation. Policy changes to increase and equalize education funding trigger countermovements to shift public funds to private schools.

Key Terms

agenda setting, p. 235
Available School Fund, p. 250
Available University Fund, p. 253
biennial budgeting system, p. 238
block grants, p. 244
bond programs, p. 238
budget, p. 238
charter schools, p. 249
Children's Health Insurance Program (CHIP), p. 260
comptroller's certification, p. 239
dedicated funds, p. 239
economic policies, p. 233
Edgewood v. *Kirby*, p. 250
evaluation, p. 236

federal funds, p. 244
fiscal year (FY), p. 238
gross domestic product (GDP), p. 245
Higher Education Fund, p. 254
implementation, p. 235
Medicaid, p. 260
Permanent School Fund (PSF), p. 250
Permanent University Fund (PUF), p. 253
policy making, p. 235
political economy, p. 237
progressive tax, p. 246
proportional tax (flat tax), p. 246

public policy, p. 234
regressive tax, p. 246
regulation, p. 237
revenue estimate, p. 238
Rodriguez v. *San Antonio Independent School District*, p. 250
social policies, p. 233
subsidy, p. 237
Temporary Assistance for Needy Families (TANF), p. 257
tolling, p. 261
Trans-Texas Corridor, p. 261
vouchers, p. 248
West Orange-Cove Consolidated ISD v. *Alanis*, p. 251

Researching Texas Public Policy

In the Library

Bond, Michael, and Ron Lindsey. "Reforming Medicaid in Texas." Austin: Texas Public Policy Foundation, February 28, 2005.

Center for Public Policy Priorities. "Special Session Tax and School-Finance Package Creates $10.5 Billion Deficit," May 15, 2006.

———. "Texas Health Care Primer," revised 2007.

———. "Texas Poverty 101," January 10, 2008.

Education Commission of the States. *No Child Left Behind: The Challenges and Opportunities of ESEA 2001*. Denver, CO: Education Commission of the States, 2002.

House Research Organization. "Texas Adapts to Requirements of No Child Left Behind Act." *Interim News* 78-10 (November 3, 2004).

——— "State Boosts Tolls to Finance Highways." *Focus Report* 78-19 (November 12, 2004).

——— "Writing the State Budget: 80th Legislature." *State Finance Report* 80-1 (February 14, 2007).

Ibarra, Robert A. *Beyond Affirmative Action: Reframing the Context of Higher Education*. Madison: University of Wisconsin Press, 2001.

Texas Transportation Institute. *Urban Mobility Study*. College Station: Texas A&M University, 2004.

On the Web

Education trends across the states: www.ecs.org.
The Education Commission of the States studies and reports on education issues.

Public policy issues before the legislature: www.house.state.tx.us/analyses/hro/.
The House Research Organization is a staff agency of the Texas House of Representatives, providing analysis of current public policy issues.

School finance equity trends: www.equitycenter.org.
The Equity Center is a research and advocacy group for school finance equity and adequacy.

Social service adequacy in Texas: www.cppp.org.
The Center for Public Policy Priorities is a research and advocacy group for social services for lower income Texans.

Transportation policy issues: tti.tamu.edu.
The Texas Transportation Institute is a Texas A&M University research entity focusing on highways and mobility issues.

Notes

Chapter 1

1. Steve H. Murdock et al., *The New Texas Challenge: Population Change and the Future of Texas* (College Station: Texas A&M University Press, 2003), 19.
2. Murdock, *The New Texas Challenge*, 140.
3. The data for this section are from Murdock, *The New Texas Challenge*.
4. During 1994, Texas passed New York in population, replacing it as the second largest state in population. The 2000 Census officially established Texas as the second largest state. California, with 37 million residents, remained the most populous state in 2007.
5. U.S. Census Bureau, Estimates of Population by Race Alone or in Combination and Hispanic or Latino Origin in the United States and States: July 1, 2005, August 4, 2006, http://www.census.gov/Press-Release/www/2006/cb06-123table1.xls.
6. W. W. Newcomb Jr., *The Indians of Texas: From Prehistoric to Modern Times* (Austin: University of Texas Press, 1961), 22.
7. Newcomb, *The Indians of Texas*, 180–5.
8. Arnoldo De Leon, *Mexican Americans in Texas: A Brief History* (Arlington Heights, IL: Harlan Davidson, 1993), 7–19.
9. De Leon, *Mexican Americans in Texas*, 20.
10. Donald E. Chipman, *Spanish Texas, 1519–1821* (Austin: University of Texas Press, 1992), 242–60.
11. Terry G. Jordan, "A Century and a Half of Ethnic Change in Texas, 1836–1986," *Southwestern Historical Quarterly* 89 (April 1986): 392–4.
12. *2007 National Directory of Latino Elected Officials* (Los Angeles: NALEO Education Fund, 2007), 120.
13. "Hispanics Key in '98 Vote, Both Parties Say," *Corpus Christi Caller-Times Interactive* (September 22, 1998), http://corpuschristionline.com/texas98/texas20612.html; Lomi Kriel, "Dems, GOP Vie for Sought-After Hispanic Vote," *Daily Texan Online* (October 16, 2003), http://www.dailytexanonline.com/news/2004/06/03/TopStories/Gop-Convention.To.Rejuvenate.Support-684288.shtml; Will Krueger, "Hispanic Leaders Looking Ahead," *Daily Texan Online* (October 17, 2003), http://www.dailytexanonline.com/news/2003/10/17/TopStories/Hispanic.Leaders.Looking.Ahead-531638.shtml.
14. Jordan, "A Century and a Half of Ethnic Change," 400–401; Terry G. Jordan, John L. Bean Jr., and William M. Holmes, *Texas: A Geography* (Boulder, CO: Westview, 1984), 77, 79.
15. Jordan, "A Century and a Half of Ethnic Change," 402, 404; Jordan, Bean, and Holmes, *Texas*, 79.
16. David A. Bositis, "Black Elected Officials, 1994–1997," *Focus Magazine* (September 1998); Joint Center for Political and Economic Studies, http://www.jointctr.org/focus/issues/sep98.html; David A. Bositis, *Black Elected Officials: A Statistical Summary 2001* (Washington, DC: Joint Center for Political and Economic Studies, 2003), 14–15.
17. Comptroller of Public Accounts, "Lone Star Asians," *Fiscal Notes* (November 1997): 3–5; *2003–04 National Asian Pacific American Political Almanac* (Los Angeles: UCLA Asian American Studies Center, 2003), 300–302.
18. Jordan, Bean, and Holmes, *Texas*, 71, 73.
19. Steve H. Murdock et al., "Dynamic Population Change in Size and Diversity," *Texas Almanac, 2002–2003* (Dallas: Dallas Morning News, 2001), 286; Steve H. Murdock et al., "Texas Population: Growth Exceeds National Rate," *Texas Almanac, 2006–2007* (Dallas: Dallas Morning News, 2006), 337; Steve H. Murdock et al., "Texas Population: A Hurricane and Immigration," *Texas Almanac, 2008–2009* (Dallas: Dallas Morning News, 2008), 412.
20. Murdock, "Dynamic Population Change in Size and Diversity," 286–9.
21. Steve H. Murdock et al., "Texas Population: A Hurricane and Immigration," *Texas Almanac, 2008–2009* (Dallas: Dallas Morning News, 2008), 412.
22. Steve H. Murdock, Md. Nazrul Hoque, and Beverly A. Pecotte, "Texas Population: Historical Patterns and Future Trends," *Texas Almanac, 1994–1995* (Dallas: Dallas Morning News, 1993), 303–4; Texas State Data Center, *Population Projections for Texas*, February 1998; U.S. Census Bureau, Basic Facts, Quick Tables, QT-PL, Race, Hispanic and Latino, and Age: 2000, http://factfinder.census.gov/bf/.
23. The exit polls showed Bush increasing his share of the Hispanic vote in Texas from 43 percent to 59 percent (corrected to 49 percent). However, the 59 percent for Bush did not stand up when analyses of actual votes in heavily Hispanic counties in South Texas and heavily Hispanic precincts in Dallas were presented. See David L. Leal, Matt A. Barreto, Jongho Lee, and Rodolfo O. de la Garza, "The Latino Vote in the 2004 Election," *PS: Political Science and Politics* 38 (January 2005): 41–49.
24. See Pew Hispanic Center, "Latinos in California, Texas, New York, Florida, and New Jersey," Survey Brief, March 2004, http://www.pewhispanic.org/site/docs/pdf/LATINOS%20IN%20CA-TX-NY-FL-NJ-031904.pdf.
25. Louis DeSipio, "Latino Civil and Political Participation," in Marta Tienda and Faith Mitchell, eds., *Hispanics and the Future of America* (Washington, DC: National Academies Press, 2006), 454.
26. Harold Meyerson, "The Rising Latino Tide," American Prospect, Online Edition (November 18, 2002), http://www.prospect.org/web/page.ww?section=root&name=ViewPrint&articleId=6611.
27. Louis DeSipio, *Counting on the Latino Vote: Latinos as a New Electorate* (Charlottesville: University Press of Virginia, 1996), 48–56; *Public Broadcasting Latino Poll 2000*, State Tabulations, July 27, 2000, http://www.latinopoll2000.com.
28. Robert S. McIntyre et al., *Who Pays? A Distributional Analysis of the Tax Systems of All 50 States*, 2nd ed. (Washington, DC: Citizens for Tax Justice and the Institute on Taxation and Economic Policy, 2003), 102.
29. "The Texas Health Care Primer," Center for Public Policy Priorities, revised 2007, http://www.cppp.org/files/3/booklet%20for%20web.pdf.
30. T. R. Fehrenbach, *Seven Keys to Texas*, rev. ed. (El Paso: Texas Western, 1986), 3–4.
31. T. R. Fehrenbach, "Seven Keys to Understanding Texas," *Atlantic Monthly* (March 1975): 123–4.
32. Fehrenbach, *Seven Keys to Texas*, 22.
33. T. R. Fehrenbach, *Lone Star: A History of Texas and the Texans* (New York: Macmillan, 1968), 472–6.
34. Fehrenbach, *Seven Keys to Texas*, 29.
35. Fehrenbach, *Seven Keys to Texas*, 24–25.
36. Fehrenbach, *Seven Keys to Texas*, 76.
37. Alwyn Barr, *Texans in Revolt: The Battle for San Antonio, 1835* (Austin: University of Texas Press, 1990), 1–4.
38. William C. Brinkley, *The Texas Revolution* (Austin: Texas State Historical Association, 1952).
39. Quoted in Mark E. Nackman, *A Nation Within a Nation* (Port Washington, NY: Kennikat, 1975), 27.
40. Joe B. Frantz, *Texas: A Bicentennial History* (New York: Norton, 1976), 69.
41. Walter Lord, *A Time to Stand: The Epic of the Alamo* (Lincoln: University of Nebraska Press, 1961), 54.
42. Lord, *A Time to Stand*, 82.
43. Paul Andrew Hutton, "The Alamo: An American Epic," *American History Illustrated* (March 1986): 24.
44. Lord, *A Time to Stand*, 142.
45. Lon Tinkle, *The Alamo* (New York: McGraw-Hill, 1958), 118.

46. Gilbert M. Cuthbertson, "Individual Freedom: The Evolution of a Political Ideal," in Robert F. O'Connor, ed., *Texas Myths* (College Station: Texas A&M University Press, 1986), 179.
47. David Montejano, *Anglos and Mexicans in the Making of Texas, 1836–1986* (Austin: University of Texas Press, 1987), 305.
48. Fehrenbach, *Seven Keys to Texas*, 95.
49. Fehrenbach, *Seven Keys to Texas*, 128.
50. Samuel P. Huntington, *American Politics: The Promise of Disharmony* (Cambridge, MA: Harvard University Press, 1981), 13–60.
51. William S. Maddox and Stuart A. Lilie, *Beyond Liberal and Conservative: Reassessing the Political Spectrum* (Washington, DC: Cato Institute, 1984), 7–21.
52. Maddox and Lilie, *Beyond Liberal and Conservative*, 14–15.
53. Roscoe Martin, *The People's Party in Texas* (Austin: University of Texas Press, 1970), 31–52.
54. Martin, *The People's Party in Texas*, 82–112.
55. The Gallup Polls conducted in Texas during 2007 indicated that 43.6 percent of the respondents identified themselves as conservative, 36.8 percent identified themselves as moderates, 18.5 percent identified themselves as liberal, and 1.1 percent would not identify themselves ideologically.
56. V. O. Key Jr., *Southern Politics* (New York: Vintage Books, 1949), 261.
57. Fehrenbach, *Seven Keys to Texas*, 50–52; *Texas Almanac, 2002–2003* (Dallas: Dallas Morning News, 2001), 596.
58. Fehrenbach, *Seven Keys to Texas*, 52–54; *Texas Almanac, 1986–1987* (Dallas: Dallas Morning News, 1985), 212.
59. Fehrenbach, *Seven Keys to Texas*, 58–60; Donald A. Hicks, "Advanced Industrial Development," in Anthony Champagne and Edward J. Harpham, eds., *Texas at the Crossroads: People, Politics, and Policy* (College Station: Texas A&M University Press, 1987), 49–50; *Texas Almanac, 1994–1995*, 608; Comptroller of Public Accounts, *Fiscal Notes* (January 1994): 1, 14; "The Texas Economy Online," Texas Department of Economic Development Web site, October 26, 1999, http://www.bidc.state.tx.us/overview/2-2te.html.
60. Comptroller of Public Accounts, "The Texas Economies: What Makes Them Tick," *Fiscal Notes* (December 1993): 7–10.
61. Comptroller of Public Accounts, *Fiscal Notes* (January 1994): 16–17.
62. Comptroller of Public Accounts, "Texas Economic Update: Looking 10 Years Back and 10 Years Forward" (Winter 2000), http://www.window.state.tx.us/ecodata/teu00/teu00_1.html.
63. Comptroller of Public Accounts, "The Rebound Is Here," *Texas Economic Update* (Fall 2004), http://www.window.state.tx.us/ecodata/teufall04/; Ali Anari and Mark G. Dotzour, "Monthly Review of the Texas Economy: January 2006," *Texas Economic Review*, http://www.recenter.tamu.edu/econ/.
64. "Texas Economy: Employment Growth and Low Inflation," *Texas Almanac, 2000–2001*, 577–9; Comptroller of Public Accounts, *Fiscal Notes* (July 1999): 10–11; Comptroller of Public Accounts, "Texas Economic Update."
65. "Overview of the Texas Economy," Texas Business and Industry Data Center, http://www.bidc.state.tx.us/overview/2-2te.htm; Anari and Dotzour, "Monthly Review of the Texas Economy: January 2006"; U.S. Department of Labor, Bureau of Labor Statistics, Texas Unemployment, December 2007, http://data.bls.gov/cgi-bin/surveymost.
66. Comptroller of Public Accounts, "The Texas Economy: Employment Growth Continues"; *Texas Almanac, 2002–2003* (Dallas: Dallas Morning News, 2001), 547; Office of the Governor, Economic Development and Tourism, "Overview of the Texas Economy: International Trade," http://www.governor.state.tx.us/divisions/ecodev/bidc/overview#internationaltrade.
67. Comptroller of Public Accounts, *Fiscal Notes* (January 1994): 12–13.
68. Economic Policy Institute/Center on Budget and Policy Priorities, "Pulling Apart: A State-by-State Analysis of Income Trends," January 26, 2006, http://www.cbpp.org/1-26-06sfp.pdf.
69. U.S. Census Bureau, Current Population Surveys, "Educational Attainment of the Population 25 Years and Over, by State, Including Confidence Intervals of Estimates: 2004," Table 13, released March 2005, http://www.census.gov/population/www/socdemo/education/cps2004.html.
70. "Poverty 101," Center for Public Policy Priorities, Policy Brief, January 2008, http://www.cppp.org/files/8/BRP%20Pov101%20Jan%2008.pdf.
71. George Norris Green, *The Establishment in Texas Politics* (Westport, CT: Greenwood, 1979), 17; Chandler Davidson, *Race and Class in Texas Politics* (Princeton, NJ: Princeton University Press, 1992), 105.
72. See Christine Carroll, "The 100 Richest People in Texas," *Texas Monthly* (September 1992): 118–43.
73. Daniel Elazar, *American Federalism: A View From the States*, 3rd ed. (New York: Harper and Row, 1984).
74. Lawrence M. Mead, "State Political Culture and Welfare Reform," *Policy Studies Journal* 32 (May 2004): 271–296.
75. "TANF at 10: Has Welfare Reform Been a Success in Texas?" Center for Public Policy Priorities, Policy Brief, August 22, 2006, http://www.cppp.org/files/3/pop%20TANF%20at%2010.pdf

Chapter 2

1. Juan B. Elizondo Jr., "Ratliff: Time to Rewrite Constitution," *Austin American-Statesman* (October 28, 1999): B6; Bill Ratliff and Rob Junell, "A New Constitution for the New Millennium," *Austin American-Statesman* (December 9, 1998): A15; Osler McCarthy, "Poll Shows Support for New Constitution," *Austin American-Statesman* (February 13, 1999): B3.
2. Ralph W. Steen, "Convention of 1836," *Handbook of Texas Online*, http://www.tsha.utexas.edu/handbook/online/articles/view/CC/mjc12.html.
3. Joe C. Ericson, "Constitution of the Republic of Texas," *Handbook of Texas Online*, http://www.tsha.utexas.edu/handbook/online/articles/view/CC/mhc1.html.
4. Walter L. Buenger, "Constitution of 1861," *Handbook of Texas Online*, http://www.tsha.utexas.edu/handbook/online/articles/view/CC/mhc4.html.
5. S. S. McKay, "Constitution of 1866," *Handbook of Texas Online*, http://www.tsha.utexas.edu/handbook/online/articles/view/CCmhc5.html.
6. Claude Elliott, "Constitutional Convention of 1869," *Handbook of Texas Online*, http://www.tsha.utexas.edu/handbook/online/articles/view/CC/mjc4.html.
7. Seth S. McKay, "Constitution of 1869," *Handbook of Texas Online*, http://www.tsha.utexas.edu/handbook/online/articles/view/CC/mhc6.html.
8. John Walker Mauer, "State Constitutions in a Time of Crisis: The Case of the Texas Constitution of 1876," *Texas Law Review* 68 (June 1990): 1638–9.
9. Joe E. Ericson, "The Delegates to the Convention of 1875: A Reappraisal," *Southwestern Historical Quarterly* 67 (1963/1964): 22–27. Ericson's reappraisal of the delegates is based on Nat Q. Henderson's *Directory of the Officers and Members of the Constitutional Convention of the State of Texas, A.D. 1875* (Austin: n.p., 1875).
10. Mauer, "State Constitutions in a Time of Crisis," 1646–7.
11. Patrick G. Williams, "Of Rutabagas and Redeemers: Rethinking the Texas Constitution of 1876," *Southwestern Historical Quarterly* 106 (October 2002): 250.
12. Williams, "Of Rutabagas and Redeemers," 250–3.

13. Although the content of the section was deleted, the title remains to prevent confusion with the numbering of the remaining articles.
14. *Texas Constitution*, Article 1, sections 12 and 29, respectively.
15. Donald S. Lutz, "The Texas Constitution," in Kent L. Tedin, Donald S. Lutz, and Edward P. Fuchs, eds., *Perspectives on American and Texas Politics*, 5th ed. (Dubuque, IA: Kendall/Hunt, 1998), 45.
16. Lutz, "The Texas Constitution."
17. Janice C. May, "Constitutional Revision in Texas," in Richard H. Kraemer and Philip W. Barnes, eds., *Texas: Readings in Politics, Government, and Public Policy* (San Francisco: Chandler, 1971), 318.
18. See *Texas Constitution*, Article 16, section 44.
19. Dick Smith, "Constitutional Revision, 1876–1961," in Fred Gantt Jr., Irving O. Dawson, and Luther G. Hagard Jr., eds., *Governing Texas: Documents and Readings* (New York: Crowell, 1966), 53.
20. The amendment accounts for sections and articles of the current constitution that have only the title or section number appearing in the text. For example, Article 3, section 3a (repealed August 5, 1969).
21. Legislative Council, Analysis of Proposed Constitutional Amendments, November 2, 1999, Election (Austin, TX: Legislative Council, 1999).
22. Smith, "Constitutional Revision," 55.
23. Informational Booklet on the Proposed 1976 Revision of the Texas Constitution, 64th Legislature, 1975, 3–7; Janice C. May, *The Texas Constitutional Revision Experience in the 1970s* (Austin, TX: Sterling Swift, 1975), 25–30; Dick Smith, "Constitutional Revision," 51–55.
24. See Texas Advisory Commission on Intergovernmental Relations, *The Texas Constitutional Revision Commission of 1973* (Austin: Texas Advisory Commission of Intergovernmental Relations, 1972), on the importance of the commission to the convention's success.
25. Janice May, *The Texas Constitutional Revision Experience*, 160–200.
26. Texas Legislative Council, Analysis of Proposed Constitutional Amendments, November 8, 2005 (Austin: Texas Legislative Council, 2005): 17–22.
27. University of Michigan Government Documents Center, Ballot Measures and Initiatives, 2005, http://www.lib.umich.edu/govdocs/elec2005/elec2005index6.html.

Chapter 3

1. The fifteen counties are Bexar, Brazoria, Collin, Dallas, Denton, El Paso, Fort Bend, Galveston, Harris, Hidalgo, Jefferson, Montgomery, Smith, Tarrant, and Travis.
2. Samuel J. Eldersveld and Hanes Walton Jr., *Political Parties in American Society*, 2nd ed. (New York: Bedford/St. Martin's, 2000), 106.
3. Frank B. Feigert, Dawn Miller, Kenda Cunningham, and Rachel Burlage, "Texas: Incipient Polarization?" *American Review of Politics* 24 (Summer 2003): 192–3.
4. Feigert et al., "Texas: Incipient Polarization?"
5. Paul Lenchner, "The Party System in Texas," in Anthony Champagne and Edward J. Harpham, eds., *Texas Politics: A Reader*, 2nd ed. (New York: Norton, 1998), 165–7.
6. Louis Dubose, "Kay Bailey Finds Religion," *Texas Observer* (July 12, 1996): 4–8.
7. A. Phillips Brooks, "GOP Lieutenant Gets Close Look," *Austin American-Statesman* (August 9, 1997): B1, B7.
8. Nate Blakeslee, "Farewell to Barry G.," *Texas Observer* (July 3, 1998): 13–15; Sam Dealey, "Bush-Whipped: The Texas GOP Undergoes a Little Soul-Searching," *American Spectator* (August 1998): 58–59.
9. Jake Bernstein, "Elephant Wars: The Christian Right Flexes Its Muscle at the Republican Convention," *Texas Observer* (July 5, 2002): 8–9, 19, 29.
10. "2006 State Republican Party Platform," Republican Party of Texas, http://www.texasgop.org.
11. Barbara Norrander, "Determinants of Local Party Campaign Activity," *Social Sciences Quarterly* 67 (September 1986): 567.
12. Frank B. Feigert and Nancy L. Williams, "Texas: Yeller Dogs and Yuppies," in Charles D. Hadley and Lewis Bowman, eds., *Southern State Party Organizations and Activists* (Westport, CT: Praeger, 1995), 84–85; Feigert et al., "Texas: Incipient Polarization?" 193–4.
13. The Scripps-Howard Texas Poll question is: "Generally speaking, do you usually think of yourself as a Democrat, a Republican, an independent, or something else?" According to state law in Texas, a party member is anyone who participates in the party's primary election.
14. James A. Dryer, Arnold Vedlitz, and David B. Hill, "New Voters, Switchers, and Political Party Realignment in Texas," *Western Political Quarterly* 41 (March 1988): 155–67; Kent L. Tedin, "The Transition of Electoral Politics in Texas: 1978–1990," in Kent L. Tedin and Donald S. Lutz, eds., *Perspectives on American and Texas Politics: A Collection of Essays*, 3rd ed. (Dubuque, IA: Kendall/Hunt, 1992), 129–51; James A. Dyer, Jan E. Leighley, and Arnold Vedlitz, "Party Identification and Public Opinion in Texas, 1984–1994: Establishing a Competitive Party System," in Anthony Champagne and Edward J. Harpham, eds., *Texas Politics: A Reader*, 2nd ed. (New York: Norton, 1998), 108–22.
15. "Republican Party of Texas Growth Chart," Republican Party of Texas, http://www.texasgop.org (percentages calculated by the authors).
16. Gregory S. Thielemann and Euel Elliott, "Texas: Same As It Ever Was?" *American Review of Politics* 26 (Summer 2005): 236.
17. Thomas L. Whatley, ed., *Texas Government Newsletter* (January 24, 1983): 2.
18. Keith E. Hamm and Robert Harmel, "Legislative Party Development and the Speaker System: The Case of Texas," *Journal of Politics* 55 (November 1993): 1145–6.
19. Hamm and Harmel, "Legislative Party Development and the Speaker System," 1146.
20. See R. Bruce Anderson, "Party Caucus Development and the Insurgent Minority Party in Formerly One-Party State Legislatures," *American Review of Politics* 19 (Fall 1998): 191–216.
21. *Texas Lawyer* (May 1994): 1, 28.
22. Paul Allen Beck and Frank J. Sorauf, *Party Politics in America*, 7th ed. (New York: HarperCollins, 1992), 420; Walt Borges, "The Court's Big Chill," *Texas Lawyer* (September 4, 1995): 1; Walt Borges, "The Texas Supreme Court in 1998–1999: Moderating the Counter-Revolution," A Report of Court Watch, Project of Texas Watch, http://www.texaswatch.org; "Decade of Watching and Waiting: Texas Supreme Court Year-in-Review 2005–2006," Court Watch Annual Review, March 29, 2007, http://www.texaswatch.org.
23. Because lobbyists are only required to report their income to the Texas Ethics Commission in broad categories (e.g., $10,000–24,999), the exact amount paid to lobbyists for their services is unknown. Figures are from Texans for Public Justice, "Austin's Oldest Profession," September 2008, http://www.tpj.org.
24. Texas Administrative Code, title 1, part 2, chapter 34, specifies the requirements for registration.
25. Kevin Bogardus, "Statehouse Revolvers," Center for Public Integrity, October 12, 2006, http://www.publicintegrity.org/hiredguns/report.aspx?aid=747.
26. Osler McCarthy, "Minority Lobbyists Increase Their Presence at Legislature," *Austin American-Statesman* (April 12, 1999): A1, A12.
27. Quoted in Robert Bryce, "Access Through the Lobby," *Texas Observer* (February 24, 1995): 16.

28. Quoted in Bryce, "Access Through the Lobby," 16.
29. Alan Rosenthal, *The Third House: Lobbyists and Lobbying in the States* (Washington, DC: CQ Press, 1993), 190–9.
30. Texans for Public Justice, "Austin's Oldest Profession," September 2008, http://www.tpj.org.
31. Rosenthal, *The Third House*, 182–90.
32. Stuart Eskenazi, "Ring Ma Bell," *Dallas Observer Online*, May 20–26, 1999, http://www.dallasobserver.com.
33. Bryce, "Access Through the Lobby," 16.
34. Texans for Public Justice, "Texas PACs: 2006 Election Cycle Spending," October 2007, http://www.tpj.org.
35. Keith E. Hamm and Charles W. Wiggins, "Texas: The Transformation from Personal to Informational Lobbying," in Ronald J. Hrebenar and Clive S. Thomas, eds., *Interest Group Politics in the Southern States* (Tuscaloosa: University of Alabama Press, 1993), 169; Texas Ethics Commission, GPAC disclosure records, computed by the authors.
36. Lynn Tran and Andrew Wheat, *Tort Dodgers: Business Money Tips Scales of Justice* (Austin: Texans for Public Justice, 1997).
37. Jeffrey M. Berry, *The Interest Group Society*, 2nd ed. (New York: HarperCollins, 1989), 154–7.
38. Fred Gantt Jr., *The Chief Executive in Texas: A Study in Gubernatorial Leadership* (Austin: University of Texas Press, 1964), 269–71.
39. Dave McNeely, "GOP Voters Switch to Fight Richards," *Austin American-Statesman* (April 5, 1994): A11.
40. Richard Murray, "The 1982 Texas Election in Perspective," *Texas Journal of Political Studies* 5 (Spring/Summer 1983): 49–50; Paul Burka, "Primary Lesson," *Texas Monthly* (July 1986): 104–5.
41. W. Lance Bennett, *The Governing Crisis: Media, Money, and Marketing in American Elections* (New York: St. Martin's, 1992), 84–111.
42. Texans for Public Justice, "Money in Politex: A Guide to Money in the 2006 Texas Elections," September 2007, http://www.tpj.org.
43. National Institute on Money in State Politics, "State at a Glance: Texas 2006," http://www.followthemoney.org.
44. Kaye Northcott, "Getting Elected," *Mother Jones* (November 1982): 18.
45. Quoted in Northcott, "Getting Elected," 19.
46. Texans for Public Justice, "Money in Politex," http://www.tpj.org.
47. See Jon Ford, "Texas: Big Money," in Herbert E. Alexander, ed., *Campaign Money: Reform and Reality in the States* (New York: Free Press, 1976), 78–109.
48. Quoted in David Elliot, "Image Is Everything: How TV Has Reshaped Campaigning," *Austin American-Statesman* (October 16, 1994): A1, A8.
49. For an excellent article on Texas campaign consultants, see Juan B. Elizondo Jr., "Political Consultants: How They Do It," *Austin American-Statesman* (October 18, 1998): H1, H5.
50. Everett Carll Ladd, ed., *America at the Polls, 1994* (Storrs, CT: Roper Center for Public Opinion Research, 1995), 78.
51. Jerry Hagstrom and Robert Guskind, "Calling the Races," *National Journal* (July 30, 1988): 1972–5; Elliot, "Image Is Everything," A8.
52. Peggy Fikac, "Texas Governor: The Democratic 'Dream Team' Bites the Dust," in Larry Sabato, ed., *Midterm Madness: The Elections of 2002* (Lanham, MD: Rowman and Littlefield, 2003), 259.
53. Delbert A. Taebel, Nirmal Goswami, and Laurence Jones, "The Politics of Early Voting in Texas: Perspectives of County Party Chairs," *Texas Journal of Political Studies* 16 (Spring/Summer 1994): 43–44.
54. Robert M. Stein, "Early Voting," *Public Opinion Quarterly* 62 (Spring 1998): 57–69; Paul Gronke, Eva Galanes-Rosenbaum, and Peter A. Miller, "Early Voting and Turnout," *PS: Political Science & Politics* 40 (October 2007): 639–45.
55. Ruy A. Teixeira, *The Disappearing American Voter* (Washington, DC: Brookings Institution, 1992), 12–13.
56. Morris P. Fiorina, "The Electorate at the Polls in the 1990s," in Sandy Maisel, ed., *The Parties Respond: Changes in American Parties and Campaigns*, 2nd ed. (Boulder, CO: Westview, 1994), 124–5. Angus Campbell, Philip E. Converse, Warren E. Miller, and Donald E. Stokes, *The American Voter* (Chicago: University of Chicago Press, 1960), 523–31, provides the classic statement of the influence of these factors.
57. *Texas Poll Report* (Fall 1986): 4; Kent L. Tedin, "The 1982 Election for Governor of Texas," *Texas Journal of Political Studies* 5 (Spring/Summer 1983): 29.
58. John C. Henry, "Poll Shows Anti-White Sentiment," *Austin American-Statesman* (December 5, 1986): B2.
59. Arthur H. Miller, Martin P. Wattenberg, and Oksana Malanchuk, "Schematic Assessments of Presidential Candidates," *American Political Science Review* 80 (June 1986): 521–40.
60. Thomas L. Whatley, ed., *Texas Government Newsletter* (November 17, 1986): 2.
61. Zogby Ten-State Post Election Poll: Texas, November 11, 2002.
62. Fox News Election Day Poll: Texas (Governor), November 8, 2002, http://www.foxnews.com.
63. Jeanie R. Stanley, "Party Realignment and the 1986 Texas Elections," *Texas Journal of Political Studies* 9 (Spring/Summer, 1987): 8–9.
64. Morris Fiorina, *Retrospective Voting in American National Elections* (New Haven, CT: Yale University Press, 1981).
65. Gardner Selby, "Texas Voters Might Be Spectators As Parties Choose Presidential Nominees," *Austin American-Statesman* (December 30, 2007).
66. Gardner Selby, "Whose Fault Is It That Our Tuesday Won't Be Super?" *Austin American-Statesman* (September 27, 2007): B1.
67. State of Texas, Office of the Governor, Message, "Veto of H.B. 770," May 25, 2007, http://www.lrl.state.tx.us/scanned/vetoes/80/HB770m.pdf.

Chapter 4

1. Sources for this story include Dave McNeely, "'Otto Craddick' Holds on to Speakership—for Now," *Abilene Reporter-News* (June 3, 2007); Lisa Sandberg, "Speaker Race Heats Up, All Behind the Scenes," *San Antonio Express-News* (December 23, 2006); Laylan Copelin and W. Gardner Selby, "Colleagues Launch Blitz for Craddick," *Austin American-Statesman* (December 31, 2006); Karen Brooks and Robert T. Garrett, "Pitts Guarantees He'll Dethrone Craddick," *Dallas Morning News* (January 5, 2007); Elizabeth Hernandez, "House Votes Against Speaker over Guillen Bill," *McAllen Monitor* (May 9, 2007); Jay Root, "Rumors Fly About Effort to Oust House Speaker," *Fort Worth Star-Telegram* (May 15, 2007); Steve Taylor, "El Paso Republican Leads House Walkout Against Craddick," *Rio Grande Guardian* (May 28, 2007).
2. Lisa Sandberg and Peggy Fikac, "Open Vote May Be Craddick's Hope," *San Antonio Express-News* (January 6, 2007).
3. W. Gardner Selby and Laylan Copelin, "Craddick Prevails," *Austin American-Statesman* (January 10, 2007).
4. W. Gardner Selby, "Was Script Behind Race for Speaker?" *Austin American-Statesman* (January 11, 2007).
5. HB 4068 Point of Order and Appeal of Point of Order, *House Journal*, May 7, 2007, 3316–3317.
6. Jay Root, "Craddick Asserts Power as Members Shout 'Anarchy!'" *Fort Worth Star Telegram* (May 26, 2007).
7. Karen Brooks, "Craddick Tells Lawmakers They Can't Overthrow Him," *Dallas Morning News* (May 26, 2007).

8. Legislative Reference Library, "79th Legislature Statistical Profile," http://www.lrl.state.tx.us/legis/profile79.html.

9. Texas State Historical Association, "Mexican Government of Texas," *Handbook of Texas Online*, http://www.tsha.utexas.edu/handbook/online/articles/MM/ngm1.html.

10. Texas State Historical Association, "Convention of 1833" and "Republic of Texas," *Handbook of Texas Online*, http://www.tsha.utexas.edu/handbook/online/articles/CC/mjc10.html and http://www.tsha.utexas.edu/handbook/online/articles/RR/mzr2.html.

11. Texas State Historical Association, "Congress of the Republic of Texas," *Handbook of Texas Online*, http://www.tsha.utexas.edu/handbook/online/articles/CC/mkc1.html.

12. Texas State Historical Association, "Lorenzo de Zavala," *Handbook of Texas Online*, http://www.tsha.utexas.edu/handbook/online/articles/ZZ/fza5.html.

13. See J. Mason Brewer, *Negro Legislators of Texas*, 2nd ed. (Austin: Jenkins, 1970).

14. New Hampshire, Pennsylvania, Georgia, Missouri, Massachusetts, Connecticut, and Maine have larger lower houses. National Conference of State Legislatures, "Population and Legislative Size," http://www.ncsl.org/Programs/legismgt/about/Legis_Size_Chart2.htm.

15. Impeachment is just one of the constitutional means by which state officials may be removed from office. See Article 15 of the Texas Constitution.

16. See House Research Organization, "Constitutional Order-of-Business Provision," *Daily Floor Report* (January 30, 2007): 2; Enrique Rangel, "House Members Block Rules for Bills," *Amarillo Globe-News* (January 31, 2007).

17. National Conference of State Legislatures, "Legislator Compensation in 2007," http://ncsl.org/programs/legismgt/about/07_legislatorcomp.htm; Council of State Governments, *Book of the States 2007*, vol. 39 (Lexington, KY: Council of State Governments, 2007), 93–94.

18. National Conference of State Legislatures, "2008 State Legislative Session Calendar," http://www.ncsl.org/programs/legismgt/about/sess2008.htm.

19. See National Conference of State Legislatures, "Full and Part Time Legislatures," http://www.ncsl.org/programs/press/2004/backgrounder_fullandpart.htm (updated October 2007).

20. James R. Jensen, "Legislative Apportionment in Texas," *Social Studies* 2, University of Houston Public Affairs Research Center, 1964; David Richards, "So Long, Oscar," *Texas Observer* (November 17, 2000): 11.

21. Texas Legislative Council, "Population Analysis with County Subtotals," January 31, 2003, http://www.tlc.state.tx.us/redist/pdf/h1369/red200.pdf and http://www.tlc.state.tx.us/redist/pdf/s1188/red200.pdf.

22. See National Conference of State Legislatures, *Redistricting Law 2000* (Denver, CO: National Conference of State Legislatures, 1999).

23. House Research Organization, "New Districts in Place for 2002 Elections," *Interim News*, no. 77-4 (January 14, 2002).

24. See Jim Riddlesperger, "Redistricting Politics in Texas 2003," paper prepared for presentation at the Southern Political Science Association Convention, New Orleans, January 8–10, 2004, http://www2.gasou.edu/spsa/conference.htm.

25. Ralph A. Wooster, "Membership in Early Texas Legislatures, 1850–1860," *Southwestern Historical Quarterly* 69 (October 1965): 163–73.

26. Data from National Conference of State Legislatures, "2004 Election Turnover in State Legislatures," unpublished table.

27. Tenure calculated by authors from individual member data (2007–2008 legislature) provided by Office of the Chief Clerk (House) and Office of the Secretary of the Senate.

28. Thomas H. Little, Jennie Drage Bowser, and Keon S. Chi, "Term Limits: Legislatures' Adaptation," *Book of the States 2007*, vol. 39, 70–74. For more information on initiative and referendum, see Shaun Bowler, Todd Donovan, and Caroline Tolbert, eds., *Citizens as Legislators: Direct Democracy in the United States* (Columbus: Ohio State University Press, 1998).

29. Categorization is difficult, as legislators use different terms to report their occupations. Business, for instance, includes business, insurance, finance, real estate, construction, etc. Members can also list more than one occupation. Calculated by the author based on House biographical profiles provided by Office of the Chief Clerk (House) and Senate Media Services, "Texas Senators 80th Legislature," 2007.

30. National Conference of State Legislatures, "Women in State Legislature 2008," http://www.ncsl.org/programs/wln/WomenInOffice2008.htm.

31. National Conference of State Legislatures, "Numbers of African-American Legislators 2007," http://www.ncsl.org/programs/legismgt/about/afrAmer2007.htm, and "Latino Legislators 2007," http://www.ncsl.org/programs/legismgt/about/Latino2007.htm.

32. Senate Media Services, "Texas Senators, 80th Legislature, 2007"; House profiles from Biographical Data, Office of the Chief Clerk.

33. National Conference of State Legislature, "2008 Partisan Composition of State Legislatures," http://www.ncsl.org/statevote/partycomptable2008.htm.

34. See, for instance, "Sierra Club Environmental Voting Record," http://www.texas.sierraclub.org/conservation/SierraClubVotingRecordAnalysisTXHouse2007.pdf; and Young Conservatives of Texas, "Legislative Ratings for the 80th Legislatures," http://yct.org/files/YCT-LEGISLATIVE-RATINGS.pdf.

35. Any such ranking is partly an artifact of the votes chosen. Different record votes could have produced different results, and absences can influence one's ranking. For a description of the earlier votes, see Stefan Haag, Rex Peebles, and Gary Keith, *Texas Politics and Government: Ideas, Institutions, and Policies* (New York: Addison Wesley Longman, 1997), 272; Stefan Haag, Gary Keith, and Rex Peebles, *Texas Politics and Government: Ideas, Institutions, and Policies*, 2nd ed. (New York: Addison Wesley Longman, 2001), 239, and 3rd ed. (2003), 249; Gary Keith and Stefan Haag, *Texas Politics and Government: Continuity and Change* (New York: Pearson, 2006), 107, and 2nd ed. (2008), 111.

36. Michael King, "The House Adjourns to Oklahoma," *Austin Chronicle* (May 16, 2003), http://www.austinchronicle.com.

37. Michael King, "Endangered Species?" *Austin Chronicle* (July 18, 2003), http://www.austinchronicle.com.

38. Malcolm E. Jewell and Marcia Lynn Whicker, *Legislative Leadership in the American States* (Ann Arbor: University of Michigan Press, 1994), 194.

39. For a description of this nonparty speaker system and the current birthing of parties that threatens to undo that system, see Keith Hamm and Robert Harmel, "Legislative Party Development and the Speaker System: The Case of the Texas House," *Journal of Politics* 55 (November 1993): 1140–51.

40. Patricia Kilday Hart, "Speakergate," *Texas Monthly* (May 2004): 78, 95.

41. *Dallas News* (December 30, 1971).

42. Gary Moncrief, "Committee Stacking and Reform in the Texas House of Representatives," *Texas Journal of Political Studies* 2:1 (1979): 47.

43. *Dallas Times-Herald* (December 1, 1980); *San Angelo Standard Times* (February 13, 1983); *Austin American-Statesman* (January 11, 1981).

44. Jewell and Whicker, *Legislative Leadership in the American States*, 79.

45. Data from caucus filings with the Office of the Chief Clerk (House).

46. The three were James Wilson Henderson, Hardin Richard Runnels, and Coke Stevenson. Texas Legislative Council, *Presiding Officers of*

the Texas Legislature, 1846–1995, revised ed. (Austin: Texas Legislative Council, 1995), 21, 25, and 77.

47. Council of State Governments, *Book of the States 2007*, vol. 39 (Lexington, KY: Council of State Governments, 2007), 199.

48. For more detailed information, see House Research Organization, "How a Bill Becomes Law: 80th Legislature," *Focus Report* (February 1, 2007); Rules and Housekeeping Resolutions, *Daily Floor Report* (January 12 and 13, 2005); and Hugh L. Brady, *Texas House Practice*, 2nd ed. (Austin: Capitol Hill Books, 2007).

49. The Local and Consent Calendar is supposed to be reserved for noncontroversial bills (though sometimes a controversial matter will be sneaked through on it). Bills on this calendar are not usually debated; if they are contested, they will be pulled from this calendar.

50. This daily calendar actually includes several calendars. Bills are considered on Major State, General State, Emergency, Resolutions, Constitutional Amendments, Local and Consent, or Senate Calendars.

51. For an account of the incident, see Robert Heard, *The Miracle of the Killer Bees* (Austin: Honey Hill, 1981).

52. See Clay Robison, "Texas Democrats Bolt Again," *Houston Chronicle* (July 28, 2003), http://www.chron.com/cs/CDA/printstory.mpl/topstory2/2015694; Michael King, "Albuquerque or Bust!" *Austin Chronicle* (August 8, 2003), http://www.austinchronicle.com/issues/dispatch/2003-08-08/pols_capitol.html; Gary Scharrer, "Demo Breaks Ranks: Senator's Return Could End Standoff," Elpasotimes.com (September 3, 2003), http://www.borderlandnews.com/stories/borderland/20030903-16807.shtml.

53. Technically, the rules only require that a majority of members of the conference committee from each chamber sign the report. This loophole allows "phantom" meetings—some conference committees never meet. The chairs simply negotiate the language behind closed doors, then present it to the others for their signatures.

54. Council of State Governments, *Book of the States 2005*, vol. 37 (Lexington, KY: Council of State Governments, 2005).

55. See the General Laws of Texas, 42nd Legislature, Regular Session, chap. 206; Stuart A. MacCorkle and Dick Smith, *Texas Government*, 2nd ed. (New York: McGraw-Hill, 1952), 99, 160.

56. Fred Gantt Jr., *The Chief Executive in Texas: A Study in Gubernatorial Leadership* (Austin: University of Texas Press, 1964), 99.

57. MacCorkle and Smith first commented on this occurrence in the 1951 session. See MacCorkle and Smith, *Texas Government*, 99.

58. Governor Rick Perry, "Proposed 2008–09 State Budget," January 2007; Legislative Budget Board, "Legislative Budget Estimates for the 2008–2009 Biennium."

59. Council of State Governments, *Book of the States 2004*, vol. 36 (Lexington, KY: Council of State Governments, 2004), 362.

60. These limits are in Article 3, sections 49(J), 49A, and 51-A, as well as Article 8, section 22.

61. Alan Rosenthal, "The Legislature: Unraveling of Institutional Fabric," in Carl E. Van Horn, ed., *The State of the States*, 3rd ed. (Washington, DC: CQ Press, 1996), 111, 124.

62. Rosenthal, "The Legislature"; Thad Beyle, *State Government: Congressional Quarterly's Guide to Current Issues and Activities, 1998–99* (Washington, DC: CQ Press, 1998), 71.

63. 2007 List of Registered Lobbyists, Texas Ethics Commission, as of December 31, 2007, http://www.ethics.state.tx.us/tedd/2007_Lobby_List-Lobbyist_Only.htm.

64. *Fort Worth Star-Telegram* (January 13, 1983).

65. See, for instance, Texans for Public Justice, "Austin's Oldest Profession: Texas' Top Lobby Clients and Those Who Service Them," August 2006, http://www.tpj.org/reports/austinsoldest06/index.html.

66. See, for example, Texans for Public Justice, "Capitol Spending: Officeholder Expenditures in 2007," January 2008, http://www.tpj.org/reports/capitolspending/index.html.

67. A 1999 constitutional amendment allows the Senate president pro tem, in the event of a vacancy in the office of lieutenant governor, to call the Senate into special session for the sole purpose of electing a lieutenant governor. The December 2000 special session of the Senate was called in this fashion.

68. Steven Kreytak, "Pulling the plug on 'ghost votes'," *Austin American-Statesman*, (June 27, 2008), 1.

Chapter 5

1. Sources for this story include Janet Elliott and Todd Ackerman, "Perry Orders Cancer Virus Vaccine for Young Girls," *Houston Chronicle* (February 3, 2007); Janet Elliott, "Critics Rip Perry's Vaccine Mandate," *Houston Chronicle* (February 6, 2007); Corrie MacLaggan, "Governor Defends HPV Decision," *Austin American-Statesman* (February 8, 2007); Corrie MacLaggan, "Furor over HPV Vaccine Shocked Perry" *Austin American-Statesman* (February 23, 2007): A01; Corrie MacLaggan, "Panel Challenges Hawkins on HPV," *Austin American-Statesman* (March 1, 2007): B01; Clay Robison, "Committee Debates Cancer Vaccine Plan," *Houston Chronicle* (February 20, 2007); Janet Elliott, "House Votes to Block HPV Order," *Houston Chronicle* (March 15, 2007).

2. Executive Order RP-65, February 2, 2007, http://www.governor.state.tx.us/divisions/press/exorders/rp65/view.

3. John Moritz, "Senators Urging Perry to Rescind Order on Vaccines," *Fort Worth Star-Telegram* (February 8, 2007).

4. Linda Johnson, "Merck Ends Push in States to Get Girls Immunized," *Austin American-Statesman* (February 21, 2007): A06.

5. Fred Gantt Jr., *The Chief Executive in Texas: A Study in Gubernatorial Leadership* (Austin: University of Texas Press, 1964), 15–16. Charles Polzer lists thirty-one Spanish governors of Texas from 1717 to 1823. *Documentary Relations of the Southwest*, in Biographical Files—Governors of Texas (Austin: Center for American History, University of Texas, 1977).

6. Larry Sabato, *Goodbye to Good-Time Charlie: The American Governorship Transformed*, 2nd ed. (Washington, DC: CQ Press, 1983), 2–4.

7. See constitution of 1845 and amendment of 1850. Also see Gantt, *The Chief Executive in Texas*, 20–27.

8. Gantt, *The Chief Executive in Texas*, 30–31.

9. The 1827 constitution included a four-year term, with a one-term limit. The constitution of the Texas Republic limited the president to a single three-year term (Sam Houston served two nonconsecutive terms). The 1845 and 1861 constitutions included a two-year term, with a limit of no more than four years in a six-year period. The 1866 constitution included a four-year term, with a limit of no more than eight years in a twelve-year period. The 1869 constitution had the most liberal provisions—a four-year term of office, with no term limits. Gantt, *The Chief Executive in Texas*, 335.

10. Allan Shivers served part of Jester's term and three of his own terms, for a total of seven and one-half years; Clements's total of eight years were not consecutive terms.

11. The president of the Texas Republic was paid $10,000 a year, as specified in the constitution. The salaries for the governors under the constitutions from 1827 until 1876 varied from $2,000 to $5,000. The 1876 constitution reduced the salary from $5,000 to $4,000. Gantt, *The Chief Executive in Texas*, 335.

12. Gantt, *The Chief Executive in Texas*, 38; Council of State Governments, *The Governor: The Office and Its Powers* (Lexington, KY: Council of State Governments, 1972); December 2004 comparisons from Council of State Governments, *Book of the States 2007*, Table 4.3, 166.

13. Richard Hubbard became governor when the first governor under the new constitution, Richard Coke, resigned in 1876 to become a U.S. senator; William Hobby did so when Governor Jim Ferguson was removed from office in 1917; Coke Stevenson did so when Governor O'Daniel won a special election to the U.S. Senate in 1941; Allan Shivers did so when Governor Jester died in 1949; and Rick Perry did so in 2000 when George W. Bush resigned after winning the presidency.
14. Gantt, *The Chief Executive in Texas*, 151–2.
15. Joseph Schlesinger, "Politics, the Executive," in Herbert Jacob and Kenneth Vines, eds., *Politics in the American States: A Comparative Analysis* (Boston: Little, Brown, 1965), 220–9.
16. Sabato, *Goodbye to Good-Time Charlie*, 4–6.
17. Citizens Advisory Committee on Revision of the Constitution of Texas, "Interim Report to the 56th Legislature and the People of Texas," March 1, 1959, 20–21.
18. See Gantt, *The Chief Executive in Texas*, 29–33; and Seth McKay, "Making the Texas Constitution of 1876," Ph.D. diss., University of Pennsylvania, 1924.
19. In Maine, New Hampshire, New Jersey, and Tennessee, the governor is the *only* statewide elected official. Council of State Governments, *Book of the States 2007*, Table 4.6, 173, and Table 4.10, 181.
20. Schlesinger, "Politics, the Executive," 1965; Schlesinger, "Politics, the Executive," in Herbert Jacob and Kenneth Vines, eds., *Politics in the American States: A Comparative Analysis*, 2nd ed. (Boston: Little, Brown, 1971), 225–34.
21. Virginia Gray, Herbert Jacob, and Robert Albritton, *Politics in the American States*, 5th ed. (New York: HarperCollins, 1990), appendices 6.1–6.7; Thad L. Beyle, "Governors: The Middlemen and Women in Our Political System," in Virginia Gray and Herbert Jacob, eds., *Politics in the American States: A Comparative Analysis*, 6th ed. (Washington, DC: CQ Press, 1996); Thad L. Beyle, "The Governors," in Virginia Gray and Russell Hanson, eds., *Politics in the American States: A Comparative Analysis*, 8th ed. (Washington, DC: CQ Press, 2004), 194–231. Beyle's latest ranking is discussed in Pamela Prah, "Massachusets gov rated most powerful," www.stateline.org March 9, 2007.
22. Beyle, "The Governors," in Gray and Hanson, *Politics in the American States*, 8th ed.
23. It is not clear exactly how many appointments a governor makes. A 1982 analysis states that there are about 4,000 appointments, with about 2,000 subject to confirmation. Yet, a 1989 Senate study counted only 1,389 appointees. Governor George W. Bush made about 3,400 appointments in just over four years in office. See Senate Nominations Committee, "Analysis of Gubernatorial Appointees to Agencies, Boards and Commissions," December 8, 1989, 1; Charles Wiggins, Keith Hamm, and Howard Balanoff, "The 1982 Gubernatorial Transition in Texas," in Thad L. Beyle, ed., *Gubernatorial Transitions: The 1982 Elections* (Durham, NC: Duke University, 1985), 396; Wayne Slater, "Bush Steps Up Number of Hispanic Appointees," *Dallas Morning News* (October 12, 1999): A1.
24. The case is *Denison v. State*. Texas Legislative Council, "Staff Memo to Senate Committee on State Affairs, Subcommittee on Nominations," January 26, 1981.
25. George Braden, *The Constitution of the State of Texas: An Annotated and Comparative Analysis*, vol. 1 (Austin: Texas Legislative Council, 1977), 327–31. See also Texas Legislative Council, "Staff Memo," 4 and 13.
26. Bruce Hight, "Senator Blocks Utility Official," *Austin American-Statesman* (September 28, 1999): C1, C2; Bruce Hight, "Senator: PUC Decision Was 'Difficult,'" *Austin American-Statesman* (September 29, 1999): D2.
27. Wiggins, Hamm, and Balanoff, "The 1982 Gubernatorial Transition," 396.
28. See Chandler Davidson, *Race and Class in Texas Politics* (Princeton, NJ: Princeton University Press, 1990), 237.
29. Peggy Fikac, "Bush Appointing Many Females, Minorities," *San Antonio Express-News* (July 9, 2000); Kelley Shannon, "Minority Appointments Rise Slightly: Perry Has a Higher Rate than Bush, but Lower than Richards," *San Antonio Express-News* (November 28, 2003); Wayne Slater, "Perry's Picks Offer Glimpse at Priorities: Donors, Minorities Among Appointees," *Dallas Morning News* (July 3, 2001). Perry appointment figures from Governor's Office (May 19, 2006) and from Texans for Public Justice, "Governor Perry's Patronage," April 1, 2006, http://www.tpj.org.
30. Charles Wiggins, Keith Hamm, and Howard Balanoff, "The 1982 Gubernatorial Transition in Texas," in Thad L. Beyle, ed., *Gubernatorial Transitions: The 1982 Elections* (Durham, NC: Duke University, 1985), 398.
31. Wayne Slater, "Bush Steps Up Number of Hispanic Appointees," *Dallas Morning News* (October 12, 1999): A1.
32. Texans for Public Justice, "Governor Bush's Well-Appointed Texas Officials," October 2000, and "Governor Perry's Patronage," April 1, 2006, http://www.tpj.org.
33. Gantt, *The Chief Executive in Texas*, 327.
34. Richard Murray and Gregory Weiher, "Texas: Ann Richards, Taking On the Challenge," in Thad L. Beyle, ed., *Governors and Hard Times* (Washington, DC: CQ Press, 1992), 186.
35. For descriptions and examples of governors' legislative prowess, see Gantt, *The Chief Executive in Texas*, 42, 237–8, 244–54.
36. William E. Atkinson, "James Allred: A Political Biography, 1899–1935" (Ph.D. diss., Texas Christian University, 1978), 275.
37. See John Connally, *In History's Shadow: An American Odyssey* (New York: Hyperion, 1993), 226; Ann Fears Crawford and Jack Keever, *John Connally: Portrait in Power* (Austin: Jenkins, 1973), 183–6; Ben Barnes, *Barn Burning, Barn Building: Tales of a Political Life, from LBJ to George W. Bush and Beyond* (Albany, TX: Bright Sky, 2006), 77–79.
38. Council of State Governments, *Book of the States 2007*, vol. 39, Table 3.2, 76–78.
39. *Ferguson v. Maddox*, 1924. Gantt, *The Chief Executive in Texas*, 221.
40. Gantt, *The Chief Executive in Texas*, 39. Twenty-five states require a two-thirds vote of the total membership to override, twelve require a vote of two-thirds of those present, six require three-fifths of the total membership, and one requires three-fifths of those present, while six require just a majority of the total membership. Council of State Governments, *Book of the States 2005*, Table 3.16, 161–2. The Texas Constitution is confusing in its language about overrides of vetoes. It says that an override requires a vote of two-thirds of the members present in the chamber that passed the bill first, and two-thirds of the elected members of the chamber that passed the bill last—or, if it is a line-item veto, two-thirds of the members present in each chamber.
41. The president of the Republic of Texas had pocket-veto authority—if he refused to sign a bill passed in the last five days of a session, the bill died. No constitution since statehood has included pocket-veto authority. Braden, *The Constitution of the State of Texas*, 333.
42. House Research Organization, "Vetoes of Legislation," *Special Legislative Report*, no. 193 (1995); "Vetoes of Legislation—75th Legislature," *Special Legislative Report*, no. 75-16 (1997); "Vetoes of Legislation—76th Legislature," *Focus Report* (June 25, 1999); "Vetoes of Legislation—77th Legislature," *Focus Report* (June 26, 2001); "Vetoes of Legislation—78th Legislature," *Focus Report* (August 5, 2003); "Vetoes of Legislation—79th Legislature," *Focus Report* (July 29, 2005); Vetoes of Legislation—80th Legislature," *Focus Report* (July 9, 2007).

43. Texas Legislative Council, "Gubernatorial Veto: Powers, Procedures, and Override History," staff memorandum, May 22, 1990. See also Fred Gantt Jr., "The Governor's Veto in Texas: An Absolute Negative?" *Public Affairs Comment* 15 (March 1969), University of Texas Institute of Public Affairs; *Senate Journal*, May 23, 1990, 149; *House Journal*, May 29, 1990, 192.

44. See Gantt, *The Chief Executive in Texas*, 39; Council of State Governments, *Book of the States 2005*, Table 3.16, 161–2.

45. House Research Organization, "Texas Budget Highlights Fiscal 2004–05," *State Finance Report*, 78-3 (November 17, 2003): 5; "Texas Budget Highlights Fiscal 2006–07," *State Finance Report*, 79-3 (January 30, 2006): 2.

46. Kendra A. Hovey and Harold A. Hovey, *Congressional Quarterly's State Fact Finder 2007: Rankings Across America* (Washington, DC: CQ Press, 2007), D-12, 113. (The book erroneously lists only five positions for Texas; apparently, the book lists only the constitutionally designated offices, omitting the elected agriculture commissioner and three railroad commissioners.)

47. Texas Watch Foundation, "Consumers Question Attorney General Priorities," July 8, 2002, http://www.texaswatch.org.

48. Virginia H. Taylor Houston, "Surveying in Texas," *Southwestern Historical Quarterly* 65 (October 1961): 216.

49. How much land this represented is uncertain, since even the boundaries of the state were in dispute.

50. For a history and analysis of the Railroad Commission, see David Prindle, *Petroleum Politics and the Texas Railroad Commission* (Austin: University of Texas Press, 1981).

51. Prindle, *Petroleum Politics and the Texas Railroad Commission*, 20, 112, and 117.

52. For a more detailed analysis of the SBOE, see House Research Organization, "State Board of Education: Controversy and Change," *Focus Report* (January 3, 2000).

53. These figures do not include regional agencies, such as river authorities, or local agencies created or funded by the state, such as the fifty community college districts.

54. See Terrence Stutz, "Court Overturns Farmers Insurance Settlement," *Dallas Morning News* (January 22, 2005).

55. Comptroller of Public Accounts, *Breaking the Mold: New Ways to Govern Texas*, 1991, 43.

56. William Gormley Jr., "Accountability Battles in State Administration," in Carl E. Van Horn, ed., *The State of the States*, 3rd ed. (Washington, DC: CQ Press, 1996), 162.

57. Gormley, "Accountability Battles in State Administration," 162.

58. Texas Sunset Advisory Commission, "Sunset Review in Texas: Summary of Process and Procedure," October 1993, 23; "Report to the 80th Legislature," May 2007.

59. Texas Sunset Advisory Commission, "Report to the 80th Legislature," May 2007, 9.

60. Texas Sunset Advisory Commission, "Summary of Sunset Legislation, 80th Legislature," 1.

61. Sabato, *Goodbye to Good-Time Charlie*, 169; U.S. Census, "State Government Employment Data," March 2006 http://ftp2.census.gov/govs/apes/06stus.txt.

62. Kathleen O'Leary Morgan and Scott Morgan, eds., *State Rankings 2007: A Statistical View of the 50 United States*, 18th ed. (Lawrence, KS: Morgan Quitno Press, 2007), 344–5.

63. See Texas Ethics Commission, "Revolving Door: Leaving a State Agency? A Texas Ethics Commission Guide to the Revolving Door Provisions in Chapter 572 of the Texas Government Code," May 28, 1999, http://www.ethics.state.tx.us.

64. Marver Bernstein, *Regulating Business by Independent Commission* (Princeton, NJ: Princeton University Press, 1955), 90.

65. *Texas Almanac 1972–73* (Dallas: A. H. Belo, 1971), 397.

66. See House Research Organization, "Major Issues of the 80th Legislature, Regular Session," *Focus Report* (July 17, 2007): 8.

67. ACCORD Agriculture v. TNRCC (1999).

Chapter 6

1. Sources for this story include Ralph Blumenthal, "Texas Judge Draws Outcry for Allowing an Execution," *New York Times* (October 25, 2007); April Castro, "Texas Judge Fosters Unsparing Reputation," *Boston Globe* (October 24, 2007); "Closing Time at the Death Chamber," *Austin American-Statesman* (October 6, 2007); "Justice in Texas? Not on Her Watch," *Austin American-Statesman* (October 13, 2007); Rick Casey, "Death Judge Broke Rules," *Houston Chronicle* (December 15, 2007); Christy Hoppe, "Criminal Appeals Court Creates Emergency Filing System," *Dallas Morning News* (November 18, 2007).

2. Quotation in R. G. Ratcliffe, "Appellate Judge Called 'Out of Control,'" *San Antonio Express-News* (October 28, 2007).

3. Paul Womack, "Judiciary," *Handbook of Texas Online*, http://www.tsha.utexas.edu/handbook/online/articles/view/JJ/jzj1.html.

4. Figures for all of the courts in the chapter are from the Office of Court Administration, *Annual Statistical Report for the Texas Judiciary, Fiscal Year 2007* (Austin: Office of Court Administration, 2007).

5. Texas Research League, "The Texas Judiciary: A Structural-Functional Overview," *Texas Courts: A Study by the Texas Research League*, Report 1 (Austin: Texas Research League, 1990), 41.

6. The operation of the court is described in James A. Vaught, "Internal Procedures in the Texas Supreme Court," *Texas Tech Law Review* 26:3 (1995): 935–58.

7. The following figures are from the Profile of Appellate and Trial Judges in the "Annual Statistical Report for the Texas Judiciary," Office of Court Administration, December 2007, 13.

8. Walt Borges, "The Court's Bill Chill," *Texas Lawyer* (September 4, 1995): 1.

9. "Tort Reform Passes," *Texans for Lawsuit Reform*, http://www.tortreform.com/1995.html.

10. Anthony Champagne, "Judicial Reform in Texas," in Anthony Champagne and Judith Haydel, eds., *Judicial Reform in the States* (New York: University Press of America, 1993), 107.

11. Texans for Public Justice, "Payola Justice: How Supreme Court Justices Raise Money from Court Litigants," February 1998, http://www.tpj.org/reports/payola/conclusions.html.

12. Texans for Public Justice, "Checks and Imbalances: How Texas Supreme Court Justices Raised $11 Million," April 2000, http://www.tpj.org/reports/checks/warchests.html.

13. Texas Watch Foundation, *The Texas Supreme Court by the Numbers: A Statistical Analysis of the Texas Supreme Court (2005–2006)*, October 5, 2006, http://www.txwfoundation.org/TWF/index.cfm?event=showPage&pg=release100506 and *Shifting Sands for Consumers: 2002–2003 Texas Supreme Court Year-in-Review*, October 30, 2003, http://www.txwfoundation.org/courtwatch/Review_2002_2003.pdf.

14. Thomas R. Phillips, "State of the Judiciary," March 29, 1999, http://www.supreme.courts.state.tx.us/soj99.html.

15. Office of Court Administration, *Public Trust and Confidence in the Courts and Legal Profession in Texas* (Austin: Office of Court Administration, 1998); Office of Court Administration, *The Courts and the Legal Profession in Texas—An Insider's Perspective: A Survey of Judges, Court Personnel, and Attorneys* (Austin: Office of Court Administration, 1998).

16. John Williams, "Name Game Cost GOP Candidate," *Houston Chronicle* (March 25, 2002), http://www.chron.com/cs/CDA/story.hts/metropolitan/williams/1307892.

17. Pamela Fridich et al., *Lowering the Bar: Lawyers Keep Texas Appeals Judges on Retainer* (Austin: Texans for Public Justice, 2003), 2; updated by the author.
18. David M. Horton and Ryan Kellus Turner, *Lone Star Justice* (Austin: Eakin, 1999), 169–205; Ken Anderson, *Crime in Texas* (Austin: University of Texas Press, 1997). In 2005, the Texas legislature made life without parole the only alternative to the death penalty for sentencing persons convicted of capital offenses.
19. Texas Chief Justice's Task Force on Judicial Reform, *Justice at the Crossroads: Court Improvement in Texas* (Austin, 1972).
20. Texas Research League, *Texas Courts: A Study by the Texas Research League*, three reports (Austin: Texas Research League, 1990–1992).
21. Texas Research League, *Texas Courts: A Study by the Texas Research League*, Report 2, "The Texas Judiciary: A Proposal for Structural-Functional Reform" (Austin: Texas Research League, 1991), 25–27.
22. See House Research Organization, "Court System Reorganization and Administration, SB 1204 by Duncan," in *Focus Report: Major Issues of the 80th Legislature, Regular Session* (July 17, 2007), 136–8.
23. John J. Goodson, "Judicial Selection: Options for Choosing Judges in Texas," House Research Organization, *Session Focus* (March 10, 1997), 2.
24. Anthony Champagne, "Judicial Selection in Texas," in Anthony Champagne and Edward J. Harpham, eds., *Texas Politics: A Reader*, 2nd ed. (New York: Norton, 1998), 95–104.
25. SJR 33, 78th Legislature, regular session, http://www.capitol.state.tx.us.
26. For an overview of revision attempts, see American Judicature Society, *Judicial Selection in the States, Texas, History of Judicial Selection Reform*, http://www.ajs.org/js/TX_history.htm.
27. Supreme Court of Texas Judicial Campaign Finance Committee, "Report and Recommendations," Office of Court Administration, February 23, 1999, http://www.supreme.courts.state.tx.us/JCFSC/campaign1.htm.
28. See, for instance, Texans for Public Justice, "Payola Justice: How Supreme Court Justices Raise Money from Court Litigants," February 1998, http://www.tpj.org/reports/payola/conclusions.html; and "Checks and Imbalances: How Texas Supreme Court Justices Raised $11 Million," http://www.tpj.org/reports/checks.

Chapter 7

1. Ruth Rendon, "Perry's Disaster Order Questioned," *Houston Chronicle* (March 23, 2006); Bill Murphy and Salatheia Bryant, "City Hurries to Find Shelter for Onrush of Evacuees," *Houston Chronicle* (September 3, 2005); Kristen Mack, "Running Shelter Is Giving Noriega Little Time to Rest," *Houston Chronicle* (September 13, 2005); Arnold Hamilton, "Last Wave of Residents Flees As Rita Barrels In," *Dallas Morning News* (September 24, 2005); Matt Stiles, "Mayor Stayed Mum on Last-Resort Plans," *Houston Chronicle* (September 25, 2005); "Refining Rita," *Houston Chronicle* (September 27, 2005); Rad Sallee, "Evacuation Picked Apart in Houston," *Houston Chronicle* (October 27, 2005); John F. Kennedy Foundation, "Acceptance Speech by Houston Mayor Bill White," May 21, 2007, http://www.jfklibrary.org.
2. U.S. Census Bureau, "Local Governments and Public School Systems by Type and State 2007," March 5, 2008, http://www.census.gov/govs/cog/GovOrgTab03ss.html.
3. Dick Smith, "County Organization," *Handbook of Texas Online*, http://www.tsha.utexas.edu/handbook/online/articles/view/CC/muc10.html.
4. George D. Braden, *The Constitution of the State of Texas: An Annotated and Comparative Analysis*, vol. 2 (Austin: Texas Advisory Commission on Intergovernmental Relations, 1977), 505.
5. See Dick Smith, "The Development of Local Government Units in Texas" (Ph.D. diss., Harvard University, 1938). See also Herman James and Irvin Stewart, "County Government in Texas," *University of Texas Bulletin*, No. 2525 (July 1, 1925).
6. Texas Association of Counties, "About Counties: County Government History," http://www.county.org/counties/history.asp; and "About Counties: County Government: Some Facts About Texas Counties," 2003, http://www.county.org/counties/facts.asp.
7. Terrell Blodgett, "Texas Cities: The Bulwark of Democracy," 1999 William P. Hobby Jr. Distinguished Lecture, Southwest Texas State University, http://www.swt.edu/cpm/lectures/blodgett_txt.html.
8. Braden, *The Constitution of the State of Texas*, 505.
9. Today, those boundary disputes continue. In 2000, a court declared in favor of Denton County in its boundary dispute with Tarrant County over the now lucrative real estate between the Dallas–Fort Worth area and Denton. On appeal, the decision was reversed, and the Supreme Court upheld Tarrant County's claim. See "Boundary Battle Puts Two Counties at Odds," *County* (September/October 2003).
10. Terrell Blodgett, "City Government," *Handbook of Texas Online*, http://www.tsha.utexas.edu/handbook/online/articles/view/CC/mvc2.html. See also Egbert Cockrell, "Municipal Home Rule with Special Reference to Texas," *Southwestern Social Science Quarterly* 1 (1920/1921): 147; and "Do Statewide Planning and the Consistency Concept Infringe on Home Rule Authority," *Journal of Planning Literature* 11 (May 1997): 564–74.
11. See Roscoe C. Martin, "County Home Rule Movement in Texas," *Southwestern Social Science Quarterly* (March 1935): 1–11; John P. Keith, "City and County Home Rule in Texas," University of Texas Institute of Public Affairs, 1951; Braden, *The Constitution of the State of Texas*, 652; and W. E. Benton, "The County Home Rule Movement in Texas," *Southwestern Social Science Quarterly* 31 (1950): 108.
12. Steve Bickerstaff, "Voting Rights Challenges to School Boards in Texas: What Next?" *Baylor Law Review* 49 (Fall 1997): 1017.
13. Based on U.S. Census Bureau's 2005 and 2007 population estimates, "Annual Population Estimates 2000 to 2007," http://www.census.gov/popest/states/NST-ann-est.html and "100 Largest Counties," http://www.census.gov/popest/counties/CO-EST2005-08.html.
14. See Jim Lewis, "The County Advocates," *County* (January/February 2003).
15. While the correct punctuation for this term would be commissioners' court, constitutional and legal references designate it as commissioners court, with no apostrophe, so we will use the official method throughout this chapter.
16. *Gray* v. *Sanders*, 372 U.S. 368 (1963); *Wesberry* v. *Sanders*, 376 U.S. 1 (1964); and *Reynolds* v. *Sims*, 84 S.Ct. 1362 (1964).
17. *Avery* v. *Midland County, Texas, et al.*, 390 U.S. 474 (1968).
18. The office of county treasurer has been abolished for Tarrant, Bee, Bexar, Collin, Andrews, Gregg, El Paso, Fayette, and Nueces counties.
19. Judon Fambrough, "County Regulation of Rural Subdivisions," Land Development, Publication 1195, October 1997 (rev. 2000), http://recenter.tamu.edu/pdf/1195.pdf; "Counties Achieve 'Sea Change' on Development Authority," *County* (July/August 1999), http://www.county.org/resources/library/county_mag/county/114/issue.html.
20. Paul Sugg, "Last Year, Counties Were Granted Greater Authority to Address Unbridled Development. So What Happened?" *County* (November/December 2000), http://www.county.org/resources/library/county_mag/county/126/issue.html.
21. Jim Lewis, "Election Reform: Will the Prayers Be Answered?" *County* (July/August 2001), http://www.county.org/resources/library/county_mag/county/134/issue.html.
22. 78th Texas Legislature, HB 1549, Regular Session, 2003, http://www.capitol.state.tx.us.
23. Jim Lewis, "Budget 2005," *County* (September/October 2005): 41–43.

24. "Are Legislators Too 'Fee Bill' Minded?" *County* (January/February 1997), http://www.county.org/resources/library/county_mag/county/091/issue.html; Cheryl Smith, "If It Moves, Put a Fee on It," *County* (January/February 2004): 18–21; Maria Sprow, "It's About the Money, Honey: State Mandates Countywide Collections Offices for Court Fees, Fines," *County* (November/December 2005): 40–42.

25. House Research Organization, "Constitutional Amendments Proposed for November 2001 Ballot," *Focus Report* (August 13, 2001): 55.

26. See Elna Christopher, "Unfunded Mandates: County Officials Uniting Behind Initiative," *County* (March/April 2004): 32–35.

27. Terrell Blodgett, "Municipal Home Rule Charters," *Public Affairs Comment* (University of Texas, 1996), 1–7; Blodgett, "Home Rule Charters," *Handbook of Texas Online*, http://www.tsha.utexas.edu/handbook/online/articles/view/HH/mvhek.html; Delbert Taebel, Susan Horton, and Jay Stanford, *A Citizen's Guide to Home-Rule Charters in Texas Cities* (Arlington: University of Texas at Arlington, Institute of Urban Studies, 1985); Terrell Blodgett, "Texas Cities: The Bulwark of Democracy," 1999 William P. Hobby Jr. Distinguished Lecture, Southwest Texas State University, http://www.swt.edu/cpm/lectures/blodgett_txt.html.

28. Almost all general-law cities have fewer than 5,000 people. However, even a few home-rule cities have fewer than 5,000 people. At one time, those cities had more than 5,000 people and achieved home-rule status. They then lost population. There is no requirement that a city give up its home-rule charter if it drops below 5,000 in population. For a list of home-rule cities, see *Texas Almanac 2006–2007* (Dallas: Dallas Morning News Corporation, 2006), 453–64.

29. Article 3, section 53, of the Texas Constitution prohibits the legislature from passing "any local or special law . . . regulating the affairs of counties, cities, towns, wards or school districts."

30. For Type A and Type B general-law cities, the Local Government Code specifies an aldermanic form of government. However, cities are allowed to change their charters and could adopt the council–manager form. In 2003, the legislature changed the Local Government Code to allow cities to assign duties to city officials, a provision that allows cities to create a city administrator, who performs the functions that a city manager performs in the council–manager form of government. Type C general-law cities are required to incorporate with the commission form of government. In practice, Texas cities do not incorporate as Type C cities.

31. Dale Krane, Platon Rigos, and Melvin Hill Jr., *Home Rule in America: A Fifty-State Handbook* (Washington, DC: CQ Press, 2000), 401; Blodgett, "Texas Cities."

32. "Hurricane That Wrecked Galveston Was Deadliest in U.S. History," CNN, September 8, 2000, http://www.cnn.com/2000/WEATHER/09/07/galveston.backgrounder/index.html.

33. Blodgett, "Texas Cities"; Bradley R. Rice, "Commission Form of City Government," *Handbook of Texas Online*, http://www.tsha.utexas.edu/handbook/online/articles/view/CC/moc1.html.

34. Laurence F. Jones, Nirmal Goswami, and Ralph Warren, "An Assessment of Capital Budgeting in Texas Cities: A Research Note," *Texas Journal of Political Studies* 19 (Spring/Summer 1997): 59.

35. Jones, Goswami, and Warren, "An Assessment of Capital Budgeting in Texas Cities," 54–57.

36. For a history of the annexation statutes and policy battles, see Scott Houston, "Municipal Annexation in Texas: 'Is It Really That Complicated?'" Texas Municipal League, January 2008.

37. A city may carry over some of this allowance from one year to another but may expand no more than a total of 30 percent of its area in one year.

38. The ETJ ranges from one-half mile for those cities with fewer than 5,000 citizens, up to five miles from the corporate limits for cities with more than 100,000 citizens.

39. Local Government Code, chap. 42.

40. Local Government Code, section 43.121, Limited Purpose Annexation (planning, zoning, health, and safety). Section 43.130 states that citizens in a limited-purpose annexation area may vote in city council races but not bond elections. Section 43.122 limits strip annexation to at least 1,000 feet wide and no more than three miles, in most cases.

41. Senate Interim Committee on Annexation Interim Report, 76th Legislature, October 1998.

42. Local Government Code, chaps. 41–43.

43. See, for instance, Craig Smyser, "Houston's Power: As It Was," *Houston Chronicle* (June 27, 1977): 6.

44. Joe Stinebaker, "Special Districts a Cause of Houston Tax Revolt," *County* (March/April 2005): 22.

45. "State Buffs Up County Statutes," *County* (July/August 1999), http://www.county.org/publications/county/archiveindex.html.

46. Bill D. Dugatt III, "How to Create a Groundwater Conservation District," Bickerstaff, Heath, Smiley, Pollan, Kever, and McDaniel, April 8, 1999, http://www.bickerstaff.com; Sugg, "Last Year, Counties Were Granted Greater Authority."

47. U.S. Census Bureau, "Local Governments and Public School Systems by Type and State 2007," March 5, 2008, http://www.census.gov/govs/cog/GovOrgTab03ss.html.

48. Texas Education Agency, *Snapshot 2005–2006*, http://www.tea.state.tx.us.

49. National Center for Education Statistics, U.S. Department of Education, State Education Data Profiles, http://www.nces.ed.gov/programs/stateprofiles.

50. National Center for Education Statistics, Overview of Public Elementary and Secondary Students," 2004-2005, Table 2, http://nces.ed.gov/pubs2007/overview04/tables/table_2.asp?referer=list.

51. Bickerstaff, "Voting Rights Challenges," 1021.

52. Bickerstaff, "Voting Rights Challenges," 1024 and 1056, fn 49.

53. "Communities in America Currently Using Proportional Voting: Cumulative Voting," Center for Voting and Democracy, http://www.fairvote.org/?page=2101.

54. "Communities in America Currently Using Proportional Voting"; also see Jennifer Wilson, "Professor's Analysis: Cumulative Voting OK; Study Shows Voters Understand Process," *Amarillo Globe News* (August 19, 2004).

Chapter 8

1. Gaiutra Bahadur, "Education Board Votes to Reject 2 Textbooks," *Austin American-Statesman* (November 9, 2001).

2. Julia Malone, "Norquist Keeps GOP on the Same Page," *Austin American-Statesman* (November 27, 2003).

3. "State's Leaders Right in Distancing Themselves from Solicitations," *Austin American-Statesman* (January 4, 2003), editorial; quotation in "Foundation Is Entitled to Its Views, but Not Our Public Offices," *Austin American-Statesman* (January 7, 2003), editorial.

4. Laylan Copelin, "Texas Think Tank's Time Has Come," *Austin American-Statesman* (December 10, 2002); Ken Herman, "Ethics Agency Investigates Perry's Trip to Bahamas," *Austin American-Statesman* (January 30, 2003); www.texaspolicy.com.

5. Virginia Gray and Peter Eisinger, *American States and Cities*, 2nd ed. (New York: Addison Wesley Longman, 1997), 358.

6. See William E. Atkinson, *James V. Allred: A Political Biography, 1899–1935*, dissertation, Texas Christian University, 1978; Robert Martindale, *James V. Allred—The Centennial Governor Texas*, M.A. thesis, University of Texas, 1957.

7. Stephen B. Thomas and Billy Don Walker, "Texas Public School Finance," *Journal of Education Finance* (Fall 1982): 223–6. See also

Richard Gambitta, Robert Milne, and Carol Davis, "The Politics of Unequal Educational Opportunity," in David Johnson, John Booth, and Richard Harris, eds., *The Politics of San Antonio: Community, Progress, and Power* (Lincoln: University of Nebraska Press, 1983), 133–56.

8. See George Braden, The *Constitution of the State of Texas: An Annotated and Comparative Analysis*, vol. 2 (Austin: Texas Advisory Commission on Intergovernmental Relations, 1977), 505; Carl H. Moneyhon, Republicanism in Reconstruction Texas (Austin: University of Texas Press, 1980): 183–96.

9. James Soukup, Clifton McCleskey, and Harry Holloway, *Party and Factional Division in Texas* (Austin: University of Texas Press, 1964), 9–11.

10. George Norris Green, *The Establishment in Texas Politics* (Westport, CT: Greenwood, 1979), 17; Chandler Davidson, *Race and Class in Texas Politics* (Princeton, NJ: Princeton University Press, 1990), 105.

11. Lester Thurow develops this argument in *The Zero-Sum Society: Distribution and the Possibilities for Economic Change* (New York: Basic Books, 1980).

12. David Osborne, *Laboratories of Democracy* (Cambridge, MA: Harvard Business School Press, 1988), 5. See also Martin Saiz and Susan Clarke, "Economic Development and Infrastructure Policy," in Virginia Gray, Russell Hanson, and Herbert Jacob, eds., *Politics in the American States: A Comparative Analysis*, 7th ed. (Washington, DC: CQ Press, 1999), 474–505.

13. Osborne, *Laboratories of Democracy*, 14.

14. Gray and Eisinger, *American States and Cities*, 355.

15. Council of State Governments, *Book of the States 2004*, vol. 36 (Lexington, KY: Council of State Governments, 2004), 359.

16. U.S. Census Bureau, "State Government Finances: 2006," http://www.census.gov.

17. House Research Organization, "Writing the State Budget," *State Finance Report* 77-1 (February 1, 2001): 13.

18. Comptroller of Public Accounts, *Breaking the Mold: New Ways to Govern Texas*, vol. 1 (July 1991), 21.

19. The estimate actually provides detail by source rather than just one total figure. Comptroller of Public Accounts, *Biennial Revenue Estimate 2008–2009*, January 8, 2007.

20. House Research Organization, "Texas Budget Highlights Fiscal 2006–07," *State Finance Report* 79-3 (January 30, 2006), 3.

21. Advisory Commission on Intergovernmental Relations, *Significant Features of Fiscal Federalism 1993: Budget Processes and Tax Systems*, M-185, vol. 1 (Washington, DC: ACIR, 1993), 34.

22. Tax Foundation, "State Tax Collections and Distribution by Type of Tax," Fiscal Year 2002, http://www.taxfoundation.org.

23. U.S. Department of Commerce, Bureau of the Census, *Statistical Abstract of the United States 2008*, Table 439, State Government Tax Collections, by State: 2005, http://www.census.gov.

24. U.S. Department of Commerce, Bureau of the Census, *Statistical Abstract of the United States 2007* (Washington, DC: Government Printing Office, 2007), 432.

25. These and following tax rates and rankings are from Commerce Clearing House, *2008 State Tax Handbook* (Chicago: CCH, Inc., 2007), 520.

26. Comptroller of Public Accounts, *Forces of Change: Shaping the Future of Texas* (March 1994): 165.

27. Martin Katzman and Patricia Osborn, "Energy Policy," in Anthony Champagne and Edward Harpham, *Texas at the Crossroads: People, Politics, and Policy* (College Station: Texas A&M University Press, 1987), 135.

28. Comptroller of Public Accounts, *Forces of Change*, 164.

29. Kendra A. Hovey and Harold A. Hovey, *Congressional Quarterly's State Fact Finder 2007: Rankings Across America* (Washington, DC: CQ Press, 2007), 126.

30. Gray and Eisinger, *American States and Cities*, 304.

31. Comptroller of Public Accounts, *Texas Annual Cash Report Fiscal 2007*, https://fmx.cpa.state.tx.us/.

32. Tax Foundation, "Texas' State and Local Tax Burdens, 1970–2006," http://www.taxfoundation.org.

33. Scott Moody, ed., *Facts and Figures on Government Finance*, 33rd ed. (Washington, DC: Tax Foundation, 1999), 287.

34. Richard Murray and Gregory Weiher, "Texas: Ann Richards, Taking on the Challenge," in Thad Beyle, ed., *Governors and Hard Times* (Washington, DC: CQ Press, 1992), 180.

35. Tax Foundation, "State and Local Sales and Gross Receipts Tax Collections Per Household and Per Capita, Fiscal Year 2005," http://taxfoundation.org.

36. Tax Foundation Tax Data, http://taxfoundation.org.

37. Osborne, *Laboratories of Democracy*, 255–6.

38. Paul Brace, *State Government and Economic Performance* (Baltimore, MD: Johns Hopkins University Press, 1993), 114.

39. Comptroller of Public Accounts, *Tax Exemptions and Tax Incidence* (January 1999, quotation at 44; January 2007).

40. Michael P. Ettlinger et al., *Who Pays? A Distributional Analysis of the Tax Systems in All 50 States* (Washington, DC: Citizens for Tax Justice and the Institute on Taxation and Economic Policy, 1996), App. 1, 44; Robert S. McIntyre et al., *Who Pays? A Distributional Analysis of the Tax Systems in All 50 States*, 2nd ed. (Washington, DC: Citizens for Tax Justice and the Institute on Taxation and Economic Policy, 2003), 102.

41. D. Martinez, "Don't Tax Me, Tax the Fella Behind the Tree: Partisan and Turnout Effects on Taxes," *Social Science Quarterly* (December 1997): 895.

42. Gray and Eisinger, *American States and Cities*, 314.

43. U.S. Census Bureau, "States Ranked by Revenue and Expenditure, Total Amount and Per Capita Amount, 2004," February 1, 2006, http://www.census.gov.

44. Capital budgets include large-cost items with long lives, such as buildings, highways, and bridges. Capital expenditures are not included in the operating budget of many states; rather, the state borrows the money (by selling bonds), and only the annual principal and interest payments on the bonds are included in the operating budget expenses. States spend about 4 percent of annual operating budgets on principal and interest payments on debt. Gray and Eisinger, *American States and Cities*, 325.

45. House Research Organization, "Texas Budget Highlights, Fiscal 2000–01," *State Finance Report* 76-3 (October 21, 1999): 25–26; "Texas Budget Highlights, Fiscal 2004–05," *State Finance Report* 78-3 (November 17, 2003); "Texas Budget Highlights, Fiscal 2006–07," *State Finance Report* 79-3 (January 30, 2006).

46. U.S. Census Bureau, "State Government Finances, 2004," http://ftp2.census.gov.

47. Hovey and Hovey, *Congressional Quarterly's State Fact Finder 2007*, 187; Morgan and Morgan, *State Rankings 2006*, 300.

48. Gray and Eisinger, *American States and Cities*, 325.

49. These and following statistics come from Texas Education Agency, *Snapshot 2007*, http://www.tea.state.tx.us/; National Center for Education Statistics, U.S. Department of Education, "Digest of Education Statistics 2007: Chapter 2, Elementary and Secondary Education," Table 33; Enrollment in Public Elementary and Secondary Schools, by State or Jurisdiction: Selected years, Fall 1990–Fall 2007, http://nces.ed.gov; Public Elementary and Secondary Teachers, by Level and State or Jurisdiction: Fall 2000–Fall 2005,

http://nces.ed.gov; Staff Employed in Public Elementary and Secondary School Systems, by Type of Assignment and State or Jurisdiction: Fall 2005, http://nces.ed.gov.

50. Hovey and Hovey, *Congressional Quarterly's State Fact Finder 2007*, 210.

51. Kathleen O'Leary Morgan and Scott Morgan, eds., *Education State Rankings 2007–2008*, 6th ed. (Washington, DC: CQ Press, 2008), 5, 19.

52. National Center for Education Statistics, U.S. Department of Education, "Digest of Education Statistics 2007, Table 172; Total and Current Expenditures Per Pupil in Fall Enrollment in Public Elementary and Secondary Education, by Function and State or Jurisdiction: 2004–05, http://nces.ed.gov; Estimated Average Annual Salary of Teachers in Public Elementary and Secondary Schools, by State or Jurisdiction: Selected Years, 1969–70 through 2005–06, http://nces.ed.gov.

53. Richard Lavine, "School Finance Reform in Texas, 1983–1995," in Robert Wilson, ed., *Public Policy and Community: Activism and Governance in Texas* (Austin: University of Texas Press, 1997), 121.

54. Calculated from data in TEA, *Snapshot '94: 1993–94 School District Profiles*, 1995 and *Snapshot '95*; see also Comptroller of Public Accounts, *Fiscal Notes*, Special Public School Issue (March 1991).

55. See Texas Education Agency, *Snapshot 2007*, Summary Tables: Property Wealth, http://www.tea.state.tx.us/.

56. Center for Public Policy Priorities, "Special Session Tax and School-Finance Package Creates $10.5 Billion Deficit," May 15, 2006, http://www.cppp.org.

57. Jason Embry, "Districts Shelve Challenge to School Finance System," *Austin American-Statesman* (May 26, 2006): B1; House Research Organization, "Local Voters Asked to Approve Higher School Taxes," *Interim News* 80-1 (October 30, 2007).

58. Gray and Eisinger, *American States and Cities*, 465–6.

59. See House Research Organization, "Texas Adapts to Requirements of No Child Left Behind Act," *Interim News* 78-10 (November 3, 2004).

60. These and following data are from Texas Higher Education Coordinating Board, "Texas Higher Education Data," http://www.txhighereddata.org; "Statistical Report 2004," http://www.thecb.state.tx.us.

61. The University of North Texas is also a "system," though it consists only of the university and its medical school. The other schools not affiliated with a system are Midwestern State University, Stephen F. Austin State University, Texas Southern University, and Texas Woman's University.

62. Lawrence Redlinger et al., "Funding Higher Education," in Champagne and Harpham, *Texas at the Crossroads*, 187, 188.

63. Texas Higher Education Board, "College Student Budgets, FY 1999 to FY 2006," http://www.thecb.state.tx.us/.

64. Hovey and Hovey, *Congressional Quarterly's State Fact Finder 2007*, 226.

65. Texas Higher Education Coordinating Board, "Closing the Gaps by 2015: 2007 Progress Report," http://www.thecb.state.tx.us/.

66. Texas Higher Education Coordinating Board, "Report on the Effects of the *Hopwood* Decision on Minority Applications, Offers, and Enrollments at Public Institutions of Higher Education in Texas," http://www.thecb.state.tx.us/.

67. Osborne, *Laboratories of Democracy*, 301.

68. Tami Swenson, Steve White, and Steve Murdock, "An Examination of Change in the TANF Caseload and Characteristics of TANF Recipients in Texas, October 1995 Through June 1998," Texas A&M Center for Demographic and Socioeconomic Research and Education, August 1998.

69. See Liz Austin, "State Might Fine Contractors for Call Center Costs," *Austin American-Statesman* (May 25, 2006): B1; "Critics Say Call-in System Changes Aren't Enough," *Austin American-Statesman* (May 23, 2006); John Young, "Texas' Premature Push to Privatize Its Services," *Austin American-Statesman* (May 16, 2006).

70. Gray and Eisinger, *American States and Cities*, 443–45.

71. *Olmstead* v. *L.C.*, 527 U.S. 581 (1999). See House Research Organization, "The Olmstead Challenge: Community Care for the Disabled," *Focus Report* 77-9 (March 27, 2001).

72. Kathleen O'Leary Morgan and Scott Morgan, *Health Care State Rankings 2008* (Lawrence, KS: Morgan Quitno Corp., 2007), 260, 364; Morgan and Morgan, *State Rankings 2006*, 249, 401.

73. Morgan and Morgan, *Health Care State Rankings 2008*, 248.

74. Health and Human Services Commission, "Estimated Number of Persons Without Health Insurance in Texas by County in 1999," June 4, 1999, http://www.hhsc.tx.us/.

75. For a history of the 1985 indigent health care bill, see Pat Wong, "The Indigent Health Care Package," in Robert Wilson, ed., *Public Policy and Community* (Austin: University of Texas Press, 1997), 95–118; see also House Research Organization, "Indigent Health Care and Treatment Act of 1985: A Burden on Counties?" *Interim News* 78-7 (July 22, 2004): 1.

76. See "Health Care for Undocumented Immigrants: Who Pays?" House Research Organization *Focus Report* 77-13 (October 29, 2001).

77. Hovey and Hovey, *Congressional Quarterly's State Fact Finder 2007*, 251; Texas Health and Human Services Commission, "Final Count: Medicaid Enrollment by Month," September 2007, http://www.hhsc.state.tx.us/.

78. Center for Public Policy Priorities, "Medicaid: More Are Uninsured and Eligible, Yet Fewer Are Served," and "Five Years into Welfare Reform: Shift in Emphasis to Problems Facing the Working Poor Has Yet to Occur," November 19, 2000, http://www.cppp.org; House Research Organization, "Texas Budget Highlights Fiscal 2004–05," *State Finance Report* 78-3 (November 17, 2003): 11.

79. Texas Health and Human Services Commission, "CHIP Caseload Fact Sheet," Spring 2004, and "CHIP Enrollment by CSA, Plan, and Age Group," April 2008, http://www.hhsc.state.tx.us/; House Research Organization, "Texas Budget Highlights Fiscal 2004–05," *State Finance Report* 78-3 (November 17, 2003): 13.

80. Hovey and Hovey, *CQ's State Fact Finder 2007*, 303–4; Health and Human Services Commission, "TANF (AFDC) Grants: Total," November 26, 2001, http://www.hhsc.state.tx.us/. See also Center for Public Policy Priorities, "The TANF Challenge: Strategic Use of the Temporary Assistance for Needy Families (TANF) Block Grant in the 2002–2003 State Budget," February 15, 2001, http://www.cppp.org.

81. Hovey and Hovey, *CQ's State Fact Finder 2007*, 305, 311; Morgan and Morgan, *State Rankings 2006*, 522–6.

82. See Texas Department of Transportation, "Trans-Texas Corridor," http://www.keeptexasmoving.com.

83. Glenn Robinson, "Highway Policy," in Champagne and Harpham, *Texas at the Crossroads*, 203, 215.

84. See House Research Organization, "State Boosts Tolls to Finance Highways," *Focus Report* 78-19 (November 12, 2004).

85. House Research Organization, "Major Issues of the 77th Legislature, Regular Session," *Focus Report* (July 2, 2001), 174–5.

86. House Research Organization, "Texas Budget Highlights, Fiscal 2004–05," *State Finance Report* 78-3 (November 17, 2003): 29.

87. Trans-Texas Corridor, "Overview," http://www.keeptexasmoving.com.

Glossary

A

Administrative Procedures Act: A stature containing Tesas's rule-making process.

agenda setting: The constant process of forming the list of issues to be addressed by government.

agriculture commissioner: The elected state official in charge of regulating and promoting agriculture.

the Alamo: A San Antonio mission that was defended by Texans during their war for independence.

American Creed: A set of ideas that provide a national identity, limit government, and structure politics in America.

Anglos: Non-Hispanic whites.

annexation: Enlargement of a city's corporate limits by incorporating surrounding territory into the city.

application for discretionary review: Request for Texas Court of Criminal Appeals review, which is granted if four judges agree.

at-large-by-place: An election system in which all positions on the council or governing body are filled by city-wide elections, with each position designated as a seat, and candidates must choose which place to run for.

attorney general: The elected official who is the chief counsel for the state of Texas.

Available School Fund: Annual investment income from the Permanent School Fund, used to pay operating expenses of schools.

Available University Fund: Annual investment income from the Permanent University Fund, used to pay expenses for the University of Texas and Texas A&M Systems.

B

balanced budget: A budget in which the legislature balances expenditures with expected revenues, with no deficit.

bicameral Texas legislature: The legislature has two bodies, a House of Representatives and a Senate.

biennial budgeting system: A budget covering a two-year period.

biennial legislature: A legislative body that meets in regular session only once in a two-year period.

bill: A proposed law.

block grant: Broad grant with few strings attached; given to states by the federal government for specified activities, such as secondary education or health services.

bond programs: Specific programs for which the state borrows money by selling bonds to investors.

budget: A plan for how much money one expects to take in and how one proposes to spend that money.

budget execution authority: The authority to move money from one program to another program or from one agency to another agency.

C

captured agency: A government regulatory agency that consistently makes decisions favorable to the private interests that it regulates.

charter school: Public school sanctioned by a specific agreement that allows the program to operate outside the usual rules and regulations.

chief budget officer: The governor, who is charged with preparing the state budget proposal for the legislature.

chief executive officer: The governor, as the top official of the executive branch of Texas state government.

chief of state: The governor in his or her role as the official head representing the state of Texas in its relationships with the national government, other states, and foreign dignitaries.

Children's Health Insurance Program (CHIP): Federal block grant program, with states providing matching revenue to provide health care to children in low- to medium-income families who have no other insurance.

city commission: A form of city government in which elected members serve on the legislative body and also serve as head administrators of city programs.

clemency: The governor's authority to reduce the length of a person's prison sentence.

cockroach: A member of a constitutional convention who opposes any changes in the current constitution.

commander in chief: The governor in his or her role as head of the state militia.

commissioners court: The legislative body of a county in Texas.

committee: A subunit of the legislature, appointed to work on designated subjects.

comprehensive revision: Constitutional revision through the adoption of a new constitution.

comptroller of public accounts: The elected official who is the state's tax collector.

comptroller's certification: A document signed by the comptroller certifying that the budge adopted by the legislature will be within expected revenues.

concurrent resolution: A legislative document intended to express the will of both chambers of the legislature, even though it does not possess the authority of law.

constitutional amendment: A change, addition, or deletion to a constitution.

constitutional county court: Constitutionally mandated court for criminal and civil matters.

Constitutional Revision Commission: Group established to research and draft a constitution for a constitutional convention.

constitutionalism: Limits placed on government through a written document.

council–manager: A form of city government in which the city council and mayor hire a professional manager to run the city.

county attorney: Elected official serving as the legal officer for county government and also as a criminal prosecutor.

county auditor: Official appointed by a district judge to audit county finances.

county chairperson: Party leader in a county.

county clerk: Elected official who serves as the clerk for the commissioners court and for county records.

county commissioner: Elected official who serves on the county legislative body, the commissioners court.

county convention: County party meeting to select delegates and adopt resolutions.

county court at law: Statutory county court to relieve county judge of judicial duties.

county executive committee: Precinct chairpersons in a county that assist the county chairpersons.

county judge: Elected official who is the chief administrative officer of county government, serves on the commissioners court, and may also have some judicial functions.

county tax assessor-collector: Elected official who collects taxes for the county (and perhaps for other local governments).

county treasurer: Elected official who serves as the money manager for county government.

court of appeals: Intermediate appellate court for criminal and civil appeals.

criminal district attorney: Elected official who prosecutes criminal cases.

cumulative voting: A method of voting in which voters have a number of votes equal to the number of seats being filled, and voters may cast their votes all for one candidate or split them among candidates in various combinations.

D

debt: The total outstanding amount the government owes as a result of borrowing in the past.

dedicated funds: Monies restricted to designated programs.

deficit spending: Government spending in the current budget cycle that exceeds government revenue.

district attorney (DA): Elected official who prosecutes criminal cases.

district clerk: Elected official who is responsible for keeping the records for the district court.

district court: Court of general jurisdiction for serious crimes and high-dollar civil cases.

E

economic policies: Public actions that affect economic activity or have economic consequences for individuals or groups (e.g., regulations, subsidies, taxing, and spending).

Edgewood v. *Kirby*: Texas Supreme Court case resulting in a decision that the state's school finance system violated the state constitution's provisions for "an efficient education system of public free schools."

engrossed bill: A bill that has been given final approval on third reading in one chamber of the legislature.

equality: The belief that all individuals should be treated similarly, regardless of socio-economic status.

evaluation: The process of examining the results of policy actions and coming to conclusions about whether goals are met or not.

executive commissioner of health and human services commission: The official appointed by the governor to oversee the state's multi-agency health and human service programs.

extraterritorial jurisdiction (ETJ): The area outside a city's boundaries over which the city may exercise limited control.

F

federal funds: Grants of money from the federal government to the states.

filibuster: A formal way of halting action on a bill by means of long speeches or unlimited debate in the Senate.

first reading: The Texas Constitution requires three readings of a bill by the legislature; first reading is when the bill is introduced, its caption is read aloud, and it is referred to committee.

fiscal year (FY): The period used for accounting purposes (September 1 to August 21 for the State of Texas).

frontier era: The period when Texas constituted a border between American civilization and an area inhabited by a hostile, indigenous population.

full-time equivalent (FTE): A unit of measurement for number of employees.

G

general-law cities: Cities with fewer than 5,000 residents, governed by a general state law rather than by a locally adopted charter.

general ordinance-making authority: The legal right to adopt ordinances covering a wide array of subject areas, authority that cities have but counties do not.

germane: Related to the topic.

good government: A term used for policies that open up agencies to public participation and scrutiny and that minimize conflicts of interest.

governor's message: Message that the governor delivers to the legislature, pronouncing policy goals, budget priorities, and authorizations for the legislature to act.

gross domestic product (GDP): The total market value of all goods and services produced in a country during a year.

H

Higher Education Fund: A constitutionally dedicated fund providing money for capital projects for colleges and universities not a part of the University of Texas or Texas A&M Systems.

home rule: The right and authority of a local government to govern itself, rather than have the state govern it.

I

impeachment: The power delegated to the House of Representatives in the Constitution to charge the president, vice president, or other "civil officers," including federal judges, with "Treason, Bribery, or other High Crimes and Misdemeanors." This is the first step in the constitutional process of removing such government officials from office.

implementation: The process by which a law or policy is put into operation by the bureaucracy.

individualism: The belief that each person should act in accordance with his or her own conscience.

insurance commissioner: The official appointed by the governor to direct the Department of Insurance and regulate the insurance industry.

intent calendar: The Senate calendar listing bills on which the author or sponsor has given notice of intent to move to suspend the regular order of business in order that the Senate may consider them.

J

joint resolution: A legislative document that either proposes an amendment to the Texas Constitution or ratifies an amendment to the U.S. Constitution.

justice of the peace court: Local county court for minor crimes and civil suits.

L

land commissioner: The elected official responsible for managing and leasing the state's property, including oil, gas, and mineral interests.

Legislative Budget Board (LBB): A joint legislative committee (with a large staff) that prepares the state budget and conducts evaluations of agencies' programs.

Legislative Council: A joint legislative committee (with a large staff) that provides legal advice, bill drafting, copyediting and printing, policy research, and program evaluation services for members of the legislature.

legislative party caucus: An organization of legislators who are all of the same party, and which is formally allied with a political party.

liberal constitution: Constitution that incorporates the basic structure of government and allows the legislature to provide the details through statutes.

liberty: The belief that government should not infringe upon a person's individual rights.

local election: Election conducted by local governments to elect officials.

Local Government Code: The Texas statutory code containing state laws about local governments.

M

Medicaid: An expansion of Medicare, this program subsidizes medical care for the poor.

municipal corporation: A city.

municipal court: City court with limited criminal jurisdiction.

N

nonparty legislative caucus: An organization of legislators that is based on some attribute other than party affiliation.

O

overrepresentation and underrepresentation: Higher and lower numbers, respectively, than would be expected from a group in comparison with that group's numbers in the general population.

P

per diem: Legislators' per day allowance covering room and board expenses while on state business.

permanent party organization: Party organization that operates throughout the year, performing the party's functions.

Permanent School Fund (PSF): The state fund consisting of revenue from state-owned lands (often paying lucrative oil and gas royalties), dedicated to public education.

Permanent University Fund (PUF): The fund consisting of revenue from state-owned lands (often paying lucrative oil and gas royalties) dedicated to the University of Texas and Texas A&M Systems.

petition for review: Request for Texas Supreme Court review, which is granted if four justices agree.

piecemeal revision: Constitutional revision through constitutional amendments that add or delete items.

plural executive: An executive branch in which power and policy implementation are divided among several executive agencies rather than centralized under one person; the governor does not get to appoint most agency heads.

policy making: The creation of public policies (through passage of legislation or local ordinances, winning gubernatorial support and leadership, passing agency rules and regulations, or winning judicial decisions).

political economy: The web of economic, social, governmental, and political institutions and processes.

populists: People who support the promotion of equality and of traditional values and behaviors.

precinct chairperson: Party leader in a voting precinct.

precinct convention: Precinct party meeting to select delegates and adopt resolutions.

president of the Texas Senate: The lieutenant governor of Texas, serving in his constitutional role as presiding officer of the Senate.

progressive tax: A tax in which the percentage of a person's income paid for the tax increases as the person's income increases.

proportional representation: A voting system that apportions legislative seats according to the percentage of the vote won by a particular political party.

proportional tax (flat tax): A tax that collects the same percentage of each person's income for the tax, regardless of level of income.

pro-tempore (pro-tem): A legislator who serves temporarily as legislative leader in the absence of the Senate president or House Speaker.

public counsels: Officials appointed by the governor to represent the public before regulatory agencies.

public policy: An intentional course of action followed by government in dealing with some problem or matter of concern.

Public Utility Commission: A full-time, three-member paid commission appointed by the governor to regulate public utilities in Texas.

Q

quasi-judicial: Partly judicial; authorized to conduct hearings and issue rulings.

quorum: The minimum number required to conduct business (as in a legislative body).

R

Railroad Commission: A full-time, three-member paid commission elected by the people to regulate oil and gas and some transportation entities.

redistrict: Redraw election-district boundaries.

regressive tax: A tax in which the percentage of a person's income paid for the tax decreases as the person's income increases.

regular session: The biennial 140-day session of the Texas legislature, beginning in January of odd-numbered years.

regulations: Rules that govern the operation of a particular government program that have the force of law.

revenue estimate: A prediction of how much revenue the state will collect in the coming biennium, made for the legislature by the comptroller of public accounts.

revisionist: A member of a constitutional convention who will not accept less than a total revision of the current constitution.

revolving door: An exchange of personnel between private interests and public regulators.

Rodriguez v. San Antonio Independent School District: U.S. Supreme Court case resulting in a decision that the Texas school finance system did not violate the U.S. Constitution

S

second reading: The Texas Constitution requires three readings of a bill by the legislature; the second reading is when debate and consideration of amendments occur before the whole chamber.

Senate two-thirds rule: The rule in the Texas Senate requiring that every bill win a vote of two-thirds of the senators present to suspend the Senate's regular order of business, so that the bill may be considered.

senatorial courtesy: Process by which presidents, when selecting district court judges, defer to senators of their own party who represent the state where the vacancy occurs; also the process by which a governor, when selecting an appointee, defers to the state senator in whose district the nominee resides.

Sharpstown scandal: The legislative scandal of 1969–1972, which resulted in a bribery conviction of the House Speaker and others and set the stage for the 1973 reform session.

sheriff: Elected official who serves as the chief law enforcement officer in a county.

simple resolution: A legislative document proposing an action that affects only the one chamber in which it is being considered, such as a resolution to adopt House rules or to commend a citizen.

single-member district: An election system for legislative bodies in which each legislator runs from and represents a single district, rather than the entire geographic area encompassed by the government.

social policies: Actions that guide our development as human beings and our relationships to other humans and to our broader environment (e.g., education).

Speaker of the Texas House: The state representative who is elected by his or her fellow representatives to be the official leader of the House.

Speaker's lieutenants: House members who make up the Speaker's team, assisting the Speaker in leading the House, either informally, or in a role as a committee chair or other institutional leader.

Speaker's race: The campaign to determine who shall be the Speaker of the Texas House for a given biennium.

Speaker's team: The leadership team in the House, consisting of the Speaker and his or her most trusted allies among the members, most of whom the Speaker appoints to chair House committees.

special election: Election held at a time other than general or primary elections.

special (called) session: A Texas legislative session of up to thirty days, called by the governor, during an interim between regular sessions.

staggered terms: Terms of office for members of boards and commissions that begin and end at different times, so that a governor is not usually able to gain control of a majority of the body for a long time.

State Board of Education: The fifteen-member elected body that sets some education policy for the state and has limited authority to oversee the Texas Education Agency and local school districts.

state convention: Party meeting held to adopt the party's platform, elect the party's executive committee and state chairperson, and in a presidential election year, elect delegates to the national convention and choose presidential electors.

state executive committee: Sixty-two-member party committee that makes decisions for the party between state conventions.

state party chairperson: Party leader for the state.

state senatorial district convention: Party meeting held when a county is a part of more than one senatorial district.

statutory constitution: Constitution that incorporates detailed provisions in order to limit the powers of government.

strong mayor–council: A form of city government in which the mayor has strong powers to run the city by hiring, managing, and firing staff and controlling executive departments; the mayor also serves on the council.

Subsidy: A grant of economic resources.

succession: The constitutional declaration that the lieutenant governor succeeds to the governorship if there is a vacancy.

sunset law: A law that sets a date for a program or regulation to expire unless reauthorized by the legislature.

T

Tejanos: Native Texans of Mexican descent.

Temporary Assistance for Needy Families (TANF): Federal-state cash assistance program adopted in 1996 to replace Aid to Families with Dependent Children.

temporary party organization: Party organization that exists for a limited time and includes several levels of conventions.

term limits: Restrictions that exist in some states about how long an individual may serve in state or local elected offices.

Texan Creed: A set of ideas—primarily individualism and liberty—that shape Texas politics and government.

Texas Association of Counties: Professional association and lobbying arm for county governments.

Texas Commission on Environmental Quality: As of 2002, the new name for the Texas Natural Resource Conservation Commission.

Texas Court of Criminal Appeals: Court of last resort in criminal cases.

Texas Education Agency: The state agency that oversees local school districts and disburses state funds to districts.

Texas Municipal League: Professional association and lobbying arm for city governments.

Texas Rangers: A mounted militia formed to provide order on the frontier.

Texas secretary of state: The state official appointed by the governor to be the keeper of the state's records, such as state laws, election data and filings, public notifications, and corporate charters.

Texas Supreme Court: Court of last resort in civil and juvenile cases.

third reading: The Texas Constitution requires three readings of a bill by the legislature; third reading is the final reading in a chamber, unless the bill returns from the other chamber with amendments.

tolling: Financing highway construction or operations by requiring motorists who use them to pay tolls (fees).

Trans-Texas Corridor: A proposed statewide network of transportation routes for passenger vehicles, large trucks, rail, and utilities.

V

veto: The formal, constitutional authority of the chief executive to reject bills passed by both houses of the legislative body, thus preventing their becoming law without further legislative action.

vouchers: Appropriations of public money for use in payment of tuition and expenses at private schools.

W

weak mayor–council: A form of city government in which the mayor has no more power than any other member of the council.

West Orange-Cove Consolidated ISD v. Alanis (2004): A school finance case pitting property-poor districts, property-rich districts, and the state against each other in state court, challenging the state's tax cap and the equity of revenue distribution, litigating the question of whether the system had become so unequalized that it again violated the state constitution.

Glosario

Ley de Procesos Administrativos (administrative procedures act): Estatuto que contiene los procesos normativos del Estado de Texas.

Anglos (Anglos): Personas de raza "blanca" no Hispanos.

Anexión (annexation): Ampliación de los límites de una ciudad o pueblo incorporando territorios o poblados circundantes.

Petición de revisión discrecional (application for discretionary review): La petición de que la Corte de Apelaciones Criminales de Texas revise la dictaminación o el veredicto de una corte inferior, aunque se requiere que cuatro jueces así lo convengan.

"En general y por lugar" (at-large-by-place): Un sistema electoral en el cual todos puestos del cabildo o cualquier otro cuerpo de gobierno se eligen en una elección general y luego a cada puesto se le llama "una curul" y cada persona debe elegir por qué distrito se quiere lanzar.

Procurador de Justicia (attorney general): El funcionario electo para servir como el abogado del Estado de Texas.

Legislatura bienal (biennial legislature): Un cuerpo legislativo que se reúne en la sesión ordinaria solamente una vez cada dos años.

Proyecto de ley (bill): Una propuesta de ley ante una legislatura o congreso.

Agencia gubernamental "capturada" (captured agency): Una agencia del gobierno que constantemente toma decisiones favorables a los intereses privados de aquellas personas u organizaciones que se supone debe regular y vigilar.

Escuela particular (charter school): Una escuela pública creada mediante un acuerdo específico que le permite que funcione fuera de las reglas y normatividades generalmente aplicadas a las escuelas públicas regulares.

Oficial de Hacienda (chief budget officer): Término para designar al gobernador que se encarga de la elaboración del presupuesto del estado para que luego la legislatura lo discuta y apruebe.

Jefe del Ejecutivo (chief executive officer): El gobernador del estado, a quien se le considera como el funcionario máximo del poder ejecutivo del Estado de Texas.

Jefe de Estado (chief of state): El gobernador en su papel como la cabeza oficial que representa al Estado de Texas en sus relaciones con el gobierno nacional, con otros estados, y con dignatarios extranjeros.

Comisión Municipal (city commission): Una forma de gobierno local en la cual se leige a los miembros del cuerpo legislativo o cabildo y, al mismo tiempo, cada uno de éstos sirve también como administrador de una dependencia del gobierno municipal.

Comandante-en-Jefe (commander-in-chief): El gobernador(a) en su papel como cabeza de la milicia de un estado.

Corte de los Comisionados (commissioners court): El cuerpo legislativo de un condado en el Estado de Texas.

Comisión (committee): Una subunidad de la legislatura que trata los proyectos de ley sobre un tema específico.

Revisión total (comprehensive revision): Término que significa la adopción de una nueva constitución en vez de simplemente hacerle cambios a la que ya existe.

Recaudador de impuestos (comptroller of public accounts): Es un funcionario electo cuya función es recaudar los impuestos en un estado.

Resolución conjunta (concurrent resolution): Un documento legislativo que expresa la voluntad de ambas cámaras legislativas simultáneamente pero que no necesita la firma del presidente porque no es ley.

Corte constitucional de un condado (constitutional county court): Una corte designada por mandato constitucional como el foro oficial para desahogar material penal y civil.

Comisión constitucional de revisión (Constitutional Revision Commission): Un grupo que se establece para que investigue y redacte el borrador de una constitución; este documento sirve como base de los debates en una convención constitucional.

Abogado del condado (county attorney): Un oficial electo por un condado que funge como el representante legal del condado y al mismo tiempo como el fiscal del mismo condado.

Auditor del condado (county auditor): Un funcionario designado por el juez de distrito para fiscalizar las finanzas del condado.

Líder del condado (county chairperson): Líder de un partido político a nivel condado.

Oficial del condado (county clerk): Un funcionario electo que funge como secretario del gobierno del condado y que es responsable de de los registros y archivos del condado.

Comisionado del condado (county commissioner): Un funcionario electo que forma parte del cuerpo legislativo de un condado; al cuerpo legislativo de un condado se le llama la corte de comisionados.

Convención del condado (county convention): Una reunión de los miembros de un partido político a nivel de un condado con el propósito de elegir delegados y adoptar resoluciones.

Corte del condado (county court at law): La corte de un condado creada por un estatuto legal y diseñada para auxiliar al juez del condado en el desempeño de sus deberes judiciales.

Comité ejecutivo del condado (county executive committee): Los jefes de las secciones de un partido político en un condado que ayudan a los jefes del partido político en sus labores políticas en el condado.

Juez del condado (county judge): Se le llama así al funcionario electo pero que funge no como juez sino como presidente del cuerpo administrativo del gobierno del condado, al cual se le llama la corte del condado; el juez del condado puede o no tener también algunas funciones judiciales.

Recaudador de impuestos del condado (county tax assessor-collector): Un funcionario electo cuya función es hacer cumplir las leyes impositivas y recaudar los impuestos del condado (tarea que a veces desempeña también para otros gobiernos locales).

Tesorero del condado (county treasurer): Un funcionario electo que se encarga de la administración de los recursos financieros del gobierno del condado.

Tribunal de apelaciones (court of appeals): Es la corte inmediata superior ante la cual se interponen apelaciones en materia de derecho penal y civil.

Fiscal del Distrito (criminal district attorney): Es un funcionario electo que procesa los casos penales, fungiendo como parte acusadora.

Elección crítica (critical election): Una elección que representa un cambio de preferencias partidistas del electorado de un partido a otro debido al surgimiento de nuevos temas que polarizan a los votantes y los hacen cambiar de partido.

Votación cruzada (crossover voting): Una elección interna de un partido político donde votan personas no afiliadas a ese partido político.

Realineación electoral (dealignment): Un declive general en la identificación y la lealtad partidistas en el electorado en contra de un partido político y a favor de otro.

Fiscal de distrito (DA or District Attorney): Funcionario electo que representa al gobierno ante la corte en todos los casos penales.

Secretario de distrito (district clerk): Funcionario electo responsable de mantener los archivos de la corte de distrito.

Proyecto de ley inscrito (enrolled bill): Un proyecto de ley que ha ya aprobado por las dos cámara de una legislatura y que se ha enviado ya al gobernador para su firma y proclamación en ley.

Jurisdicción extraterritorial (ETJ or extraterritorial jurisdiction): El área fuera del fundo legal de una ciudad en la cual el gobierno municipal puede ejercer ciertas facultades limitadas.

Política fiscal (fiscal policy): El conjunto de políticas públicas del gobierno federal que tienen que ver con los impuestos, el gasto, y la deuda, y cuyo propósito es dar forma a las metas macroeconómicas del país con respecto al empleo, la estabilidad de los precios, y el crecimiento económico.

La era de la frontera (frontier era): El período histórico en el que Texas era un territorio fronterizo entre los Estados Unidos y las zonas del suroeste del país habitadas por los mexicanos y las tribus indias.

Equivalencia de tiempo completo (FTE or full-time equivalent): Unidad de medida mediante la cual se determina el número de empleados.

Autoridad para constituir estatutos propios (general ordinance-making authority): El derecho legal de las ciudades de adoptar sus propios estatutos municipales en una amplia gama de asuntos públicos; esta autoridad la poseen las ciudades pero no los condados.

Vinculado (germane): Que está relacionado a un cierto asunto.

El buen gobierno (good government): El conjunto de políticas que abren las burocracias a la participación y al escrutinio del público y que reducen al mínimo los conflictos de intereses.

Gobernador (governor): La persona electa que ocupa el puesto de jefe de gobierno en un estado.

Mensaje del gobernador (governor's message): Mensaje que el gobernador entrega a la legislatura y que anuncia los objetivos de sus políticas públicas, las prioridades de su presupuesto, y las acciones que recomienda a la legislatura.

Gobierno autónomo (home rule): El derecho y la autoridad de una comunidad local de gobernarse a sí misma, sin la interferencia del gobierno del estado.

Enjuiciar políticamente (impeach): Un voto de la cámara de diputados mediante el cual se acusa formalmente a un político o juez del gobierno haber cometido un delito oficial.

Implementación (implementation): El proceso mediante el cual una ley o una política pública se pone en operación por la burocracia.

Individualismo (individualism): La creencia que cada persona debe actuar de acuerdo a su propia conciencia.

Comisionado para la Regulación de la Industria de Seguros (insurance commissioner): Un funcionario designado por el gobernador para dirigir el Departamento de Seguros, cuyo objeto es regular la industria de seguros, ya sea automovilísticos, médico, de vida, de propiedad, etc.

Calendario de intenciones (intent calendar): El calendario del Senado que enumera los proyectos de ley e indica que sus autores o patrocinadores han dado notificación de que desean suspender las reglas generales para que el proyecto de ley pase inmediatamente al pleno del Senado.

Triángulos de hierro (iron triangles): Las relaciones y los patrones de interacción relativamente estables entre las agencia gubernamentales, los grupos de intereses, y las comisiones o subcomisiones del congreso.

Redes temáticas (issue networks): Las relaciones informales que existen entre una gran cantidad de actores que trabajan en una área de la política pública.

Resolución conjunta (joint resolution): Un documento legislativo que propone una enmienda a la constitución de Texas o que ratifica una enmienda a la constitución de los Estados Unidos.

Corte de un juez de paz (justice of the peace court): Corte menor de un condado local que tiene jurisdicción en delitos y demandas civiles menores.

Comisionado de la tierra (land commissioner): El funcionario electo responsable de manejar y de arrendar las propiedades del estado, incluyendo las concesiones del petróleo, del gas, y de los recursos minerales.

Comité presupuestario legislativo (Legislative Budget Board or LBB): Un comité legislativo conjunto (con un personal numeroso) que prepara el presupuesto estatal y conduce evaluaciones de los programas de las burocracias.

Consejo legislativo (legislative council): Comité legislativo conjunto (con un personal numeroso) que proporciona asesoría jurídica, ayuda a redactar proyectos de ley, edita, e imprime trabajos de investigación sobre políticas públicas y servicios de evaluación de programas para beneficio de los miembros de la legislatura.

Grupo legislativo de un partido (legislative party caucus): Una organización de legisladores que pertenecen a un mismo partido político, y que se alía formalmente con un partido político.

Proceso legislativo (legislative process): El proceso que sigue una legislatura en la consideración y aprobación de legislación.

Elección local (local election): La elección organizada por funcionarios electorales locales para elegir a funcionarios de los gobiernos locales.

Código de los Gobiernos Locales (Local government code): El código estatutario de Texas que contiene las leyes del estado que rigen a los gobiernos locales.

Administrador o gerente (manager): Un ejecutivo profesional empleado por el cabildo o la corte del condado para manejar las operaciones diarias de la entidad y recomendar cambios en las políticas públicas.

Programa de salud pública (medicaid): Programa creado como parte del Seguro de Salud Pública. El programa es subsidiado por el gobierno federal de los Estados Unidos y provee asistencia económica a las personas con bajos recursos económicos para cubrir sus gastos de salud.

Seguro de Salud Pública (medicare): Programa federal mediante el cual se otorga asistencia médica y tratamiento hospitalario a personas mayores de 65 años de edad, aunque la cobertura es sólo parcial.

Corporación Municipal (municipal corporation): Término legal utilizado para referirse al gobierno local en alguna ciudad, pueblo, condado, aldea, etc.

Corte municipal (municipal court): Corte de la ciudad con una jurisdicción limitada a sólo ciertos delitos menores.

Asociación legislativa no partidista (nonparty legislative caucus): Una organización de legisladores que se basa en una cierta característica o interés común entre sus miembros y no en la afiliación partidista de éstos.

Acuerdo de Libre Comercio de Norteamérica (NAFTA): Acuerdo que promueve la libre circulación de mercancías y de servicios entre Canadá, México, y los Estados Unidos.

Sobrerrepresentación y subrepresentación (overrepresentation and under-representation): Se dice de una situación en la cual los números de representantes de un grupo social en un cuerpo son más altos o más bajos, respectivamente, que los números de ese grupo en la población en general.

Organización permanente del partido (permanent party organization): Organización del partido que funciona todo el año haciendo el trabajo necesario para mantener el partido.

Petición para la revisión (petition for review): Petición de reconsideración de una decisión tomada por una corte inferior hecha ante la Suprema Corte de Texas; esta la petición se concede si cuatro de los magistrados de la Suprema Corte de Texas votan a favor de reconsiderar la decisión.

Revisión fragmentaria (piecemeal revision): Cambios a la constitución llevados a cabo mediante enmiendas pequeñas a la misma constitución que agregan, abrogan, o modifican partes de ésta.

Ejecutivo plural (plural executive): Un tipo de poder ejecutivo en el cual las facultades de un gobierno se dividen entre varias agencias ejecutivas, cada una con su titular autónomo e independiente, en lugar de quedar todas bajo una sola persona. En este tipo de poder ejecutivo, el gobernador no nombra a la mayoría de los miembros del gabinete.

Veto de bolsillo (pocket veto): Situación en la cual un proyecto de ley se considera permanentemente vetado si el presidente no firma ni rechaza el proyecto de ley aprobado por el congreso y éste entra en receso dentro de diez días hábiles.

Comité de Acción Política (PAC): Comité sancionado por la ley y oficialmente encargado de recaudar fondos para hacer campaña a favor de un candidato; estos fondos generalmente pertenecen a un grupo y representan sus intereses en el proceso político.

Convención seccional (precinct convention): Reunión de los miembros de un partido político en la sección territorial que cubre una casilla electoral con el motivo de seleccionar delegados y adoptar resoluciones.

Presidente del Senado de Texas (President of the Texas Senate): El vicegobernador de Texas al momento de fungir en su papel constitucional como presidente del senado del estado.

Elección primaria o interna (primary election): Elección en la cual los votantes deciden cuál de los precandidatos de un partido va a ser el candidato oficial del partido en la elección general.

Representación proporcional (proportional representation): Un sistema de votación que reparte las curules legislativas según el porcentaje del voto recibido por cada partido político.

Pro-tempore (pro-tempore): Un legislador que sirve temporalmente como líder legislativo ante la ausencia del presidente del senado o del presidente de la cámara de diputados.

Consejos públicos (public counsels): Funcionarios designados por el gobernador para representar al público ante ciertas agencias gubernamentales, principalmente aquellas agencias reguladoras.

Comisión de servicios públicos (public unity commission): Una comisión de tiempo completo con tres miembros pagados y que es designada por el gobernador para regir los servicios públicos que provee el gobierno de Texas.

Cuasi-judicial (quasi-judicial): Audiencia semi-judicial; cuerpo autorizado para llevar a cabo audiencias y emitir veredictos.

Quorum (quorum): El número mínimo de miembros requerido para conducir una sesión (como en un cuerpo legislativo).

Comisión Ferroviaria (Railroad Commission): Una comisión de tiempo completo compuesta de tres miembros electos por el pueblo y a quienes se les paga, cuya misión es regular la industria del petróleo, el gas, y algunas agencias del transporte.

Sesión regular (regular session): La sesión bienal de 140 días de la legislatura de Texas que comienza en enero de los años nones.

Puerta que gira (revolving door): Un intercambio de personal que sucede entre intereses privados y reguladores públicos—o sea entre compañías privadas y agencias gubernamentales.

Segunda lectura (second reading): La constitución de Texas requiere que se le den tres lecturas a un proyecto de ley en la legislatura; la segunda lectura es cuando se lleva acabo la discusión y se proponen enmiendas ante el pleno.

Regla de los dos tercios del senado (Senate two-thirds rule): Regla en el senado de Texas que requiere que cada proyecto de ley obtenga dos tercios del voto de los senadores presentes para poder suspender el orden regular de la sesión y debatir el proyecto.

Escándalo de Sharpstown (Sharpstown Scandal): El escándalo de corrupción de 1969 a 1972 que resultó en un veredicto de culpable de soborno del presidente y de otros miembros de la cámara de diputados; sirvió de base para las reformas de 1973.

Alguacil (sheriff): Funcionario público electo como el principal oficial que aplica la ley a nivel de un condado.

Resolución simple (simple resolution): Un documento legislativo que propone una acción del cuerpo legislativo que le compete solamente a la cámara en la cual se presentó dicho documento; por ejemplo, una resolución para adoptar o modificar las reglas de la cámara o para dar un reconocimiento a un ciudadano.

Distrito uninominal (single member district): Un sistema de elección en el cual cada legislador es electo por y representa a un solo distrito.

Presidente de la Cámara de Diputados de Texas (Speaker of the Texas House): El representante o diputado estatal que es electo por sus compañeros para fungir como el líder oficial de la cámara en tu totalidad.

Lugartenientes del Presidente de la Cámara de Diputados (Speaker's lieutenants): Diputados que forman parte del equipo del Presidente de la Cámara de Diputados. Asisten al presidente en el mantenimiento el orden en la cámara formal o informalmente y fungen como presidentes de las comisiones.

Equipo del Presidente de la Cámara de Diputados (Speaker's team): El equipo de liderazgo en la Cámara de Diputados o Representantes. Consiste del Presidente de la Cámara y sus aliados, a los cuales el presidente designa como jefes de las comisiones legislativas.

Sesión especial (special session): Una sesión legislativa de Texas de hasta treinta días, convocada por el gobernador, durante el período en el cual la legislatura se encuentra en receso.

Términos escalonados (staggered terms): Períodos de servicio público que no están empatados sino que comienzan y terminan en distintos tiempos, de modo que un gobernador no puede generalmente tener control de una mayoría del cuerpo legislativo durante mucho tiempo porque por lo menos algunos miembros de éste terminan su período de servicio.

Comisión de Educación del Estado (State Board of Education): Comisión que consta de quince miembros electos para fijar la política educativa del estado. La comisión tiene también facultades limitadas de supervisión sobre la Agencia de la Educación de Texas y los distritos escolares del estado.

Convención Estatal (state convention): La reunión de los miembros del partido para adoptar la plataforma de éste y para elegir al comité ejecutivo y al presidente del partido y, en un año donde hay una elección presidencial, para elegir a los delegados a la convención nacional y a quienes serán miembros del Colegio Electoral.

Comité ejecutivo del estado (state executive committee): Comité de un partido político que consta de sesenta y dos miembros, el cual toma las decisiones del partido entre convenciones estatales.

Presidente Estatal de Partido (state party chair person): Líder del partido en el estado.

Convención senatorial de distrito (state senatorial district convention): Reunión del partido cuando un solo condado es parte de dos o más distritos senatoriales.

Constitución estatutaria (statutory constitution): Constitución que incorpora provisiones detalladas para limitar los poderes del gobierno.

Alcalde Fuerte y Cabildo (strong mayor-council): Una forma de gobierno local en la cual el alcalde tiene poderes fuertes para gobernar la ciudad, mediante sus facultades sobre el personal y los departamentos del gobierno; en este sistema el alcalde también es miembro activo del cabildo.

Sucesión (succession): La declaración constitucional que dice que el vicegobernador puede asumir la gubernatura si el puesto estuviera vacante.

Tejano (tejanos): Texanos con orígenes mexicanos.

Organización temporal del partido (temporary party organization): Organización de un partido político que existe por un tiempo limitado e incluye varios niveles de convenciones.

Comisión Texana sobre la Calidad Ambiental (Texas Commission on the Environment): Nombre que se le dio en el 2002 a la antes Comisión para la Conservación de los Recursos Naturales de Texas.

Corte Suprema de Texas para Casos Criminales (Texas Court of Criminal Appeals): Corte del último recurso en casos tipificados como un delito o crimen grave.

Agencia de Educación de Texas (Texas Education Agency): La agencia del estado que supervisa a los distritos escolares locales y reparte fondos del estado a aquellos que lo necesiten.

Liga Municipal de Texas (Texas Municipal League): Asociación profesional y brazo de cabildeo de los gobiernos locales en Texas.

Guardabosques de Texas (Texas Rangers): Una milicia montada que se formó para proporcionar orden a lo largo de la frontera con México.

Secretario de Estado de Texas (Texas Secretary of State): El funcionario del estado designado por el gobernador para que se encargue de mantener los archivos del estado, por ejemplo, las leyes del estado, las estadísticas referentes a éste, datos y registros sobre las elecciones, las notificaciones públicas, y las cartas corporativas.

Suprema Corte de Texas (Texas Supreme Court): Corte de último recurso en casos civiles y juveniles.

Tercera lectura (third reading): La constitución de Texas requiere tres lecturas a un proyecto de ley en la legislatura; la tercera lectura es la última lectura en una cámara antes del voto, a menos que el proyecto provenga de la otra cámara con enmiendas.

Sistema de Alcalde débil y Cabildo Fuerte (weak mayor-council): Una forma de gobierno de una ciudad en la cual el alcalde no tiene ningún poder por encima de los miembros del cabildo.

Index

Abbott, Greg, 159, 166
Abortion, 13, 19, 23, 68
Administrative Procedures Act, 164
Advertisements, 86
African Americans, 9–10, 12, 102, 186, 187, 223
Agenda setting, 100, 235
Agriculture commissioner, 161–162
AIDS, 259
Aid to Families with Dependent Children (AFDC), 29, 258
Alabama, 46
Alabama-Coushatta tribe, 7
The Alamo, 17–18, 18*f*
Allred, Jimmie, 155*f*, 234
American Creed, 20
American Indians. *See* Native Americans
American Legislative Exchange Council, 232
The American Voter study, 92–93
Anchía, Rafael, 8*f*
Anders, Larry, 153
Anglos
  appointments of, 152
  explanation of, 11
  historical background of, 16
  as judges, 187
  in legislature, 102
  population of, 12
  in Texas Republican Party, 72
Annexation, municipalities, 221–222
Apache, 6
Arizona, 26
Asian and Pacific Americans, 10–11, 13*f*, 152
Association of Texas Professional Educators (ATPE), 76
At-large elections, 222, 223, 226, 227
Attorney general (Texas), 36, 38, 42, 53, 100, 158–159
Austin, Stephen F., 17, 179
Austin, Texas, 217, 219*f*, 227
Austin American-Statesman, 33, 121, 190*f*
Available School Fund, 250
Available University Fund, 253
Avery v. *Midland County* (1968), 210

Bailey, Kevin, 80
Balanced budget, 129–130, 238, 239
Barkley, Dean, 62
Barnes, Ben, 156
Barrientos, Gonzalo, 151
Barton, David, 68
Bay Area Center for Voting Research, 23
Bell, Chris, 62, 63*f*
Benkiser, Tina, 66*f*
Bennett, W. Lance, 83
Bentsen, Lloyd, 29
Bernstein, Marver, 172
Beyle, Thad, 147–148
Bicameral legislatures, 102
Biennial budgeting system, 238
Biennial legislature, 105
Bilingual education, 26–27
Bilingual Research Journal, 27
Bills, legislature, 124–129
Binder, Bob, 224

Blanton, Annie Webb, 163
Block grants, 244
Blogs, 85
Blum, Micheline, 85
Board of Pardons and Paroles, 165
Bond programs, 238
Bonham, James, 18*f*
Border fence, 220
Bowie, Jim, 17, 18, 18*f*
Brace, Paul, 245
Braden, George D., 209
Brennan, William J., Jr., 103
Brimer, Kim, 126
Briscoe, Dolph, 53, 54, 158
Brown, George, 29, 236
Brown, Herman, 236
Brown, Jerry, 223
Brown, Lee, 223
Brown, Willie, 223
Budget, 238, 247
Budgetary process, 129–130, 238–240
Budget execution authority, 129–130, 239
Bullock, Bob
  as comptroller, 73, 103, 160
  Connally and, 156
  on judicial selection reform, 198
  as lieutenant governor, 123, 127, 171, 198
  as secretary of state, 165
  on sunset laws, 161
Bunton, Lucius, 198
Burka, Paul, 8*f*
Burnam, Lon, 178
Burns v. *Richardson* (1966), 103
Bush, George W.
  as governor, 68, 144–145, 151, 152, 154, 155*f*, 156–158, 161, 163, 166, 167, 189, 198, 243, 251
  Hispanic Americans and, 12–13
  Houston contributors to, 29
  No Child Left Behind Act and, 252–253
  as wealthy Texan, 29
Business groups, 75
Business taxes, 244. *See also* Taxes

Caballero, Raymond, 223
Cabinet, 55, 141, 145*t*, 147, 148–149
Caddo Lake, 6*f*
Caddo tribe, 6–7
Calendars Committee, 126
California
  budget in, 247
  governor salary rate, 145
  legislative staff, 131
  legislator per diem, 104–105
  lobbyists in, 78
  multi-state comparisons, 6*t*, 38*t*, 69*t*, 145*t*, 193, 205*t*
  nonpartisan redistricting proposals in, 110
  partisan elected mayors in, 223
  Proposition 13, 56
  Proposition 77, 110
  Proposition 227, 26
  public school enrollment in, 248
  social and economic demographics of, 235

Calvert, Robert W., 52
Cameras, traffic intersection, 214–215
Campaign contributions, 84, 199
Campbell, Robert, 189
Capital punishment, 176–178
Carrillo, Victor G., 8, 162, 163
Carroll, Jimmy, 191
Casinos, 7–8, 7*f*
Caucuses. *See* Party caucuses
Center for Public Policy Priorities, 252
Center for Voting and Democracy, 110
Centers for Disease Control and Prevention (CDC), 138
Charter schools, 226, 249. *See also* Public schools
Chew, Linda Yew, 10–11
Chicago, Illinois, 218
Chief budget officer, 146
Chief executive officer, 146
Chief of state, 146
Children's Health Insurance Program (CHIP), 247, 260
Chinese Americans. *See* Asian and Pacific Americans
Chisum, Warren, 56
Christian Coalition politics, 68
Cigarette taxes, 252
Cisneros, Henry, 223
Cities. *See also specific cities*
  for conservatives, 23
  general-law, 213
  for liberals, 23
  overview of, 213–215
City commission, 216, 217
Clark, Harley, 43
Clayton, Bill, 54, 77, 119, 133
Clements, Bill
  appointments of, 75, 152, 189
  campaign for governor, 93–95, 133
  executive orders of, 157
  as governor, 151, 245
  party loyalty and, 134
  Republican House and, 74
  social conservatives and, 68
  support for George W. Bush by, 29
  television show of, 154
  use of veto power by, 156, 157
  White and, 93, 158
Clinton, Bill, 161
Clinton, Hillary Rodham, 95
Cochran, Cathy, 184*f*
Cockrell, Lila, 223
Cockroach, 53
Coke, Richard, 39
Colleges. *See* Higher education
College students, 169, 224
Colorado, 110
Colquitt, Oscar B., 155
Colt, Samuel, 16
Comanche, 6
Combs, Susan, 106, 160, 162, 239
Commander in chief (Texas), 36, 146
Commissioner of health and human services, 168
Commissioners court, 208

291

Commission on Judicial Conduct, 178, 185, 188
Comprehensive revision, 48
Comptroller of public accounts, 73, 159–160
Comptroller's certification, 239
Concurrent resolution, 124
Connally, John, 49, 156
Connecticut, 249
Connor, Geoffrey, 165–166
Conservatives, 22f, 23, 68
Constables, 210–211
Constitution, U.S., 41, 240
Constitutional conventions, state provisions, 51
Constitutional county courts, 182–183
Constitutionalism, 18–20, 41
Constitutional Revision Commission, 49, 51–52, 52f
Cornyn, John, 7, 67, 159
Corte, Frank, 104
Corte, Valerie, 104
Council-manager government, 216, 217
County attorneys, 210
County auditors, 211
County chairpersons, 66
County clerks, 210
County commissioners, 208, 210
County conventions, 65
County courts, 182–183
County courts at law, 183
County executive committee, 66
County judges, 208
County tax assessor-collectors, 211
County treasurers, 211
Court of appeals, 184
Courtroom security, 183
Craddick, Tom, 113f, 232
  ghost workers and, 121
  on party caucuses, 122
  as Speaker of the House, 98–100, 119, 134
  staff and, 132
  support for, 80
  Wilson's support for, 115
Criminal district attorneys, 210
Crockett, David, 17–18, 18f
Cuellar, Henry, 165
Cumulative voting, 223

Dallas, Texas, 218
Dallas News, 120
Daniel, Price, 53, 155f
Davis, Edmund J., 40–41, 147
Death penalty, 176–178
Debt, 129, 238
Deceptive Trade Practices Act, 159, 188
Dedicated funds, 239
Defense of Marriage Act (Texas 2003), 56, 114
Deficit spending, 129
Delaware, 150
DeLay, Tom, 120
DeLee, Alexis, 121
Democracy, 18–20
Democratic Party, 9, 63–64, 66, 67, 70–75, 70f, 72f, 73f
Demographics. *See* Population
Department of Agriculture, 161
Department of Insurance, 167
Department of Justice, 226–227
Department of State Health Services, 247

Deshotel, Joe, 10
Dewhurst, David, 29, 109, 113f, 123, 127, 161, 232
Dietz, John, 43
District attorney, 210
District clerks, 210
District courts, 183–184
DNA tests, 195
Doggett, Lloyd, 190
Duncan, Robert, 197, 198
Dunnam, Jim, 121
Dutton, Harold, 10, 178

Eagle Forum, 139
Earle, Ronnie, 80, 119–120
Eckels, Robert, 202–204
Economic policies. *See also* Finance; Public policy
  Depression era, 234
  explanation of, 232
  school finance and, 249–252
  state government, 237–248
  in Texas, 25–27
Edgewood v. *Kirby* (Texas 1989), 43, 250
Education. *See also* Higher education; Public schools; *specific schools*
  bilingual, 26–27
  reform of, 263
  in Texas, 206–207
Education Code, 263
8-F Crowd (Houston, Texas), 29, 236
Eisenhower, Dwight D., 261
Elazar, Daniel, 29
Elections
  at-large, 222, 223, 226, 227
  presidential, 89, 95, 212
  in Texas, 79t, 81–84, 188–189, 192t, 222, 223, 226, 227
Electric Reliability Council of Texas, 166
Electronic voting systems, 90–91
Elgin Bank v. *Travis County* (Texas 1999), 211–212
Elkins, Gary, 173
Elliott, Euel, 71
Ellis, Rodney, 131, 198
El Paso, Texas, 10f
El Paso Herald-Post, 209
England, Kirk, 114
Engrossed bills, 128
Enrolled bills, 129
Equality, 20
Equal protection clause, 103
Equal Rights Amendment (ERA), 20
Equity Center, 132, 265
Ericson, Joe E., 40
Espinosa, Gary, 81
Ethics Commission, 76–77, 84, 105, 133, 199
Evaluation, policy, 236
Evans, Donald, 153
Executive branch, 36, 37–38, 47, 55, 73–74, 140, 146
Expenditures
  comparisons of state, 247–248
  policy areas of state, 246–247
Extraterritorial jurisdictions (ETJs), 221–222

Farmers' Alliance, 22
Farrar, Jessica, 121
Father's Day Massacre, 156, 258

Federal Emergency Management Agency (FEMA), 203
Federal funds, 244
Federal Highway Act of 1956, 261
Federation for American Immigration Reform, 21
Fehrenbach, T. R., 14, 16, 20
Ferguson, James E., 50, 139, 145, 155, 156
Ferguson, Miriam "Ma," 138, 139, 145, 155
Filibuster, 128
Finance. *See also* Economic policies
  city government, 219–220
  county government, 212–213
  public policy and, 237–248
  public school, 249–252
First reading (legislative bills), 127
Fiscal year (FY), 238
Flat taxes, 246
Flores, Kino, 80
Florida
  lobbyists in, 78
  multi-state comparisons, 6t, 38t, 69t, 145t, 193, 205t
  presidential election of 2000 in, 212
  social and economic demographics of, 235
Food and Drug Administration, 138
Fourteenth Amendment, 103
Franchise tax, 244. *See also* Taxes
Frantz, Joe, 17
Free Market PAC, 57
Frew v. *Hawkins* (2002), 159
Friedman, Jeff, 224
Friedman, Kinky, 62, 63f
Frontier era, 15–16
Frost, Martin, 121
Full-time equivalent (FTE), 171

Gaines, Thomas, 22
Gallego, Pete, 199
Galveston, Texas, 24, 217–218
Gantt, Fred, 154
Garcia, Buddy, 166
Garcia, Gus, 223
Gardasil, 138–140
Garner, Tyron, 19
Garza, Ed, 165, 223
Garza, Tony, 8
Geeslin, Mike, 167
General-law cities, 213
General ordinance-making authority, 211–212
Georgia, 90, 110, 148
Germane, 128
Gerrymandering, 108, 110–111. *See also* Redistricting
Ghost voting, 135
Giddings, Helen, 10
Gonzalez, Raul, 191
Good government, 170
Goolsby, Tony, 121
Governors. *See* Texas governors
Governor's messages, 146
Gramm, Wendy, 232
Grange, 40
Granger, Kay, 223
Great Society, 234
Gross domestic product (GDP), 245
Guerrero, Lena, 152

Haas, Rene, 191
Harris County, Texas, 10, 202, 208, 224, 228
Hawaii, 15
Hawkins, Albert, 168, 258
Health and human services
  adequacy of, 260–261
  federal government and, 257–258
  food, shelter, clothing and protection and, 259
  function of, 14, 122, 168, 211, 256
  privatization of, 256–257
Health and Human Services Commission (HHSC), 168, 247, 256
Health care
  costs of, 259
  explanation of, 259–260
  vaccines and, 138–140
Health maintenance organizations (HMOs), 167
Heath, Richard, 153
Hecht, Nathan, 191
Heflin, Talmadge, 11, 232
Help America Vote Act (2002), 90, 212
Hervey, Barbara, 184f
Higher education. *See also specific schools*
  access to, 254–255
  funding for, 253–254
  statistics regarding, 253
  student government opportunities in, 169
Higher Education Fund, 254
Hightower, Jim, 67, 162
Hill, Fred, 100
Hill, John, 19, 158, 165, 189
Hispanic Americans
  Democratic Party and, 9
  health insurance for, 15
  political ideology of, 13–14
  Republican Party and, 9
  support for George W. Bush, 12–13
  in Texas, 8–9, 13f, 152, 186, 187, 223
Hobby, Paul, 74, 160
Hobby, William P., 54, 123, 145
Holcomb, Charles, 184f
Holmes, Zan, 152
Holt, Peter, 153
Home rule charters, 206, 209, 213–214, 216–218, 221–222
Hopson v. *Dallas ISD*, 251
Hopwood v. *Texas* (Texas 1996), 159, 254–255
House Study Group (HSG), 122
Houston, Sam, 143f
Houston, Texas, 10, 12, 25, 31, 76, 202–204, 217, 218f, 222
Houston Independent School District, 226, 249
Hubbard, Richard, 145
Hudson, Paul, 166
Hunt, Nelson, 236
Huntington, Samuel, 20
Hurricane Katrina, 202–204
Hurricane Rita, 202–204
Hutchison, Kay Bailey, 60–62, 68, 106, 162

Idaho, 89
Ideology. *See* Political ideology
Immigration, 21, 27f
Impeachment, of governors, 145
Implementation, policy, 235–236
Income distribution, 28–29, 28f

Income taxes. *See* Taxes
Incumbency, 109–110
Individualism, Texas Creed, 14–16
Initiatives, 56–57
Insurance commissioner, 167
Intent calendar (legislative), 119f, 126
Interest groups. *See* Texas interest groups
Internet, 85
Internships, 131
Iron triangles, 173
Isett, Carl, 104
Isett, Cheri, 104

Jamail, Joe, 188–189
Jefferson, Wallace B., 9, 9f, 10, 187
Jester, Beauford, 50
Jewell, Malcolm, 115, 122
John Hopkins University, 90
Johnson, Cheryl, 177, 184f
Johnson, Lyndon B., 29, 234
Joiner, C. M. "Dad," 25
Joint resolutions (legislative), 124
Jones, Anson, 36
Jones, Elizabeth Ames, 162, 163
Jowett, Garth, 21
Judges, 187, 208, 210–211
Judicial Campaign Fairness Act (Texas 1995), 199
Jumano tribe, 6
Junell, Rob, 33, 48, 54, 54f, 197
Jury pool, 194
Justice, William Wayne, 26
Justice of the peace courts, 182

Kalmbacher, Colin, 224
Kansas, 150
Keasler, Michael, 184f
Keffer, Jim, 100
Keller, Sharon, 177–178, 184f
Kelley, Russell T., 77
Key, V. O., Jr., 24
Kickapoo Lucky Eagle Casino, 8
Kickapoo tribe, 7
Kilgarlin, William, 188
Kilgarlin v. *Martin* (1966), 103
Kim, Jennifer, 11
Kiowa tribe, 6
Kirk, Ron, 10, 152, 165, 223
Kurita, M. Sue, 11

Labor unions, 76
Land commissioner, 160–162
Laney, David, 153
Laney, Pete, 55, 74, 119, 120, 134, 171
Latinos. *See* Hispanic Americans
Lau v. *Nichols* (1974), 26
Lawrence, John Geddes, 19
League of United Latin American Citizens (LULAC), 222
League of Women Voters, 49
Legislative Budget Board (LBB), 129, 130, 132, 238, 239, 246
Legislative Council, 132
Legislature. *See* Texas legislature
Leininger, James, 163, 230–232, 265
Lewis, Gib, 134
Liberal constitutions, 41
Liberals, 22f, 23–24
Libertarianism, 21–22, 22f, 41, 68

Libertarian Party, 21–22
Liberty, Texas creed, 17–18
Licensing fees, 245
Lieutenant governors, 123
Limited English proficiency (LEP), 26–27
Lobbying. *See also* Texas interest groups
  by "astroturf" interest groups, 79
  in Texas, 76–79, 77f
Lobbyists
  retired legislators as, 78
  in Texas, 76–79, 77f
Local elections, 82–83
Local Government Code, 211, 213–215
Local governments. *See also* Texas city governments
  college students as elected officials of, 224
  multi-state comparisons, 205t
Loeffler, Tom, 153
Los Angeles, California, 218
Lottery revenues, 244, 250
Lucas, A. F., 25

Magallanes, Rudy, 80
Maine, 89, 158
Mansfield, Steve, 198
Mansour, James, 80
Martin, Crawford, 165
Martinez, Mike, 227
Martin v. *Hunter's Lessee* (1816), 248
Maryland, 90
Massachusetts, 15
Mattox, Jim, 67, 81, 159
Mauro, Garry, 67, 74, 158, 161
May, Janice, 47, 52
Mayors, 216, 217, 223
McCall, Brian, 98–100
McClendon, Ruth Jones, 10
McDonald, Craig, 80
McDonald, Michael, 88
McKinnon, Mark, 84
McKnight, Peyton, 83
McLean, In re, 19
Medicaid, 4, 15, 19, 158–159, 168, 260
Medicare, 258
Medina, David, 9, 187
Merck, 138–140
Messer, Bill, 77
Mexican American Legal Defense and Education Fund (MALDEF), 76, 222
Mexican Americans. *See* Hispanic Americans
Mexico, and Texas, 8, 11, 16–17
Meyers, Lawrence E., 184f
Michigan, 105, 131, 242
Mid-Continent Oil and Gas Association, 75
Milburn, Beryl Buckley, 52
Militias, 16
Miller, Geraldine "Tincy," 232
Miller, Laura, 223
Miller, Vance, 232
Minnesota, 89
Minorities
  and redistricting, 103, 108
  in Texas judiciary, 186, 187, 191, 198
  in Texas legislature, 113
Minton, Roy, 80
Miranda rights, 193
Mississippi, 148
Missouri, 213
Morales, Dan, 67, 94, 159

Mosbacher, Robert, 29
Motor-voter laws, 87–88
Mowery, Anna, 49, 55
Municipal Annexation Act (Texas 1963), 221–222
Municipal corporations, 205–206
Municipal courts, 182
Municipalities, annexation in, 221–222
Murdock, Steve, 4
Murphy, Paul, 190
Murray, Richard, 191
Mutscher, Gus, 119

National Association for the Advancement of Colored People (NAACP), Legal Defense and Education Fund, 222
National Association of Criminal Defense Lawyers, 178
National Center for State Courts, 183
National Network for Immigrant and Refugee Rights, 21
Native Americans, 6–8, 16
Nau, John, 232
Neeley v. *West Orange-Cove CISD* (Texas 2005), 43
Nelson, Jane, 139
New Hampshire
  governors office in, 158
  same-day voter registration in, 89
  state legislature in, 105
New Jersey, 158, 249
New York City, 218
New York State
  budget in, 247
  income taxes in, 242
  legislature in, 105, 130
  lobbyists in, 78
  multi-state comparisons, 6*t*, 38*t*, 69*t*, 145*t*, 193, 205*t*
  social and economic demographics of, 235
No Child Left Behind Act (NCLB), 252–253
Nonparty caucuses, 122
Noriega, Melissa, 104
Noriega, Rick, 104, 202–204
Norquist, Grover, 232
Northcott, Kaye, 83

Obama, Barack, 95, 165
Odom, Elzie, 223
Office of Court Administration, 185
Ohio, 110
Oklahoma, 148, 180
One-person, one-vote, 210
Organization of Petroleum Exporting Countries (OPEC), 25
Organized labor. *See* Labor unions
Osborne, David, 237, 245, 256
Overrepresentation in appointments, 151–152
Owen, Priscilla, 191

PACs. *See* Political action committees (PACs)
Parrott-Oliver, Alice, 191
Parsley, Julie Caruthers, 166
Partial-birth abortion, 68. *See also* Abortion
Party caucuses, 118
Party identification, 12–13, 70–72, 70*f*, 92–95

Party realignments, 71–72
Patterson, Jerry, 106, 161
Pena, Aaron, 80
Pennsylvania, redistricting plan in, 110
People's Party, 22–23
Per diem allowance, 104–105
Perkins, Bob, 185*f*
Permanent party organization, 65–67, 67*f*
Permanent School Fund (PSF), 250
Permanent University Fund (PUF), 253, 254
Perot, H. Ross, 252
Perot, Ross, 29
Perry, Bob, 80
Perry, Rick
  appointments of, 8–10, 75, 152, 153, 158, 163, 165–168, 191
  campaign funds and, 83, 84, 232
  corporate contributors to, 153
  executive orders of, 138–140, 157–158
  as governor, 60–61, 94, 95, 106, 127, 134, 145, 204, 239, 252, 258, 261
  as agriculture commissioner, 162
  as lieutenant governor, 123
  negative ads of, 86
  party switching of, 67
  public opinion leadership, 154
  use of veto power by, 156, 157, 167, 173
Personal Responsibility and Work Opportunity Reconciliation Act (PRWORA) (1996), 29–30
Phillips, Thomas R., 191, 197
Piecemeal revision, of Texas Constitution, 49–50
Pilgrim, Lonnie "Bo," 84, 133
Pitts, Jim, 98–100
Plural executive, 47, 140, 147, 148, 158–163
Policy making, 235. *See also* Public policy
Political action committees (PACs), 79–81, 79*t*, 83–84. *See also* Texas interest groups
Political cartoons
  on judicial selection, 190*f*
  on voter choice, 92*f*
Political economy, 237
Political ideology
  explanation of, 22*f*
  of Hispanics, 13–14
  in Texas, 13–14, 20–24, 114–115, 115*f*
Political parties. *See* Democratic Party; Republican Party; Texas political parties
Polunsky, Allan, 153
Population, of Texas, 2–14, 13*f*
Populist Party, 23
Populists, 22–23, 22*f*, 41, 233–234
Poverty rate, 28–29, 28*f*, 256, 259, 260
Pragmatism, 68
Precinct chairpersons, 66
Precinct conventions, 64
Presidential election
  of 2000, 212
  of 2004, 89
  of 2008, 95
Price, Daniel, Jr., 53
Price, Tom, 184*f*
Primaries, 81–82
Progressive taxes, 246
Proportional representation, 223
Proportional taxes, 246
Protest, 21, 27*f*
Public counsels, 168

Public hearings, 125
Public interest groups. *See* Texas interest groups
Public opinion, 84–85, 154
Public policy
  background of Texas, 230–232
  explanation of, 234
  finance and, 237–248
  health and human services, 256–261
  higher education and, 253–255
  public education and, 248–252
  reform efforts for, 263, 265
  roots of Texas, 233–234
  transportation and, 261–263
Public policy process
  explanation of, 235–236
  outcomes in, 237
  policy actors in, 236
Public school districts, 45, 226–228, 249
Public schools. *See also* Education
  charter, 226, 249
  constitutional mandate for, 248–249
  enrollment in, 4, 248
  finance issues for, 249–252
  quality of, 252–253
  reform of, 263
  structure of, 249
Public Utility Commission, 165, 166, 168

Ramsey, Ben, 123, 162
Ratcliffe, Debbie, 45
Ratliff, Bill, 33, 48, 54, 54*f*, 123, 197
Ray, C. L., 188
Rayburn, Sam, 106
Raymond, Richard, 114
Redistricting
  impact on minorities, 103, 108
  by nonpartisan commissions, 110–111
  Supreme Court on, 107–110
  in Texas, 100, 103, 106–111
Red-light running, 214–215
Reform Party, 29
Regional Mobility Authorities (RMAs), 262
Regressive taxes, 246
Regular session, 105
Regulation
  explanation of, 237
  land-use, 227
  utilities, 234
Republican Party
  Hispanic voters and, 9
  in Texas, 60–63, 68, 70–75, 70*f*, 72*f*, 73*f*, 202–195
  youth voters and, 71
Republic of Texas, 9, 101–102, 141–143, 148–149, 160–161, 180, 205–207, 234
Resolutions, 124
Revenue
  federal funds as, 244
  miscellaneous sources of, 244–245
  sources of, 241
  taxes as, 241–246
Revenue estimate, 238–239
Revisionist, 53
Revolving door, 172
Reynolds v. *Sims* (1964), 103
Richard, Michael, 176–178
Richards, Ann
  appointments of, 75, 152, 153, 160, 161
  on campaign finance reform, 84

as governor, 67, 108, 134, 156, 245, 250
health and human services and, 167
ideology of, 155f
in primary elections, 81
public opinion leadership, 154
on sunset laws, 171
vetoes by, 156
Richie, Boyd, 66f
Rieff, Susan, 152
Robbins, Brooke, 232
Rodriguez, Demetrio, 250
Rodriguez, Xavier, 191
Rodriguez v. San Antonio Independent School District, 250
Rohack, James, 15
Roosevelt, Franklin D., 234
Rose, Patrick, 45
Rouvell, Kerdon, 224
Rowlings, Robert, 153

Saibara, Seito, 10
Sales taxes. *See* Taxes
Same-sex marriage, 55–57
Sanchez, Tony, 29, 86, 94, 95, 153
Santa Anna, Antonio López de, 17
San Vicente Independent School District, 226
Schlesinger, Joseph, 147
Schools. *See* Education; Higher education; Public schools; *specific schools*
School vouchers, 248, 249
Schwarzenegger, Arnold, 110
Scott, Robert, 45
Second reading (legislature), 127, 128, 135
Secretary of State (Texas), 165–166
Seltzer, Cathy, 50, 51f
Senate two-thirds rule, 126, 127
Senatorial courtesy, 150–151
Severance taxes, 243–244. *See also* Taxes
Sharp, Frank, 133
Sharp, John, 25, 74, 160, 167
Sharpstown scandal, 84, 133, 220
Shaw, Bryan, 166
Shea, Gwyn, 165
Sheriffs, 210
Shivers, Allan, 129, 145
Simple resolution, 124
Single-member districts, 107–109, 222–223, 227
60 Minutes, 188–189, 190f
Slavery, 9, 20
Smith, Dick, 49
Smith, Steven Wayne, 191
Smitherman, Barry, 166
Social conservatives, 68
Social policies. *See also* Public policy
explanation of, 232, 234
school finance and, 249–252
Social Security, 258
Social Security Act, 258
Socio-economic comparisons, 6t
South Carolina, 148, 198
South Dakota, 89, 247
Soward, Larry, 166
Speaker of the House (Texas), 116, 119–121
Speaker's lieutenants, 120
Speaker's team, 120
Speaking Rock Casino, 7, 7f
Special (called) sessions, 105
Special districts, 224–228, 225t

Special elections, 82
Spector, Rose, 191
Staples, Todd, 106, 162
State Bar of Texas, 185–186
State Board of Education (SBOE), 158, 163, 226, 230, 231
State conventions, 65
State executive committees, 66
State governments, 51. *See also* Texas government
State party chairpersons, 66
State senatorial district conventions, 65
Statutes, 124
Statutory constitutions, 41
Sterling, Ross, 155
Stevenson, Coke, 145, 155
Strauss, Annette, 223
Strayhorn, Carole Keeton, 10, 60–62, 63f, 73, 158, 160, 223, 239
Strong mayor-council government, 216, 217
Subsidies, 237
Sunset Advisory Commission, 170
Sunset laws, 170–171
Supreme Court, U.S.
on affirmative action, 255
on death penalty, 176–178
on redistricting, 107–110
on voting laws, 210

Taft-Harley Act (1947), 53
Task Force on Homeland Security (Texas), 161
Taxes
business, 244
cigarette, 252
consumption, 242–243, 251
effects on individuals of, 245–246
income, 241–243
levels of, 245
severance, 243–244
types of, 43, 44, 146, 237
Technological advances. *See also* Internet
political protest and, 21
traffic safety and, 214–215
Teixeira, Ruy, 89
Tejanos, 18
Temple, Buddy, 83
Temporary Assistance for Needy Families (TANF), 29–30, 256–261
Temporary party organization, 64, 67f
Tennessee, 566
Tennessee v. Lane (2004), 104f, 163
Tennessee Valley Authority (TVA), 232f
Term limits, 104, 109–110
Terrell Election Law, 81
Texans for a Republican Majority, 119–120
Texans for Lawsuit Reform, 189
Texans for Marriage PAC, 57
Texans for Public Justice, 80, 153, 199
Texas
abortion and, 13, 19, 23, 68
African Americans in, 9–10, 12, 102, 186, 223
Anglos in, 11, 13f, 16, 72, 102, 152, 187
arguments for and against bilingual education in, 26–27
Asian Americans in, 10–11, 13f, 152
border fence, 220
cattle industry, 24

conservatives in, 23
contemporary economy of, 25–27
cotton crops in, 24
education, 26–27, 206–207
election reform in, 95–96
frontier era, 15–16
general elections, 82
Grange, 40
health insurance in, 14, 15
Hispanics in, 8–9, 12–14, 13f, 152, 186, 187, 223
historical background of, 5–12, 63–64
immigration and, 21
income distribution in, 28–29, 28f
liberals in, 23–24
libertarians in, 21–22
local elections, 82–83
marriage legislation in, 55–57
Mexico and, 8, 11, 16–17
motor-voter laws in, 87–88
multi-state comparisons, 6t,38t,113
Native Americans in, 6–8, 16
petroleum resources in, 25
political blogs, 85
political campaigns in, 83–86, 95–96
population trends of, 11–14, 13f
populists in, 22–23
poverty in, 28–29, 28f, 256, 259, 260
primary elections, 81–82
public opinion polling in, 84–85
public school enrollment in, 248
redistricting in, 100, 103, 106–111
revenue in, 241f, 242f
same-sex marriage in, 55–57
school enrollments in, 4
Sharpstown scandal, 220
social and economic demographics of, 235
sodomy statutes in, 19–20
special elections, 82
Texas Register, 165, 173
timeline of voter requirements, 86–87
voter choice, 92–95, 92f
voter turnout, 46f, 64, 86–92, 93f
Texas Alcoholic Beverage Commission, 165
Texas A&M University, 238, 253, 254
Texas Assessment of Knowledge and Skills (TAKS), 252
Texas Association of Builders, 172
Texas Association of Business, 119–120, 133
Texas Association of Counties, 206f, 208
Texas Association of Realtors, 76
Texas Association of Taxpayers, 75
Texas Automobile Dealers Association (TADA), 75, 79
Texas Bankers Association, 75
Texas Bilingual Education Act (1973), 26
Texas Bill of Rights, 41–42, 46, 51, 56
Texas Center for Actual Innocence (TCAI), 195
Texas Chemical Council, 75
Texas Citizen Action, 76
Texas city governments. *See also* Local governments
annexation and, 221–222
at-large-by-place elections in, 222, 223, 227
authority and functions of, 218–219
council managers, 216, 217
cumulative voting in, 223

finances of, 219–220
forms of, 216–218, 216*t*
functions of, 218–219
general-law, 214
overview, 213–216
politics and representation in, 222–223
proportional representation, 223
red-light cameras, 214–215
single-member districts in, 107–109, 222–223, 227
strong mayor-council, 216, 217
Texas Civil Justice League (TCJL), 189
Texas Civil Rights Project, 178
Texas Classroom Teachers Association, 76
Texas Commission on Environmental Quality (TCEQ), 78, 165, 166–167, 226
Texas Conservative Coalition, 74, 122
Texas Constitution
  attempt to reform, 32–34, 196–197, 197*f*
  amendments to, 46–47, 46*f*, 47*f*, 54, 55–57, 100, 104, 130, 180
  articles of, 41–47, 41*t*, 88, 103, 142, 146, 150, 180, 209
  current version, 39–40
  Bill of Rights, 41–42, 46, 51, 56
  Citizens Advisory Committee, 49
  cockroach, 53
  comprehensive revision of, 48–55
  Constitutional Revision Commission, 49, 51–52, 52*f*
  counties, 207*f*
  of 1836, 35–36, 37*f*, 103, 180
  of 1845, 36–37, 37*f*, 103, 141
  of 1861, 37, 141
  of 1866, 37–38, 143
  of 1869, 37*f*, 38–39, 143
  of 1875, 39–40
  of 1876, 40–48, 103, 143–146, 180, 206–207
  on executive branch, 36, 37–38, 73–74
  on judicial qualifications, 186
  on legislators, 104–105
  marriage amendment, 55–57
  multi-state comparisons, 38*t*
  piecemeal revision of, 49–50
  revisionist, 53
  as statutory form of, 41–42
  timeline of, 34–35
  on voting, 88
Texas Constitutional Convention of 1868, 102
Texas Constitutional Convention of 1875, 39–40, 39*f*, 43–44, 102
Texas Constitutional Convention of 1974, 51–53, 52*f*, 53*t*
Texas Constitutional Revision Commission, 49, 51–52, 52*f*
Texas county governments
  auditors, 211
  commissioners, 208, 210
  commissioners court, 208
  county attorneys, 210
  county clerks, 210
  criminal district attorneys, 210
  district attorneys, 210
  district clerks, 210
  finances of, 212–213

general ordinance-making authority, 211–212
land-use regulations in, 227
Local Government Code, 211, 214–216
provision for, 207*f*
sheriffs, 210
tax assessor-collectors, 211
Texas Association of Counties, 208
Texas Association of Counties, 206*f*
treasurers, 211
Texas Court of Criminal Appeals
  application for discretionary review, 185
  justices, 184*f*
  murder cases reviewed by, 195
Texas Creed
  constitutionalism and democracy, 18–20
  equality, 20
  individualism, 14–16
  liberty, 17–18
Texas Department of Public Safety, 87, 214
Texas Department of Transportation (TxDOT), 261–263
Texas Eagle Forum, 139
Texas Education Agency (TEA), 45, 163, 226, 228, 249
Texas Enterprise Fund, 154
Texas Equal Rights Amendment, 19
Texas Ethics Commission, 84, 105, 132, 199
Texas Federation of Business and Professional Women, 19
Texas Federation of Teachers, 76
Texas Good Roads Association (TGRA), 261
Texas government
  Administrative Procedures Act, 164
  agencies and private interests, 172–173
  agriculture commissioner, 161–162
  attorney general, 36, 38, 42, 53, 100, 158–159
  boards and commissions, 168–170
  Capitol, 165*f*
  captured agencies in, 168
  Commission on Environmental Quality, 166–167
  comptroller of public accounts, 159–160
  executive commissioner of health and human services, 168
  full-time equivalent employees in, 171
  good government recommendations, 170
  health and human services commission, 167–168
  home rule in, 206, 209, 213–214, 216–218, 221–222
  human services in, 4
  insurance commissioner, 167
  land commissioner, 160–162
  local governments (*see specific types*)
  modern bureaucracy in, 164–165, 164*f*
  municipal corporations, 205–206
  partisanship and, 73–75
  public counsels, 168
  Public Utility Commission, 166
  quasi-judical roles in, 166
  railroad commissioners, 162–163, 172
  Residential Construction Commission, 172–173
  revolving door in, 172
  Secretary of State, 165–166
  staggered terms, 162

State Board of Education, 163
state employees, 171
Sunset Advisory Commission, 170, 171, 171*f*
welfare reform in, 29–30
Texas governors. *See also specific governors*
  appointments of, 150–153, 151*t*, 152*t*
  as chief budget officer, 146
  as chief executive officer, 47, 55, 140, 146
  as chief of state, 146
  clemency power of, 146
  as commander in chief, 36, 146
  executive orders of, 138–140, 157–158
  historical background of, 141–143
  history of (1876–2009), 144*t*
  ideology of, 155*f*
  impeachment provisions for, 145
  legislature and, 134, 146
  lieutenant governors, 123
  multi-state comparisons, 145*t*, 148–150, 150*t*, 158
  as plural executive office, 140
  and public opinion, 154
  relations with legislature, 134, 146, 154–157
  restrictions on, 147
  roles of, 146–154
  salary, 145
  senatorial courtesy, 150–151
  staff and budget, 153–154
  succession provisions for, 145
  term length, 143–145
  veto power of, 142, 156, 173
Texas Higher Education Coordinating Board, 253, 254
Texas interest groups
  business groups, 75
  electioneering by, 79–80
  labor groups, 76
  litigation and, 80–81
  lobbying by, 76–79
  multi-state comparisons, 69*t*
  PACs and elections, 79–81, 79*t*, 83–84
  professional associations, 75–76
  public-interest, 76
  racial and ethnic groups, 76
  trade associations, 75
Texas JOBS PAC, 80
Texas judges
  county judges, 208
  judges and constables, 187, 210–211
Texas judiciary
  appeals, 195, 196
  application for discretionary review, 185
  arguments for and against judicial elections, 188–189, 192*t*
  arraignment, 194
  arrest and searches, 192–193
  booking, 193
  civil justice process, 195–196
  constitutional county courts, 182–183
  county courts at law, 183
  court of appeals, 184
  criminal justice process, 192–195
  death penalty, 176–178
  district courts, 183–184
  explanation, 48
  graded penalties in, 192*t*
  grand jury indictments, 183

historical background of, 179–180
judicial campaign finance reform, 199
judicial qualifications, 186–187, 186*t*
judicial selection, 187–192, 198
jury selection, 194
justice of the peace courts, 182
magistrate appearance, 193
minorities in, 186, 187, 191, 198
multi-state comparisons, 193*t*
municipal courts, 182
petition for review, 185
pretrial motions, 194
pretrial procedures, 195–196
reform proposals, 196–199, 197*f*
structure of, 181*f*, 182–185, 196–197, 197*f*
Supreme Court, 180, 184–185
trial *de novo*, 183
trials, 194–196
Texas Legislative Internship Program, 131
Texas legislative process
  arguments for and against initiative process in, 56–57
  bills, 124–129
  concurrent resolutions, 124
  engrossed bills, 128
  enrolled bills, 129
  filibusters, 128
  first reading of bills, 127
  germane amendments, 128
  governors' role in, 134
  House Calendars Committee, 126
  joint resolutions, 124
  partisanship and, 74–75
  quorum, 127
  rules and procedures, 124
  second reading of bills, 127, 128, 135
  Senate calendaring, 126–127
  Senate intent calendar, 119*f*, 126
  Senate two-thirds rule, 126, 127
  simple resolution, 124
  steps in, 125*f*
  sunset laws, 170–171
  third reading of bills, 127, 128
Texas legislature
  agenda setting in, 100
  Anglos in, 102
  balanced budget, 129
  bicameral, 102
  biennial session, 105
  budget execution authority, 130
  budgeting process, 129–130
  committees, 116*t*, 117–118, 117*t*
  compensation for, 104
  daily calendar of, 119*f*
  debt, 129
  deficit spending, 129
  election reforms in, 212
  Ethics Commission, 84, 105, 132, 133, 199
  functions of, 100
  ghost voting by, 135
  governors and, 134, 146
  hiring of "ghost workers," 121
  historical background of, 101–102
  Killer Bees incident, 127
  Legislative Budget Board, 129, 130, 132
  Legislative Council, 132
  lingo, 118*t*
  lobbying ethics and, 133
  member characteristics, 110–115, 112*f*
  member ideology, 114–115, 115*f*
  Militia Bill, 40
  minorities in, 113
  nonparty caucuses, 122
  opposition to leadership of, 122–123
  party caucuses, 118
  political parties in, 113, 114–115, 118, 120, 121–122
  president protem, 116
  Proposition 10, 50, 51*f*
  regular session, 105
  relations with lobbyists, 132–133
  relection rates in, 109–110
  Senate coalitions, 123
  senatorial courtesy, 150–151
  Speaker of the House, 116, 119–121
  Speaker's lieutenants, 120
  Speaker's team, 120
  special (called) session, 105
  staff, 130–132
  State Board of Control, 129
  temporary acting legislators, 104
  term length, 104, 106
  voting patterns of, 115*f*
  women in, 113
Texas Medical Assistance Program (TMAP), 19
Texas Medical Association, 75–76, 80, 190
Texas Mobility Fund, 262
Texas Monthly, 8*f*
Texas Municipal League, 219
Texas Natural Resource Conservation Commission, 166
Texas political parties. *See also* Democratic Party; Republican Party
  county chairpersons, 66
  county conventions, 64–65
  county executive committees, 66
  effectiveness of, 68–69
  formal organization of, 64–66
  functional organization of, 66–67
  legislature and, 113, 114–115, 118, 120, 121–122
  multi-state comparison, 69*t*
  party identification, 70–72, 70*f*, 92–95
  permanent party organization, 65–67, 67*f*
  precinct chairpersons, 66
  precinct conventions, 64
  realignment in, 71–72
  redistricting and, 108–109
  state conventions, 65
  state executive committees, 66
  state party chairpersons, 66
  state senatorial district conventions, 64–65, 65*f*
  temporary party organization, 64, 67*f*
Texas primaries, 81–82
Texas Public Policy Foundation (TPPF)
  background of, 230–232
  function of, 132, 236, 265
Texas Railroad Commission, 162–164, 166, 172, 234
Texas Rangers, 16
Texas Register, 165, 173
Texas Research League, 196–197, 230, 236
Texas Residential Construction Commission (TRCC), 172, 173
Texas Revolution, 141
Texas Rural Legal Aid, 223
Texas Senate Agenda, 119*f*
Texas special districts
  school, 226–228
  water, 225–226
Texas State Bar, 198
Texas State Teachers Association, 76
Texas Sunset Act (1977), 170–171
Texas Supreme Court
  civil procedures established by, 195
  explanation of, 180, 184–185
  petition for review, 185
  on school finance, 251, 252
Texas Transportation Commission, 261–263
Texas Trial Lawyers Association, 75, 80, 188
Texas Watch Foundation, 159
Texas Workforce Commission, 165, 170
Thielemann, Gregory, 71
Third reading (legislature), 127, 128
Tigua tribe, 7
Tobacco settlement funds, 245, 246
Tobacco Settlement Permanent Trust Account, 246–247
Tolling, 261
Tonkawa tribe, 6
Toomey, Mike, 139–140
Top 10 Percent Law, 255
Trade associations, 75
Traffic safety, 214–215
Transportation policy, 261–263
Trans-Texas Corridor, 262, 263
Travis, William Barret, 17, 18, 18*f*
Travis County, Texas, 57, 209
Tuition Equalization Grant Program, 254
Tunnell, Byron, 156
Turner, Sylvester, 10
Turnout. *See* Voter turnout

Underrepresentation in appointments, 151–152
Unemployment rates, 26–27
University of Michigan, 255
University of Texas, 195, 238, 253–255
Urban areas. *See* Cities
U.S. v. *Texas* (1981), 26
Utah, 249

Vaccines, 138–140
Value added tax (VAT), 242
Van de Putte, Leticia, 139
Venire, 194
Veterans Land Program, 161
Vetoes, 142, 156, 157, 167, 173
Vieth v. *Jubelirer* (2004), 109
Villagarosa, Antonio, 223
Vo, Hubert, 11
Voir dire, 194
Vote choice patterns, 92–95, 92*f*
Voter registration, same-day, 89
Voter turnout, 46*f*, 64, 86–92, 93*f*
Voting Rights Act (1965)
  effects of, 203, 226
  redistricting and, 108, 110
Voting Rights Act (Texas 1975), 13
Vouchers, school, 248, 249

Wainwright, Dale, 10, 187
Wallace, James, 189
Wallace, Mike, 188–189
Waller, Texas, 216, 216*f*

Walsh, Judy, 151
Water Code, 225
Water districts, 225–226
Watson, Kirk, 223
Watson, Mark, 153
Weak mayor-council city government, 216, 217
Weddington, Susan, 68
West Orange-Cove Consolidated ISD Alanis, 251
Whicker, Marcia Lynn, 115, 122
White, Bill, 202–204, 223
White, Mark
    as attorney general, 103, 158, 165
    as governor, 73, 93–94, 151, 153, 252
    ideology of, 155*f*
    in primary elections, 81
    as secretary of state, 165
    State Board of Education and, 163
    television show of, 154
White Oak, Texas, 217, 217*f*
Whitmire, John, 109, 127
Whitmire, Kathy, 223
Wichita tribe, 6–7
Williams, Clayton, 29
Williams, Michael, 10, 162
Williams, Patrick, 41
Williams, Roger, 62, 166
Wilson, Phil, 166
Wimberley Independent School District, 45, 228
Wisconsin, 89
Wohlgemuth, Arlene, 232
Womack, Paul, 184*f*
Women
    as state and local officials, 223
    in Texas legislature, 113
Women, Infants, and Children nutrition program (WIC), 259
Women in Government, 140
Wong, Martha, 10
World Wide Web. *See* Internet
Writ of *certiorari*, 184
Wyoming, 89

Yarborough, Ralph, 67
York, Dwain, 45
Young America's Foundation, 224
YouTube, 135

Zavala, Lorenzo de, 102